Criminal investigation : a practical textbook for magistrates, police officers and lawyers.

Hans Gross

Criminal investigation : a practical textbook for magistrates, police officers and lawyers.
Gross, Hans
collection ID CTRG98-B2883
Reproduction from Yale Law School Library
Includes index.
London : Sweet & Maxwell, 1924.
xvii, 606 p. : ill. ; 27 cm

The Making of Modern Law collection of legal archives constitutes a genuine revolution in historical legal research because it opens up a wealth of rare and previously inaccessible sources in legal, constitutional, administrative, political, cultural, intellectual, and social history. This unique collection consists of three extensive archives that provide insight into more than 300 years of American and British history. These collections include:

Legal Treatises, 1800-1926: over 20,000 legal treatises provide a comprehensive collection in legal history, business and economics, politics and government.

Trials, 1600-1926: nearly 10,000 titles reveal the drama of famous, infamous, and obscure courtroom cases in America and the British Empire across three centuries.

Primary Sources, 1620-1926: includes reports, statutes and regulations in American history, including early state codes, municipal ordinances, constitutional conventions and compilations, and law dictionaries.

These archives provide a unique research tool for tracking the development of our modern legal system and how it has affected our culture, government, business – nearly every aspect of our everyday life. For the first time, these high-quality digital scans of original works are available via print-on-demand, making them readily accessible to libraries, students, independent scholars, and readers of all ages.

The BiblioLife Network

This project was made possible in part by the BiblioLife Network (BLN), a project aimed at addressing some of the huge challenges facing book preservationists around the world. The BLN includes libraries, library networks, archives, subject matter experts, online communities and library service providers. We believe every book ever published should be available as a high-quality print reproduction; printed on-demand anywhere in the world. This insures the ongoing accessibility of the content and helps generate sustainable revenue for the libraries and organizations that work to preserve these important materials.

The following book is in the "public domain" and represents an authentic reproduction of the text as printed by the original publisher. While we have attempted to accurately maintain the integrity of the original work, there are sometimes problems with the original work or the micro-film from which the books were digitized. This can result in minor errors in reproduction. Possible imperfections include missing and blurred pages, poor pictures, markings and other reproduction issues beyond our control. Because this work is culturally important, we have made it available as part of our commitment to protecting, preserving, and promoting the world's literature.

GUIDE TO FOLD-OUTS MAPS and OVERSIZED IMAGES

The book you are reading was digitized from microfilm captured over the past thirty to forty years. Years after the creation of the original microfilm, the book was converted to digital files and made available in an online database.

In an online database, page images do not need to conform to the size restrictions found in a printed book. When converting these images back into a printed bound book, the page sizes are standardized in ways that maintain the detail of the original. For large images, such as fold-out maps, the original page image is split into two or more pages

Guidelines used to determine how to split the page image follows:

- Some images are split vertically; large images require vertical and horizontal splits.
- For horizontal splits, the content is split left to right.
- For vertical splits, the content is split from top to bottom.
- For both vertical and horizontal splits, the image is processed from top left to bottom right.

CRIMINAL INVESTIGATION

A PRACTICAL TEXTBOOK

FOR

MAGISTRATES POLICE OFFICERS AND LAWYERS

ADAPTED FROM THE

SYSTEM DER KRIMINALISTIK

OF

DR. HANS GROSS

Professor of Criminology in the University of Prague

BY

J. COLLYER ADAM, BARRISTER-AT-LAW

Public Prosecutor, Madras

LONDON
SWEET & MAXWELL, LIMITED,
3 CHANCERY LANE, W.C.2

| TORONTO | SYDNEY, MELBOURNE, BRISBANE |
| THE CARSWELL COMPANY, LTD | LAW BOOK CO. OF AUSTRALASIA, LTD |

1924

(*Printed in England*)

YALE LAW LIBRARY.

Printed in Great Britain by
The Eastern Press, Ltd Reading

(iii)

TABLE OF CONTENTS.

	PAGE
TABLE OF CONTENTS	iii
LIST OF ILLUSTRATIONS	vi
INTRODUCTION	xiii

PART I.—GENERAL.

CHAPTER I

The Investigating Officer.

i —General considerations	1
ii —The duties of the Investigating Officer	3
iii —Procedure of the Investigating Officer	3
iv —Preconceived theories	10
v —Certain qualities essential to an Investigating Officer	15
vi —Knowledge of men	21
vii —"Orientation"—Finding his bearings	25
viii —Jurymen	30
ix —The "Expeditious" Investigating Officer	32
x —Accuracy and precision in details	33

CHAPTER II

Examination of Witnesses and Accused.

i —General considerations	36
ii —Examination of witnesses	39
A When the witness desires to speak the truth	39
1 Fundamental considerations	40
(a) Perception	40
(b) Memory	49
2 Special considerations	52
(a) Strong feeling as a cause of inaccuracy of observation	52
(b) Inaccurate observations following wounds on the head	55
(c) Differences in the observing powers, resulting from differences in the natural qualities and intellectual culture of the observer	59
B When the witness does not wish to speak the truth	66
C Pathological lying	74
iii —Examination of the accused	75

CHAPTER III

Inspection of Localities.

i —Preparation	84
ii —What to do at the scene of offence	86
iii —The actual description of the scene of offence	89
iv —Search for hidden objects	95

CHAPTER IV

Equipment of the Investigating Officer.   PAGE
                                              99

CHAPTER V

The Expert and how to make use of him.

i — General considerations	103
ii — The Medical Jurisprudent	107
A In cases relating specially to Medical Jurisprudence	109
B Preservation of parts of a corpse	110
C Tattooing	112
D Mental affections	115
E Hypnotism	121
F Colour-blindness	126
G The teeth	127
iii — The Microscopist	128
A For traces of blood	129
B For excrement	131
C For hair	131
D For other cases relating to medicine	138
E For falsification of writing	139
F For examination of cloths, etc	140
G For examination of stains	142
1 On weapons and tools	142
2 Dust	144
3 On clothes, etc	146
4 Mud on footwear	147
iv — The Chemical Analyst	148
v — The Expert in Physics	150
vi — Experts in Mineralogy, Zoology, and Botany	153
vii — The Expert in Firearms	155
viii — Handwriting	157
ix — Photography	169
A Importance of photography from a judicial point of view	169
B Particular cases of the employment of photography	171
C Recognition of criminals from their photographs	180
x — Finger prints	185
A Practical application of finger-prints	186
B The manner of recording finger-prints	195
xi — Geometrical Identification	196

CHAPTER VI

Legitimate Sphere of the Public Press   198

PART II.—KNOWLEDGE SPECIAL TO THE INVESTIGATING OFFICER.

CHAPTER VII

Practices of Criminals.

	PAGE
i.—Disguising the face	203
ii.—False names	208
iii.—Pretended illnesses and pains	215
A Illness of witnesses or suspects summoned before the Court	215
B Sudden illness of accused or witnesses when under examination	216
1 Shamming blindness	217
2 Do deafness	218
3 Do epilepsy	219
4 Do paralysis	221
5 Sham Fainting Fits	221
6 Pretended insanity	222
7 Shamming catalepsy	223
iv.—Signs and signals	223
A Graphic signs	224
B Hand signals	231
C Signals of recognition	235
D Acoustical signs	237
1 Calls and cries of warning	237
2 Phonetic communication in prison	238
E Marks of stigmata on the face	240

CHAPTER VIII

The Slang of Criminals   242

CHAPTER IX

Wandering Tribes

i.—General considerations	243
ii.—Their methods of stealing	247
iii.—Child-stealing	251
iv.—Their good points and their superstitions	252
v.—Instruments used for theft, poisoning, etc	254
vi.—Attitude before the authorities	256
vii.—Their corporal characteristics	258
viii.—Gipsy proverbs	260

CHAPTER X

Superstition.   261

i.—Superstition attaching to dead bodies and to objects abandoned at the place of the crime	262
ii.—Superstition attaching to objects carried on the person	263
iii.—Divination and fortune-telling by cards, etc	267
iv.—Treasure-finding, dreams, and chiromancy	271
v.—Superstitions regarding oaths	274

CHAPTER XI

Construction and use of Weapons.

	PAGE
I.—Fire arms	276
A General considerations	277
B Different kinds of fire-arms	278
1 Guns (including Rifles)	278
(*a*) Shot guns	278
α The Barrel	280
1 The material of gun barrels	280
2 Number of barrels	281
β Explosive action	282
1 Muzzle-loaders	282
2 Breech-loaders	284
(*b*) Bullet guns	285
α Muzzle-loaders	287
β Breech-loading rifles	290
2 Pistols	291
3 Revolvers	291
C Ammunition	294
1 Powder	294
2 The Projectile	294
D Objects hit by a projectile	295
II.—Cutting and stabbing weapons	297
A General considerations	297
B Cutting and stabbing weapons properly so called	299
1 Sword-arms	299
2 Arms in the form of a knife	300
3 Arms in the shape of a lance or spear	300
4 Indian weapons	300

PART III.—CRAFTS SPECIAL TO THE INVESTIGATING OFFICER.

CHAPTER XII

Drawing and Allied Arts.

I.—General considerations	301
II.—Drawing	301
A Plan of the interior of a house	304
B Sketch of a dwelling	305
C Sketch of the environs of the house	307
D Sketch of a larger portion of country	311
III.—Drawing on squared paper	314
IV.—Modelling	315
V.—Moulding and stereotyping	317
VI.—Reproduction of drawings, etc	319
VII.—Piecing together torn paper	319
VIII.—Preserving and deciphering burnt paper	322

TABLE OF CONTENTS

CHAPTER XIII

Footprints and Other Impressions.

	PAGE
I —Footprints	325
A General notions	325
B How to observe footprints	325
1 Preparatory	325
2 Observation in an actual case	329
C Origin of the footprints	336
1 Speed	336
(a) Walking	337
(b) Running	344
2 The "Trace" itself	346
(a) The walking image	346
α The line of direction	346
β The line of march	347
γ The line of the foot	347
δ The length of the step	350
ε Other kinds of walking	352
(b) The image of the foot	354
D Measurements to be taken	357
E Reproduction of footprints	363
1 General	363
2 Various methods	364
3 Methods recommended	367
II —Other impressions	371

CHAPTER XIV

Traces of Blood

I —Search for traces of blood	374
II —How to register and describe traces of blood	382
III —How to detach traces of blood	385
IV —Search for traces of blood which there has been an attempt to remove	391
V —Finger-prints in blood	395
VI Preservation of blood marks	400

CHAPTER XV

Ciphers and other Secret Writings.

I —General considerations	403
II —Various kinds of ciphers	407
A Numerical ciphers	408
B Alphabetical ciphers	409
C Syllable and word ciphers	413
D The Stencil or Black-line cipher	414
E Miscellaneous ciphers	415
III —Suggestions as to deciphering secret writing	417

PART IV.—PARTICULAR OFFENCES

CHAPTER XVI

Bodily Injuries and Poisoning

	PAGE
i.—General considerations	419
ii.—Wounds by blunt instruments	420
iii.—Wounds made by a sharp instrument	422
iv.—Wounds caused by fire-arms	428
v.—Marks on the bodies of persons strangled or hanged	437
vi.—Bodies found in the water	440
vii.—Injuries to corpses	445
viii.—Poisoning	446
ix.—Abortion	453

CHAPTER XVII

Theft.

i.—General considerations	454
ii.—Thieves' scouts and spies	455
iii.—Other preparations for the theft	460
iv.—Thieves' equipment	462
v.—Accomplices	463
vi.—The theft itself	478
A Burglary and Housebreaking	482
1 General	482
2 Entering by the window	490
3 Entering by the door	495
(a) Attacking the door itself	496
(b) Attacking the lock	501
4 Entering in other ways	509
B Pocket-picking	511
C Sneak thefts	513
D Thefts in bazaars and shops	516
E Domestic thefts	516
F Thefts through superstition	518

CHAPTER XVIII

Cheating and Fraud

i.—General considerations	520
ii.—Falsification of documents	521
A Falsification of documents in general	521
B Examination of false documents	524
iii.—Counterfeiting seals, stamps, and coins	532
A Counterfeiting employment stamps	532
B Seals on letters, etc	539
C Coining	540

		PAGE
IV.—Horse Frauds		540
A. General		540
B. Special methods employed		541
1. The horse is shown under the most favourable conditions		542
2. Utilisation of certain physiological circumstances		545
3. Do. do. psychological circumstances		546
4. Fraud properly so called		549
(a) Frauds relating to the age of the horse		549
(b) Fraud concerning the temperament of the horse		550
(c) Faking the colour		551
(d) Hiding defects		552
(e) Concealment of illnesses		553
5. Employment of assistants		555
V.—Cheating at games		557
A. General		557
B. Methods of the sharp		559
VI. Frauds relating to antiquities and works of art		564
A. Prehistoric objects		567
B. Egyptian antiquities		567
C. Antique pottery		567
D. Glassware		568
E. Old coins and medals		569
F. Jewellery in precious metals		570
G. Pictures		570
H. Artistic engravings		571
I. Enamels		571
J. Articles of earthenware, stone, and porcelain		571
K. Manuscripts, books and bindings		572
L. Furniture and upholstery		572
M. Weapons		573
N. Miscellaneous		574

CHAPTER XIX

Arson.

I.—General considerations		576
II.—Quasi-spontaneous combustion		578
A. Through physical causes		578
B. From chemical causes		579
III.—Spontaneous combustion proper		580

CHAPTER XX

Serious Accidents and Boiler Explosions.

I.—General considerations		582
II.—Technical problems		585
III.—Causes of boiler explosions		586
A. False theories		586
B. Admissible theories		586
INDEX		589

LIST OF ILLUSTRATIONS

			PAGE
Figure	1	Investigating Officer's Satchel	101
,,	2	Method of preserving hair	133
,,	3	Drawing to accompany same	133
,,	4	Specimen of writing	166
Plate	I	Finger prints	188
,,	II	Specimen Hand	189
,,	III	do	190
,,	IV	Corresponding portions enlarged of 1st and 2nd fingers	191
,,	V	Skeleton Chart of Plate IV	192
Figure	5	Chart of Geometrical identification	195
,,	6	Tramp's Graphic Signs	224
Figures	7 to 11	do	225
,,	12 to 14	do	226
,,	15 to 22	do	227
,,	23 and 24	do	228
,,	25 and 26	Gipsy Signs	229
,,	27 and 28	Hand signals	235
Figure	29	Owl's song	233
,,	30	Gipsy's hook	255
Figures	31 and 32	Fortune telling diagrams	269
Figure	33	Lines of the hand	273
,,	34	Moplah powder horn	284
,,	35	Section of rifled barrel	285
,,	36	Colt revolver	291
,,	37	American style of aiming	293
,,	38	Star by bullet on glass	296
,,	39	Diagram, firing through window	297
,,	40	Sections of daggers	300
,,	41	Plan of room	304
,,	42	Plan of house	305
,,	43	Plan showing tapering wall	306
,,	44	Conventional sketch of curtilage	308
,,	45	Conventional sketch-plan of country	312
,,	46	Drawing on squared paper	314
,,	47	Contour lines	316
,,	48	Scheme of legs running	337

			PAGE
Figure	49	Scheme of sole of foot	340
,,	50	do. do	341
,,	51	Height of centre of gravity	344
,,	52	Scheme of legs	345
,,	53	Scheme of lines of march and of foot	346
,,	54	Scheme of feet walking	348
,,	55	Footprints	355
,,	56	Print of great toe	358
Figures	57 and 58	Skeleton footprints	360
Figure	59	Bowl and Plaster	368
,,	60	Mode of preserving footprint	359
,,	61	Impression of cart wheel	372
,,	62	Blood under table	378
,,	63	Blood splashes	382
,,	64	Sketch showing positions of blood marks in room	383
Figures	65 to 67	Details of Fig 64	384
Figure	68	Blood on corner of waistcoat	392
,,	69	do boards	394
Figures	70 and 71	Modes of protecting blood on hatchet and beam	402
Figure	72	Specimen of picture writing	406
,,	73	Section of bayonet	425
,,	74	Position of knife when cutting	427
,,	75	Gipsy mode of fastening door	490
,,	76	Comparative width of head and body	491
,,	77	Modes of forcing barred windows	491
,,	78	Modes of forcing barred windows	493
,,	79	How to apply a screw-jack	493
,,	80	Door hinges (in position)	496
,,	81	Modes of cutting through wooden doors	496
Figures	82 and 83	do do	497
Figure	84	do do	498
,,	85	Mode of cutting through a ceiling	500
,,	86	Padlock neatly removed	502
,,	87	Collection of skeleton keys	503
,,	88	do swell-cracksman's tools	504
,,	89	do crowbars	506
,,	90	Braces and bits for safe-cutting	507
,,	91	Collection of safe-cutting tools	508
,,	92	Safe, cut open and rifled	509
,,	93	Modes of abstracting purse from pocket	512
,,	94	Method of arranging chain or strap to catch flats	564

INTRODUCTION

This book is a practical textbook of instruction for all engaged in investigating crime. It not only deals in detail with subjects coming directly within the province of a criminal investigator, but also informs that official in what cases and in what manner specialists may or must be resorted to At what stage of the inquiry the rôle of the expert begins, depends almost entirely upon the person conducting the inquiry. If the latter is unaware, for example, that a chemist can bring out with the help of his science an almost invisible impression of a finger upon a drinking-glass, there is small chance of the drinking-glass either being examined or ever reaching the chemist's hands. An investigator with a fair equipment of knowledge will be aware, almost instinctively, just when to invoke the assistance of experts in many cases wherein another would not dream of doing so

We of course foresee and meet on the threshold the charge of encroaching upon the province, and thereby attempting to dispense with the help, of specialists Nothing could be more harmful than such advice, nothing could so expose the investigator to mistakes as such fancied independence. But there is a vast gulf between permitting an Investigating Officer to undertake work beyond his sphere and instructing him how to recognise *when he ought to resort to experts, what experts should be chosen*, and *what questions must be submitted to them*. *Cuilibet in suâ arte perito credendum est*.

As a rule, these three considerations alone will present themselves But there are also cases, nor are they extremely rare, where the Investigating Officer must *himself* play the rôle of expert.

(1) In all cases where no real experts exist and where a little reflection alone is required, *e.g.*, in cases of falsification of documents, observation of footprints, the deciphering of writing, questions concerning superstition, etc. (2) In the numerous cases where, no expert being at hand, it is necessary for the Investigating Officer to act without delay, for example, make an arrest, conduct a search, or revisit the scene of a crime. The Investigating Officer is often placed in such a situation He has, for example, to decide whether an incinerated corpse is that of a murdered man or of one accidentally burnt in a fire. He has no medical expert

with him—he has no means of getting one within a reasonable time—he is under the necessity of at once coming to some conclusion on the matter—he must rely entirely upon his own special knowledge; his method of procedure at this moment will have the very greatest influence upon the result of the inquiry. (3) Finally and not the least important, especially as regards India and the Colonies, experts of the first rank are not always to be found. Frequently medical men, even men of long experience, have never learnt the art of drawing up a satisfactory report in a criminal matter. They may know their trade thoroughly and be able to give most useful information, but are incapable in a criminal matter of applying their knowledge and answering questions put to them with any precision. Finally a workman, a hunter, or a cultivator cannot be expected to find just the correct expression or to put into words exactly what he desires to say, especially from the point of view of the Investigating Officer. It must never be forgotten that the best of experts is far from being a criminalist. The Investigating Officer must therefore know something more than what is set out in the Codes, if he wants to obtain answers to the point. And if he is entirely ignorant on all matters connected with outside knowledge, he cannot gain that assistance from specialists which they would otherwise be able to afford.

No doubt the Investigating Officer can find much of the requisite information in a mass of books, yet some is to be found nowhere; as to the books themselves, they are not always to his hand, and when he has them at his disposition, he speedily realises that a man without some knowledge of a subject cannot intelligently use a scientific manual. It is impossible for him to find the notions he is in need of, united in one systematic whole; and he has often neither time nor opportunity to question anyone in a position to give him information. He is thus generally compelled to fall back on his own resources, or on some guide easy to consult and capable of giving him the starting-point necessary in the majority of cases that arise. In fact he wants a book of "First Aid." The present volume is intended to be such an auxiliary; in any event we trust that the beginner will find in it a practical guide, at least for the outset, on his journey, and possibly even through the inevitable Slough of Despond.

For various reasons some subjects of interest to an Investigating Officer have not been treated of exhaustively: a full discussion would encroach too extensively upon subjects outside his province, would be beyond the compass of a single book, or perhaps prove profitable to the criminal classes and harmful to the public.

The object of the book then is to show how crime is to be handled, investigated, and accounted for, to explain the motives at work and the objects to be attained. The legal aspect of arson, for example, and the punishment appropriate thereto, the principles of the criminal law, the laws of evidence, and the rules of procedure to be followed in the trial of a case are barely within our limits; but how the arson was accomplished, what means and assistance the incendiary had at his disposal, how its origin may be accounted for, the character of the criminal and—here comes in criminal psychology—the weight to be attached to the testimony of the witnesses, the consideration of errors in observation and deduction, to which judge, jury, and all who have to deal with crime, are exposed,— these things are part and parcel of our subject.

Abstract legal knowledge is practically worthless where the Judge, Magistrate, or Policeman cannot make it fit in with facts, when he does not understand the witnesses, or appreciates them erroneously, when he assesses wrongly the worth of sense perceptions, when he is led astray by every bit of roguery, when he does not know how to make use of traces left behind by the criminal, and especially when he does not know the numberless facts systematised in *Criminal Phenomenology*.

It must be admitted that at the present day the value of the deposition of even a truthful witness is much over-rated. The numberless errors in perceptions derived from the senses, the faults of memory, the far-reaching differences in human beings as regards age, sex, nature, culture, mood of the moment, health, passionate excitement, environment—all these things have so great an effect that we scarcely ever receive two *quite similar* accounts of one thing; and between what people really experience and what they confidently assert, we find only error heaped upon error. Out of the mouths of two witnesses we *may* arrive at the real truth, we may form for ourselves an idea of the circumstances of an occurrence and satisfy ourselves concerning it, but the evidence will seldom be true and material; and whoever goes more closely into the matter will not silence his conscience, even after listening to ten witnesses. Evil design and artful deception, mistakes and errors, most of all the closing of the eyes and the belief that what is stated in evidence has really been seen, are characteristics of so very many witnesses, that absolutely unbiassed testimony can hardly be imagined. If Criminal Psychology teaches us this much, so the other parts of the subject show us the value of facts, where they can be obtained, how they can be held fast and appraised—these things are just as important as to show what can be done with the facts when obtained. The trace of a crime discovered and turned to good account, a correct sketch be it ever so simple, a microscopic slide, a deciphered correspondence, a photograph of a person or object, a tattooing, a restored piece of burnt paper, a careful survey, a thousand more material things are all examples of incorruptible, disinterested, and enduring testimony from which mistaken, inaccurate, and biassed perceptions, as well as evil intention, perjury, and unlawful co-operation, are excluded. As the science of Criminal Investigation proceeds, oral testimony falls behind and the importance of realistic proof advances; "circumstances cannot lie," witnesses can and do. The upshot is that when the case comes for trial we may call as many witnesses as we like, but the realistic or, as lawyers call them, circumstantial proofs must be collected, compared, and arranged beforehand, so that the chief importance will attach not so much to the trial itself as to the *Preliminary Inquiry*

We venture to hope that this book will be of use to many besides Investigating Officers properly so called. Throughout the work the expression "Investigating Officer" is used as a compendious term to include all persons engaged in the investigation, official or non-official, of criminal cases. To all these, as well as to judges of all ranks and medical officers of all grades, this work is intended to appeal.

This volume is designed to be a working hand-book for all engaged or interested in Criminal Investigation. It was, by special permission, translated and adapted from the well-known work of *Dr. Hans Gross*, Professor of Criminology in the University of Prague and special lecturer on that subject in the University of Vienna. Translations have appeared in various languages, including French, Spanish, Danish, Russian, Hungarian, Servian, and Japanese. *Dr. Gross* has been for many years "*body and soul*" an Investigating Officer. As *M. Gardeil*, Professor of Criminal Law at Nancy, says, in introducing the French translation to French Criminalists, *Dr. Gross* is "an indefatigable observer, a far-seeing psychologist, a magistrate full of ardour to unearth the truth, whether in favour of the accused or against him, a clever craftsman, in turn, draughtsman, photographer, modeller, armourer, having acquired by long experience a profound knowledge of the practices of criminals, robbers, tramps, gipsies, cheats, he opens to us the researches and experiences of many years. His work is no dry or purely technical treatise, *it is a living book, because it has been lived.*"

The book, following the author's arrangement, has been divided into four parts. Part I. is designed, in the first place, to enunciate general principles and qualities, inform the investigator in a general way of what assistance science can afford in the investigation of crime, and in a more detailed manner to show in just what cases expert knowledge may be effectively brought to bear. Advice is also given regarding the examination of witnesses and accused and the inspection of localities. Parts II and III. deal respectively with various heads of knowledge and certain handicrafts with which every Investigating Officer should be thoroughly well acquainted, while Part IV. gives information upon the methods of criminals in committing particular offences.

In the first edition the references amounted to no fewer than 1242, and were collected in an appendix. They utilised 67 pages of small type. This has now been omitted, as the majority of these references were to foreign and not easily accessible treatises. A number of references to standard works have, however, been retained in the text itself. In this adaptation of *Dr. Gross's* book many works of experts have been referred to and from some of these excerpts have been made, but to no unreasonable extent. No quotation or extract has been taken from any author without acknowledgment *in loco*.

J. COLLYER ADAM.

CRIMINAL INVESTIGATION.

PART I.—GENERAL.

CHAPTER I

THE INVESTIGATING OFFICER.

Section i.—General Considerations.

Of all the duties that an official can be called upon to perform in the course of his service those of an Investigating Officer are certainly not the least important. That his services to the public are great and his labours full of interest will be generally admitted, but rarely, even among specialists is full credit given to the difficulties of the position. An Investigating Officer should possess the vigour of youth, energy ever on the alert, robust health and extensive acquaintance with all branches of the law. He ought to know men, proceed skilfully and possess liveliness and vigilance. Tact is indispensable, true courage is required in many situations, and he must be always ready on emergency to risk his health and life, as when dangerous criminals are dealt with, fatiguing journeys undertaken, persons stricken with infectious diseases examined, or dangerous *post-mortems* attended. He has to solve problems relating to every branch of human knowledge, he ought to be acquainted with languages, he should know what the medical man can tell him and what to ask the medical man, he must be as conversant with the dodges of the poacher as with the wiles of the stock jobber, as well acquainted with the method of fabricating a will as with the cause of a railway accident, he must know the tricks of card-sharpers, why boilers explode, how a horse-coper can turn an old screw into a young hunter. He should be able to pick his way through account books, to understand slang, to read ciphers and be familiar with the processes and tools of all classes of workmen.

But it is not on the day of his appointment alone that an Investigating Officer can learn all this or acquire the activity and perspicacity requisite for his work. It should therefore be a fundamental rule only to nominate as Investigating Officer those who, besides being mentally and bodily fit, possess a veritable encyclopædic culture, who know the world, have observed life, and have undergone many experiences, finally, who are ready to place at the service of society with all the energy of which they are capable the knowledge thus painfully acquired. Every criminalist knows that the Investigating Officer in the exercise of his functions may be compelled to draw on all, absolutely all, the varied knowledge he has amassed, and that he will feel at least once in his life a profound regret for his ignorance of what he has neglected to acquire.

If an Investigating Officer is wanting in such general information the cause is lack of interest in the work, and in this case he will never make a good Investigating Officer. He will do well to seek without delay to utilise his legal knowledge, which may perhaps be of great value, in other branches of judicial work. As an Investigating Officer he will not only fail to play his role well but his life will be miserable, he will be definitely forced to busy himself with affairs that do not interest him and, being deficient in the necessary information, he will never secure good results. He will be obliged to confess, sooner or later, that he is not occupying a situation suitable to him, and nothing is more discouraging to a man than work under such conditions. He who would spare himself such disappointment ought to make sure of possessing the qualities indispensable to an Investigating Officer before entering on this thorny and difficult career.

But knowledge alone is not everything. The Investigating Officer must possess not only legal and other acquirements, a general training, special fitness, and ideas ever ready for development, but also such a complete devotion to his profession that even outside the exercise of his official functions he will be always seeking to learn something calculated to extend his knowledge. He who seeks to learn only when some notable crime turns up will have great difficulty in learning anything at all. His knowledge should be acquired beforehand by constant application in his ordinary life. Every day, nay every moment, he must be picking up something in touch with his work. Thus the zealous Investigating Officer will note on his walks the footprints found on the dust of the highway, he will observe the tracks of animals, of the wheels of carriages, the marks of pressure on the grass where someone has sat or lain down, or perhaps deposited a burden. He will examine little pieces of paper that have been thrown away, marks or injuries on trees, displaced stones, broken glass or pottery, doors and windows open or shut in an unusual manner. Everything will afford an opportunity for drawing conclusions and explaining what must have previously taken place. For what we call "adducing proof" consists only in concluding from the knowledge of one fact the knowledge of other facts which must have followed or preceded it. And these lessons must be learned in advance in connection with matters of small importance and not waited for until some murder has to be investigated. Quite insignificant words uttered by passers-by, striking the ear by chance, or little suspicious acts accidentally observed, may afford precious opportunities for putting two and two together. It is equally useful to get others to relate events, insignificant or important, at which they as well as oneself have been present. These recitals, supposing that those who make them really wish to speak the truth, are extremely interesting on account of their variations, and this is the simplest and indeed only way of learning how the depositions of witnesses should be appreciated.

Nor ought the budding Investigating Officer to neglect any opportunity of obtaining information concerning any profession, the work of an artisan, technical processes, etc, etc, nor, *last not least*, of learning to know men For this every man with whom we come in contact may be taken as an object of study, and whoever takes the trouble can always learn something from the biggest fool

Section ii.—The Duties of the Investigating Officer.

If we now ask "How should the Investigating Officer set about his work?" we can come to but one conclusion His whole heart must be set upon success" It not, he reduces his work to the mere dispatching of documents and firing off reports as fast as he can If he would succeed in each inquiry his work will be by no means easy, smooth, or peaceful, on the contrary, he will have to devote himself completely and continually to his task, working with all his might and never pausing for rest

Nervous people are useless as investigators Success in a mission means the complete elucidation of the business in hand No matter what may be his profession, a man must, if he be conscientious, bring his task to a successful termination But here is not a task in which one can advance little by little, along a natural and clearly demarcated route, terminating when one has completed a certain amount of work mapped out in advance, there is always a new problem to unravel, the investigator whose work is half done has accomplished nothing Either he has solved the problem and quite finished the work, that means success or he has done nothing, absolutely nothing

Obtaining a result" must not be confused with "producing an effect" The work of the investigator ought to make neither noise nor sensation suffice it that the culprit must be discovered at any price To succeed in his mission the Investigating Officer must just commence his work at the start with the resolution of devoting to it every effort humanly possible and the determination not to pause till it is finished The end has not been attained simply by the elucidation of the affair in an ordinary way It is very easy and convenient to say, "It is impossible to go further" But if one says continually, "Another step forward must be taken," one finally advances several leagues In every case that he has to solve the Investigating Officer has first to obtain facts, often not without worry and trouble As adversaries he has the accused, and often the witnesses, circumstances, natural events, difficulties that crop up from time to time, and if he loses sight of the proverb, 'If you don't allow yourself to be beaten to-day, you are saved a hundred times over," then on the first difficulty arising he will throw up the sponge He will take a difficulty for an impossibility and say "Thus far and no further"

Section iii.—The Procedure of the Investigating Officer.

When he starts work, the most important thing for the Investigating Officer is to discover the exact moment when he can form a definite opinion The importance of this cannot be too much insisted upon, for upon it success or failure often depends If he should come to a definite conclusion too soon a preconceived opinion may be formed, to which he will always be attached with more or less tenacity till he is forced to abandon it entirely by then his most precious moments will have passed away, the best clues will have been lost—often beyond the possibility of recovery. If on the other hand he misses the true moment for forming an opinion, the inquiry becomes a purposeless groping in the dark and a search devoid of aim. When will the Investigating Officer find this true moment, this psychological instant of which we speak? It is impossible to lay down a general rule all that can be said is, that the Investigating Officer will of necessity always find it if he set to work under the guidance of fixed and immutable principles, never losing sight of the fact that a "definite opinion" *on an affair as a whole* will not come to him all of a sudden, to arrive at it he must advance step by step while making use of such "definite opinions" as may be prudently formed about phenomena, facts, and isolated events *as they arise.*

The case must be taken up from the start with an open mind. The complaint or information received by the Investigating Officer ought to have no more value in his eyes than this statement, "It is said that such and such a crime has been committed at such and such a place." Even if details about the perpetrator, the injury, the motive, etc., are published, he should attach no more importance to them than if he had heard the remark, "It is said that the affair must have happened thus." Supposing that an important crime is involved and he repairs to the scene, certainly a great number of strong and lively impressions will bring themselves to bear upon him and the task of ordering them in his mind will be hard enough. In addition he will receive communications from all quarters, officials, authorised and unauthorised, desire to make statements more or less important, he does not wish to dismiss them for they may tell him something which he will be able to turn to account in forming at once, if he is so disposed, a definite opinion. His work at this important stage of the inquiry must enter into great detail, just as if he gathered up with a sponge one by one all the drops of water he sees, in order, when it is quite soaked, to squeeze into a basin all the drops that have been collected. No matter for the moment whether the drops are clear liquid or dirty slush, he gathers them all in. Little by little as the work advances, certain opinions and ideas become separated and fixed such or such a witness makes a good impression and one begins to believe what he states, an idea is obtained of the way in which the criminal has reached the spot account is taken of the instruments he has employed, or certain indications appear which restrict the period of time in which the deed must have been committed.

When a certain number of ideas on the incidents of the case, considered individually, seem at length determined, the Investigating Officer will seek to obtain a precise idea of the way in which everything has happened, even if only the most general view be possible. Perhaps the conclusion will be forced on him that the real facts are not what they appear on the surface and that a false complexion has been given to them, or on the other hand he may be enabled to say with certainty that a crime of such or such a nature has been committed. In short the Investigating Officer will be sufficiently advanced to erect a framework on which a provisional theory or scheme may be developed. To set out this scheme beforehand would be superfluous and dangerous superfluous because it may have to be changed at any moment, dangerous because with a prematurely formed plan one can easily get off the track and proceed in a wrong direction. We do not imply that the Investigating Officer must not at the beginning establish a classification to be followed in his operations, for without that he would only grope about, finding nothing and advancing nowhither, but between a provisional classification to guide inquiry and a definite scheme of the crime there is a great difference.

But if it is difficult to construct the plan of campaign, it is still more difficult to conduct the inquiry according to that plan. A scheme of inquiry cannot be compared with a scheme devised in view of circumstances which can be brought into existence and modified at will. It is drawn up in view of circumstances which alter of themselves, which are often unknown and which do not depend on the person applying the scheme. It resembles, not the design of a house to be built, but a plan of campaign. It is based upon data which the Investigating Officer possesses, or believes himself to possess, when he constructs it. It must be rigidly adhered to as long as these data are unchanged or have undergone only their natural development, but it must be modified in part or in whole as soon as these data are found to have changed or to be false. One would imagine that this could be done quite naturally and spontaneously, but such is human nature that so simple a principle is rarely conformed to.

The greater difficulty there is in securing anything, the more one holds on to it, that is why fools are so obstinate. They never willingly abandon an idea, because they have had trouble in getting it into their heads. Now the scheme of an inquiry is difficult to follow out, and, when one has already worked in conformity therewith, it is not willingly abandoned, but still pursued unthinkingly and almost automatically. It happens at times that one perceives all of a sudden that one is following with exact minuteness a plan based upon data the falsity of which should have become apparent long ago, or which are so modified that the work constructed, if not built altogether in the air, is quite crooked. This advice may seem pedantic, yet, however unimportant an inquiry may be at each step (examination of witnesses, visits to localities, technical or expert reports, etc.), the information upon which a scheme has been based, must be verified anew, to ascertain if the data remain unchanged and, if not, in what way the scheme must be modified.

It will therefore be not only the easiest but usually also the best and safest way to construct the hypothesis in the simplest possible manner. Strange and extraordinary suppositions should be disregarded. And never forget the one great stupid fault which a criminal nearly always commits, especially in big crimes. It has happened hundreds of times that criminal investigators, already on the right track, have left it thinking "The man who has committed this crime cannot have been so foolish as to do that," but innumerable cases prove that he *has* been so foolish. It matters not whether he was confused, suddenly frightened, has made a miscalculation, acted hastily, or what not. It is therefore always best for the Investigating Officer to take the simplest view at the outset.

Pfister in his "Curious Criminal Cases" rightly says :—' The greatest art of the Investigating Officer consists in conducting the inquiry in such a way that the initiated at once perceive that there has been 'a directing intelligence,' while the uninitiated imagine that everything has fallen into place of its own accord." But in order to perceive this 'directing intelligence,' the whole must rest upon a scheme continually verified and thoroughly carried out. How often do we not come across inquiries where the Investigating Officer has started on an excellent plan, but has adhered to it with desperate tenacity even when the data upon which it was based have long since changed. Thus to continue to follow a line the falsity of which has been demonstrated, may sometimes prove more fatal and more dangerous than to grope about with no plan at all: in the latter case it is still possible to hit the right clue, in the former it is impossible. The case for instance, where an inquiry runs the greatest risk of failure is when the scheme supposes a certain person to have been the author of the crime, and after having worked entirely with this idea it suddenly becomes evident that that person is innocent.

When an almost incalculable amount of time has been lost on such a false scent, it may be concluded as a general rule that the inquiry will prove abortive. The Investigating Officer has expressed his ideas on the manner in which things have come about, he has utilised the elements of proof in view of a predetermined result, and, what is graver still, he has allowed time to slip away. And now his original supposition has been found to be false, he has first to combat his own discouragement and that of his assistants. If a new scheme is drawn up he cannot muster the same degree of interest, and the elements of proof seem neither so certain nor so useful. Many have disappeared and can no longer be found, and with each production of new proofs he will make the objection, or others will make it for him, that in the original scheme they would have borne another meaning and pointed to another conclusion. There is only one way to obviate such a danger, never to allow himself to be dominated exclusively by one idea and never to follow exclusively that sole idea.

In the preceding pages the title 'Investigating Officer' has, as explained in the preface, been used in a comprehensive sense, but it will be well to point out that there may be two or more Investigators. In many countries criminal procedure, in addition to taking care that the Magistrate possessing jurisdiction should be kept constantly in touch with the labour of the police, provides both for an "Investigation" by a police officer and an 'Inquiry" by a Magistrate. These may be going on simultaneously, and if there be friction or jealousy between the two authorities, only the most sanguine would hope for success. But let us assume—and we trust the assumption is permissible—that both are working together with a single eye to promote the ends of justice. That he may develop or modify his plans in the way described, the Magistrate, to economise his forces, must *have, understand,* and *know how to make use of,* his associates and subordinates. It is common enough to hear the remarks, "The Magistrate is not a policeman" 'That is police work', 'The Magistrate has something else to do'. Those who adopt this tone can hardly quote in its favour success scored by them. The Magistrate of course ought not personally to interfere in matters which do not concern him but he should keep the reins in his hands and guide the whole team, whatever the police do ought to fit in with the scheme of the Magistrate The actual work may at times have to be done by the police alone, but the police should work strictly under the directions of the Magistrate

The police are sometimes found in a false position in being placed either too high or too low Too low when the Magistrate deems it useless to march abreast of the police does not desire to work with them, and draws, between their work and his, too deep and inflexible a line of demarcation Too high, when the Magistrate accords the police complete independence, lets them have all their own way and afterwards accepts as absolutely definite and certain what has been done solely on their own responsibility The police will be found in their proper place only when the Magistrate co-ordinates the efforts of both, works sympathetically with them in the recognised interests of justice keeps them well acquainted with all he has done and all he intends to do, when in short he has but one ambition, to bring the work to a successful conclusion But if on the one side the Magistrate thus marches hand in hand without jealousy, he must on the other firmly demand that the control of the inquiry be placed immediately and completely in his hands, that nothing be done without his knowledge, and that everything he has ordered be carried out in the way prescribed Every police officer who has his duty at heart, should willingly accept this situation The ends of justice will be furthered, and the Magistrate will have at his disposal men devoted to him, and, because they have confidence in him, working well and expeditiously But the Magistrate must *know* his men, not only know their worth in a general way, but know what they are thinking about in each particular case

Suppose that sufficient light has been thrown in an important case to arouse suspicion against a particular person or to give an accurate idea of the nature of the offence (for instance, whether it be a theft or a pretended theft for the purpose of hiding a breach of trust) The Investigating Officer in the course of the inquiry ought to come to a conclusion one way or the other and form his opinion Admit that the proof is strong enough for suspecting X to be the perpetrator of the crime and for ordering his arrest As we have said, the Investigating Officer ought not to follow blindly and solely the idea that X can alone be the author of the crime, but neither ought he, under risk of complicating the case, to set out at the same time in several other directions It is at this moment he must *possess* his men, *know* them, and *see that they serve him* He will *possess* them if, as we have indicated he is on good terms with them he will *know* them if he has constantly kept in contact with them, and he will *know they will serve him* if in choosing them he takes into consideration first their character and education and then the ideas they have on the case in hand, for some concession ought to be made to a man's ideas and he ought to be employed on a suitable task

Now suppose that certain police officials have been the first strongly to suspect X The best way to make use of their zeal and good will will be naturally to make them continue to follow the same track and search for other motives for suspecting X If the suspicions against X are not overwhelming the Investigator will not forget that some police officials are of a different opinion and have even suspected another person. As these latter officers must have some grounds in support of their opinion, he will ask for these reasons, and, if they do not appear to be altogether ill founded by reason of other grounds that contradict them, those very officials who have conceived the idea ought to be entrusted with the duty of following their own clue. If other officers take yet another view of the matter, these again will be charged with watching that idea, the fruit of their own reasoning, that it will be the object of the most careful attention we may be quite certain. When the Investigating Officer has taken care to employ upon every imaginable clue which promises to bring forth some discovery the men most fitted to each, he is then free to direct all his efforts to the point where in his own opinion the correct clue is to be found. He will from time to time collect the reports of those searching in other directions, will examine their information, and compare it with his own results. Should he not even then be convinced that another clue is the right one, this method of proceeding will spare him many disagreeable surprises. It often enough happens that the real criminal is supposed to be found and is actually handed over to justice, the police assume that all is over and fold their arms. But the Magistrate goes on with his inquiry and is finally obliged to release the supposed "real criminal," to the discomfiture of the police; there is nothing more to be done, the matter is ended till "further orders," and immediately sinks into oblivion.

Another important matter relating to the police is, How to act when things have gone wrong? It is quite natural that the Investigating Officer should not spare himself, but he must treat with equal severity all who work with him and are under his orders, to ensure their performing their duty to the end; he must act with rigour every time he discovers a breach of duty. But if the faults committed turn out to be only mistakes, he should treat them with the greatest indulgence, letting his subordinates clearly understand that nowhere is it so necessary to acknowledge as soon as possible a mistake which has been committed, as in the service of public order and justice. Above all it must be well recognised, that as nowhere else is it easier to make a mistake, so nowhere should mistakes be more readily pardoned. It cannot be repeated too often that nowhere is a mistake more fatal and more dangerous than where the question is that of discovering a crime and its perpetrator; but it must also be said that nowhere can a mistake be more completely repaired, provided it is discovered at once and frankly acknowledged. An individual cannot be expected never to make mistakes, but those occupied in criminal matters must be honest and conscientious enough to immediately recognise and freely confess their errors.

If the question be asked, To what points the Investigating Officer should direct the attention of the police? the answer will depend entirely upon the case in question, for no general rule can be laid down on the subject. But we may say that the Investigating Officer ought to attempt to delineate to his subordinates the salient characteristics of the case. Only the man possessed of psychological training can carry out the task. The most experienced police officer may very well perform to perfection everything necessary to his own functions, but he can rarely specialize the characteristics of a given case. This is the work of the Investigating

Officer. He will distinguish the present from similar cases in the past. He will look for its special character by reference to the actual crime, to the victim, and to the suspect, drawing indications therefrom as to the directions in which, at least for the moment, search need not be made. The police officer finds it just as easy to accept views pointed out to him and grasp the details of a crime when his attention has been drawn to them, as he finds it difficult to form the first picture of a given case.

Finally it is part of the business of the Investigating Officer to indicate to the police (we are speaking now specially with regard to towns or large villages) the principal persons who can give information about important crimes,—drivers of public conveyances, messengers, prostitutes etc. Though the importance of these persons is well recognised yet recourse to them is often neglected. Their importance is manifest for three reasons *firstly*, they are not in regular employment and generally possess time and opportunity during a great part of the day to observe their neighbours business. Their districts and resorts are habitually fixed and during their hours of idleness they can notice anything that takes place out of the ordinary. From these persons information will in most cases be obtained as to the customary conduct of such and such an individual, be he the victim or the criminal, what he used to do and used not to do, with whom he associated, what were his earnings, how much he spent, when he went out, and when he came in, and so on. They may also be able to tell of something unusual that happened at the time of the crime either as regards money paid, meetings, goings and comings, or the demeanour of the parties. The *second* ground for the importance of these classes of persons relates not so much to themselves as to the criminal himself, who will in a very great number of cases have had relations with them before and perhaps after the crime. Often after the commission of a crime a suspect will be in funds and will try to get away quickly and without being seen from the neighbourhood of the crime. This is when he will engage a public conveyance. He will employ a messenger to send off letters, raise money, or make purchases for him. And finally he will need amusement and distraction and will have recourse to a prostitute. The *third* ground for the importance of this category of persons is that each class forms a body of which the members have very extended relations with one another. A hackney carriage driver in towns of ordinary size, knows nearly all the others of the same fraternity, a commissionaire knows the other commissionaires, a prostitute other prostitutes. In consequence of the relations existing between these persons, what one knows the others learn, and the police officer can therefore generally obtain from them the information he wants. But in this he will not succeed if he only starts on the day following some great crime to make the necessary acquaintance with these classes. This he must have done long before, he must know these people and possess their confidence, then alone can he obtain information on the points he wishes to know about. But it is the Investigating Officer that ought previously to draw the attention of the police to the importance of these points. He ought not indeed to manufacture satellites and spies, but simply take measures to bring a number of persons into co-operation with himself in the service of justice.

There is an old adage that the Investigating Officer can often remember to good purpose, namely, "*Cherchez la femme,*" "Seek for the woman." Sounding rather like a phrase in a novel every practitioner of experience will certify that it contains a large portion of truth. Mistakes however can be made in relying on it, either by believing that the crime, no matter what, has been instigated by a woman, or by declaring the explanation sufficient only because the name of some woman has been mentioned during the inquiry. In the first case one goes too far, in the second the goal has not yet been reached. The proper procedure is to endeavour, without any pedantic obstinacy, to look for a woman as having been an influencing factor in the crime. The suggestion of a crime does not always of necessity emanate from a woman, but one will frequently find that the most important deeds done before or after the crime itself have been done at the instigation of a woman or on account of a woman. This is assuredly not a minor point. We never feel sure of our case when we can assign no motive for some important action revealed by the inquiry, and we are not disposed to believe that such an action has taken place so long as we do not know what the motive is. The Investigating Officer will therefore always do well to admit at the beginning that a woman may have something to do with the crime; it is not necessarily so, but inquiry in that direction is recommended. Take the simplest of facts, a farm servant steals wheat in order to buy a pair of shoes for his young woman, an honest woodcutter has turned poacher so as to be able to cut a dash in new buckskin breeches before his girl, or let us go further and take a great political trial, in which we see how an offended beauty stirs up partisans to carry out projects tending to the overthrow of the State, everywhere we find a woman.

Offences against property are committed for the purpose of getting married or spending the proceeds on prostitutes. At balls, dancing parties, and public assemblies of all kinds, brawls for the most part break out on account of women. The safest hiding-place for stolen objects is with a woman of apparent innocence. It is almost always with the aid of a woman that criminals succeed in escaping and concealing themselves. In frauds and coining on a large scale, women are almost always the agents for putting false goods into circulation. The worst gambling dens are invariably run by women, crimes of passion innumerable have been committed on account of women, and many men have turned criminal through associating with them. Every criminal expert almost without exception, having a certain amount of experience, is wont in criminal matters to go in search of the woman as a matter of course. Doubtless mistakes and errors may arise from that procedure, but for all that one must never forget the old adage.

Section iv.—Preconceived Theories.

The method of proceeding just described, that namely, in which parallel investigations are instituted, which to a certain extent mutually control each other, is the best, and one is tempted to say the only, way of avoiding the great dangers of a "preconceived theory"—the most deadly enemy of all inquiries. Preconceived theories are so much the more dangerous as it is precisely the most zealous Investigating Officer, the officer most interested in his work, who is the most exposed to them. The indifferent investigator who makes a routine of his work has as a rule no opinion at all and leaves the case to develop itself. When one delves into the case with enthusiasm one can easily find a point to rely on, but one may interpret it badly or attach an exaggerated importance to it. An opinion is formed which cannot be got rid of. In carefully examining our own minds (we can scarcely observe phenomena of a purely psychical character in others), we shall have many opportunities of studying how preconceived theories take root, we shall often be astonished to see how accidental statements of almost no significance and often purely hypothetical have been able to give birth to a theory of which we can no longer rid ourselves without difficulty although we have for a long time recognised the rottenness of its foundation.

Nothing can be known if nothing has happened and yet, while still awaiting the discovery of the criminal, while yet only on the way to the locality of the crime one comes unconsciously to formulate a theory, doubtless not quite void of foundation but having only a superficial connection with the reality, you have already heard a similar story, perhaps you have formerly seen an analogous case; you have had an idea for a long time that things would turn out in such and such a way. This is enough the details of the case are no longer studied with entire freedom of mind. On a chance suggestion thrown out by another, a countenance which strikes one a thousand other fortuitous incidents above all losing sight of the association of ideas, end in a preconceived theory, which neither rests upon juridical reasoning nor is justified by actual facts.

Nor is this all often a definite line is taken up, as for instance by postulating, "If circumstances M and N are verified then the affair must certainly be understood in such and such a way." This reasoning may be all very well, but meanwhile, for some cause or other, the proof of M and N is long in coming, still the same idea remains in the head and is fixed there so firmly that it sticks even after the verification of M and N. has failed, and although the conditions laid down as necessary to its adoption as true have not been realised.

It also often happens that a preconceived theory is formed because the matter is examined from a false point of view. Optically, objects may appear quite different from what they really are, according to the point of view from which they are looked at. Morally, the same phenomenon happens, the matter is seen from a false point of view which the observer refuses at all costs to change and so he clings to his preconceived theory. In this situation the most insignificant ideas, if inexact, can prove very dangerous. Suppose a case of arson has been reported from a distant locality immediately in spite of oneself the scene is imagined, for example, one pictures the house, which one has never seen, as being on the left-hand side of the road. As the information is received at headquarters the idea formed about the scene becomes precise and fixed. In imagination the whole scene and its secondary details are presented, but everything is always placed on the left of the road. this idea ends by taking such a hold on the mind that one is convinced that the house is on the left, and all questions are asked as if one had seen the house in that position. But suppose the house to be really on the right of the road and that by chance the error is never rectified, suppose further that the situation of the house has some importance for the bringing out of the facts or in forming a theory of the crime, then this false idea may, in spite of its apparent insignificance, considerably confuse the investigation

All this really proceeds from psychical imperfection to which every man is subject. Much more fatal are delusions resulting from efforts to draw from a case more than it can yield. Granted that no Investigating Officer would wish by the aid of the smallest fraud to attach to a case a character different from or more important than that which it really possesses, yet it is only in conformity with human nature to stop the more willingly at what is more interesting than at what belongs to every-day life. We like to discover romantic features where they do not exist and we even prefer the recital of monstrosities and horrors to that of common every day facts. This is implanted in the nature of everyone, and though in some to a greater, in some to a lesser extent, still there it is. A hundred proofs, exemplified by what we read most, by what we listen to most willingly, by what sort of news spreads the fastest, show that the majority of men have received at birth a tendency to exaggeration. In itself this is no great evil, the penchant for exaggeration is often the penchant for beautifying our surroundings, and if there were no exaggeration we should lack the notions of beauty and poetry. But in the profession of the criminal expert everything bearing the least trace of exaggeration must be removed in the most energetic and conscientious manner; otherwise, the Investigating Officer will become an expert unworthy of his service and even dangerous to humanity. We cannot but insist that he should not let himself slip into exaggerations, that he should constantly with this object criticise his own work and that of others, and that he should examine it with extra care if he fail to find traces of exaggeration. These creep in in spite of us and when they exist no one knows where they will stop. The only remedy is to watch oneself most carefully, always work with reflection, and prune out everything having the least suspicion of exaggeration. It is precisely because a certain hardihood and prompt initiative are demanded of Investigating Officers that one finds in the best of them a slight leaning towards the fictitious; one will perceive it in careful observation of oneself and get rid of it by submission to severe discipline.

Krafft-Ebing, a psychologist of repute, has stated that great artists, poets, and actors are "mostly neuropathic individuals." We are sure that in saying this he does not intend to suggest that the occupations connected with art, poetry and the stage are conducive to madness, but that a certain neuropathic nature leads those who follow them to become what they have become, *i e*, their nature is the cause and not the effect of their occupations. But not only those who are called poets, artists and actors have this neuropathic nature, many other people in less poetic professions possess it. Though in an unpoetic profession they may be so highly intellectual that they may be called (as *Krafft-Ebing* has called them) "neuropathic people." Their nerves, it may be said, are of such a nature that they are poetically inclined. Those gifted in this way are the greatest amongst us, but at the same time they have the heaviest responsibility in using such gifts.

A special variation of the preconceived opinion consists in holding to the characterization first given to a fact. This characterization is based on the first impression and may be entirely justified by that impression, but another consideration comes in namely, to see if what has been noticed at the beginning continues to bear the same aspect throughout the inquiry. It is self-evident that details must be modified, but we do not here refer to these; we confine our attention to the nature of the crime.

The most important examples to be noticed here are those where the problem is whether a violent death is caused by suicide or by unknown causes. Too much attention cannot be given to cases of this kind; they will be treated of later e.g., *Chapter XVI, Section* vi. "Poisoning", *Section* iv. "Death by firearms", *Section* v. "Death by strangulation". Above all a minute examination must be proceeded with where persons are believed to have been drowned, to have fallen from a height, to have been suffocated, or to have died of sudden illnesses (with vomitings, diarrhœa, cramp, etc.)

It is safe to affirm with certainty that an enormous proportion of such cases is due to the hand of another. Many other crimes are often in reality quite different from what one wanted to take them for. The Investigating Officer of experience will disregard at first sight quite a series of crimes and will enquire whether he does not find himself in the presence of something quite different; to this category belongs robbery with violence, or armed with deadly weapons. People often pretend to have been victims to this grave crime where they wish to cover up the loss of money. The Investigating Officer must therefore be on his guard when a person declares that a sum of money has been stolen from his custody, even the grave wounds which the victim of the theft will pretend to have received may be disregarded. Often a man who has gone wrong, lost at cards, dissipated or hidden money held in trust will inflict such wounds upon himself. The author has met with two cases of this kind in which a peasant, having lost at play the money received for the sale of his cattle, made pretence of robbery merely to avoid the reproaches of his wife.

Rape again, is often set up to hide the downfall of a young girl who wishes to avoid her shame, by turning the pity and sympathy of everyone towards her; girls often enough invent attacks by quite unknown persons or, graver still, they bring false accusations against persons named. In such cases the real seducer is hardly ever accused of the rape,—he is spared —and no charge is made until the fact of pregnancy is certain. Then the woman allows herself to be seduced by a second person and the latter only is accused of the rape. Unhappily in this case the proof of the falsity of the charge can often only be made later on; at the birth of the child, the date of this shows that conception must have occurred long before the pretended rape. In such a case therefore, one must never neglect immediately after the birth to have the child examined by experts in order to know whether or not it has attained its full term, for, as we have supposed, at the time of the pretended rape the woman was already a long time enceinte.

It is not uncommon to find people who inflict wounds on themselves, such are, besides persons pretending to be the victims of assaults with deadly weapons, those who try to extort damages or blackmailers, thus it often happens that after an insignificant scuffle one of the combatants shows wounds which he pretends to have received. To this category also belong people who declare that certain named persons have recently caused them wounds which in reality date from a long time before the profit made in such cases from dislocations, old sores on the eyes or ears, and above all from rupture, is well known. Ninety per cent of affections of this kind, alleged to be the outcome of recent quarrels, bad treatment, etc., date from long before. Profit is also made from wounds received from machinery, etc., they are exaggerated or fraudulently mixed up with old complaints: the cure is also purposely delayed. We are acquainted with not a few cases where, when the author of the wounds is rich, all sorts of means are employed to keep them open or aggravate them in order to obtain a bigger indemnity. Railway and insurance companies are particularly exposed to frauds of this description.

It is only too little known that many quacks follow the profession of helping people who require "an artificial sickness." In some countries in which conscription exists, these gentlemen drive a roaring trade in giving young men illnesses to free them from military service. They can confer heart disease, carbuncle, jaundice, boils, skin diseases and injuries of every kind.

Singular, but not so very rare, are cases where individuals castrate themselves and impute these mutilations to nomads, gypsies, tinkers, pedlars, &c., but always to unknown people. It is characteristic of these voluntary mutilations that most frequently those who perform them do not quite complete the operation, and that they are for the most part men who manifest excessive piety, or lead a solitary life, as shepherds, gamekeepers, &c.

Among wrongs to property, theft and arson are the most frequently simulated. In the first case, loss of fortune and breach of trust are most frequently sought to be accounted for by the pretence of theft: as a rule it is not very difficult to prove the falsity. The most important point is for the Investigating Officer to remind himself continually that the theft may have been a sham. In many cases the point must be elucidated, it is not necessary to make a noise about it straight away, but let him keep this idea ever before him and examine from this aspect each of the circumstances. After considering what any fact would signify if there had been a real theft, let him ask himself what the fact would signify if the theft were only concocted. The Investigating Officer ought never to permit himself to abstain from making this examination by the rank and situation of the supposed victim of the theft, by the cleverness of the *mise-en-scene*, or by any other consideration. Not only must the self-made victim be exposed, but innocent people who may be suspected must be protected.

It often happens that people set fire to their own property in such a way as to arouse a suspicion that a fire has been started by others; their aim is often to obtain the amount for which they are insured, often to hide the bad state of their affairs, often to get rid of the traces of a murder or some other crime. In many cases the proof of these facts is not so difficult as it appears. The important point is always to remember that it is possible that they may have wished to hide something; this ought not to be from the start a suspicion amounting to strong probability, but only a door open to every explanation. In order to know exactly the attitude to be maintained towards what has passed, all the circumstances of the crime must be clearly taken into account and submitted to strict logical examination from their commencement to their last stage. If at a given moment something has not been explained, suspicion is justified and pause must be made at the point where the logical sequence is broken, for the purpose of examining if there is no better way of explaining the fact. If one is found the rest of the inquiry is easy.

Section v.—Certain Qualities essential to an Investigating Officer.

It goes almost without saying that an Investigating Officer should be endowed with all those qualities which every man should desire to possess —indefatigable zeal and application, self-denial and perseverance, swiftness in reading men and a thorough knowledge of human nature, education and an agreeable manner, an iron constitution, and encyclopædic knowledge. Still there are some special qualities the importance of which is frequently overlooked, and to which attention may be peculiarly and forcibly directed.

First and above all an Investigating Officer must possess an abundant store of energy, nothing is more deplorable than a crawling, lazy, and sleepy Investigating Officer. Such a man is fit to be a gentleman-at-large. He who recognises that he is wanting in energy can but turn to something else for he will never make a good investigator. Again the Investigating Officer must be energetic not only in special circumstances, as when, for example, he finds himself face to face with a witness or an accused person who is hot-headed, refractory, and aggressive, or when the work takes him away from office and he proceeds to record a deposition or make an arrest without having his staff or office bell to aid him, but energy must always be displayed when he tackles a difficult, complicated, or obscure case. It is truly painful to examine a report which shows that the Investigating Officer has only fallen to his work with timidity, hesitation and nervousness, just touching it, so to speak, with the tips of his fingers but there is satisfaction in observing that a case has been attacked energetically and grasped with animation and vigour. The want of special cleverness and long practice can often be compensated by getting a good grip of the case but want of energy can be compensated by nothing. Those incomparable words of Goethe, true for all men, are above all true for the criminal expert,

> "Strike not thoughtlessly a nest of wasps,
> But if you strike, strike hard"

The Investigating Officer must have a high grade of real self-denying power. It is not enough for him to be a clever reckoner, a fine speculator, a careful weigher of facts, and to possess a good business head, he must also be self-denying, unostentatious and perfectly honest, resigning at the outset all thoughts of magnificent public successes. The happy-go-lucky apprehension of the policeman, the effective summing-up of the judge, the clever conduct of the case by counsel, all meet with acknowledgment, astonishment and admiration from the public but such triumphs are not for the Investigating Officer. If the latter be working well, those few people who have had an opportunity of really studying the case as it goes along will discover his unceasing and untiring work from the documents on the record and will form some correct idea of the brain work, power of combination and extensive knowledge which the Investigating Officer has employed. The Investigating Officer will be held responsible for the smallest and most pardonable mistake, while his care and his merits are seldom acknowledged. Let him be conscious of having done his duty in the only possible way. Beyond this we can only say, "Virtue is its own reward."

Another quality demanded at any price from the Investigating Officer is absolute accuracy. We do not mean by this that he must set out details in the official records exactly as they have been seen or said, for it goes without saying that this will be so done. The quality indicated consists in not being content with mere evidence of third parties or hearsay when it is possible for him to ascertain the truth with his own eyes or by more minute investigation. This is to say no more than that he should be accurate in his work, in the sense of being "exact," as that word is used in its highest scientific signification. Indeed the high degree of perfection to which all sciences have to-day attained is entirely due to "exact" work, and if we compare a recent scientific work, whatever the subject, with an analogous book written some decades ago, we shall notice a great difference between them arising almost wholly from the fact that the work of to-day is more exact than that of yesterday. Naturally in all inquiries a certain amount of imagination is necessary, but a comparison between two scientists of our time will always be to the advantage of the one whose work is most exact the brilliant and fruitful ideas of the scientist which astonish the world being often far from sudden and happy inspirations but the outcome of exact research. In close observation of facts, in searching for their remotest causes, in making unwearied comparisons, in instituting disagreeable experiments, in short, in attempting to elucidate a problem, the Investigating Officer will observe it under so many aspects and passing through so many phases that new ideas will spontaneously come to him which, if found to be accurate and skilfully utilised, will certainly give positive results. Since "exactness," or accuracy of work, is of so much importance in all branches of research, this accuracy must also be applied to the work of the Investigating Officer. But what is to be understood by accurate work? It consists in not trusting to others but attending to the business oneself, and even in mistrusting oneself and going through the case again and again. By so proceeding one will certainly bring about an accurate piece of work. A thousand mistakes of every description would be avoided if people did not base their conclusions upon premises furnished by others, take as established fact what is only possibility, or as a constantly recurring incident what has only been observed but once. True it is that in his work the Investigating Officer can see but a trifling portion of the facts nor can he repeat his observations. He is obliged largely to trust to what others tell him and it is just here that the difficulty and insufficiency of his work lie. But this inconvenience can to a certain extent be remedied, on the one hand by wherever possible, making sure of things for himself instead of accepting what others tell him, and on the other hand by trying to give a more exact form to the statements of others, by comparison, experiment, and demonstration, for the purpose of testing the veracity of the deponent's observation and obtaining from him something exact, or at least more exact than before. In endeavouring to verify the facts for himself the Investigating Officer must personally examine localities, make measurements and comparisons, and so form his own opinion. If a small matter which can only be established by accurate observation is in question, not *data* furnished incidentally, but only ascertained facts and investigations specially carried out, must be relied upon.

In an important case the circumstantial evidence had been brought together and conclusions thereby suggested drawn, results which might have been of decisive importance in clearing up the case. At the last moment it came into the head of some outsider to ask if the distance between two points was really two thousand paces. That was one of the grounds of the argument so artistically built up; in fact two witnesses had declared the distance to be two thousand paces. It was decided to send a policeman to visit the ground, and when the distance was found to be only four hundred and fifty paces the new conclusions rendered necessary contradicted the former ones. This is a typical example among hundreds of similar instances.

It is much more difficult to point out how depositions can be rendered more exact, when they cannot be verified by actual inspection, *de visu*. Let it be granted that the witness is really desirous of speaking the truth and is merely a bad observer. In general the matter should be elucidated by experiment, by ocular demonstration. Suppose a witness affirms that he was beaten by H for ten minutes. Let a watch be placed before him and ask him to take good note of how long ten minutes lasts and then say whether it was really ten minutes. After a quarter of a minute he will exclaim, " It certainly did not last longer than that." Again, a witness asserts that he is perfectly certain that he heard a cry coming from below, but trials on the spot prove that he never can guess correctly whether a cry comes from right or left, above or below. Again, a witness says that, though he did not look very closely, H held at least twelve coins in his hand, that he can swear to. " Very well," he is asked, " How many coins have I at present in my hand?" " Also about twelve," he answers. But there are twenty-three. Again, a witness declares, " When once I see a man I always recognise him again." " Did you see the witness who went out as you came in?" you ask him. " Certainly I saw him very well," he answers. " All right, go and pick him out from ten other persons."

A witness estimates an important distance at, let us say, 200 yards; let him be brought out of doors and say how far might be 100, 200, 300, 400 yards. If now these distances be measured, one can easily judge if and with what degree of accuracy, the witness can judge distances. As this judging of distances is often necessary, it becomes important to measure beforehand from a convenient window certain visible fixed points and to note the distances for future examinations. For years the author had many occasions for doing so from his office-room window and knew for instance — to the left corner of the house—65 yards, to the poplar tree—120, to the church spire—210, to the small house—100, to the railway—950. By these distances he has often tested witnesses. If the witness proves fairly accurate in his estimates, his evidence may be considered important for the case under investigation. One can even rectify wrong estimates, if for instance we find out that the witness is accustomed to estimate always too high or too low we can correct them by a species of personal equation

Such checks give the most instructive and remarkable results, whoever practises them will soon be convinced that their importance cannot be exaggerated

If accuracy of work is necessary in even the most insignificant cases, it becomes in the highest degree important in serious cases where increased working material must be laid out for the future and a base of operations established. Here often the most incomprehensible things happen. While perusing the papers connected with grave cases one often remarks that, the base of operations once established, the work has been carried on with the greatest care and accuracy and much sagacity has been expended. But all this has been a dead loss, for in establishing the base of operations an accessory circumstance of seeming insignificance has not been accurately observed or estimated, a false premise has been included, and the whole of the stately fabric built up so laboriously reposes on a tottering and yielding foundation. Two cases will be described giving a clear idea of what has been said

In the first, interesting for more than one consideration, the singular fact came to light that the Investigating Officer actually stood for a long time above the corpse of the murdered man without being able to find him. A blood-stained coat was found on the bank of a river in a fairly large town, about the same time a man named J S who lived not far from this place disappeared. On inquiries being made the coat was discovered to be that of J S. The latter could not be traced Fifteen days later an old saw-setter turned up and declared that one morning (just after the disappearance) he had noticed traces of blood at a certain spot near the river in question but not on the bank where the coat had been found. The saw-setter could not read and was very deaf, so that he had not heard till some time afterwards about the disappearance of J S and of his probable murder. The place where the traces of blood were found was beside a bridge and at that point the river was banked up to a considerable depth and bordered by a very high wall. Behind this wall the snow gathered from the streets of the town was usually thrown. After every snowfall great masses of snow were thrown over at this place, and, as in winter the river hardly ever came up to the foot of the wall, a bank of snow twelve feet long and twelve feet deep often became heaped up and did not melt till late in the spring. From the blood discovered by the saw-setter, which had long since disappeared, it was supposed that the dead man had been thrown over the spikes that crowned the wall on to the bank of snow below, and that he had been immediately buried beneath the sweepings of a heavy snowfall that had taken place on the night of his disappearance and which had been collected and thrown over in the early morning. This took place on the 15th December. It had snowed again on the 20th and 27th December, and on each occasion fresh quantities of snow had been thrown on to the bank in question, but during that winter no snowfall was so heavy as the first. The investigators began to shovel these masses of snow into the river for the purpose of finding the corpse of the murdered man. Representatives of Justice were present in order to draw up reports in the event of a discovery being made. Now the Investigating Officer desired to know whether the first snowfall had really taken place on the 15th December, that is to say, on the night of the disappearance of J S, he himself having no exact recollection on the point. He was informed that the 15th December was the date of the *second* snowfall, which was not nearly such a heavy one as the first, so that the body ought to be found resting on a bed of snow of a considerable depth formed by the first very abundant snowfall. It was added that on the 15th, this bed must have been 6 to 8 feet in height. It was then decided to dig until they had arrived approximately at the first bed of snow, where the murdered man ought to be found. They dug and shovelled away the snow, and when what remained was no more than four feet in depth and it was certain that they had long before reached the first bed the work was abandoned. But the sawsetter though old and deaf was not mistaken, for when the late spring had melted away the snow, the corpse of the murdered man was found quite at the bottom, on the ground bordering the river and at the very spot over which the Investigating Officer had stood for hours when the snow was being shovelled away. The explanation was simply that the people questioned by the Investigating Officer concerning the date of the first snowfall were mistaken, the fall of the 15th December was not the second but the first of that winter, the corpse had been thrown over the wall when as yet no snow had been deposited beneath it, and it was therefore necessary to search below and not above the first bed. If the Investigating Officer had been more accurately informed about the date of the first fall, he would have removed that bed as well and the corpse would have been found. But much time had run on and to this day the author of the crime is unknown.

The second case also relates to a murder and points out how inexact indications furnished by a large number of witnesses might have turned suspicion from the real criminals and let it fall upon an entirely innocent person. Two peasants of evil reputation and involved circumstances, Sp and B, had induced a third peasant T, an old man, to accompany them to a cattle market, some considerable distance away, for the purpose of purchasing cattle. They left their common residence at S together in the early morning and walked as far as L where they rested during the middle of the day. At three o'clock they set out again with the object of going by way of V to D there to pass the night, so as to arrive the morning after at M the place where the market was to be held only a league distant. The next day T was found stretched in the ditch beside the road between the places L and V but nearer to V. He was badly wounded in the nape of the neck and was unconscious, in the course of the following day he came to himself and declared that all three had, as we have said, left L after their midday meal just as the hour of three was striking on the church clock, and had continued on their way, after having walked for about an hour, Sp and B all at once asked whether the market would not be forbidden owing to cattle plague and said that information about it would have to be obtained in a village some distance from the road. But T had declared that there was nothing to support their idea and besides that the information could be obtained at any inn along the road. Those on the road, he had added, were better informed than those away from it, and it was useless to further lengthen their already long journey by making a detour by that village. But Sp and B were so obstinate about it that T supposed that they had something to do there which they wished to hide from him, probably the purchase of a beast which they did not want him to know about, and so he had told them to go to the village while he would slowly continue on his way until his two companions should rejoin him on the road after their detour. But the two were away a long time and he sat down to await them on a milestone, turning his back to the road, for the wind was violent and raised up a great dust. All at once he received a tremendous blow from behind on the head and he remembered nothing more. The money set aside for the purchase of the cattle had disappeared.

Some days later T died of his wounds without the possibility of being again questioned. Sp and B declared, in a way that certainly bore out each other's statement, that they had really been to the village for no other purpose than to obtain information regarding the market, that they had even at an inn questioned two wayfarers about it and that they had then started to rejoin T, but had not found him on the road and had seen nothing of him lying in the ditch. They had then come to the conclusion that he had gone on to V or D, but as they had not found him they had proceeded to the market at M. They had not heard of a man having been half killed until they were on their way back. They had even been invited to go and see him at the house of a peasant, because he had been identified by no one. They had then recognised their comrade T. That they had not seen him when he was already doubtless wounded and stretched in the ditch beside the road was explained by the fact that when they passed the scene of the crime it was already night, being in the last days of autumn. Preliminary inquiries pointed to the fact that Sp and B had the intention of attacking T at nightfall and of killing him and stealing his money. In order to plan at their ease the details of the attack, they had made the pretext of going to the village to ask for information concerning the market, for they very well knew that T, who was the worst walker of the three, would not agree to the detour. They could not possibly know that T would sit down on the stone and turn his back to them, but they would probably have chosen for the place of the crime a forest to be passed through after dark. But having seen him in a position so favourable to their scheme and the road being at that part very deserted and quiet, they had immediately seized the opportunity of striking him down from behind and plundering him.

There was but one circumstance in favour of the accused, namely that the story as told by them was not improbable. A stranger might have killed T and plundered him and the two men would have been unable to see him in passing, because it was already dark. In fact many of the country people were questioned and unanimously stated that at that time of the year, if one left L at three o'clock and made the detour by the village in question, one could not, at the slow pace of persons fatigued as the three men in question then were, arrive at the scene of the crime before it was quite dark. That the departure from L took place at three precisely, was spoken to not only by the two accused but also by many other persons with whom they had kept company at the inn. One of the former had even remarked "There goes three o'clock, we must be off as we have still a long way to go." In spite of this weak point in the prosecution, Sp & B were found guilty.

At the beginning of spring the accused demanded a revision of the case, they succeeded in effect in to some extent shaking the case for the prosecution. They fastened suspicion on a young man of bad character who used to roam about in the neighbourhood of the scene of the crime and as the point in favour of the accused already indicated, namely, whether they could have seen T lying wounded in the ditch, always preserved its importance, they proceeded to arrest the young man and revise the case against Sp and B. At this juncture the Investigating Officer took it into his head to investigate the incident on his own account. It was naturally impossible to await the end of the autumn, which was the time of year at which the crime was committed, so he asked two astronomers to indicate that day in spring which as regards light, sunset, etc., would most closely correspond with the day in autumn on which the crime took place. he then repaired to the scene on the given day accompanied by a magistrate. They left L at three o'clock precisely, walking slowly, as Sp B & T were supposed to have walked, they made a detour by the village and remained there as long as Sp and B said they had remained, in order to give the accused the benefit of all the circumstances in their favour. When they arrived on the scene, it was still broad daylight! They then made every imaginable trial. They lay down by turns in the ditch on the side of the road where T had fallen from the milestone on receiving the blow and where he had been found on the following day. They then alternately went back along the road, turned round, and advanced, and came to the conclusion that from no matter what side of the road, and even at a considerable distance, one could not miss seeing that a man was lying in the ditch and no one could possibly pass without perceiving him. Only after lengthy experiments did night fall. It was thus settled that the statements of all the witnesses rested on false suppositions and the only circumstance which had shown in favour of the accused did not, after exact verification, exist at all.

A number of analogous examples could be cited; every Investigating Officer has come across them during his career. Just because they are so frequent they cannot be too strongly insisted upon, and the decisive importance of having the base of operations very firmly established cannot be too frequently pointed out. Besides, as has been indicated, it is the nature of mankind to cling to points of support which have but little solidity; one hears of a circumstance (often but incidentally referred to by a witness) and is easily disposed on its verification to base an argument upon it. Perhaps this argument is not without merit and, giving satisfaction, another and yet another argument is made to cling to it. The case grows interesting and a successful result is in sight. All the points thus gathered together are most minutely and carefully gone into, but meanwhile the re-verification of the primary fact on which the whole structure is based has been neglected. Carried away by zeal and the desire to bring the case to some conclusion, the Investigating Officer has proceeded too fast and without the calm and prudence requisite to such inquiries, and so all his work has been in vain. There is but one way to avoid this: to proceed "steadily," be it at a walk, at a trot, or at the charge; but in such inquiries a halt must from time to time be made and instead of going forward he must look back. He will then examine one by one the different points of the inquiry, taking them up in order from the beginning. He will analyse each acquired result even to the smallest factor of those apparently of the least importance, and when this analysis is carried to its furthest limits, will carefully verify each of these factors, from the point of view of its source, genuineness, and corroboration. If the accuracy of these elements be established, they may then be carefully placed one with another and the result obtained examined as if viewed for the first time. The case will then generally assume quite another complexion, for at the outset the sequence was not so well known; and if it has a different aspect from at first each time the matter is so revised, the question must be asked whether it is in proper adjustment with the whole argument which has been formulated and whether there is any mistake to rectify. If the whole result is defective the Investigating Officer must have sufficient self-denial to confess: "my calculation is false, I must begin all over again."

Section VI—Knowledge of Men.

One of the requisites necessary to enable an Investigating Officer to work with accuracy is a profound knowledge of men, for after all he cannot advance a step without utilising the agency of men. The people who play a role in an inquiry are only useful to furnish proofs; they render just as much or just as little service to the Investigating Officer as he knows how to exact from them. The impression of a foot found on the scene of a crime is absolutely of no significance to an ignorant Investigating Officer, but it is a decisive proof if he knows how to make use of it. A witness will tell nothing or make but inaccurate and unimportant statements to an incompetent Investigating Officer while the very same witness will make precise, true, and important statements to an Investigating Officer who can read him at a glance and knows how to handle him. And if an Investigating Officer who has no knowledge of men by chance discovers the truth, it is worthless to him. There are witnesses who really desire to tell the truth, but when witnesses do not wish to do so the result is truly lamentable. The record shows only how the Investigating Officer has let himself be duped by the witnesses and led by them just where they chose. A treatise on the knowledge of human character, teaching how really to know men has never yet been written and probably never will be; we can but indicate certain methods available in particular cases, few though these unfortunately are.

When the accused is an old offender, a most important and really valuable means is the study of documents, if there be any, forming the record of his career. One can then start with more confidence. If the matter is of some importance the old record must be studied as if bearing on the case in hand. It is not sufficient for example to merely read through the statements of the accused and to look up a few important registers,—the record must be studied in its entirety, the whole history must be gone through step by step and in its fullest development, in order to see how the accused has defended himself on previous occasions and compare that defence with his present one. It is astonishing how men stick to the same defence and justification of their conduct even after a long space of time. This is not to say that an individual who pleads guilty once will do so always, or that if he has once endeavoured to vindicate himself by throwing suspicion upon the witnesses, that he will repeat the charge upon every occasion; nothing in life repeats itself with such servile accuracy, but the broad lines of the picture, the whole impression that the examination has produced, will be renewed as often as he is examined. Every Investigating Officer who, following the procedure indicated, studies at the outset the antecedent record of the accused will receive at the commencement of the new examination the impression that the accused is striking out a new line, but as the examination advances he will regain, little by little but very accurately, the impression as a whole and will be definitely convinced that his man has not changed. The process is indeed identical, only perhaps with the difference that the individual has in the meantime acquired more experience, has become more cunning and more circumspect, or on the other hand that he has become older and has fallen away somewhat in craftiness and address. The picture previously seen has become tarnished but the broad lines stand out quite plainly. If one is in possession of the records in several cases relating to the accused and if they have been carefully studied, one will know his man so well as to be able to say in advance how he will behave and what explanations he will give, on what points he may be believed, about what he will lie, and how he must be handled in order to extract the truth from him. The study of old records is very important not only in the case of the accused, but also as regards important witnesses who are themselves old offenders or who have given evidence in other cases. In this way one often discovers how easiest to handle the witness, what to say to him, how far to believe him, and the readiest method of proving him to be a liar

Another guide to the knowledge of men consists in bringing to the examination the closest attention and in seeking all the time to read the very soul of the man. If the Investigating Officer wishes to know men, every individual who enters his room must become an object worthy of study from the first moment. The manner in which he presents himself looks around allows himself to be questioned, replies, asks questions in return, in a word the way in which he behaves, ought never even in the most insignificant affair, to be a matter of indifference to the conscientious Investigating Officer. He must always make himself form an idea as to whether the person has spoken the truth and the whole truth, or whether he has lied or passed over something in silence. He must also look for the motives prompting the individual to act in the way in which he has done, how his statements fit in with the circumstances which have to be taken into account the effect he has desired to produce, what was of importance to himself, and what means he has employed to make his testimony appear sincere and accurate. The Investigating Officer ought to remember, or better still note down, what he has thus observed or believes he has observed. This will be of use to him during the course of the inquiry. If in its course he finds a circumstance proving the accuracy or inaccuracy of the previous observations, he secures in the first case confirmation of the view taken and in the second will endeavour to find out why he has been deceived and discover where and how the error has taken birth

Before finally leaving a case the Investigating Officer has a fresh opportunity at the time of the general revision, always necessary on other grounds, of going over all he has observed and comparing it with the results obtained, this work costs much time and trouble but great profit is obtained from it in the shape of valuable and interesting observations for future guidance. Above all, where the Investigating Officer has succeeded in completely elucidating an intricate case and has arrived at an unexpected result then it is most useful to go again over the inquiry and verify all the depositions of the witnesses noting how they accord with the now known course of events. He can then understand why such a witness spoke with so much hesitation or why another was so embarrassed, and he comprehends a mass of equivocal and uncertain statements. Many things which appeared to be quite contradictory now fit in together neatly he can explain the tone of voice, the doubt, or the assurance, shown by the witnesses while giving evidence, for future cases this task is most valuable

Yet it is not in the exercise of his duty that the Investigating Officer can best acquire this knowledge of men, but in his daily and ordinary life, in his relations with his fellows, and in the course of ordinary events. He does indeed learn while working and every case teaches him something new, but his necessary occupations give him so much to do and in so many ways that they are not precisely the best suited for imparting instruction. In following his profession he must always be in possession of pre-acquired knowledge, this may be perfected and increased, but the true time for studying is gone. The principal reason is that nothing can be properly learned without actual experience. "Practice is better than precept," rightly says a popular proverb. But experience can be very well gained in private life, while it is not always convenient to acquire it during the exercise of one's profession. To this end everything in life can be utilised. Every conversation, every concise statement, every word thrown out by chance, every action, every aspiration, every trait of character, every item of conduct, every look or gesture, observed in others, be it only for a moment or during a long course of years, and compared with events as they arise, ascertained facts, and realities. The Investigating Officer ought indeed to keep a balance sheet for every man with whom he comes into contact, noting down therein his observations upon his acts, his words, and physiognomy, balancing them with events, making comparisons, and controlling and verifying them. The best way to fill his diary, if he keeps one, will be to write down observations on himself and others. But many things can be learned without written notes. As a rule we find no difficulty in remembering the impression made upon us by the actions of others and do not easily forget the discovery of the mistakes we have made as regards them. To him who goes through life with no desire to enlighten himself, these disillusionments only produce a painful impression, but he who wishes to profit by his experiences in life can obtain from them lessons of utility. "The best employed money," says a philosopher, "is that of which we have been defrauded, because with that money we have purchased the circumspection necessary to life."

The Investigating Officer can also profit by those painful experiences which are the most numerous in life. They invariably arise from false ideas we have acquired and, when the mischief comes, we may yet derive great profit from it, if, instead of bewailing our loss, we look upon it as an "interesting problem" and try to find the cause. He will in such a case revive the idea first formed, attempt to discover how he formed it, and compare it with the experience just undergone; the mistake committed may then be recognised, he will not repeat it, and will be able to make use of the acquired results of experience in his profession.

Other experiences than those in which we ourselves take part may prove valuable. The smallest observation may some day be of decisive importance. We are told something and believe it and later we discover its inaccuracy; something is told us which we do not believe and afterwards find to be quite true. This sort of thing appears of little importance in life but there is matter for instruction in it if we care to find out how we have allowed ourselves to fall into error, how the mistake arose —whether voluntarily or not,—how we might have been able to discover the truth at the time, and why we did not discover it. Perhaps subsequent events will even enable us to find out the exact reason why the truth was kept dark, how our mistake came about, and finally the truth itself. Let us place ourselves in our former position and consider what our conclusion would then have been. By acting frequently in this way we will be the less liable to make mistakes when analogous cases crop up.

What is above all of importance in private life is to ferret out the motive for a lie. When a story about something has been related either to ourselves or to others, false in some particular which we only discover later on, we more often than not carry the matter no further, because it is of no importance in itself but if we wish to gather a lesson therefrom we will try—by a direct method for preference, as by frankly and honestly asking the question—to discover why the lie has been told. Most often we will find that the lie has been started out of human weakness rather than through real perversity. Throughout life we will find that lying is infinitely more common than is generally believed. We shall be much less disposed to be indignant about falsehoods if we recognise that the motives for them are most often perfectly childish and foolish. What an Investigating Officer has thus learned in private life can often be utilised in important cases. He will understand that a man is not necessarily in league with a thief because he has not spoken the truth, and that if he has told a falsehood it is often out of vanity or some other little human weakness

Section vii.—"Orientation"—Finding his Bearings.

The Investigating Officer is "oriente," that is, "has found his bearings" (the metaphor is derived from the mariner's compass), when he knows his department, his district, his subordinates, his auxiliaries, the means at his disposal for facilitating his work, his possible difficulties, in short when he is acquainted with everything he may come across in his official career and what may be of service or disservice to him. He must not forget that every case of even ordinary complexity presents or may present so many difficulties that when he comes to attack it he has neither time nor opportunity for studying the means calculated to lighten his labour or solve his difficulties. All this ought to have been seen to beforehand.

Suppose that an Investigating Officer has just arrived at his post. His first duty is to make the acquaintance of his superiors and subordinates. It is self-evident that the most important person to him is his principal assistant—the magisterial clerk, or police sub-inspector, or station-house officer, as the case may be—for all depends on this man's intelligence, willing co-operation, and knowledge of the district and people. When he can be trusted, his information is most valuable more especially if the assistant happens to have been for a long time in his post. The Investigating Officer will then try to obtain information about the other officials so as to know what to expect from them. Every official under Government, no matter what his duties, is bound to promote the general welfare and it is incumbent on him in important cases to lend assistance to officials in other services. But in order to command the help of other officials when needed, the Investigating Officer ought to be on good terms with them beforehand and in his own sphere to show himself as serviceable to them. This co-operation may be most varied and extend to every imaginable branch of information. As a rule the most important thing to know is, to what extent one can rely upon and trust people with whom one has business.

In the district in which the author started work, there was an old tax collector who knew the people and country thoroughly, in whom he could repose the most absolute confidence, and who rendered him inestimable services. Nearly every day the author used to overwhelm him with questions and his kindness in answering them was inexhaustible. He had lived in the district for a long time, was a tireless walker, and, knowing the smallest village and its inhabitants, was acquainted with everything he could be asked. "Can A be relied on?" "Can you also get from X to Y by way of Z?" "If someone steals a cow at M and brings it to N, can he go by way of the mountain at O?" "What would be the weight of the largest trout that can be poached from the stream P?" "Has Q really the reputation of being a man of violence?" To a thousand questions of this kind, he would reply accurately and without hesitation.

There are men of this description everywhere, only they must be discovered. With such men at his disposal, much labour and trouble and many mistakes may be obviated. One such person is naturally not enough to give information; the Investigating Officer must have them in every village and in each district. He ought naturally to procure certificates of good character and good conduct and other information respecting different persons from the local police authorities which should find their allotted place among his records. But anyone who has any experience knows full well that the value of such documents is in most cases very small. In theory these certificates should come from the members of the community itself whereas they are in practice drawn up by officials and frequently a mere clerk prepares them. In such cases but more especially in the latter, personal opinion, favour and disfavour, relationship and friendship, enmity and jealousy, play a great part.

If the Investigating Officer knows this, and he ought to know it, he cannot in good conscience base his opinions or decisions entirely upon a certificate thus drawn up. To act conscientiously and wisely he ought to have men in whom he can trust, to whom he can have recourse in difficult cases. It must not be thought the act of a spy to obtain information from people in whom we have confidence concerning individuals whose testimony is for the time being of importance. But it is not only when the need makes itself felt that such persons must be sought out, they must be already known for a long time and have been often tested, so that implicit reliance may be placed on them. Perhaps he will not be ready at first sight to admit the utility of these people, but when he has to appreciate the effect of an important but uncorroborated statement, or compare the value of two contradictory depositions, or still more to come to a conclusion as to the possibility of someone committing a crime of which he is accused, then will he be thankful to find in honest, serious, and trustworthy person, who knows the situation and can give information concerning the character of the persons in question. In European countries the most trustworthy information will generally be derived from the parish priest. The opinion of the military authorities upon old soldiers furnished in discharge notes and other documents is also of great importance. The officer in command of the company of the man in question has had sufficient opportunities of observing him and that at a time when his character is revealed most forcibly and clearly. The accuracy and justice of the notes made by military officers, even when recorded a long time previously, is often most striking.

The Investigating Officer ought to study as accurately as possible the local topography. From the moment an official becomes an Investigating

Officer, he is no longer anything but an Investigating Officer. All that he does, observes, studies, or hears, ought to be subordinated to the single aim of knowing how he can make use in his work of what he has learned. He ought not exclusively to occupy himself with one side of things; his knowledge ought to be extensive,—as extensive as possible. Everything can be of service to him, and it is exactly for this reason that he ought to obtain information about everything—but always with the view of making use of it as an Investigating Officer. He will be indeed unable to " go for a walk," in the sense of strolling with mind at rest, enjoying peacefully the beauties of Nature. He cannot go to the band merely for the pleasure of listening to the music. In all the walks he makes either for pleasure or duty, an ordnance or survey map should be in his hand so as to study thereon all the roads, hills, and watercourses, engraving their names upon his memory. He ought to know to whom the smallest hut belongs, to make note of every road traversed, to seek out known localities, and establish their relative situation, their distance apart and the means of communication between them, to know what can be seen therefrom and how far the view extends. When he sets out he should look at his watch and should afterwards mark on the back of his map the time it takes from point to point. A peasant can but give in measures of time the distance from his house to the church, the market, the nearest railway station, etc., etc., for he finds it inconvenient to arrive late at a religious ceremony, miss his train, etc. If he is questioned upon any other distance, he will no doubt always answer promptly but also invariably inaccurately; and this may often be the source of grave mistakes. It is not always possible when necessity arises to have the distance measured by an official and therefore a note of it should be taken in advance as opportunity presents.

There are localities which the Investigating Officer must examine in the light of future events—hotels and drinking-shops and brothels, because of brawls that may take place in them, mortuaries because of *post mortems* that may be carried out there, ponds and wells in villages on account of possible accidents by drowning, forests because of poaching and illicit felling, etc. He must try to become acquainted with the local police stations, the organisation of forest guards, the beats of the perambulating police force, customs circles, irrigation systems, the manner of closing doors, windows, stables and outhouses. Within the distance of a league one often finds quite dissimilar practices.

Attention must also be paid to industrial works and technical installations, which vary greatly according to localities, because, when the case arises, one often finds very great difficulty in understanding them from the descriptions given of them, which are always more or less defective. A flour-mill, an oil-mill, a saw-mill, a blacksmith's forge, a stone quarry, a coke furnace, a brick and tile kiln, and many other industrial establishments differ in appearance in different localities and cannot be pictured from mere description; to know what they are really like they must have been seen. Everyone has found by experience that he can form but a very inexact idea of one of these places from a mere verbal description; on the other hand it is thoroughly comprehended if seen only once. A great many educated people have never entered a flour-mill or a saw-mill in their lives, and yet such establishments have considerable interest. This is all the more surprising as everyone must have passed say an oil-mill, hundreds of times and could have inspected it without any inconvenience. The Investigating Officer should never let slip an opportunity of visiting an industrial establishment or factory, of having everything shown and explained to him in the most detailed manner; he will generally find the management ready to afford every information. Every man, especially the plain man, is pleased when interest is shown in his work and what he happens to be doing; when he can teach and explain anything, he always exhibits willingly and readily whatever there is to be seen. If one already knows something of what he is showing you, so much the better; he will be the more disposed to speak. If one knows nothing, care must be taken in questioning him, for ordinary folk cannot imagine that educated people know nothing of such every-day things. He may become distrustful and circumspect, fancying that he is being played with. One must be contented in such a situation with examining, asking short questions and listening; on the next occasion things will work better.

If the Investigating Officer has some technical knowledge of this kind he can in many cases facilitate his work. Take for example a mill, not a very rare thing, and suppose that the Investigating Officer has never in his life set foot in one. An accident takes place in the mill, or a burglary, or a fraud or embezzlement by the staff, or a fire, etc. Each of these cases will have some connection with the technical construction of the mill. The accident has been brought about for instance by a fault of manufacture, or material, or want of supervision in some part of the building; the burglar will also have profited by some portion of the machinery; the staff could not have carried out the frauds without knowing the plan of the interior and the relative position of the various departments; as regards fire one cannot possibly find how it has taken place without knowing the complete fitting up of the mill. How can an Investigating Officer conduct the inquiry in such a case when he possesses not the slightest assured base for his investigations? Let it be again remarked that the recollection of places once seen is easily retained—most men find little difficulty in remembering places, even when the details have been forgotten, the memory is soon refreshed when a witness begins to speak about them.

Another important point is that of the means of communication in a district, main roads, ordinary roads, cart-tracks, footpaths, etc. It is not difficult to become acquainted with these. The Investigating Officer has only to find and mark on the map all the roads he has passed over and see whether they are correctly set down, which will probably be the case. As regards the principal arteries, corrections will mainly show where a main road has degenerated into a side-track through the making of a new main road, or where a second-class road has been promoted to the position of a main road. He will also note down any other changes that may have taken place, such as new buildings, houses abandoned, changes in the nature of the crops, alterations in watercourses etc., in short his map must always be kept up to date. Nor should ordinary footbridges newly made or disused be forgotten nor wells, tanks, marshes, ponds, or other pieces of water be overlooked. To these latter special attention must be given. On a map the extent and direction of the water may be seen, but this is not enough. We must note the depth, nature of banks, change in the volume of water, sluices fords and dams, in short all particulars in connection with the water. For water plays a role in many a criminal case, and it is not easy to do good work while unacquainted with its usual aspects.

Finally, attention must be paid to the interior of houses. When in the country the Investigating Officer has examined in full detail several peasant's houses, big and small, he knows practically all others, for they are constructed in accordance with a small number of types. But these several types must be known. The various parts of the houses and the uses they are put to must be noticed. Otherwise great difficulties would be encountered in the very first case of theft or burglary.

It is also of the greatest importance that the Investigating Officer should be thoroughly posted up about the experts that he will have at his command when the occasion arises. Naturally he ought to be perfectly well acquainted with the special talents, singularities, and weaknesses, of the most important experts—the medical jurisprudents. But experts in other departments ought also to be known to him, such as experts in fire-arms, building, valuations, etc. All these should be known beforehand, he must learn what to expect from them and how they may be usefully employed. But for this it will not suffice merely to know their profession, this can be done by reading, their particular talents and singularities must be accurately ascertained.

When a person is a good linguist, or has travelled, is a numismatist, has knowledge of horses, possesses a microscope or a well-trained dog, he does not publish it to all the world but each of these circumstances may be of the greatest utility. In the first case he can act as an interpreter, in the second make sure whether a criminal is speaking the truth about his supposed travels, in the third he can examine false coin, in the fourth discover a horse fraud, in the fifth lend his instrument to the medical man and in the last lend his dog to track down some criminal. A photographic camera will always be useful. And even where an individual has no other peculiarity than that of having been born in a different country, he may still be useful in exposing some foreigner or stranger pretending perchance to belong to that very same country but actually speaking quite another dialect. In the smallest towns there are always certain people in possession of knowledge which may subsequently when occasion arises prove to be most valuable.

If in towns the police force and its auxiliaries are of great value to the Investigating Officer, the rural police are none the less so for without them he could do little and often nothing at all. But the result obtained with the aid of the police will in fact depend on the Investigating Officer himself. If he is on good terms with the police force and knows how to make use of it he will obtain good results, otherwise the result will be negative, and in the latter case the Investigating Officer is always at fault and not the police. But a subordinate is not a machine, even a policeman, put into uniform and subjected to military discipline, preserves his individuality, you cannot kill it and must therefore submit to learn how to make use of it. This is why the Investigating Officer should possess the most accurate information as to the humour, character, and education of his assistants. One officer is distinguished for tact, another for energy, another for unusual physical strength; if in a difficult case one of these qualities is specially demanded, everything may be lost if the right man is not employed. If he knows his men he will have the right officer sent to him, explain the case, and give him his opinions and plans, he will listen also to the views of the other, he will take precautions against incidents which may crop up, he will discuss with him the various ways of setting to work, in a word he will explain the whole matter as clearly as possible.

Thus posted up the officer will certainly do his best; his self-conceit, thus awakened, will prove a powerful stimulant. And if his work is well done, he should be congratulated on his success: a cordial word of encouragement and praise is so quickly given and goes so far. Think of the difficulty of a policeman's work: often heavily laden, often insufficiently protected from cold or heat, he has to tramp many miles to fulfil a mission for which he is solely responsible, strictly tied down by the innumerable ligaments of red tape, unable to take counsel with anyone. He must display the finest tact, indomitable courage, do neither too much nor too little, and finally reduce the whole to the limits of a complete and accurate report. If he has done all this without a mistake, his co-operation must prove most valuable, and it is only common justice on the part of his superior whom he has saved so much trouble and work and whom he has provided with so useful a foundation for his further inquiries, to tender his devoted assistant a word of acknowledgment and thanks. He should also express his satisfaction in presence of the man's comrades and superiors, honour to whom honour is due. Well-earned praise is the best stimulant of zeal; nothing discourages a man so much as to find his superior always discontented, constantly finding fault, and never having a good word to say of anyone or anything; this must be kept in view in all our relations with subordinate officials.

Section viii.—Jurymen.

It will be useful for the Investigating Officer to bear in mind that his work may at times be submitted to a body of men whose decisions often can be explained by no discoverable principles and whose intellectual and moral faculties work in mysterious ways. Considering also that his labours will be presented to this body by a third person, it is all the more incumbent on him to endeavour, before the case leaves his hands, to eliminate every possible cause of error discernible by the eye of ordinary human intelligence.

In this view, the Investigating Officer will endeavour to present the case to himself as it would appear to a person absolutely devoid of the experience he himself possesses. He possesses knowledge of legal theories, of substantive law, and of procedure. The juryman knows nothing of these things and the Investigating Officer should therefore never forget that his work may one day be placed before a jury of the uninitiated. These bestow great attention upon the mode in which an inquiry has been conducted, they are always trying to find out if the Investigating Officer is worthy of belief or not. As judges they are also incompetent; an inexact though absolutely unimportant piece of information, an insignificant contradiction, an unimportant gap, which a juryman has himself discovered in the inquiry, is sufficient motive for distrusting the whole case for the prosecution; it loses all value in their eyes, and the accused is acquitted in face of the most overwhelming proofs of his guilt. On the other hand a smart bit of procedure, the revelation of an accessory fact, or some other circumstance, will so please a jury that it will condemn the accused simply from confidence in the Public Prosecutor.

Again, the Investigating Officer should be careful to arrange all the documents that may have to be read at the trial in as simple, clear, and comprehensible a manner as possible. Above all, the proofs of evidence must be taken down from the witnesses with scrupulous accuracy, and it should be impressed on the witness to say *exactly* what he has seen or heard and not merely something like it. Many persons suppose it is a matter of indifference which of several synonyms is employed; frequently it is of no importance, and an experienced judge knows it does not matter if a witness who has spoken of "breeches" now uses the word "trousers." But the juryman is often much more particular.

It is dangerous for a Public Prosecutor to put forward conclusions, trusting to the Investigating Officer. Both he and the judge may have the best of grounds for placing confidence in the Investigating Officer. But it is otherwise with that amateur judge,—the juryman,—the slightest contradiction or mistake will destroy all confidence, all the more if the juryman be an expert or imagine himself to be one.

All this is very human and easily explained; we are ever ready to put forward our own knowledge, professional or special, particularly when we know nothing about the matter really at issue. The words, "Allow me, I know this class of business," constantly used even when there is no question of business at all, is regularly in evidence among jurymen, often entailing most unfortunate results. For the same reason care must be taken to guard against any mistake even in the minutest detail; if one of the jurymen discover a mistake, however irrelevant to the issue, the result of the whole case may depend on that and that alone.

Finally, as has already been indicated, the case must be put before the jury with the greatest simplicity attainable. The mistakes and misunderstandings that arise when documents are read out, pass all belief. The juryman sees and hears during the case so many things he has never seen or heard before; he is introduced into a strange world where he has to strain every nerve to comprehend but a little of what is going on. If the case is badly put before him, his trouble is increased and he sees everything awry.

The best method to adopt in every case that is to go before a jury is to arrange everything as if one were dealing with a child; stick to the truth, draw no conclusions, exclude everything that may appear contradictory, use the simplest words, and be absolutely clear. In this way failure may sometimes be avoided.

Section ix.—The "Expeditious" Investigating Officer.

The struggle with crime is after all only a war for which the first necessity is plenty of money, money is the best aid for the conduct of criminal justice. But if the service is undermanned and the pecuniary allotment is insufficient, what is to be done? In answer to this query we have the invention of "the Expeditious Officer." Every inquiry may be closed extremely quickly if one wishes if one considers it unnecessary to take the evidence of certain persons who have been named, there is no need to enter their names in the list of witnesses for the prosecution, and if they are not on the list, there is no necessity to question them, here is time gained at once! Let some ignorant persons be asked whether a visit to the spot will help to clear up the case and they will reply no, here then is sufficient excuse for not paying the visit and here again time is saved. A band of thieves is accused of having committed a dozen burglaries. There is quite enough evidence to get them convicted and one is not absolutely obliged to start the police upon investigations which may perhaps bring to light another dozen which the same band has committed; here again time is saved. Suppose there is a big cheating case, it is quite the thing to pick up certain "well established" facts and stop there, doubtless to do the thing well one ought to place the matter on a wide basis and to study and clear up in its entirety the procedure of the person who has committed the fraud and examine the whole business from the point of view of loyalty to one's employers but is one under any obligation to do so? By not doing so more time is saved. Again what a lot of work there is to fix the real blame in an accident case. What endless consultations with experts, what repeated visits to the spot, what minute questionings, all taking up such an enormous amount of time, by fixing the responsibility upon the first workman who is found at fault, the whole case is ended like a shot. These examples might be multiplied without end; a little time saved in each inquiry ends in the gain of a considerable amount in the long run, the inquiries run on all right and when our artistic Investigating Officer is sufficiently skilled in suppressing the difficulties and obstacles that may prove troublesome in quick work, he will well deserve the title of "expeditious."

Let the Investigating Officer who has no qualms of conscience when gathering such laurels, act thus if he so desires. It would be useless to try to turn him from his course. Whether he will be able to look back without remorse upon his work even though his fame for being "expeditious" has brought him many substantial advantages, is another question. No one will suggest that inquiries should languish or be conducted slowly, that it is necessary to write or do what is absolutely superfluous, but in a serious inquiry we *must* seek out what may however indirectly furnish or corroborate proof of the guilt or innocence of an accused. The Investigating Officer who neglects this primary duty incurs a very great responsibility. The conduct of every inquiry costs much time and trouble, the smallest piece of forgetfulness or the most pardonable carelessness may have the gravest and worst consequences. to do good work and to be "expeditious," are two things which mutually exclude each other. Every Investigating Officer should renounce the vain glory of being considered "expeditious"

Section x.—Accuracy and Precision in Details.

We shall now notice certain details which, small in themselves, are of importance when taken together. It seems superfluous to state that the Investigating Officer should avoid all disorder, and yet it too often happens that an Investigating Officer who has not a natural instinct for order and neatness does not keep his eye close enough to many small matters, especially when he is much worried in his work.

Notes must be kept in most minute order, the most insignificant things must be written down at once, so as not to accumulate for a future date fully occupied with unexpected work. Mistrust the hourly expression, "I will not forget." It is just the more important things which one thinks will never be forgotten, and in consequence it is just the important things that are forgotten. Appointments with witnesses, things to be attended to on a certain day, adjournments, and in short all those things that have to be done at a certain fixed date must be carefully noted down. Further the notes already made must be run through so as to find out not only what time remains free, but also what has been assigned to the following days, otherwise one may be disagreeably surprised at the last moment by an adjournment which is about to expire or a formality absolutely necessary to be accomplished.

The Investigating Officer should be inexorable in demanding from his clerk a legible handwriting and should himself cultivate a clean hand. Anyone, given the will, can write legibly.

Equal care must be taken with regard to paging and numbering, the marking of exhibits, and marking for identification other objects not exhibited but connected with the case. The best descriptions of objects are good for nothing if they cannot be referred to at need. It may appear almost incredible, but we have heard the statement, "According to the photograph, this is certainly the man," and yet no one knows what photograph has been shown to the witness. Or again the witness on being brought into the presence of A and B says 'It is the taller of the two that committed the crime,' but no one who has not the pleasure of knowing A and B can say which is the taller. Again on reading the letters dated 1, 3, 5, 10, Jan., the witness affirms, "of these letters only those in the good handwriting were written by me," and whoever has the task of getting up the case is forced to pick out the letters indicated by examining the handwriting. The perpetuation of inaccuracies is not only a mark of disrespect towards those who may afterwards have to go through your work, but it is far from conscientious, for grave confusion and error may result therefrom.

In certain cases it is necessary for a tabular statement to be drawn up. This is specially recommended wherever there are several charges against the accused, or where several accused are involved. This table will miss its aim if only drawn up when the work is over or if it contains merely a few inadequate headings. The Investigating Officer must not forget that his table has a double aim; it ought to facilitate the work of anyone who has to go through the record subsequently to the Investigating Officer, and it ought also to enable him to take in at a glance the case as a whole, give him a lead as to whether his work is complete, and enable him to revise it if necessary. But to attain this end he ought at the outset to draw up a table divided into a greater or less number of headings. This he fills in as the work advances and opens headings corresponding to all the important points of the inquiry. These headings ought not in any particular case to refer only to the questions, " Who? Why? Where? When? How? With what?" but ought also to indicate the accomplices, the circumstances for and against, the different criminal characteristics, a confession or offer of damages, and other important circumstances. If these headings are filled in as the case goes on, the Investigating Officer in the course of or at the end of the inquiry has but to cast his eye over the table to know if all is complete or if there is yet some point to clear up. To judge of the care and accuracy of an Investigating Officer it often suffices to see how he has drawn up a tabular statement.

Of very great importance are plans or tables on which the result of the enquiry is shown in a graphic way, so that the connection of the most important incidents can be gathered by a single glance at the plan. The possibility of using such plans happens very often and especially when the enquiry deals with the movements of a person or a thing; this occurs for example if an accused has had important meetings at several places, or if at a big affray many injuries (especially to several persons) have been inflicted, or if a connected proof against one man has to be constructed out of many rather trifling incidents which only by being linked up show their real value. For example: A arrives at X on the 16th January, he meets B on the 17th January, sells his coat on 18th January, he asks for work from the person C on the 19th January, he buys a black hat on the 20th January, etc.

Below is a tabular statement in a forged bank note case. The inquiry had the result of showing that the notes were traced back to one man, who again had received them from several people in Italy, where (near Adine) a big gang of forgers was detected, the members of which circulated these notes.

(AND B)	(Note C)	(Note D)	(Notes E AND F)
Ulli Marco Tb Nr 12	Tullio Verdi in Celle Tb Nr 115	Annibale Formi in Manila Tb Nr 17	Paolo Verme in St Maria Tb Nr 94

ANTONIO SAGLIO

	Mario Schwarz Tb Nr 7	Conrad Peter Tb Nr 2	Carl Weiss Tb Nr 18	Emil Brun Tb Nr 11	Joh Ellz Tb Nr 20
	Emil Franz Tb Nr 19	Gustav Edler Tb Nr 21	Franz Schulz Tb Nr 30 (Note D)	Anton Muller Tb Nr 26	Alois Truh Tb Nr 23 (Note F)
	Oskar Gelb Tb Nr 15 (Note B)	Josef Terrer Tb Nr 31		Cajetan Spat Tb Nr 32	
		Police Station in Huthdorf (Note C)		Baldum Berger Tb Nr 31	
				Tax Office in Klettendorf Tb Nr 3 (Note E)	

CHAPTER II

EXAMINATION OF WITNESSES AND ACCUSED.

Section 1.—General Considerations.

The object of the examination or interrogatory is to inform the Investigating Officer of the occurrence and all its details, as if he had been present in person. If the witnesses examined have actually been present, they should tell what they have seen or heard in such a manner that the Investigating Officer may imagine that he himself has seen or heard. If the witnesses only give indirect circumstantial testimony, the facts they speak to as being connecting links should produce on the Investigating Officer the same effect as if he himself had witnessed them. If the person suspected confesses, his testimony will practically have the same weight as that of an accomplice; if he denies, his statements will complete the information obtained in other quarters.

Finally, the testimony of the expert enables the Investigating Officer to view the whole case, not alone with his own eyes, but with the assistance of the expert's knowledge. In short, the result of the testimony recorded should be such as to enable the Investigating Officer to understand the case, as if he had himself been present and in possession of the necessary knowledge. If this result is attained, the inquiry is at an end. If not, of two things one, either it was in reality impossible to collect sufficient proof, or, if it was possible, the Investigating Officer could not find it. In the latter event either the inquiry is *incomplete*,—in which case the gaps may at some future time be filled up, or it has *failed*, and the mistake cannot be set right. In the former case the Investigating Officer has been baulked by fate, in the second he has bungled. An Investigating Officer may be said to do well in proportion as he is able to reduce the number of inquiries in which the necessary basis of proof cannot be secured. Further, to form an opinion as to the ability of an Investigating Officer, it is necessary to see *whom* and *how* he interrogates, for witnesses are, so to speak, the skeleton of an inquiry, their evidence being the flesh and blood; if, among the persons necessary to be questioned, some have been omitted, the skeleton is incomplete and unstable; if all have been examined but their testimony is defective, there is indeed a body, but it is lifeless or at least weak and good for nothing.

The Investigating Officer frequently decides in a very easy manner the question as to whether any specific person should be examined as a witness or as an expert in any matter; he has before him the complaint or the police occurrence reports in which certain persons are named as able to furnish information; they are summoned and interrogated; they and the accused introduce the names of other persons, who are examined in turn, and who may introduce perhaps a third lot of names. This process goes on until no one is mentioned or at least no one not yet examined. The Investigating Officer will then perhaps find it necessary to examine experts; all these statements are collected together to form the record, and the inquiry may be considered at an end. The whole business has gone forward easily and naturally; one conclusion has led step by step to the next; every person whose name has been mentioned has been heard; the whole is complete, there is no gap in the inquiry. All this is true, in a certain sense; naturally an Investigating Officer who has worked in this way, cannot be charged with laziness or negligence. But he can be reproached with having simply turned the handle and played the tune on a barrel organ, of having been the sport of events like a morsel of wood carried along by the stream, of having followed all the formulæ without directing or conducting to its close the inquiry. Let the Investigating Officer who is insensible to such reproach go on in his old way; that is his affair; but he who has sworn to do his duty and to do his very best, should face the matter otherwise and look upon it, above all, as a systematic whole. He must always keep clearly before him the fact that in the natural development of things nothing happens *per saltum* by fits and starts, nothing comes about which is inexplicable, isolated, incoherent; every result follows naturally on its cause; every fact can be explained, is one among many united facts, has a plain story to tell. Humanity had a beginning, it has been fashioned, without interruption, without gaps, not by chance but by design. The same may be said of everything springing from man, his language, his actions, his will and his capacity, his efforts and the results he obtains; all is a living organism developing gradually and naturally,—an organism put together with the greatest care, and in which everything that exists in any specified place has its reason for being there and must of necessity be found there. So is it with all human actions; not one of them happens by pure chance unconnected with other happenings, none are incapable of explanation, they are fruits which must of necessity develop under the influence of nature and individual culture, fruits whose formation is explained by the organism producing them. They are attached to the individual, as the leaf is attached to the tree on which it has grown; they emanate from the individual as naturally and as surely as the fruit emanates from the tree. We do not look to gather grapes from thorns or figs from thistles.

If the Investigating Officer is penetrated with this idea, then, in regard to every crime in which he is interested, he will remember this, that the people mixed up in the affair are necessarily and naturally connected with it, whether their role be active or passive, whether they be complainants or accused or only outsiders. Not chance meetings nor the readiness of the persons first questioned, should guide the Investigating Officer, but the systematic re-building up of the case, the clear and first conception of its natural development. Of course he will interrogate those who have seen how the criminal set to work; that will form part of the first statement of facts. But how did the affair start, why did it happen in this particular way, what were the motive and the final object, what obstacles were there, how were they surmounted, what were the antecedent facts, and how connected with the catastrophe? All that has to be built up, and to answer such questions, the Investigating Officer must not trust to the windfalls of chance and the cordiality of the witnesses. And then what is to be done if no one has seen anything, if there be no witness to the deed itself and consequently no connecting thread? Here comes in the supposed art of heaping testimony on testimony, of making the necessity for one witness spring from the testimony of another, and if the Investigating Officer have recourse to this plan, summoning the persons first seen in the vicinity or who have heard any rumour, and then interrogating all the mortals named by them, he will be almost always led astray and found wandering from the goal. The Investigating Officer must in such a case reconstruct the occurrence, build up by hard labour a theory fitted in and co-ordinated like a living organism, and just as on seeing the fruit he will recognise the tree and the country of its growth, so from the scrutiny of the deed he can presume how it has been brought about, what have been the motives, and what kind of persons have been employed in it, the secondary characters in the picture will find themselves.

How can one acquire the necessary precision of glance and how form the picture in any particular case? No precise rules can, indeed, be laid down on this point; but certain it is that even in the most difficult case, if one conjure up in the mind's eye, quietly, prudently, and thoughtfully, the way in which events have occurred, one will always arrive at a safe conclusion as to the circle or class in which persons who know something will be found, it is for the police to get a hold of their names. These persons will be examined as witnesses, but whenever an advance has been made one must begin anew, making fresh deductions and rectifying previous conclusions, so as to hit upon new circles where persons likely to furnish information can be found. But an Investigating Officer must never and under no circumstances allow himself to follow the paths along which he is pushed, be it designedly or accidentally, by the various witnesses. Apart from the fact that the reconstitution of the crime for oneself is the only effective method, it is the only interesting one, the only one that stimulates the inquirer and keeps him awake at his work.

While experience and capacity, zeal and readiness, are essential qualities, the possession of instinct is indispensable—the Investigating Officer is indeed born not made—as also the development by assiduous study of knowledge of men, while often a perspicuous mind, clear and penetrating, will alone effect the desired solution. Tact—that faculty which nothing can replace—to light instinctively upon the best way to set to work, is a natural gift. Whosoever does not possess it will never make an Investigating Officer, though he be endowed a hundredfold with all the other necessary qualities, with the best intentions in the world, he will stumble against everything without discovering anything, he will intimidate the witness who wishes to give him important intelligence, he will excite the babbler to babble still more, he will encourage the impudent, confuse the timid, and let the right moment slip past. Whoso has tact can instinctively distinguish what is purely individual from what is general; whoso is devoid of tact never can. Now an Investigating Officer who cannot do this is not fit to question a witness, for every man differs essentially from his neighbours, every man has a presence of his own,

GENERAL CONSIDERATIONS

sees, hears, and feels differently from others, relates what he has perceived in his own way, yet men are all the same and individual differences disappear and are swallowed up in broad common outlines. The groundwork is always the same, the form alone differs. We see the differences clearly if we adhere only to the form but on examining the groundwork we find things identical and invariable. Fortunate is he who can distinguish the merely formal from the fundamental. The advice that can be given under this head is intended more particularly to direct the attention of the Investigating Officer to special circumstances likely to give rise to difficulties and mistakes. What is here supplied is extracted from the larger work of the author on "Criminal Psychology."*

Section ii.—Examination of Witnesses.

There is but little real difference between the testimony of witnesses and the statements of suspected or accused persons. But they are arrived at by different routes in the case of witnesses the truth should be directly deducible from their depositions, in the case of the accused it can be inferred only indirectly from the manner in which he endeavours to justify himself taken along with information gathered from other quarters. Therein lies the essential difference and not in any external formalities. But this difference is so important that it will be well to treat the two classes separately and confine ourselves in this section to witnesses alone.

In the examination of witnesses the principal task of the Investigating Officer is twofold, he must watch carefully that all the important points of the case are taken up and dealt with, none being omitted, and he must further make sure that the witnesses speak the truth, the plain truth, the whole truth. We have already shown how to ensure the former end, to obtain the truth from his witnesses the Investigating Officer has still to contend with two classes of difficulties, on the one hand the witness may have the best intentions of telling the plain and entire truth, but it is absolutely impossible for him so to do. He has observed badly or has badly comprehended what he has observed. On the other hand the witness may have the deliberate intention of lying. The method to follow and the precaution to adopt, differ in the two cases. The difficulties in the former case are greater and harder to overcome than those in the latter.

A. When the witness desires to speak the truth

Let us place ourselves at a perfectly general point of view. We note at once that in daily life in connection with the most ordinary occurrences different persons perceive them differently and describe them differently. Many matters of this kind can be cleared up by making all the witnesses give faithful accounts of the events in which each has taken part, or which have occurred in the presence of several persons. It is a small matter whether the fact be important or insignificant, for frequently witnesses who have to depose to the most important circumstances in a sensational case, do not imagine at the time that something apparently so insignificant will one day be of first importance. Take any occurrence in which you

---

* "Criminal Psychology," by Hans Gross.

yourself have taken part along with others, and make these others describe it, one by one and separately, you will be amazed to find how differently the occurrence will be reported by each, without the slightest hesitation or uncertainty on the part of any of them. To profit by such an experiment, you must at the time of observing the occurrence intend to make the experiment subsequently, and consequently must have yourself followed the course of events with scrupulous accuracy, so as to be able later on to decide which of the witnesses are the better observers. It is not sufficient to attend to the mere words of the recital, you must note the greater or less assurance with which each tells his tale, and endeavour to discover the cause of the inaccuracies of each: false perception, temperament, age, social position, interest in the matter, these considerations and a crowd of others influence the narrative, and when after a series of observations you have noted how certain classes of people (people of sanguine temperament, children, professional men, etc), commit the same inaccuracies in their observations and statements, you will be driven to believe, when a real case arises, that the inaccuracies of a witness belonging to one of the categories already observed and registered are produced in the same way.

We shall now discuss the fundamental principles underlying the deposition of a witness—his power of perception and his memory, and shall then treat of certain *special* points connected with inaccurate statements.

1. Fundamental Considerations

(a) *Perception*

If we wish to ascertain the facts in accordance with the depositions of the witnesses we must constantly insist that each witness shall tell us absolutely, only what he has seen or what he has heard, and leave to us the work of drawing conclusions. But the great error is frequently committed of accepting the story of what has been seen or heard as if the witness himself excluded all reasoning, all induction: that is to say, to consider as accurate what he has told us from the moment that we are convinced that the witness wishes to speak the truth. Now if we believe that the account given of the sense-perceptions of the witness excludes all reasoning there is no motive for seeking this "ratio concludendi," certainly more important than the "ratio sciendi," a matter with which every jurist must occupy himself. But in the record of almost all the perceptions of sense there is found not only a reasoning but a series of reasonings. A simple example will show this. When for instance I say "There is a glass," I would appear to report a very simple sense-perception. But let us look at it a little closer. To express myself exactly I should have to say something like this: "As I have never known myself to be the victim of hallucinations, as I have not been, so far as I know, in bad health, as further I have no reason to suppose that anyone has been trying to deceive me by an optical illusion by means of mirrors or some physical trick, as besides I have no ground for surmising that there is upon the table a picture so artistic as to make a painted glass appear a real glass, as finally I cannot imagine that the people of this house have their table glass of rock crystal, I feel entitled to state that what I saw on the table was an ordinary glass.

Of course it is not suggested that one should go so far and give such a complete series of reasoning every time that a deposition is taken down; everyone knows what is intended by the words I have seen a glass. But everyone ought to know also that such an affirmation contains reasoning, and reasoning the correctness of which must be frequently examined. What is necessary is not to set down on the record the whole chain of reasoning, but to bear constantly in mind that the depositions suppose such reasonings and that in such reasoning, mistakes and even important mistakes may be committed. Let us place morbid phenomena on one side for the present and consider only what happens daily when our senses and spirits are in a perfectly normal state. We have only to think of the way in which our senses perceive a thing and the manner in which we come to present it to ourselves, to be convinced that we very seldom in examining an object take note of all the details which characterise it and which really cause us to have such and such an idea of it. The best example is offered by figures which we call "figures of harmony," and which, having typical forms, that is to say, forms corresponding to known types render superfluous the accurate analysis of their different parts. When we read we do not spell out every letter we seize at the first glance the whole word we only take to spelling if we come across a word in a foreign language or with a novel grouping of syllables hence it comes that we constantly fail to notice small printer's errors especially if the words are rather long and if the mistake does not modify essentially the appearance of the word. In the same way a clever pianist seizes only the general look of the notes, especially chords, without examining each in particular. But it is especially at cards or dominoes that this can be best observed: the player does not count the pips on the cards one by one but seeing before him the group, he says, "It is a seven or a nine." If these images did not conform to a known type, if the pips were arranged in different ways or in a perfectly arbitrary manner the player would be obliged to count every time, at least for the high cards.

Something analogous occurs in all perceptions and more frequently than we ordinarily suppose what enables us to seize more easily the aspect of a whole is that we seek and store up in our memory certain characteristic features from which we can immediately spot the object. When in a room I see a clock-face, I am convinced that there is a clock there, even if I have not seen it very clearly and even if the look of the clock-face and the objects around it give but a vague idea of the clock; later on I shall perhaps recall exactly what the clock was like, and if in a menagerie I can see only indistinctly a big beast with a long trunk, I am sure it is an elephant. It is not always as easy as this to draw conclusions from characteristic signs; the nature and the education of the person drawing the conclusion makes such estimates very different and of varying degrees of correctness. The specialist for example knows very well the true characteristic feature of objects entering into his speciality and will not be deceived even if he has seen but one of these features. The medical man knows for instance that there is a consumptive or a strong smoker in his consulting room, if he hears the one coughing or the other walking about. But it is not the same in all cases and curiously enough it is particularly the objects of ordinary life of whose characteristic features we are completely ignorant. We may here learn much from scene painters in theatres who with a few telling daubs of colour conjure up before us the most beautiful images. Scene painters work in a purely empirical manner, which is proved by the fact that they cannot correct any mistakes. If their basket of roses does not produce the intended impression they never try to touch it up, for that would be always useless, they just make another one. We may conclude from this that every person does not recognise an object by the same distinguishing features, if the painting representing a basket of roses were placed alone upon the scene probably one part of the public would think it very well painted while the other would wonder what in the world it was. But on the evening of the representation, when all the necessary decorations are on the scene, the whole public will find the basket of roses very good indeed. The reason of this fact is that in certain circumstances the senses can be "prepared." In the present case we will admit then that the painter has been able to give in a typical way for one part of the public the characteristic features of a basket of roses, for the other those of an old castle, for another those of a wood, and for the rest those of the background. But it is sufficient if but one part of the scenery be exactly represented, for the sense of sight is already prepared to be captured and therefore disposed to find the whole of the scenery correct, the idea created that one object is well represented extends and applies itself to other objects by a kind of induction, thus the person who thinks the painter has rendered the old castle excellently well, will at once find that the basket of roses, the wood, and the background are equally well represented. This psychological phenomenon is very clearly shown in panoramas, the principal trick of these consists in putting in the foreground real objects (stones, trunks of trees, wheels, etc.) which become to all appearance parts of the picture. The eye of the spectator is attracted by these real objects, is convinced of their materiality, and immediately transfers this impression to the portion that is only paint and canvas, so successfully that the whole appears real.

These phenomena of the inductive faculty are of first importance for the expert in criminology. Frequently in our daily work we come across analogous impressions of the same class as just described, perhaps less sharply accentuated, a circumstance which renders such an image or *eidolon* all the more dangerous, because the illusion more readily escapes attention. It must not be forgotten that a witness, at the moment of being an actual spectator of the occurrence, or at the time of reporting it, is frequently in a state of agitation and over-excitement which leads him to glide easily from one conclusion to another. Once these inductions are in full swing, it is difficult to say where they will stop, and if this is the case with impressions arising under normal conditions, the reality is enormously accentuated when certain things have strongly struck the sensations and especially that of sight.

This kind of vision is nothing but an inference or induction. We conclude that what appears to stand out in solid relief, does really so stand out, because we have proved a thousand times by actual touch, that objects bearing exactly the same appearance are material and solid

But we push our conclusions still further, and by the same visual illusion accept as real not only bodies of which we have seen the like a thousand times, but those which we come across for the first time. We may not have seen a living whale, but if we came across one in the Arctic Seas we should never for a moment doubt that it was a real whale. This, however, is only an inference based upon similarity; on our hypothesis, it would be absurd to suppose that the whale was painted on canvas, but in numberless cases, the conclusion will by no means be so certain, and frequently the spectator, on more or less good grounds, draws a false inference based on appearances, without the slightest suspicion of the reality of what he believes himself to have seen. This can be easily seen in most optical illusions.

It is all the more necessary to take note of errors springing from this first false idea or conception, because we are never really aware of its presence, or at best forget it at once. In any given case we must with the aid of known facts segregate the idea or notion which served as a starting point; we must then by a scrupulous inquiry verify whether or not there is any ground for suspecting a mistake in that idea, if there is, we must then endeavour to find the cause. This has an importance of its own, and when we have discovered wherein certain assertions are incorrect, we must not rest content with a mere statement of the facts. Indeed in most cases we can directly discover only the incorrectness of subsidiary statements; but, in working backwards to the idea which is then cause we can sometimes find by the mere process of reasoning, amongst the other important statements, some which can only arise from fundamentally incorrect ideas or conceptions. This is all the more important because frequently as the result of certain perceptions which we believe we possess, we arrive at conclusions which are not in accordance with our own experience.

Note also that we have not as yet taken into account what may be called "illusions of the senses." If it be admitted that almost all sense perceptions are based upon inductions, it follows that only those arising from a physical cause in the body itself of the individual ought strictly speaking to be called "illusions of the senses." Thus there will be an "illusion of sense" if owing to a lateral pressure on the eyeball images are seen double; or again if two points of a compass separated a little distance be placed on the top of the thigh or on the back or on some other part of the human body deficient in nervous tissue, instead of feeling the two sensations of touch the person believes that there is only one. Apart from cases of this kind, what is commonly called an "illusion of the senses" is in no sense an *illusion* but only a *false induction*. If on looking through a red glass we see the landscape red, our eye is not deceived, we have only made the mistake of not taking the red glass into account. If a little before rain falls, the mountains appear nearer, it is not because the eye is deceived but because in calculating the distance we have forgotten that air charged with humidity refracts the light. In the same way if a stick is held slanting in the water refraction makes the portion submerged in the water appear to be raised up, so as to form an obtuse angle with the other portion. There is no error of the senses, for if the stick be photographed it will appear in the photograph also broken in an obtuse angle. There will be no mistake unless we believe that the stick is really broken; if we do so, it is only an error of reasoning owing to having forgotten that the refraction of light is not the same in water as in air. There are a great many similar cases: it is only necessary to mention the numerous phenomena of radiation of light, phenomena in which light surfaces appear larger than dark ones on account of their greater power of radiation. A line with divisions appears shorter than a continuous line. A square divided by a diagonal appears broader than high, while a square divided by a vertical appears higher than it is broad. Lines which go in a parallel direction, such as railway tracks, avenues, &c., appear to converge, and vertical lines cut across by short oblique parallel lines always appear to diverge from the vertical in the direction opposite to that of the cutting lines. But in all these cases our senses are not in error, only we do not take into account the optical laws which come into play and consequently accept the appearance for the reality. Yet all these illusions and a crowd of others may exercise a decisive influence on the depositions of witnesses and the grossest mistakes may slip into the inquiry if we simply accept a deposition without looking for the deductions of which it is the result. And here we have not only to deal with simple cases as *e.g.*, where a person clothed in white and seen by night is depicted by the witness as a very tall man, when in fact he was only a boy. False conclusions of this sort may be the starting point of a whole series of facts falsely conceived, because from one sense-perception falsely interpreted may hang a whole series of mistakes, both in the idea which we have of things and in the way in which we report them. It is not always so easy to establish the cause of error *i.e.*, how the perception has been led astray; an explanation by a technical term such as refraction, radiation, etc., is not always enough. We have often to do with very complicated psychical phenomena. We know, *e.g.*, that if objects appear unexpectedly at night, especially on a dark and misty night, they are seen prodigiously enlarged. This phenomenon is a fairly complicated one: suppose that on a foggy or misty night I see unexpectedly a horse whose outline appears very indistinct on account of the mist. I know from experience that objects which appear to have indefinite outlines are usually at a great distance; I know further that very distant objects appear smaller than they really are, so when this horse which I fancy to be very far away seems to have ordinary dimensions, I can only suppose that its real proportions are enormous. The train of ideas is then as follows :—I do not see it distinctly, therefore it is very far away; but in spite of the distance it retains its natural size, therefore if I were to see it close at hand it would be immense.

It is self-evident that a person does not reason in this way, slowly and step by step; his conclusions are produced with the rapidity of lightning and without reflection, and he arrives direct at the conclusion without stopping at the intermediate stages; it is therefore frequently very difficult to discover the train of ideas and how the mistake has been committed. If the man who has seen, finds in past events an inexplicable gap, the affair will appear to him strange and mysterious simply because he cannot explain it, and this is how arises that tendency towards the mysterious which often plays such a great game in the depositions of witnesses. Thus if we see, of course in disagreeable circumstances, a horse galloping without hearing the sound of his hoofs, if we see the trees swaying without perceiving any wind, or if we meet on a fine moonlight night a man, apparently without a shadow, every such thing will appear mysterious and disquieting because there is something wanting which ought logically to be there. We know also what a state of mind a man gets into when he believes he has seen something mysterious. When a person has become thus unsettled not a single one of his sense-perceptions can inspire confidence, we must even suspect the truth of what he professes to have seen or heard before he became the victim of terror. It therefore becomes all the more necessary to throw light upon the subsequent inferences made by the witness, because that is the only way of finding out the unsettled state of mind in which he has been and which may be the cause of serious mistakes.

An important source of error arises from the way in which observations are joined together or split up. This frequently happens in observing moving objects we know well the many blunders to which we are exposed when it is a matter of deciding which body is moving often we do not know whether it is the railway carriage in which we are that is moving or whether it is the carriage upon the parallel line of rails. Again from the top of a bridge, if we look for a long time at the running water, at last it appears to us that the bridge is moving up stream.

The cause of these phenomena is, that we are incapable of appreciating anything else beyond the displacement of one object relatively to another. But it is a different matter when we wish to split up a movement into its component parts. How often do we come across facts like the following: The witness is incapable of saying whether the accused has thrown the glass of beer at his victim's head or whether he has struck him with it, and often enough one set of witnesses say one thing and one set the other. It by no means necessarily follows that one set of the witnesses has lied, provided we take into consideration the relative slowness of perception, if we may use such an expression, i.e., that a certain time is necessary for a visual impression to be fixed on the retina. In our example the witnesses have seen the glass raised and they have seen it fall on the head of the victim but all the intermediate facts have escaped them, they followed each other too swiftly for each to make its own separate impression. This gap is filled up with the help of inductions and the way in which each witness fills it up depends on his individuality or the humour in which he happens to be at the moment generally the witness sticks to the idea which he formed at the beginning of the incident seeing the accused raise the glass one witness says to himself "He is going to strike him", another says "He is going to throw it at him", and when the complainant has got the glass on his head, each witness has filled up in his own way what had escaped his observation and imagines he has seen the action in the way in which he expected it would happen.

Of equal importance, but less capable of analysis, are acoustical illusions or mistakes of hearing. They are undoubtedly more frequent amongst sick persons than optical illusions, but of these we shall not here treat. Let us only say in passing that the Investigating Officer should satisfy himself even more minutely than for optical illusions, whether there is any question of acoustical illusion due to morbid conditions of the body, if so, anything further must be left to the physician. We can here only consider mistakes which may be committed by persons in good health or who, although supposed to be in good health, are temporarily in a state different from the normal. We refer in particular to people who have been greatly terrified or have fancied themselves in danger of death. This abnormal condition must be taken into account, especially when questioning people who have been dangerously wounded in a riot, robbery with violence, attempted murder, etc.

Fear, terror, pain, produce all sorts of mistakes on their own account, all the more will they do so when people find themselves in a condition practically equivalent to the morbid state. They suffer real hallucinations and hear words which have never been pronounced. Thus they hear voices of people pursuing them and threats which have never been uttered, and at the same time they hear the voices of persons offering them assistance, although there is no one in the neighbourhood.

In this connection there are some remarkable illusions. Sometimes certain words long forgotten appear suddenly to strike upon the ear. A case is reported of a sailor who, when on the point of drowning, heard distinctly before losing consciousness these words pronounced by his mother "Johnny! Have you eaten your sister's grapes?" He had heard these words in infancy and had never thought of them since. In this case nobody could for a moment imagine that these words had been really spoken to the drowning sailor. But suppose that a person, the victim of a crime and severely wounded, declares that he heard some remark or other, there is perhaps at the moment no sufficient reason for doubting the truth of the statement. Further it is necessary to be extremely careful not to admit without verification statements of witnesses concerning the direction, the distance, or the intensity of the human voice. One has only to make certain experiments and examine the hearing faculty of a few people to discover the strangest things. The majority of people cannot tell you whether a voice comes from above or below, from the right or from the left, from before or from behind, from a distance or close at hand, and very few people know how defective their power of observation is in such matters.

Further, everyone does not possess the gift of hearing sounds distinctly and the majority of people understand what they hear not from the exact words themselves but from the general tenor of the phrase. There would be nothing serious in that, if everybody picked up the true meaning, but people give what they believe to be the true meaning, so that we are compelled to take into account their manner of comprehension and in consequence endeavour to reconcile an infinite diversity. If instead of one witness we have several who tell us what they have heard, we can at least compare their different statements and correct one by the other, but if we have only a single witness, we often commit the mistake of accepting his deposition as absolutely correct, simply because it is not contradicted by that of another witness.

Thus even in ordinary circumstances we must be cautious and accept only with reserve what a witness pretends to have heard. All the more must it be so if there are special difficulties in the way,—if for example the voice comes from a great distance, if it is shrill, muffled, or presents any other abnormal peculiarity. The same is true if the person whose voice has been heard is of a different nationality from the listener, if he speaks another dialect, or is better or less educated. Prudence is also necessary if the witness hears the voice unexpectedly or if he does not mark the connection between the words he has heard and the action, still more if there is any ground for supposing that the witness has been mistaken as to this connection. We must remember that here memory is not yet in question, we are dealing only with inaccurate perceptions, where the witness is giving an incorrect account of what he has seen or heard immediately afterwards. Note also that stupid or uneducated people not only find it difficult to repeat word by word what they have heard, especially when the sentences are of some length, but also they constantly distort the sentences when they are compelled to repeat word for word. We must therefore be content with getting them to tell us the general sense of what they have heard, but we must of course from the first instant take care that the witness really knows all about the affair, otherwise in reproducing the sense of the words he has heard he will certainly twist the meaning according to the idea he has taken.

There is not much to be said about mistakes of the other senses, their place being of secondary importance. Everyone knows that the sense of touch gives rise to many mistakes, such mistakes are of great importance for the criminal lawyer when it is a question of wounds. We know for instance that wounds made by a dagger or a bullet give only the impression of a shock, and that insignificant contusions cause extreme pain while we hardly feel a mortal wound. People who have in the course of a riot received a number of slight wounds and one severe one, are generally incapable of telling when they received the severe wound. Further such wounded persons cannot as a rule state exactly how they received the blows. In short the statements of wounded people, where the sense of touch is involved, must be received with great caution.

Another fact frequently overlooked must be taken into consideration, it is that the different parts of our body fulfil their functions normally only when they are in ordinary positions. If for example we take up a pea between the thumb and the first finger, we feel only one pea although the tactile impression has been conveyed by two fingers, but if we cross the third finger over the fourth and place the pea between the extremity of these two, we feel it doubled, as if there were two peas, because the fingers are not in their natural positions and thus transmit to the brain a double tactile impression.

To defective sensations, due to touch alone, must be added a species of transmissibility of tactile impressions. If for example ants are running about near where one is seated, one immediately feels the sensation of ants running about under one's clothes, and when one sees or hears the description of a wound, one sometimes feels pain in the corresponding part of one's own body. It may be taken for granted that, with witnesses of an impressionable nature, this tendency may be the cause of serious mistakes.

This want of independence, so to speak, of the sensation of touch, is intensified by the fact that all sensations are relative, and most markedly in this case. We feel a cellar to be hot in winter and cold in summer, because we perceive only the difference between its temperature and that of the outside atmosphere, and if, after having plunged one hand in cold water and the other in hot water, we place both in tepid water, the former will have the sensation of heat and the latter of cold. We have frequently in magisterial reports, to deal with *tactile* sensations, we must be always careful to take into account their lack of certitude.

Certain strange phenomena may here be alluded to, the *raison d'être* of which is to be found in the irregular structure of the human body, e.g. walking in a circle instead of straight. This phenomenon is especially noticeable when walking in a fog in an unfamiliar locality, or in the forest at night time, and particularly if the person be to some extent out of his senses, as sick, frightened, intoxicated, stunned, or weak from loss of blood. It appears very strange that sometimes a murderer or robber instead of running straight away walks in a circle round the place of the deed, a fact which may be proved by footprints or witnesses. Nobody nowadays would assert that a person who has been running round in a circle in this way is for that reason alone incapable of telling the truth.

As to taste and smell they are frequently perverted by illness, and even a man in good health finds it difficult to say if his senses of taste and smell are normal, for it is impossible to submit them to any standard of comparison.

The parts played by these two senses in our life is less important than those of sight and hearing. We can readily ask a person if he sees well or hears well, and even test his ability; but it would be useless to ask him if he can taste or smell properly and with normal accuracy, for we have no means of testing the correctness of his reply. Besides extraordinary changes take place in these senses. If for example in judging of food by its look alone, we conclude that we have before us a dish of sweets when in reality it is a plate of salted viands, we shall on tasting have the sensation of neither, but only a horrible taste in the mouth. The savour of the sweets is mixed with that of the salted provision, just as if we had really mixed up the two meats on the plate.

It must be particularly noted that in the case of smell, the sensations of pleasant and unpleasant are most diverse. One person delights in the smell of rotten apples, another in that of a wet bath sponge, what one calls the horrible smell of carrion, another hails as a delicious gamey odour. Some women consider *assafœtida* to be the best perfume, most people would say the smell was stinking. The odour of garlic, it is universally known, is very diversely appreciated; and many people cannot endure such common perfumes as musk and patchouli.

Thus when it is a question of determining the correctness of a smell-perception, great care is necessary, and all the more because the sensibility of the organ varies so much with individuals. Some people can smell a cat in a room, others can recognise persons by the mere odour of the clothes they are wearing, while others are unaffected by the strongest stenches. At the same time, the sense of smell is of an extraordinary persistence. An odour, scented but once, is recognised ten years afterwards, it raises up before our eyes with the greatest fidelity all the objects perceived at the same time. This fact may occasionally be of importance in testing the recollection of witnesses.

(b) *Memory*

The second faculty to be taken into account in the psychical life of a person under examination is his memory. Memory is a thing so marvellous and so complex, manifesting its activity in so many diverse ways, that the Investigating Officer can never study it enough. All the facts of a case must in the end be established by the truthfulness and accuracy of the memories of the witnesses.

According to *Forel*, the province or function of memory is three-fold:

(1) The fact observed must produce an impression;
(2) That impression must be recalled;
(3) The impression must be recognised as identical with the fact observed.

"I saw yesterday," he says, "a white bear for the first time in my life, and to-day I think thus, (1) the white bear yesterday made an impression on me, (2) I have to-day reproduced within me the image of the white bear, and (3) I am assured of the identity of the image seen yesterday with that reproduced to-day." This example really tells us everything that is to be said as to the activity of the brain in the case of memory, and all we have got to do is to show how it works out in particular cases. We have already dealt with accuracy of perception, upon which naturally the other operations, and especially that of reproduction, depend.

The second stage then is the reproduction of the impression. Its accuracy depends on the degree of precision with which what has been perceived, whether well or ill, re-appears, and the mode in which the inevitable gaps are filled up. One may fill up these gaps accurately by comparison with the whole picture, or inaccurately by fanciful imaginings. Sometimes they are never filled up at all.

It is only some time after this second operation that we begin to establish the identity of the perception with its reproduction, by examining if the two correspond and to what extent the greater or less certainty of a statement depends on the success of this examination. To return to *Forel's* example, the accuracy of the first stage will depend on the precision and care with which one has looked at the white bear. The second stage, that of reproduction, gives its picture more or less imperfect. For instance the image of the white bear may be very accurately reproduced but the observer has not noticed whether it had a tail or not. If the conclusion drawn from the whole look of the bear is accurate this gap will also be accurately filled up, but if the observer gives reins to his imagination he may confer upon the animal an appendage which it has no right to possess. But if neither analogy nor imagination comes into play, the gap is not filled up, and the witness does not remember what sort of a tail the beast had or whether it had a tail at all.

After the reproduction comes the establishment of identity between the two pictures and here accuracy depends on the greater or less stringency of our examination.

The Investigating Officer must, in every important case, carefully distinguish between these three operations of the mind, whenever he has reason to suspect that the memory of a witness is not trustworthy. If he searches at random in the hope of finding the weak spot he will certainly fail, but will almost certainly succeed if he examines separately the three stages enumerated. Thus he will first question the witness as to how long the perception lasted, the way in which it was produced, the circumstances accompanying it; he will thus, leaving aside all questions of accuracy, discover the 'solidity' of the perception. Next he will ask how the reproduction was made and particularly how the gaps were filled up; and lastly he will devote his attention to the way in which the identity between the perception and reproduction was established; it is almost always during this last examination that the mistake is found. Do not say that this procedure will take up too much time; in every case less time is lost in establishing, even with the greatest trouble, the accuracy of our facts, than in allowing a mistake to slip in and in consequence futilely examining a host of witnesses.

We must distinguish between the conscious and the unconscious activity of the memory. G. H. Lewes shows by a physical example the unconscious activity of the memory. If a key be placed on a sheet of white paper exposed to the sun, and afterwards the key be removed and the sheet of paper placed in the shade, the image or rather the shadow of the key will re-appear before the eyes on looking at the sheet of paper even after a considerable time. There are even memories that influence us and make us, without knowing why, act in one way or another. Forel says: "If, while absorbed in a philosophical problem, I avoid a pail of water, I have unconsciously in going round it made a whole train of thoughts." This remark is of great importance in the present connection. Indeed we are able on many occasions to explain a person's actions by this theory of unconscious memory. Yet how frequently do we fail to take account of this factor, sometimes through forgetfulness, sometimes through ignorance, sometimes through sheer stupidity. Further it appears to us most improbable that a man could perform unconsciously actions which we could perform only after mature consideration. We must therefore know a person's nature, for then only can we judge whether we have in fact to deal with a question of unconscious memory, and, if so, to what extent. We may take it, in a general way, that the unconscious memory is the most trustworthy, because it is based on a long line of experience.

Another point of great importance in dealing with the recollections of other persons, is to find the connecting link between the different remembrances. We all know how we, so to say, help our memory. One associates different reminiscences with each other, one fact remembered furnishes *data* which lead directly to the recollection of other facts. For example, suppose one desires to know when he has bought a certain object, being perfectly unable to call to mind the purchase. He remembers that on the day of the purchase he carried the parcel in his hands until his fingers were cold; hence the season was winter. Then he remembers that he put it in the inside left-hand pocket of his overcoat; therefore it must have been last year, because in the preceding year his overcoat had no pocket on the left hand side; then he remembers that on arriving home he found his friend X there; therefore it was a Wednesday, because X came only on that day of the week. X admired his new overcoat; therefore it had just been purchased. Then he finds from the tailor's bill that this overcoat was sent home early in November, and thus, keeping in mind that the day of the week was Wednesday, the exact date of purchase may be fixed.

We are constantly forming such trains of association but stupid people do not do so readily, and to obtain from them accurate information it is not enough to give them time to think and reflect, they must be helped, and upon the skill with which they are helped will depend the accuracy and precision of the information obtained from them.

Naturally we take into account the physical surroundings and social position of the witness. We refresh the memory of a countryman by talking to him of interesting agricultural happenings; we wake up an old woman by recalling to her mind religious festivals; we remind the loafer of some scandal running round the town at the time. But even when we have not to do with such typical characters the best method still is to get into conversation with people and thus try to arrive at more assured information. Here once more practice makes perfect.

A method of great importance in assisting the memory is to replace the witness in the same surroundings. This is a common phenomenon in our daily life. Sitting in my study I think of certain business I have to transact in a certain direction when I walk abroad. When I get into the street I have completely forgotten all about it, and all my efforts to stir up my memory are useless. But if I return to my study and seat myself as before, I shall recollect everything. Here is the undoubted explanation, I again unconsciously experience all my former sense-impressions, the same aspect of my writing table, the same tick-tack of the clock, the same soft and easy chair, and what I was thinking of then returns spontaneously. As Professor *Grashey* says "there is a very remarkable law impressions which act simultaneously on the cerebral envelope are linked or, so to say, associated with each other."

Such linked ideas are most important: we know that certain sense impressions, as the sound of bells, certain effects of light, and—most persistent of all—odours or smells, have the faculty of evoking in our minds memories long since forgotten. Such observations are as interesting as important. Reminiscences which have wholly disappeared from our minds are thus reconstituted, slowly and with difficulty, by the aid of such sense impressions.

But what use can we make in practice of this well-known fact? The answer is that the best way to make a witness remember with accuracy and detail a certain occurrence, is to place him in exactly the same circumstances as when he first made his observations. But it is not enough simply to take him to the place, we must reproduce the surroundings as they were at the moment of observation. We should select if possible the same hour and the same season and, without attempting a purely theatrical display, remember that the more accurate is the "reconstitution," the more useful it will be. We specially recommend this procedure in complicated transactions, when, for example, the order of events is important, or when there are several actors in the drama and the part played by each has to be determined.

We are often powerless, relying on memory alone, to recall the different scenes of an occurrence, but find no difficulty if we place ourselves on the spot and among the surroundings which we occupied at the time.

Following this course we often obtain the most astonishing results: people who in the Magistrate's chambers will remember nothing, change completely when they find themselves on the spot, they recall first the accessory details and subsequently some most important fact. Of course we must not expect that the witness, when taken to the spot, will be seized with a sudden inspiration. Give him time to collect his thoughts and find his bearings, talk to him about the scenery and matters of no importance, bring up casually the missing links in the story, or the portions he has already remembered, and thence you can lead him on by degrees to recollect all he has seen. But here there is a danger, and a great danger, to be shunned, nothing must be suggested to the witness so as to lead him to testify to matters of which he is ignorant. The danger will be less, if, without giving him special information, the witness be interrogated by simple questions to which he can reply by a plain 'Yes' or 'No.' Nor must we ever forget that memory itself has its illusions. We frequently imagine that we have formerly seen something which in reality we have never seen. It is a well-known fact that this is no proof of mental aberration, it happens to men in a perfectly normal condition of mind when suffering from mental or physical fatigue. Such mistakes happen most frequently in connection with localities; how often has one the feeling, "I have been in this place before," knowing well that one never has been. Such hallucinations are easily produced in emotional witnesses and may lead to most dangerous results.

Such errors (*Paramnésie*) may be explained in various ways. Leibnitz (" Perceptiones Insensiles ") was one of the first to study these questions and was followed by Dugas, J. J. Van Biervliet, J. Sury, A. Lalande, Bourdon, Anjel, W. Sander, Jensen, Langwiser, Wiedemeister, Huppert, Krapelin, Wigan, Maudsley, Neuhoff, etc., and every modern handbook of psychology. This literature shows that the phenomenon is of frequent occurrence and for that reason it is important in criminal investigations. Dickens even introduces it in "David Copperfield." One explanation has been given as follows:—the brain works in two parts and when the subject is not in a perfect state of health one of these sometimes receives an impression the fraction of a second before the other. This first impression gives one, at the time of receiving the second impression, the idea that he has been somewhere or seen something at some former time, though his memory immediately corrects him and his reasoning power proves the absurdity and impossibility of his imagining. We believe that the majority of people are ashamed to mention having experienced this mental illusion, for we have very seldom heard the subject opened, though when asked whether they have ever experienced it, people frequently reply in the affirmative.

2. Special Considerations

(a) *Strong Feeling as a cause of inaccuracy of observation*

If men perceive the most insignificant facts in the most diverse manner, even when it is impossible that these facts should produce on the observer any emotion preventing him from observing with absolute calm, how much more will their impressions be diversified under circumstances calculated to produce in the onlookers excitement, fear, or terror. The fact is that in such a state they are absolutely incapable of observing accurately. Examples are innumerable, we may cite one of historical interest relating to the execution of Mary Stuart Queen of Scots. When, between 1830 and 1840, the coffin was opened, it was discovered that the Queen had at her execution received two strokes of the axe, one of which had only slashed the nape, while the second had separated the head from the trunk. Now we possess a series of accounts of this execution, dating from the period itself and all distinguished by abundance and exactitude of details, but not one of these accounts mentions the first blow which merely injured the nape of the neck. Yet judging from the careful way in which these accounts have been recorded, this detail would certainly have been reported had it been noticed by any of the spectators, but all were evidently in such a state of agitation that not even one of them observed the false blow and would all if questioned in a court of law have probably sworn that only one blow was dealt.

Recently the author had the opportunity of verifying this by an analogous circumstance. He was present at an execution at which for some reason or other the executioner wore gloves. After the execution he asked four officials who were present what was the colour of the executioner's gloves. Three replied, respectively, black, grey, white, while the fourth stoutly maintained that the executioner wore no gloves at all. Yet all four were in close proximity to the scaffold, each replied without hesitation, and all four are still perfectly confident that they made no mistake.

Again a man of reserved and calm temperament, an old soldier, reported the day after a railway accident which he had witnessed, that there were at least one hundred dead, that he had himself on extricating himself from the smashed carriage seen many human heads, cut off by the wheels of the vehicles, rolling along the track. As a matter of fact, one man was killed and five persons wounded, all the rest was due to the imagination of a man ordinarily most composed but at the moment suffering under strong excitement due to fear. Another railway accident furnishes an example of what a man in a state of terror can see and hear. A brewer, a veritable Hercules, in the prime of life and in no way nervous, having jumped from the smashed carriage, took to running across the fields to the neighbouring town, three-quarters of an hour's distance, in the full belief that he saw and heard the locomotive of the train puffing and blowing after him. This man, the prey to his imagination, ran so hard that he caught an inflammation of the chest from which he died some months afterwards. The fact that he thus ran with such excess of vigour, proves conclusively that in his imagination he had really seen and heard the pursuing locomotive.

Some time ago it was related in the papers that in a prison in Norway a famous criminal named Gudor had escaped, during his walking exercise, by suddenly attacking his warder. The latter, seeing a long knife glittering in the hand of Gudor fled. Gudor fled also. On being recaptured, it was found as the result of a minute inquiry that he had brandished a *bloater* in the air, and this bloater the poor man in his terror mistook for a long knife.

It is interesting to note that in the murder of President Carnot by the Italian Caserio not a single person saw the blow struck though the murderer had jumped upon the foot-rest of the carriage, pushed aside Carnot's arm and thrust the dagger into his abdomen. In the carriage three gentlemen were seated, two grooms were standing behind, mounted officers were accompanying on either side, and yet no one saw the President stabbed and the murderer would have easily escaped if he had refrained from calling out in a loud voice while running away — ' *Vive l'anarchie!* ''

Each one of us has probably made similar observations on ourselves or our friends, but we often fail, in the practice of our profession, to appreciate their value. In the cases just described it is easy to discover the cause of the error. If several persons have observed the same fact at the same time and one alone amongst them has seen something extraordinary there is a good ground for suspicion as to what he pretends to have seen. But how frequently does it not happen that there is only one witness who, through excitement, observes incorrectly, without the circumstances being such as to betray the falsity of his impression. How many times is an Investigating Officer compelled to draw from such an '' observation,'' due entirely to the imagination, conclusions of the gravest nature. We cannot, indeed often demonstrate in criminal matters that such observations are false. But we may safely conclude that they often are so.

How can the mistakes which may spring from this faulty observation on the part of witnesses, be avoided? The only thing is to check every deposition inconsistent with the others and presenting the slightest trace of improbability. We must never go to sleep, lulling ourselves to repose with the thought '' In spite of everything this is how it must have happened, however unlikely the story may be, for the witness—so absolutely worthy of confidence—must be telling the truth.'' In such a fix only one course can be followed, we must '' reconstitute'' the whole affair in all its details, taking no account whatever of the statement of the exceptional witness. If before introducing this deposition it was easy to build up the case, while afterwards inconsistencies and improbabilities spring up, the statement of the witness must be accepted with extreme caution and that all the more, if it is the only thing which inculpates the accused.

If the statement of the witness appears improbable and if at the time of the occurrence he was in a state of excitement, his story must be criticised with the most minute and scrupulous care. If the improbability of the statement is glaring, there is no difficulty, because we are at once put upon our guard. The danger arises when the observation of the witness has been at fault, when he tells in perfect good faith a most likely story, and thus creates great confusion. A long investigation ensues, and only at the end of it, if at all, is the mistake discovered. Fortunately this rarely happens except when a witness is in an unusually excited state, when he is perfectly collected he rarely hears or sees what is absolutely non-existent. It is therefore always safe to commence by being incredulous of a single uncorroborated statement and taking steps to ascertain the condition of the witness at the time. If he has suffered from excitement, we must further enquire as to its duration, whether momentary or whether producing a permanent effect.

The author himself has been witness of a fact which had nothing to do with criminal matters, but was of the greatest importance in preventing a too ready credulity. A young peasant whom the author had known from his infancy and believed to be absolutely incapable of lying, had for the first time in his life visited a large town and gave a most animated description of all the wonders he had seen. What had impressed him most was a menagerie of wild beasts, he spoke of all the beasts, described their appearance told how they had been fed and how the trainer had managed them at last, said he there came a gigantic serpent which rushed on the lion to devour him, suddenly naked savages jumped up who fought with and killed both the lion and the serpent. The explanation was simple, the scene described was represented on a huge picture hung at the entrance to the tent to attract the public as is usual with travelling menageries. But the peasant had seen that day so many new and marvellous things, that the scene had appeared to him perfectly real, and when relating it the picture became reality, so that he reported in perfect good faith what the picture represented just as if it had really taken place. How many times has it not happened in criminal cases that we have been led astray in a similar manner.

Here is an analogous case, a peasant a man of intelligence, retired from active work told the author one day when on business in the Law Courts, that the medical expert had cured him of deafness in the most remarkable manner. The doctor had he said looked into the interior of his ear and with much difficulty extracted bit by bit a large beetle, whose several parts were collected on a piece of paper and shown to him, the body head and legs were all there, and the deafness had disappeared. A little while after the medical man was asked how he had brought about this marvellous cure and explained that he had only withdrawn from the peasant's ear an obstruction of wax. The peasant had been much run down and worried by his deafness and very frightened at the operation. The joy of being cured had so played upon his emotions that this creature of his imagination is quite explicable. He was certainly not lying but really the victim of a false perception.

In a criminal case, where an incident as related is not absolutely unbelievable, no one would have doubted in the least the veracity of a man of excellent reputation who had no reason to tell a lie.

(b) *Inaccurate observations following wounds on the head*

Great prudence must be observed in examining witnesses who have received wounds on the head. It frequently happens, and for that reason is of primary importance, that the wounded person is the principal and at times even the only witness. Care is all the more necessary in that the doctor himself is never able to say with certainty whether or not the wound has had any influence upon the mental condition of the patient. The question of the nervous "centres" is far from being definitely solved.

Speaking generally we may say with *Forel*, The seat of memory for *visual* images is in the occipital lobe of the brain, for *auditory* images in the temporal lobe, for *co-ordination* of movements between the vertex and the frontal lobe.

The books which treat of this subject furnish numerous examples of intellectual disorders due to wounds in the head. *Holland* relates in his "Mental Pathology," that one day he completely forgot the German language, owing to great fatigue. *Abercrombie*, the surgeon, one day injured his head by a fall from his horse, there being no medical man at hand, he dressed and bandaged the wound himself, in a perfectly professional manner but he had absolutely forgotten that he had a wife and children. *Carpenter* tells of a child, who having fallen on his head, remained unconscious for three days. On regaining consciousness he had forgotten everything he knew before except music. The author will cite several criminal cases and others within his own experience, which go to show what care must be exercised in recording the depositions of persons who have been wounded in the head.

The first of these deals with a peasant who, on his way to a fair, had been set upon, severely wounded, and robbed of his money, intended for the purchase of a cow. When interrogated the next day this man was perfectly conscious; he related his story with the most minute accuracy, and his account was in absolute accord with the results of the enquiry. But he affirmed obstinately and regardless of all objections, that the purchased cow had been stolen and not the money destined for the purpose. It was pressed upon him that he was going to the fair and that the robbery took place the evening before the fair, that people had seen him 15 minutes before the attack and he had no cow with him then, etc., he would reflect a moment and always make the same reply: "That does not matter, the cow was stolen, I do not know what she was like nor how much she cost, but I had a cow." In this case the inaccuracy of the statement could be easily proved, but what would have happened had the consequences been different and the Investigating Officer set off on the quest for the unlawful possessor of a cow that had never been stolen?

A miller's man had received in a riot a blow on the head from a stick, so violent that his skull was fractured and he remained for a long time in an unconscious state. Questioned two days afterwards he stated with perfect confidence that the man who struck him was very tall and had a long black beard. Fortunately among all the persons mixed up in the affair there was none that in the slightest degree answered this description, besides several witnesses affirmed that the culprit was a short young man with a fair moustache. If there had been no eye-witnesses, and if a man answering the description given had been mixed up in the affair, he would certainly have been arrested on the strength of the clearness and certitude of the statement made by the wounded man. The latter, it may be remarked in passing, had no motive for shielding the guilty man, as they were perfect strangers. On his restoration to health, he was again questioned, when he described the same person as the other witnesses, but explained that it appeared to him, stretched in a semi-conscious state on his bed, that a tall man with a long black beard was trying to drag him from the bed.

The next is a case which, though not a criminal matter, is most instructive on more than one ground. It concerns a friend of the author's, a man absolutely trustworthy. This gentleman, Mr S , visited one day with several friends the estate of his uncle. To get there, they had to cross a chain of mountains and profited by the opportunity to do a little chamois hunting. In descending, Mr S fell from the top of a rocky wall and received severe injuries,—a broken leg and fractured skull—so that he was carried in an unconscious state to his uncle's house, where he remained a whole week in the same condition. What is most remarkable is that Mr S has not the least recollection, not only of his fall, but of everything that happened during the hour and a half preceding it. He remembers the smallest details, of the start, of the ascent, of the talk he and his friends had on the way, &c., up to the moment when, just before reaching the summit he pointed out to the others a tree which recalled certain memories of the chase From that moment all recollection vanished, although they had spoken of several important matters On reaching the summit they breakfasted, drinking only spring water, and spoke of getting up a hunting party, later on when S advanced along the rocky wall his friends cried out to him to be careful, and at that moment he fell so unfortunately But S is ignorant of all that, the fall has entirely effaced every recollection of what passed during the hour and a half On waking up after the seven days during which his unconsciousness lasted, his memory reverted directly to the talk about the tree mentioned above

Suppose that a similar thing had happened to a criminal seriously wounded during the commission of an offence, he would affirm that he knew nothing at all of what had passed during the hour and a half preceding the moment of his wound Who would believe him? and, if he were a witness, who would credit him straight off? People would simply say it was impossible, and he would be pressed with questions—cross-examined in short—until he began to recount all sorts of things, which might very well have happened but of which in reality he knows nothing

Another remarkable feature of this case is that Mr S although unconscious made several quite sensible utterances On leaving home his mother had entrusted him with a message for the uncle he was about to visit Now when he was carried unconscious to his uncle's house and the latter in alarm called out his name, S delivered his message accurately and clearly, although it was rather complicated, and immediately relapsed into his state of absolute unconsciousness

If it had been a criminal matter, absolutely no importance would have been attached to the utterances of the injured man, they would have been put down to delirium and allowed to pass unheeded; further if the wounded man were inculpated in the crime, there would have been suspicion of his simulating or at least exaggerating, this unconscious state, since otherwise he could not have suddenly recovered consciousness so as to speak for an instant in a reasonable manner

We learn from this case that in such matters the most unlikely things are quite possible, that isolated facts have no value in themselves, but must be considered in their connection with each other, and that every important notion arising during an inquiry, must be submitted to a special investigation before being recorded as an ascertained fact

Here is another characteristic case A high official, Mr C, was returning in a carriage from a round of inspection, the horses took fright, C was thrown out of the carriage, seriously wounded on the head, and remained lying unconscious on a little-frequented road About half-an-hour later he recovered his senses went on foot to the country house of a friend close at hand, entered the dining room without announcing himself to anyone and there remained seated on a sofa An hour afterwards—this happened in the afternoon—the master of the house found him there and C spoke to him quite sensibly In the course of conversation the host noticed that C was under the impression that he had been in the house since morning and had breakfasted there When at last the wound on his head was observed, he professed to know nothing, neither of his injury, nor of his fall from the carriage, nor of any accident whatever, and persisted in his statement that he had been there since morning. Not until evening, when he was seized with traumatic fever accompanied by delirium, did he wholly lose consciousness. Here again the same thing would have happened as in the previous case had a crime been in question: no one would have believed an accused person a proved thief, for example, in his pretence of having entered the house without knowing how; and if C had been the victim of an act punishable by law, as an attack by a robber, he would probably have known no more about it than he did of his fall, and by his statement would have led the Investigating Officer completely astray.

Such cases are by no means rare. An engineer was passing an inn accompanied by an old gentleman, when a soldier suddenly rushed out and threw himself upon him. Some drunken soldiers had been fighting in the inn, several of them had been "chucked out," and one of them inflicted on the unsuspecting engineer as he passed a blow with a sabre in the head which knocked him down. As the fight went on in the road, the old man ran away to obtain assistance from a neighbouring village. When he returned to the inn, accompanied by some of the villagers, he met the engineer; the latter knew nothing of the occurrence and wondered where his companion had got to. He would not allow him to speak of the attack or of his wound, and yet the wound was so serious that when he came to be examined surgically, the brain itself was found to be exposed.

It may also be remarked that according to *Oesterlen* this oblivion of incidents happening before a wound also occurs with persons who have been struck by lightning and have subsequently recovered.

The following case is most instructive on several grounds; it caused great excitement and no wonder, early in the year 1893. On 28th March, 1893, a murder, having theft for its motive, was committed in the house of one M. Brunner, a school-master at Diebkirchen in Lower Bavaria. Two children of the school-master had been killed with blows of a hoe and his wife and the servant had been mortally wounded with the same instrument and were found unconscious. The school-master, who occupied a room apart from the others, had when first questioned shown himself so upset and given such extraordinary answers that he was taken to be the guilty person, nor was this presumption dispelled until his wife recovered consciousness and could be questioned. She told the Investigating Officer that on awakening from a deep sleep, she found the bed all wet, as day was just breaking she saw that it was blood and again became insensible. Besides that, she could tell nothing in spite of many questions put to her; she was absolutely ignorant of when, how, and from whom she had received such severe wounds, all on the head; and had even to be told by a third person that she was wounded at all. When the record was prepared, she signed without the slightest hesitation the name, "Martha Guttenberger," instead of her own "Martha Brunner." The Investigating Officer inquired of the neighbours if by chance "Guttenberger" were her maiden name, but was told "no." He then inquired if there were any other person of that name, and found that a former sweetheart of the nurse was so called, and that the school-master had forbidden him to enter the house on account of his misconduct. The Investigating Officer jumped at this casual indication, Guttenberger was pursued, arrested at Munich, and immediately confessed.

Thus, and Madam Brunner subsequently confirmed it, the school-master's wife had recognised her assailant at the moment when he struck her, but she had forgotten the circumstance owing to the serious wounds in her head. But not altogether. The picture of the crime of Guttenberger had in reality entered into her consciousness but in the lower sphere, so that she had only a vague idea that the name Guttenberger was of primary importance, and she felt she had sufficiently met this demand by declaring his name instead of her own. This proves once more that *Max Dessoir* was right in supposing that there are at least two spheres of consciousness,—the first or higher, and the second or lower, in the latter of which are received always or almost always facts of which we take only partial account or which are wholly distorted.

But there is yet another point of view from which we must consider wounds in the head: that is in the case of criminals long since cured. *Sander and Richter* rightly call attention to the fact that even in our days medical men are slow to look for such influence, although *Delbruch*, for example, out of 58 prisoners attacked by mental maladies, found 21 with old head wounds, and *Knecht* found 73 similarly marked out of 214 criminals examined by him.

The "*Friedrichs Blätter*" reports a case which inculcates prudence. The subject had been guillotined; a *post-mortem* examination disclosed the existence of grave cranial defects. Radiating scars were found on one half of the cranium, which, arrested in its development, was one-third less than the other. These scars coming from fractures of the skull had been produced by a kick from a horse received at the age of 14, which had prevented the natural expansion of the cranial sutures. *Gaulke* reports an identical case. In making a *post-mortem* examination on a man who had been imprisoned for strangling his wife, he found that a complete hemisphere of the brain was wanting, the space being filled by a hydatid. This had been caused by a fall on the head. For other cases see *Dr. Paul Guder*, etc.

The net result of the foregoing is that it is the bounden duty of the Investigating Officer to consult a medical expert, on every occasion on which he learns that the accused had been wounded on the head. He will often be informed of this if he notices on the person interrogated scars on the head, a striking asymmetry of the cranium, etc.

(e) *Differences in the observing powers, resulting from differences in the natural qualities and intellectual culture of the observer.*

In the examination of witnesses the principal difficulty for the Investigating Officer is to appreciate the value of their depositions. If he is content with satisfying himself as to whether or not the witness be trustworthy, and has a character as a well-behaved and moral man, he will have followed the usual formulas but will have made no true investigation. He can only truly investigate by means of hard work, taking into account the differences in the fashion in which the various witnesses have observed, and by then going on to try to establish what these differences really are, and how the different groups of persons see things. Here he has abundance of materials; he finds them in every inquiry, in every examination, and if he only knows how to use them he must of necessity attain positive results of great general value. This has not yet been generally achieved and the reason is that the psychologists have not these observations at their disposal, while the jurists who possess them have abandoned the work of inference and deduction to the psychologists. Thus each of us has to-day at his *disposal* only the materials which he has himself painfully gathered together, but the leading principles, the general rules have as yet been propounded by no one. However, with a stout heart and hard work each of us can localise a certain number of starting points which later on will be of great utility.

The root of the matter is, as we have already indicated, to establish this fact,—that the witnesses, however anxious they may undoubtedly be to speak the truth, have told different stories, while if they had observed accurately, they should have all given absolutely identical accounts. This done, we must endeavour to discover the *cause* of the difference between their statements. Here the Investigating Officer will do well to begin by trying to find out whether the fault does not lie with himself and his bungling way of setting to work. Let him consider above all whether he has not pressed the witnesses too far. No one in the world is by nature an exact observer and if he has not noticed a particular detail, all the questions in the world are worthless. Moreover it frequently happens that a detail, which to day is of decisive importance, could not appear in any way material at the moment when the occurrence was observed. This importance is discovered only afterwards, and the Investigating Officer, who himself knows to-day how important it is, is too often powerless to place himself in the situation in which the witness found himself at the moment when he witnessed the occurrence, which to him then appeared absolutely insignificant. For example, the witness has seen a man come out of a house and has looked at him, just as we are in the habit of glancing at any passer-by. Later on it turns out that he or someone has committed a crime in the house, then the *inquisition* of the unfortunate witness begins, and every attempt is made to force him to know that of what he is perfectly ignorant, " But you have at least seen if—', ' But you must at least know that—", and so on. As a matter of fact, we know no more at the end than at the beginning, and that is the best thing that can happen, the worst result is, if the witness be harassed into making a false statement. If there are many truthful witnesses and their statements differ, of two things one—either they have not been examined after the same fashion or, if they have, the method was a bad one.

In the first case, what ordinarily happens is this: we question the first witness quietly and if he does not know much, we do not lose patience but console ourselves with the thought that the others will be better posted up. But as we go on with witness after witness this hope dwindles, then we lose temper and press the witness, with the result it is true that he tells a long story, but the accuracy of the statements becomes less and less. When then we come to compare the recorded depositions it is seen that there is no agreement, solely because the witnesses have been pressed in different directions. The witnesses have observed right enough but the Investigating Officer has examined them badly.

We do not of course mean to say that an Investigating Officer should question in an indifferent and dry manner, for there are many people, and especially country people, who at the beginning of an examination know "absolutely nothing", and what they really do know can be extracted only by cross examination. The witness must be questioned with care and accuracy but not driven and compelled to give out what he does not know; these are two very different modes of proceeding.

But if after having really treated all the witnesses in the same way, we still obtain different statements, the origin of such differences must not always be looked for solely in differences of observational powers, for frequently the primary cause is to be found in the office of the Investigating Officer himself. This is important from a psychological point of view when we come to estimate the value of depositions.

It constantly happens that for one reason or another witnesses take it into their head that we want to make them responsible for the crime; it may be that they are afraid of being suspected of being themselves the perpetrators, or that they are conscious of negligence which may have facilitated the perpetration, or that they may be considered as abettors or accessories of the accused, &c. In all these cases and in a hundred such, the witnesses will, despite their best intention to speak the truth, fashion it the way apparently most useful to themselves. They will rely on certain details, they will slur over others, they will arrange the various incidents in a new manner, and if the Investigating Officer examines attentively all the depositions he will recognise the existence of a group of persons deposing inaccurately, the group of frightened people, always imagining themselves suspected and constantly shuffling.

The Magistrate befogs himself and confuses the whole inquiry, if, being himself a man of imagination, he has in hand a witness as highly endowed with that quality as himself, and knowing something of the affair. Often in such a case he allows himself to come to rash conclusions, which he does not conceal from the witness. The latter, yielding to his own inclination, willingly accepts these, and goes on to pad them out in his own way. The judge proceeds to build, on the fresh details added by the witness, new hypotheses, and thus each in turn giving the other a lift up, both are lost in the clouds. In the result, the Magistrate no longer knows what the witness has told him, and the witness cannot distinguish between what he knew before and what he has picked up from the Magistrate; so that the resulting deposition is for the most part the product of the combined imaginations of Magistrate and witness.

We must not imagine that an honest witness will, at all hazard, stick to the truth. It is difficult to believe how far the imagination of emotional, though highly intellectual, persons will carry them. Besides, in such cases, each of the parties clings to the authority of the other, the Magistrate to that of the witness, who, he thinks, must know all about it; the witness to that of the Magistrate, who is deemed to be well versed in the law. Thus each, just as he desires, finds in the authority of the other room to give a loose rein to his imagination, and both are highly gratified.

To be convinced of this fact it is only necessary to note how easily emotional persons can be made to relate occurrences which they have never seen nor heard and that without any recourse to suggestion. In spite of their earnest desire to stick to the exact truth, on the first opportunity they strike off to the right or left, and at last can no longer distinguish between what they have really seen and what they have only imagined. With such persons the Investigating Officer cannot be too careful or reserved, especially if he himself be of an imaginative turn.

But the plan to be adopted will be just the opposite, with a reserved laconic witness, one who weighs his words and, simply through indifference, says no more than he is obliged to say. We do not for a moment suggest that the witness should be cross-examined or bullied into saying what is wanted. No, he must be piloted very differently; we must gently lead him along with us, show him the deep interest we ourselves are taking in the matter and the time we have devoted to it, explain to him the importance of his own statements, make him understand how important it is that he should tell everything and describe everything in exact conformity with truth. Then we see the witness brighten up little by little, when he begins to understand the Magistrate and his business; when he has got to that stage, he realises the importance of careful reflection, of remembering, and of communicating everything which returns slowly to his memory. Thus the Investigating Officer may obtain, not without difficulty it is true, the most valuable testimony from the most indifferent witness. Hence we must always begin by making sure of the natural characteristics of the witness beforehand, treating him in accordance therewith.

But it is not enough to take into account the natural disposition and characteristics of the witness; his environment, his idiosyncrasies, his opinions, &c., are of equal importance. Many persons even in the gravest emergencies allow themselves to be influenced, more or less, by their religious, political, or social standing, by considerations of family, of profession, perhaps even of club or society, and that without the slightest intention of departing by a hairbreadth from the truth; there are many details which they wish neither to see nor to hear, or they see and hear them otherwise than the actual happening, so that a witness who would naturally be for the prosecution, becomes one for the defence, and *vice versa*.

More than once it has occurred to the author, in consequence of a strange answer given by a witness, to make enquiries as to his personal status, and as a result of these enquiries to value his statements very differently.

Finally the age and the sex of the witness are of importance. Of course we cannot fix absolutely the age at which witnesses are more or less worthy of credit; we must in addition and even to a greater extent take into account all the other elements which go to make up a man, his natural qualities and intellectual culture. But still certain broad rules may be laid down as to age.

Children.—In one sense the best witnesses are children of 7 to 10 years of age. Love and hatred, ambition and hypocrisy, considerations of religion and rank, of social position and fortune, are as yet unknown to them; it is impossible for preconceived opinions, nervous irritation or long experience to lead them to form erroneous impressions; the mind of the child is but a mirror that reflects accurately and clearly what is found before it. These are great advantages, accompanied however by certain corresponding drawbacks. The greatest is that we cannot place ourselves at the point of view of the child; it uses indeed the same words as we do, but these words convey to it very different ideas. Further, the child perceives things differently from grown-up people. The conceptions of magnitude—great or small, of price—

fast or slow, of beauty and ughness, of distance—near or far are quite different in the child's brain from in ours, still more so when facts are in question. Facts to us perfectly indifferent, delight or terrify the child, and what for us is magnificent or touching does not affect it in the least. We are ignorant of the impression produced on the child's mind.

There is yet another difficulty: the horizon of the child being much narrower than ours, a large number of our perceptions are outside the frame within which alone the child can perceive. We know, within certain limits, the extent of this frame, we should not for instance question a child as to how a complicated piece of roguery was committed or how adulterous relations have developed, we know it is ignorant of such things. But in many directions we do not know the exact point where its faculty of observation commences or stops. At times we cannot explain how it does not understand something or other while at other times we are astonished to see it find its bearings easily among matters thought to be well beyond its intelligence. We are as a rule too distrustful of the capacity of a child. We have rarely found too much expected of it, while we have often discovered that it knew and noted much more than anyone imagined.

The same experience occurs to us in daily life. How many times do not people speak in its presence of things a child is not supposed to understand only to discover later on that it has not only understood very well but has combined the information with other things heard before or after. Again it must not be forgotten that a child is peculiarly exposed to external influences whether designed or accidental. Anyone knowing that a child is to appear as a witness in a court of justice if he is interested in its statements and has the chance of influencing it himself, will almost certainly exert that influence. The child, as yet devoid of principles, places great faith in the words of grown-up people, so if a grown-up person brings influence to bear on it, especially some time after the occurrence, the child will imagine it has really seen what it has been led to believe. This result is obtained with certainty if the man proceeds slowly and by degrees, leading the child to the desired goal by repeated simple questions as, 'Is it not so?' 'It was not so, was it not thus?'

The result is the same, when the influence is undesigned. An important event happens, it is naturally much talked of, all sorts of hypotheses are started, there is gossip of what others have seen or might in certain circumstances have seen. If a child, which has itself seen something of the occurrence hears these conversations they become deeply engraved on its young mind, and ultimately it believes it has itself seen what the others have related.

We must therefore be always careful in questioning children, but their statements if judiciously obtained, generally supply material of great value.

In passing from the child to the succeeding age, it becomes necessary to distinguish sex, for just as sex differentiates in external appearance the youth from the girl, so are they differentiated in their methods of perception.

Boys.—An intelligent boy is undoubtedly the best observer to be found. The world begins to take him by storm with its thousand matters of interest, what the school and his daily life furnish cannot satisfy his overflowing and generous heart. He lays hold of everything new, striking, strange; all his senses are on the stretch to assimilate such things as far as possible. A change in the house, a bird's nest, anything out of the way in the fields, remain unnoticed and unobserved; but nothing of that sort escapes the boy; everything which emerges above the monotonous level of daily life gives him a good opportunity for exercising his wits, for extending his knowledge, and for attracting the attention of his elders, to whom he communicates his discoveries. The spirit of the youth not having as yet been led astray by the necessities of life, its storms and battles, its factions and quarrels, he can freely abandon himself to everything which appears out of the way; his life has not yet been disturbed by education though he often observes more clearly and accurately than any adult. Besides, he has already got some principles; lying is distasteful to him, because he thinks it mean; he is no stranger to the sentiment of self-respect, and he never loses an opportunity of being right in what he affirms. Thus he is, as a rule, but little influenced by the suggestions of others, and he describes objects and occurrences as he has really seen them. We say again that an intelligent boy is as a rule the best witness in the world.

Girls.—It is a different affair with a young girl of the same age. Her natural qualities and her education prevent her acquiring the necessary knowledge and the breadth of view which the boy soon achieves, and these are the conditions absolutely indispensable for accurate observation. The girl remains longer in the narrow family circle, at her mother's apron strings, while the boy is off with his playmates, picking up in the fields and the woods all sorts of knowledge of the ordinary aspect of common things, which is the best training for discovering, distinguishing and observing anything extraordinary or out of the way when it turns up. With his father and his playmates the boy learns to know the great sum of practical things of which life is composed, and which one must know before being able to talk about them. The girl has no training of this sort; she goes out less, she has little to do with workmen, artizans, or tradesmen, who are in many ways the school-masters of the boy anxious to learn; she sees little of human life, and when anything extraordinary happens she is incapable, one might almost suggest, of seizing it with her senses, that is to say, of observing accurately. If beside there be danger, noise, fear, all which attract the boy and serve to excite his curiosity, she gets out of the way in alarm and either sees nothing or sees it indistinctly from a distance.

A young girl may even in certain circumstances be a dangerous witness, when she is interested in the matter or is herself perchance the centre. In such a case strong exaggerations and even pure inventions are to be feared. Natural gifts, imagination, dreaming, romantic exaltation, such are the natural degrees by which the girl, too young yet to have had any interesting experiences of her own, arrives at last at "Byronism." Now Byronism is a sort of *ennui* or weariness of life, always urging one to seek for change; and what happier variety could there be than a criminal matter in which the little lady finds herself mixed up. It is interesting enough in itself to appear in the witness box, to make a deposition and to intervene in the destiny of another; but how much more noteworthy is it when an important matter is in question, when the attention of everyone is turned upon the witness, when all the world is breathless to learn what she has been asked, what she has replied and how the case is going to turn. Thus an insignificant theft is easily magnified into a robbery with violence, the witness, out of a miserable swindler, manufactures a pale and interesting young man, a coarse word becomes a blow, an insignificant event develops into a romantic abduction, stupid chaff turns up as a great conspiracy. A young girl is also a very dangerous witness at, and often previous to, the period of her first menstruation. Many women remain similarly influenced throughout their whole life before and during each period of menstruation. Climate is frequently a factor in causing this aberration. In short too great care cannot be observed in interrogating a young girl, to whatever class of society she belongs.

But, to be just we must recognise on the other hand that no one notices and knows certain things more cleverly than a young girl. If her imagination does not carry her away, she can furnish information more valuable than any grown-up person. The reason is the same as we have given for her exaggerations and inventions. Her school, her life, her daily tasks do not afford sufficient nourishment for her imaginations and her dreams; the sexual instinct begins to awaken, she searches around her, almost unconsciously, for incidents touching, however remotely, this sphere. No one discovers more rapidly than a sprightly young girl approaching maturity the little carryings-on and intrigues of her neighbours, the delicacy of her sensibility enables her to seize the least shade of sympathy which the pair she is observing have for each other, and long before they have found it out themselves, she knows what their true feelings are for each other. She notes accurately the birth of the intimacy, she knows when they spoke for the first time. And she anticipates long before what the result will be, reconciliation or rupture; in short she knows everything earlier and better than anyone else in her circle.

Connected with this is the trick young girls have of spying on certain people. An interesting beauty or a young man acquaintance have no more vigilant watcher of all their goings on, than their neighbour—a little girl of twelve to fourteen. No one knows better than she, who they are, what they do, what company they keep when they go out, and how they dress. She even notes the moral traits of those coming under her supervision,—their joy, their grief, their disappointments, their hopes, and all their experiences. If one desires information on such subjects the best witnesses are school girls—always supposing that they are willing to tell the truth.

Adults.—From youth we pass to adults, who though in the flower of their existence are far from furnishing the best witnesses. The adult is in general the worst of all observers. Finding himself in the happiest epoch of his life, full of hope and ideals, interested only in himself and his desires, the young man finds nothing important but himself. Childhood is far away; middle-aged and old men have long ago ceased to exist for him; what they do is of no importance, the world is the empire of youth, what interests it is alone of value, nothing else is worth troubling about.

The ideal representative of this age is the young lady to whom the disappearance of the world would be a matter of no moment compared with the momentous matter of a ball, or the student to whom his club or society is the most serious thing under the sun. All this of course changes with time, but youth with its plenitude of force is the personification of that robust egoism which takes possession of the world and in all its diversions sees only itself. Anyone who has critically watched himself and watched others, knows all this, whoever has had the opportunity of questioning young people about important facts happening in their neighbourhood, is at once irritated and delighted at the sublime indifference exhibited.

But if perchance the young man has observed, his deposition will be true and trustworthy, he has preserved his good principles, not yet scattered by the storms of life.

In *middle age*, man employs all the forces with which he has been endowed by nature his good and bad qualities alike have reached their fullest development, and what the middle-aged man and woman want to perceive, they can perceive and describe. Then career the goal of their labours is fixed, then likes and their dislikes are formed and that decisively, the middle-aged man thus has a clearly defined position in all circumstances, when it is a question of testimony as to justice or injustice he advances with a firm and decided step.

True this is the case only with the man of sound moral principles. For there is no period of life in which man is assailed more violently by his passions, malevolence, egoism, self-seeking, discord, than when he mounts to the highest plane of his life, when he is the most active but also the most unreasonable. These passions never exert their influence on him more strongly than at this age, their omnipotence makes him an unconscious liar, and there is no witness more difficult to tackle, or more dangerous, than the man in full possession of all his faculties, both good and bad.

If you ask the difference between the word of a man and that of a woman, we can only reply in the words of the poet, ' man has great ideas woman profound sentiments, for the man, the world is his heart, for the woman, her heart is the world." This explains the vast difference between the standpoints of observation of the man and the woman. We can even say beforehand how a man and a woman will assimilate a fact which they have both seen. And what is interesting and instructive, and at the same time right to establish with certainty, is exactly that one anticipates what one is going to hear. We are then armed against anything which may lead us astray or befog us, and moreover we can go straight to the point, before an inaccurate and distorted statement has been definitely recorded.

The *old man* comes last, he is either sweet and conciliatory or sour and cynical according to his luck in life. His senses and faculties of observation are weakened but experience tells him by a sort of insight what his eyes do not catch, and frequently his opinion may be summed up in the words, ' To understand, is to forgive.'

In fact, the old man has become a child again, accurate perception of external objects is wanting, but also his passions are dulled. He sees simply and without cunning, the difference between the sexes is again accentuated the old man and the old woman see and understand things like children and the suggestions of mother in favour of this or that regain their power, just as when they were young.

B When the witness does not wish to speak the truth

It is impossible to lay down a rule for preventing witnesses lying, but they would lie much less, if Investigating Officers would only give themselves more trouble. This is a fact which everyone must admit who knows with what rapidity Investigating Officers frequently interrogate the most important witnesses. It is true they have generally no time to do otherwise. But it is just this rapidity which is the cause of the numerous false depositions to be found on our records. The only means of remedying this evil which eats into the very vitals of the State and society, is for the Officer to carefully prepare his interrogatory, not to be afraid to remind the witness at length that he must speak the truth, and to probe him to the bottom, especially if he has the slightest suspicion that his statement is false. But to enable the Investigating Officer really to manage the affair in his own way in the interests of the State, he should have much more time at his disposal than he generally has. Whoever is acquainted with the progress of an inquiry, knows that a minute examination may preserve the Investigating Officer from the gravest blunders.

The importance of a minute interrogatory is clearly shown in the case where a complicated plot has been laid to deceive the Investigating Officer and the falsity of the depositions must be exposed. Take the following case concocted in a very short time and by absolutely ignorant women. It was a case of affiliation in which the attempt was made to father a child on a well-to-do but mean peasant. The fraud was discovered and the mother of the child, as well as her mother, were prosecuted for defamation, both denied it and appealed to the testimony of a woman, who, so they asserted could give important evidence in their favour. As soon as this woman was summoned they tried to get her to give false testimony. She would not consent, but consented to sell them the summons. Another woman appeared in the witness-box, fortified by the summons of the real witness. Fortunately the Investigating Officer examined this woman carefully and at length, and when he came to speak of matters that the real witness must have known, she got into difficulties, hesitated and could give no satisfactory replies as to certain personal details, &c. Thus the Investigating Officer succeeded, not it is true without difficulty in establishing that the person in the box was not the person that should have been there.

The author has come across at least two other cases where a substituted witness has so appeared. In one case the deception was discovered by minute examination; in the other the witness gave himself away at the end of his examination, by signing his deposition in his own name.

Now if within a narrow circle one knows no fewer than three cases in which this trick has been somewhat cleverly attempted, how frequently must it be tried on and how few must there be who can detect it. Often too the most detailed and meticulous examination fails to disclose the falsity of a cleverly got-up statement, the problem then is, which is the craftier, the Investigating Officer or the witness? But the Investigating Officer always holds the best hand of trumps in this contest. He is the calmer of the two, for after all the witness is playing a dangerous game and risks his liberty, while the worst that can happen to the Investigating Officer is once more to be made a tool of. Besides he knows the whole record of the case, he knows approximately what may be true and what must be false, the depositions of the witnesses as the inquiry advances are stones which should fit into the whole building, he can denounce them as false when they do not so fit in. Above all he is in the happy position of being able to ask questions which the witness, unless in very exceptional circumstances, cannot do. By questioning, and questioning thoroughly, he always arrives at a point of which the witness has not dreamed, and on which he has not consulted his accomplices; the slightest indication of contradiction betrays to the Investigating Officer the weak point of the convention between the witnesses and the accused, and he has only to follow up on the same lines to pierce the whole tissue of lies. But to arrive at this result he must take full advantage of the superiority of his situation; he must question freely and record every reply. The growth of these useful materials does not, or need not, materially swell the record, if the Officer has well studied the matter, if he knows clearly what he wants and the goal he has in view; if he interrogates only on points of real importance and records the replies briefly and concisely, he will have fewer words but more matter, and the record will be no longer. This task, of course, is not always very pleasant, but he is not there to amuse himself, and he who is afraid of such worries should not become an Investigating Officer.

As an example we may take the case where an Investigating Officer has to combat a false *alibi*, certainly the most dangerous obstacle to the conviction of the real malefactor. *Karl Stener* it was, we believe, who truly said, "to be a good poacher, three things are indispensable—a gun that takes to pieces, a blackened face, and a good *alibi*." That is just what happens in countries where poaching is common. In the mountains, things almost always happen thus: a wood-cutter goes poaching, the keepers surprise but cannot catch him because he has got the start of them; the gun is concealed in a crevice in the rock, and the cattleman and his wife swear that at the very hour when the keepers pretend to have seen him, he was in their hut patching his working clothes. Everything is carefully and beautifully arranged beforehand, and all goes well so long as the Investigating Officer does not poke his nose into details, does not put questions too precise and troublesome, and asks everything he is at liberty to ask—how they were seated, how long they were together, what they did, what they said, in what order things occurred, &c. If the Officer has taken the indispensable precaution of summoning the accused and his witnesses at the same time, and of so ordering his examination that a witness once examined cannot communicate with those yet to come, it will be very odd if he cannot get contradictory statements. The most complicated proofs of *alibi*, concocted by the most experienced scoundrels, are just the same. The only difference is that they are perhaps got up more carefully, yet we believe it is always possible to prove the falsity of a false *alibi*; the job sometimes involves a lot of trouble, necessitating wearisome and repeated examinations, but cannot fail to bring to light contradictions.

The most difficult cases to deal with are those in which an *alibi* is set up all the incidents attaching to which are perfectly true, the time or date alone having been changed, i.e., if the crime has been committed on a Monday, a meeting which has taken place on a previous day is transferred to the Monday. Then of course all the details given by the different witnesses will fit in. If this procedure be suspected the best plan is to cross-examine the witnesses regarding the incidents of previous and subsequent days. In other words, having satisfied oneself that the alibi is false, the next problem and the only one will be, how to break down the witness as to date? As all the incidents deposed to actually occurred, cross-examination as to them will be not only waste of time but will tend as well to establish the truth of the story. We must consequently proceed to incidents *outside* the witnesses' story. Richard Harris K C , in his book " Hints on Advocacy " discusses this question at considerable length. He points out that such questions as, Where were you the day before? or The day after? are useless. You must take the witness entirely out of the circumstance and ask something which he does not anticipate. You must ask about dates as much previous or as much subsequent to the day in question as possible.

Even if the accused be in prison we must not imagine that all necessary precautions have been taken. So long as one cannot keep each accused by himself, compel him to solitude even in his walks, surround him with absolutely incorruptible warders, it will be impossible to prevent him communicating with his friends outside. The greatest danger in this respect comes from his co-prisoners, especially when they are " under remand," for one never knows when the inquiry against any one of them will not suddenly break down and the man be set at liberty. In such circumstances the accused always take the necessary precautions, they arrange among themselves what each shall tell the friends and relations of the other, if he ever gets outside the prison walls. Thus it is that, as we all know, it frequently happens that an accused suddenly starts an *alibi* which he has just thought of. We cannot understand how this man could be so indifferent to his fate, as not to have bethought himself sooner of so easy a means of at once proving his innocence. But we understand it all when we find out that another accused, confined in the same cell as this man " of the bad memory," has just been set at liberty, to him has been entrusted the working up of the *alibi*.

If we cannot show that a person so detained has been liberated, we may be sure that the accused has managed to get a letter smuggled outside, giving the particulars of his scheme, for who would have so poor a memory as to forget for so long so important a defence?

As a general rule it is more difficult to unmask false witnesses when their evidence has nothing to do with an *alibi*, then the chief weapon of the Investigating Officer, the discovery of contradictions, becomes useless. Whoever wants to prove an *alibi* always takes care to have at least two witnesses, for he knows it is not likely that one will inspire confidence. But in other cases, especially when an accused wishes to present the whole circumstances of a case, it is often difficult for him to produce more than one witness for each particular moment. If then we have to combine the evidence of several witnesses, the contradictions which may appear in small details and especially in incidents of very short duration, do not count for much. For instance, if a man wishes to prove that he has not taken part in a row, and that three witnesses can corroborate his statement, they will naturally be questioned only as to the moment at which the complainant was wounded. The false witnesses will be careful not to enter too much into details or to affirm anything too positively, it will be enough for them to swear that at the moment at which the complainant was wounded, their friend was not near him. But they cannot say exactly how everything happened—the row was too great," and " the whole affair was over in a minute." It is difficult to say how in such a case we can discover contradictions, but if that method does not succeed we must try another.

The preceding rules of course lose none of their value: study and get up the case as minutely as you can, and cross-examine thoroughly. But another rule may be added, discriminate as closely as possible the various portions of a witness's deposition. It is not sufficient to wait until the deposition becomes, for some reason or other, suspicious, for as soon as such reason arises we have the end of the thread in our hands and can ordinarily unravel it with ease. But it is necessary to face in advance the possible falsehood of every statement of witnesses. To do so is not to display exaggerated mistrust, but is only a proof of prudence and experience, for one has often found false depositions slip into an enquiry in the most innocent and least suspected form.

Starting from this principle, we first try to see if for some reason the witness is not speaking the truth, though desirous of doing so. If no ground is discovered for adopting this hypothesis, we must ask ourselves if perchance the witness does not wish to tell the truth, this will lead us to search for some reason for his desire, a search which may indeed lead to the conclusion that no such reason exists. Such a ground may perhaps be found in the personal relations of the witness with the accused or the wounded man, or perhaps in some real connection between the witness and the occurrence itself. In the former case it may not be difficult to establish friendship, relationship, or some other tie, but in the latter, an accurate knowledge of all the circumstances can alone show if the witness is to any extent interested in the result of the investigation, if he has himself been an accomplice, or if he is afraid of being considered an accomplice, of the accused.

If we find that the witness has any sort of connection with the affair, we must, to some extent, accept with mistrust all that he says and verify every one of his statements, we must spare no trouble to ascertain the point of view at which the witness stations himself. This is not so difficult as one would think, the witness almost always betrays himself, if only by a word. We can in this connection learn much from the novelist, by compelling ourselves when reading a romance to guess which will be the hero and which the villain of the story, and that from the very beginning before the author has expressly pictured them as such. Almost always our guess will be correct, often thanks to a single word. The hero may have the very worst character but he will never be avaricious, stingy, envious, untruthful, or spiteful, he will not always be depicted as an ideal of masculine beauty, but he will never be bald, he will not squint, he will not have bad teeth, or if he has, the teeth will be left out, and he will possess instead " a broad and lofty forehead," or " a piercing glance ", he may be clad carelessly or out of the fashion but his linen will always be scrupulously clean. The villain will perhaps be presented to us at the outset gifted with every physical and intellectual good quality, under the mask of an honest man, he will insinuate himself into the heart of the ingenuous reader, until he finds that the author makes him speak with " harsh " voice, or " cast a furtive glance " or appear " dressed with a tawdry elegance." Our man would never have received such epithets, had not the author intended later on to unveil him as a scoundrel.

This is precisely the procedure of a witness who desires to save the guilty and inculpate the innocent. In the former case he will be careful, especially if he is apt at the work, to attribute to the accused some bad qualities and prudently to admit those traits in his character which it is impossible to deny, but he will guard himself against saying anything likely to render the accused contemptible or to permanently injure him in our estimation. On the other hand, does he wish to prejudice the accused? At the start he will be genial, he will excuse, he will embellish; then all at once he will make use of some epithet which will attract the attention of the Investigating Officer and remind him to be prudent; the witness imputes to the accused matters too grave to be considered as stated conscientiously.

For observations of this kind one need not be a great psychologist; with good will and sustained attention almost everyone will in time arrive at the exact moment at which the witness lets slip the word that betrays him. Of course, we have not yet indisputable proofs, but the Investigating Officer has strong foundations for suspecting the sincerity of the witness's statements. It is not as a rule difficult to verify the justness of the suspicion. He has only to relate or describe to the witness some fact having an important bearing on the innocence or guilt of the accused, and of which the Investigating Officer is certain, either from having witnessed it himself, or heard it from absolutely trustworthy witnesses.

It often happens, especially when we are dealing with people not particularly obdurate, that the witness attempts more or less impudently, to lie to the Investigating Officer, then turns round and tells the truth as soon as he sees that the Investigating Officer is not going to allow himself to be taken in. We may assert indeed that it is all the fault of the Investigating Officer, for if he had paid better attention from the very beginning he would have easily prevented the development of the whole tissue of falsehoods. There also he must open his eyes and especially note carefully the contradictions in the deposition of the witness, and those between the deposition and the facts, for there is no check more powerful and more surprising to such a witness than a clear and striking "ocular demonstration."

Of course attention must also be paid to small details, for instance, the witness pretends that a certain man has read him something whereas the man in question can neither read nor write. Again a witness affirms that his house was in danger of catching fire, although it was not in the direction in which the wind was blowing at the time, or he asserts he remained out of doors half-an-hour with naked feet although the snow was knee-deep. The witness states that the river frequently rises so high that it overflows; we have only to look at the stones emerging but a little above the water, to see that they are covered with a thick bed of moss which would not be there if the stones were frequently submerged. The witness says his son had already drawn his attention to something; a small calculation shows that at the time in question the son was only four years old.

Similar examples of contradictions and self-evident impossibilities are frequently met with in our records, they supply the surest method of demonstrating to the witness the falsity of his deposition—but we must first discover them. This is never very difficult if one gives sedulous attention to the examination, listens carefully to the reading of the record, and always pictures to oneself in imagination what the witness has related. The last is indispensable and of the greatest assistance. Words alone do not contradict each other so strongly or clearly as facts, or at least one does not notice so clearly the contradiction in the words. But if we compel ourselves to build up in our mind the scene as the witness has described it, or as we know it from previous recitals, and to adjust what we are told with what we already know, if in the course of the narrative of the witness we follow closely the facts and allow in thought the whole scene to unroll itself at the very spot where, according to our previous information, it must have taken place, it is almost impossible for an improbability or an impossibility to escape us. We must always abandon ourselves wholly to the business, thus only can our task be fully accomplished.

We have already mentioned cases in which the wrong man comes forward as a witness. Sometimes when a medical examination has to be undergone a substitute is sent. *Caspar Liman* refers us to the historic case of the Countess of Essex (Lady Francis Howard) who sent another young person instead of herself to prove her virginity. Such cases happen very often nowadays. The author remembers a case where A injured B with a stick but without fracturing a bone. B, summoned to appear in Court, sent C, who happened to have fallen from a tree and broken his arm. C appeared, gave the name of B, was examined and cross-examined, and the fraud was not detected until much later, by which time B had succeeded in obtaining much heavier compensation from A. In another case instead of a woman A, a pregnant woman B was sent to Court to personate A and prove that she was pregnant. Sometimes the wrong person comes forward as the accused. The person D suspected of forgery sends E, who personates D, and states that he is half blind and therefore unable to commit forgery. He undergoes medical examination, his blindness is proved, and the prosecution of D is dropped. In another case F, accused of concealment of birth, declared herself to be too ill to appear at Court. A commissioner was sent to the house, where an old woman showed him her daughter lying in bed. A medical examination took place, the result of which established that the girl had never had a child at all, certainly not within a few days. Later on doubts arose, leading to the suspicion that the sister of the girl had taken her place in the bed and been examined in her stead. In another case H was summoned for fraud, and sent J, who was arrested as H. After J had been in jail for four or five days, H succeeded in leaving the country and J declared his real identity. In another case K had been allowed out on bail, and on the day of the first remand L appeared in his stead and was committed to jail. Advantage was taken of a change of Magistrates, but the clerk of the Court observed something different about the appearance of the man. It turned out that K had gone to bed and was too lazy to get up, so he sent L, who was also on bail for another offence. K fully intended to give himself up but wanted to have another day's leave.

All these cases prove how easily and how often such substitution can and does happen, although the consequences may be of the greatest importance

It is difficult to avoid them altogether as each witness cannot in all cases be properly identified. But if anything strange appears in the case, such as peculiar behaviour on the part of the witness, we must make it a rule to be specially careful.

A question which in many cases assumes great importance is as to the value to be attached to the statements of dying persons. These statements may have to be taken into account in various ways: thus the Investigating Officer may have to question wounded persons or those suffering from poison, he may have to record the depositions of persons who on their deathbed betray secrets long safely guarded and accuse someone of a crime, sometimes dying persons salve their consciences by accusing themselves of crime, perchance they may testify to the innocence of one who has been convicted. In many such cases the dying statement has a special importance because on account of lapse of time or some other circumstance, every other proof is wanting. If the Investigating Officer has been able himself to question the dying person the difficulty is less, because he has had the opportunity of noting for himself the way in which the deposition has been given and so forming an opinion on its value. But very often it has been impossible to secure the presence of the Investigating Officer, and the statement is made to third persons who hand it on to him.

Naturally such witnesses must be questioned with special accuracy and appropriate precautions, particularly in every case the medical expert should decide whether the dying person is in a fit condition to make a sensible statement. If the medical man gives an absolutely affirmative reply to this question, another arises,—does the fact of being at the point of death exercise any special influence over the truth of the statement? The opinion of lawyers varies greatly on this point, some declare that the words of a dying man are true and infallible in all cases, others are of opinion that they must be valued on the same footing as those of any other man.

Clergymen, and especially Catholic priests, who have heard a thousand times the last secrets of the dying must have had much greater experience than lawyers on so important a question. The opinion of enlightened and unprejudiced priests is that the answer depends upon whether the dying man is or is not a true believer. In the former case every credence can be given to his statement, since, in the firm conviction that he is about to appear before the Supreme Judge, he will certainly not burden his conscience with a grave sin. The difficulty is to know whether the dying man is or is not a true believer.

Assuming that he is not a believer a further distinction must be drawn. In the first case the dying man has no need to be cautious because his memory cannot be injured by what he says, or because it matters little to him if it be, so long as he is sure that no injury can befall his relations in honour, fortune, or any other fashion. Here the deposition made in presence of death is true, even if the deponent has not been in life one to whom absolute credence could be accorded. But when it can be proved that the unbeliever still takes an interest in his own memory and his relations' welfare, and that interest is affected by his statement, then the latter is of no more value than if made at any other period of his life. If he was an honest man, he will speak the truth also on his death-bed, but if not, he may well have lied, even at the supreme moment.

C Pathological Lying

Between the state of a person who desires to speak the truth and that of another person who does not so desire there are what may be called intermediary positions, such is the case where a person, not having at a given moment the intention of lying, yet under the influence of habit presents his facts in such a manner that their falsity becomes at once apparent

This is not as a rule due to sickness or disease. But there must have been undoubtedly a train of circumstances causing the individual to be, at least temporarily, in an abnormal state of mind leading him to accept falsehood as truth. Such cases present great difficulties to the Investigating Officer, for while these lies are without motive, at least any apparent motive, yet the impression produced by such persons is absolutely normal, and their statements are always so cleverly and clearly presented that one would never, apart from extraneous circumstances, suspect their falsity. Such cases, which may be called "pathological," occur particularly among persons gifted with a lively imagination, among women and children, and pass through every grade from the small exaggeration to the complete invention of the whole story.*

The Investigating Officer encounters his greatest difficulties when he has to deal with people whose character is what *Forel* calls "Ethico-Idiotic," which renders them absolutely incapable of speaking the truth. This may go further than one would suppose, take for example, the case of the woman, hysterical it is true, cited by *Reinhard*, who wrote herself false letters, sent to herself anonymous messages, and finally at last became thoroughly convinced of the genuineness of all she had herself written. In this connection *Rupping* recommends extreme caution in the interrogation of women who are enceinte or have been recently confined, these frequently give long accounts of things that never happened although at ordinary times absolutely truthful and worthy of credence

Even in the simplest circumstances, the Investigating Officer himself may be the cause of much difficulty; if for example he has to do with timid or conscientious witnesses he may by his mere questioning drive them into making false statements, by bringing them to believe at last that they have really witnessed things that have never taken place. To this feature *Bernheim* has given the characteristic name of "retro-active hallucination." Great care and caution is in such cases the best support of the Investigating Officer

---

* The most interesting example is furnished us by Goethe, he says in the second book of his work "*Truth and Falsehood*," that he often related stories he had himself imagined, as narratives of events that had really happened to him. He concludes thus 'If I had not learnt gradually and in conformity with my natural bent to transform these imaginings and braggings into works of literary art, such a beginning would undoubtedly have had very serious consequences for me." The first to treat of normal sources of errors of memory was *Maudsley*, followed in order by *Sully*, *Krapelin* and *Delbruck* The last, who has dealt with the matter exhaustively, cites a great many cases in which people have told false stories through an instinctive impulse to lie but in spite of there being lack of discernment between true and false these cases cannot be classed with those we have described as "pathological". Evidently, we must put on one side all instances in which there is real disease, to which *Delbrück* has given the name '*Pseudologia phantastica*" It must be left to the medical expert to decide whether the impulse to lie and deceive is developed to such a point as to enter into the domain of "hysteria" and 'moral insanity'

Section iii.—Examination of the Accused

As is probably known to most of our readers, the examination of an accused person in Europe is legally much more thorough than is contemplated by English Law, and is occasionally in practice carried to a pitch which shocks our sense of fairness. Yet we have to deal with statements and confessions of accused persons, and the following section will furnish suggestive hints to those whose business it is to interrogate, or record the statements of an accused.

The examination of an accused person is the most difficult of all tasks for an Investigating Officer who appreciates its value. We can here give only a few hints. He who knows men, who is gifted with a good memory and presence of mind, who takes pleasure in his work and zealously abandons himself to it, who keeps always scrupulously on the legal platform and who sees always in the accused a fallen brother or one wrongfully suspected, he will question well. But an officer who is wanting in a single one of these qualifications will never do any good.

And yet even these qualifications are not all; there are other conditions which the Investigating Officer ought indeed never to lose sight of, but which are exceptionally necessary in the examination of an accused.

Thus the officer must compel himself to be sincere even to the limits of pedantry, impenetrable by any shock. It appears supremely natural that an honest man should speak the truth, and yet the Investigating Officer is tempted only too often, by excess of zeal, to alter, be it but in the minutest detail, the deposition of a witness, the report of an expert, or some other document, which he communicates to the accused—"to assist him in making a clean breast of it," often, too, he is led to pretend to know something of which he is ignorant, or knows only imperfectly, or to affirm something without substantial grounds.

But how terrible are the consequences! the fear that the falsehood may be discovered, the confusion if the accused remains incredulous, the lifelong torments inflicted by conscience! What at the moment appeared but a slight "inaccuracy," lives in our recollection as time goes on, as an infamous lie, its effect, if it had any, seems to us a success unfairly obtained, and the man whose guilt was certain will be transformed into an innocent victim. Calm and absence of passion are also indispensable. The officer who becomes excited or loses his temper delivers himself into the hands of the accused, if the latter, wiser than the officer, preserves his *sangfroid*, or even with happy foresight, sets himself deliberately to exasperate his questioner so as to get the better of him. Certainly it is not always easy to maintain a calm demeanour, the crime may be of a nature to justify disgust or hatred, the accused may deny everything too impudently, may be always evading the real object of the question, may be unwilling to understand, or may talk only nonsense, but in spite of everything the Investigating Officer must never forget that he has to do his duty and that his duty enjoins on him not to allow himself to be beaten by the accused. A conscientious officer, however, naturally irascible, will not allow himself to be carried away, he will be constantly repeating to himself these words, "It is my duty."

Further an Investigating Officer who is afraid of the accused is lost.

It is difficult not to feel fear when one is naturally timid, but as we have already said, whoever is wanting in courage has no business to be an Investigating Officer. Besides, we have all seen examples of men by nature cowardly who, thanks to their own determination and force of long habit, have quite forgotten that there was a time when the rolling eyes of an accused made them feel very uncomfortable.

We would not assume for ourselves the responsibility of advising that an Investigating Officer should *never* take precautions for his safety as regards the accused, as having him put in irons, guarded during his examination, &c. let each man do what he thinks necessary. The author's opinion is that such inquietude is always and without exception superfluous. Will not a mortifying impression be produced upon the accused when he finds himself dragged in chains into the office of the Investigating Officer and by excess of precaution surrounded by warders, or if he notices that, before he has been brought in, scissors, heavy ink bottles, paper knives, and all dangerous utensils which he might snatch up and use as weapons of offence have been carefully put aside, or even if the officer maintains a respectful distance and changes his tone whenever the accused raises his voice or clenches his fists? The officer will not by this means convince him by his arguments.

And even when all precautions have been taken, even if the accused be brought shut up in an iron cage, if he really *wishes* to do anything he can always do it. But that is of no importance. It is as rare to see an accused raise his hand against an Investigating Officer, as to see a meteor kill someone in its fall; should any mischief befall an Investigating Officer at the hands of an accused person, the former can always console himself with the reflection that it is certainly his own fault.

There are other and better means of self-protection which the Investigating Officer has always at his disposal, among these are perfect composure, prudence, and procedure in strict conformity with law and humanity. There are, it is true, extremely dangerous prisoners, with whom extreme caution is never out of place. One must become accustomed in such a case never for one moment, not even one single moment, to remove one's eyes from the individual, to cease following and watching all his looks, all his movements. Further, one must never sit down near a suspicious character; both in attack and in defence one should always be standing, for if one is seated when attacked, the mere getting up and putting oneself on the defensive causes considerable loss of time. If the accused be seated—as he ought to be—and the officer be standing, the latter has the advantage whatever happens.

Further, one should stand as near the accused as possible without attracting his attention. One observes him better, does not forget constantly to keep an eye on him; he is not so tempted to do anything if he sees the officer close to him, and if the worst come to the worst, one is in the best possible attitude for seizing him.

But all that is only to frighten him. The author has interrogated hundreds of accused and has never come across one who made as if to attack him. There are, indeed, but few cases where such an attempt would have been of any use, for example in a very small court or office room, with no warders or police in the passages or at the doors, the accused might try to get away in this manner. If in such a case the Investigating Officer is not accompanied by a clerk or attender, or if the latter is at a distance, he must never for an instant take his eye off the accused, as for instance to search for some document on the record, for then if the accused be armed he may very well endeavour to strike down the officer and attempt to fly; but here there are so many "if's" and so many imprudences, that such a concatenation of circumstances is almost impossible.

Another case in which the accused may raise his hand against the Investigating Officer is where the latter shows himself unfair, passionate, rude, or contemptuous towards the accused, thus exciting his anger. If, in such circumstances, one of those misfortunes to which human nature is exposed befalls the Investigating Officer, it is only what he deserves. Do not say "There must have been a mistake, perhaps the accused fancied that he was being treated or judged in an unjust manner, when in reality it was not so." That does not usually happen. The accused, to whatever class of society he belongs, is most precise, and just like a child, if one treats him with unjust severity. He will never rebel against severity, and the most perverse is impressed when he sees the official doing his duty zealously; the harshest severity will not affect the accused if he finds the Investigating Officer at the same time exhibiting towards him a humane good-will and not endeavouring solely to crush him whenever possible, but setting out in relief as zealously everything which can establish his innocence or attenuate his offence.

The very technique of the examination demands a knowledge and understanding of the man with whom we have to do. If the previous history of the accused has been registered only at the end of the record to which he has been a party, we need not expect any good to come of the whole inquiry, for the Investigating Officer has not taken the trouble to study the accused before setting to work, and if he has not done so he must have omitted many points absolutely necessary. But if we find the antecedents of the accused carefully registered at the beginning of the record, the whole inquiry will be conducted at least carefully and intelligently.

In thus setting out his antecedents with accuracy we learn above all what sort of man is before us; we can hark back to events of long ago and establish, with the help of questions, many things which, if not strictly relevant to the matter in hand, often enable us to form an accurate estimate of the character of the accused. As a general rule the accused here speaks the truth, at least to a great extent, and if he does not do so, we can learn thereby to recognise his usual style of lying. In addition, we can quickly pick out the lies. We take notes and establish certain periods, then we make him go over the story again a little later, and then note the impossibilities, the contradictions, the gaps; also we can often pick up from the old records antecedents incidentally mentioned by the accused and compare them with his story. If we recall them to the accused, at the same time letting him see that we are not going to allow ourselves to be imposed upon, he may not unfrequently be led to renounce his intention of lying about the matter in hand, and penitently admit his guilt, when the affair under inquiry is imperceptibly introduced. It is a good plan not to draw too accurate a line between the antecedents and the examination strictly so called, but rather, proceeding in chronological order to arrive gradually at the moment at which the crime has been committed, in the hope that he will begin himself to speak about it.

We do not assert that in this way a confession should be dragged out of the accused; that would be both dishonest and useless. What we say is that nothing is gained by making his confession a painful task to him. We are convinced that in rendering his avowal easy, we are acting in his best interest, for it is always to his interest to confess: his actions appear in less sombre colours, he is sure of a less severe punishment, and the disburdening of his conscience is a blessing to the most hardened criminal.

It is needless, or rather psychologically wrong, to expect anyone boldly and directly to confess his crime, perhaps an abominable offence; persons with an extensive acquaintance with men of the lowest character know only too well what repugnance they feel in employing the correct expression even after a complete avowal. Persons of a somewhat higher moral grade, often shrink from using the word 'steal', while the number of periphrastic expressions employed to avoid uttering the simple word 'kill' is extraordinary. Now if it is repugnant to such people to pronounce a single characteristic word, it must be much more painful for them to make without ceremony a confession of their misdeeds in a connected recital. We must smooth their way, render their task easy. Often also we must seize the exact moment when confession is easiest to the guilty man; we must often have abundance of patience, we must advance slowly, step by step; we must make troublesome investigations, if the guilt is only partially admitted or if from a number of facts the accused recognises only some. We must often in such a case make very accurate distinctions; frequently an accused admits only up to a certain point, that is to say, as far as he can go without compromising an accomplice, or again up to the time when his conduct becomes criminal, or perhaps when a less serious crime may be transformed into one carrying a heavier punishment, as *e.g.*, theft in a dwelling-house into house-breaking and theft.

There often exists, even among the vilest specimens of humanity, a certain standard of honour, which it is most important the Investigating Officer should appreciate at its true value. Frequently the attempts of the accused to prevent his crime appearing worse than it really is, are very like an attempt to deny everything that can possibly be denied. We cannot, hardly without exception, be absolutely certain as to what is true and what is not true, unless, in the course of our examination, we come to know the character of the accused sufficiently well to enable us to judge what line he is most likely to take.

To sum up, we must never shrink from any trouble which will help us to *know* the accused, his history, and the necessary details of the matter in hand, for nothing will so entirely and so definitely sweep away any ascendancy we may have acquired over him as to betray ignorance of details, even the most insignificant. If the accused notes any gap, any mistake, any piece of ignorance on the part of the Investigating Officer, he at once intrenches himself behind it, and all the labour, all the sagacity of the officer are powerless to make him abandon his asylum.*

---

* With regard to an important point in connection with "Confessions," referred to in the author's "Criminal Psychology," we can only mention here that false confessions are very often made through insanity. Such cases are very dangerous, for the insanity is

We may here add a few words on the question of physiognomy. There are few sciences the value of which has been more exaggerated by its partizans and more unjustly depreciated by its adversaries. The balance seems to incline in favour of those who attribute to it considerable value. Certainly it is going too far to fix certain types of the human face and to pretend that one can deduce from certain features, structures, colours and their relations with one another definite mental and moral characteristics, but it is beyond doubt that the experienced critic can learn from the lines of the face and play of the features much more and more satisfactorily, than anyone could tell him. We cannot of course give here a précis of physiognomy, but we know enough to enable us to recommend strongly to an Investigating Officer the study of the subject both theoretically and practically. We certainly do not pretend that he should take in his hands the antiquated *Lavater* and pin his faith to him. But whoever studies attentively the works of modern writers on this subject, will find that even to-day we can learn much from the founder of the science. It is not easy always to say when he is deceived, and when he is right. He is deceived, as we have just said, when he exaggerates the value of typical characters; he is instructive when he teaches us how to read the general character of a physiognomy.

It was his fate, for instance, to mistake for a portrait of *Herder*, a portrait he had long looked for, that of a murderer executed in Hanover and to read in the features all the qualities he had supposed to exist in *Herder*. But again he is invaluable when he says, e.g., "I chiefly recognise the true sage and the truly honest man by the mode in which they listen. They have a certain brightness in the eye, a clearness of vision, in which serenity and liveliness appear to unite, something intermediate between the lightning flash and the extinguished glimmer of a dying eye." No one can even to-day give an Investigating Officer a more precise lesson. To observe how the person questioned listens is a rule of primary importance, and if the officer observes it, he will arrive at his goal more quickly than by hours of examination. Undoubtedly the features must not be wholly neglected. *Rubers* is quite correct when he says, 'suppose that one of your intimate friends covers his face so as to conceal the forehead, the chin, and half the cheeks. The eyes, the nose, and the upper lip are alone visible, and yet you will recognise him at once. But if he puts on a mask which covers the half of his forehead and the small space between the eyes and the upper part of the nose, you will no longer recognise him."

These rules and a hundred others of great value, the Investigating Officer cannot discover for himself, however hard he tries, even in the course of a long experience; he must seek them in books where they are laid down scientifically; then in his practice he can extend and perfect his knowledge and the time devoted to his preliminary studies will certainly not be thrown away.

It is impossible to leave this question of the treatment of an accused person by the Investigating Officer, without saying a word as to what is

---

sometimes quite unnoticeable, the confessing person appearing perfectly normal to the non-professional. In several cases of poisoning (by gas and mushrooms) very strange false confessions have been made and the Investigating Officer cannot be too careful.

called "the school of *Lombroso* Indeed the works of *Lombroso* are to be found to-day in the hands of all criminal experts and have exercised on all of them some, at times great, influence The high authority wielded by *Lombroso* is due not only to the abundance of the materials provided by him, to the number of new ideas and the captivating audacity of his reasoning, it is due also to the fact that his theory is in absolute accord with the nihilistic tendency which, to-day, penetrates everywhere This modern tendency to bring everything to the same level consists in the negation of distinctive characteristics, as just as the social ideas preach equality, so the natural sciences profess that all living beings have the same origin, physical science propounds the identity of forces, and medical science affirms the impotency of a thousand remedies once deemed to be infallible Why then should we be surprised if this nihilist tendency penetrating into *our* science has created this doctrine —there is no difference in nature between the criminal and the honest man, the former is only a hereditary degenerate, gifted with a morbid constitution, and if we do not go on to draw the logical conclusion— there is no difference between good and bad—it is only because we do not dare If *Lombroso* did not exist, there would be a gap in the logical evolution of modern ideas

Let us examine a little the basis of this new doctrine One of the German authors, *Dr Kurella*, summarises it thus ' According to this doctrine all true criminals possess a continuous series (of the nature of cause and effect) of physical characteristics, the existence of which is proved by anthropology, and of moral characteristics the existence of which can be proved by psychophysiology, these characteristics constitute of criminals a particular variety, an anthropological type of the human race, and those who possess them are criminals by the stern decree of fate—even if they are never found out,—and that too independently of all social and individual conditions Such a man is born to be a criminal, he is as *Lombroso* puts it, *delinquente nato*, the genuine original sinner This hypothesis does not pretend to deny that acquired qualities or social influences (education, habit, temptation, poverty) will not occasionally make a man a criminal, on the contrary, the theory may be developed to recognise the existence of criminals by passion, by chance, or by habit, but it seeks to explain the existence of criminals by nature, by an innate disposition The indications of this disposition are certain physical peculiarities not the result of bodily disease, and its elements are certain fundamental qualities of character and morality, clearly distinct from the symptoms of mental disease, and the knowledge of which enables the psychologist to declare that those possessing them cannot help becoming criminals "

Now the School of Lombroso sets itself to discover and establish the anatomical variations to be found in criminals, their primary characteristics, variations in rudimentary organs, variations in secondary sexual characteristics, variations in multiple organs, variations resulting from a stoppage or diversion in development, and finally, acquired characteristics

It cannot be denied that the "school" has succeeded in proving the existence of these anatomical variations in a certain number of criminals but it has been impossible to push the demonstration far enough to establish a *determinate* type of criminal This has been proved by

Dr Kirn in a most convincing manner in a brief brochure. He shows that, truly enough, one can in examining carefully a certain number of convicts discover some mental anomalies and various marks of degeneracy, but these never appear in identically the same fashion and far from being typical appear in the greatest diversity, setting all rules at defiance. Further one frequently finds one symptom of intellectual weakness, but very rarely in combination all the symptoms characteristic of "moral insanity." Thus there being no correspondence in individuals taken one by one there can be no question of a criminal type.

The theory of *Lombroso* has been completely demolished by *Dr Nacke* in his dissertation on "The methodology of a scientific anthropology" in which he comes to the conclusion that the works of *Lombroso*, with their arbitrary processes, their exaggerations and premature conclusions, in no way answer to what one has a right to expect in a scientific work." The truth is "there is neither criminal born nor type of criminal."

The chief dogma of the positive school is thus destroyed, but we may pause to ask whence has it drawn the materials necessary to these seductive conclusions. It has noted and utilised the statistics furnished by prisons, and here it cannot be denied that the numbers cited and furnishing such and such percentages are here and there pretty high, but only here and there. Often the percentage is so low that no conclusion can be drawn from it, for whenever the percentage is very low we are always liable to find that chance has had something to do with the calculation of the statistics. Further it is frequently overlooked that the percentage obtained for a particular criminal anomaly must be compared with the corresponding percentage among non-criminals. Ordinarily this comparison is impossible, for one can carry on investigations only upon criminals confined in gaols, occasionally, on certain points, we may make enquiries among men, but not among women, so that no one can say in what proportion any particular anomaly is met with among others than convicts. The enquiries undertaken in schools, barracks, and hospitals, and the notes made at *post-mortem* examinations, can furnish but approximate information, for it cannot be imagined that a definite and representative section of the whole human race is here dealt with. But if it cannot be asserted that a certain anomaly is met with in a well-established percentage of the whole race, then the percentage found for criminals is of very doubtful scientific value, however accurate the enquiry may have been. Suppose for example it has been established that a certain anomaly is found among 10 per cent of all criminals, that is of no value unless it can be shown that a different percentage prevails among non-criminals. But if it is pretended that this anomaly is found among only 5 per cent of non-criminals because that proportion has been found to exist in schools, barracks and hospitals, it is only an approximate *supposition* for no one knows in what proportion the anomaly might be met with among that other section, and far the larger section, of men who are *outside* schools, barracks, and hospitals. Besides the materials at disposal in each of these inquiries are special and do not represent the bulk, at school we find youth, in the barracks picked men from a physical point of view, in the hospital, the poorest portion of the populace. But approximate suppositions are not scientific proofs.

In truth the weak point of the conclusions derived from statistics by *Lombroso* and his followers arises from the theoretically false way in which he builds up his figures, whereby the whole basis of his system crumbles away. Admit what *Lombroso* says. The anomaly A is found among $x\%$ of the convicts in all the prisons of the world, the anomaly B in $y\%$, the anomaly C in $z\%$ and so on; then to conclude that these anomalies will be found in the indicated proportions among all the criminals of the world, is false. We could only draw this conclusion if we could divide all the inhabitants of the world into two camps, criminals and non-criminals, sheep and goats; if then we could examine all the people in the two camps, establish the percentages of anomaly, and compare the results, we should be safe. But here the materials are not only uncertain but inaccurate. *Lombroso* has examined convicts in prison; that his materials may be complete, he must examine all who have been previously in gaol, all who commit crimes without being caught, and all who would naturally become criminals if favourable circumstances had not by chance snatched them from a criminal career, *e.g.*, those who would have been thieves if they had not been well off, or poachers if they had not been lucky enough when young to be appointed game-keepers.

Thus we cannot say that convicts represent an unfluctuating and certain proportion of criminals, for that cannot be proved. No more can we tell, even approximately, the number of old offenders now at liberty, the number of living criminals who will be punished some day, the number of undiscovered criminals, and the number of those who naturally disposed to crime, will never for one reason or another enter the criminal ranks. But if such numbers cannot be fixed even approximately, there is nothing to rest on to establish the proportion in which an anomaly will be found among convicts, in comparison with criminals at liberty.

The arithmetical error committed by *Lombroso* is thus a double one; on the one hand he does not take into account all the criminals which he should include, and on the other he counts the criminals at liberty among his honest men. Thus if convicts be C, honest men H, and criminals at liberty X, he compares C with H and X, instead of comparing C and X with H. And he cannot help himself, because X is an unknown quantity.

We do not deny that the general researches of *Lombroso* have awakened a crowd of ideas and established many important facts. Nor do we deny that *Lombroso* has shown, better than any of his predecessors, that our prisons contain more than one moral wreck or individual of stunted mental development, who would be far better in a hospital for incurables. To *Lombroso* belongs the immortal merit of having insisted on the care with which we should proceed in dealing with such individuals. But his theory reaches no further. That persons of feeble intelligence, full of hereditary defects and morally shipwrecked, fall into crime more readily than others, has been known for ages, and when we are advised to be more careful of them than we have been up to now, when it is a question of their punishment, we receive the advice with many thanks, but that is no ground for the criminal expert suspending his work and yielding up his place to the medical man alone.

Sir Basil Thomson, the Chief of the Criminal Investigation Department in Great Britain, writing in 1923, says: 'One has only to take charge of a great convict prison for a few weeks to realise that there are as many varieties of human character within its walls as you will find in any collection of human beings in the world outside,' and having pointed out how false generalisation is the weakness of the age he goes on to add ' We have all formed a conception of the criminal physiognomy—the kind of face that one rarely sees in the convict prison and which one may any day come face to face with in the pulpit, just as one may find the face of an angel gazing pensively at the judge from the dock. My own experience has been that about ten per cent of the convicted criminals in any prison have been predestined to commit anti-social acts through some mental or moral defect. There is the young person who is a congenital liar and may begin a life of crime at a very early age; there is the educated man who seems to have been born without any moral sense at all, and there is the mental defective who is just cunning enough to make a living from dishonest courses, and the man of inflamed temper who sees red on the smallest provocation. The other ninety per cent are the ordinary men and women of whom most have begun their careers under the age of twenty-one" (Foreword to Goodwin's "Sidelights on Crime" op cit infra)

CHAPTER III

INSPECTION OF LOCALITIES

Section i.—Preparation.

His report of an inspection of localities is a real touchstone for the Investigating Officer. In no other duty are address, power of observation, logical reasoning, methodised energy and keeping the end ever in view so clearly revealed, and nowhere else can more striking examples of awkwardness, feebleness of observation, disorder, vagueness and hesitation be found. An unskilful Investigating Officer will never furnish a good report of this description, while on the other hand such a document will reveal a good Investigating Officer at his true value. In a judicial inspection of localities it is necessary to conform to a sort of technical formula (*technique*) in the method of procedure and this formula is acquired only by conscientious preparation, complete absence of excitement, and by dispassion. The latter must be obtained at all price and must be divested of all affectation. Above all he must take care to be well prepared and have everything arranged—even to the smallest details. Local inspection is only ordered in the most important cases, but then the gravity of the case, the unlooked-for incidents, the feeling of heavy responsibility, the emotion produced by horrible and sorrowful sights, in addition to other circumstances in themselves act so violently upon the Investigating Officer that he has no need of other difficulties of an incidental nature to distract his attention, already sufficiently absorbed, even though these lesser difficulties may have an importance of their own.

In the first place then the Investigating Officer must be careful to obtain a clerk or assistant who is willing, brisk, and clear-headed. Should the clerk or assistant find his task tedious or work with an ill grace, the Investigating Officer runs the risk of being himself unconsciously influenced by him and may neglect to make so minute an inquiry as he otherwise would do in order not to further dishearten him. If the assistant be a slow writer the best part of one's time is lost and the most zealous of Investigating Officers begins to feel himself becoming disgusted or impatient,—according to his temperament. Moreover the time allotted to each excursion is nearly always limited, and the Investigating Officer is often hindered in making the necessary observations for the sole reason that the assistant is a dawdler. Further he should be intelligent so that he may seize with rapidity the information dictated by the Investigating Officer, be able to assist him, and devote his attention to details pointed out to him by the Investigating Officer, to observe on his own account and point out to the Investigating Officer what may have escaped the latter—four eyes are better than two

The author always recalls with a feeling of thankfulness the services of one of his assistants who during five consecutive years seconded him when attached to one of the largest and most important Provincial Courts. At first it took a deal of trouble to knock this man into shape, for all his schooling had been acquired at but a primary school, but to his indefatigable zeal, sincere attachment, unceasing wakefulness, and natural gift of observation, the author owes most valuable discoveries, and more than one success obtained in important inquiries should be entirely attributed to this honest and simple minded subordinate. It is true that in the smaller Courts one has not always good material at his disposal, but the Investigating Officer should be given the best at hand when he is setting out to examine the scene of a crime.

Being then in possession of a useful assistant, care should be taken to make him perfectly conversant with the matter in hand, all the facts, theories, and possible solutions should be explained to him, he must be told to observe for himself things that the Investigating Officer foresees he will be unable to attend to, and in short the whole scheme of the inquiry must be discussed with him. To try to make mysteries with one's assistant is not only ridiculous but can in no case be of any utility whatsoever. If he be unworthy of confidence, he is unfitted for his post and must be at once got rid of, but if he is worthy of confidence, he may as well be made acquainted a little in advance with what he cannot fail to see when he comes to carry out his personal duties.

The author has made a point of not communicating his plans too soon to the assistant but only immediately before carrying them into execution, when it was certain that he would not be leaving again before the work was begun. However worthy of confidence a man may be, his tongue is frequently stronger than his head and heart, and his chatter may do a great deal of harm. It must not be forgotten that the assistant by virtue of the law itself, is not a mere writing machine, he is employed by Government to help the investigation, and has the right to give an opinion. It is self-evident that he cannot be allowed without restraint to put his spoke into every wheel, for then the Investigating Officer would lose his authority. Such conduct would also be productive of disorder and in many cases the thoughtless boasting of the assistant might upset all the master's plans. Where the Investigating Officer is thus in the habit of informing his assistant of his projects and initiating him into his schemes, it is a good plan to arrange that should the assistant wish to inform the master of anything he should write it down on his writing pad. When the Investigating Officer notices that the assistant is starting to scribble, he should, so as not to draw the attention of anyone, stop dictating for some excuse or other and then when he sees that he has finished he will start reading over his shoulder (as if looking for the thread of his ideas for the purposes of continuing his dictation) all that the assistant has written. Often the most precious information will be found thus written down, as for instance, "you have forgotten to search such and such a box," or "the accused is throwing uneasy glances towards the fire-place," or even, "it seems to me that the person is holding an open knife behind his back," all which had been overlooked.

Further all necessary tools and aids should be kept in continual readiness, these we shall discuss minutely later on. But there are other details no less important. Care must be taken to have the means of transport quite ready, to be properly equipped for the time that will be taken up, and to give the necessary notices to witnesses and assistants, as for example in an exhumation to the grave-digger and the persons who will identify the body, etc., so that they may be found on the spot. This also applies to experts, municipal representatives, and the like. It is almost always a priceless advantage to have with one from the outset a representative of the Detective Department. He can be made use of in a thousand ways, and many a difficulty and much loss of time may be avoided: if nothing else, rogues and idlers must be kept at a distance, arrests made, articles and localities watched, necessary inquiries pursued in the neighbourhood, conversations between accused persons and witnesses prevented, houses and persons searched, and many other similar details often of decisive importance attended to.

Section ii.—What to do at the Scene of Offence.

On arrival at the scene of the crime certain things must be attended to which are common to all cases, be they of simple theft, robbery, murder, arson or misdemeanour. The first duty is to preserve an absolute calm. With it everything is won, without it everything is compromised. An Investigating Officer who fusses about, sets to work aimlessly, starts a plan only to drop it, asks everybody useless questions, and gives orders only to cancel them, makes a most painful impression on those engaged with him in the inquiry and destroys any confidence they may have had in his successful management. In such a case, it is all up with the zealous co-operation and sustained attention of his assistants. But if the Investigating Officer shows perfect confidence with no trace of excitement, and acts as with a sure prevision of the results, everyone willingly submits to his orders and each does his very best and the result of the enquiry is assured. Thus when the Investigating Officer reaches the spot, he must beware of speaking at random and starting to do something without rhyme or reason. Man indeed is naturally the victim of excitement and in the presence of an important event can find no better way to control his agitation than by issuing orders wholesale, altering them, and at all hazards making things hum. In the same way soldiers are more at ease on the field of battle when they can themselves join in the actual fighting, fire off their rifles and make a noise, but the superiority of a company is proved less in the fight than when it is held in reserve, observing quietly what is going on, allowing the bullets to rain upon it, and watching the wounded carried to the rear. The first point is therefore quietly and attentively to take stock of the situation; the Investigating Officer ought to find his bearings, correct if need be the impression that he has already formed about the case on its first being reported and modify his plans accordingly.

These latter considerations are of importance. As soon as the Investigating Officer is informed about a case it absorbs all his thoughts (or at least, ought to do so), he immediately makes a mental picture of the case itself and all connected with it, in a definite form, with precise outlines; when travelling to the spot he bases upon this idea his conjectures as to how the offence has been committed, and builds, upon his mental picture of the spot the plan of inquiry to be pursued. The idea may take root in his mind to such an extent that he cannot rid himself of it either in part or in whole even when the scene is actually displayed before his eyes, and frequently causes him to go wrong in his reckonings. For this reason the faults of his first impression must be corrected on the spot and his plans and intentions modified accordingly. The scene of the crime must then be inspected both in its general aspect and in detail and must be considered as far as possible in relation to the facts. The time allotted to this close examination is far from being lost and the results compensate largely for any apparent delay.

After this the Investigating Officer must find out the persons best able to give information about the case, which will enable him to become at least approximately acquainted with its circumstances. If the case is one of slight importance or the investigation but an incidental one found necessary in the course of the main inquiry, he is already aware of what it is all about. But if it is a first inquiry with reference to some important crime, such as murder, or arson, or some big accident such as a railway collision, boiler explosion, etc., he should endeavour to find a representative of the authorities, a policeman, a municipal inspector, or a person directly interested in the matter, as for example a relation of the murdered man the sufferer by the fire, a skilled workman, from whom to obtain preliminary information. Habit above all helps the Investigating Officer in examining people with a view to obtain this preliminary information, he learns little by little not to waste time over details, while forgetting nothing of importance, and however inexperienced he will commit no grave mistake if he always remembers the old and precious maxim of the jurist

> Quis, quid, ubi, quibus auxiliis, cui, quomodo, quando?
> Who, what, where, with what, why, how, when?
>
> "What was the crime, who did it, when was it done, and where,
> How done, and with what motive, who in the deed did share?"

If these words be always kept prominently before one in one's office, they will be impressed on the memory and imagination, and prevent many a grave mistake.

When the information that can be gathered up rapidly has been obtained, the next care should be to make a selection among the people interested in the case. The Investigating Officer must watch that all who have given or who can give information do not go too far away but remain on the spot. If possible it is as well to submit the witnesses to a certain surveillance so as to prevent them from gossiping uselessly with one another. For witnesses and more especially people of little education, women and children cannot help discussing the case and the case only, and telling one another what they have seen to such an extent that they do not exactly know in the end what each does know, i.e., they mix up what they have themselves seen and heard with what has been told them by others.

True, the witnesses may have talked to each other and heard each other's stories beforehand, but in every case nothing leads them to talk to such an extent and exclusively about the case as then being collected together on the scene of the crime in the very presence of the Investigating Officer, thus making the affair, as it were, stand out in full relief. While taking these measures, the Investigating Officer should attend to the preservation in as complete a manner as possible of existing vestiges of the crime and take care that they are interfered with as little as may be. he must at once establish, e.g., whether the corpse of the person who has been murdered is still in the same position as when the crime was discovered. he must distinguish among the marks of footsteps those made before the discovery from those made afterwards by the curious, etc. The exclusion of everything happening after the moment when the crime was committed is a very special task for the Investigating Officer, all the more so as the most regrettable errors may arise from the neglect of it.

There are known cases where the Investigating Officer has described with the most minute accuracy the position of the corpse and drawn therefrom the most ingenious conclusions, while unhappily the evidence pointed out that the corpse had been turned several times by different persons before his arrival and had therefore been placed in quite a different position. Again, a jacket of rough cloth found on the corpse played an important part in the case until the discovery was made that it had been simply placed over the body to hide from passers-by the horrible sight of a fractured skull. Bayard as far back as 1817 related a case in which the physician who was summoned stepped in the blood and then walked all over the building, leaving blood-stains everywhere, which subsequently caused so much trouble and confusion as to completely spoil the investigation. Here is an instance where the consequences might have been much graver. In a case of arson a footprint was discovered which undoubtedly corresponded with that of the accused. It was indeed his, but it had not been made at the time of the crime, but subsequently, when on his speedy arrest he had been taken to the place by a policeman.

We shall describe yet another case which forcibly points out what danger may arise from the introduction into the examination of localities, of <u>details which are purely accidental</u>. The story seems almost incredible, but it is absolutely true, and all who were connected with it will remember it perfectly well. The extraordinary combination of circumstances which characterise it, render it all the more instructive. A lady, the proprietress of a factory, in counting out her money, had made up five little packets of 1,000 florins in paper and placed them, so she believed, in the cash box. Next day she found only four packets there, although the cash box was as well secured as it had been the previous night. The lady suspected her maid-servant, who, on being arrested, protested her innocence and it was only after a search that lasted a week that her trunk could be discovered. This trunk was carefully searched in the office of the Investigating Officer and its contents, consisting for the most part of old and valueless articles, were exposed on the table and carefully examined without discovering anything suspicious. It was only on lifting up the lot that a strip of paper was found underneath on the table on which were printed besides several letters the words "1,000 florins in 1 florin notes." It was one of the strips that the Austro-Hungarian Bank was in the habit of using, for rolling up round sums of money paid out. The complainant declared that she often received her money wrapped up in such strips, and frequently made use of them when she counted up her cash, but she could not say whether the packet in question had one or not. Fortunately the Investigating Officer discovered written on the ribbon the date 22/8 in very small and almost imperceptible characters. It was established that this date was written by the clerk in the bank who had counted out the bundle of 1,000 florins that was wrapped round by this particular ribbon, but as the accused was arrested on the 22nd August it was inexplicable how this ribbon came among her things. At length it all came out. The examination of the trunk took place on September 1st in the office of the Investigating Officer, and while it was going on a clerk brought that official his monthly salary. Now he had received the packet of 1,000 florin notes from the bank and after taking off the unlucky cover had carelessly placed it upon the table, then covered by the belongings of the accused. The Investigating Officer and the clerk had not noticed this and so the strip of paper assumed such enormous importance. But suppose that by some chance the date on the strip had been but a few days earlier, a perfectly innocent person might have been convicted simply because an object which had nothing to do with the case had not been eliminated.

Section iii.—The actual Description of the Scene of Offence.

Having established with all necessary prudence what does and does not form part of the subject matter to be examined, all connected in any way with the case must be definitely ascertained and described.

In this connection there is one golden and inviolable rule.—*Never alter the position of, pick up, or even touch any object before it has been minutely described in the report.*

It very rarely happens to the Investigating Officer to find everything clear and distinct from the beginning. As a rule he has not the slightest idea of what turn the case will take, he does not know what may be of importance, or what will be denied and therefore have to be proved. At this early stage everything may be of importance and nothing too small or insignificant to have a decisive bearing upon the case. The situation of an object—an inch or two to left or right, to front or back—a little dust, a splash of dirt easy to efface, may all turn out to be of the first importance. The natural impulse is to immediately touch any object of apparent significance, as e.g., an object left on the scene of the crime by the criminal. It is laid hold of and moved about, and only afterwards is it recognised that the object in itself signifies very little, but that everything depends on its position—which can no longer be fixed.

Again the involuntary impulse is at first to seize the hands of the murdered person to see if there is any hair or scraps of clothing of the criminal in them, but it may turn out that some little detail, such as a smear of blood upon the hands effaced in seizing them so heedlessly, would have been of much greater importance. Now in order to follow the important rule—" never to change in any way the condition of the scene before it is described in the report "—it is necessary to make sure of the preservation of that condition. Footprints should be protected by coverings of little boxes or small planks resting on two or three stones. Traces of blood and forgotten or discarded objects should also be carefully covered up, especially if they are in the open air and the hour is late, and moreover lines should be drawn round objects which may be confused with others (such as footprints, etc.). When all this is in order and everything useless has been eliminated, the report can be commenced.

No one supposes that a report should be a model of style, but a certain grammatical accuracy and logical sequence are indispensable. This is in the first place important to the person dictating the report, for he will only be able to do good work if he is convinced of the accuracy of what he states without having to wait for its confirmation afterwards, if he deals carefully with each point on its own merits and without connecting it with those that follow, and lastly if it proceeds logically and according to a determined plan, passing from the general to the particular and so avoiding the treatment of the same point twice over. Secondly, the arrangement is of importance to the reader, for he will only understand the matter clearly if he finds the style of the report lucid and logical. Anyone who has perused many such reports knows how difficult it is to make use of them when badly drawn up, how little convincing they are, or how easy it is to miss important points from the difficulty of understanding what the Investigating Officer intended to express.

Nor is it very difficult to establish a determinate form remaining always the same in its principal features. It will suffice to recall the rules laid down for drawing up an inquest report. In all cases a general description of the spot must be set out, stating where it is and how it is reached. Then state whether it is a house, field, wood, etc., that is in question; next indicate the neighbourhood precisely, and then describe the actual scene in detail, always having regard to its connection with the case under inquiry.

The extent of the description in the first place naturally depends on the nature of the crime. In all cases (we are not dealing with accidents) the following must be described:—

i. the place itself;
ii. the direction from which the guilty person came;
iii. that in which he went away;
iv. the spot whence the witnesses have seen, or could have seen anything;
v. all points where traces of the crime are to be found or where they might have been expected to be found, but where in fact there are none.

The notification of even purely *negative* facts should not be neglected, for on the one hand they may lead to positive inferences and on the other reassure the reader and show him that they were not forgotten altogether. Suppose, *e.g.*, traces of blood are mentioned as having been found in the room of a murdered man, it is not sufficient merely to enumerate these but what has *not* been found must also be stated, as, *e.g.*, that there was no bloody water in the wash-hand basin nor any imprints of blood stained fingers—or hands; or if the report concerns a search for compromising papers which has been without result it must be expressly stated that no ashes of burnt paper were to be found in the fireplace. The special circumstances attaching to each particular crime must of course be set out, *e.g.*, in cases of arson the objects more especially exposed to danger or anything that may have assisted or impeded the wind—in riots, places from which weapons have been taken (such as a fence, pile of wood, thatched roof of a hut, etc.)

After the general sketch, the actual place of occurrence must be described in detail, as e.g. in cases of murder the room containing the body of the victim, in cases of burglary the place where the house was broken into, or in arson the place where the fire first started. And here a certain order must also be observed. With a room or other enclosed space the door should be taken as a starting point and the same direction followed as the hands of a clock i.e. standing in the entrance and facing into the room, start from the left hand and go round the room towards the right hand. In this way one will be certain that nothing has been forgotten. First describe the size, shape, height, and other peculiarities of the space in question. Then go from the entrance towards the nearest left corner, then the left-hand wall, then the wall facing the entrance, then the right-hand wall, then the remainder of the wall to the right of the doorway, and finally the objects in the middle of the room. In the course of this description the windows and the doors will be noticed. Next describe any alterations in the state of the moveables in the room consequent upon the crime in question, damage done by blows, blood-stains, changes in the situation or position of objects, damage to windows, doors etc., and finally a minute description of the subject-matter of the crime (e.g. a broken safe, a dead body etc.) with all the particulars necessary to a detailed description.

In doing this the Investigating Officer must proceed step by step examining minutely at the same time its description as written down. A piece of cloth for instance lying on the ground will be primarily described according to the impression it produced when first observed, as e.g.—

"Quite near the corpse, an inch from the left hand, a red cloth rolled up in a ball, apparently of cotton and about the size of a pocket-handkerchief, one corner sticking out, lying on the ground in the direction of the head of the body. On picking up this piece of cloth it is found not to be cotton but half silk. It is a three-cornered scarf with hemmed borders and each side 17 inches (43 cms.) in length. It is unmarked, and has a hole in the middle about the size of a farthing, probably due to use. Under the scarf is no trace of blood or anything remarkable. It is not identified by anyone present (naming those present, A B, C etc.) it probably, therefore did not belong to the murdered person."

He then passes on to all the important details that may serve to throw light on the case, footprints, marks caused by fire-arms or tools, impressions of all kinds, in short everything which may have been produced by the guilty person, and everything which may have been left behind by him.

In these sub-divisions, as well as in the general preliminary description, an invariable order must also be rigidly adhered to. The same order or direction followed at the beginning must be continued when treating of the details. If, for example, the description of a corpse has been commenced by proceeding from the head to the feet, it is best first to describe any important objects found in the neighbourhood of the head and finish with those near the feet. In making an abstract of these details a measuring rule must as far as possible be used and the distances indicated exactly, for one never knows at the time what may be of use subsequently. All expressions should be avoided which only serve to fill up a sentence without giving an exact idea of anything. Expressions such as "not far from there,"

' some little distance away,' ' a little higher,' ' further behind,' ' away at the bottom' ought on *no condition* to occur in a report. That such expressions should be used is easily understood, for the Investigating Officer has everything before his eyes, and such an expression as ' quite near' is perfectly clear to him—but the person who has to read the report may have quite different ideas of the distances. Anyone who has paid attention to this detail will allow that there are few reports where such expressions are not to be found and that these very expressions have often rendered it difficult for him to properly appreciate the case.

The expressions ' on the right ' and ' on the left ' may only be used when they admit of no ambiguity, as for instance ' on the right hand of the corpse ' or ' on the left bank of the river.' In all other cases these words must be totally discarded, for even such expressions as " to the right of the spectator " or " to the left of the entrance " may give rise to ambiguity if the position of the spectator is not stated or if it is uncertain whether the Investigating Officer is within or without the entrance and in what direction he is facing. But if all this has to be stated at length, the description becomes tedious and obscure. Therefore, be exact. *The points of the compass* should be used as far as possible to describe the position of objects, for then no doubt can arise in the mind and the description can always be checked subsequently. But in a building, and above all in a room, it is in certain cases more convenient to choose, if possible, fixed points which have already been noted down and to state, *e.g.* ' on a line extending from the head of the corpse to the corner of the room where the fire-place is situated and at a distance of two feet from this latter.' In this case the distance should *without exception* be taken as starting from a point which remains fixed. It would not do to say, for example, ' on a line extending from the head of the corpse to the corner where the fire-place is situated and at three feet from the head of the corpse ' for the corpse will be removed and on subsequent measurements being taken it may be difficult to find this point again. In addition to this the direction of measurement must be in most cases indicated. It is not enough simply to say ' at 12 feet from the apple tree in question was found——' but say ' at 12 feet from the apple tree in question in the direction of the corner of the house situated to the north-west——.'

This sometimes necessitates a very long description, but the Investigating Officer must not be disheartened by that ; it may be necessary to say at length as follows :—' This door, single, not double, is 3 feet 3 inches broad. Starting from the hinge side which is towards the north and going towards the lock side which is towards the south, measure 18 inches along the bottom where the door touches the floor. From this point draw a perpendicular to the line formed by the bottom of the closed door and from this perpendicular measure off 7 inches starting from the door. At the spot thus obtained was found a piece of watch chain.'' When the situation of an object is of essential importance the distance must be fixed by two measurements. This will be absolutely necessary where there are, for example, splashes of blood on the wall, from which the position of the accused, or of the person attacked, and the kind of blood, may be deduced. In such a case, where a horizontal and a vertical are involved the floor should always be taken as the horizontal, for a spirit level would be necessary to lay a horizontal on the wall. The vertical may easily be found with the aid of a thread to which a knife, stone, or some such object is attached. *E g*, for a drop of blood on the wall a plumb-line should first be constructed (a line with some small heavy object hanging from it) then hold this plumb-line at the point where this blood-stain is to be found (taking care not to touch or graze it) and make a mark where the line touches the ground.

Before completing the description of an enclosed space the Investigating Officer must be well assured that nothing connected with the crime has been neglected or forgotten. For this it is not sufficient to throw a rapid glance around, but every object must be carefully and attentively reconsidered so as to make certain that nothing important has been overlooked and to see whether or not, after all that has been done, the matter does not bear a different aspect from that which it bore previously or some detail which at first appeared to be of no consequence is not now of some importance. In a recent case a cigar-holder with an amber mouthpiece was found near the corpse of a murdered man and the marks of the teeth upon it brought about the detection of the murderer (see *Chapter V, Section* II G, "The Teeth").

If any independent person who knows the room in question be near at hand he should be sent for and asked to help in the examination of the room and its contents. Such a person will be better able to notice any changes that may have taken place than the Investigating Officer who now sees the room for the first time.

It is impossible to notice everything which may subsequently turn out to be of importance even though folio volumes be written, there are always certain details which will be passed over owing to the difficulty of foreseeing their value. In one case it turned out to be of great significance to know whether the sun shone into a certain part of the room at a certain hour of the day, and for this purpose the locality had to be specially revisited though very far distant from the place where the court was sitting. In another case everything depended upon whether any sand was strewn about on the floor of the room, a point that no one had thought it worth while to observe. Such an omission will never be a reproach to an Investigating Officer, for only chance would make him think of noting down such details, but it would be a grave fault for the Investigating Officer to neglect details of which, though insignificant in themselves, the subsequent importance might have been foreseen. The old axiom of the Civil Law "De minimis non curat lex" does not hold good for the Investigating Officer. Only too often he must seek the strongest proof in the smallest details. Everyone has seen, everyone has read in thousands of criminal tragedies how some trifle has become the pivot upon which the whole case turned, and yet the capital fault in inspecting localities very often consists in the neglect of small details, the importance of which would have been apparent if a proper and sustained attention had been brought to bear upon them.

The following cases are cited from the author's own experience. On one occasion everything rested on whether or not at the hour of the crime the latch of the door was oiled or made a noise, on another, whether a half-burnt cigar was in an ash tray or beside it, again whether there was a spider's web near a nail in the wall, on another whether there was still some kerosine in a lamp (i.e. whether it had been extinguished or had burnt itself out), in a murder case the assailant would certainly have gone undiscovered if the Investigating Officer had not thought of examining the top of a wooden partition about eight feet in height and not reaching to the ceiling. He saw that the top of the partition was covered with a thick coating of dust save in one place where the dust had been displaced, and naturally concluded that a man must have quite recently climbed over the partition at the spot. He made a search and discovered the accused among people living in the room separated from the scene of the crime by the partition in question.

When the description has to be made in the open, the same method should be followed. It is distressing to see how badly the work is sometimes done. In reading certain reports one can clearly see what trouble the Investigating Officer has taken in writing down the result of his labours and what difficulty he has had in finding a starting point—generally the most unfortunate point of all is chosen—how painfully he has made his way through his description and how, recognising the insufficiency of his work, he has attempted to remedy it by making all sorts of conditions, modifications, and explanations, which have but served to completely obscure what before had perhaps some approach to clearness. For all that the matter is not really so difficult, but the Investigating Officer must first perceive clearly what the matter is about and what is to be described. He must, moreover, remember that the reader will not have the scene under his eyes and cannot, therefore, represent it to himself in the same way as the Investigating Officer who has seen it all, and he must make up his mind to proceed according to a definite plan and not jump about, now here, now there. If he has a principle and remains faithful to it, not only will the description be comprehensible and useful but his task will be greatly facilitated, one thing following from another, and he will not have the trouble of making every few lines additions and references which he himself has brought about, and of having to face difficulties of his own making. What principle to choose will be indicated by the nature of the case, yet it would be well for the Investigating Officer before actually commencing his work to consider how the case will proceed if he acts according to such and such a plan. If he foresees difficulties, he must set to work in some other way.

The systems followed by an Investigating Officer may be divided into "subjective" and "objective."

The mode of procedure will be "subjective" where the various objects and places are described in the order they presented themselves to the Investigating Officer or to the accused himself, i.e., in the order in which the Investigating Officer sees them as he comes from a certain direction or in following the direction taken by the accused at the times of his arrival and of his departure and flight. This method is not always a very good one because e.g. the accused may perhaps have come and gone on the same side though by different roads. But it is very convenient in certain circumstances and specially when it is thought that by this method the report will better adapt itself to an enquiry on the spot.

The procedure is "objective" when the Investigating Officer deals simply with the localities themselves without having regard to the direction followed, as e.g. beginning at the east and advancing step by step towards the west, or by choosing some fixed point such as a street or house and advancing from it in other directions as towards a street, river or boundary.

Let it be repeated that no method can be absolutely recommended for every case: the choice must ultimately depend on the case itself. It will be easier to decide by first making a sketch plan (*Chapter XII.*) which should *always* be made before the written description. With this always before his eyes, the Investigating Officer will soon find out what is the best method to follow in each case.

Section IV.—Search for Hidden Objects.

If one desired to call attention to every place where objects bearing in some manner upon a case might be found hidden, a list would have to be drawn up of all objects situated either in houses or in the open air, and large enough to shelter a *corpus delicti*. There is little probability of finding anything of importance if the attention be confined to safes, beds, boxes, stoves or chimneys. Absolutely everything must be examined, for there is no place where important objects cannot be hidden. The following for example are a few of the hiding places discovered by the author or his friends:—the horsehair stuffing of a sofa, a birdcage, the space between the back of a picture and its protecting board, the hole of an old key, the manger in a stable, a pot in which soup was actually boiling on the fire (it contained 28 gold coins), a prayer-book, old boots, a dog kennel, the space between two upright millstones, wine barrels, a spectacle case, a pill-box, old newspapers, a cuckoo clock, a baby's clothes, and on one occasion the criminal himself was discovered in a dung heap, a small opening having been made to give him air in the side nearest to the stable wall. Weapons and even other objects are constantly concealed in the thatch of houses or sheds, jewellery and small portable objects are buried, either tied up in a cloth or in a pot, in grain heaps and in wells. In one case where a large number of documents were stolen solely for spite, it is understood that they were boiled to pulp in the caldron used for boiling the cattle food and were then run off through the town drain.

Moreover the accused himself must *always* be carefully searched. This the Investigating Officer often neglects to do, either out of regard for the accused, or from timidity or some other motive. Certainly search is a grave affront to the liberty of the subject, and such a measure should only be resorted to after mature consideration and in the last extremity, but if resolved on, it must be carried out energetically and not only the house but the man himself must be searched. In the great majority of cases the hidden object will be found upon him, for everyone is naturally inclined to carry on his person suspicious or dangerous objects—just as he is wont to carry objects of value—believing they are more secure. The task is greatly facilitated if it is known what is to be searched for, for then many places where it *cannot* be hidden may be excluded. Unfortunately the objects searched for are often small and easy to hide, such as money, jewels, papers, poison,—such things can be hidden almost anywhere. The presence of the accused may render the task easier, for his face and glances often indicate to a keen observer whether the search is in a likely place or not, whether the searcher is " hot or cold." If objects of some size are sought for and it is ascertained that they are not hidden in places easy to be got at, they must be looked for in the structure of the building itself. But as it is scarcely ever practicable to make a thorough search by demolishing the building, the Investigating Officer may employ certain artifices of the simplest kind and keep his eyes well open.

Suppose that the objects have been walled up. It is useless to take into account those parts of the wall which can be easily seen, for it is scarcely probable that anything is hidden there—at least when there is no reason to suppose that the plaster has had time to dry. As a rule the walling up is behind mirrors, or boxes, or in cellars and the place may be recognised by the freshness or inequality of the plastering. If the place is not found thus and there is still room to believe that the objects are hidden in the walls there is nothing else to be done but to knock and tap the walls and listen for the hollow sound indicating a cavity, noting whence such sound is produced. This work is really quicker to execute than might be supposed. The search for a hiding place under a wooden floor is more difficult and, as the floor cannot be completely taken up, indications of a recent disturbance must be sought and such indications do, as a rule, exist. In an ordinary plank, the heads of the nails driven into the boards must be examined. When the floor is first constructed the nails holding the planks to the cross beams are driven in as far as possible so that the heads of the nails are a little below the surface of the floor, to prevent the feet from catching upon them. This being the case, it is difficult to pull out the nails, especially if the floor has been often scrubbed and the nails have become somewhat rusted with the wet. With the nails holding so tenaciously to the floor it is impossible to extract them without damaging the wood round them and traces of such damage cannot be effaced. If therefore the wood round the nails appears to be bruised or damaged in any way, it can with certainty be presumed that something is hidden in that place. It is useless to hit the planks where no such indications are to be seen.

A frequent case is where something has been buried in an earthen or mud floor. Here water should be poured in fairly large quantities on the suspected surface. *The place where the water filters through more rapidly than elsewhere and where at the same time bubbles make their appearance, is the place where the soil is broken and where digging has been recently carried on.* It is the same when the covering is of bricks, flag-stones, or such like. In time a quantity of dust or sand gathers between them which by its own weight and humidity forms a kind of firm cement. If then water be thrown over this paving it sinks in but slowly, being as it were drunk up little by little. But if the flagstones, etc., have recently been taken up and laid down again and the interstices have been filled up by sweeping in sand or dust, which does not as yet hold together like cement, the water will penetrate very rapidly and air bubbles be seen mounting to the surface.

It is always difficult to carry on such searches in the open air. The large expanse of space hinders methodical procedure and success must often depend on luck. There is one possible expedient when the object is to discover a corpse—to make use of a good bloodhound. But it is useless to take the first setter or bloodhound that comes along. Few dogs have a good enough scent. If the Investigating Officer needs help in such cases it will be of little good to him to issue an order for a hunting dog, for he is pretty sure not to get one of any use. In this case again, as we have said before, preparation for war must be made in time of peace. This is the more necessary since helps of this kind are often met with when not looked for while generally not to be found on the spot when they are wanted and where, owing to the nature of the case, one might have hoped to find them. A tanner was the owner of quite a common watch dog having absolutely no resemblance to a hunting dog, but which—out of pure voracity —could even from a great distance scent out any carrion. The local sportsmen used to borrow him after each shoot to look for the game killed which had been undiscovered by the dogs. The tanner's dog would find anything animal, alive or dead, and he would pull up just as quickly before a recently killed deer as the body of a cat dead long since, but he would find both. One day when they were seeking the body of an idiot who had disappeared and who was suspected of having been murdered by his brother-in-law, this dog discovered the body a long way off in a wood. At that moment it was yet possible to establish that the idiot had succumbed to an attack of epilepsy, but some days later a *post mortem* would have been unable to prove that no violence had been used and the brother-in-law would have gone through life with the suspicion of murder hanging over him.

But this matter can also be managed in a systematic way. In Paris, where every year an astonishing number of people disappear, especially children, the police keep dogs which are trained like the bloodhounds of Cuba, where they used to be employed for tracking fugitive slaves. In such cases some clothes, etc., belonging to the person to be caught are placed to the nose of the dog, which is then brought on the trail. If this trail is fairly fresh, the dog will follow it without caring for the hundreds of other trails crossing the right one until the fugitive is reached. A short time ago a dog was mentioned in a Paris paper as having succeeded in finding for the police its twenty-fifth lost child. If we compare this with the splendid results of the Austrian and German war dogs it must be allowed that dogs can help us in many cases. We do not claim that the State should keep official dogs of this kind, but if a policeman or any other official should show special interest in training dogs for this purpose, Government should give him some assistance. Here we may also repeat that it is very helpful to study Nature. We have mentioned that a considerable number of murdered people are buried in rather deserted places, a great number of these are often dug out by animals who easily scent out such spots. When a corpse is not completely covered, it is of course easy for dogs or even men to find it. In the Province of West Prussia in the summer of 1867 two murder cases were discovered through the murdered bodies having been uncovered by foxes. Moreover, crows, ravens, kites, and above all vultures, etc., will at once collect and so it is not unprofitable to watch for this sign. The body of a murdered woman was once found in the following way: the teachers of the surrounding schools told the children to report as soon as they saw many crows, ravens etc. gathering anywhere. Some of them made such a report, with the successful result that the murdered person was traced.

A most instructive incident arose during the search of a dwelling-house. A poacher had fired upon a game-keeper, who thought he recognised his assailant. The house of the suspected person was searched, the principal object sought for being the gun. The search was carried out with the greatest care, the house being turned out from top to bottom. But no trace of gun or ammunition was to be found, and the inquiry was declared closed. During the search a heavy rainstorm came on and the search party remained in the house waiting for it to stop. The house in question was built like most peasants' houses. It had a ground floor divided by a corridor, at one end of which was the front door and at the other the back door, while the doors of the kitchen and living rooms opened on to it. The front and back doors, except in winter, remained open all day. It was in this corridor the search party awaited the end of the storm. The rain coming down heavier and heavier and beginning to come in at the front door, they shut the latter and there they found, hanging on the inside of the door, which had up till that time been leaning against the wall, the gun and a pouch containing powder and shot.

A similar case (communicated by M. *Stelal*, Vicar of Glem) also related to a poacher. Numerous thefts of game had taken place for some years in a certain part of the country and the bell-ringer of a little church was suspected. No proof however could ever be obtained, the most minute searches in his house being without result. It was only after his death that his gun and accessories were discovered hidden under the high altar of the church, where no one seems to have thought of looking.

CHAPTER IV

EQUIPMENT OF THE INVESTIGATING OFFICER.

The work of the Investigating Officer is like all other pursuits, the material side, the tools necessary, are of inestimable importance. More than one great success, more than one great failure, have been due exclusively to the fact that on the one hand the Investigating Officer had ready on the spot all the aid necessary for his investigation or, on the other, that he either had no implements at all, or those which he had were defective or unsuitable.

Perhaps some will consider what follows useless or trivial, but experience has shown that an Investigating Officer who possesses a travelling office box or bag, in perfect order and provided with all necessaries, will find his work much facilitated, and will ensure greater speed in his labours. Such an outfit has been at times the sole cause of a great success.

First, let us consider in detail what is indispensable.

1. *A supply of paper* is of course a necessity. This should include several sheets of writing paper of the best quality. In an inquiry the ordinary Government official paper should never be used, it is generally of very bad quality and you may have to repent employing it.

2. *Several envelopes of various sizes.*

3. *Several sheets of blotting paper.*

4. A certain number of all the usual *official printed blank forms*, as inquest reports, warrants, summonses to witnesses, etc. One must not wait for the time of starting to put these in order, they should be replenished immediately on the return from each inquiry.

5. *A good map* of the district in which one is about to travel. To save space it is better to have an unmounted map as its use is comparatively infrequent.

6. The Investigating Officer will also be provided with *pens and pencils.* These should be of the best quality. Good pens mean quick and legible writing, whence economy of time and consequently greater care and accuracy in the inquiry. For steel nibs a good globe or ball-pointed pen is the best, as it does not penetrate or catch the paper and thus permits swift and easy writing. The use of fountain pens is now almost universal among officials. The advice to be given as to them is, to shun cheap imitations by unknown makers. Nothing is more trustworthy than a fountain pen by a reliable maker—everyone has his own fancy—but a pen without such guarantee and previous trial should be rigorously discarded.

7. *For ordinary pens a pocket ink-bottle is necessary.* Care should be taken to see that it shuts closely and is re-filled *after each investigation.* 1 *Swan fountain pen ink-filler* should be carried.

8. 1 *yard measure.*

9. 1 *pair of compasses.*

10. 1 *pedometer,* though not perhaps indispensable is most useful, it is the shape and size of a watch. If one wishes to measure a long distance one sets the needles on all the dials (units, tens, etc.) at zero, puts the instrument in the pocket and walks off. For greater certainty one may put the instrument in one's boot, when every step will certainly be registered.

11. *Tracing paper and cloth.* The cloth is useful for removing traces of blood, and in all circumstances when paper is not strong enough.

12. 1 *bottle of plaster of paris and another of oil.* These are mainly of use for preserving footprints and impressions (see *Chapter XIII.*)

13. 1 *brush.* The brush is useful for taking impressions of solid objects and surfaces in relief with moistened blotting paper, such as marks made by a tool, as a chisel, cuts by a knife or hatchet, damage to material objects, etc. As to the method of doing this, see *Chapter XII.*

14. *Sealing wax.*

15. *Two small glass test-tubes.* These tubes should be of clear thin glass, closed at one end, from three to four inches long, and the thickness of a lead pencil (see *Chapter XVI.*)

16. *Two wax candles* of the length and thickness of one's finger are often useful.

17. 1 *compass.*

18. *An iron box with matches.* If smokers themselves often forget their matches, how much more careful should Investigating Officers be in making sure of being always provided with this indispensable accessory.

19. *A piece of soap.* Soap is useful to take small impressions, as of keys, teeth (in case of bites) etc. It is also a great comfort to have a wash after a search, handling dirty clothes, perhaps dirty bodies, etc.

20. 1 *good magnifying glass.* This most useful friend should be mounted in a broad rim, so as to be protected from scratches.

21. 1 *camel-hair brush.* This is useful for oiling footmarks before taking the impression, and also for removing traces of blood, etc.

22. *Some gum arabic.*

23. *Some thick, smooth notepaper.* Ordinary notepaper is too coarse and rough for preserving small articles, while glazed paper contains too many foreign admixtures.

24. *The office seal.* For greater convenience this may be used without a handle, so that it takes up no more room than a coin.

25. 1 *few sheets of manifolding paper.* The use of this is too well known to require explanation. The best appliance to use when travelling is a hard and sharp lead pencil.

26. *Some tissue paper.* This is handy for taking impressions of fine surfaces, as of wood, a stone, etc. where blotting paper would be too rough.

27. 1 *good watch.*

For the carriage of all these indispensable accessories we strongly recommend a leather bag like a courier bag or military sabretache (See *Fig 1*) This will hold everything required, protect the contents from damp, and be easy to carry. Military experience shows that if well balanced and resting on the correct spot, which can always be found after a few trials, its existence is forgotten after a march of a quarter of an hour. It should be about ten inches long by eight inches broad, divided by partitions lengthways and with an outside pocket. At the top two leather loops about five inches long should be firmly sewn, through which passes an ordinary belt. The latter must be so adjusted that the bag hangs or rests on the top of the left thigh behind, there it will remain immovable, even on a quick march. The best fastener is by means of a ring passing through a slit in the flap, and secured by pin and chain.

Fig 1

One compartment should be reserved solely for paper, the sheets being folded, where necessary, first lengthways and then crossways.

All the accessories, together with the bag, should then be taken to a saddler or binder who will fix them by means of slips of leather or linen on pieces of stout cardboard, the size of the bag, just as is done with toilet articles in a travelling bag. These boards can then be slipped into the divisions of the bag and withdrawn at will. But we must repeat that it should be made a rule to replenish the bag *on the return* from every journey and not wait until the next setting-out. These sudden starts are generally made only in important cases, but it is just in such cases that one has plenty to think about and cannot be bothered with remembering if all the little necessary articles are in order; one should be able just to take up the bag and be ready. This advice may appear puerile, but no one who has once experienced what it is to be without the necessary article at the critical moment will so consider it.

It will greatly assist in keeping the receptacle in perfect readiness, to have a list of all the articles it should contain legibly written and gummed inside the flap of the bag.

Other things may be usefully carried according to the fancy of the officer. In particular a few simple medicines should always be handy, early rising, a hot journey, bad food, may always bring on a headache, diarrhœa, etc. In these days of tabloids and concentrated medicines this requirement is easily satisfied. Aspirin, chlorodyne, sal volatile, and quinine, or better some reliable fever pill containing opium, and a few similar common remedies, are easily carried and may make all the difference between comfort and misery, that is, between success and failure. When starting on an expedition which may last many hours, the precaution of taking a few preserved provisions, two or three bottles of aerated waters and a flask of best brandy should never be omitted. It seems almost absurd to indite a warning against drinking unfiltered water drawn from country wells or tanks, yet we have known the most valuable lives thrown away by absolute disregard of the simplest precautions, and even in spite of specific warning.

Smokers should always have a few cigars in reserve, for how often does not one in his haste forget his cigar case. A *post mortem*, for instance, is not a very pleasant thing for the layman, if he cannot smoke, even the brandy flask may be a very present help in such circumstances.

Carry, as a rule, a supply of copper coins. Travellers either give no tips, which leads to dire discomfort, if not worse, or give far too much, being generally thought fools for their pains. A small copper coin here and there, especially if given to the real helpers, will work wonders, far more than as many silver ones given to an officious loafer.

The following is what is known as the Thorndyke equipment:—

The detective to whom a difficult murder or homicide case is submitted is provided with a kit containing the following list of articles:—

Steel tape measure 100 feet long	Six dozen metal bound paper tags for marking exhibits
Compass	
Six test-tubes	Small file for marking metals
Electric lamp	Ball of twine and glass cutter
Six towels and soap	Two inch rubber roller with handle
Magnifying glass	Tube of printer's ink
Bottle of iodine	Glass slab
Small saw, jemmy, and wrench	Two camel's hair brushes
Small mirror and pair of scissors	Pound of lampblack
Rubber gloves	Pound of chemists' grey powder
	Twelve inches sealing-wax

In case of murder the body will be photographed. When the nature of the crime indicates that blood tests may be necessary, the test tubes may be used to take fluid directly from the wound, and the saws and other tools will enable the police to take stains from the floor or even from glass.

The rubber gloves and the disinfectant iodine are for use in such work to avoid infection. The mirror has been placed in the kit so that the police may determine whether life is extinct. The kit also contains a complete outfit for taking finger prints.

CHAPTER V

THE EXPERT AND HOW TO MAKE USE OF HIM.

Section 1.—General Considerations.

Experts are the most important auxiliaries of an Investigating Officer, in some way or other they nearly always are the main factor in deciding a case. True it is that the Investigating Officer has not skilled experts always at his immediate disposition, but, in important cases, he is able to refer to experts at headquarters on the other hand, experts of even very small value can give excellent results, but everything depends upon knowing how to make use of them. Indeed it is often less important to know *who* is to be questioned than to know *how*, *upon what*, and *when* questions must be put.

But it is also important for the Investigating Officer to know just whom he ought to apply to, *i e*, what kind of expert he ought to select moreover he must know what the expert is capable of telling him in each case, that is to say where his knowledge begins and what are the natural limits to it, and finally he must seize the proper moment for putting his questions, *i e*, the moment when he is in possession of sufficient material to render any further research superfluous. He will for instance only be in possession of the best information on interrogating an observer at the microscope in cases where medical men are incapable of enlightening him; at other times sportsmen will be able to give him satisfactory replies where learned experts in arms may fail him. In this connection the explanations of the latter may be of little use, some special knowledge being required in each case.

As regards the limits of the expert's knowledge, the Investigating Officer must be particularly careful not to ask too much, for if he were to do so he might look ridiculous, on the other hand if he does not ask enough he may deprive himself of information of great value. A case is recalled in which the Investigating Officer desired to know whether the blood-stain on a piece of cloth was that of a boy or of a girl, another Investigating Officer took a stove to pieces and sent it carefully packed to the chemical examiner with a request to know whether bank notes had been burned in it or not, and a colleague of the author recently met with a case in which it was asked whether the arsenic found in the corpse could be identified with that found in a sausage. On the other hand every Investigating Officer knows of cases in which the solution of almost insoluble problems has been obtained, in this way experts in physics will discover, by a magnetic process, traces of iron, where chemical experts have found nothing, botanists once furnished the author with certain proof that some branches of hops had been cut with a particular knife. What can be performed with the assistance of electricity, the refinements of photography, radio-active rays, Röntgen rays and other acquisitions, is simply illimitable.

As regards the moment at which advice should be asked, care must be taken not to lose too much time, but knowledge of the circumstances attending the crime must be given to the expert. It is often stated that the expert has only to occupy himself with the object to be examined, on a wound for example being shown to him, he should determine its nature, the time necessary for its healing and say generally what will be its consequences,—but this is not all, he ought also to tell us the weapon, position of the criminal, and mode in which the blow has been delivered. The numerous difficulties which such cases present and the number of different causes which may produce the same effect must not be forgotten. That a conscientious expert is aware of all the circumstances attending a crime, has read the depositions of the witnesses, and has seen the supposed weapon, etc., is no reason for his coming to a precipitate conclusion, but, thus informed, it will be possible for him to weigh every circumstance, obtain a general idea of the occurrence, and affirm more clearly, with more certainty, and, what is very important, less discursively, than if the aids in question had been refused to him. It must not be forgotten that to-day, in spite of, and perhaps because of, the great progress of science people make statements with much less assurance than formerly. One has only to compare books on medical jurisprudence written 40 years ago with those of to-day to see that the writers of those days, acting upon a small number of cases at their disposal, did not hesitate to state general principles the correctness of which is now much shaken, for experimental science, now much more extensive, has found out so many exceptions that in the long run they sometimes become more numerous than the so called rules.

This principle must be applied to other domains and we must not boast of our own knowledge which is always more or less incomplete if we do not know the exceptions ourselves we have but to demand them of specialists. By conforming to this rule we will obtain astonishing results. The specialist will refute a well-established conviction leading us to say "I believe it is always thus," with a series of exceptions in which it is *not always thus*. In a recent case medical experts who on examination in the witness-box affirmed positively that it was impossible for a cavity to form in lobar pneumonia, when confronted with authorities in cross-examination admitted that such a thing was quite possible. If therefore experts themselves may be mistaken, how much more should the Investigating Officer be unashamed to question others upon things which seem beyond all doubt. Moreover the circle of experts must be enlarged as much as possible. Some Investigating Officers in many years have never made use of any other experts than doctors, analysts and gunsmiths, it has never crossed their minds to consult workmen and artisans of all kinds. They have not thought that they might be able to obtain the most precious information from such sources.

The author must confess that he has often had business with experts without knowing at the outset what they might be able to tell him. He once sent for a cutler and gave him a knife found in the wound of a murdered person and asked him whether he could give any information about it, the cutler replied that such knives were only manufactured in the north of Bohemia. And this information brought about the discovery of the criminal. A turner pointed out that an article the criminal had left behind must have been turned by a left-handed person. The person arrested (who denied the

GENERAL CONSIDERATIONS

crime) came from a distant town. Search was made in that place for a left-handed turner, who when found, identified the accused as the person who had bought the article from him. Linguists have indicated the nationality of the writer of a letter; a schoolmaster has guessed the age of a bank-note forger, then unknown, from the mistakes in writing which he made; and astronomers have given the day in spring which, as regards the evening light, corresponded with a certain day in autumn. In the last case, the Investigating Officer was able to visit a locality in *spring* in order to find out if the criminal would be able to see, and must have seen, such and such a thing at a certain hour on a certain day in the autumn. (See *Chapter I*, p. 20).

A numismatist was able to play an even more important role as an expert. A coin with a figure of St. George was found on the scene of a crime (on the face St. George, on the reverse a ship with Christ and His disciples); a witness was able to swear that the accused owned a coin which had a ship on one side (he had not seen the other side). The numismatist affirmed that this coin was most probably a St. George coin, for there are very few other coins bearing a ship, and besides, it was impossible for the accused to be in possession of any of those others.

It is self-evident that numerous consultations with specialists have no results, but one must not allow oneself to be disheartened by the number of consultations made, nor discouraged by the key in any particular case. If one is content to examine and measure accurately the instrument of the crime in conjunction with the expert without going any further, the result would be hardly appreciable. If one entered upon a fairly long technical discussion with the specialist, especially if he is a simple-minded person, and if the case is related and explained to him little by little, much useful information will be obtained.

Often quite a series of workmen, etc., will have to be consulted when it is believed that some peculiarity is due to a certain kind of skill connected with some particular trade. One day, for example, an important theft, extremely skilfully carried out, was committed in the following manner. A thief, a former servant of a banker who lived alone, had slipped during the daytime into the room next to the bedroom of his old master. The thief was aware that the banker was in the habit, before going to bed, of locking the door between his bedroom and the room where the former was hidden. He therefore resolved to wait until the old gentleman was asleep, then slip into the bedroom, take the key of the safe from the bed-table, open the safe and complete the theft, which indeed he did. But, so as not to be shut out in the room where he was hiding, it was necessary to make the banker believe that he had already locked the door of communication. The thief therefore shaped a small piece of wood to block up the slot or square opening into which the bolt of the lock penetrates.

When the banker went to lock the door before getting into bed, the bolt was unable to enter the hole in the door-post, thus producing the same effect as if the door had been already locked, and, indeed, the banker declared afterwards his belief that he had already locked the door without remembering having done so. The door therefore remained unlocked and the thief was able to carry out his project, but he had left the little piece of wood, which was prismatic in shape, in the slot, and it was shown to various experts

The first was a locksmith, who very sensibly remarked, "the person who made this works more minutely than we do; it was not necessary to cork the hole with so much care, quite an ordinary little piece of wood would have done well enough provided that it was of the proper length." A turner was then questioned, who on seeing the piece of wood was of opinion that its workmanship indicated a man who knew how to carve. A turner turns but does not carve, and so it could not have been a turner who was concerned in the theft. A wood-carver was next questioned and he was able by chance to indicate an instrument used exclusively by makers of boot and shoe trees. This instrument was procured and the Investigating Officer was easily convinced of the accuracy of the wood-carver's statements, and, on the result being communicated to the victim of the theft, the thief was easily found; in fact, the last servant whom the banker had dismissed had formerly been a tree-maker and indeed went back to that trade whenever he was out of a place.

It is, besides, astonishing to note the difficulty which people have, especially persons of the working classes, in getting rid of their usual manner of working; it seems quite natural to them and seeing nothing out of the way in it themselves they have no fear of discovery. They imagine that it appears quite as natural to others; thus a weaver makes a weaver's knot, a miller one like those with which he ties up his sacks of flour, a sailor makes a sailor's knot, a fisher a fisherman's knot, a butcher makes the same kind of knot as that which he uses to tie the cord to the horn of the animal to be slaughtered, and the gipsy who, in breaking into a room, fastens the door to avoid surprises, ties the stick which he employs for that purpose with a cord in quite a singular manner. *Tardieu* tells of a case regarding a so-called "artillery knot," and *Hoffman*, in his 'Legal Medicine,' of a case of suicide of a silk worker who used a knot such as he employed in making shawl fringes. It goes without saying that there are no professional experts in the science of knot-making; the only thing to be done is to question people whom one believes to have some special knowledge until the right man is hit upon. Cases of this kind are numerous: a new-born child had been killed with a knife thrust in the back of the head (at the place where the head joins the spinal column) " in the same way as one kills a partridge " said the *Mayor* who was an experienced sportsman, and indeed the lover of the dead child's mother was a young sportsman. In the case of 'Madame Henri,' in which a body was found in a sack in the river, it was shown by a police officer that the sack had been sewn up by a woman and then bound and tied up by a man.

But if experts are capable of informing the Investigating Officer on many points care must at the same time be taken not to ask them (and especially medical ones) for too many or for too precise explanations. The author has no intention of reprobating the ridicule with which the Investigating Officer is covered when he asks a doctor foolish questions or requests information which cannot, in the present state of science, be conscientiously given. He would merely recall the fact that a medical man, like all other men, sums up the person who questions him from the way in which the questions are put. Profound medical knowledge is certainly not required of the Investigating Officer, but it is necessary that his questions be not too absurd; it is only too easy for the medical man to be placed in such a position that he is forced to ask himself how, in spite of all the knowledge he has so laboriously acquired, such infantile questions can possibly be answered. If he persist in demanding answers which cannot be given to him, not only does the Investigating Officer deprive the medical man of all pleasure in his work but he also exposes the whole case to an irremediable check. It must be repeated that the Investigating Officer has not always at his beck and call the medical jurisprudents and experienced professors provided with all necessary instruments who are to be found in great cities. He is often obliged to work with doctors who are quite young, very old, or with little training. They may be the best practitioners in the world in general practice but they are not medical jurisprudents in the proper sense of the word. Only those who have had long experience of them can know what qualities a good medical jurisprudent should have; he ought certainly to be a specialist in all branches of medical knowledge, ought to know all the difficulties to be met with, and have special experience of criminals. It would not be fair to the medical jurisprudent, who represents all branches of medical science, to pretend that any country doctor, even the very best, can be a medical jurisprudent absolutely worthy of confidence.

It is for this reason that the Investigating Officer should take care not to ask the medical man for too much. It is natural for a man to prefer to say "the thing is so" rather than "I do not know," and sometimes, the doctor will make precise replies when pressed by an Investigating Officer, replies which will not bear the examination of science. It has been necessary for the best-known professors in medical jurisprudence to boldly avow —"We do not know this, nor yet that, and many other things besides"— and yet the scientists of former times used to make the most categorical statements. Take but a few examples. With what certainty did they not use to distinguish *ante mortem* from *post mortem* wounds? And yet every medical jurisprudent of to-day points out most convincingly that the so-called distinctive signs are not always infallible. Again, medical jurisprudents used to determine very accurately the beginning and the end of a gash or cut, a point perhaps very important in a case of murder or suicide; modern medical men dare not in most instances form an opinion from the mere sight of the wound. And with what certainty they used to distinguish between the blood of wounds and that of menstruation. Yet it is now admitted that this distinction is one which is not to be depended on and which can only be made in particular cases. Formerly the possibility of ruptures of the larynx, of precipitate birth, and rupture of the umbilical cord in living persons was absolutely denied. To-day these possibilities can be no longer doubted.

Section ii.—Rôle of the Medical Jurisprudent.

Of all the experts an Investigating Officer has to deal with the most important and the most frequently questioned are medical jurisprudents; with them therefore the Investigating Officer should enter into very intimate relations. It may be that the relations between the Investigating Officer and the medical jurisprudent have no *direct* value in a case yet they are of the very highest importance. If they are purely professional in the sense that they are *exterior*, the manner of treating the most important and the greater number of cases in which medical jurisprudents play a role will be also *professional* and *exterior*. But if the connection between the Investigating Officer and the medical jurisprudent is closer and more amicable by reason of the interest taken in a common cause, the mode in which that cause is treated will bear witness to the lively enthusiasm and active co-operation of both persons. It must of necessity be presumed that the Investigating Officer and the medical jurisprudent are interested in their respective professions, for if they have no interest in them, they are as much to be pitied as they are unfit to render any service whatever: all they can do is to turn to some other career. If on the contrary they have zeal and energy, working together will encourage their efforts, and their collaboration will considerably aid the solution of the problem.

The author always recalls with a feeling of thankfulness a deceased friend who was like himself attached to a large provincial court: he as District Medical Officer and medical adviser to the court and the author as Investigating Officer, we worked five years together and settled not a few cases. Many of these cases necessitated journeys of some distance, not one of which was made without freely discussing the case in question and obtaining from a medico-legal point of view every possible explanation concerning it. The cases in which he took part were considered common property and one as much as the other used to do his best to throw light upon them. It is impossible to imagine how work was stimulated, what lessons were obtained for the future, how the task was lightened, and the author does not hesitate to say, what success crowned this collaboration. Neither the Investigating Officer nor the medical jurisprudent, especially the latter, can do good work if the relations between them are not close and intimate. To the advantages indicated above, another must be added: it is thanks to these relations that the Investigating Officer can more easily learn to know the occasions when he ought to consult a medical man. In many cases he neglects to question an expert even when the latter may be able to furnish him with important information, the reason being that he is incapable of exactly appreciating the extent of the knowledge the expert or medical man possesses. This is a difficult thing to learn professionally, but it is easily learned privately.

In cases into which medical knowledge enters, the medical man must always be questioned even when the solution of the problem appears to surpass the limits of human knowledge *e.g.*, when a long space of time has elapsed since the commission of the crime. Thus *Liman* relates that from the corpse of a man so extensively decomposed that it had become black and green, it was possible to determine by the condition of the heart that death was due to a stroke of apoplexy and that in consequence the man must have died a natural death. The same professor reports that the bones of King Dagobert which were disinterred at St. Denis twelve hundred years after his death were so well preserved that it was possible to observe every mark of violence committed on his person.

We may also mention the six thousand skulls contained in the crypt of the St. Florian Convent near Ems in Upper Austria. They date from an unknown battle which is supposed to have taken place towards the end of the great migration, and are so well preserved that historians have been able to determine, from the wounds upon them, the shape of the weapons of the period *e.g.*, one skull bears a wound made by an arrow which could have had only one sharp edge. It goes without saying that such old facts as these can scarcely be of interest to the Investigating Officer, but they prove that it is never too late to furnish proof of some particular fact; a medical jurisprudent ought always to be questioned before hazarding such an assertion.

We now pass to the role of the medical jurisprudent in particular and will first speak of the manner in which he must be utilised.

A Cases relating specially to Medical Jurisprudence

To this category of cases belong *post mortem* wounds, illnesses, offences against morality, shamming or malingering, questions concerning the force and skill required for and the age of certain acts, and a great number of other questions which crop up every day. Practice alone can teach us what are the questions themselves and the way to attack them, and if in the course of time one has succeeded in reducing the number of these questions, one notes that it is precisely the good information obtained from the medical jurisprudent to which that reduction is due. Let us be content with a prudent reply, a little vague rather than too precise, but let us question the medical man in all cases where there is room to suppose that he can see further than an outsider. If one accepts a hypothetical reply from the medical man, one will know that he has replied in that manner on purpose, especially if, later, one comes to the conclusion that his answer could not have been more definite. Between A and not-A there is more than the whole alphabet although each letter may have its own importance; the medical man should therefore not be pressed and should be allowed sufficient time; when he examines a wounded man on the first occasion he is not perhaps quite sure what to say,—allow him a second or even a third examination. One is certainly less exposed to mistakes when the medical man draws up no report at all, than when, pressed by the impatience of the Investigating Officer, he makes a report which he would have drawn up quite otherwise if the wounded person had been submitted to him for a second examination after a sufficient interval.

This is still more true as regards *post mortem* examinations. If the medical man can say nothing immediately, he must indicate the investigations to be made to complete what the *post mortem* has brought to light. We repeat that it is incorrect to say that the medical man has but to pronounce upon the actual situation and that the investigation has nothing to do with him; the medical man only sees in a medical examination or in a *post mortem*, the result and in many cases, he hardly occupies his mind with the means that have brought about that result.

In most cases it is the manner in which the circumstance has come about that is the important thing, and the medical man can after all only arrive at a conclusion if he knows the facts. Besides there is no fear that this knowledge of the case may beguile him into error, for he knows the result and if, by chance, the indications contained in the papers he has read lead him on to a false path he will always have a constant check in the fact itself; he will indeed perhaps be able to point out inaccuracies in the statements of the witness to the Investigating Officer. The interrogatory and the inquiry are one. Each completes the other and, if the medical man knows that the Investigating Officer is not so foolish as to require from him mathematically incontrovertible replies, the knowledge he may possess of the facts of the case will induce him to make a prudent statement rather than draw up a hasty and precipitate report.

Besides those cases in which the Investigating Officer necessarily requisitions the assistance of the medical man, there are others in which he may be of assistance. We will now mention some of these.

B. Preservation of parts of a corpse

It often happens that a corpse cannot be identified on account of decomposition being too far advanced and neither the structure of the body nor the articles of clothing, etc., found on the deceased showing any peculiarity to aid identification. And yet the identification may perhaps in certain circumstances be of the greatest importance. Let us suppose *e.g.*, that we wish to establish that a corpse is really that of a man seen two weeks before in an hotel, no one knows him, but the witnesses state that they would be sure to be able to recognise him on seeing the features. They cannot remember *e.g.*, his clothing, and they do not recollect having seen his watch or pocket-book, etc., they cannot say whether he had a particular cicatrix on the thigh, or other exterior marks of identification. But if his features are so disfigured by decomposition that no man is able to recognise them, the medical specialist must be asked to carry out the "regeneration process" described by *Professor von Hofmann*.

Professor von Hofmann says:—

"The head is cut off, the brain removed and several deep cuts made in the back and sides of the head, it is then placed in pure running water. In twelve hours' time the green colouring of the skin of the face will for the most part have disappeared or have got blanched, and the swelling greatly diminished, the top of the skull is then replaced and the skin of the head sewn up again. The head is then plunged into a concentrated solution of alcohol. After another twelve hours the green colouring and the swelling of decomposition will have so completely disappeared that the face will finally assume its normal condition and present the appearance of a corpse newly embalmed. Instead of the above solution, chloride of zinc may be employed with equal success. Of course the possibility of reconstructing a face has its limits, especially when the hair has already fallen off and the skin of the face begun to be perforated with holes—in such a case nothing can be done."

This process is all the more valuable in that the head when rendered recognisable may be preserved, at least until the hearing of the case, and may be again shown to the witnesses. Attention has been called to it here as it is probably unknown to many medico-legal men though it is often necessary to make use of it. Two things should be mentioned *firstly*, when recourse is had to this process in localities where running pipe-water cannot be obtained (and this happens more often than not), all that need be done is to plunge the head into some stream or flowing river, taking care to do so at some spot where contamination to the water will not be a source of danger, but in this event precautions must be taken to prevent the head being damaged by the animal life of the water (such as fish, etc.), which may in a single night destroy nearly all the skin,—thus causing the loss of all our trouble. A box of convenient size may be pierced in its four sides with four large holes and covered with duck cloth, or better still the netting of a very fine sieve the water will then enter and leave freely and even the smallest animals will be excluded *secondly*, there cannot be in these days many places so isolated that the chloride of zinc cannot be procured during the twelve or fifteen hours the head is in the water

For forensic purposes formalin is also very useful It acts like spirits of wine but with much stronger effect It may be used both for preservation and disinfection It completely removes the smell of a corpse in a very advanced state of decomposition

In wounding cases preservation of pieces of bone is of equal importance It is even often necessary to preserve bones of people not yet dead when *e g*, splinters of bone (generally bones of the head and the tubular bones) have been abstracted either by operation or in the course of healing The medical jurisprudent must always attend to the preservation of such pieces of bone, as they may sooner or later form material for conviction When the wound has caused death it is especially necessary to preserve such pieces of bone and in most cases the wound is to the skull *The damaged skull itself should be most carefully preserved* Wounds will be much better seen upon a prepared and macerated head than upon one still covered with bloody skin and scraps of flesh which render observation extremely difficult If the head be neat and clean, it may be taken in the hand as often as necessary, accurate and minute measurements can be taken, and even experiments may be made with the view of determining the instrument employed Moreover, if new information be obtained the skull may always be re-examined to more advantage than when the inquest took place Finally, the damaged skull may play an important rôle at the trial itself and may be the means of proving the innocence or guilt of the accused

Two remarks should be made —In University cities it is the business of the laboratory attendant to look after the maceration and preparation of the bones which may be seen heaped pell-mell in the water-troughs and upon the drying-shelves The assistant is even allowed to prepare what may be, from a legal point of view, an important skull But the Investigating Officer should on no condition tolerate this, for small splinters of bone may be lost new wounds made, or bones mixed up, or even the whole *corpus delicti* itself may be lost It is the Investigating Officer and the official expert who are responsible for the identity and integrity of the *corpus delicti*, the laboratory assistant is in no way responsible The *corpus delicti* loses all its authentic character and demonstrative value if it leaves the hands of the Investigating Officer or the expert, the Investigating Officer ought therefore to insist upon the manipulation of a skull being made either by the expert himself or, if by one of his servants, then under his direct supervision, and such work should never be executed contemporaneously with any other work

Secondly as regards the manner in which skulls should be mended, it is very instructive to gather and carefully put together all the parts of a skull in fragments On the one hand one acquires the conviction that no piece is missing, on the other one may observe how, in what direction, or with what instrument, etc, the wound was given The author remembers the effect produced on one occasion upon the jury by a medical jurisprudent in showing them a skull which seemed quite intact He had carefully gummed cigarette papers over it, then, with a slight pressure of the hand, he broke it into a thousand pieces, just as it had been smashed by the blow it had received; that is the way a wounded skull should be put together for demonstration to the jury; it is an incorrect process to join the pieces solidly. The author once saw a skull which had been broken into a quantity of little pieces by the head of a hatchet and carefully stuck together by the laboratory assistant with the best fish-glue; neither the fractures themselves nor the direction of the sutures could longer be seen. And the worst of it was that it was impossible to remedy the mistake, for the glue refused to melt even when steeped for a long time in water.

As has been stated, splinters of bone ought to be put back in their places and held together on the inside with very fine gummed paper.

Certain hints regarding age and sex may nearly always be found from an anatomical examination of the skull.

In conclusion we must point out the danger of attempting to identify solely by means of clothes, dress, and papers found on a corpse. There are many known cases in which such articles have been employed purposely to mislead the Investigating Officer.

It is always good to hand over a head to a medical man for preservation in formalin (formic aldehyde solution) or spirits of wine, etc. That it is important to be careful in identifying corpses is proved by many mistakes which have been made—even by wives of their husbands.

In cases of corpses swollen out by drowning, the corpse of a thin old man has often been taken for that of a stout young man (see also Section in (C), " Hair ").

C Tattooing

Tattooings which exist or which have existed on the bodies of living or dead persons may be very important in determining identity; they must therefore be examined and described in detail. Let it also be stated that attention must be paid to tattooings which are no longer visible; there is no doubt that they may disappear from view; they fade away either through lapse of time or, if the work has been badly done or unstable colours have been used, even after a short time. They may also be made to disappear artificially by submitting them to the corrosive action of an acid, especially indigo extract (indigotin disulphonic acid).

Dr Tarnot mentions a device whereby nothing but a scar is left: the application of a paste containing salicylic acid and glycerine (for about a week's time) will make the tattoo mark disappear. Another method has lately been suggested as the best; a strong solution of tannin is put on the tattoo mark, which is then treated with a needle in the same way as in tattooing, and finally a strong solution of nitrate of silver is used. *Tardieu* also tried the following: acetic acid and fat, then potash, hydrochloric acid and finally solution of potash. But the result of all these methods must always be that a scar, however slightly visible, will be left.

If it has been artificially removed, even the naked eye will discover very noticeable cicatrices, the form, size etc., of which are easily described.

In regard to the time which tattooing takes to disappear, *Caspar Liman* says that even on old invalids he found the marks clearly to be noticed after 40 or even 50 years. Amongst 36 tattooed persons he found two with the marks faded, two half and four completely disappeared. Hutin found among 3,000 invalids more than the sixth part (506) tattooed. Tardieu found even more striking numbers, as the people he examined mostly had used chalk, 96% of the tattooed marks had not vanished. The materials employed will disappear in the following order: cinnabar, gunpowder, washing-blue, ink, chalk mixed with lampblack will keep longest.

About the age of the tattoo mark in general, not much can be said. The scar after the operation is soon healed and does not change much for a long time. More or less strength in the colouring does not prove anything. A fresh tattoo with little pigment and an old tattoo with much pigment look nearly alike, but when the tattooing has been performed can rarely be laid down afterwards. Only in a few cases can one judge this, i.e., if a child has been tattooed on the back, the design will lose its form as the child grows up, the same will happen with a circle tattooed on the arm of a strong young man, as he becomes old, the mark of the inoculation will often move far away from its original place as years go on. Lately a young American girl was shown in many European centres with beautifully tattooed designs over the whole body. These were certainly genuine and interesting, but it was false to state as was done to the audience that her father did them when the lady was a child, as the designs would have lost their correct forms and become irregular and distorted if they had grown with her.

If the tattooing has disappeared naturally the medical man will in most cases be able to discover, with a strong magnifying glass, the cicatrices in the form of pricks or marks of a needle, or stitches. In many cases these cicatrices are so well preserved that it is easy to reconstitute the whole design, this reconstitution is rendered easier if the part of the skin in question be vigorously rubbed with some colouring matter such as ink, lampblack, or oil, etc., the colouring matter will adhere better to the cicatrised places, which becoming blacker than the other parts of the skin causes the tattooing to show up distinctly.

In proving the existence of tattooing upon a corpse the same method is followed, we have even a further important proof in cases where it has disappeared long before. The small colouring particles penetrate as far as the lymphatic glands nearest to them, where they remain and go no further, they lodge for preference in the periphery of the gland and on enlargement may be observed as much in the whole gland as in certain sections of it. They can, naturally, be better seen through the microscope, but the cinnabar so often employed as colouring matter looks reddish when rays of light fall upon the gland and has a black aspect when they traverse it. The examination of the gland should in such cases be always made by a medical man. It must also be remarked that tattooings upon wet corpses and upon mummified and dried-up corpses are not easily recognisable, in the first case the parts of the skin in question must be taken off and dried and in the second they must be soaked in water.

Let us now call attention to the general importance of tattooing. It is not necessary to go as far as a number of specialists who, following the example set by Lombroso in 1874, consider tattooing the characteristic sign of habitual criminals. Be that as it may, tattooing is very important. Kurella has clearly demonstrated this in finding tattoo marks upon 14 per cent of his subjects.

It may be laid down as a general proposition that tattooing is almost exclusively met with among people of an energetic disposition, a disposition already revealed in the career such people have chosen. Tattooing will generally be seen upon soldiers, sailors, butchers, fishermen, wood-cutters, smiths, etc., rarely on tailors, weavers or waiters. Not only can energetic people better support the pain caused by tattooing, but their character leads them to the display of something uncommon and difficult of acquisition. In this connection sexual sensuality plays an important role—why, it is difficult to say, but the motive seems to be that strong and sensual natures find pleasure in placing their bodies on view; they admire their own persons and love others to admire them also; it is for this reason that among persons of the feminine sex tattooing is in Europe generally only found among prostitutes; though it should be noticed that women of the cultivating classes are also frequently tattooed; in Bosnia for instance, a girl or woman of the Catholic peasant class is seldom to be found without it. It mostly consists of a more or less decorated cross on the forehead, the chest, or the upper part of the arm.

Mashka examined all prisoners before and after detention and found that most of them were not tattooed before but only after leaving the prison; this shows that the chief reason is the tediousness of the incarceration. *Ginter* asked 24 tattooed persons for the reason of undergoing this operation, and the reply in nearly all cases was—tediousness or imitation.

If we add to what we have stated that this rude body toilet is found chiefly among common people (*Lombroso* says among people of Celtic origin) we shall have collected all that concerns tattooing among criminals. We will be able to conclude that we only meet with tattooing among people of energy such as murderers, hooligans, housebreakers, etc., and on the other hand among people of a sensual nature, such as bullies, sodomites, ravishers, and others who commit crimes against morality, but not among cheats and thieves. It should further be noted that the simple and honest man is content with certain characteristic figures; the sailor carries an anchor or dates and initials, soldiers, swords or rifles, the butcher, crossed axes, etc., and the tattooing is generally placed on the inner aspect of the right forearm. A grosser and less honest nature is not content with that, it adorns itself with allusions to its crime or signs of vengeance, accompanied with resigned or frivolous indications of its probable end (e.g., "le bagne m'attend" or a gallows, etc.) If the person is by nature of obscene imagination it is revealed by the character of the design or by the place in which he is tattooed (the sexual parts or the buttocks).

Now it is very natural that among people of gross and energetic natures and doubtful morals many criminals exist. If, therefore, many criminals are tattooed it is that the same reason (natural grossness and immorality) has produced two effects, tattooing and crime. In this lies the whole correlation existing between tattooing and a criminal.

That not only criminals and those of criminal instincts tattoo themselves is shown by the fact that recently among the young English nobility tattooing was the height of fashion. This was not done in the usual way with hot needles, but by professional artists with the help of electrical apparatus (the galvanometer system).

D Mental Affections

A question, the value of which is not sufficiently appreciated is to know in what cases the Investigating Officer is morally obliged to submit an accused person or an important witness to medical examination or observation. It goes without saying that a furious madman, idiot, or person of undoubted melancholic character should be placed in the hands of the medical expert; this, indeed, has been done for centuries. But the progress of mental and legal science demands nowadays that attention also be paid to mental maladies which an outsider is incapable of recognising; care must be taken that people who are really ill be not punished for acts committed in an access of madness. It is only by the most minute attention and the most conscientious strictness that we are able to avoid those terrible errors formerly committed when numbers of weak minded persons were punished on the ground of their perversity or monstrous infamy.

Such cases are as difficult to deal with as they are sad to think of and, everything considered, the mental condition of *every* accused person and *every* important witness who makes a statement must be examined. Reasons of convenience and the exigencies of time and money alone prevent us from making the obligation to have medical examinations in every case a statutory one; but if it is impossible for this to be done, science, conscience, and humanity order us to act with generosity when the least doubt of the responsibility of an accused person for his acts arises, to study our man carefully when his mental condition appears suspicious, and not to refuse to allow his re-examination by doctors even when they have already declared perfectly sane a man whom we believe to be somewhat wanting. When a jurist makes a mistake upon a medical question—and it is not impossible for him to do so—and he has interrogated a lunacy doctor without obtaining any result, his conduct can only do honour to his conscientious scruples; every medical man will tell him that it is far from easy, even for a specialist, to decide whether an individual is sane or not; every honest man will be of opinion that it is better to examine, from the point of view of their responsibility, many sane people than punish a single person who is rendered irresponsible by mental illness.

Looking into the matter more closely, we find that here again the Investigating Officer ought to be something of an expert and consider and observe to a very considerable extent. He ought at least to be sufficiently informed to know, without committing absurd blunders, when a medical man ought to be consulted.

The ways of procuring the information the Investigating Officer requires in this connection are numerous. He should study quite a number of treatises on medical psychopathology. But the knowledge so acquired would be a dead-letter if one were to stop there; the Investigating Officer who takes his profession seriously should attend a course on mental diseases at some medical college. It is only by seeing and studying the demonstration and explanation of different cases in relation to every subject that he will become capable of making use in practice of what he has imbibed from books; only then will he really be able to understand the phenomena described. Even the best books are incapable of giving the reader an exact idea of what the author means when he uses phrases to express varying degrees of intensity with regard to any particular phenomenon. Such phrases as "a wild look," "incoherent speech," "slow thinking," and other similar expressions convey to a person who has no acquaintance with such peculiarities, either too much or too little. He takes the troubled look of a sane person which is of no consequence for a "wild look," worthy of mistrust, or else he imagines the expression to imply a horrible rolling of the eyes etc., while the real wild look, the psychopathological look, seems perfectly normal to him. The truth in such a case can only be pointed out by a lunacy doctor and with living subjects, books alone are insufficient.

The most instructive cases for the Investigating Officer are those which he has had to elucidate himself; in such cases he is able to see the manner in which the doctor examines the patient, he can gather information upon a mass of things, and finally he considers the report the expert has drawn up. If he scans only the last lines of this carefully composed certificate for the sole purpose of finding the word *mad* or the words *not mad* the reading of the report, or for that matter of a thousand reports, will teach him absolutely nothing. But how easy it is for him to learn something: the report treats of the case which he has managed from the start, he had to deal with the patient when he believed him to be "sound," he remembers how the first traces of suspicion came into his mind, he knows what he himself thought of the case in general and all the symptoms in particular, and now he has the expert's detailed report in his hands, in it he sees described and scientifically explained the observations he has made as an outsider, and is thus enabled to correct his opinion. If certain details still remain obscure and doubtful it is possible for him to procure enlightenment and information from the expert, and his own judicial experience will at least show him how he ought to go on with the case. He must be able to say afterwards that he has minutely observed the patient, carefully studied the report, asked the expert for explanations, and read certain cases in point in special books.

Well-known specialists have essayed to facilitate the Investigating Officer in dealing with the cases where he ought to consult a medical jurisprudent: to this end they have enumerated the distinctive characteristics of mental derangement, characteristics easy of observation and capable of making even a person who is not a specialist in mental diseases suspect a mental affection. According to *Caspar Liman* the medical man should always be consulted in cases in which the following characteristics appear:—

1. Hereditary dispositions, where it is known that the parents or family or relations of the family (including children) of the individual are or have been attacked with mind troubles.

2. Wounds affecting the brain (wounds on the head), severe illnesses accompanied with brain complications, such as puerperal fever, brain fever from over-study, etc.

3. Nervous diseases, epilepsy, hypochondria, hysteria, etc.

4. Alcoholism.

5. Various maladies of the body (headache, insomnia, giddiness, cramp, paralysis, delirium tremens, etc.)

6. Hallucinations.

7 Visions
8 Enfeebled intelligence
9 Periodical return of certain phenomena
10 Peculiar bearing
11 Extraordinary manner of writing

Professor *Krafft-Ebing* mentions several points which might lead us to consider a man sane when he is really not so:—

1 A madman's act may have a motive just as well as that of a perfectly sane man
2 The fact that the action is an isolated one in the life of its author can only allow of practical conclusions in an abstract way
3 Premeditation, cunning, and prudent calculation are not incompatible with insanity
4 Nor are consciousness of guilt and responsibility for it
5 Nor even repentance after the act
6 The insane person may speak perfectly rationally
7 Even in madness there is method and logic

Besides these he gathers together important particulars of which notice must be taken in considering mental affections, such as the antecedents, the report of the crime, the complaint drunkenness, knowledge of the act, the manner of its commission and accessory circumstances not in direct conformity with the object of the action, e g, a particular exhibition of cruelty, useless acts of destruction, etc. Moreover, the alleged crime must be particularly examined objectively when it is a case of spontaneous confession made by a man of melancholic and reserved temperament, for such confessions may themselves be false

There is room to suppose that a person is mentally diseased when he commits, with no apparent motive, crimes against his parents and those dear to him, or friends, or public officials, etc, also when he tries to make out that his act is much worse than it really is, or seems apathetic in the face of most moving events, or again when he is extraordinarily excited or violent, loquacious or taciturn, or when he absolutely refuses to hear the action itself spoken about In such cases it must be remembered that an individual struck with temporary madness may have lucid intervals when his words are perfectly rational

Other suspicious phenomena are a radical and inexplicable change in the manner of living and character of a person accompanied with indifference for relations formerly of great importance (i e, business and family relations), irritability, sudden taking to drink, vagabondage, sexual excesses, feebleness of memory, rapid cerebral fatigue, denunciation of morality, negligence in bearing and person, pugnaciousness, destructiveness, irritation, jealousy, complaints of slanders uttering threats—even before the Court, complaints of bodily illness and pain—especially of nervous varieties, anxiety, apprehensiveness, headache insomnia, fear of becoming mad, imaginary troubles, melancholy or excessive good spirits being tired of life, attempts at suicide, complaints of being troubled with peculiar thoughts exaggerated religiousness formerly foreign to the character, apprehension of something terrible happening with vague indications as to the misfortune, menacing warnings or threats to friends, attempts to deprive himself of means that offer to commit a crime *Krafft-Ebing* also mentions other inquiries to be made where there exist in the family of the accused, e g grave brain, nerve, or mental maladies suicides, chronic drunkards, or peculiarly immoral or criminal manner of living, again where the age of the accused disposes him to commit such and such an action, e g certain crimes against morality at the beginning of old age, or false accusations of imaginary crimes at the age of the development of puberty, or where at the period of menstruation a woman generally acts in some abnormal way and the crime has been committed during such a period there are women who do things at the period of menstruation which would never enter their minds at any other time

The author would especially call attention to "the peculiar manner of writing" spoken of by *Caspar Liman*. This manner of writing is peculiar to mad persons and of great importance to the Investigating Officer who has more occasion to observe it than the lunacy doctor and to whom it is easier to discover an anomaly in handwriting than in the expression on a face The Investigating Officer has occasion to read so many things written by sane persons that he acquires great experience by doing so and can notice better than other people anything out of the ordinary in handwriting

Certain people afflicted with mental troubles are very fond of writing especially when misanthropic, they are prone to substitute letters or petitions for personal relations. Moreover, people suffering from the monomania of persecution are particularly fond of appearing before the courts believing they are safest there

We have all had experience of habitues among this latter class of unfortunate madmen who come from time to time to seek news of their suit, legacy, fortune, etc It sometimes happens that these persons will on no account appear before the court for fear of being shut up, deceived, or even executed, they prefer to make their accusations in writing, such accusations of imaginary crimes come before every court and cause most disagreeable confusion, when, led astray by apparently perfectly reasonable explanations, cases are rashly taken up against the parties accused

When an urgent matter comes before an Investigating Officer and a doctor is not always at hand, he will be obliged to go on with the inquiry himself it is therefore desirable that he should be acquainted with these special ways of writing peculiar to insane persons They may be found in the office of every registrar and a registrar of any experience will immediately recognise them, the young Investigating Officer has but to read them with great care in order to discover their characteristic signs One can hardly define in what the originality and the distinctive features of these documents consist, the habit of dealing with them will, so to speak reveal their sentiment It is especially to be noted that these petitions are generally of great length and repeat themselves over and over again, amplifications and exaggerations are generally to be found and in themselves are certain indications of the falseness of the complaint (e g, the petitioner says he has had his head split or has been shut up for three months with only a small piece of dry bread each day) The construction of the phrases is often involved, incomprehensible, and stiff, often again short and full of little prepositions —but it is never natural It is a striking fact that a man afflicted with a mental disease, almost always makes use, when writing, of words of extraordinary formation and inordinate length. He is often betrayed by this.

But what an insane person may say or write is not always devoid of truth or inaccurate, and *every accusation, even coming from a person notoriously mad, is worthy of examination*. It only too often happens that people profit by the circumstance of an individual's madness to say "all the same no one will believe that madman." If this be so the unfortunate lunatic is at the mercy of the whole world and exposed to the exploitation, teasing, and bad treatment of ill-conditioned and ill-minded people, especially when they find out that their victim's repeated complaints have not been believed. It is therefore the duty of the Investigating Officer to verify the accuracy of all the statements of a lunatic; on every occasion he should make sure that there is really no truth in the case even where the evil complained of has been found on previous occasions to be false. We remember a case in which a crazy old peasant had made innumerable representations to the authorities in which he declared that "his enemy" had made pits, traps, and similar contrivances, before his house or on his way, by which he would be killed or injured. Many of these representations were furnished with clear sketches of the asserted pitfalls, etc. These representations became known to the people of the neighbourhood and on one occasion the village boys played a practical joke and really made a pit before his front door and filled it with manure. The unfortunate man fell into it and was nearly drowned.

We shall now direct attention to some points which the Investigating Officer should carefully note:—

1. LUNATICS.—It is often necessary to cite lunatics as witnesses, they should never be sent away merely on the ground that they are demented, for they can sometimes render considerable assistance. It has been frequently remarked that madmen, especially certain varieties of madmen, are excellent observers; they are not nearly so adverse to telling the truth as many people who rejoice in all their faculties, for they do not allow themselves to be guided by considerations of propriety; they have also more opportunities for observation, for things are done and said in the presence of a lunatic which would not be done or said before others; it is self-evident that the statements of a madman must be well weighed before being utilised as evidence in a case.

2. DELIRIUM.—Everyone knows that delirium causes a man to commit all sorts of actions; we often believe we have to do with deliberate acts when they are but the result of an attack of intermittent fever; in such a case errors are easily made, for the invalid generally conducts himself in quite a normal manner and it is only during the short intervals of an attack that he performs acts for which he cannot be held responsible. When therefore the Investigating Officer learns that the accused suffers from time to time from these attacks he should not neglect to consult a physician.

3. DREAMS.—*Krafft-Ebing* remarks that very vivid dreams often continue their effect after the sleeper awakes, in such cases the incidents in dreams are often taken for realities. Numerous inaccurate statements are explained in this way—perhaps also more than one piece of supposed perjury. It is said that such dreams are especially common among epileptics.

4. SOMNAMBULISM.—Not less important are acts committed in a state

of somnambulism. Somnambulists mostly attack the objects nearest at hand, generally people they suddenly meet, and they often develop a strength which bears no comparison with that of their waking state. This phenomenon is especially noticeable among young people in their first sleep, and after great intellectual or corporeal efforts. The recollection of these acts is either completely effaced or else preserved in the vaguest possible way.

5. IMITATION.—Just as the satisfaction of certain corporeal needs (such as eating, drinking, sleeping, smoking, yawning), is contagious, so certain acts of the insane may arouse imitation among people of perfectly normal condition. Especially noticeable is the contagion of hysteria, epilepsy, and other psychological epidemics—at one time so frequent. But the imitation of an isolated action of a lunatic may also take place, especially by young persons who have been for a considerable time in his society.

6. When the accused declares that he has only committed a great crime with the intention of being executed, and under the pretext that he is too cowardly to commit suicide, his declaration must not be brushed aside without further examination; it may have some foundation, especially when we have to deal with people who are melancholic by nature or mentally deficient. All such cases should be referred to the medical expert.

7. MANIA.—The theories regarding "moral insanity," "fixed ideas" and other species of mania, are so important to the Investigating Officer that it is absolutely necessary for him to familiarise himself with them and study some leading work on the subject. This kind of brain trouble is so uncommon that it often remains unperceived, and if the Investigating Officer does not detect it, the medical jurisprudent is not consulted, and as such kinds of affections hardly ever show themselves during the course of the trial, the accused is condemned though not really responsible for his actions.

8. REFLECTED ACTS.—Nowadays the theory of reflected acts has assumed some importance. By a reflected act is meant one coming between a pure reflex act wholly independent of volition and an act done with full consciousness, and only realised when reflected upon in the sub-consciousness (through habit, analogy, etc.)

9. HABITUAL DRUNKENNESS.—An objective and sure sign of drunkenness and its degrees is given by H. Gudden. It is to be particularly remarked that genuine habitual drunkards are most untrustworthy. They can be judged from their tearful whimpering and accusations. When the question of the conjugal fidelity of his wife is ostentatiously brought forward by a man, he is almost always a chronic alcoholist.

10. HOMOSEXUALITY.—It should be decided in each case whether we have to deal with a disease of the mind, a vice, or an innate peculiarity. One has to put before oneself a long chain of developments which begin with the normal sexual man and extend over the man and woman of light character, to the effeminate and the virago, and from these to the declared hermaphrodite. The unnatural character of the hermaphrodite and the repugnance we feel towards him must lead us to look on him as a being for whom punishment is not the proper treatment.

11. EPILEPSY.—The numerous and for us often weighty signs (twilight conditions) are well handled by Morchen in treating of the characteristics of the true and masked epileptic (nightly wetting of the bed), and the frequent,

prominent, and inexplicable skin bleedings on the neck, shoulders and behind the ears (stigmata). Nearly every epileptic fit is violent, and a bigot.

12. MASOCHISM, SADISM and FETICHISM are treated in text-books on Psychiatry, Psychopathology, etc. Only a suggestion of their important appearances is given here.

(a) *Masochism* appears when the afflicted person allows himself to be ill treated by his partner, in order to be wholly sexually excited or to attain the full enjoyment of the act of generation.

(b) *Sadism* conversely is when the afflicted person for the same object ill-treats his partner, chokes, bites, pricks, beats, etc. Hereby alone many murders can be explained, the man or woman having for once gone too far.

(c) *Fetichism* appears when for sexual objects or for sexual stimulus a person purloins such things as plaits of hair, cloth-bags, shoes, stockings, apron strings etc. As a rule this peculiarity accompanies masturbation.

(d) *Saliromania* is the name given to the desire to soil and spoil clothes of women with ink, acid, etc. One concludes this behaviour has a sexual origin, a sort of fetichism bound up with sadism.

E. Hypnotism

The jurist who glances through the flood of books on this subject can no longer hold aloof as an outsider from the question of hypnotism.

If we desire to obtain an idea of the value of hypnotism for ourselves we must study however superficially, its very essence, otherwise the Investigating Officer will be incapable of knowing when he is face to face with a case of hypnotism and must consequently have recourse to an expert.

We must at the outset agree with *Max Dessoir* ("Das Doppel-Ich" Berlin, 1889) that human personality divides itself into at least two spheres which are theoretically, quite distinct, namely "the waking state" (the superior consciousness) and the "dream state" (the inferior consciousness). The latter state is by no means unknown to us, it exists whenever we dream or when, in a fit of sleepwalking or distraction, we act without knowing what we are doing. It is in the sphere of this inferior consciousness that all the acts of a person under the influence of hypnotism are placed, and by arranging these phenomena in a category of known facts we attempt to form a clear idea of that state. Hypnotism has most resemblance to sleep. Suppose we were to see a person asleep for the first time—the phenomenon would appear much more strange than anything seen or heard with regard to hypnotism. But we may distinguish sleep from hypnotism by designating the latter (as does *Forel*), by the phrase "state of suggestibility." To "suggest" is to produce a dynamic change in the *nervous system* of a person under the influence of another person, inducing in the subject an idea that this change is taking or has taken place. As to auto-suggestion it is the suggestion a man effects upon himself either consciously or unconsciously. We can therefore distinguish as determining motives:—

1. *A supernatural agent.*—Magnetism, mesmerism, telepathy, presentiment, visions, etc.

2. *Suggestion.*—As formulated since the time of *Braid*, 1843 and *Liébault*, 1864.

3. All somatic, corporal, or materialistic theories which presume peripheric influences on the extremities of the nerves (fixity of look, rubbing of the forehead, etc.)

The second theory (suggestion) alone has any scientific value. Only one kind of hypnotism is then established by science, i.e. that consisting of the suggestion of ideas.

It would be superfluous to analyse the way in which it takes place in practice; whoever feels any disposition for these questions, dangerous as they are, may find the necessary information in almost any work on hypnotism, but it is better to leave such experiments to medical men.

In the hypnotic state itself three stages may be distinguished:

(1) SOMNOLENCE,—state in which the subject can still open the eyes.

(2) LIGHT SLEEP,—(hypotaxis, charm)—state in which he partly submits to the influence of suggestion.

(3) DEEP SLEEP.—somnambulism with amnesia (forgetfulness) after waking.

Müller also differentiates between deep sleep with or without post-hypnotic hallucinations, i.e., the subject may, after coming to, remain under the influence of what has been suggested to him while in the hypnotic state.

We have also to distinguish:—

(a) MENTAL SUGGESTION.—Here the thoughts of one person act upon other persons. *Peronet* relates how he ordered a person to play the piano until it was suggested to him to stop. He placed himself behind the pianist while he was playing and began to wish energetically that he would stop playing, and, at that very moment, he stopped.

(b) RETROACTIVE HALLUCINATION.—By which a person is persuaded that certain facts have happened. The person believes these facts though they have never taken place.

(c) NEGATIVE HALLUCINATION.—By which it is suggested to a person that certain objects present have disappeared (e.g., that a person present has gone away: the subject no longer sees the person though he is still there).

If it be asked up to what point people can be hypnotised we learn that a man with a healthy mind may be hypnotised when there is no "auto-suggestion" not to be hypnotised, i.e., where the patient does not battle against the hypnotiser. According to *Obersteiner*, one person in every three is absolutely proof against hypnotism, one in three is moderately affected and one in three is perfectly hypnotisable. *Liébault* and *Bernheim* have hypnotised thousands of persons, very few of whom have opposed any resistance. *Wetterstrand* found 97 refractory persons out of 3,148, *Renterghem* and *Eeden* found 395 out of 414 susceptible to hypnotism. Speaking generally it may be said that from 80 to 95 per cent. of men may be hypnotised. People having mental illnesses are not included in this figure; they are hardly ever hypnotisable.

The effects of hypnotism have been established scientifically. *Forel* says:—By suggestion in hypnotism one may produce, influence and impede all the subjective phenomena known to the human mind as well as a large number of the objective functions known to the nervous system, only the functions of the ganglions and the reflexive movements of the spine, as well as those of the base of the skull, seem to escape the influence of suggestion. Suggestion may even act upon the so-called somatic functions, such as digestion, perspiration, and menstruation.

The post-hypnotic effect, i.e. ulterior obedience to orders given during the hypnotic state, does not occur with all persons. It may last minutes or days and *Liegeois* even mentions a case where suggestion was effective at the end of a year. The hypnotised, says *Muller*, may be in the most abject state of submission to the hypnotiser; from the point of view of phenomena of the mind and the nervous movements he may be in a condition of absolute dependence.

In the hypnotic state it may be suggested to people that they are ignorant of certain languages, that they are animals, that they are of another sex or age to what they really are. The senses and memory may be sharpened, the subject may recognise the owner of an article by the smell of it; the servant of a clergyman was able to recite Latin and Hebrew passages, which she was unable to do in the waking state. An old lady transformed herself in turn into a peasant, a general, a little child, a young man (*Richet*). If it is suggested to a hypnotised person that certain acts be done within a certain time, the suggestion is coercive in character, it must be done as suggested but always with the idea that another has constrained the subject so to act, and the latter is generally aware that he has been so constrained by the person who has hypnotised him; but again if it is suggested that what he does is of his own accord he believes so. If all this be true, the whole question is a very serious one.

As regards the handwriting of a person while in the hypnotic state we find that such writing hardly differs from the subject's writing in the waking state. *Ames* discusses this at some length. He tells of an experiment tried in the following circumstances. A trial was made upon a young man, Mr Guy Oppelt Mason, who had never been hypnotised. He was put under hypnotic influence, and was requested to write two specimens of his handwriting. After being awakened, he wrote a specimen in his normal state. He said that he had not written the hypnotised specimens, at least he did not remember anything about it. A comparison of the two specimens showed that about the only difference was the size. Mr Mason, while in the hypnotic state, had been told that he had the toothache, etc., and consequently was more or less agitated when he sat down to write. While there were a few slight differences in some letters and in the pictorial effect, on the whole the two specimens were wonderfully alike, and are most convincing that hypnotism, and no doubt other forms of double consciousness, cannot destroy the characteristics in handwriting.

We are thus driven to ask what importance the question of hypnotism has from the criminal point of view. Either, says *Ryger*, the whole question is of no importance in criminal law, having existed and having been known for long but meriting no attention from that standpoint, or, it has become important solely by reason of great discoveries made since the drawing up of our present criminal codes. If we combine these two opposing phrases we may perhaps discover the truth; the thing has existed for long, has had its influence, but its criminal importance has not been appreciated at its true value and is only now becoming recognised by us. The effects of hypnotism were formerly well known, but not as such; *Delbruck*, indeed, shows that they have been utilised in poetry, *e.g.*, *Gattfried-Keller* in his book "Le vert Henri" relates the history of a child of seven years old who disgracefully slandered several boys older than himself by a quite imaginary story suggested to him.

To understand the complications we meet in connection with hypnotism we have but to consider some results obtained by specialists in that science. If for instance operations and accouchements may be painlessly performed in these days under the influence of hypnotism we may also be allowed to presume that common and immoral assaults may be performed upon hypnotised persons; thus a man is said to have been castrated during an hypnotic sleep. *Liegeois* made a lady confess before an audience to debts to the extent of six thousand francs; he suggested to her that he had lent her that sum some time before. At the Congress of Jurists at Zurich a hypnotised boy swore that one of the gentlemen present had stolen his handkerchief, and after a new suggestion he swore he had never made such an accusation.

Liebault and *Bernheim* state that more than one case of illness and even cases of death must be put down to "suggestion" and they recall "the ordeals and judgments of God" of the Middle Ages. The thing seems almost unbelievable, but really it is not so; doctors and especially military doctors have often observed that the will of a man may in certain circumstances prolong life; people dangerously ill live until the happening of such and such an event, *e.g.*, the arrival of an expected relative; soldiers gravely wounded on the field of battle live until the moment when someone finds them—thanks to the energy of their will. In the Russian and Austrian wars it was several times noticed that soldiers whose character was weak and resigned often succumbed to wounds which were not really mortal while the energetic character and love of life of others enabled them, in spite of grievous wounds, to struggle with death until the moment when help arrived.

But if the influence of the will upon life and death is so great even in a normal state, it must be admitted that this influence may be increased in certain circumstances by the will of another.

The effect of suggestion upon daily life cannot be presumed to be the culminating point that may be attained by hypnotism. That goal will be reached when hypnotism is able to bring about certain purely somatic phenomena; these phenomena are not only very remarkable but from a criminal standpoint may be full of the most enterprising consequences. If, *e.g.*, it is possible, as stated above, to retard or advance menstruation, it is natural to suppose that abortions may take place by suggestion, and in consequence, by hypnotism. It is even stated that blisters may be made to appear on the body of a hypnotised person by telling him that a strong plaster has been put on him, whereas in reality it is only a piece of wet paper. The same phenomenon is produced by touching a person with a cold object and suggesting that it is burning.

In this connection another question naturally arises. Is it not possible to bring about in like manner all kinds of ecchymoses, traces of strangulation, etc., which may have the gravest consequences? In another sense is there not room for fear that in certain circumstances all sorts of abuses are committed on persons susceptible to hypnotism? It is related that one of the Baronesses Rothschild was hypnotised and robbed in a railway carriage.

Many professors of hypnotism fear that Investigating Officers may suggest false depositions or false confessions to a witness or accused person by bending their recollections by unconscious suggestion or retroactive hallucination. It is certain that this happens, the explanation is quite natural, since, by persuading oneself and others, one is liable to commit very grave mistakes without its being possible to say that there is wilful suggestion. In all cases it is possible to control the accuracy of a witness's statements by exercising an excess of complacency. One has only to question him in the same manner as before upon facts which one knows have not happened, if the individual in question still replies in the affirmative it is very probable that all that he has stated before is also untrue.

As to acts done by the hypnotised person after hypnotism (post-hypnotic action), they do not appear to be very dangerous. The hypnotised person when asked to do so while under the influence of hypnotism will drink e.g., a glass of water, bow to a person, etc., but he will show repugnance and embarrassment when he is told to overturn a chair, throw ink about or do other absurd things. But if he is asked to do something serious, e.g. to throw someone out of the window, to give a blow or to seize a person by the body, he will not do it, for as the absurdity of the demand increases so also the resistance of his own will grows, for *that will* must triumph over the *foreign will* which has suggested these things in proportion to the absurdity of the exactions of the foreign will. In relation to this another question arises:—To what extent are the statements of a hypnotised person to be believed? We cannot trust them very far. Foul has recently said (in a private letter) that it must not be forgotten that when all is said and done it is always the same cerebral substance which is dictating the statements in the waking as well as in the hypnotised condition, so that the force of will not to speak the truth can only be paralysed to a certain extent. If one wishes therefore to undertake experiments which in themselves are not allowable, i.e., to try to find out the truthfulness of hypnotised witnesses or accused persons, the results obtained will be little worthy of reliance.

If we sum up all the cases imaginable in which the criminal expert has to deal with hypnotism we can say:—

1. It may affect the property or moral character of the person hypnotised.

2. Every kind of extortion may be committed with its assistance.

3. It may suggest crimes to be committed.

4. It may suggest illnesses, etc.

5. The courage necessary for the performance of a crime may be suggested with its help.

6. Persons who have committed no crime may be unjustly accused by a person under its influence.

7. On the other hand a person who has knowingly committed a crime may plead suggestion by another.

8. Traces of wounds and strangulations may be produced by suggestion and subsequently serve as proofs.

9. Abortion may be brought about by suggestion.

10. All kinds of illnesses—especially of the nerves, and convulsions—may be the consequence of illicit or awkward hypnotising.

11. Involuntary suggestion may be practised by the Investigating Officer himself or other persons to be questioned.

We may say, generally speaking, that the dangers of hypnotism are not so very great and are better known than formerly, thanks to new theories which have carried us a considerable way forward. Difficulties always become less as we learn to know them better. All the Investigating Officer need keep well in mind is that he should call in an expert on every occasion when he discovers the least trace of hypnotism.

One of the clearest statements on the subject was that put forward by *Professor Hut* of Breslau in the *Czynsky* case. He said: "One can compare the superficial part of the brain, where according to the observations of to-day the memory, feelings, and sensations play, so far as concerns a conscious normal thoughtful person, with a sheet of paper which is ornamented with thousands of letters—these letters are the thoughts. When I by some means or other, as for example was done by the accused with Baroness Z., by sharp looks and strokes with the hand before the face, put the victim into a sleeping condition, then the letters fade more and more, as the individual gets tired, and are finally imperceptible in deep hypnotism, indeed altogether wiped out. When I then suggest something to the patient I write new characters and signs on the piece of paper, which the sleeper hears, reads, and without criticism believes to be true, that is to say takes for his own thoughts. The clearer the writing of the suggester, the more impressive the suggestions that follow, and on waking they cleave to the consciousness of the hypnotised subject, he takes them home with him and works with them. The more frequently the suggestions are repeated, and the deeper the hypnotic sleep is, so much the clearer and lasting are the characters which belong to it, and so much the more likely to influence the actions of the person sent to sleep (post-hypnotic suggestion)."

The question of the working of post-hypnotism is not nearly so interesting as it once appeared to be, as the strength and length of the effect are shown to be very insignificant. This is best illustrated by a well-authenticated case related by *Ernest Naville*, in which *Dr. Liébault* suggested to an idle stubborn child the desire to work. This lasted, however, only a short time, the child became once more idle, and attempts at the same suggestion did not succeed. This case is well established.

Without doubt we shall continue to study the question with the greatest care and call to our help the expert when a case of hypnotism comes before us, but the complicated importance which the matter was formerly believed to possess no longer exists.

F Colour Blindness

Colour blindness is more widespread and more important than is generally believed. Since 1777 when *Joseph Huddart* first mentioned this peculiarity when writing to Joseph Priestly, and *John Dalton* dealt with the subject more deeply in 1794, colour blindness has been the object of most extensive study and investigation. The number of persons who ought to be considered victims of colour blindness to a greater or less degree cannot be established. The percentage given varies from 3·25% to 8%. We may assume the average to be 5%, thus making one man in every 20 to some extent colour blind; this is probably a very conservative estimate. It should be added that colour blindness is much more frequent among men than women and its most usual form is a confusion of red with green or yellow.

Futhof Holmgren draws the following distinctions:—

1. *Total colour blindness*, i.e., the individual in question can only distinguish that a colour is dark or light. He can only see, e.g., red on red or grey on grey; we cannot say how he really sees the colour for we are unable to discuss it with him owing to our having no corresponding notion of it ourselves.

2. *Partial colour blindness*—(A) *Typical*, i.e., the individual cannot distinguish certain determinate colours:—as a rule he cannot see (a) red, (b) green, (c) violet.

(B) *Incomplete*, i.e., he distinguishes with some hesitation either all or only certain colours.

The importance of colour blindness arises in many contingencies. In the first place it is rarely admitted by those who are its victims. Most men are unaware that they are thus afflicted and when they do know they hate to confess to it as though they were guilty of some crime. It is beyond doubt that it may be very important to an Investigating Officer; it is especially dangerous in all cases where colour signals are in question, for it may bring about grave accidents on railways, ships or in mines; it must be taken into account when there is a question of the colour of, e.g. a garment, in identifying persons (the man in a green coat) or when looking for traces of blood. A colour-blind man can see blood only on a green background (as for instance on the grass or on green or yellow clothes), and that with difficulty. If therefore the Investigating Officer has the slightest suspicion that he has to deal with such a person and if the designation of the real colour is of importance, he will hand over the witness to a medical expert.

G. The Teeth

The very important help which can be given by the experienced dentist is far too little appreciated. He should always be consulted when any traces caused by teeth are discovered, e.g., wounds caused by biting, forgotten or discarded smoking materials (cigar ends, pipes, cigar or cigarette-holders etc.) marks on pens or pencils, etc. In questions of identity, dentists in cities can frequently help by making sketches of teeth they have operated upon. When one considers the assistance a dentist can give we cannot help thinking that he is called in far too seldom.

Some time ago a banker was murdered in Petrograd and near him was found a cigar-holder with an amber mouthpiece. The holder was so shaped that it could only be held in one position in the mouth and a close examination showed that it had two marks which must have been made by two teeth of unequal length. The banker had no such irregular teeth, but his nephew had and, then suspicion aroused by this simple but important discovery, the authorities soon learned enough to warrant them in arresting him on the charge of murder

Section iii.—The Microscopist.

However perfect the construction of the microscope may be, however great the services rendered by this admirable instrument, it is not yet much employed by the Investigating Officer. To examine blood, establish the existence of sperms, to compare hair is about all the good at present the microscope observer is to the Investigating Officer. Other examinations are the exception, although there are innumerable cases where the microscope expert might be able to give the most interesting information and even clear up more than one dark mystery. And the explanation of this is that the Investigating Officer does not know what the observer at the microscope is capable of telling him and that the latter is unaware that the Investigating Officer requires his help or in what way he requires it. The result is that they remain strangers to one another where they should, in many a case, walk hand in hand together. This ignorance of one another goes so far that in the numerous works upon microscopes and their employment, all the services they are capable of rendering are mentioned, with the exception of those they are capable of in the domain of criminal law. If we consider the benefits we owe to the microscopist in the domain of hygiene we are almost forced to say that the microscope alone has rendered this science practicable. Bacteriology, examination of water, air, soil, or food, the determining of the nature of a large number of illnesses, and many other important branches of the science of hygiene, would have absolutely no existence unless it were for the microscope. And the reason is simply that the hygienist knew the services the microscope was able to render him, he asked for those services and received them, just as the Investigating Officer would have obtained them if he had thought of questioning the microscope expert. If these two persons come into contact so rarely, it is the fault of the Investigating Officer and not of the other, for the observer at the microscope is in no way obliged to ask the Investigating Officer what he wants. Besides he cannot even know, in spite of the best will in the world, when his existence will be of utility for the domain of the criminal law is too much out of his line, and he does not know the difficulties and requirements of the Investigating Officer.

To remedy this difficulty nothing can be done but to collect in practice as many cases as possible in which the Investigating Officer has invoked the help of the observer at the microscope with success, and thus inform him not only of isolated examples of cases in which the microscope expert can help him but also furnish him with a list of these cases systematically grouped and co-ordinated. Speaking quite generally it may be said that the microscope expert is useful in all cases where it is desirable to see anything more clearly than with the naked eye, also where it is necessary to establish the composition of an object without destroying or deteriorating it—which the chemist is nearly always obliged to do, finally, in cases where it is necessary to distinguish and differentiate the physical (as opposed to chemical) parts of a body, that is to say, when mechanical separation and not chemical analysis is desired (e.g., determination of various powdered bodies of a mixture, apart from the elements of which those bodies are constituted).

In the following paragraphs a small number of cases will be cited in which the Investigating Officer has a right to hope for the help of the microscopist. It should be remarked that these examples are not intended to form a complete or nearly complete list of all possible cases; the object of the author is to encourage and to continue this work in the same sense and ask his colleagues to call in a microscopic expert on every occasion he may be of any use—and thus greatly benefit criminal justice. The reader is, moreover, warned that practically no difference is made with respect to examinations made with a magnifying glass; such a distinction cannot be drawn, for in certain cases the one instrument is employed and in others the second, while both are often used together. Both examinations are united in the term " microscopic examination."

A Traces of Blood.

When the existence of blood-stains is to be determined, it is the Investigating Officer's duty to look for them with the utmost attention, collect and preserve them with the greatest care, and hand them over to the expert as soon as possible. What the Investigating Officer should do in such a case will be considered in *Chapter XIV*—" Traces of Blood ", here we simply point out how and at what stage the expert must be utilised. It will be especially important to obtain his co-operation at the outset so that he may be of assistance in discovering the traces.

This search is to be made methodically and nothing omitted which may possibly prove to be a blood-stain. A saving of time and trouble will also be effected by not bothering with articles which bear no traces of blood. It must not be forgotten that traces of blood do not always bear the aspect given them in criminal romances; a blood-stain may, according to its background, assume all imaginable colours. It may also have been hidden by something which chance or premeditation has placed there. In fact, the search for blood traces in extensive areas such as large rooms, fields, or woods, is not so easy as one might imagine. In the way of example it is cited that blood-spots which were quickly exposed to the sun, according to the experiments of *Hammerl*, even after five days became fawn-grey. Special experience and knowledge such as an expert alone possesses are necessary. For this reason his help must be invoked as often as possible, but if the expert is being made use of, his advice and experience must also be utilised to preserve and pack up the objects. This is important because the expert, when examining them, knows from having seen with his own eyes exactly what procedure has been followed, what measures have been taken, and what the aspect of the objects was immediately on their discovery. He can thus form a fair opinion of changes which sometimes take place. It is the Investigating Officer who should actually attend to this business, at the same time mentioning in his report that he has done so under the supervision of the expert, i.e., the medical officer. This procedure guarantees the truth and increases the value of the operation; it also points out the auxiliary rôle of the expert. As to his primary rôle, we must try to find out what the

Investigating Officer should ask the microscope observer, that is to say, what he has the right to ask and what it is his duty to ask.

Above all it must be recollected that the fresher and more intact are the traces the better the expert can reply.

It goes without saying that a large number of objects facilitate the work, and, though small quantities may give a satisfactory result, yet it will be the duty of the Investigating Officer to give the expert as large a quantity as possible. He ought never to leave behind any objects under the pretext that there is already enough of them. One never knows what turn the case may take, one cannot say at the outset that different objects will not give different results. It is certain that the expert can in nearly every case distinguish blood stains from other stains. Even when the stains might lead us into error by their more or less perfect resemblance to blood, science possesses sufficient means of enabling an indisputable judgment being formulated.

However great the resemblance between blood-stains and marks of paint, rust, chewing tobacco, and the mouldiness of certain mushrooms, the expert cannot be deceived. It is not the same, however, if he be asked whence the blood comes. Science of to-day can distinguish the various kinds of blood by the shape and colour of the blood globules; it is known that those of amphibious animals, fish, birds, the camel, the dromedary and the lama are elliptical, and those of all other mammifers are quite round. But, as a matter of fact, the size of the globules of blood varies in the different mammifers; they are largest in man.

Further, and what is most important, science can now distinguish with the greatest certainty between human and mammalian blood.

Another question that may be asked is whether the blood in question is arterial or venous blood? This question is generally confounded with the following "Do traces of blood which have been discovered proceed from a large or small wound?" Venous blood may indeed also spout out (e.g., if a brisk movement is given to a wounded member or if it is contracted strongly and suddenly), but as a rule only arterial blood comes out with any force. If therefore there are large splashes of blood upon an article, especially upon a plane surface, e.g. a wall, it is natural to suppose that an artery of a wounded or killed person has been severed in the neighbourhood of those splashes. The medical man can therefore say not only that it is arterial blood, but he may also be able to indicate at what distance and in what position the individual was at the moment when he received the wound.

In certain circumstances one can and even ought to ask other questions. Does the blood come from a wound, or piles or an abscess? Is it the blood of menstruation or blood lost during defloration? Is the blood mixed with brain or other matter of the body? Is it due to bites of fleas, bugs, or mosquitos? But it is not always possible to answer these questions. A definite decision can only be arrived at when foreign matter characteristic of the actual case is found in the blood, e.g., absence of fibrine, presence of oxyhemoglobine or blood particles in cases of flea and bug bites. In this connection the expert may be able to furnish very precious information—but not in every case.

As regards the age of a blood-stain the question may be put, but in most cases the reply will be vague. The general impression of the case, the examination of accessory circumstances and all the material available, may perhaps enable the expert to form an opinion on this subject. Success is sometimes obtained by employing arsenic or chlorine water. The reply in every case will be very approximate, at least when there are no other particularly significant circumstances which can be taken into account (See also *Chapter XIV*.)

B Excrement

The expert can give the most valuable information on this subject. Two very instructive cases are usually cited in the books. In the first of these a person had been murdered—it was probably a *crime passionel*. Suspicion fell upon a young man the outside of whose trousers was stained with human excrement; the examination of these stains and of the fœcal matter of the intestines of the murdered person showed conclusively that there was no connection between the two fœcal matters, one coming from meat and the other from vegetable food. The second case gave decisive results. Near a small town there was discovered floating down a stream the corpse of a young woman who had been robbed and murdered. The *post-mortem* was carefully performed and the fœcal matter examined with attention; seeds of fresh figs were found in it, but in the small town in question there were fresh figs in the garden of only one house; with the aid of this clue it came out that the servant of that house had enticed the young girl into the garden, given her figs and then raped and killed her. The state of digestion of the figs exactly corresponded with the time which had elapsed between the eating of the figs and the murder of the girl.

In a recent case, an old woman was murdered, and fœcal substance found at the scene of the crime contained ascarides (thread-worms). The excrement of six men suspected of the deed was examined and only in that of one man (and that after repeated and varied experiments) were ascarides found. He was charged and convicted of the crime. Excrement is also important in other ways. *Moller* recounts that it was turned to good purpose in the case of an arrested criminal whose excrement was submitted to microscopic examination after he was taken into custody. Although such examination cannot be entirely relied upon, yet it can be recommended in some cases. When, for example, in the case of an important criminal the suspected person is arrested very soon after the crime, his last dwelling place and nourishment may be of importance, and then the examination of his first stool after his arrest is to be recommended.

In treating of superstition (*Chapter X*.) we see that wrong-doers not unusually deposit their motions on the place of the crime. In such cases the preservation of fœcal matter may be of much importance.

It is recommended that these questions should at least be taken into consideration.

C Hair

Hair may be found under all manner of circumstances and more may be learnt from it than is generally supposed. Here again the Investigating Officer's business is not to make the necessary examination of the hair when found, but in all cases where there is any possibility of finding hair which may serve to detect an unknown criminal, to look for it and pass it on to a medical man or a microscopist

As to examination of hair it would be out of place to detail here all the results of science on the subject but the author desires, guiding himself by the text-books, to indicate from what points of view the microscopist may be useful to the Investigating Officer when the latter sends him an important hair

We should in the first place not lose sight of the faculty of absorption possessed by human hair, it is capable of absorbing gases, odours, etc, with extreme facility and retains them for a relatively long time This detail is of importance when it is desired to determine whether a man, be he alive or dead at the moment of examination, has been in a place impregnated with a gas or smell, a point upon which the whole case may turn It is true that these gases do not remain for a long time, the examination ought therefore to be undertaken immediately or, if that cannot be done, the hair must, as far as possible be protected from exterior influences The Investigating Officer ought to take the precaution of placing the hair in a perfectly clean receptacle of small size and hermetically closed

It is hardly necessary to remark that in all such cases the receptacle should be clean, it ought besides to be of relatively small dimensions, as superfluous space will absorb the gas of the hair, finally the manner of its closing must be such as to prevent the air escaping Such details are frequently overlooked The hair should be taken with absolutely clean hands and placed in a bottle having a wide neck and fitted with a close-fitting cork, or better still in a receptacle of white metal, or in case of need in an ordinary bottle The stopper or cork and the inside of the lid of the metal receptacle, as the case may be, should be slightly rubbed over with *absolutely* pure fat this fat will render the closing more secure, will attract and absorb the escaping gases, and may itself be an object for examination

Here again the Investigating Officer ought to do what an expert would do He ought to describe with scrupulous exactitude the manner in which he has proceeded The expert will then be able to know if the methods followed by the Investigating Officer in preserving the objects do not sufficiently guarantee the correctness of his examination, or if on the other hand they exclude the possibility of error, in this way, by stating clearly his procedure, the Investigating Officer will be fortified against the common objection that such examinations cannot be satisfactory as no one knows what has happened to the object while in his hand

If the hair is preserved in a box of white metal, the lid may be soldered on, an operation which the most awkward tinsmith of the village will be capable of performing, but special care must be taken to see that he does not heat the box or its contents On the box being handed to the expert, he must be minutely informed of all that has been done, it is then his task to ascertain whether the hair has absorbed and retained smoke, perfumes, poisonous vapours, or characteristic odours and gases, etc

Another important rôle of the microscopist consists in examining hair which has been found in suspicious places for the purpose of ascertaining whether or not it belongs to a particular individual The commonest case is where hair has been found in the hands of persons who have been killed This happens more frequently than one would believe, indeed, if the hands

HAIR

of the victims were more carefully examined it would be found even more frequently.

It is often irritating to see how the first constable who arrives or the doctor who first inspects the corpse examines the hand of the dead person carelessly and imperfectly, they sometimes even wipe it or seize it briskly; they notice the hair perhaps if it is in tufts in the hands, but they most certainly miss isolated hair when they act in this manner. The hands must therefore be examined in the most minute manner and that only by authorised persons. The preservation of the object when found ought to be commenced at once and with all possible care; the best thing to do is to fold it in a piece of clean paper and enfold the latter in a second piece. On the first or inner cover write at once how and by whom the hair has been found. It is not sufficient to state:— "hair found in the right hand of X X," the situation of the hair must be expressly indicated, e.g., "between the thumb and first finger" or "lying obliquely across the root of the first finger and the ball of the thumb."

The best method is to make a drawing—as minute as possible. This is not difficult. The Investigating Officer has but to place his hand with fingers extended upon a sheet of paper and then trace its outline with the pencil. Whether the fingers of the corpse were contracted or not is indifferent in the present case; the important thing is to have a sketch of a hand on which the length and position of the hair may be indicated with a stroke of the pencil. Anyone is able to make a drawing of that kind.

It may also be important for the expert to know where the end and the root of the hair lay. There are two ways of indicating this:—

1. If the particular hair is not to be handled on account, for instance, of blood attaching thereto. The only thing then to be done is to place the hair on a sheet of paper and fix it thereto with bands of paper gummed over it (Fig. 2). These bands should not be gummed all over but only at the extremities, so as not to injure the hair with the gum; a sketch is then made as before and the extremities of the hair set out on the paper carrying the hair itself as well as upon the sketch, using the same letters (Figs. 2

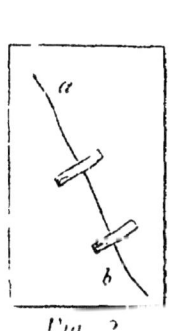
Fig 2

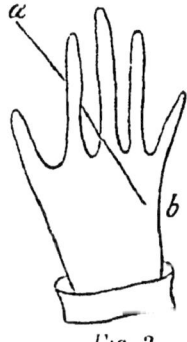
Fig 3

and 3). There can then be no doubt of the position of the hair on the hand of the murdered person.

2. If it is unnecessary to take such precautions, e.g., in the case of a hair found in the hand of a strangled or drowned person, the position of the root and the tip of the hair may be decided at once; the procedure followed is the same as that of wig and plait makers who are obliged to arrange the hairs so that all the roots and all the tips respectively come together. The hair should be therefore seized between the thumb and the first finger so that the hair is perpendicular (of course the position of the hair in the hand of the dead person has previously been well determined).

Keeping the first finger immoveable, the tip of the thumb is rubbed gently up and down the hair using the tip of the first finger as a rest, the root of the hair is then of necessity in the same line as the hair itself if the hair moves downwards the root is below and moves down, if the direction in which the hair moves is upwards the root must be above and moves upwards, but the tip of the hair must finally be between the finger and thumb.

The hair has corticiform prominences which run from the root towards the tip, when it is between the fingers which rub upon one another it can only move if the corticiform prominences catch upon the unevennesses of a finger, the hair therefore moves along the root always going away from the finger. When the tip has thus been determined, or to speak more accurately the direction of the tip, and when the root, or rather the direction of the root, has been established, it is noted on the sketch (thus in *Fig 2*, instead of *a* and *b* we put T and R).

If several hairs are found the same procedure must be followed for each of them, each one should be separately preserved (presuming that they are not stuck together with blood), and each one is placed aside there and then. The beginner should take warning not to think that he will be able to keep everything in his memory and that it is unnecessary to note down and describe everything, for we do not remember everything particularly after a certain time has elapsed and when the emotions which are always produced in an important case interfere with and confuse one's impressions.

The examination of hair may assume an important rôle in various sexual crimes. Two instances are generally cited in the books, in both of which the acts were committed with animals. In the first case a horse's hair was found between the fore-skin and the glans of an individual suspected of having committed an unnatural crime upon a mare. In the second case a servant woman was accused of having had connection with a large dog and when the hair of her sexual parts was examined the black hair of a dog was discovered.

The same phenomenon sometimes occurs in cases of rape, it is possible that during violent sexual intercourse the hairs of the sexual parts of one person come out and get mixed with those of the other, and it may even happen that on account of uncleanliness they remain there for a fairly long time. In such case therefore, it is recommended that an examination be made with the object of discovering such strange hairs on both persons (that is of the accused as well as of the victim), and if any be discovered they should be handed over to an expert for examination.

It must be remembered that every hair discovered during the course of an inquiry may be of the greatest importance when it is possible to prove beyond all doubt that it belongs to the accused person.

Pfaff cites a very instructive case which well illustrates this. A man was gravely wounded by an unknown person on a very dark night. The author of the crime, whose appearance was absolutely unknown, dropped his cap in his flight and it was brought to the authorities. Inside the cap two hairs were sticking. These hairs were sent to the medical jurisprudent for microscopic examination. Pfaff found that the hairs were light grey but that they had in the medullary substance a large number of pigmentary cells which were as black as jet, he concluded from this that the hairs belonged to a dark man still fairly young but who was beginning to grow grey. It was also established that the individual must have had his hair cut very shortly before the crime, for the sections of the hairs were still sharp. Finally he found the roots of the hairs were very much wasted; he concluded from this that these hairs which carried in ampullary prominences in their epithelial parts which must have been produced owing to perspiration, must have grown at the edge of a kind of tonsure caused by the beginnings of baldness; and he further concluded that the individual in question was inclined to stoutness since he had perspired freely in the head. The observer at the microscope thus gave the following description of the criminal:—" A man of middle age, of robust constitution, and inclined to obesity; black hair intermingled with grey hair recently cut; commencing to grow bald."

Similar deductions may be obtained in many cases; one must never be prevented by the trouble that is necessary nor the cost which must be incurred in making them.

It happens fairly often that a criminal while taking flight or in the course of the struggle loses his head covering and that the latter is handed to the Investigating Officer, but how often is this head covering examined to see whether or not hairs may be found there and how many times when hairs have been found are they sent to a skilled microscopist?

Examination of hair is also necessary when we may establish thereby the identity of a corpse or the age, constitution, etc., of a dead person, which information owing to advanced decomposition would not otherwise be obtainable. If there be the least suspicion of crime a little of the hair of the corpse should always be taken and handed to a microscopist in order that anything which can be established may be established.

If the question be asked what in a general way the observer at the microscope can teach us concerning the distinctive characters of hair, the answer will be that he is above all and with absolute certainty able to distinguish between the fibres of plants and between the hair of animals and the human hair. He also knows how to distinguish between the hair which grows on the various parts of the human body. The books set out the distinctive signs which characterise the various kinds of hair, e.g., the hair of the head of a man and the hair of the head of a woman, eyelashes, eyebrows, the hair of the nose and ear, of the beard and moustache, of the hair in the arm-pits and on the back of the hand, on the forearm, on the shoulder, on the chest, in the pit of the stomach and the umbilical parts of a man, also between the hair on the upper and lower parts of the buttocks, on the foot, and on the sexual parts of a man and woman, on the perinæum, the anus, and the scrotum.

All these different kinds of hair have their distinctive characteristics, which prevent any error being made in differentiating between them; the expert may therefore be asked if necessary upon what part of the body the hair in question has grown and further whether the said body is that of a man or a woman.

The expert is also able, within certain limits no doubt, to determine the age of a person by examining some of that person's hair; it is especially easy for him to do so if the hair be given to him with its root, for the root of a hair dissolves in a solution of caustic potash, and the younger the owner of the hair the more easily does it do so; the hair of children will dissolve immediately, but that of old people will resist the action of the solution of caustic potash for hours. With several hairs of the same person various experiments may be made and the average time necessary for the dissolution of their roots be established; it may then be determined what are the persons of a known age whose hair will dissolve in the same space of time, and the approximate age of the person whose hair is the subject of examination may be thus determined.

There are indeed other means of determining the age of a person from the hair, e.g., by the diminution of the pigmentary cells, of the medullary substance, and the spaces or gaps thereby produced; thanks to this means we can tell whether perfectly white hair belongs to a young man who is growing grey early in life or to a really old man. The hairs of the sexual parts of a young girl have the tips very fine, while the tips of those of an old woman are calviform; in both sexes the hair in the arm pits is very slender in youth and as the subject ages it will in that locality reach a diameter of .15 millimetres and even more; in a word the observer at the microscope has at his disposal, besides the methods of the dissolution of the roots of hair by a solution of caustic potash, the means of furnishing at least approximate information as to the age of a person. Moreover, as we have seen, a medical jurisprudent can at least in certain cases indicate with more or less accuracy the characteristics of a person from an examination of hair; sometimes indeed he will be able to say in what manner the hair has been looked after (use of various pomades, dyes, etc.), from which many an important clue may originate; even the exterior aspect is able to teach us whether it has been drawn out, cut, or chopped, and this in some cases is of the greatest importance. For instance, an examination of hair cut at the place where a wound has been made on the head often teaches us more concerning the weapon employed than an examination of the wound itself.

The Investigating Officer should therefore never neglect to hand over the hair to a medico-legal expert for microscopic examination when a wound on the head is in question and the weapon employed is unknown. Some other circumstances also merit the attention of the Investigating Officer; on every occasion that he notices any peculiarity whatsoever about the hair of a corpse either at an inquest or an exhumation, he ought to immediately question a medical expert. For instance, a common symptom in cases of poisoning by arsenic or mercury or narcotics is the ease with which the hair can be torn out, especially the hair of the private parts.

Hair is of great importance legally from another standpoint; it resists decomposition for an extremely long time. It is evident that we cannot cite as an example mummies and mummified bodies preserved in vaulted tombs or other favourable places, nor even the example of dried pericrania; it is natural that the hair will remain preserved when the conditions of preservation are so favourable that those parts of a body which putrefy easily, such as the muscles, tissues, skin, etc., do not decompose; but we speak of that large number of corpses which found in extremely unfavourable conditions of preservation still carry the hair astonishingly well preserved. If then the question be whether a corpse ought to be exhumed or whether the time which has elapsed leaves no room for hope that an important result will be brought about, the exhumation must always be decided upon when there is a chance that an examination of the hair of a corpse will furnish any information about the individual, as for instance, his very identity. If the death of the individual has taken place not very long before it must be presumed, if the conditions as to the soil, etc., of the place of interment are in any way favourable, that the hair is well preserved. Here it may be noted that the hair of young persons decomposes more rapidly than that of old persons, that dark hair keeps longer than fair hair, and that the hair of the head keeps best of all; the hair of the sexual parts putrefies the most rapidly.

Guder states that hair mixed with substances in putrefaction changes colour to no considerable extent; at the most it will become a little lighter or a little darker. This observation is of importance when the identity of a person is sought to be established.

But *Caspar Liman* draws attention to a case in which the hair of a person buried for two years had so altered that his relations would have failed to recognize him had not his false teeth precluded any doubt. Under such circumstances attention should be drawn to the fact that in decay not only temperature, moisture, surroundings and so on, but also very essential individual peculiarities work together, so that conclusions drawn from the degree of the decay as to the time of death will be seen to be very important. For the decision of this time the appearance of certain insect larvae may be of great importance. A complete discussion of the questions relating to *Rigor Mortis*, *Putrefaction* etc., and the deductions to be drawn therefrom will be found in the standard work on Medical Jurisprudence by *Taylor*, edited by *Stevenson*.

However great the services which are rendered by the microscope may be, the jurist must not always count too much upon its assistance. Especially is it of help when the identity of hair is in question or the determination of whether a particular hair belongs to a particular person. If the reply is in the negative, the matter is completely elucidated; in this case we have an absolute proof of the innocence of a man, and that is one of the finest triumphs science can bring about; for the observer at the microscope is able to say with absolute certainty that a tuft of smooth fair hair does not come from a black curly head, and this single piece of evidence should suffice to solve the question. But the same cannot be said when the question is answered in the affirmative and it appears that the two samples of hair are identical. There is indeed but one identicality, whereas non-identicality permits of innumerable differences, and in this case chance may take a much more important place than in the former, and we criminal lawyers know better than anyone what chance is capable of doing. Recently an old woman whose business was the pledging and redeeming of articles at the pawn shops was murdered. In the hand of the corpse were found three hairs which the woman must have torn from her aggressor during her desperate resistance. Suspicion fell upon the victim's own son and the three hairs found upon the corpse as well as some samples of the hair of the son (who was in custody) were sent to microscope experts. The latter happened to be two scientific celebrities whose names were known all over Europe; they went into the matter with the greatest care and with all the aids of modern science and circumstantiated their result in the most detailed manner. The three hairs found in the hand of the corpse were from six to seven centimeters in length, were dark brown in colour, had been torn out (the roots were preserved) and seemed to have belonged to a man of from twenty to forty years old. Under the microscope two of the hairs were brown but the third had some parts brown and others black, a fact which immediately struck the specialists as well as the outsider. Just above the root it was brown, half a centimetre further on it became black, then again brown, and half a centimetre further towards the tip it became black again. This is a phenomenon which specialists tell us is most extraordinary and very rare. Hair of the accused person was then taken from three different parts of his head, it being cut just above the roots; this individual was twenty-nine years old, his hair measured from six to seven centimetres in length, it was dark brown in colour, and examined under the microscope was about the same thickness as the three hairs. Finally they counted the hairs and placed them one by one under the microscope; about two thirds of the hairs were brown and the other third presented absolutely the same peculiarity as the brown and black striped hair mentioned above. And yet the son, in spite of the strange coincidence of this phenomenon, which according to these experienced medical men is so rare, was not the assassin of his mother; when subsequently the murderer of the old woman was discovered it was found that his hair was also striped in the same way and was astonishingly like that of the son of the deceased woman. We learn from this case that even the fact that distinctive signs of quite exceptional character are to be found in both the specimens examined does not always prove that the hair under comparison is indeed hair coming from the same head.

Almost every man has on his head a few of the other essentially different hairs, for instance, blonde persons have almost always a few dark thick hairs. The author knows a lady who has rich wavy soft hair, but on one place, on account of a scar caused by a wound received early in life, the hair is straight, rough to the feel, and noticeably lighter in shade. No one would believe that a hair from the scarred place and one from another portion of the head belonged to the same person.

When proof of the "identicality" of hairs is to be considered, the matters with which they are artificially coloured must not be forgotten; this colouring matter may be got rid of in various ways, *e g*, washing in water, dilute hydrochloric acid, nitric acid, or chlorine water.

D Other cases relating to Medicine

Besides the cases already mentioned, which are frequent enough, the Investigating Officer will order microscopic examination in cases relating to *post-mortems* and other medico-legal inquiries. Suppose for instance that the question is to establish whether an individual has been in an atmosphere filled with dust, smoke, or other substance, or in a liquid other than pure water, the microscopic examination of the respiratory channels and also often of the hair will generally furnish accurate information; the spittle of living persons and the contents of the respiratory channels of dead persons should be examined. Even a microscopic examination of substances contained in the stomach (obtained by vomiting or at the *post-mortem*) often gives better results than a chemical examination will, when it is desired to determine, e.g. the nature of the food absorbed, the same holds if organic poisoning be suspected—especially vegetable poisons the presence of which cannot always be proved chemically.

The author is firmly convinced that a great number of murders by poison would be discovered if the contents of the stomachs of people dying by 'suicide' or whose cause of death is set down as doubtful were examined. Considering the great number of poisonous plants which grow freely on the earth, and remembering that their properties are known to everyone and that the alkaloids of a certain number of them can hardly be determined we cannot help being convinced that many plants are employed for criminal purposes much oftener than is officially known.

If we take the first work on toxicology to hand (as *Blyth* on 'Poisons') or a treatise on the poisonous plants of a country or even a work on legal chemistry, we will find a number of noxious plants enumerated of which it is said that the proof of their having been absorbed by a human organism can only be determined by botano-microscopic means, that is to say, that the botanist ought to search for particles of the plants in evacuated and digested matter and examine and determine their nature. We cite but a few of these plants —the water hemlock (*Cicuta virosa*) the little hemlock (*Aethusa cinapium*) the water oenanthe (*Oenanthe crocata*) the spurred rye (*Secale cornutum*), the black hellebore (*Helleborus niger*), the sabine (*Juniperus sabina*) and all the poisonous mushrooms and toadstools, etc. All these plants may be easily found anywhere in Europe in one evening ramble enough may be collected to poison a whole village.

The microscopic proof will not be very difficult to carry out, if the plant has been given in its entirety—that is to say, as a vegetable or even as a dish (e.g., toadstools served up as mushrooms). It is usually easily discovered in the stomach, intestines or vomited matter etc., if it has been given as a decoction it will perhaps be possible to find in the urine a more or less large particle of the plant. The greater number of these noxious plants have so characteristic an aspect that a small piece such as the point of a leaf or the fragment of a thorn is sufficient for the microscopist and botanist to recognise (see *Chapter V, Section* vi, *Chapter XII, Section* vi).

As to microscopic examination applied to Fire-arms and Ammunition, see *Chapter XI*, and *Chapter XVI, Section* iii.

E Falsification of Writing.

The first examination to which writing supposed to have been falsified is submitted is that of the microscope the microscope in no way damages the object and in every case brings us very near the solution of the problem. Manipulations made upon the paper, such as erasures, obliterating with water, the employment of corrosives, etc., which are invisible to the naked eye, become astonishingly clear under the microscope.

Differences between makes of paper may be discovered with complete certainty, as when for instance a false sheet of paper which has an absolute resemblance to the other sheets, at least as regards its exterior aspect, is inserted into a document, false seals, water-marks, false grease-spots, and yellow-stains, may all be at once discovered under the microscope, the ink of genuine writing will resemble, to the naked eye, that of the forged part, but under the microscope differences will appear so clearly that they will be recognised by the naked eye, attention having been thus directed to them. Even the nature of the pen employed may be deduced and it may be determined whether the pen had a sharp point and entered the paper deeply, or whether it had a broad and soft point which glided lightly over the paper. Writing executed with a steel pen may be distinguished from that done with a quill, or that with a hard pencil from that with a soft one etc. (See "Falsification of Documents," *Chapter XVIII, Section II*, and the present chapter *Section VIII*.)

F. Examination of Cloth, Woollens, Linen, Paper, &c

Cloth. —The examination of cloth stuffs is of some importance when the question is the identification of woollen cloth, linen, thread, paper, &c. In these cases the advice of a merchant or manufacturer will in the first place be taken when it is desired to know whether a piece of cloth belongs to such and such a weaving or a piece of paper bearing a certain trade-mark has been made by a particular mill etc. In ordinary thefts that is what will have to be done, but if the case is one of great importance the advice of a manufacturer, merchant etc., will not be sufficient, but an expert will have to be questioned. With the help of a microscope the latter will be able to judge of the fineness of a stuff by the number and the strength of the threads (counts) which cover a square centimetre of the texture, as well as by the manner in which they are twisted, as regards each individual thread he will determine its substance and state whether it is of cotton, flax, wool, or silk, etc. finally, he will be able to say by studying other details whether the fragment found is part of a particular garment, whether a handkerchief has been taken from a certain dozen of handkerchiefs, whether the threads with which a *corpus delicti* has been sewn are the same as those which have been employed in mending the coat of a person suspected, or whether the paper forming the wad of a fire-arm is the same as that found in the house of the presumed murderer, etc.

The cases in which examination is necessary are more numerous than one would believe. But it will be always well when the identity of material is in question not to be content with an exterior resemblance however similar the articles in comparison may appear to be, the observer at the microscope ought always to be examined before forming a conclusive judgment. Experience teaches us that many things which are really identical are thought to be different and inversely many things appear to be absolutely similar which are in fact not at all so.

The identity of a thread is often of extreme importance and may be established by the microscopist with very great accuracy. It must not be forgotten that to obtain his results it suffices to have almost imperceptible little ends of threads and such are always at our disposal whenever a wrong-doer leaves some object behind him on the scene of the crime. In one case some threads had been sewn into an apron which had been left behind by some burglars. The apron was of the same blue linen used in the aprons of innumerable workmen, but the thread of the hem was without doubt the same as the only sewing thread found in the house of a suspected individual. Here is another example the thread with which the exercise book of a schoolboy had been sewn together established the identity of the corpse of a child. There was no doubt that an outrageous and murderous attack had been made upon the child, whose corpse was found in a nude and half-decomposed condition under some branches in a forest. The school books of the child were missing; at a short distance from the corpse was found an exercise book in fairly good preservation; the cover and the written pages had been torn away and no definite indication could be obtained from the book. But the mother of the child knew with what thread she had sewn up the last exercise book of the child and she handed it to the Investigating Officer and microscopic examination proved the two threads to be the same. In another case a thread with which some strips of tinder had been sewn together was compared with a thread in a fur cap of the accused and brought about his conviction.* In another case a microscopic particle of thread had remained attached to a chisel at the place where the blade meets the handle. The experts were able to affirm that the particle of thread must have belonged to the upper border of the pocket of a waistcoat worn by the supposed criminal on the day of the crime.

The observer at the microscope can also give us much information as regards linen from which the marks have been unpicked. Extreme care and special skill are required for this operation, to enable him to tell that at such and such a place a mark has been unpicked; but in the majority of cases he will be able to give us the most ample information and discover what has been unpicked at the place. This information is of great importance when it is desired to establish whether the unpicked mark is identical with that on another garment. In this case the observer will look for the little traces of the thread with which the mark was made; he will nearly always find these traces, especially when the linen has been washed and ironed several times; if the piece of thread found is then compared under the microscope with the thread with which the other articles have been marked it is possible to establish its identity with almost absolute certainty.

Paper.—It is often of great utility to make an attentive examination of paper in serious cases of forged documents, libels, threats, and all other crimes committed with or on paper; domiciliary search is frequently indispensable and will always bring about the discovery of a more or less large quantity of paper belonging to the accused. If paper presenting the least resemblance to the subject matter of the crime be found, it should always be submitted for examination. The objection will be often wrongly made that the majority of the people of a locality buy their paper at the same establishment or at least at a very small number of establishments, so that the most certain proof of the identity of two papers cannot serve for very much. But in these cases it is characteristic that nearly every individual who commits a forgery is afraid to make use of paper sold in his own neighbourhood. Experience teaches us that if such a document be shown to sellers of paper near the house of the accused the result will nearly always be negative; the paper in question will not be found to form part of the recent stock in such shops, for the author of the crime is afraid to use this

---

† For the detailed account of this case see under Arson *Chap XIX*

paper, in most cases the *corpus delicti* is torn from an exercise or other book or is the second page of a sheet of paper of which the first sheet has been already used. If the other half is found at the residence of the accused the proof of identity made by the observer at the microscope will be practically conclusive.

G. Examination of Stains

The observer at the microscope can obtain the most decisive proof from the smallest and, in appearance, the most insignificant objects, but in this class of cases the Investigating Officer also has an opportunity of showing his skill in carefully preserving the *corpus delicti* in its original condition and without in any way damaging the stains. But will he be able generally speaking, to fix his attention upon these little objects, and, from the results furnished by the expert, draw the conclusions which proceed from them? Here again it is the old question, all the skill of an Investigating Officer consists in knowledge how to conclude, combine, and utilise. Let us take a few examples haphazard showing the great value of the examination of stains.

1. *On Weapons and Tools*

Besides those cases in which blood is the object of search the examination of weapons is important for other reasons, the weapon may for instance while being cleaned or carried about be dirtied by contact with various substances. The following case has come to the knowledge of the author. A drunk and swearing individual entered the garden of a café, where he met a dragoon who split his skull with a blow of his sabre. At the request of the Investigating Officer all the sabres of the dragoons who had leave from barracks on the previous day were collected next morning and submitted to microscopic examination. No trace of blood was found upon any of them, but one had a tiny little notch in its cutting edge in which was a fragment of a blade of grass which was hardly visible in spite of considerable enlargement under the microscope. As the inquiry had been commenced at once and as the blade of grass in the notch had been sufficiently protected by the sheath of the sabre to prevent it from drying, it was possible to say that this blade of grass could not have been sticking to the sabre for any length of time, since it had preserved its freshness. The dragoon to whom the sabre belonged must have, as indeed he afterwards confessed, cleaned his blade upon the wet grass after having delivered the blow, he had then wiped it with a cloth, but the fragment of grass had remained in the notch. This case is instructive, for it shows that the examination should not be restricted to the search for a single object (as in this case traces of blood) but it ought to be extended to all the isolated or extraordinary peculiarities which the object may possess; but the work of the expert is of no real utility if he be not instructed as widely as possible by the Investigating Officer upon the course of the case and its smallest details. If in the above case the expert had received an order only to look for traces of blood upon the sabre he would have fulfilled his task by merely giving a reply in the negative. But here he knew the case in detail and he was able at the first sight of the blade of grass to make up his mind as to how it came there and say that it was of the greatest importance.

In the same way traces of earth, dust, fibres, and dried-up liquids, etc, may furnish excellent clues

The Investigating Officer will, of course, never dispense with the obligation to order microscopic examination for the sole reason that he can see nothing particular upon the weapon in question, etc, in the first place the microscope will be able to bring about the discovery of many important things which have not been perceived by the naked eye, and in the second place every expert knows that he ought to take the weapon or instrument to pieces and search for suspicious substances in the joints and places of adjustment. Thus a hatchet may have been cleaned in the most careful manner, so that nothing will be discoverable even with a microscope, but if the iron be separated from the handle perhaps objects of great importance will be found either in the aperture or on the part of the handle where it meets and joins the iron

The following instance may be cited. In a district where hops are grown with much success a large quantity were cut down one day, a short time before the harvest, to about the height of a metre from the ground. These hops belonged to one of the most skilful cultivators and the plants dying, he suffered damage to the extent of more than a thousand florins. Suspicion fell upon a neighbour who also grew hops but with much less success that he envied his more skilful and industrious competitor was well known, for he had made no attempt to hide his feelings. The police officer who made the first inquiries had already on the day following the crime taken possession of the pocket-knife of this person and handed it to the Investigating Officer. It was a large knife with a very strong bent blade such as is used by gardeners and vinetenders; there was only one peculiarity about it, it had been quite newly sharpened. One could not help thinking on seeing it that it would be an excellent instrument for easily and quickly in passing so to speak, cutting down strong branches of hops. The knife was handed to a medico-legal man, who was a thoroughly good operator with the microscope, and he was completely instructed upon the case. The inquiry necessitated preliminary study, consisting of the examination under the microscope of the structure of the hop plant and especially of its rind. It was found that the branches of hop were covered with little and big spurs of a very characteristic nature, the rind or peel of a large number of other plants which also have these little spurs was then examined and the spurs thereon were found to be so different that it was absolutely impossible to confound them with those of hops when placed under the microscope. Even those spurs which resembled them the most, namely, the spurs on the branches and stalks of the melon, the cucumber, and the pumpkin, have distinctive signs which exclude all possibility of mistake. The outside of the knife was examined, but nothing was discovered; the rivets were then taken out and on a close examination of the place where the end of the blade is joined to the handle a large number of such spurs were found. on examination under the microscope they were found to be spurs of the hop plant and it was impossible for anyone to doubt that the knife had been used quite recently to cut hops

On another occasion the microscope was instrumental in furnishing an important proof that a bar of iron, in the form of a crowbar carried traces of brick dust. This piece of iron had a rusty place about 4 or 5 inches from its sharp end and there a red stain was noticed. Under the microscope it was found that this stain was the remains of some brick dust incrusted in the iron; there was no manner of doubt that this rusty part of the crowbar had been brought down with force upon a brick. Now in the case of the burglary in question a similar instrument had been made use of as a lever in attacking a wall; it could therefore be presumed that the crowbar had been inserted into the wall and had been pressed with force against a brick, thus causing the stain in question. Moreover this particular crowbar had been in constant use so that the brick dust could not have been of long standing; it was therefore practically certain that this instrument had been employed in this burglary.

Very often one can also decide with regard to instruments for working in wood, whether they have been used for certain work, as by notches in pickaxes, hatchets, large knives, chisels, etc., in which may be seen with the magnifying glass remains of the material. In the same way it can be decided what sort of wood has been sawn by the teeth of a saw. Thus it was once shown by microscopic examination that certain sawdust in the teeth of a saw proceeded from pine-wood not cherry-wood, although the bystanders could not be sure about it with ordinary eyesight.

The dirt under the finger-nails of the victim and of the alleged author of the crime should also be examined under the microscope. This dirt teaches us in the most definite way what has taken place, for it is composed of what has last come into contact with the individual in question. If the latter be a living person no time should be lost in taking possession of the dirt.

We remember a case in which there was grave suspicion that the dirt under the finger-nails of a criminal proceeded from blood. The microscopic examination (carried out at the Investigation Bureau in Nuremberg, 1896) decided that the colouring substance was berlin blue.

2. Dust

According to Liebig, dirt is matter in the wrong place, so we may say dust is our environment or surroundings in miniature. An object covered with dust gathers to itself infinitesimal particles of bodies which happen to be at a greater or less distance from it. Neither dirt nor dust is a determinate body; the former is composed of small particles which come into contact with an object and remain there for some reason or other, while the latter is composed of small particles ground up to form the powder deposited upon the object. Dust may indeed be brought from great distances by the wind, but in the majority of cases it comes from the immediate neighbourhood; thus by recognising the constituents of the dust upon a specified article it is possible to indicate approximately the objects surrounding it.

The dust of the desert will contain little besides pulverised earth, sand, and small particles of plants; the dust of a ball-room, crowded with people will in great measure proceed from the fibres from which the clothes of the dancers are woven; the dust of a smith's shop will be for the most part composed of pulverised metal; and that upon the books of a study nothing but the reunion of the particles of earth carried in on the boots of the master of the house and the servants with very tiny particles of paper. Examining more closely, we find that the coat of a locksmith contains a different kind of dust to that on the coat of a miller; that accumulated in the pocket of a schoolboy is essentially different from that in the pocket of a chemist; while in the groove of the pocket-knife of a dandy a different kind of dust will be found to that in the pocket-knife of a tramp. All these examples are drawn from the author's own practice and in all of them neither a determinate body nor a particular particle of a determinate body was being searched for, but the dust was collected for microscopic examination and in each case new clues were found therefrom enabling the inquiry to proceed.

One day, for instance, there was found upon the scene of a crime a garment from which no information could be obtained as to its owner. The coat was placed in a strong and well-gummed paper bag which was beaten with sticks as vigorously and for as long a time as could be done without the paper tearing, the packet was left alone for a short time and then opened, the dust being carefully collected and submitted to a Chemical Examiner. Examination proved that the dust was entirely composed of woody fibrous matter finely pulverised; the deduction drawn was that the coat belonged to a carpenter, joiner, or sawyer etc. But among the dust much gelatine and powdered glue was found; this not being used by carpenters or sawyers the further deduction was drawn that the garment belonged to a joiner,—which turned out to be in fact the case.

The dust which collects so quickly and in such quantities in the pockets of clothes is also very important; this is especially so when the clothes are not frequently brushed and shaken. It tells us from its composition the whole history of a person during the time he has worn the garment. In the first place it is no doubt composed of pulverised particles of the material of which the pocket is made; to this is added the dust of the atmosphere in which the person lives, which may enter the pocket directly or through the cloth or other fabric; then there is the dust deposited by articles placed in the pocket, such as crumbs of bread, tobacco dust, particles of paper, metallic powder, wood dust, etc., finally we have the dust covering the hands so often placed in the pockets. All this forms a composition which will contain at least one element from which the quality, trade, and occupation of a person may be determined.

Just as important is the dust in the groove of a pocket-knife, i.e., in the space between the two sides of the handle in which the blade lies when the knife is shut. However clean a pocket-knife be kept, an astonishingly large quantity of dust and even larger particles will collect in it. In almost all cases the nature of this dust can be accurately determined, and it indicates with the greatest certainty where the knife has been and what it has done. All such articles, always or nearly always carried on the person give the same information, e.g., the leather folds of the outside of a purse or card case; the outside edge of a watch case as well as the interior edge (which is indeed called the "dust catch"), also the jewels of watches with the incrustations thereon, which pick up all manner of dust. Examinations of this description should be undertaken in all cases where it is desired to establish the identity of a person who carries such articles about him, and also when the articles are found by themselves and information is sought regarding their owner, and finally when the articles are found in the possession of people who have evidently no right to them and then true owner is being searched for

3. Stains on Clothes, etc.

Here again microscopic examination is generally restricted to the search for stains of blood and spermatozoa, and yet what precious information can we not obtain in other directions. In a crime of any importance no stain on the clothes of a suspected person should be permitted to pass unnoticed, nor must one allow oneself to be drawn into forming a preconceived opinion and asserting "who knows from what time this stain, which has moreover no connection with the crime, dates?" But it is impossible to distinguish with the naked eye whether a stain is really too old to be of use, while with a microscope the matter may perhaps assume quite a different complexion. We cannot then assert *at first sight* that a stain has no connection with the crime; microscopic examination is alone capable of telling us this, and even the connection may not be discovered at once but only on subsequent investigation; besides it is not necessary for the stain to have direct connection with the crime to make its composition a matter of interest. Thus we may instance the discovery, in a murder case, upon the trousers of the suspected murderer, of a large stain of singular aspect which had thickened and stiffened the material at one place. The microscopist who was examining the trousers for blood stains, examined this stain under the microscope and was able to establish that it was composed of a mixture of ashes, sawdust and glue; it was therefore putty with which joiners fill up cracks and other inequalities in wood. This stain could not possibly have any connection with the crime for investigation of the *locus in quo* proved that there was none of this fresh putty about. But the Investigating Officer questioned the suspected individual upon the origin of this stain and received, though in a slow hesitating manner, what seemed to be a fairly satisfactory explanation, which however he proceeded to verify. As the inquiry became long drawn out and no further proof could be adduced against the suspect, he was on the point of being released when it was found that his explanation was completely false. It was presumed that his conscience was not perfectly clean as he had attached importance to a stain of whose origin perhaps even he himself was unaware, and had thought fit to recite an entirely false story about it. His release was postponed and he was subsequently convicted of the crime.

Microscopic examination of marks of dirt will often be regarded as the only experiment possible when one has no halting-place for the purpose of carrying out a long and costly chemical examination, and it is necessary at least partially to decide the question. By a microscopic examination little or nothing is lost. It costs little, can be quickly performed and perhaps a decision can be arrived at. For example, marks taken for stains of spermatozoa might under microscopic examination prove to be paste, food, etc. Even if the microscope gives no sure information, one can always have recourse to chemical examination.

Speaking generally it may be said that what has been stated above concerning dirt and dust applies equally to stains on clothes; they proceed from the place where the wearer of them has been and also from those substances with which he comes in contact. In many criminal trials, the work of the Investigating Officer consists entirely in establishing at what place the accused was at a specified time. The stains which he discovers and the nature of which he can identify will perhaps enable him to determine at least some stages of the road followed by the accused.

1. Mud on Footwear

Mud or sand attaching to feet and footwear often indicates more readily than the most minute investigations the place where the individual carrying it has been. Such examinations are of the greatest interest when we have to deal with dead bodies or suspected persons; it is desired, e.g., to know whence come the former and where they have stopped last, or again whether the latter have been at the place of the crime.

It goes without saying that such an inquiry has small chance of being conclusive if the ground is everywhere of uniform nature, e.g., the same clayey soil for several leagues around, or mud in the streets of a city, etc. But even in these cases it would be imprudent to neglect the examination of the mud upon footwear and on feet, for such examination may possibly bring about the discovery of fresh details sufficient at least to indicate the direction in which subsequent information may be employed.

Suppose the case of a man found dead in a town; there is every reason to believe that he has not left the town; there is no other mud upon his shoes than that of the streets, which is practically identical throughout the town. If it is important to know where the individual has last been, e.g., whether he has been killed far from or near to the place where his body has been discovered, it will be well, at all hazards, to hand over his shoes to the microscopist, who will examine the various elements of the mud upon them; it is even possible for these elements to allow of certain conclusions, e.g., manure, vegetable debris, the fruit of trees, to be found only in certain roads and lanes in the city, may be discovered, also fragments of minerals only employed in the composition of certain roads, or chalk, or brick dust, which permit of the deduction that the man has been in a workshop or manufactory.

The matter is easier and has more chances of success when the investigation takes place in the country; there the nature of the soil is more varied, the rooms of the houses are not paved and the floors are often covered with characteristic materials. The author is acquainted with two cases of this kind. In one it was desired to convict a man of theft in a mill; in the other the accused was suspected of having hidden a large sum of stolen money in a hollow willow tree near the bank of a stream. In both cases the mud on the boots of the accused was examined and in both cases two layers of mud were found separated from one another; in the first case by flour and in the second by fine sand. In the former the accused had walked with muddy boots in the flour lying about the mill; in the latter he had also walked first in the mud, then in the sand of the river bank, and then again in the mud. In both cases the two layers of mud and the intermediate substances were identified so thoroughly as to preclude all doubt as to their origin.

Prof. Jeserich gives a third case in which diatoma were found in the sand sticking to the shoes of a murdered person, whereby the place where the man must have been was ascertained.

Section iv — The Chemical Analyst.

Here we may be brief, in effect, the chemist will be employed in all cases in which the microscopist may be called in. In many cases both are necessary, for there are few cases of a purely chemical category; the analyst has frequent recourse to the magnifying glass or microscope before or after his chemical work, for the purpose of completing or checking it. Conversely, the microscopist can hardly do analyst's work, and so we can only attain satisfactory results from the combined action of the microscopist and chemical analyst. Speaking generally we may say that the Investigating Officer does not employ the analyst or chemical examiner frequently enough, and that many cases which have remained in a state of obscurity would have taken another turn if the expert had been consulted. This is especially true in all cases of poisoning, where recourse to a chemist is sometimes had only where pieces of arsenic as big as a pea, or a strong odour of phosphorus, opium or other substances which exclude all doubt, are found in the stomach. Yet we feel we cannot be reproached with looking at the dark side of things when we assert that the Chemical Examiner should be resorted to in every case of sudden death which the inquest has not completely explained, every case of a disease appearing without natural reasons has ended in death, and this especially if any possibility of a criminal prosecution arises. When one skims through a work on medical jurisprudence and notes the numerous substances which, in relatively small doses, are capable of causing a man's death, when one remembers the uncertainty of the signs of poisoning as revealed by the history of the patient's illness and the death-certificate, and when, finally, one thinks of the modern extensive diffusion of superficial chemical knowledge, and the facility with which nearly all chemical products, even the most dangerous, are procurable, one is astonished that many cases of poisoning even more difficult to discover do not occur. The Investigating Officer ought therefore always to pay attention to the possibilities in these cases and considerations of money and trouble should not be allowed to enter into the question.

Nor should the other side of the matter be lost sight of. Often death remains unexplained and is believed to indicate a crime, whereby suspicion may rest for long years upon the innocent. It is the duty of the Investigating Officer to prevent the happening of such a state of things just as much as it is his duty to bring about the conviction of the guilty. We are aware of a large number of substances not venomous by nature which, when they become tainted, are harmful or deadly; they may be absorbed through imprudence or without anyone being to blame, so it is allowable to presume that these substances have caused inexplicable and suspicious deaths. But the chemist if consulted would clear up the matter. Take, for example, poisoning by coal gas, trichinous or tainted meat, poison developed in sausages or cheese, poisoned shell-fish, oysters, lobsters, tainted fish, wine, beer, vinegar or other articles of everyday use, in fact the whole range of ptomaine poisons, finally the frequent cases of poisoning through culinary utensils.

The ptomaine alkaloids (e.g. collidene) lead to the most serious mistakes; they may arise entirely through the decomposition of the dead body, are often highly poisonous, and in many cases bear a great resemblance to the plant alkaloids. Their behaviour under physiological tests may also lead to confusion. For full details the reader will refer to such standard works as Lauder Brunton's "Materia Medica" and Blyth on "Poisons." Equally important in this connection is poisoning by carbon-monoxide fumes. A case is related in which a man was killed through gas fumes in a lime-kiln. His wife though innocent was condemned as a murderess and detained in prison for some years.

In short every suspicious death requires minute investigation by the Investigating Officer: it is not sufficient merely to ask the analyst whether there be poison in such and such a stomach, without giving him any indication of the direction his researches should take; if he has no starting point his examination becomes difficult and costly; but if he knows all that the Investigating Officer has been able to learn in his inquiry, he will easily, quickly, and surely complete his share of the work.

If we wish to know what the Investigating Officer can demand of the chemist, we should say: the Investigating Officer ought not to have too many scruples in this connection especially as regards the question of time. We know that after a long space of time the existence of certain poisons particularly arsenic is ascertained, and the interval during which organic poisons may be discovered after their absorption is never so short as is commonly believed. Traces of morphia in the intestines have been discovered after 18 months, although the corpse had been buried in circumstances favouring decomposition. It is not therefore for the Investigating Officer to decide whether too much time has elapsed since the death of the victim. Let him leave the solution of this question to conscientious and experienced experts.

Moreover the Investigating Officer ought not to fear in certain circumstances, to raise the question of whether the poison has not been introduced into the body otherwise than by the mouth, but has been given perhaps in quite another manner, e.g., through a wound either already existing or made on purpose. It is related, it is true in a novel, that in a certain German military hospital (1871) a jealous woman, who was acting as a nurse, took from the wound of a soldier on the point of death a composition of blood and pus which she introduced into the wound of another soldier who was slightly wounded, with the object of bringing about his death. As we have stated, it is simply a story from a novel, but it is quite possible. Just as possible and indeed frequent are cases of death caused by the prick of a poisoned needle. These wounds are made in passing and no one pays attention to them, owing to their apparent insignificance. Such are some of the difficult questions an analyst may be asked. Besides in inquiries relating to death the Investigating Officer will also have recourse to the analyst in all those cases which belong specifically to the sphere of the microscopist. The Investigating Officer will himself get to know by practice which of the two will be capable of solving a particular question; but if he does not know, no great harm will be done: for the specialist he asks will soon tell him that the work is the business of his colleagues.

---

* Proks relates that once on the deal boards of a cell upon which a person poisoned by arsenic had spit arsenic was still found, although the floor had been scrubbed 40 times. Phosphorus has been discovered six weeks after death.

Section v.—The Expert in Physics.

If the medical jurisprudent cannot enlighten us, if the microscopist and chemical analyst are incapable of elucidating the matter, recourse must be had to the expert in physics. The cases in which one can and ought to approach him are innumerable. Here we will again repeat an observation already made, in order that the physicist may lend his aid to the Investigating Officer the latter must ask him for it. The Investigating Officer it is who must go to the physicist to ask if he can help him in a given case, it is not for the physicist to come and offer his services to the Investigating Officer. The expert in physics studies, experiments, discovers and publishes, it is for the Investigating Officer to read, weigh, and question.

The Investigating Officer ought then to recall his former knowledge, generally at once forgotten, which has accompanied him from college into practical life, he should try to complete it and keep it in touch with modern science by reading at least the reviews which always teach the reader something about the new results in various natural sciences and the services rendered by them. And also, as it is his duty to inquire of everything he sees and hears how it may be utilised in his profession (and he can utilise all science), so he ought never in reading these reviews to forget to ask what advantage may be gained from what he has just read, he must attempt to imagine practical cases in which he could call in the expert in physics to utilise the new results of the science. In real cases when they arise he will certainly remember his meditations and call in the physicist.

Indeed we require that the physicist as well as all other experts should interest himself in his business, when he has been often questioned and knows approximately what the Investigating Officer requires he ought to make inquiries on his own initiative and draw the attention of the Investigating Officer to the information which he is able to furnish and of which the Investigating Officer is ignorant.

In the following pages we shall enumerate a few cases in which the physicist can second the Investigating Officer confining ourselves to general indications and contenting ourselves with citing some examples, we simply wish to demonstrate that the physicist in many cases is really capable of giving us information and enlightenment. Speaking generally, it may be stated *the physicist must always be called in when it is important to determine the effect of the natural forces which have exercised any influence upon a matter within the purview of the criminal law. It goes without saying that every man is capable of determining this effect, but the scientist can better observe it and with more accuracy and justice especially in cases requiring special knowledge, such as those involving calculations and the use of scientific appliances.*

Let us presume for example that the fact of an article having been thrown has become of some importance in a criminal case, a stone has been hurled against a window, wall, or upon a roof, the questions now are, to establish the spot where the person who threw it was standing, the force with which he threw it, the size and weight of the stone, the direction in which it ricochetted, the time at which the event took place, and many other similar questions. True it is that anyone can draw such conclusions and make such observations, anyone, that is to say, who has "two good eyes" at his disposal and who has not forgotten what he has at other times learned concerning "ballistics" or the science of calculating the force with which things are projected; but with what accuracy and correctness will not a man do this, who all his life has been occupied with the study of these questions and who comes armed with all the special knowledge required for such a case. Where an outsider sees nothing useful the specialist perhaps observes all that is necessary to clear up the case.

The same may be said of a large series of optical questions, when, e.g. it is desired to know how a light effect has been produced, what has been its action, what amount of light has been necessary for the perpetration of determinate acts, how a certain shadow has been produced, how far it has stretched, what object has caused it, at what moment of the day the sun has produced such and such an effect, or at what hour in the night the moon has shone in a particular manner, and a thousand other questions.

In a case in India a man who was attacked in the night was said to have been lying on his left side on a cot facing the northern and open side of a chavadi or shed, the foot of his cot being a few feet from its eastern wall. It was alleged the stabbing took place about midnight and just as the moon was rising, the injured man stating in the witness-box that he was lying awake and "watching the moon rise" when his assailants came up and attacked him, and therefore he recognized them. No one was found to be able positively to say whether at that time of the year he could possibly have seen the moon, which, if his story was true, must have been a very northerly one. Had this witness's story not been completely broken down and found to be false in other directions it is probable that he would have been believed when he asserted that he saw the moon rising. It would have been impossible to have adjourned the case, which was a sessions one, to a date upon which the moon would have been in an equivalent position, and it is very doubtful whether any physicist could have been summoned for that trial. But had the Investigating Officer taken the precaution of verifying beforehand the man's story by communicating with an expert in astronomy there would have been no such difficulty as was raised in this trial upon this point.

Other information relating to the sun and moon may also be of great importance, whether for example the sun has been able to give a certain amount of heat, and at what moment of the day, and what accessory circumstances must be taken into account, whether the rays of the sun can have fallen at a particular hour of the day upon a glass of water so as to make a sort of burning glass, whether the heat of the sun can have changed the shape of certain objects, e.g., by shrivelling them up, breaking them, causing them to split, or expand. Other questions concerning the effect of light are: how long a piece of cloth must have been exposed to the heat of the sun in order to fade to a certain degree, how long would it take for a piece of paper (especially the modern kinds of paper which are full of ligneous material) to become yellow or brown with exposure to the sun's rays, or how long an object must have remained in the daylight to have undergone a certain transformation, etc.

As regards draughts, the wind, and storms, very important questions may arise, whether e.g. during a fire it is the wind or a draught caused by the heat which has carried a piece of burning straw or a wooden tile (shingle), what direction of the wind may be deduced from such or such circumstances whether a particular object has been able to resist the hurricane, that is to say, in attempting to fix the time of its having been placed in position—was it in existence before the tempest the time of which is known? Questions concerning rain and snow are at times more important still: what has been produced by their agency, from what direction they have come, how often it has rained upon a certain article, etc. In this connection also we have the effects of frost, which are of a determinate character and may lend force to certain suppositions. It may be asked whether a particular object has been acted upon by frost, and with what force, and how often; also what other atmospheric phenomena have acted upon the body in question and what has been the duration of the action.

To this category also belong the following questions:—A stolen object has been hidden and discovered, has it been buried? and if so, wrapped up or not? and for how long? what was the nature of the soil? were there other articles with it? The manner of their preservation, especially when not in the air, sometimes alters them, and these alterations are especially noticeable in objects of delicate colour and structure, so that the physicist may often draw conclusions of great importance.

There is yet another and well known branch of the physicist's business, namely cases concerning the effect and properties of water. Has an article been in the water and if so for what length of time? has it been carried along by running water or sunk to the bottom? if the latter, what is the nature of the bottom? how far has the article been carried by the river and what was the nature of the current? How long must it have taken a body of given weight, shape, and size to traverse a given distance? When the banks are irregular and covered with vegetation it may be necessary to make detailed and accurate trials and experiments. Other questions are, the effect of water upon banks or flooded places, and the length of time such places have been covered.

Investigations concerning corpses found in the water are particularly important; it is necessary, e.g., to establish the successive conditions of the corpse in the water, where it has gone, whence it has come, what obstacles and currents it has traversed, etc.; all such questions are within the sphere not of the medical man but of the physicist (see *Chapter XII, Section V, Bodily Injuries*).

To this domain also belong inquiries regarding the effect of artificial heat apart from actual burns on the body, when it is desired, e.g., to establish the length of time an object has been exposed to a more or less severe heat, and the kind of heat, i.e. whether produced by a particular stove, as by an ordinary cooking stove, or a special furnace.

Other examinations should also be enumerated bearing on breakages, tears, splits, or scratches on all sorts of articles when desirous of knowing their direction, as also the time and manner of their production (whether, e.g., naturally or artificially). This information is often of the greatest importance and can only be obtained where the observer is intelligent, knows the exact nature of the damaged article, and how to appreciate the value of other phenomena accompanying the deterioration, such as direction, force, time, etc. This is heavy work, especially in giving advice on a case of negligence and the damage resulting therefrom—railway accidents explosions, fall of buildings, landslips, etc. In such cases, minute examination of secondary details (e.g. a split screw) intricate calculations, and a penetrating eye are alone capable of elucidating the truth.

Let us finally take a passing glance at those two great motive forces of our times, magnetism and electricity. The least service magnetism renders us is the discovery of iron in cases where a chemical examination is not possible for some reason or other, as for electricity, we do not yet know all the services it can render and how far it will go or exactly what results the electrician will some day be able to afford us in criminal matters.

In forgeries also (as to ink, paper, writing materials, files of documents, etc.) the physicist can afford the chemist and the microscopist important help obtainable in no other direction.

Section vi.—Experts in Mineralogy, Zoology, and Botany.

Experts in Mineralogy and Zoology are but little consulted by the Investigating Officer, the former is only utilized for the examination of minerals and to establish their particular properties or he aids the microscopist when, e.g., it is necessary to determine the nature of a mineral so as to deduce therefrom the origin of dust, dirt, or stains etc.—and indeed these are often important points for elucidation. The zoologist is employed to determine the nature and origin of animal wool, assist in forming a judgment upon blood globules, determine the functions of certain animals, tell us what they are capable of doing and producing, give us information concerning poisons proceeding from animals, aid the medical man in many histological, anatomical, and physiological cases, and thus complement the latter's knowledge.

The zoologist finds important employment when the question arises of how long a man lying in the open has been dead, under what conditions animal life of various sorts (especially insects) appear at different times upon every corpse. If the death does not take place in the cold part of the year certain flies at once appear, somewhat later certain beetles, etc., are found, until at last, sometimes after many months, certain animals bring about the final work of destruction of the non-osseous parts. In such circumstances zoologists can often afford important and reliable information.

Finally some known attributes of animals are of importance. It is only necessary to consider this and consult a zoologist. So once in a certain case it was desired to know how many hours a drunken man had lain in water. At first it was said that he could only have been there one or two hours, because in his clothes live fleas were still found. On account of the importance of the case inquiries were made, and it was discovered that fleas can live as long as 16 hours under water. Flies, spiders, caterpillers, etc., die much more quickly under water.

It is for the botanist to play the greatest role, he can indicate poisonous or abortive plants, discovering the smallest pieces he can determine the nature of powdered substances composed of plants, seeds, and fruits, he can study the juices of these plants and the preparations made therefrom. These indications are often important, especially when such vegetable matter is discovered in a house search or upon the person, or in the stomach and intestines of deceased persons, or in the matter vomited or passed by them. It must not be forgotten that the smallest atom of leaf, the most minute piece of bark or fibre, suffices for the botanist to recognise the entire plant.

It is often of equally great interest to know how to determine the nature and origin of a piece of wood with the assistance of a small piece which has been found, when, e.g., it is desired to indicate whether a splinter of wood comes from a weapon, instrument, utensil, post, or living tree etc.; or when the nature of the piece of wood may tell us the locality where a certain person or object is to be found, the place whence it has come, or the objects with which it has been in contact. The botanist is also sometimes able to tell the age of an injury to a living plant, its aspect before healing up, the way in which it has been made, and the instrument employed; he may be able to tell us the force which must have been used to produce on a piece of dead wood such and such a mutilation or change; the time when a leaf or a fruit must have been damaged (e.g. by a shot from a fire-arm), the place of origin of certain pieces of plant, etc., the shape of an instrument which has produced such and such a cut or mark on a piece of wood (discovery of the traces of a clean cut by a knife demonstrating the absence of a toothed saw).

The intervention of the botanist may be of special importance in obtaining information regarding certain textile fibres, e.g. in determining the nature of the fibre (flax, hemp, jute, cotton), in identifying threads and parts of threads (twine, ordinary thread &c.), in studying the effect of certain liquids (paints, acids, or alkalis, etc.) upon vegetable fibres (change in shape, length, colour, and aspect), in determining the age of textile fibres and the place where they have remained (including such questions as the age of a cord, whether a piece of string has been for a long time in the water, whether a piece of linen cloth has been exposed to great heat, or whether some cotton stuff has been buried.)

A whole series of questions are connected with the chemical and physical properties of vegetable matter; in these cases the botanist should work with the microscopist, the chemist, and the physicist. Such questions are the absorption of gas, odour, and fumes, by vegetable fibres; the explosive properties of flax, hemp, and jute dust; the spontaneous combustion of vegetable fibres impregnated with oil (tow, flax, thread, engineer's paste, etc.); the hidden combustion of ignited fibres (saltpetre treatment); the duration and certainty of the combustion of materials composing wicks (arson, explosions); the dangerous combustible properties of celluloid; the spontaneous combustion of damp hay, newly carbonized paper, or vegetable carbon; the proof of the existence of the juice of plants upon metals (e.g., on a knife which has been used to cut fresh plants or fruit), or upon garments (e.g., stains made by grass upon coats, and the age and the origin of such stains). It is permissible to assert that the botanist may come to our assistance in the most difficult, important, and interesting cases.*

---

* Upon the frequently recurring mistakes concerning poisoning through mineral acids, see *Chapter XVI, Section VIII* "Poisoning".

Section vii — The Expert in Firearms.

As indicated above the examination of firearms requires more than anything else, the assistance of a whole series of different experts, as a rule only a gunsmith is called in, but this the author considers a mistake Nowadays local gunsmiths no longer exist as in former times they are as rare as the local clock-makers of old, for both the local gunsmith and clock-maker sell instruments they have received ready made from the factory, at the most they have only placed the various parts of the instrument together and know how to do certain repairs The firearm and the watch are made only in the factory and the merchant or shop-keeper cannot be expected to understand in a special manner their interior mechanism

Even when dealing with a gunsmith who knows his trade we find his knowledge restricted in most cases to being able to indicate the origin and the price of the weapon, the names of its different parts and other mechanical details which, it must be confessed, will have in most cases a certain value But he will not be able to say much regarding the use to which the instrument may be put the effects which it is capable of producing, the connection existing between the arm itself and the bullet employed, besides numerous other questions of capital importance Recourse must therefore be had to the experienced sportsman, the medical man, the inspector of musketry, the physicist, the chemist, and the microscopist in many other cases, moreover, where the question is to determine the effect of a bullet on different substances yet other experts who are conversant with these substances must be questioned, in many cases experts consulted by the author have been unable to give a satisfactory reply, when an ordinary workman has answered without hesitation The dresser of stone can tell us the resistance of the various kinds of stone, the locksmith can explain to us how a certain effect has been produced upon iron, and the botanist can indicate with accuracy the time and the season at which a bullet has struck a living tree and lodged in the wood

As regards the practical method of procedure in examining experts care must be taken not to allow different experts to make their experiments at the same time and give their advice together The Investigating Officer must obtain a clear idea of how the various experts are best to be consulted, and arrange to question *after the others* those experts who with their experiments destroy in part the documents and material objects at his disposal

Once the experiments are made and the reports sent in, the Investigating Officer will be able, following the case and the results of the reports, to bring the experts together either all at once or in several categories, in this way he will perhaps find the agreement or the explanation of doubtful questions or questions resolved in different ways, when the experts are already *au courant* with the matter and know what they have to reply they will agree together much more readily than if they have been allowed to work together from the outset This method of procedure has yet another advantage, important *corpora delicti*, serving as objects of conviction, are less exposed to being lost or injured when they are sent to but one or two experts at a time, instead of in the space of a quarter of an hour being passed through a great number of hands.

Besides examination regarding the origin of a firearm, the effects produced thereby, the mode of its employment, and its connection with such and such bullets, etc. questions relating to the science of arms properly so called, and besides those questions which it is within the province of the medical jurisprudent to decide, there are yet other examinations of decisive effect which are within the competence of the chemist. Suppose for example it is desired to establish whether a bullet has been taken from a stock of bullets found upon a suspected individual, it will certainly not suffice to establish that it is of the same size, the same shape, the same calibre and the same weight as the others, it is also necessary to prove that their chemical composition is identical. Pure lead is but rarely employed for the making of bullets, tin, zinc, antimony, bismuth, and arsenic being mixed therewith, even traces of silver may be found, if then the quantitative analysis of the chemist shows that the alloy is the same in both cases, this will be a decisive proof of identity. This examination may also be of great interest in many other cases. If, for example we have the firearm of the suspected individual and a bullet, and if the weapon be coated with fresh lead inside, it is for the chemist to withdraw this lead from the barrel and analyse it as he has analysed the bullet. if then the analysis of the bullet corresponds with that of the lead in the firearm, it may reasonably be presumed that that particular bullet has been fired from that particular firearm especially if the composition of the lead is uncommon or contains an abnormal proportion of some other element. Even when it is impossible to make these two analyses and compare the results, as for instance when we possess only the bullet, it is well to submit the latter to chemical examination, this may furnish the proof of a composition but little used, which in default of other clues, may perhaps afford some indication regarding the author of the crime. If the bullet has not been manufactured by the man himself but has been made in some factory, its chemical composition may very well lead to the discovery of its place of manufacture, for in this industry the same alloy is not everywhere employed. Finally, in certain circumstances, there may be traces of powder upon the bullet, which, chemically analysed, are capable of giving an indication regarding the explosive which has been used. Such traces sometimes remain upon a bullet even when it is lodged in the human body, they were clearly distinguishable upon the French bullet which the author's grandfather carried behind his eye for 46 years (from 1799 to 1845) and which was only extracted after his death.

Chemical analysis may be of the greatest importance when it is desired to know when or how long before a certain firearm has been fired. The Investigating Officer does not naturally have to deal with the manner in which such an examination must be made, an examination which however is very curious in that it can only indicate whether the weapon has been fired off a very short time before. *Sonnenschein & Classen* in their " Handbook of Legal Chemistry " indicate the following process it is so simple that it may be employed if necessary even in the country by any doctor or hospital assistant and frequently brings to light decisive results. It is true that this process can only be employed if the explosive has consisted of the ordinary powder which still remains in common use. The firearm in question must be withdrawn as soon as possible from the action of the air for this purpose the barrel is hermetically corked and the breach wrapped up in cloth. The examination must be carried out as soon as possible. First the discharged barrel is rinsed with distilled water and the solution obtained filtered and examined for sulphuric acid (with barium chloride), alkaline sulphides (with salts of lead), and salts of iron (with ferrocyanide of potassium). Let us presume that the barrel is dark brown, contains neither rust nor green crystals of ferrous sulphate and that the solution is light yellow in colour, smells of sulphuretted hydrogen, and with salts of lead gives a black precipitate. It follows that the firearm must have been fired within 2 hours. If the colour is clearer still and there is neither rust nor crystals but traces of sulphuric acid are discovered, more than 2 hours but less than 24 hours must have passed since the moment the weapon was fired. If the barrel has numerous stains of oxide of iron and the reagent proves the existence of iron in the water, the weapon has been fired at least 24 hours before and at most within 5 days. If the oxide of iron is in large quantity but no iron salts are found in the solution at least 10 days and at most 30 days have elapsed.

If the firearm after having been fired has been immediately reloaded without having been cleaned, the cylindrical portion of the pull-through or the cleaning rod has a dark grey colour during the first four days and during the following days it is yellowish grey and the water contains distinct traces of sulphuric acid. If the weapon has been cleaned before being loaded the second time, the colour is light red or yellow ochre during the first two days, during the following days becomes dark red, and after 12 to 15 days becomes and remains grey; the powder will have a light red colour owing to the oxide of iron attaching thereto and the reagent will show no signs of sulphuric acid. If the firearm has been reloaded immediately after firing the colour will be green but will quickly attain that described above. If the barrel be rinsed with lime-water, red colouring will also be noticed. Finally, if the wad is of paper containing alum or plaster, and the reagent shows the presence of sulphuric acid in the water with which the wad is washed, it proves nothing.

In all cases we also recommend the examination of the bullet with a magnifying glass; information is then obtained about the number, pitch, shape and depth of the rifling, the substance and structure of the wad which has left traces upon the lead, upon the manner in which a muzzle-loader has been loaded, and upon many other points of importance.

Section viii.—Handwriting.

As to the value to be placed upon the appreciation of manuscripts the most divergent opinions exist; some have made a science of it and yet do not know how to appreciate sufficiently the results of their examination, while others consider the knowledge so many persons pretend to possess is the mere product of the imagination or at least of gross exaggeration.

No lawyer is obliged to form a decision on one side or the other, but he must take up a position on the subject and form an opinion upon it whether he believes in the study of graphology or not. At least everyone will allow that the writing of an uneducated peasant looks different from the writing of an educated lady, that the child does not write like the old man, that the writing of a farmhand will not be mistaken for that of a learned man. However, as soon as one has gone so far, one has confessed that there is such a thing as graphology, in fact one has acknowledged the principles of it to be correct. If one goes further—speaks of a copied, pedantic, interesting, fickle, nervous, or energetic handwriting and recognises the writing of the aristocratic lady, the soldier, the merchant, the scholar, one has gone a long way in the rudiments of graphology, and would act inconsequently, as is done by people prejudiced against graphology, by declaring that the things established were not capable of a wider and more scientific development. If data in greater number were collected, if more cautious and more accurate experiments were made, then it would be possible to individualize, generalize, and establish rules, thus leading to the increase of knowledge, a knowledge which must inevitably go very far. That graphology when more exactly and scientifically studied can be brought to a more workable knowledge, no one can well doubt. That there is a line in some subjects beyond which we cannot go, is easy to see. Would anyone for example maintain that chiromancy, the study of the connection between the lines of the hand and the fate of the criminal, should be advanced to a science? No earnest man would maintain that, for the little we know of it, chiromancy is anything but doubtful, and where there is absolutely no truth there can be no development. But as regards graphology there are acknowledged facts, and it is therefore permissible to think that it is capable of development.

We may say at once that there are few people so well fitted to be handwriting experts as Investigating Officers themselves. 'Ames on *Forgery, its Detection and Illustration*,' states "the expert is the man who knows," and he then proceeds to briefly consider the lines of study and experience calculated to confer the highest order of skill upon a handwriting expert.

First. The study and practice of handwriting as a teacher, in the constant observation, criticism, and suggestion to learners afforded by such an occupation.

Second. The preparation of publications devoted to writing and other phases of penmanship, involving the careful preparation of models for the engraver and the critical scrutiny of plate reproductions of such models.

Third. The preparation of critical and technical, literary and scientific instructions for the student of penmanship.

Fourth. The accumulated experience arising from previous examinations of disputed writing, and the multiplied precedents of Court opinions, rulings and the verdicts of juries, in cases on which the expert has been previously employed.

Fifth. The occupation of an engraver or lithographer where the frequent reproduction of handwriting and especially autographs is involved. The careful drawing of his models upon the plates prior to engraving and the critical comparison between models and reproductions lead to nice distinctions and the detection of delicate personal or individual characteristics.

Sixth. The constant professional observation of handwriting in any line of financial or commercial business tends to confer skill. It should be said here, however, that the average bank cashier or teller bases his opinions and his identifications generally upon the pictorial effect, without recourse to those minuter and more delicate points upon which the skilled expert rightly places the greatest reliance. Such testimony cannot be compared for accuracy or value with that of the scientific investigator of handwriting. It follows, then, that one who is endowed with more than ordinary acuteness of observation, and has had an experience so varied and extensive as to cover most of these lines, is likely to be best fitted for critical and reliable expert work.

It will be seen that an Investigating Officer of experience and intelligence (and we are entitled to presume that a person in the position of an Investigating Officer is a man of experience and intelligence), must at least have followed the fourth line of preparation laid down by *Ames*. Observation and personal study, followed with zeal and regularity, will convince Investigating Officers that examination of handwriting has nowadays become a science. The examination of manuscripts is of value to the Investigating Officer in two ways it enables him in the first place to know his men and next renders it possible for him to solve the preliminary question, namely, " are the presumptions sufficient to assume that two writings are identical and to warrant the employment of an expert on the subject?" An Investigating Officer is in a better position than anyone else to obtain the knowledge necessary for this, not only has he to examine many writings, but he nearly always comes to know the author of them. He can therefore verify the conclusions he has arrived at on examining writing by personal dealings with the writer.

Every criminal record offers, from this point of view, ample material, in the notes and signatures of the Investigating Officer's colleagues and clerks, and the signatures and writings of witnesses and accused persons, and often also, in letters and other documents forming part of the papers in a case, sufficient material is to be found; all that is necessary is for the Investigating Officer to take an interest in the subject—and it must be presumed that every zealous Investigating Officer does so. The course to be followed is not difficult to point out. The writing must be studied and an attempt made to read all that can be read in it, the results obtained must then be compared with all the information obtainable from other sources as regards the individual in question, and, finally, one must try to find out, when things are not clear, how and where a mistaken judgment has been formed. All this indeed is easy to say, but the work itself requires much time and trouble, though these are largely compensated by the interesting results obtained. As regards the first part of the work, it is necessary to proceed in the most methodical way. In the first place it is necessary to become familiar with old forms of letters generally used by old people who have learnt them many years before, but in doing so it must not be forgotten that the employment of such forms is no absolute proof that the writer is an old person any more than the employment of more modern letters proves the writer to be a young person. Certain persons who have had an old writing-master and whose character is not very independent often employ for long afterwards or even throughout their whole lives, the letters they have first learned. There are also people who have taken to the habit of using antiquated letters out of sympathy for the archaic or for an old person. In the same way there are old people who have preserved their youthful character and who like to do everything as young people do; they follow the fashions of the day; they reject the old letters as they would an old-fashioned garment and adopt new forms of letters as soon as they come in. But this is exceptional, and as a general rule people do not change the writing to which they have become accustomed—especially when well advanced in life. *Ames* cites two cases of character reading from handwriting which show what store he lays by fashion in writing. He states as follows:—Not long since the writer was present with a party of ladies and gentlemen where the reading of character from handwriting was the subject under discussion, when one of the ladies took from her pocket two letters, and handing them to him, asked an expression of his opinion respecting their authors. Inspecting one of them, he said: "The writer was upward of sixty years of age, a careful, methodical, experienced business man, and probably the head of some corporation or large business." Inspecting the writing of the other letter he said: 'The writer of this is between thirty and forty years of age, a keen, active man of affairs, probably the secretary or chief clerk of a corporation or a large business house." The lady who had solicited the opinion at once clapped her hands exclaiming that nothing could be more truthful, adding that the one was president of a savings and loan company and the other was secretary of a corporation. "Now," she said, 'I would just like to have you explain to me how you could tell that." The reply was taking the first one: 'Here is a strong, clear, legible, and practised hand very methodical, without blot, change, or erasure from beginning to end, and is written in a round-shaped hand, which must have been learned more than forty-five years ago, as that school of writing has not been taught in this country within that period. This, with the dignified deliberate appearance of the writing fixes his age at over sixty years, while the practised style of writing indicates a large experience in the business world. The good judgment, taste, and accuracy manifested in the writing show corresponding traits in business; while the concise, clear, and intelligent statement of the subject-matter is indicative of an able, lucid, and comprehensive grasp of business affairs."

As to the other letter he said: "This is an elegant Spenserian hand, which must have been learned at a much more recent date and hence by a younger man. It is written with great facility, indicating young and trained muscles in immediate practice, and the composition and subject-matter is such as to indicate a mind trained and familiar with the business world. Here therefore is a man not above medium life and possessed of the requisite qualifications for the active duties of the secretary or chief clerk of some large business enterprise."

Having determined this outside question the next thing to be done is to see whether the writing examined is by one who writes little or much. This presents no difficulty, and though it may not be easy to express in words what is meant by a "running" hand everyone knows how to distinguish an awkward, heavy, and embarrassed script from a free practised, and flowing one. But the result of this is of great importance, for hereby whole groups of persons may be eliminated and it may be once for all decided that the writing in question is not that of a person belonging to such and such a group

A more difficult question is to discover the sex of the writer, yet even when one is not accustomed to examining writing one may in the majority of cases make this distinction without mistake. A little experience and practice will soon make it almost impossible to commit an error, and herein lies the groundwork of much success, for when one has obtained a certain sureness one will be also able to discover feminine traits in the handwriting of a man and masculine traits in that of a woman which will always materially contribute towards the characterisation of an individual.

The next problem concerns mainly the exterior form of the writing and consists in classifying the writing of men according to their professions, thus it is easy to recognise the rapid, light, uniform, and legible writing of the tradesman. The writing of learned men usually presents this peculiarity that although often very illegible, the characters bear a certain resemblance to print, the reason perhaps being that owing to his continual reading the writing of a savant begins to bear a certain likeness to print. The writing of soldiers is more like that of tradespeople, but it is clearer and more energetic—more sure of itself. The schoolmaster, who finds himself obliged to set beautiful copies to his scholars, is incapable of permitting himself the luxury of a writing of his own, even in everyday life he still writes copies. Finally, medical men who are always busy write their letters very much like their prescriptions.

Nationality, moreover, is brought out in handwriting, a Frenchman or an American writes like no other person, and when one studies their handwriting carefully one comes to the conclusion that a man with the national character of a real Frenchman or a real Yankee could not possibly write otherwise than he actually does write.

Of course there are exceptions, but one is tempted to agree with *Dr Frederic Scholz*, who says "When a professor writes like a copyist and a merchant like an artist they have missed their vocation", no doubt here also secondary influences must be considered the imitation of the writing of a revered person, *e g*, one's father, or one's school teacher, the imitation of some strange hand or other which one has found convenient, pretty, or original, heredity also plays its rôle in this matter as well as certain physical conditions of the body, short-sighted people write as a rule very minutely. But all the secondary influences act either only upon the purely exterior phenomena (size of writing distance between the lines, etc), or else they indicate certain qualities of character (spirit of imitation want of personality, etc)

To know how to distinguish these peculiarities of character is the most difficult as it is the most important operation in examining handwriting —' We write not only with the hand, but also with the brain," says Scholz, and in this he is right. Another experienced graphologist states —" Writing is not a mere chimerical art, but is an outburst of the heart, an exponent of life and character, more reliable than the delineations of the countenance of the physiognomist " The most difficult thing to do is to compare, not the writings of persons of different character, but those of the same person in different moods. With much reason the various signatures of Napoleon are usually cited in this connection, few men have experienced so strongly is he the whole gamut of impressions, few men have seen so many events as he 1801, 3rd December, 1805, 1806, 21st September, 1812, 6th October, 1812, 13th October, 1813, abdication, 4th April, 1814, St Helena. What changes of destiny, what changes in disposition, what changes in writing! The study of these eight signatures is more instructive than "a whole shelf full of books." It seems quite impossible to confound the dates of the various signatures, and mistake those of the zenith of the fortunes of Bonaparte for that made by him at St Helena.

We need not deal with peculiarities of handwriting which are the outcome of an illness, such cases are for the medical man. It is the duty of an Investigating Officer to question a doctor wherever he finds extraordinary phenomena in the handwriting of an accused. Such phenomena are for example letters and words in the wrong place, inability to transcribe words and writing without making mistakes, peculiar and disused forms of letters, letters and words which can easily be confused, in short, anything unusual and unnatural. There is no doubt that many brain diseases (e g, paralysis) are discoverable in writing long before any trace of the infirmity is otherwise noticeable. It is important for the lawyer to remember that stutterers, when they are idiots, write as they speak. In the first place they frequently make needless and incomprehensible scratchings in the middle of the writing and in the second place they leave out letters, e g, for "the frog is green" they write "the fog is geen." In anonymous, threatening, insulting, and stupid letters and writings received from idiots such lapses alone frequently betray them. There are also certain exterior phenomena, not so difficult to determine, the influence of which upon writing is very important for Investigating Officers. They may be easily discovered if one has at one's disposal for purposes of comparison one or several specimens of the writing of a man when these influences have not been acting, but they may also be determined when one has no such independent writing for comparison, that a writing has been dictated may be established by the presence of certain faults which could only exist through words having been badly heard, or because the writing and spelling show a degree of culture inferior to that of the wording of the document and above all, because it is evident that the writing has been done without thinking. What this means can hardly be expressed in words but it may be understood by examining a writing which one is certain has taken much trouble to execute. It will be noticed that there is a particular connection between the writing and the work of the mind which is always missing in a writing which has been dictated.

The same may be said of a copy, which, as a rule, is more carefully done than a writing done straight away, corrections are few and the writing has a certain appearance of completion. The same is also noteworthy in forgeries which have the character of copies owing to the way in which the pen is dipped in the ink. Let us first consider a piece of dictation or a rough draft having no erasures and written right off with no considerable pauses for reflection. When writing with the same pen and the same ink, etc, each time a dip is taken the same quantity of ink is taken on the pen and about the same number of words written. when the ink on the pen is nearly done the letters become paler and are clearly distinguishable from the other and blacker letters. But nervous and excitable persons do not wait till there is no more ink on the pen they take more ink long before they need, thus betraying by the total absence of pale places their state of nervous excitability. The paler parts may be easily discovered with a magnifying glass and once found we know when the writer has dipped his pen in the ink. These places should then be marked and the letters written with each dip counted. If the number of letters between the dips is almost identical the writing may be presumed to have been written at once or from dictation the writer has dipped his pen in the ink at the moment when there was no more ink on it to go on with. But if a noticeable difference be found between the number of letters in each group, the counting must be continued, let us suppose that the number of letters in several groups is the same and that all at once the number becomes very much greater the conclusion to be drawn is that the writing has been interrupted as e g , for reflection. He has stopped writing when there was still ink on his pen, he has then reflected, or taken a pull at his pipe or his peg, re-dipped his pen in the ink and started writing again, so that there are no pale letters at that particular place and the distance between the two pale places is therefore considerable. Of course a person dictating may also make pauses but the dictated matter has other characteristic signs which prevent any confusion. These remarks do not of course apply to those who use fountain pens

It is quite otherwise with a copy, the copyist dips his pen not only when he needs ink, but also frequently does so on reading over and assimilating portions of the matter he is copying. If a person be observed while copying it will be noticed that he takes more ink whenever he begins a new paragraph though he does not really require it. The consequence is that pale places are either entirely wanting in a copy or come at very irregular intervals. As regards very exact copies, as, e g , in imitating a writing, the personal experience of the author is that pale places do not exist at all. The forger makes each stroke slowly, one after the other (or else but one or two at a time) looking at the model continually as he does so, he therefore takes advantage of these natural pauses to dip his pen in the ink with the result that pale letters do not exist at all

Another phenomenon, the effect of which is also not difficult to recognise, consists in haste or marked carefulness. Haste in writing is characterised by large irregular letters with the angles round rather than sharp, the writing quickly loses its primary direction, straight writing becomes sloping and sloping writing straight. The distance between the lines is irregular, the final strokes of the words, especially at the end of a paragraph, are elongated, and the position of the writing on the page is not observed, as may be seen from the margins at the top, bottom and sides of the paper

Converse phenomena may be observed in writing where special care has been exercised. The first thing to notice is that a new pen has been taken on beginning to write the letters written therewith being unmistakably sharp and fine the writing is much smaller, the angles of the letters more pronounced, the full stops are round (i e , do not tail towards the right) the paragraphs are well separated from one another, in short the exterior form of the writing has been carefully attended to

A person who is forging a document finds it necessary to take special care over each detail and the more he attempts to hide this care the more is it betrayed his desire is to make believe that he is writing with a running hand when in fact he is taking the greatest trouble in the world. An individual who is capable of falsifying a writing so that it really has the appearance of a running hand knows his business *au fond* and is a past master in the art of forgery. But every imperfection in his writing will at once reveal a contradiction although at first it may be difficult to say in what it consists. Only after further consideration will it be possible to say "The writing is by a running hand—and yet it is not so." Once this result is attained the answer to the puzzle is clear the writing is made to pass for a running hand but has not in fact been written with a running hand. It is much the same with a transcript, it is generally carefully done and there are few corrections, but the whole has a certain stiff appearance.

As important and moreover, not difficult to recognise is when a person has written under conditions different from those to which he is accustomed. We all write quite differently when sitting at home at our own desk and using our own writing materials undergoing no strange influence, than we do when with a wretched office pen we have to sign our name, on our feet, bending over unaccustomed paper. To find out such derangement in accustomed habits it is unnecessary to proceed to comparison, one has only to note the form of the letters to become convinced that the writer is accustomed to use the pen but at the same time that the whole writing shows a certain awkwardness. It is of course true that if a person is not a practised writer it will be very difficult to say whether or not he has written in normal conditions. This is very common in India in the case of signatories and witnesses who frequently can write only their names and a few common words.

The most important thing an Investigating Officer can extract from a writing is, in every case, the character of an individual. To be able to do so is partly a matter of natural disposition and partly a matter of experience. Proceeding methodically the learner must first make a collection of manuscripts of persons whose character, age, occupation, etc., are well known to him. These manuscripts should be taken one by one and read *ad hoc*, i.e., with the intention of finding some definite peculiarity, e.g., in an old man's writing everything which may be considered as the result of age, such as antiquated expressions, trembling script, awkwardness, archaic forms of letters etc. All such indications will be noted and similar peculiarities searched for, first in manuscripts written by persons of the same age and afterwards in all the others at one's disposal. If in the latter, phenomena are also met with which one has so far believed to be signs of advanced years one will try to find out the reason for their existence in the writing of the younger persons, and will leave on one side all the characteristics not specially belonging to the writing of old persons. If, later, one comes into possession of another of these latter mentioned writings it will be verified with respect to these characteristics and the new data obtained will be added to the list already commenced. This register will undergo many alterations, new distinctive signs will often be discovered, but on the other hand peculiarities also found in the handwriting of young persons will continue to crop up and must be struck out of the list. The same procedure will be followed in making lists from every imaginable point of view —from the point of view of age sex, size nationality, position profession occupation, intellectual condition, natural disposition benevolence or penuriousness, boldness or timidity, morality, inclinations qualities character, physical and mental organisation situation in life and often the intention of a writer, in sum all those qualities which go to make up human nature And this work will be double in the first place the point of departure will be the writer and the writing must be searched for signs of some special tendencies really forming part of the character of an individual we know for instance that he is a weak man and we look for indications of a weak character in the writing When we believe we have discovered such signs they must be noted and accurately verified as was done when drawing up the list of distinctive signs of old age In the second place our point of departure will be the writing itself, and in it we will try to discover everything that can be discovered and verify it until the results arrived at coincide with those we have obtained from our study of the individual When this work has been practised for some time the result obtained may be that the information concerning the individual will not correspond with the indications drawn from the writing but at the same time it will be found that it is not the latter indications but the former that are inaccurate Writing never lies, and it will prove our former opinion to have been fallacious

After having examined in this way all the manuscripts at one's disposal it is necessary to group them, we should compare them, keeping in view the questions of age, sex, special peculiarities, and finally the kind of manuscript (hurried notes, careful work etc) As soon as a grouping from a particular point of view has been made, the writings should be attentively examined for such common characters as may be easily remembered, it is in the highest degree suggestive and interesting to make and study such groups and manuscripts, when one has begun to become interested in this kind of work one soon gives oneself up to it with a passion which grows all the more as little by little one discovers the enormous profit to be obtained therefrom, this profit increases in proportion to the skill of the operator and the pleasure the latter finds in his occupation increases in like proportion

Criminalists have at their disposal material of high value only accessible to themselves, such as the signatures of persons who have been judicially examined along with their general description and depositions When carrying on this study of manuscripts a document such as a deposition should never be handled without an attempt to gain some profit by that study First look at the signature and read all that can be read in it, then, relying on the facts set out in the deposition itself, the accuracy of the opinion formed therefrom may be verified with a little practice this does not take long and the minutes lost are largely compensated for by what is otherwise gained one soon begins to do this out of habit and does not neglect it even when in a hurry A glance taken at the end of the deposition and we immediately conclude —
"Artisan 40 or 50 years old, open-hearted, trustworthy, honest, small in stature, careless" then the description, profession, age, etc, is looked at and our opinion found to be accurate Then the tenor of the

document is examined and our opinion again borne out. More time is required when the opinions formed do not agree with the facts found, for then the fault must be sought for, but soon one seldom or never makes a mistake. This study takes up but little time, presents a variety of surprises, and becomes as interesting as it is useful. The author advises everyone to study handwriting in this way.

When the identity of two writings has to be established, there is nothing else to do but to apply to a particular case what one has already learned from an appreciation of handwriting. He who in comparing two writings only places them side by side in order to find resemblances or differences will discover absolutely nothing or if he do discover anything it will be in an exceptionally easy case. The only correct method is to study, examine, and determine the characteristics of each writing apart and then to compare the results obtained, but not the writings themselves; only after having carefully done this can the two documents be compared together for resemblances and differences. Now for this it is necessary to have special notions of what is meant by the words "resemblance" and "difference", we do not understand by this mere similarity or dissimilarity in the form of the letters. Everyone makes the same letter in quite a different way at different times, even indeed often in the same line, and besides it is easy to imitate each letter, even the most characteristic. The identicality of letters really only exists if the same brain has formed them, if they proceed from the same thought, the same character, and the same nature. Two letters may have a marked air of resemblance but they are always different from one another if the same brain has not dictated them or if they have not been written in the same mood. This is the alpha and omega of all appreciation of writing, the man who is capable of finding this difference will be able to formulate a correct judgment. It is true that in addition to this, other processes exist which may help us in judging a writing.

Fig. 1

It is useful, for instance, whenever writing is to be examined critically, to draw certain lines which enable characteristic peculiarities to be discovered. These lines are horizontal or demarcating lines four of them should be drawn, such as we see in the first writing books of children, but instead of being straight these lines will be broken (*Fig. 1*) joining exactly the upper and lower extremities of all the letters. The straightest line will be that joining the lower edge of the letters without loops or tails (a c e m n o etc) taken together the four lines will present characteristic peculiarities very important for comparison.

But if a writing has been forged and in consequence written slowly and with many pauses the direction of the line alters in a most noticeable way for the pen after each pause no longer finds the exact point at which it would have continued to write had no interruption taken place. The line will therefore be markedly interrupted though the characteristic distances between the lines may not at all be lost. If the case is an important one the documents should be, and are as a rule, photographed, these photographs may then be handled at will and many things are often discovered in them which are missed when examining the document itself

Further, interruptions in words taken singly are very important. As a rule words are written without stopping and in one continuous stroke. There are, however, exceptions: —

1. When the word is so long that one is obliged to move the forearm which rests on the table, the pen is also moved.

2. When, also in long words, near the commencement of the word an i has to be dotted or t stroked. When these signs come at the end of a word one, as a rule, writes the whole word before placing the sign; in other cases the word is usually interrupted in the middle, the sign being placed and the word continued. Take for example, the word "misunderstanding," one probably stops after the first s and dots the i and then goes on to the end of the word before dotting the i in ing and finally stroking the t.

3. When certain letters do not join easily with others, as c q, s, or after certain capital letters, B, Z, D, etc., sometimes also after certain small letters, g, d, l, and finally one sometimes breaks off in the middle of a letter itself, c q, m p, d, k.

4. When the person writing has got into a habit of breaking off frequently without any particular reason.

In every case such interruptions are characteristic of all writings and must on that account be minutely studied both in the undisputed and the disputed documents. If there is forgery or falsification in the latter it will be noticed that the interruptions are few and unnatural, that is, they cannot be explained by one of the above-cited reasons. The interruption is made simply to look at the model and for reflection. This, indeed, is the infallible sign of the forged writing.

The way in which the pen is held should also be considered, i.e., whether both points of the pen are pressed equally, or whether one of the points is pressed more or less heavily than the other; as a rule it is difficult to change the way in which one holds or presses a pen, finally, the observations which have already been made above with regard to dipping the pen in the ink and the interruptions consequent thereon are very important.

As to the spelling, upon which too much value is often placed, it proves absolutely nothing. The forger may know how to spell and yet intentionally introduce mistakes into what he is writing, he may also make many mistakes in his ordinary writing while in the forged document he may have looked up some of the words in a dictionary; besides, nothing prevents him from having it corrected by another person. If there are faults both in the undisputed as well as in the disputed writing and these faults are not identical, this also proves nothing; it must not be forgotten that only a person who writes without mistakes observes the rules of grammar, a person who cannot spell follows no rule (at least generally speaking), sometimes he makes one fault, sometimes another, and sometimes he will write the word correctly just by chance. Those who, like Investigating Officers, are accustomed to read letters from all sorts of people know how much the spelling of uneducated persons differs

Ames gives some interesting information regarding tracing. There are, he says, two general methods of perpetrating forgeries: one by the aid of tracing, the other by free-hand writing. These methods differ widely in detail, according to the circumstances of each case.

Tracing can only be employed when a signature or writing is present in the exact or approximate form of the desired reproduction. It may then be done by placing the writing to be forged upon a transparency over a strong light, and then superimposing the paper upon which the forgery is to be made. The outline of the writing underneath will then appear sufficiently plain to enable it to be traced with pen or pencil so as to produce a very accurate copy upon the superimposed paper. If the outline is with a pencil, it is afterwards marked over with ink.

Again, tracings are made by placing transparent tracing-paper over the writing to be copied and then following the lines over with a pencil. This tracing is then pencilled or blackened upon the obverse side. When it is placed upon the paper on which the forgery is to be made, the lines upon the tracing are retraced with a stylus or other smooth, hard point which impresses upon the paper underneath a faint outline, which serves as a guide to the forged imitation.

In forgeries perpetrated by the aid of tracing, the internal evidence is more or less conclusive, according to the skill of the forger. In the perpetration of a forgery the mind, instead of being occupied in the usual function of supplying matter to be recorded, devotes its special attention to the superintendence of the hand, directing its movements, so that the hand no longer glides naturally and automatically over the paper, but moves slowly with a halting, vacillating motion, as the eye passes to and from the copy to the pen, moving under the specific control of the will. Evidence of such a forgery is manifest in the formal, broken, nervous lines, the uneven flow of the ink, and the often retouched lines and shades. These evidences are unmistakable when studied with the aid of a microscope. Also, further evidence is adduced by a careful comparison of the disputed writing, noting the pen pressure or absence of any of the delicate unconscious forms, relations, shades, etc., characteristic of the standard writing.

Forgeries by tracing usually present a close resemblance in general form to the genuine documents, and are therefore most sure to deceive the unfamiliar or casual observer. It sometimes happens that the original writing from which the tracings were made is discovered, in which case the closely duplicated forms will be positive evidence of forgery. The degree to which one signature or writing duplicates another may be readily seen by placing one over the other and holding them to a window or other strong light, or by close comparative measurements.

Traced forgeries, however, are not, as is usually supposed, necessarily exact duplicates of their originals, since it is very easy to move the paper by accident or design while the tracing is being made, or while making the transfer copy from it, so that while it serves as a guide to the general features of the original, it will not, when tested, be an exact duplication. The danger of an exact duplication is quite generally understood by persons having any knowledge of forgery and is therefore avoided. Another difficulty is that the very delicate features of the original writing are more or less obscured by the opaqueness of two sheets of paper, and are therefore changed or omitted from the forged simulation and their absence is usually supplied, through force of habit, by equally delicate, unconscious characteristics from the writing of the forger himself. Again, the forger rarely possesses the requisite skill to exactly reproduce his tracing. Many of the minutiæ of the original writing are more or less microscopic and for that reason pass unobserved by the forger. Outlines of writing to be forged are sometimes simply drawn with a pencil and then worked up in ink. Such outlines will not usually furnish so good an imitation as to form, since they depend wholly upon the imitative skill of the forger.

Besides the above-mentioned evidences of forgery by tracing, where pencil or carbon guide-lines are used, which must necessarily be removed by rubber, there are liable to remain some slight fragments of the tracing lines, while the mill finish of the paper will be impaired and its fibre more or less torn out, so as to lie loose upon the surface. Also the ink will be more or less ground off from the paper, thus giving the lines a grey and lifeless appearance. And as retouchings are usually made after the guidelines have been removed, the ink, wherever they occur, will have a blacker and fresher appearance than elsewhere. All these phenomena are plainly manifest under the microscope. Where the tracing is made directly with pen and ink over a transparency, as is often done, no rubbing is necessary, and of course the phenomena arising from rubbing do not appear.

In concluding this section the author would add that there are distinguished experts in handwriting who often proceed in conformity with really scientific principles; to these we may confide without apprehension work within their competence, but we must not neglect to make our own observations in order to compare them with those of the expert, in the interests of our inquiry. On the other hand there are experts who proceed in an unscientific and cut-and-dried way; when we have only such at our disposal, it is much better to do the work ourselves.

Section ix.—Photography.

A Importance of Photography from a judicial point of view

Especially brilliant are the services rendered by photography to the criminal law; however recent the applications of photography in criminal matters may be, yet to-day they are none the less multitudinous and there even exists a whole series but dimly foreshadowed. We know approximately that we are able to employ photography in certain circumstances and *how* we ought to do so, and yet we know but an infinitesimal number of the cases in which it may be useful. The number of these cases will increase for we are not content with having direct recourse to photography properly so called but profit besides by all the applications of photography in other sciences. *E g.*, to-day Röntgen rays have become of immeasurable importance to us. For it can be said that they in certain cases bring the same certainty as to the living body that in the dead only *post-mortem* examination can afford. That thus extraordinary results are achieved need not be insisted upon.

Let us first deal with the personality of the photographer who comes to the aid of the Investigating Officer here we are able to make a distinction at least in theory many cases occur where it is merely necessary to photograph without worrying whether the result is more or less successful, it is always possible to rectify and correct in the report of the case even grave faults in a photograph. Such photographs may be, e.g., the place of a fire, the position of an individual who has been killed, the scene of a railway accident, landslip, or explosion, etc. If the photograph does not produce an exact impression it may be stated in the report as follows: ' The distance between the buildings A & B does not seem so far to the eye as on the photograph, it only extends according to measurements to double the length of the house A,' or ' The position of a corpse was not so perpendicular as might be believed from the photograph, the grass upon which it lay was sloping about 12 degrees.' *

Such photographic proofs, where it is only required to give an idea of localities or reproduce the position of objects, the general impression, or certain details, may be made by anyone who has taken up photography; it is not necessary to call in the professional photographer expressly for the purpose, the amateur photographer is more than sufficient. And as it is often embarrassing, or at least costly, to engage a professional photographer, it is desirable that the greater number of Investigating Officers become amateur photographers; in this way photographs may be obtained in numerous criminal cases, thus elucidating the case and facilitating the work.

It is in this way that the well-known chemical legist *Dr. Paul Jeserich* has worked for many years. On commissions which he has attended he has never ceased to insist upon the importance of photographs from a criminal point of view; photography, he says, is entirely objective and always impartial, it is capable of fixing certain details which may perhaps be of subsequent importance and of which no one has dreamed at the time of the inspection of localities. It is for this reason that the sensible advice is given of taking several views from different sides, for it frequently happens that at the time of the visit to the scene of the crime the important and decisive side cannot yet be indicated.

And, indeed, many Investigating Officers have already recognised the importance of photography; we often find appended to the report of an inspection of a locality a photograph made by an Investigating Officer in his capacity of amateur photographer, and it is needless to add that the report has gained enormously in clearness and simplicity thereby. No doubt the State cannot order every Investigating Officer to buy a photographic camera and its accessories, to procure all the necessary chemicals, and impose upon him the always wearisome duty of developing, printing, washing, fixing, and mounting. But little by little it will recognise the importance of photography from a criminal standpoint. The State ought to facilitate the use of photography and furnish photographic apparatus not only to criminal courts but also to all important police stations; almost everywhere will be found an Investigating Officer or head constable who will learn to work it and who will take over the business. It is quite otherwise in cases in which the scientific photographer, or rather the photographic scientist, comes in. It is these latter cases which give to photography the important and unexpected place which it occupies in criminal investigations; it has already assumed this position though it may as yet be in its infancy, and every day may bring to light

---

* Concerning the objectivity and the apparent untruthfulness of photography too much cannot be said. We must try and find out why photographs frequently create a wholly wrong impression (see *infra*, p. 180).

a new side of its importance. Perchance in a little while we shall hardly be able to understand how we were able formerly to conduct any case without invoking at each moment the aid of *scientific* photography. It seems absolutely impossible to exaggerate the importance photography will assume several years hence.

It is difficult to indicate the line of demarcation between the work of the ordinary photographer and of the scientific photographer. This depends on the one hand upon the case itself and on the other upon the photographer. In the following pages some examples will be cited in which recourse may be had to photographers, but no distinction will be made between the work of the ordinary and that of the scientific photographer.

B Particular cases of the employment of Photography

It is hardly possible to exhaust by complete enumeration the number of cases in which photography may be employed. Speaking generally it may be said that it should always be employed when it is desired to obtain absolutely objective, permanent, and easily controlled proofs capable of bringing about a conviction the sensitized plate is the new retina of the man of science (*Prof H Vogel*), it may then be said that photography may be employed every time that there is room to suppose that the camera sees further than the eye, or, if it does not see further, each time that an object should be fixed for future reference. A painter, and especially a portrait painter after having worked for a certain time, places his portrait before a mirror and considers the image which the latter reflects, he often discovers great faults which he was incapable of seeing upon the portrait itself. The reason is that when one looks for a long time at an object, especially when one has been doing so since its origin, and been assisting at the whole of its development, one always sees it under the same aspect, which prevents certain defects being noticed, but when the image is reflected by the mirror one sees the object under lateral inversion and in consequence under another aspect, details may then perhaps be discovered which have formerly escaped notice. In photography exactly the same may be said, an object has been observed with great minuteness and application a whole series of observations have been made regarding it, nothing striking has been noticed about it because one has become accustomed to its appearance, but if it be photographed, the new colour the new situation, and the new aspect enable us to see it from another point of view and reveal fresh details which have not yet been discovered.

Here, then, we have to start with quite a number of cases in which photography may be useful, that is to say, each time that an object and its particular relation and position with respect to other objects is difficult or impossible to explain *e g*, in the case of an accident supposed to have been caused by a criminal hand but which cannot easily be explained in its entirety, the photograph of the scene of the accident may be able perhaps at once, perhaps later, to furnish the desired explanation. It is the same when one has doubts regarding the manner in which thieves have set to work in a burglary, when the position of a corpse is unnatural, when conclusions may be drawn from that position without having sufficient proof for doing so at one's disposal, and finally when it is question of the appearance of wounds, writings results of arson, etc. We have all had occasion to say,

'This position ought to give an important clue for finding the correct point of view.' Such a reflection ought always to make us photograph the object. The photograph in fact procures us another point of view, another way of looking at things, and often the desired explanation. And if the Investigating Officer, who has himself seen the surroundings of the offence, does not find the solution, perhaps another to whom the photograph is subsequently shown will find it therein; but if no photograph exists, no one will any longer have the exact position of the object before his eyes and we shall never obtain the explanation we are looking for.

Another class of cases exists in which objects may be photographed, first, on every occasion on which it is the duty of the Investigating Officer to see and describe an object and its position in such a manner that persons who have subsequently to deal with the case may be enabled to form as clear an idea thereon as possible. Theoretically, the Judge trying the case, the Public Prosecutor, the expert, the counsel for the defence, and the jury or assessors, ought to see everything the Investigating Officer has seen. As this is generally impossible, the Investigating Officer has to supply the lack of the direct view by description. But how much clearer, more convincing and more objective this description would be, if he supplemented it with photographs. In cases such as the following we ought to photograph: places where a man has been killed, where there has been a quarrel, where a child has been abandoned, where a person has been the victim of an accident, the scene of a fire, the scene of an important railway smash, boiler explosion, collapse of a bridge, house, or other building, the scene of a burglary, highway robberies, a disputed water channel in cases of rioting connected therewith, and many others which will occur to the mind as occasion arises.

We will here cite a typical example demonstrating that photography may aid us even without our knowledge. During the riots at the time of the marriage of Prince Croy at Brussels, several young men were arrested who pretended that they had taken no part in the affray, and had been carried into the crowd by chance and against their will. But a policeman happened to notice that an amateur photographer had not allowed the occasion to escape of taking an instantaneous photograph of the riot from his window; the photographer was asked for a proof, which was immediately enlarged, and it turned out that several of the young men under arrest, the so-called "passive spectators," were in the photograph; they were distinctly recognisable, and as unhappily they were represented with mouths wide open to shout and arms in the air brandishing sticks, they immediately gave up the line of defence that they had been dragged into the disturbance against their will.

A report of a similar case appeared in the "Daily Express" at the time of the assassination of *President McKinley*. During that fatal visit of the murdered President to the Buffalo Exhibition, the kinematograph was, of course, in constant activity. An exquisite series of pictures shows the President as he delivered his address and shook hands with the people who approached him. All his movements shortly before the moment when the fatal bullet struck him were fixed upon the films. When some days later these photographs were developed at the Edison Laboratory and examined by officers of the Criminal Investigation Department, a discovery was made of the greatest importance. Among the closely packed multitude surging around McKinley, one face and figure stood out with striking distinctness. It was Czolgosz. The first pictures of the series show the President as he steps on the platform and begins his speech. A man is next seen making his way with difficulty through the crowd. Various people whom he pushes recklessly aside turn round on him with angry looks. Undisturbed, however, he forges ahead and seems to succeed in making his way through the living wall. Then he stands still for a second and turns his face unsuspectingly towards the camera. Desperate resolution can be seen in his eyes. Then he goes on further, pushing and thrusting, until he is almost immediately before the President. Again he faces the camera. At this moment he seems agitated and excited. Now his hat is knocked over his eyes and hastily he puts it back. He then looks wildly around, and appears as if waiting for someone in the multitude and expecting a signal. Thousands of people are in the picture with him, but most of them stand with their backs to the camera. The features of all who turned round are clear enough to make them recognisable in the photograph. From these films drawings were taken for the secret police service, with the object of discovering by their help some clue to the confederates of the murderer.

Acquittals have also been brought about by 'accidental photography.' The 'Amateur Photographer' relates how an Englishman was accused in Rio de Janeiro of the murder of a Brazilian friend. A few days before, the two had a violent quarrel but this was stated to have been amicably made up, and on the day in question they went together for a sail in the harbour in a small yacht. In the evening the Englishman returned with the dead body of his friend on board, and stoutly maintained that death was due to an accident, his companion having fallen from the mast-head on to the deck. An oar was missing and the medical experts gave it as their opinion that death was the result of a blow on the head with a stick and that an oar might probably have been the weapon used. An inquiry was proceeded with, and the previous quarrel made things look very black against the accused. Now, a passenger on a steamer had happened to take a snap-shot of the harbour and on developing it, a dark spot was noticed on the white sail of a small yacht which chanced to be in the neighbourhood. On this being enlarged the spot proved to be the body of a man falling from the mast, thus conclusively proving the truth of the Englishman's story and bringing about his acquittal.

Apart from such situations, perishable objects and those likely to change their appearance should also be photographed. Firstly, *wounds*, especially when the instrument with which they have been made is unknown, or when the relative position of the aggressor and the victim is doubtful, or when it is not certain whether the wound has been inflicted upon a person while living or after death. Secondly, *footprints*, impressions of which cannot be taken and whose relative position is of some importance; it may even be said that all footprints ought to be photographed before the impression of them is taken; thus provision would be made against every eventuality, for the impression may not succeed and the footprint may be destroyed. Thirdly, the same holds with *finger-prints* upon the body of the victim of an assault or upon other objects; apart from their scientific interpretation, the size, shape, and general appearance may be of great importance (see *post*, Section X, *Finger-prints*). Fourthly *the position of a person killed* ought always to be photographed, and from different sides, if one is sure that the corpse is still in its original position and has not been moved by earlier comers.

A whole series of important clues will, the author believes, be furnished by the following property of the photographic process. This process renders red and brown darker and clearer than they appear to the eye, and the photographic plate also reproduces the colours red and brown even when a human eye cannot see them at all. This peculiarity explains the often cited case of "The small-pox woman." A woman, apparently in the best of health, had her photograph taken, and when the photographer developed the negative he noticed that the face and the neck were spotted over with a multitude of dark marks; yet the photographer did not remember having seen such marks upon the skin of the woman; his astonishment increased when he learnt that the woman had become ill some days later and that her illness was small-pox. This fact is only explicable on the assumption that the marks of the illness were already existent when she posed for her photograph, but that they were as yet but slightly red and that the sensitized plate had registered them when the human eye was unable to perceive them.

Experts in colours are also aware of similar phenomena. Photographs sometimes show marks on the face, e.g., on the cheeks, which are not noticeable naturally. These are old injuries which the lapse of years has rendered invisible to the eye, but they have left a little redness which is clearly brought out by photography.

These remarkable facts lead us to believe that it is possible in a general way to render *brown and red marks yet in a latent state visible by photography*. Every pressure exercised on the skin of a man results in the breaking or at least in the inflaming of the small veins, and each time redness is produced. If the pressure has been very feeble the redness will exist but will not be discernible by the eye. This redness is particularly common after scratches, attempts at strangulation, blows with the fist, falls, squeezing, and also after inflammation caused by poison, heat, rubbing, etc., when the attacks are not severe. But in most cases the important thing is, not to prove that there has been an attack of a particular violence, it suffices to know that there has been an attack, and the traces must be looked for both on the victim and on his aggressor, who no doubt wishes to pass them off as marks of resistance in a case of legitimate defence. The question is specially serious if the victim has been wounded when already at the point of death and when the beats of the heart are already weakened. In these cases the blood can no longer spurt forcibly from the injured blood-vessels, and even an energetic attack may produce only a slight redness.

It is easy to conjecture cases which may be met with in practice, e.g., a person has been suffocated by cushions or other soft articles, so that no exterior trace of violence can be perceived. The verdict would most likely be "natural death," but the photograph will perhaps discover very distinct traces of strangulation or perhaps indicate that the individual in question has been firmly held and then stifled. In the same way there may be found on an individual who has apparently committed suicide by hanging, bruises or effusions of blood towards the skin which the eye will not notice but which the photographic plate will render visible; these contusions will often permit of the supposition that death has been preceded by a struggle (see *Chapter XVI, Section v*).

It is also important to establish the existence of traces of resistance on the person of the supposed aggressor; the person assaulted may have given him blows or scratches, or attempted to choke him, but so feebly that the camera is alone able to discover the marks. Moreover, the redness produced (we are, of course, always dealing with white-skinned persons) may have been very distinct at first and have disappeared by the time of arrest, so that only photography can establish its existence. It therefore seems the right thing to do, in all cases of suspicious death of white persons, to have the corpse photographed as well as the suspected assailant, when resistance is believed to have been offered, and to search on the body for traces of redness. Nor ought we to forget objects from which an attempt has been made to obliterate marks of blood, e.g., linen, floors, walls, etc. It is difficult to submit large surfaces to chemical and microscopic examination, but if they be photographed, perhaps the places where such marks exist will be discovered; and the particular spot once found microscopic and chemical examination may be proceeded with (see *Chapter XII, Section iv*). In certain circumstances the photographing of internal organs may also be recommended, e.g., the brain, mucous membrane of the respiratory channels or stomach, when it is not known whether such redness is natural or not. In poisoning cases it may be possible to determine with greater accuracy the moment when the poison has been absorbed. When, e.g., fairly large particles of arsenic remain for some time attached to the mucous membrane of the stomach, the latter becomes inflamed at the places where the arsenic has remained longest. If this redness is imperceptible to the eye it is possible for photography to discover it, and therefrom can be deduced the length of time the arsenic has been in the stomach.

With respect to this it should be remarked in a general way that on an ordinary photographic plate colours do not come out as in the reality; that is to say, they do not make the same light and dark impression as they make in nature; red and brown become, as has been said, darker, blue and violet generally appear lighter but also at times darker according to the chemical nature of the colouring matter. Fluorescent bodies influence the shades of colours in various ways; green generally becomes somewhat darker, yet bodies are known, e.g., the green flower of the gooseberry, which come out quite light; natural colours photograph better than artificial; the photograph of a bouquet of natural flowers will give a much more accurate impression than that of a painted bouquet, however faithful the painting may be. In many cases these small details must not be overlooked.

We should also mention that in some circumstances it is good to take several photographs of a person who is shamming. For example, when dealing with an accused who constantly contracts the muscles of his face, rolls his eyes, makes impossible grimaces, etc., and thus leads us to suspect shamming, he should be placed in a room lending itself to photography, well lit and furnished with a trap permitting observation without being oneself seen; a sufficient opening is also arranged to hold the camera which is brought into play when the person under observation is in a good position and is behaving naturally; needless to say the photograph must be an instantaneous one.

Nor must it be forgotten that magnesium-light photographs are often necessary. When e.g. a corpse has been found on a busy road and it is not advisable to wait for daylight (owing to the heavy day traffic) to photograph blood or footprints, the spot must be photographed with the aid of artificial light.

We now come to photography of objects observed under the microscope; this is not the business of the Investigating Officer but in some cases he ought to absolutely insist on its being done. We suggest that the microscopist should sign no report without adding thereto a photograph of what he has observed under the instrument. Dr Paul Jeserich was probably the first to draw attention to the necessity of such photographs. The idea came to him when during the argument of a case, he heard the objection raised that what the experts had seen under the microscope and taken for blood was perhaps only mushroom mould or grains of starch. This objection could not then be refuted, since the objects microscopically examined had long before decomposed and been destroyed being thus incapable of further use in the case. This drawback is easily got over by asking the microscopist to prepare and exhibit photographs of his experiments. Any mistake on the part of the expert may thus be excluded, for in his zeal he may perhaps see many things which are non-existent. He presents his photograph saying as much for his own peace of mind as for that of others: 'look at the photograph and form your opinion.'

Proof of this kind may be given at any moment—even after many years, provided that the record of the case is still in existence, and is particularly easy to lay before a Judge and jury. The Parisians in 1871, when sending letters and despatches by pigeon post, gummed them side by side upon a wall (like tapestry) and then made a photographic reduction of the whole surface (measuring several square metres) upon a sheet of paper several centimetres square. This reduction was then rolled up inside a quill and attached to the pigeon's tail. On arriving at its destination the little photograph with its hundreds of letters was enlarged by the microscopic lantern and projected on a screen or white wall and anyone who expected a letter had but to go and read it. Let us apply this process to judicial photography, the microscopic photograph of the object in question as well as of the objects which it is to be compared with or differentiated from may be enlarged in open court, thrown upon a wall, and explained to the Judge and jury by the expert. By this means the possibility of error will as far as possible be averted.

This procedure will be adopted not only in determining the presence of blood, semen, poison or one or other of those numerous substances which the microscope is capable of recognizing and which can be seen directly, but also in connection with other microscopic phenomena. Here is a most interesting case: in a house destroyed by fire the half-carbonised corpse of the landlord was discovered and there was room to believe that a murder had taken place; we know that fresh blood has certain microscopic properties which alter greatly under the action of certain chemical agents. But if blood be submitted to the action of carbon monoxide, which is most poisonous, it does not alter under the influence of chemicals; the question was whether the person had been suffocated in the fire or killed before it began. In the first hypothesis the blood would present the characteristics of blood that has absorbed carbon monoxide, and one breath of this gas undiluted is quite sufficient to affect the whole blood of the body in a most marked manner. Dr *Paul Jeserich* experimented with a few drops of the blood which still remained in the heart of the corpse and was able to establish that death was due to suffocation. At the same time he took a photograph of the spectrum and exhibited it at the trial, when the *corpus delicti* had already been long in a state of putrefaction.

The same expert has also exhibited in Court photographs of his experiments with hair; the jury were then in a position to consider the case just as if they had seen the material objects mentioned by the expert.

The use of magic-lantern slides or even of radiographs (sciagraphs) may yet play a great role in the Law Courts. Anyone who has had to show and explain a very small object in Court is aware of the inadequacy of present methods. The explanation has to be given over and over again, to the several witnesses, the Public Prosecutor, the complainant or plaintiff, the defendant and his counsel, and the Judge and jury. All who have business in Courts know how tedious and defective is this method. But with a whitewashed wall or a sheet, or piece of white paper stretched on a frame or on the wall, the objects may be shown enlarged by means of the lantern; not only can transparencies be shown but also wood-engravings, photographs, prints, handwriting, etc., in short everything on paper which transmits the light and whose size permits of its entering the apparatus. The necessary darkening of the Court would be a difficulty which a little ingenuity would soon overcome. Theoretically this idea has been widely approved and has already been turned to practical account.

Photography is also of great importance from the point of view of the examination of manuscripts. We have already mentioned that in comparing handwriting recourse should be had to photography so as for example to be able to make drawings upon the photographs, which would be impossible on the original. But photography can also furnish direct proofs, for it brings to light things which could not be seen by the naked eye. In this connection *Jeserich* of Paris, *Gobert* of Berlin, and *Eder* of Vienna were the initiators; since their first experiments it is known that photography is the easiest method of discovering erasures, obliterations, and rubbings out, which cannot be seen with the naked eye. By choosing a suitable position the contrast may be increased, so that the parts of the writing which remain appear to us with a darker tint. It is also easy to determine the employment of various chemical products, indeed those parts of the paper where they have been applied have a different colour when photographed. Very often writing effaced by an acid becomes quite readable in the photograph.

Photography is also able to detect the presence of various kinds of ink which may have been employed; in this way we are frequently able to prove a forgery. The forger often finds (with great trouble) an ink with the same colour as the original, but to the eye alone does it appear identical. If a suitable light be chosen for photographing the writing (e.g., gas), and the plate be properly developed, the two apparently similar writings will come out the one light grey and the other dark brown. In comparison of handwriting, photography is also of some value in other ways. Above all it is possible to reduce the two writings, the forged and the genuine to the same scale, thus enormously facilitating comparison; again it is possible to get rid of the troublesome difference in paper, since the photos are on the same paper. If need be, comparison may be facilitated by photographing one of the two writings on a transparent film which is then placed upon the other writing. Points of resemblance may thus be very accurately compared.

Finally, work is enormously facilitated by making photographic enlargements of the two writings. These should be as large as possible. After a long examination of writing, especially very small writing, the sight becomes confused, so that it is difficult to see things clearly, and it is often necessary to interrupt the work. But with enormous letters to work with, observation is very easy; moreover, all the details, differences, resemblances, hesitations, places where a dip of the pen has been taken, stoppages, and all other points connected with a writing are better judged, and in a short time a sure and definite decision may be pronounced. Comparison by means of enlargement with the projection apparatus has succeeded admirably.

It is even sometimes possible to read, with the aid of photography, writing which so to speak does not exist. When, for example, one writes with a very hard pencil upon a writing block or upon a blotter, the writing leaves an impression on the next sheet of the block or upon the blotter; nothing is visible to the naked eye, but if the sheet or blotter be greatly enlarged by photography the writing thereon may often be very distinctly read.

Not only can written characters be observed by means of photography, but as a rule any object which has been in contact with a writing. Thus *Dr Bem*, of the Sheriff's Court of Berlin, was consulted as to whether there had formerly been a stamp upon a bill of exchange; he photographed the bill of exchange and at the same time a blank bill to which a stamp had been affixed for a very short time. The difference was astonishing, and the answer to the question asked could be given in the negative with the most absolute certainty. (*Phot. Arch. 1891, No. 681.*) Another case had to do with the forgery of the name of a deceased person to a receipt. No question of fraud had been raised when traces of obliterated writing were accidentally observed, while looking at the paper by the reflected oblique rays of the sun, on those portions of the paper not actually covered by the later writing. These traces were copied as accurately as possible and the copy superimposed on the new writing so that the blanks in the copy were filled up. Thus the original script was accurately determined. By photography the fraud was rendered unmistakable.

In a general way the fact must not be lost sight of that photographs often bear a different aspect to the real object, from the point of view of dimension, reciprocal situation, and especially general impression. It is some explanation that a good photograph reproduces objects much more distinctly than we can see them. When at some distance from a tiled roof we cannot distinguish one tile from another, a painter recognises this by representing the roof with a uniform colour corresponding to the impression. The Japanese seem to see more distinctly than we do, for they represent such objects with minute accuracy and their drawings thus appear to us very crude. It is the same with photography; it reproduces the tiled roof much more accurately than we see it; we only perceive a brown colour. It is thus that photography appears to us to some extent untrue and wanting in naturalness. Added to this, a certain depth and other effects of light and distance exist and in short the image appears unfaithful. It would be well to remember the following points: —

1. The sun should be upon the side of or behind the camera. This adds to the clearness of the photograph; if the sun is behind the object, the photograph will be flat, as if taken during cloudy weather. This latter principle must then be applied if perchance it is really desired to give an impression that the photograph has been made in dull weather.

2. When photographing persons in the open air it must be remembered that when the light comes from the front of the camera it flattens the face; when it comes from above it renders the countenance dark and forbidding, and that the direct rays of the sun cover the face with marks and give it a hard expression.

3. When it is necessary to photograph house interiors, a photograph by artificial light should be obtained, in which case the windows do not interfere. If this is quite impossible, the dark part of the room must at least be lightened by light reflected by mirrors to which some movement is given.

4. Sometimes when, for example, it is necessary to photograph rapidly in the middle of the night, if it is absolutely impossible to procure magnesium, it is possible to make use of *lightning powders* which may be prepared at the nearest pharmacy, e.g., 6 parts of saltpetre, 2 parts of sulphur, and 1 part of sulphurated antimony are reduced to powder and lightly filled into tubes of paper, or saltpetre may be melted in a vessel over a lamp and flour of sulphur added thereto in small quantities. Each time the sulphur is thrown upon the melted saltpetre a bright light results. But these powders can only be employed when the resulting gas, which has a disagreeable smell, has sufficient means of escape. If one has long enough time to have an exposure of say several hours, a few lamps may be sufficient for lighting purposes.

5. Upon every photograph the scale of reduction must be indicated; the best method is to photograph at the same time the measure of comparison. In photographing a vertical surface, which will in consequence not be deformed, since its various parts will not be at different distances from the camera, e.g., the facade of a house, it would be well to photograph a man at the same time; proportions will thus be accurately indicated.

6. With each photograph the date, hour, temperature, light, points of the compass, time of exposure, kind of camera, and the lenses employed must be indicated.

7. Shining and light objects present great difficulties to photography. We must be specially careful not to dust them, for if that is done they come out still worse. When possible shining objects should be neutralised, for example, iron and glass objects with plumbago or with a mixture of magnesium carbonate and milk, or Russian talcum mixed with essence of turpentine. These washes harm neither the photograph nor the article photographed and are easily got rid of.

8. In photographing machinery (e.g., after accidents) care must be taken not to do so when other work is in progress near by; the vibration of other machinery in motion would greatly spoil the photograph.

9. Photographs of very fine objects in relief, e.g., inscriptions, deteriorations on objects, papillary lines etc., should be taken in a very strong lateral light, for shadows augment the relief; if the latter come out too strong the fact must be mentioned in the report.

We have said above that photographs may appear to us to a certain extent to be untruthful, but it must be noted that from a theoretical standpoint it is by no means so certain that the camera is a bad reproducer of objects. We ourselves perhaps do not see things exactly from the point of view of perspective. When for example, one shows his hands to a person sitting in front of him so that one of them is about a yard nearer him than the other, they will appear to be of equal size, but if a camera be put in place of the person and the hands photographed the hand nearest the camera will appear much larger than the other. According to the laws of perspective, this latter phenomenon conforms to the reality, for the hand nearest one ought to appear larger to the eye, only we do not notice the difference because *conclusions drawn from experience* influence our observation. We know the two hands are really of equal size and this knowledge has so powerful an action that we see them of equal size although, being in perspective, they ought to appear unequal. On looking at the photograph of the hands, however, the principle of experience no longer acts with the same force; on the contrary, we remember that what we are looking at is a picture and attribute the fault to it and say it is an inaccurate reproduction, for we see upon the picture an exact reproduction from the point of view of perspective and we notice an enormous difference in size, but it does not seem to agree with the reality. Let it not be said that "wide-angle objectives" as they are called, which, for example, photograph two corners of a room at the same time, prove the entire contrary. This objective (if it does not distort) no doubt reproduces objects as they are in reality, only we cannot seize them without turning the eyes. At one glance we observe but very little of a thing at a distance of five or six yards. We only perceive distinctly an object of about the size of a chair without moving the eyes; what lies to the right and left of the chair we are looking at is seen by us only approximately; we only see it accurately if we remove our eyes from the chair. If, therefore, a "wide-angle objective" is employed to photograph two walls of a room at the same time (at a distance of five or six yards) the resulting picture appears quite strange to us, because in nature we cannot see so much at a single glance; we say the picture is inaccurate although each particular object therein is reproduced exactly and distinctly. The lens shows more objects than can be seen contemporaneously by the naked eye but these objects are not reproduced inaccurately.

C. Recognition of Criminals from their Photographs

In all countries photography is employed for the identification of persons, especially since its uses have so largely developed. But it is only done systematically in large towns where the police administration is particularly well-skilled in the method. Paris is at the head of this movement, as a perusal of "Judicial Photography," by *Alphonse Bertillon*, Chief of the Identification Department, Prefecture of Police, Paris, will readily demonstrate.

Taking *Bertillon's* book as a guide we shall refer to the most important points.

1. The best position for the individual to be photographed in depends upon the object of the photograph. For the comparison of two photographs, or of a photograph with a person, the best is beyond all doubt a sharp profile; it is in this position that outlines show up best, the various prominences of the face are not projected thereon, and it is easy to measure with accuracy the dimensions necessary for comparison. But it is quite another thing when it is desired to *identify* a person from his photograph; then a profile is absolutely useless. Indeed we only see a person's profile in one position, while we see more or less the front face in all other positions. We are often unacquainted with the profile of a person whom we know intimately. We are surprised to find that an individual we are in the habit of seeing constantly has, when we look at him sideways, quite another aspect to that which we imagined. A person's face seen from the front does not appear strange to us, but it is not characteristic, because the nose is wholly projected and thus difficult to distinguish, and because the ears, so important for purposes of recognition, are deficient in clearness of outline. The most favourable position will, therefore, be the three-quarters face, because then the nose stands out distinctly, one ear is visible, and, moreover, because in this position we are best able to recognise people. Two proofs, however, must be taken—that of the profile and that of the three-quarters face, thus doubling the expense and the number of photographs to be preserved. In England this is got over by placing the subject to be photographed in the three-quarters position and arranging a mirror beside the face which reflects the exact profile. So as to get the mirror at the wished-for distance from the face the lower right-hand corner of the mirror is cut away, thus making a place for the shoulder. In this way, on the same negative, the profile and the three-quarters face are united. *Bertillon* rejects this method; he asserts that if such a double photograph be shown about, everyone would immediately know that it had to do with a suspected individual; but in these matters everyone always does know this when a photograph is shown, and besides the method is so practical that its universal adoption must be recommended.

2. The position of the individual to be photographed leads to another question. Is it preferable to photograph the bust or the whole figure? In a general way it may be said that a face is more easily recognised the larger it is; therefore the bust is to be recommended. But if the individual in question has some peculiarity easy of recognition, the full-length photograph is to be preferred. Such a proof has also the advantage of permitting, if need be, the enlargement of the head, whereas the person is not always at our disposal to photograph his feet. We must not suppose that peculiar movements or twitchings will be reproduced in a photograph of the attitude or physiognomy of the subject. If an individual is afflicted with such movements, it is recommended only to photograph the bust, because the witnesses, and not only uneducated witnesses, always look on a full-length photograph handed to them for the particular movements they know so well, and if they do not find them they fail to recognise the photograph.

3. As regards the *format* of the photograph *Bertillon* considers reduction to one-seventh of natural size is best. This is no doubt a convenient *format*, as the long reign of *cartes de visite* demonstrates. The head reduced in this proportion is always large enough to be readily identified, even by people who seldom see photographs. We think, however,

that size is not of so much importance, and it matters little whether the natural size is reduced to a sixth or an eighth. The essential thing is to employ *the same scale* of reduction. Indeed the exchange of photographs is generally carried out when distances are great and comparison is much facilitated when the photographs are not of different sizes. It would be best to adopt a uniform scale of reduction for all photographs made for the use of justice and the police. This would not be difficult to carry out in practice.

4. As to the tone of the photographs, that is to say, whether they should be lighter or darker, and, in consequence, whether there should be a shorter or longer exposure, it is impossible to give a general answer. The face of the sitter is nearly always adapted to a particular tone and an experienced and intelligent photographer always knows on merely looking at him whether the photograph will be better (i.e., more like) according to whether the tone is lighter or darker. If the photographer cannot tell this, the best shade must be found by degrees, for the difference is often so great that the tone is no indifferent matter.

5. The usual *format* must often be departed from, especially when it is desired to compare a photograph with a particular object. If for example, the description of a person is given, the photograph must be taken so that the most important signs indicated in the description are reproduced, if a photograph already exists the new photograph will, of course, to facilitate comparison, be made in the same style (as regards size, position, tone, paper, etc.) as the old one.

6. If two photographs with different hair, beard, etc. are to be compared (if, e.g., in one photograph the individual has an abundant head of hair and beard while in the other his hair is short and he is clean shaven), those places on the photograph on which hair appears must be covered up. For this purpose *Bertillon* has specially cut papers or stencils which however, are only of use when both photographs are of equal size and the position is also identical. The simplest method is as follows:—The photograph is placed upon a window and over it a sheet of white paper is fixed, upon which is outlined with a pencil the parts covered with hair, thus beginning above the forehead where the hair starts, thence descending the temple and cheek, then passing above the moustache and under the nose and then reascending the other cheek and temple to the forehead. This line is then cut with a sharp knife. The same is then done with the clean shaven face, i.e., a line is drawn where the hair would come if the person was not clean shaven. If the photograph is gummed to a mount it must either be steeped in water and detached, or else the drawing must be done on tracing paper and transferred to ordinary paper. The two sheets having been cut they are placed on the photographs and the two compared. If they are of the same man the result is astonishing, the photographs as a whole have absolutely no resemblance, whereas when the hair on the head and face is covered the resemblance is striking. This is only in accordance with common experience. Likenesses are usually detected and persons recognised by the portion comprised between the lower half of the forehead and the upper part of the nose, including eyes and eyebrows, i.e., just the portion covered by the mask in masked assemblies or balls.

7. Examination of the photograph with a good magnifying glass is

also to be recommended in this way cicatrices, warts, scars, etc, invisible to the naked eye may be discovered, but too much must not be expected from a magnifying glass, for a too great enlargement causes the unevenness of the paper to appear and thus leads to confusion

8. Always strictly observe the principle of never retouching a photograph; professional photographers may be allowed to do this and are adepts in the art of flattery, but a judicial photograph must resemble the sitter and every retouch spoils this resemblance. There is but one case where retouching may be permitted, i.e., when the photograph is not made for personal use but for outside authorities, and when there are faults on the plate causing marks and blemishes. Such marks may be mistaken for warts, moles, cicatrices, etc., and must therefore be retouched to prevent mistakes.

9. In comparing photographs the following cases may occur:—
    (a) Comparison of one portrait with another,
    (b) Of a portrait with an accused,
    (c) Of a portrait with a person at liberty, and
    (d) Of a portrait with a person's recollection of the subject.

(a) *Comparison of one portrait with another.* In the rare cases where two photographs are of the same size, measurements may be at once taken with the compasses. If the hair and beard are in the way they should be covered up as shown above, and particular signs (warts, cicatrices, etc.) must be carefully looked for. If none of these signs appear on the photographs, the probable date of the photographs must be considered and if need be a medical jurist consulted. If the portraits are of different sizes they must be enlarged, the smaller more in proportion than the larger, and if the colour of the one is totally different from that of the other, a new photograph is indispensable. Thus both portraits are of the same size. As we have said, only really satisfactory results are obtainable by getting rid of everything interfering with the comparison.

(b) *Comparison of a portrait with an accused.* The precaution of clothing and dressing the hair of the accused as he is in the photograph is never superfluous. In a difficult and important case it will be best to photograph him in the same size as the portrait; it is always easier to compare one photograph with another than to compare a photograph with a person.

(c) *Comparison of a portrait with a person at liberty.* Here we have to deal with cases where we have to decide whether a particular person we are searching for is living in a certain locality. Let it not be forgotten that the persons sent out for this purpose will only succeed when they have the portrait firmly impressed on the memory; if they meet the suspected individual they cannot first pull the photograph from a pocket and refer to it for comparison; all the features of the photograph should be carried in the memory. The person must be made to engrave the photograph in his memory feature by feature and we must ascertain that he has done so by examining him on the various details: hair, beard, moustache, shape of eyelids, position of the eyes, cheek bones, nose, ears, etc., even peculiar gestures, manner of bearing, glance, etc., must not be overlooked. We assert that no policeman can at first answer such questions even though he thinks he has looked at the photograph very well. The art of observing must be learnt like everything else. If the policeman knows his photograph by heart he will in most cases recognize, if he meets him, the person he is after. (See the *Portrait Parlé* Chapter III.)

(d) *Comparison of a portrait with our recollection.* We generally attach importance to this method of recognition only when the witness has frequently seen the person he is supposed to recognize. Supposing he has seen him only once as, for example, an individual who has cheated, robbed, or wounded him and gone off, the witness's opinion will be of little value. His recognition will inspire more confidence when the witness is able to pick out the person from a number of similar photographs, and does not recognize him merely because he had a moustache and there is in the collection only one photograph of a person with a moustache. But the greatest precautions must be taken, for enormous difficulty is always experienced in recognizing persons from photographs, especially when the person recognizing is a simple minded fellow who has rarely seen photographs and has never before tried to find resemblances. This is clear from the following example:—in nearly all garrison towns a photographer is to be found near the barracks who has a supply of large pictures (coloured-lithographs) representing a dragoon, artillery-man, hussar, etc., galloping on horseback and brandishing a sword; the raw recruits flock to the photographer who takes their photograph the same size as the ready-made lithograph, cuts out the face and carefully gums it upon the face of the hussar or horseguard, and the warrior finds himself in possession of his portrait complete on horseback and in colours, which he sends to his proud relatives. One of these photographers related to the author how on one occasion he had photographed more than a dozen recruits who paid their money and left addresses to which the photographs were to be sent when ready, but unfortunately he lost the numbers designating each soldier, he therefore sent haphazard a dragoon to each of the addresses indicated, not a single complaint was made although perhaps not one of the fourteen or fifteen pairs of old people received the portrait of their own son; this shows the difficulty with which people recognize photographs.

10. It is appropriate here to call attention to what has been said about the distance at which we can recognize persons. Dr. Vincent in *Legrand & Saule's* "Legal Medicine" lays down that, presuming the eyesight to be normal and the light good, one is able in broad daylight to recognize:—

(a) Persons whom one knows very well at a distance of from 70 to 90 yards, when there are particular and very characteristic signs, 110 yards; in exceptional cases up to 165 yards.

(b) Persons one does not know very well and has not often seen, from 28 to 33 yards.

(c) People one has only seen once, 16 yards.

By moonlight one can recognize, when the moon is at the quarter, persons at a distance of from 21 feet, in bright moonlight at from 23 to 33 feet, and at the very brightest period of the full moon, at a distance of from 33 to 36 feet. In tropical countries the distances for moonlight may be increased.

These are only approximate indications; in practice they are of but slight value. In the first place the statements concerning good normal eyesight and good light are vague, and in addition certain supplemental circumstances often have decisive influence. The gaseous air of the town compared with the limpid atmosphere of the mountains diminishes the range of vision by at least ten per cent, the position of the sun, the background, the wind, and the temperature, also combine to affect it to perhaps the same extent, and our faculty of combination which unconsciously comes into play, may corroborate our perception so that we may be completely led into error. If a person at a distance of say 220 yards sees a man first come out and then go into the house of A, and knows that A lives alone in that house, he will suppose, if the man he has seen resembles to a certain extent the exterior aspect of A, that the man is indeed A, and will maintain the fact, as if he had seen him very distinctly. But he has not seen him properly and his perception is entirely the result of conclusions which may be false. In such cases verification must always in important and serious cases be carried out on the spot whereas in less important cases it may be carried out elsewhere but under conditions as similar as possible.

11. It is important to copy the photograph many times, Bertillon asserts that in urgent cases several thousand copies of a photograph have been made in a single night, it is useless to dwell upon the immense value that the rapid propagation of thousands of copies of the photograph of a suspected criminal may have.

12. When it is required to multiply photographs in great numbers it must be remembered that it can only be done with the assistance of zinc engravings, it is indeed easy to insert in the columns of any newspaper a zinc plate mounted on wood, for an engraving on zinc represents in a way a stamp composed of lines in relief corresponding to the lines of drawing. An engraving on zinc may be made from any drawing but not from a photograph, for a photograph only contains tints. If therefore it is desired to publish in haste in the police and other papers a man's portrait and we possess only his photograph the following process must be followed.

Someone skilled in drawing traces boldly upon the photograph the features of the person so that the outlines are clearly visible, this is a matter of a few minutes. The photograph is then decolorised with chloride of mercury which leaves only the drawing unattacked. This drawing is reproduced by photography upon a plate and engraved on zinc and the block thus obtained is inserted in the newspapers. This kind of drawing is not beautiful but is often easier to identify than a photograph.

Section x.—Finger-Prints.

The advantages of finger-prints over the Bertillon system have become so well established that the latter can with perfect safety be dispensed with altogether as unnecessary for purposes of identification. These advantages have been well set out in a memorandum published by the Dresden Investigation Department —

1. The necessary accessories—a piece of tin, a bit of indiarubber, and printing-ink, are above all cheap and easy to procure.

2. Any person can after half-an-hour's practice take clean finger-prints.

3. The finger-prints can be taken by any policeman at any place.

4. To check a sequence of recorded finger-prints, the comparison of a single impression suffices.

5. The prints of the whole 10 fingers can be taken very much more quickly than body measurements.

6. It is not necessary for a person to remove his clothes.

7. The pattern of a finger-print never alters during the life of an individual.

8. Mistakes being impossible, no second search is necessary.

A Practical application of Finger-Prints

Finger-prints are now in common use for the detection of criminals as well as the elucidation of criminal mysteries in nearly all civilised countries. It has been known for a long time that the lines on the fingers are different for each person, also that, in the course of a year they may come together or go further apart, but if nothing in the shape of a wound has taken place they do not really alter. *Welker*, the anthropologist, gives the impressions of the palm of his hand for the years 1856 and 1897 which fully confirm this. The finger-tips of a mummy in the Natural Museum of Vienna show after thousands of years clear papillary lines. They can be seen on corpses that have lain in water for a week, the lines only disappearing with mortification. Even when the tip of a finger is lost, the new tip shows the same pattern, though of course, transversal wounds disturb this.

From the most ancient times the Chinese have used the lines on the tips of the fingers of criminals for their identification. *Sir William Herschel* adopted this method in India in doing business with the natives instead of their usual signatures, and in the Indian army finger-prints of the soldiers are always taken and preserved. *Galton* was the first to see the advantages of this system and by his careful observation and collation of examples brought it into favour as a means of recognition of old offenders.

Classification of finger-prints is not really difficult. With the help of a magnifying glass the marks are examined in all possible ways and carefully noted down. It is seen that a line is broken or divides into two separate branches, or two lines come together to form one ridge. All points such as these afford excellent means of dividing the various classes of finger-prints or identifying with greater certainty two pictures of the same finger taken at different times. And here we come to the kernel of the whole question. These remarkable signs which appear on the body three months before birth and after death only disappear with the final dissolution of the corpse, maintain their formation unaltered during the whole lifetime. Take for example the two pictures of the forefinger of *Sir William Herschel*, the right hand one dating from 1860 the other from 1888. Although in the latter the lines are somewhat broader and fainter, yet the first glance shows them to be the same and closer examination proves that the lines of the 1860 finger-prints are exactly the same as those of 1888. *Galton* compared at lengthy intervals the finger-prints of eight persons and at the first examination he noticed 296 particular points which he found exactly the same at the second examination. There is no possible doubt as to the durability of these signs; the dimensions may alter a little with time but their character remains the same, just as a piece of lace can be twisted in all directions without damaging its original pattern. The accompanying plates have been kindly lent by the Madras Government. They were issued with a Government Order upon the utilisation of finger-prints in India which contained a considerable amount of information on the subject. In explanation of the plates the Order stated as follows:—

'For the information of officers, who may have occasion to examine finger-prints with a view to verifying the identity of the individual from whose hands they have been taken, it is necessary to premise that the impressions recorded form clear and distinct patterns which are constant and ineradicable. Each individual's hand presents a separate set of impressions which a slight scrutiny suffices to distinguish from the finger-prints taken from any other hand. Nor do the impressions taken from the same hand at different periods of life change with lapse of time except as has been remarked, for alterations "such as would be found in lace, which after being washed and stretched will show the same pattern and number of meshes although they may be somewhat distorted in shape." There are three main types of pattern, namely, 'arches,' 'loops,' and 'whorls,' specimens of which are shown in the accompanying *Plate I*.

'The pattern is an "arch" when the ridges in the centre run from one side to the other of the bulb without making any backward turn or twist, a "loop" when there is a single backward turn but no twist, and a "whorl" when there is a turn through at least one circle. Loops on the fingers may further be distinguished as either *inner* loops when they open towards the thumb side, or *outer* loops towards the little finger (*Plates I and II*).

'It will ordinarily suffice to examine each finger-print either by the naked eye or with the aid of a magnifying glass in order to ascertain if in each case the distinctive pattern corresponds with that noticeable in the impression previously recorded. Thus supposing *Plate II* (left hand) to represent the permanent record, it would be necessary to examine the new set of impressions in order to make certain that the pattern of the fourth or little finger was a loop, that of the third finger a whorl, and so on. A variation in any one case would be sufficient to leave no doubt that false personation was being attempted. Should the general patterns correspond, a closer examination may, if thought necessary, be made (either with or without a magnifying glass) in order to ascertain whether each line in a particular impression coincides in appearance with the corresponding line in the finger-print forming the permanent record.

'To further illustrate these rules, *Plates III to V* appended have been prepared in the office of the Inspector-General of Police. *Plate III* exhibits impressions of the thumb and fingers of the right hand taken with an interval of 2½ years. *Plate IV* represents the corresponding impressions of the first and second fingers enlarged. *Plate V* is a skeleton chart of *Plate II* and shows the axes of the ridges with the points of reference numbered.'

H*indl* divides finger-prints into four main types of pattern which he calls 'loops,' 'arches,' 'whorls' and 'composites.' This is also the classification adopted in England. To these arithmetical and algebraical values can be given so that 1024 combinations can be made therefrom. These are the bases of a very learned system introduced by F. K. King of London.

But not only are finger-prints of importance for identifying and

(188)

PLATE I

FINGER PRINTS

| ARCHES | LOOPS | WHORLS |

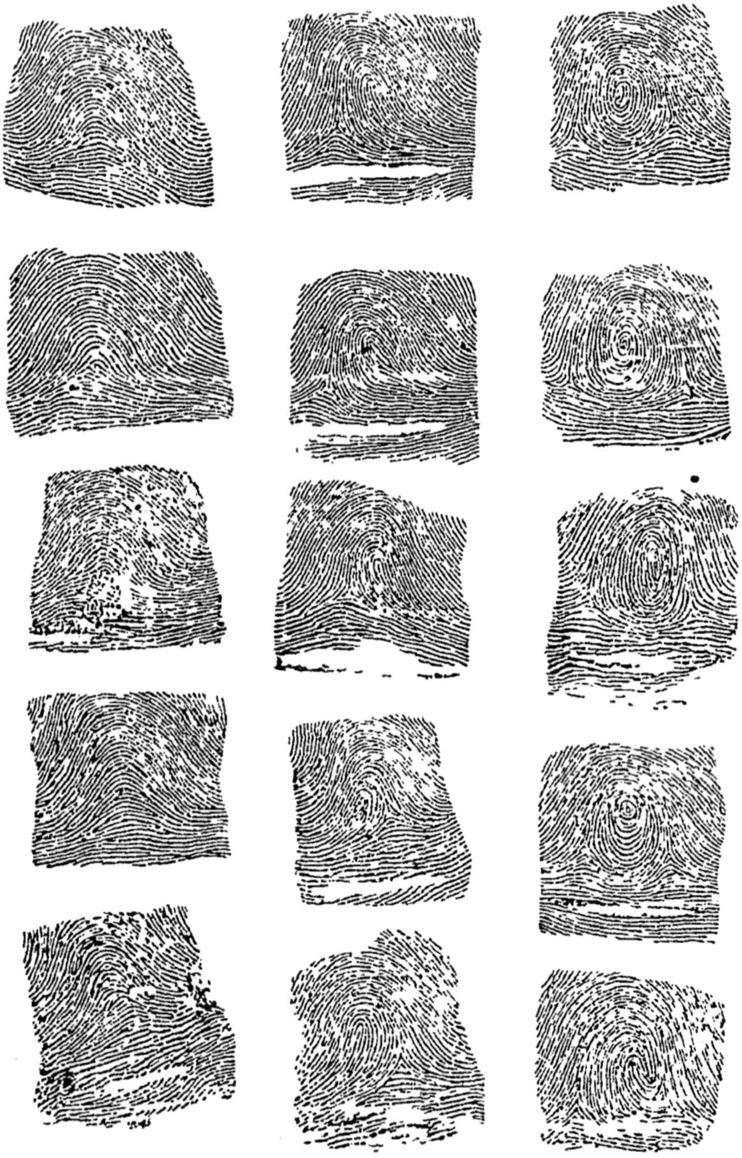

(189)

PLATE II

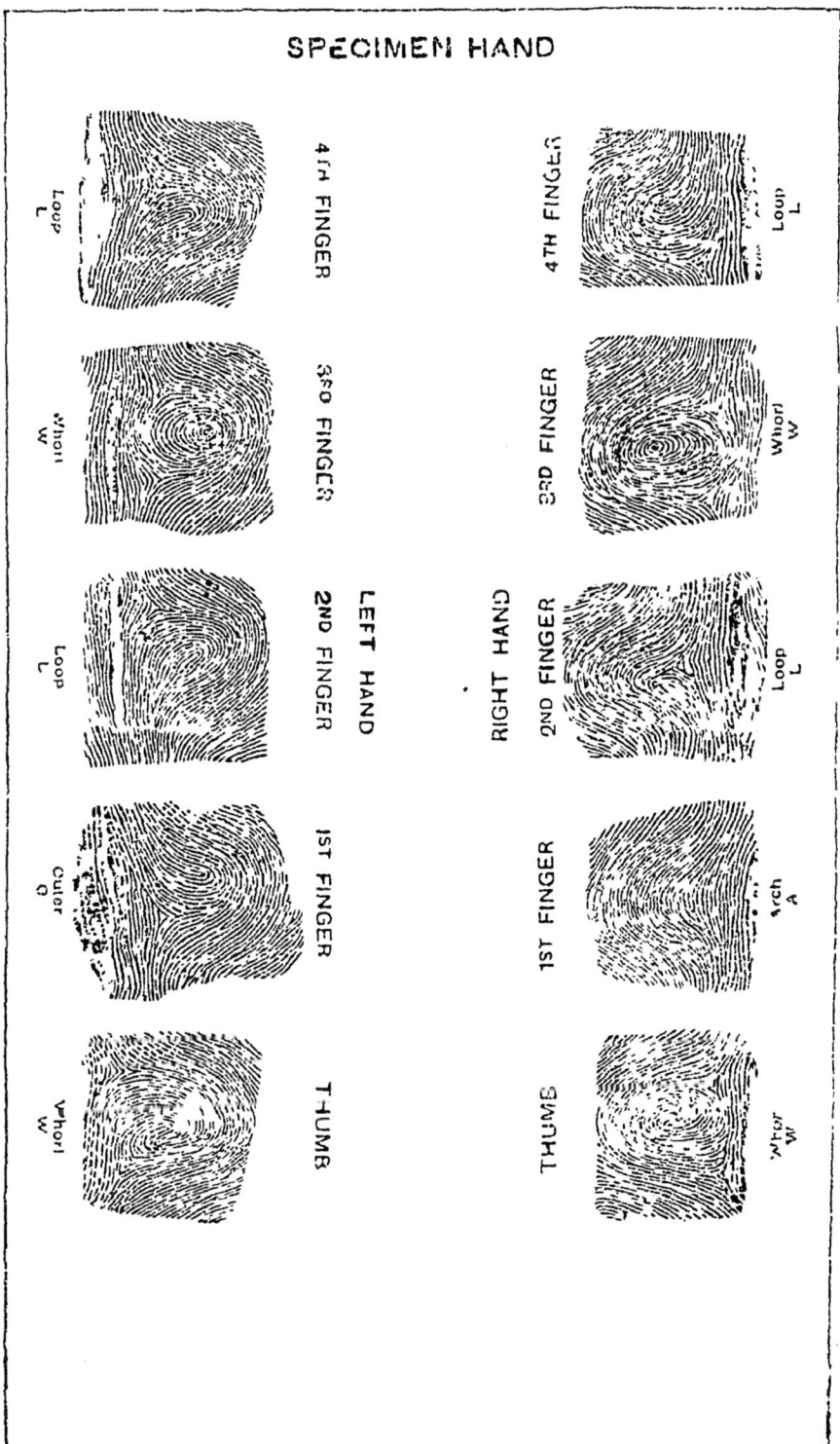

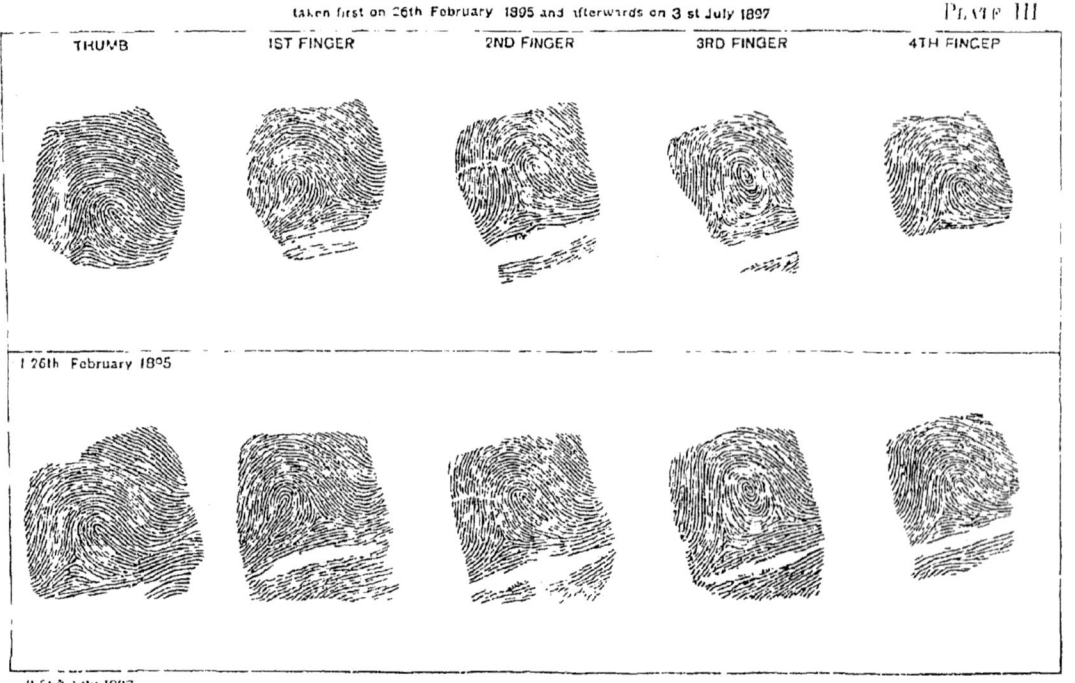

(191)

PLATE IV

CORRESPONDING PORTIONS ENLARGED
of
FIRST and SECOND FINGERS (PLATE III)

26-ii-95 & 31 vii-97 with axes of ridges

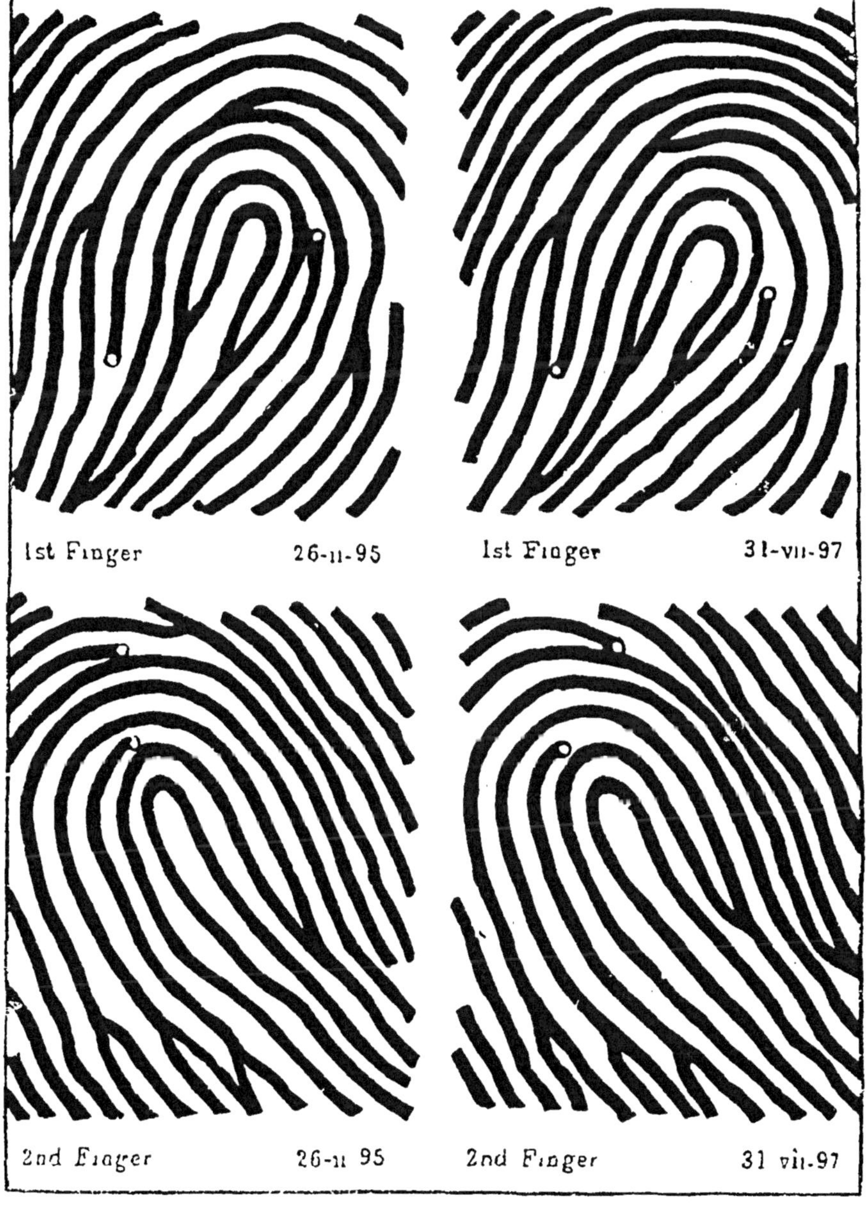

1st Finger   26-ii-95   1st Finger   31-vii-97

2nd Finger   26-ii-95   2nd Finger   31 vii-97

(192)

PLATE V

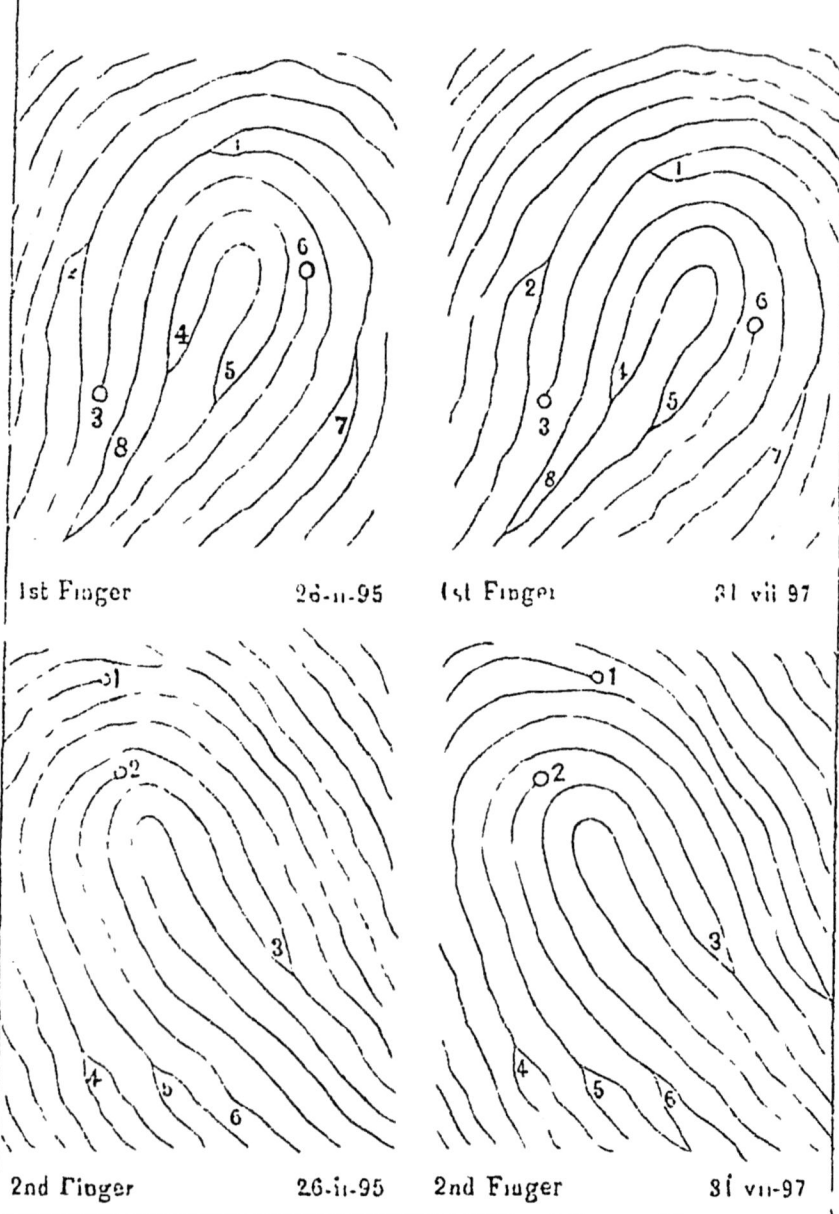

classifying old offenders but they are also of great value from another point of view, namely, the actual elucidation of particular crimes. It is to Mr. Joseph Farnside that elaboration of this branch of finger-prints is largely due, though Mr. E. R. Henry, Chief of the London Police, first brought the subject to the front in England, and the standard work on the subject is written by him, namely, "The Uses and Classification of Finger-prints." It is now established that in the detection of crimes too great value cannot be placed upon finger-prints, as the following cases cited by Mr. G. E. Mallett (*Strand Magazine*, May, 1905) will show.

The first case was in the early part of the year 1905. An office in the chief street of the city of Bradford was entered by means of breaking a glass panel in the door, and money and stamps were stolen. In pulling out the glass from the door the thief left a finger-print on the glass, which was brought away, photographed, and enlarged. Suspicion fell on a person whose finger-prints had previously been taken, and on the file being searched his left thumb was found to be identical with the impression on the glass.

In another case several burglaries had been committed in the district. The property stolen was of a kind which could not be readily identified—chiefly cash. After several of these robberies had passed undetected there came at length an instance where a small polished wood box, used to contain homœopathic medicines, had been removed from its customary position. In consequence this box was carefully examined, and the lid was found to bear a finger impression, which was photographed. A person was suspected of the offence, who had previously been in custody, and it was natural of course at once to proceed to enlarge the finger impression on the medicine box and compare it with the registered impression. When it was found that the impression on the box was identical with that of the suspected person, orders were issued for his arrest. A number of incriminating circumstances appearing against him, he was convicted.

In a case in September, 1904, cash was stolen from a club in Bradford. The thief got in through a window, and had helped himself to a bottle of beer. The finger-print on the bottle was very obscure indeed, but after being chemically treated, photographed, and enlarged, it came out clear enough for the purposes of identification. Suspicion fell on a sailor who had been observed by the police in the district. Circumstances led to his arrest, and he failed to account for some money. He was remanded and his finger-prints were taken. His right middle finger corresponded exactly with the impression on the beer-bottle. In passing it should be noted with regard to this case that without the finger-print it would have been impossible to obtain a conviction.

The next case is not without its humorous element. Two men were found in possession of a quantity of stolen property. They were arrested on suspicion. Their explanation was that the property had been given to them by a man unknown to carry away. Inquiry was made and it was found that the articles had been taken from the house of a minister who was away on his holidays. The thieves had got into the minister's residence by removing the slates over the bathroom. After getting through the ceiling of the bathroom they let themselves down on to the floor below by means of the bathroom door, which stood open. In doing so some finger-print impressions were left on the top of the door. One impression was a very plain one. The bathroom door was taken bodily but very carefully from its post. The door (seven feet high) was treated with the utmost respect, and, protected by paper, was conveyed on a cart to the town-hall, where it was carried up to the detective studio and photographed.

The last case cited by Mr. Mallett is perhaps the most remarkable of all. It was reported to the police on a Sunday that the premises of a well-known bowling-green club in Bradford had been entered on the Saturday night, and some five hundred bottles of whisky and other liquor had been carried away to an adjacent wood. The customary careful examination of the premises showed that the thieves had been helping themselves to whisky. Apparently only one vessel had been used—a small tumbler of thin glass. On this there was a finger-print, very faintly discernible. The finger-print was chemically treated with hydrofluoric acid, photographed, and enlarged. Considering that the impression was upon glass, it was wonderful how clearly the ridges of the finger were eventually reproduced. The impression was evidently of the "whorl" type. There was no clue of any kind in this case, but on looking at the register the impression of the finger of a man was found who had been remanded some time previously for another offence, but had been discharged. In this case the man whose finger-print was on the glass was at once arrested, and when he was charged with the robbery confessed to being guilty, and he gave information to the police which enabled them both to arrest another man implicated and to recover part of the stolen property.

One of the most remarkable murder cases of modern times was the trial of the brothers Stratton accused of a crime which took place on the 27th of March, 1905, and became known as the "mask murders." An old man and his wife were brutally murdered one night in their shop and their cash box rifled. All that was left behind by the burglars were three masks very roughly made from the tops of stockings and a finger-print on the tray of the cash box. This was the first time finger-print evidence was ever submitted in an English murder trial, and the criticism with which it was received is interesting. Enlargements of the photographs taken of the finger-print found on the cash box and Alfred Stratton's right thumb were produced by the Police Inspector, while copies and magnifying glasses were handed to the jury to enable them to follow the parallel characteristics of identity that the officer pointed out on a large chart which he held up. He asserted that he could find no characteristic visible in the print on the cash box which did not agree with Alfred Stratton's thumb. In cross-examination the Inspector said, 'That in points, which he could not agree with counsel were discrepancies, the pressure applied by the digit would play a large part. It was only a mark of perspiration and dust on the cash box, and a mark made on evenly distributed ink in the other. Pressure would give a curved line in the one, and lack of pressure a straight line in the other."

It was pointed out to the Inspector by the aid of the compasses that the distances between certain points of identity relied on by the witness varied as much as the twelfth of an inch on the cash box print and Alfred's thumb print. The Inspector explained this by saying that the two enlargements were on a slightly different scale, and he added that as they were thirteen times the natural size the difference of one-twelfth of an inch would have to be divided by 13, and so would be infinitesimal in the original prints. Finger-prints of the dead couple and of all who were in the habit of being in the house were also presented to the jury to show that the finger-print on the tray of the cash box could not possibly be theirs. The Judge in summing up said that, as to the finger-print identification, where the prints were taken for the purpose of identification of a criminal whose impressions the police already possessed, the system seemed to be 'extremely reliable.' But it was a different thing to apply the system to a casual mark made by the perspiration of the thumb on an object. You could not expect that it would correspond with the same degree of accuracy. It would be blurred and the other taken from the suspect would be clear. So it was in this case.

"Consequently," the Judge continued, 'this is not so satisfactory as it would have been if you could suppose the murderer had a pot of ink and made a definite impression. But there is one thing that is clear about this. If it is true that people's fingers do vary so much as has been described there is an extraordinary amount of resemblance in the two photos and to a certain extent it is corroborative evidence. None of you, I should think, would like to act on this alone. The point is not whether you will go on this alone, but the point is whether it is not substantial evidence corroborating the other statements that Alfred Stratton must have been one of the men on the scene of the murder."

Both prisoners were convicted sentenced to death, and executed.

B. The manner of recording Finger-prints

The examination of finger-prints is no easy matter. It is therefore above all necessary that good and true impressions should be taken which can be kept and compared with others. To make true and sharp copies containing no gaps *Galton* gives two methods. Firstly, a sheet of glass or a metal plate may be covered with lamp-black and a finger-print made thereon. At all parts touched by the elevations of the skin the lamp-black comes off. The following is the method now generally adopted. The finger is placed on a metal glass, or porcelain plate on which black printer's ink has been spread as smoothly as possible and the impression is then taken on a piece of paper. The ink adheres to the elevations of the skin which are thus reproduced on the paper.

The following are the rules laid down by the Indian Government for the taking of finger-prints:—

'The apparatus required for taking impressions consists of the following articles:—

A sheet of tin or copper 10½ inches by 7 or of such other size as experience may show to be most convenient, screwed down by its corners to a board one inch thick, an ordinary printer's roller and a tin of printer's ink. Both roller and slab must be thoroughly cleansed with kerosine-oil on each occasion, dried with a rag and put out of the way of dust."

The manner in which impressions should be taken is explained below:—

(1) Squeeze a drop of ink on the plate and work it with the roller till it forms an even layer over the surface. The ink must be so thin as to allow the colour of the plate to show through it.

"(11) Then take the little finger of the left hand roll the bulb slightly on the inked slab and roll it again on the paper in the space marked for that finger do the same with each of the other fingers and thumb in succession so that the imprints of them may be taken in their allotted places on the paper"

'Note.—A drop or two of kerosine oil added to the ink makes it more fluid The inked finger should only be rolled once on the card from one side to the other and then removed cleanly without smudging the pattern To afford clear scope for identification, the whole of the finger (or thumb) between the tip and first joint must be impressed'

Section xi.—Geometrical Identification.

H Matthews (British Journal Almanac 1890, p 112) makes an ingenious proposal, according to him photographs may establish the identities of persons with absolute certainty even after the lapse of a number of years since the time when the last photographs were taken His system is based on the no doubt accurate idea that certain dimensions of the face of an adult human being do not change, if, at all events, there have been no illnesses or injuries to the skull in the meantime

The photographs to be compared are first very greatly enlarged and in the same proportions. The greater the enlargement, that is to say, the larger the photographs to be compared are, the more decisive will be the proof, for the errors of measurement which may be committed will be of less importance

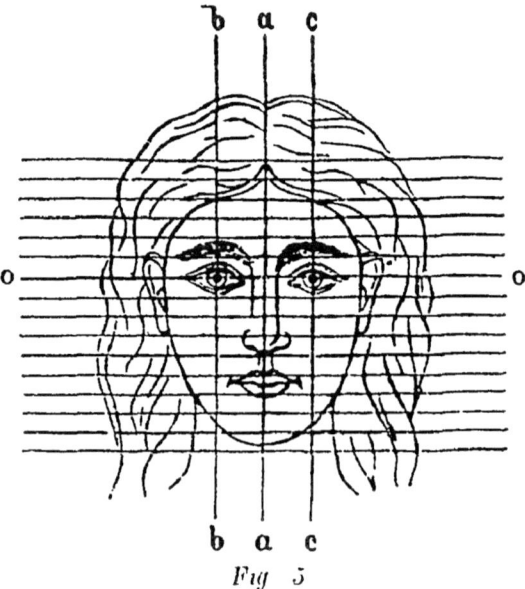

Fig 5

Next a fundamental line (Fig 5) is drawn through the pupils of the eyes, the distance separating the middle of the two pupils is divided into two equal parts through this dividing point a perpendicular a a is drawn and two parallels are drawn thereto through the pupils (b b and c c) Finally parallels are drawn to the fundamental line o o above and below that line as far as the chin and the roots of the hair, these parallels are numbered

1, 2 3, etc. The distance between the horizontal lines is exactly the same as the diameter of the iris, that is to say, of the pupil of the eye on the picture.

The verification of identity may be done in two ways: —

1. The two portraits are cut into two pieces along the line $a\ a$ and the halves of each are interchanged. If the portraits are of the same person all the other lines will fit.

2. The two portraits (unmounted) are placed one upon the other, so that the lines $o\ o$ and $a\ a$ coincide. If the portraits are identical the other lines will also coincide.

This method is to be recommended in important cases.

CHAPTER VI

THE LEGITIMATE SPHERE OF THE PUBLIC PRESS.

It is natural for the Investigating Officer to find it impossible to escape from the influence of the great power wielded by the Public Press, we have therefore to discuss the position he ought to take up as regards that influence and in what way it may be of service to him.

The connection between the Investigating Officer and the Press is based upon a community of interest, the Investigating Officer is interested in crime and everything connected with it, and the daily Press is interested in great measure in the same questions. An experienced journalist who had accurate information of what the public preferred to read in its daily paper once furnished the following list in which the heads are arranged in order of importance :—

1. Births, deaths, marriage and divorce
2. The reports of crime and criminal trials
3. Local news
4. { The serial story
     The theatrical news
     The short story
5. { Special telegrams
     Political communications
     Leading Articles
6. Scientific notes, and reviews

From this list it may be seen how much people are interested in communications relating to crime, and as the interest of the public is the interest of the journalist, the place of honour is given to these communications. The experienced and expert journalist would rather give up every other article in his paper than the first report of a criminal case. And this is where he finds himself in conflict with the law, for in all civilised States the precipitate divulgence of details connected with judicial cases is considered to be more or less illegal. True it is that there are few laws more often broken than those of which we speak; every day we read in the paper exact descriptions of crimes which have just been committed, especially when these crimes are particularly outrageous and horrible. How much truth can be found in such reports is another question; more than one of us have been unable to help saying to ourselves on reading these newspaper reports :—" I seem to have heard of a case like that ", so much had the case brought to the notice of the Investigating Officer on the previous day been disfigured.

It is easy to understand how this comes about when we observe the manner in which the news given by the paper is fabricated. The Investigating Officer and his assistants have sworn to guard their professional secrets, and in every crime the manner in which it has been committed is considered to be relevant to the matters to be embraced by this professional reticence. In consequence of this the Investigating Officer and his auxiliaries wrap themselves in the impenetrable mantle of secrecy, and tell the journalist nothing; the reporters therefore fall upon the watchman, the witnesses, and their relations, upon the jailors of the prison, upon the cabman who has driven the Investigating Officer to the scene of the crime upon the people of the house and upon other persons who have or may have some knowledge of the matter,—and then compose their narrative a narrative said to be "worthy of all belief." We may cite the case of a reporter who with particular cunning had entered into the closest relations with the housemaid of the Investigating Officer, in order to learn from her what her master related to his wife at table with reference to interesting cases. In this way are those horrible descriptions which overflow our newspapers fabricated, of which "we legal gentlemen" take no notice, saying — "these newspaper reports are all quite indifferent to us."

But they are not in reality so indifferent, and, if regarded more closely, we must be convinced that these inaccurate reports do harm; in the first place falsehood in itself is evil, and for that reason alone ought not to be tolerated. The importance and power of the press are far too great not to persuade us that it causes an immense amount of prejudice by furnishing continually, as it does, inaccurate statements of fact.

We must, moreover, consider the influence which the report may exercise upon all those persons who have something to do with the case, be it intimately or remotely. Whoever has seen or heard something of the "case in question" takes a particular interest in it. Every such man gives himself an absolutely excessive importance, and whenever an individual's eyes fall by chance upon a list of names among which he finds his own, and his attention is, as we are sure it will be, first drawn by that name, he will become particularly interested in the case, for he "has taken some part in it"; he reads minutely everything connected with it and everything which he knows better than anyone else. But, if he has some real knowledge of a case he will be called as a witness and will be no longer able to depose with an unbiassed mind since he has read inaccurate reports.

Not only the man in the street but Investigating Officers themselves have a certain confidence in everything in print and allow themselves in spite of many disillusions to be influenced by newspaper articles; "there must be some truth in it" one thinks, and if one reads several times over the account of the case otherwise than as one has seen it oneself, one ends by doubting oneself, and, in spite of the best will to speak the truth, one gives an account of the case different to what one would have given if not under exterior influence.

Newspaper reports, moreover, induce the public to form a definite opinion upon the case itself and upon the culpability of the author of the crime, so that the verdict is often pronounced by the public long before the competent authorities have delivered their judgment. The official verdict, once given is no longer in agreement with public opinion, which latter was based on erroneous information; moreover the public does not change its opinion, even in view of the light which is shed during the hearing of the case; the decision of the authorities is criticised, and it is not necessary to set out the bad effect of everything which is calculated to disturb the confidence which ought to be placed in the Powers That Be

The only means of remedying this evil is to allow the Investigating Officer to *himself* communicate the essential matters concerning criminal cases to the newspaper the latter on its part would be compelled to keep silent upon all the other details of the case There seems to be an air of censure about this, but in reality it is not so bad as that In the first place we do not mean that the question should be regulated by law, for we imagine that it will be generally very easy to come to an agreement upon this subject with the reporters of the local paper even in a large town The Investigating Officer would provide the reporters with the news in question while the latter would engage only to print the communications of the former and to insert on their part everything which the Investigating Officer desires to make public

The tact of the Investigating Officer will guide him in *what* should be printed in a given case, and *how* and *when* it should be published

We do not desire by any means to advise the Investigating Officer to give the papers inaccurate information in order to baffle the unknown criminal or inspire his accomplices with confidence, etc But it is not necessary to tell all that one knows or all that one suspects or, if one wishes to tell it, the propitious moment must be awaited The manner in which *what* may be told *should* be told is not, speaking generally, easy to indicate, and it is not even easy to express it in a particular case, but it is possible to find the correct method by taking into account all the circumstances accompanying the crime The best way to proceed will be for the Investigating Officer to himself write out the note for the paper without long hesitation or reflection, and then consider the consequences which it will have from the point of view of the author of the crime in the event of his reading it, the same applying to the accomplices, witnesses, etc, if they come to know of it, at the moment when the note is drawn up the general turn of the case will be fairly well known and after a little reflection the effects of the note will also be guessed

More than one success in important criminal cases may be traced entirely to the use that has been made of a newspaper, but on the other hand, it is also certain that one is exposed to very great dangers when an awkward use is made of the press Here is an example of this in a case of murder accompanied by theft, it had been possible owing to a series of fortuitous circumstances to describe very accurately, immediately after the crime, a number of the articles stolen, although the murdered person lived all alone and had no dealings with the world It was supposed that the author of the crime, then still unknown, was well aware of this peculiarity of the woman in question, and would not fear to sell the stolen articles at the earliest possible moment In order to rapidly inform the pawnshops the Investigating Officer resolved to publish at once the description of such of the stolen articles as were accurately known, and succeeded in doing so in the evening papers, although the murder had only been committed on the morning of the same day But this publication had a contrary result to what had been anticipated, for the author of the crime had, extraordinarily enough, got rid of no article that morning, and it came out later on that it was only in the evening, after the papers had appeared, that he sold such of the stolen articles as had not been described in the evening papers. In this case it would have been much better to have kept back the description.

On the other hand those mysterious airs so often affected by the authorities are quite ridiculous and often harmful. One will be doing the right thing if one takes into account the consequences which the divulgence of information may have. If there is no adequate reason to suppose that this divulgence will have bad consequences there need be no hesitation in speaking out.

But special care must be taken that the information published is accurate. The following cited case shows this. It is also an interesting example of the value of unprofessional expert advice (Chapter I. Section 1). Some time ago in London a lady committed suicide by poisoning in a West-End Hotel. The *Morning Leader* in its report said:—' She took the greatest care to destroy every possible trace of her identity, even to buying new clothes and underclothes which bore no apparent mark of any kind. But she missed one little detail—the red thread figuring on her dressing-jacket. This mark was given out at the inquest as a laundry mark.

E U X A O Z

' Those letters have been published far and wide—in England, France, Germany, and in America. Hundreds of laundry-keepers have been interrogated, with E U X A O Z as a clue to work upon. After a lapse of days, the President of the Laundry Association has come forward and has proved, after his expert examination, that with the exception of the E, these supposed letters are numbers stitched in angles. He, therefore, reads the inscription thus:

E 18,992

There is a possibility that the last figure may be a 0—but in his experienced eye, the others are plain. He is convinced that they do not form a laundry mark, because laundry people never use so many figures. He thinks that the mark is a dyer's and cleaner's mark. Thus, says he, it is certain that this row of figures has been entered, as a reference, in the books of some dyer and cleaner's firm, and it is possible that the name and address of the owner of that jacket may be entered alongside."

When the Investigating Officer succeeds in obtaining the good will of the reporters, he can in return for his complacency expect many kindnesses when dark days arrive. The Investigating Officer often finds it necessary to have official notes published, but official advertisements have this peculiarity that no one reads them, especially those persons whom they most concern, but if these publications are inserted among the general news of the day they are read with avidity and their object is attained. The discovery of witnesses and of the owners of the various articles, questions concerning such a state of affairs or such an event, invitations to come and inspect certain articles in the possession of the Investigating Officer, the search for people who have disappeared, and a thousand other similar communications which would fill up without result the police gazettes and papers would have some chance of success, if they appeared in the public press under the head of "actualities." When important matters are in question a few words may be added to the note requesting other papers to notice it in their columns.

In such cases the press is for the most part quite ready to assist justice, especially the more important and better class of paper. On one occasion, for example, persons a long way off were placed in a position to give information in a case about which a note had appeared in a small country paper; this note found its way into the principal papers of the capital, and finally, even American papers, which had reproduced it, were received. Some of them indeed had added a few words to the note embodying the assurance that they had been happy to be able to serve a good cause. And, what is more important from a fiscal point of view, all this costs the State absolutely nothing.

But in order for the Investigating Officer to be able to make use of the press, he must not only hold the journalists in hand and proceed with tact, but he must also be allowed complete and entire liberty by the authorities. The latter ought to know whence these notes originate and that the Investigating Officer is conducting the case as it ought to be conducted, and not come down upon the paper some fine day for the premature divulgence of secrets which are considered to be harmful to the investigation.

PART II.—KNOWLEDGE SPECIAL TO THE INVESTIGATING OFFICER.

CHAPTER VII

PRACTICES OF CRIMINALS.

In this chapter we shall deal with some of the smart tricks and dodges employed by rogues and criminals. The Investigating Officer who endeavours to learn and keep count of these will obtain the knowledge of a great number of facts, will know in what direction and in what manner he must commence and continue his investigations, and will be able, more or less, to form an idea of the personality of the individual under observation. Among modern specialists, F. Ch. B. Avé-Lallemant, in his work, *Das Deutsche Gaunerthum* ("The practices of German rogues") gives the most accurate information on this subject. Although somewhat out of date in certain parts, his book has furnished us with much valuable information, to which has been added our own observations collected from special works, from private communications, and from personal experience.

Section i.—Disguising the Face.

Criminals have constantly recourse to disguises. With what cleverness and persistency they keep on disguising themselves, and yet it is not superfluous to urge attention to the matter, for indeed there is nothing which malefactors will not try to simulate, nothing they will not try to dissimulate. Frequently the medical man alone can decide whether or not there be dissimulation, and it will be the business of the Investigating Officer to place no faith in pretended infirmities and maladies, and to call in regularly the advice of the medical man.

But here again there are numerous cases where it is impossible to fall back upon the medical man, it may be the nature of the affair excludes medical assistance or, it may be, an important decision must be come to before being able to call in the aid of the physician. We may therefore mention some of the disguises which a criminal assumes for the purpose of altering his appearance from the description given in the warrant of arrest. *As a general rule it may be laid down that a novice commits a crime and afterwards disguises himself, while the expert criminal disguises himself before the commission of the offence. The former therefore tries to escape in disguise, the latter on the contrary, in his natural appearance, and consequently he finds himself much more favourably situated than the former.* If the criminal be captured or even placed under observation, the disguise is easily detected and the individual is generally quickly convicted of having committed the offence.

Suppose then that a novice at the game commits a piece of roguery: he has no beard and wears his hair cut short: he is pursued on this description but travels disguised in a red beard and a long-haired wig. This disguise will be quickly detected and he will be compelled to dispense with it. The expert scoundrel does exactly the opposite; when committing the fraud he dons the red beard and the long-haired peruque; he is so described in the warrant; he is pursued; but immediately after the offence he throws away his beard and wig and the most minute search can no longer discover him.

When a warrant of arrest, containing a description of the "man wanted," is studied, a certain point of view must be assumed: everything which appears unnatural should be considered as suspicious and unauthentic; it matters little whether this unnatural appearance be artificial, designed only to disguise the individual or whether it be genuine. In both cases, the fugitive will get rid of it if he can. If, for example, the warrant says—"an unkempt black beard"—either it was false, or it has been shaved off after the crime and before the flight; if it is said—"he wears blue spectacles"—either they have been put on specially for the crime and then removed, or the criminal is really in the habit of wearing blue spectacles and has got rid of them during his flight, however accustomed he may be to wear them. Even special signs incorporated, so to speak, with his person will not be of much value. Thus the criminal may, at the moment of the offence, assume a very high-toned or falsetto voice, or if the timbre of his voice is naturally high he will pretend, often with great difficulty, to possess a deep-toned bass voice. He will also thus disguise his walk, carriage, mannerisms, costume, even his height.

For instance, a swindler had managed to cash with a banker a number of false coupons most cleverly forged, but the description the banker gave of the man, which was immediately published, was not true in a single particular; the beard, the spectacles, the hair, the dress, the voice, the corpulence, the height, all were false. The strangest part was that the man was described as being below middle height, although he was notably tall. As a matter of fact, on his visit he wore a long greatcoat, the banker's desk, about the height of an ordinary bank counter, was boarded up in front, hence the man could easily cover the short distance between the door and the desk and back again with his knees bent, thus in the bank he produced the impression of a short man.

Swindlers also pretend to special characteristics, clubfoot, stiffened arm, deformed hand, and if this be mentioned in the description, generally in big black type, the inexperienced constable or Investigating Officer sees only this peculiarity and pays no attention to people who do not walk lame, who have no stiff arm or withered hand. It is the same with birthmarks, warts, etc. A well-known railway pick-pocket at the moment of effecting a big theft, made on his cheek a large mole with carpenter's glue mixed with grated leather. A cash-keeper, who had committed serious defalcations, had a large natural wart by the side of his eye. This wart was specially mentioned in the warrant of arrest, but the fugitive had immediately after the offence, shaved it clean off and placed spectacles on his nose. The small cut made by the operation was horizontal, i.e. from the eye towards the ear, and when afterwards a very fine, straight reddish scar was produced, it looked exactly like a mark caused by the pressure of the arm of the spectacles.

The art of beautifying has in these days attained great perfection: warts, burns, red stains, scars, freckles etc. are removed without any difficulty; even discolorations of the skin can be removed without leaving any roughness thanks to the process invented by Dr. I. Paschkis of Vienna: the skin covering the portions affected is tattoed with special colours, it remains reddish for two or three days, but at the end of a week assumes a normal tint. We can readily understand that criminals often display a lively interest in these processes of beautification. An infallible method of making faded scars visible was discovered nearly a century ago by Devergie. The places on which scars especially of burns are supposed to have existed, are lightly beaten with the palm of the hand until the spot becomes red. The old scar will appear white and of its original shape. In all this class of business face massage now plays a great part.

The changes in physiognomy produced by changes of complexion are well known, and whoever is acquainted with the excellent composition of the pigments usually employed will not be surprised at criminals making such frequent use of them. It is especially easy to transform a dark rough complexion into one of a delicate rose tint; it is more difficult to turn the blonde into a brunette, especially when the illusion has to be effective at close quarters. A deep rouge tint can, however, in some cases be remarkably well imitated with a solution of permanganate of potash. This colour takes well, lasts a long time, and resists washing.

An artificial paleness generally goes along with a sickly appearance; the person affecting it walks slowly, painfully, and doubled-up, his neck is carefully wrapped up with a shawl and he coughs incessantly. Women are special adepts at this kind of imitation. (For *tattooing*, see Chapter I Section II, C.) The criminal is enormously assisted in his task if he comes to know the description given of himself, and that is easy enough. In important cases it appears in all the newspapers, in other cases it is inserted in the police journals and circulars, which in their very nature and to attain their object cannot remain hidden in the hands of the authorities, but must be brought to the knowledge of dealers in second-hand goods and antiquities, pawnbrokers, and the like, to acquaint them with the nature of the missing articles. But among such people, the person wanted can but too easily learn the contents of the warrant. In an extremity he applies to the authority itself either directly or through the intermediary of a comrade, who, on the pretext of giving information obtains a sight of the warrant for the arrest of his friend and his exact description.

Such impudent boldness is more common than one would suppose: in no other way can be explained the rapidity with which fugitive criminals obtain such accurate details of the description given of them. But whoever should preach prudence in this direction would do more harm than good, for we cannot overlook the files of descriptions which must remain valueless if not published as widely as possible. Besides, they pass through the hands of so many people that the individual described has little difficulty in obtaining the desired information. The only remedy for this danger, and that but a partial one, is to prepare the description of the fugitive with much thought and minute care; that is to say, in a given case we shall ask ourselves—which are the details that must be necessarily true *i.e.*, that cannot be changed *e.g.* a stature singularly short, a missing limb, the colour of the eyes, the form of the nose, etc., and which are those that can be changed. From what we have said above, the number of the members of the former class is seen to be small and cannot be too much restricted; in fact it will be well to deem any characteristic absolutely unchangeable more as an exception than a rule.

For all the other special characteristics we must ask in what manner and with what object, falsification can take place: an approximate result will soon be arrived at, and we must stick to the description thus obtained. The most difficult task is that of the police officer who with the description furnished to him must search for the criminal throughout the whole town, in hotels, in passing trains, etc., without having the time to compare persons one after the other with a description containing characteristics, some disguised, some real. He can succeed only by practice and a natural gift for taking in things at a glance. The task of the Investigating Officer is easier when an individual suspected of being the criminal "wanted" is brought before him. If the description does not agree with the appearance of the man he will in the first place bear in mind that almost the whole may be false; he will then make sure that some mistake of observation has not slipped into the description when written down; finally he will examine one by one the signs which do not correspond and verify their intrinsic value, that is to say, will see whether the divergence noted may or may not be the result of falsification. We do not say that a definite decision must be immediately pronounced, for no change can be pronounced impossible so long as the specialist has not been consulted.

The author has often believed that certain transformations were impossible but been speedily deceived by the medical man, the dentist, the orthopædist, the maker of trusses, belts, etc., the hairdresser, and woman experts in the arts of the toilette. Every experienced surgical belt maker can tell us how to conceal and how artificially to produce *e.g.* deviation of the spinal column, hunch back, deformity of the foot, etc.; every theatrical hairdresser can furnish information on the changes wrought in the visage, or as they call it, the *mask*.

Having just indicated how important it is for a policeman to have an accurate and rapid glance of identification, we may here call attention to a method introduced by *Bertillon*, of anthropometrical fame. It is called graphically the "*Portrait parle*" or speaking likeness. We all know the remarkable descriptions which are found, even in these days, on passports, licences, in police gazettes, etc.: face oval, chin round, nose medium, mouth moderate, etc. The officer, who, armed with a description of this kind, is sent in search of a criminal, may just as well stop at home. Even the aid rendered by a photograph, still sometimes employed in case of need, is very much a matter of luck, failures amount to more than 60 per cent., and for various reasons:—the defects of the photograph, difference in age, changes in hair, beard, corpulence, etc. To *Bertillon* there belongs the credit of having devised a complete process, without the aid of photography, founded solely upon a precise and scientific description of a certain number of the features which enables the officer who knows how to employ it to find and identify in the middle of a crowd, and that with certainty the individual whose "*Portrait parlé*" he possesses.

The system is taught to the police of Paris, by a teacher employed by M *Bertillon* The instruction, theoretical and practical lasts for two months, twenty men forming a class.

The theoretical course consists of lectures or classes in which the professor describes in exact and scientific terms the various characteristics of the forehead, the nose, the ear the lips the mouth, the chin, etc. The walls of the lecture-room are covered with numbered life-size photographs of heads, so that when the description is finished the pupils can look around and point out heads containing the characteristics described. Here for instance is the description of the *nose*, quoted from the "Recapitulary table of descriptive marks as entered in the new model descriptive card," which is a summary of the lectures on the "*Portrait parlé*"

THE NOSE.—*Depth of the root* small, medium, large
    Profile concave, rectilinear, convex, arched, irregular, sinuous
    Base raised, horizontal, depressed
    Height }
    Projection } small, medium, large
    Size }

PARTICULARITIES.—*The root* of the nose may be very narrow, or very large, high or low the root may be broken
    The profile may be in the shape of an S it may be flat, fine, or broad, or the nose may be broken, it may be curved to right or left
    The tip may be tapering, or thick, or bi-lobar, or flat twisted to right or left, blotched and pimpled
    The partition (septum) may be disclosed or hidden
    The nostrils may be stiff or mobile recurved, dilated, pinched up

All the features and the general contour of the head are thus examined and described in succession with perfect precision. The next lesson is on colours the colour of the iris, hair, beard, complexion then morphological characteristics, first in profile, then full-face. As the professor describes a trait he draws it on the board, and asks the students to search for it among the photographs on the walls. The eye is quickly trained, and after a two months' course of five lectures weekly of 1½ hours each the student is able to construct a speaking likeness or to search for a person by the aid of a speaking likeness which he either has written on the card or fixed in his head

Practical work also helps him. From the second month of the course a descriptive card, serially numbered and drawn up in conformity with the principles of the "*Portrait parlé*" is prepared for every person arrested and brought daily to the office for anthropometric measurement. These cards are given to the students, and when all the criminals, one or two hundred or even more are assembled in the great hall, the students are ordered to go amongst them, and pick out and bring up the person or persons whose card or cards they possess. In a very few days the students can pick out their men in two or three minutes. At the end of the second month, on leaving the school they are provided with a formidable and accurate instrument for the recognition of malefactors.

Section ii.—False Names.

The assumption of a false name or alias is one of the greatest difficulties encountered by the police and the magistracy. Whoever can appreciate at its real value this difficulty and its troublesome consequences will not perhaps be inclined to laugh at the counsel of despair, namely, to print painlessly but in indelible writing, on a part of the body not usually visible, the name and birth-place of every convicted criminal and even of every individual in general. But as this bold proposition has little chance of adoption, we must find other means of arriving at a solution in those troublesome cases where we cannot help suspecting some individual of passing under a false name. In every case such people must be shadowed, for no one desires to move about in the world under an alias merely for amusement or for some trifling offence as yet unexpiated.

Generally speaking, the reasons for assuming a false name are the following: either our man has escaped from confinement, or he is obliged to fly in consequence of some serious crime committed, or he prefers to travel under a distinguished, high-sounding name, imposing upon and living at the expense of fools. Sometimes we find in the same individual two of the reasons indicated or even all the three. Of course no definite rule can be laid down for ascertaining with certainty the true name of such a person, but one can, and not so infrequently as might be supposed, establish a man's identity in roundabout ways, provided always one does not shrink from taking a little trouble.

First, we must see if the individual in question possesses any papers of identification. If he has, they must be examined for the purpose of seeing if they have been forged in whole or part (see *Chapter XVIII., Section ii.*)

If they be wholly false, or at least false so far as names and descriptions are concerned, they must be treated simply as non-existent; perhaps a starting point may be discovered by communicating with the authorities who have issued the certificate, if, indeed, this portion of the document be authentic. It may be asked for instance on whose behalf the certificate was issued, and thus may be discovered the original owner of the paper, who can perhaps inform us how he lost it and into whose hands it has fallen.

Of course the description of the original proprietor must be carefully compared with that of the man in possession, the height, corpulence, hair, etc., but especially the trade recorded. From this point of view the person in possession of the certificate may even be examined by a specialist. Thus one can establish, with more or less certainty, that the individual is in illegal possession of the certificate, however loudly he may protest. If the suspect has got no letter of identification or if the name found on a genuine certificate is false, we must never forget that almost every man in assuming a false name tries to find some assonance or other relation with his real personality,—a strange but common obstinacy. Thus the baptismal name is often preserved or the family name is simply reversed or transformed in some manner. (See Chapter XV, 'Ciphers.')

The following are some examples of name transformation, drawn from the experience of the author. *Sonnenberg* becomes *Steinthal*, *Reinoser* becomes *Reinhuber*, *Herlog* becomes *Rehgol* (each syllable reversed), *Maudis* (Slav) becomes by permutation *Dasumi*, *Maller* reversed is *Rellam*, *Mandl* = (*Mann* = Latin *vir*) becomes *Vir*, *Mundinger* (*Mund* = *Maul* = mouth and *Ding* = *Sache* = thing) becomes *Maulsacher*.

Such transformations are not discovered at a glance. Of those quoted *Dasumi* was deciphered and *Maulsacher* suspected, the others were not observed until the real name was known. In one case a mother took her daughter's name, in another the name of the birth-place with the termination *er* was assumed, and in two cases the name of the illegitimate father slightly changed was taken—*Hohnmaier* for *Hollmaier*, and *Kreuziger* for *Krinziger*.

Each individual case will give us some information as to how to proceed to discover the individual's real name. We can evidently only give some hints upon important points. If it is of real importance to establish a person's identity, much time must be devoted to it. A method the author has found very successful is to make the suspect converse as much as possible.

This class of gentry have in general travelled much and seen much. It is a good plan, when one knows how to tickle vanity, to make them describe their travels and their career. Most often our man pretends that he was born on board ship, among gipsies, on a journey, or in some other romantic fashion; then he joins a troup of travelling comedians, bear-leaders, rope-dancers, circus performers, etc., and traverses the world with them; then he takes an engagement as servant with a dealer in cattle or horses, or goes to sea as a sailor or stoker, the vessel bears some common name (Pluto, Neptune, Venice, St. Mary, etc.) and the captain is dead, or perchance has remained in America, or else he was a disorderly sort of man who failed to maintain his registers in order. In such case it is impossible to establish if the man has really been in the service he pretends to or not.

One listens to all these tales, makes a note of them, or better still, takes them down in shorthand without being observed by the speaker; little by little a morsel of truth slips into the recital, then come descriptions of countries and people that he has really seen, at the same time come relations he has had with these people, in fine reminiscences of his past life. When his story runs dry the Investigating Officer interrupts the conversation and proceeds to gather all the information he can from books of travel, etc., as to the countries, people and things of which the man has been speaking. At the next conversation he can dwell on these descriptions and thus draw out more precise details. The truth will come to light by degrees and perhaps it will be possible to form an idea of a man's trade, of his occupation, even of his origin, of his relations, and other ties. Meanwhile the Investigating Officer will be able, by noting his language and dialect, to limit, more or less closely, the area in which he must have been born. He will then have recourse to an expert; if, for example, he has been able to determine that the man is a North German, he will call in another North German to speak to his countryman, he should be able within certain limits to determine the district where the particular dialect is spoken. Then, on some pretext, a conversation is started, and if the agent is a clever man he will always discover some of the countries with which the suspect has some acquaintance, and may, with good luck, light on the exact neighbourhood of his birth. When nothing further can be discovered by these means, the Investigating Officer will apply to the authorities of the supposed place of his birth and will send them his photograph, his description, and all the details that have been discovered, his probable trade, travels, relations, etc.) When this has been carefully done with a sufficiency of time and trouble then the Investigating Officer, if he has any luck at all, should easily establish the identity of the individual and have the satisfaction of rendering harmless a most dangerous person. An instructive case may be here related in detail.

The author was a Magistrate of a small town, about three leagues from this town was situated a watering-place or spa, celebrated throughout the world. One morning early, he rode over to this station on some magisterial business which was soon finished. But as the horse had cast a shoe and the only reliable farrier had gone out, delay in this watering-place until late in the afternoon became compulsory. The Mayor and Inspector of the Baths was an old aristocrat, a retired cavalry officer, who had accepted the appointment as something to do. He was well educated and intelligent, a bachelor, a jolly fellow, who took an interest in everything going on. The author spent the day in the Mayor's company, who pointed out a man of foreign demeanour, who had been staying in the town for some time. Very tall, of friendly manners, extremely elegant, dressed like a real dandy, he was to be found wherever anything was going on, preferred to mix in the best society, was not an invalid, and spent his money recklessly. He called himself the Baron de V——, a native of Hanover.

This young man did not look like a genuine nobleman, as also thought my companion, who was most jealous of the reputation of his town, and related all sorts of stories about him. We were both much interested and resolved to shadow him throughout the afternoon. We followed him in the park, in the saloon of the bathing establishment, in a restaurant, in a café, and observed his strange goings-on. The most striking thing about the man was the way he spent his money; he appeared to take delight, not in making purchases, but in throwing his money about. Now this is an infallible sign of a man of little cultivation, who has gained without difficulty a fortune he has not always enjoyed. This mode of spending is as characteristic as it is difficult to describe; it cannot be defined otherwise than by the words—spending money for the sake of spending. Further, we were surprised to find our man boasting, without rhyme or reason, and often in an importunate manner, of his high and noble rank, while his manners appeared to show little confidence, and even to betray a certain disquietude, far from being in accord with his boisterous gaiety. All this was so characteristic and at the same time so interesting, that we continued our study as long as possible; we came to the conclusion that our man was probably dissipating a fortune inherited from an over-selfish father, and that to fit in with his pleasures he had assumed a high-sounding and aristocratic name.

The incident had passed from the author's mind when one day a gendarme brought before him "the Baron de V——." The gendarme had learned that de V was gambling heavily and had invited him to establish his identity. De V declared that people of his rank were not in the custom of carrying about papers of identification, dismissed the gendarme abruptly and rudely, and made preparations for quitting the watering-place on the morrow. This precipitate departure, immediately after receiving the invitation to establish his identity, appeared suspicious to the gendarme, who arrested him and brought him before the Court. This excessive zeal on the part of the gendarme seemed very unlucky, for the Court did not know what answer to make to the man just arrested and who kept on demanding to be informed what fault he had committed. He showed himself polite but indignant to the highest degree at the insult inflicted on him, talked loudly of the embassy, where, he said the Magistrate would be obliged to justify his conduct and where much unpleasantness awaited him.

Soon however, we began to talk more quietly. His father he said, was a landowner in Hanover, his family was descended directly from William the Lion, and was closely connected with all the families which, little more than a dozen years after the annexation of Hanover, were still known throughout the whole world (Borries, Hodenberg, Hammerstein, etc.). After the annexation he added, his family emigrated, and since then he had spent his time in travelling far and wide. He related all this quite naturally and with just sufficient explanation, he appeared really to speak the true Hanoverian dialect, and conducted himself otherwise like a gentleman. What nevertheless made the Court doubtful was his refusal to furnish the address of anyone who by telegraph could supply information about de V. He was ashamed, he said, to allow reference to be made through the Court to his relations and friends, many highly placed, a course which would ruin his future, etc. As he was absolutely guilty of no offence, proof of his innocence would soon be forthcoming, he would therefore rather remain under arrest than telegraph as suggested.

All this not being satisfactory, he was asked to describe his coat of arms. he replied with hesitation,—' A helmet above, a shield below, arabesques all round, and plenty gold and silver everywhere." But in spite of precise questions, he could tell nothing about his real armorial bearings, crest, colours, supporters, etc. That a "Legitimist," who had with his king left his country and his fatherland, should be ignorant of his own arms was a certain proof of his being an impostor, and accordingly he was not released from custody.

Fortunately a copy of the *Almanach de Gotha*, which gives the list of all the families of Barons, was at hand, and a reference to it showed that while there certainly was a family of " Barons de V " there was no " Otto, Baron de V," the name given by the prisoner. The information he had given as to various members of the family was fairly accurate but contained blunders which no genuine member of the family could have committed. This conclusion arrived at, he was remanded under arrest, in spite of his rage and repeated threats. But what was to be done? All that we had as yet proved was that he was a liar passing under a false name, but he could not be accused of any grave offence justifying his detention.

On reflection it was remembered that there lived in the town an old master-turner a native of Mecklenburg, who had somehow or other got stranded in the little place. He was sent for, and a fairly long conversation with the prisoner took place in his presence. The old Mecklenburger gave it as his opinion that though the man spoke the Hanoverian dialect very well, yet he was a native of Hamburg, a place this expert knew from his infancy. Photographs, descriptions, etc., were then sent to Hamburg, Hanover, Bremen, Luneburg, and Oldenberg and within a week it was known that the man's real name was Otto H. that he had kept an inn in the neighbourhood of Hamburg, and was "wanted" by the authorities of Osnabruck for manslaughter, and by those at Dresden for a great theft of valuable securities. Further inquiries showed that his mother had at one time been a chamber-maid in the family of the Barons de V., thus he was able to know approximately all about the family; he had retained his own Christian name Otto.

We may here remark that information afforded by such yearly publications as the *Almanach de Gotha*, the various Peerages, Landed Gentry, etc., is often most serviceable, though not always quite complete. As the information concerning each family is for the most part furnished by the family itself its value varies. The historical part is frequently inaccurate, at least the genealogy often goes further back than serious criticism would permit. But this is a matter of little importance for the Investigating Officer. Dates concerning members of a family still alive, or recently deceased, are almost without exception accurate, for there is no reason for making false statements which would be immediately corrected by readers who knew. Even the ages of ladies are accurate, not being furnished by persons who have already reached an uncertain age but dating even from the birth of the person and being passed on from year to year.

Besides the dialect spoken by the unknown, and which almost always, with a little trouble, betrays the place of his origin, there are few devices, or rather we should say, only petty devices to fall back on. For the most part they leave us at fault. It is a good plan to make the suspect undergo a medical examination; such an examination may disclose exterior indications, as a deformity, birth-mark, etc.; one may perhaps discover signs of circumcision, indicating that the man is a Jew; perhaps also there may be tattoo marks on the arms or chest. These are very important, they may show that the person belongs to the army or navy, and sometimes display his initials, etc. It is generally easy to discover signs which are of importance as indicating the trade to which the person has belonged. Thus by constant handling of a plane, the joiner becomes lopsided; tailors and shoemakers from the sedentary nature of their occupation develop a characteristic curvature of chest and shoulders; hairdressers have one shoulder higher than the other. Many striking instances are pointed out by *Felix Hement* in an illustrated essay, *La Photographie Judiciaire* who further presses the point that photography can reveal what is hidden from the naked eye. (See Chapter V., Section ix. B.) Thus handling the reins produces *wales* on the inner sides of the fingers of coachmen; the chisel causes thickening of the skin between the forefinger and thumb of engravers, etc.; the traces of the last are seen on the right thumb and upper part of the thigh of cobblers; the skin on the ball of the little finger of printers who have to tie the type together with string is thickened; writers, students, clerks, and artists have frequently a wale on the right middle finger from holding the pen or pencil, as well as a perceptible thickening of the skin of the left elbow. Seamstresses have plentiful needle pricks on the left fore-finger, glass-blowers have the cheeks baggy and the muscles developed. Nine-pin players have a wale on the middle finger near the nail; the place where the handle of the brush comes can be easily seen on the hands of painters and varnishers.

It is also very important to examine the man's clothes, being particularly careful over the seams, unripping those portions where the cloth is folded several times, as the coat-collar, waist-band, trousers-flap etc.; we often thus discover papers that the suspect does not, for some reason or other, wish to part with, as letters, paper-money, even his true papers of identification, preserved for different circumstances. A very curious discovery was thus once made. The man had inserted in the lining of his hat, a piece of newspaper folded several times, as is frequently done to make a rather large hat fit. This bit of paper, filthy with grease and dirt, contained among other things a short account of a highway robbery which had been committed by two persons several years previously. According to the paragraph, one of the robbers had been caught and convicted, the other had escaped and had not up to that time been captured. One might easily look upon this as a mere accident, and indeed the prisoner declared in the most natural way, that he had been at school with the convicted robber, that the article in the journal had come into his hands by chance, and had been used to pack his hat bought second-hand. Besides, he added, the sad fate of his old school-fellow, fallen so low, had painfully impressed him. But on forwarding the extract with the portrait and description of the unknown to the authorities where the robbery had been committed, it was found that the man was in fact the second robber, unfound up till then; he confessed he had preserved the article out of pure " interest in his case."

Another case (September 1903) made the round of the newspapers. In Paris a certain Lemot was murdered and the police had no knowledge of the murderer. A few weeks later a policeman found a man asleep in the Jardin des Plantes on a bench, out of whose pocket a number of newspaper cuttings had fallen. The policeman read these, which were all about the case of Lemot, and when the man awoke and was questioned, in his half-waking state he confessed that he was indeed the murderer.

Even for " High Class " malefactors, *Hochstapler*, swell mobsmen, cases so frequent and so difficult, no other means can be suggested. By this designation we nowadays understand a man who knows how to give himself the manners of a person in easy circumstances and of good reputation so as to be able under this guise to commit swindles, thefts and other plants. Generally they are men who have received a good education in their youth or who at least have had opportunities of picking up the appearance of such. Without exception they are men of ability, full of dexterity and presence of mind but with a love of easy and idle life which prevents them turning to any regular and honest occupation.

The *modus operandi* of the swell mobsman is well enough known from the daily press, which is always ready to give publicity to his exploits. Fashionably dressed, he steps into a jeweller's shop and steals while pretending to select, or he causes the valuables selected to be brought to his hotel, takes delivery, and disappears through another door (see *Chapter XLII. Section v*.); he goes to the banker and collects the amount of a forged cheque, he manages to get introduced to the highest social circles, runs up heavy debts and disappears; he cheats at play and that on a large scale, he becomes engaged to one or several wealthy young ladies, and makes off with the moneys borrowed from presumptive fathers-in-law; he buys houses and estates without paying for them, mortgages them, and disappears; he gets into business relations with a merchant and runs up debts in his name; in a word, he knows marvellously well how to play upon that weakness of mankind that allows itself to be bluffed by a high-sounding name, fine clothes, easy and self-possessed manners; he knows there are fools to be found always and everywhere and lives at their expense until he is caught.

The position of the Investigating Officer with respect to this gentry is a delicate one, especially when there is no specific offence to charge them with; the Investigating Officer has always the fear of committing a mistake and arresting an honest man. We repeat, the only and safest plan is to observe whatever is not "quite the thing" in these people, and that does not as a rule demand much time; in his bearing, his dress, his way of introducing himself, his manners, his tales, his affirmations and denials, contradictions and inaccuracies can be speedily detected, and then the Investigating Officer can tranquilly set about his real work. The brassy gold, the gipsy coral, the sham ermine appear genuine only at a distance; to anyone knowing even but a little of such things the suspect can be easily upset by making him give a detailed account of his previous career; the improbabilities, the contradictions, the fantastic and concocted adventures, are not difficult to recognise; the rest of the work may be safely left to the telegraph, photography, and perhaps "Burke's Peerage."

The time expended in establishing the identity of an individual, or at least in making certain that he is not the person he pretends to be, is never lost, for, that accomplished, the crime for which he has been arrested is already discovered and half proven. If the great landholder, the self-styled "Chevalier de X," has run into debt, he will be speedily convicted of swindling when he is proved to be a man without a name or fortune; if the self-styled "Countess Y," suspected of cheating at cards, is no other than an ordinary cocotte, the proof of the cheating will not be very difficult.

In every case in which one has to do with a fashionable swindler one will naturally endeavour to fix the exact scene of the crime; but the greatest care and the most trouble will be bestowed on the identity of the swindler. Above all this rule should be rigorously followed when a false name has been given or there is a suspicion thereof. Our records show a shockingly large number of penal cases in which the most dangerous people have been mildly punished because they have chosen to conceal their real names and given themselves out as innocent. This deception succeeds most beautifully when the accused is cunning enough to take the name and parentage of some real living respectable man whom he has perhaps met in an inn and whose papers he may have purloined. The law makes inquiries at the home of the supposed accused, and receives the most satisfactory account of his previous life. The only thing to be done in such a case is to watch our man carefully; the old jail-bird belongs to such an easily recognisable type that the practised eye can scarcely be mistaken, but if there be the slightest suspicion that a false name has been given, then one must secure without fail at the alleged home of the suspect a good photograph. If the name and the person agree the question can be almost always settled with certainty.

Section III.—Pretended Illnesses and Pains

Hardly one of the afflictions to which humanity is subject has not been worked up and simulated by criminals. The reasons for such shamming are many. If the rogue is at liberty, he often assumes infirmities for the purpose of begging; blindness, deafness, paralysis, skin eruptions, and other disabilities assumed by beggars are so well known that they require but a passing reference. It is a common trick, too, for beggars to insinuate themselves into houses with stories of children sick at home, always taking care to add that the illness is small-pox, diphtheria or some other contagious malady, so that to get rid of them quickly people give them much larger alms than would usually be given. These maladies, as well as pretended cramps, epilepsy, spitting blood etc., are not particularly interesting to the Investigating Officer. The following cases are the most important from his point of view.

A. Illness of witnesses or suspects summoned before the Court.

It is often observed that of two or more persons summoned before a magistrate, only one turns up; the other is unwell, has been kicked by a horse, or otherwise prevented from appearing on the appointed day. The Investigating Officer then thoughtlessly questions the individual present and sends him away with a strict injunction to see that the other appears on the morrow without fail. Of course he does, for the person questioned to-day has learned in the course of his examination what it is all about, he knows what he has said, reports it to his friend, and the two can at leisure agree as to what statement is to be made on the morrow.

And not only do accomplices act thus, but apparently most straightforward witnesses, who for some reason or other do not wish to speak the truth—often the accused and witnesses work together for an acquittal, the latter testifying falsely in the interest of the former. In such circumstances the very fact that a witness though summoned is not present, should rouse in the mind of the Investigating Officer a suspicion that there is something unusual in the affair; either the accused or the witnesses are anxious to work together, or both have made common cause, and the only resource is to send away *every time*, the person who appears, and see to it that all the persons cited appear together, without exception.

If this sort of thing happens, one must be doubly careful to ensure that the individuals interrogated succeed each other without interruption, and that the persons to be examined are allowed no opportunity even in the courthouse or police-station for communication with each other. If only two persons are to be interrogated it is imperative that the examinations follow each other without interruption. If there are several persons, those not yet examined must be kept together in the witnesses' waiting room, and each one immediately on the conclusion of his examination must be compelled to leave the courthouse without being afforded an opportunity of meeting the persons not yet interrogated. If the matter is important it is not sufficient to pass orders to this effect, persons already examined must be carefully watched, a precaution which will be well compensated for by the accuracy of the depositions obtained.

The best plan in important cases is to hurry on the examination of the witnesses as much as possible, without giving them time to discuss the matter in detail. One will also do well to proceed with the inquiry at the scene of the crime, thus preventing the witnesses having to journey together to the courthouse. This journey is always dangerous, for on the way the coming examination will naturally form the subject of conversation, and the matter is discussed at such length that finally nobody knows what he has seen himself and what he has heard from the others. But if the Investigating Officer arrives on the spot soon after the occurrence and immediately proceeds with his inquiry, the statements he collects will not yet be disfigured. Of course the witnesses should not be collected together in a crowd so as to give them time for talk, while one is being questioned, another naturally the nearest, will be sent for so that no one knows whether he is to be called at all or has time to talk to another witness. Acting thus one will take every precaution humanly possible. To sum up, the most important maxim will always be: "the more quickly a witness is examined, the more accurate will be his statement." Lapse of time dulls the memory and gives opportunities for discussion which befog the whole matter.

B. Sudden illness of accused or witnesses when under examination.

Of course it may happen that a person under examination falls ill by chance or in consequence of great emotion and excitement, but in the majority of cases a sudden fainting fit, an epileptic attack, or some other nervous seizure is not genuine. The trick will be recognized when it is seen that the attack always occurs at a time favourable to the witness. Thus when the man is driven into a corner, when he does not find a ready answer, when he contradicts, when the Investigating Officer pulls him up sharp, that is the psychological moment. In such a case little can be done, for even if the trick be guessed, the sick man cannot be compelled to stop shamming, the scoundrel has effectively gained time and that is all he wanted.

It follows that it is not a matter of indifference to the Investigating Officer whether there be shamming or not; on the one hand, he will be convinced that there is something wrong somewhere, since simulation has been deemed necessary; on the other hand, he may induce the man to throw up the sponge, by showing him that nobody is taken in. The Investigating Officer will then always and without exception, have recourse to the opinion of a medical man, and meantime will observe closely the phenomena accompanying the faint, fit, etc., he will make a note of his observations on a sheet of paper, so that he may communicate them as completely as possible to the medical man. If the phenomena have been accurately observed the medical man may be able to give his opinion on the question of shamming with as great certainty as if he had himself seen the attack. This is the best thing to do for it will seldom be possible to have the medical man at hand quickly enough to witness the seizure, while usually the condition of the sick man improves with extraordinary rapidity on the arrival of the physician. If the latter declares the whole thing a pretence, the Investigating Officer can take a high hand if it occurs again, explaining to the person that his game is up, that it is extremely dangerous, and adds greatly to the suspicions against him.

Some recommend the use of little stratagems or tricks which they consider permissible. Thus, they say, it is a good thing to talk with the clerk, paying no attention to the individual twisting about in his attack of nerves, about matters which will be unpleasant for him to hear. Thus it may be said that he has already made a confession, or that one of his accomplices has given him away, the shammer, indignant at the lies he is hearing, will suddenly begin to listen, will twist about less, especially if one talks in an undertone. The story is told of a gipsy, suddenly fallen in an epileptic fit, who recovered at once when he heard the magistrate say that it would be necessary to send the man to an asylum for the insane where he would be compelled to sit on ice and be douched with cold water several hours a day. The gipsy was at once himself and promised to have no more epileptic fits. But such tricks cannot be countenanced however useful they may prove in special circumstances, for in no case should the Investigating Officer descend to deliberate lying, while on the other hand, if the shammer is not taken in by the trick, the Investigating Officer is completely disarmed.

One permissible device, which often succeeds quite as well when one is right in assuming simulation, is to say calmly and firmly that the whole thing is a sham and that the accused by his conduct is doing no good to himself. If the latter perceives that he is not believed he will generally give up the game.

But as we have already said, the all-important thing is to make sure that the attack is a sham, and as one cannot always have a medical man in attendance, as the attacks do not always last until a medical man can arrive, and as in so-called chronic affections (as partial deafness) one cannot await the arrival of the medical man (for example on a journey), it is useful to know some methods of treating cases of no great complication.

1 Shamming Blindness

Blindness may be simulated in many ways, some of the crudest description. Dr Litton Forbes mentions an ingenious device. He met a man in Paris who asked for charity on the score of blindness. The writer proceeds: "The man attracted attention. He walked quickly and with an air of confidence. He looked fixedly at me, and his eyes seemed to give expression to his thoughts. There was no uncertainty in his gaze, no shifty movements, no drooping or quivering of the lids. His story told of blindness from deep-seated inflammation in both eyes, which the doctors had pronounced incurable. He had at command a rich vocabulary of technical terms, some of which he misplaced absurdly. On closer looking into, the eyes did indeed present a curious appearance. In each the pupil had almost disappeared. The iris or coloured portion had absorbed the central black spot. The pupils had become mere pinholes, but what remained of them was bright and well-defined. A glance was enough for anyone familiar with eye affections. The man was an impostor. He had instilled a drug named eserine, the active principle of the Calabar bean, into each eye. This had contracted the pupils temporarily, without any permanent injury, but the appearance produced was well calculated to lend weight to his other statements." It is added that "he might with more effect have used atropine. This alkaloid is the active principle of belladonna and has the effect of enormously dilating the pupils. In fact, the pupil may be made to absorb practically the whole of the coloured portion of the eye, and the black pupils then violently contrast with and appear in relief against the white portion of the organ. A very strange and weird appearance, well calculated to move the benevolent, is thus induced. Such a deception could be suspected readily enough from the fact that the size of the pupil was greater than in any known disease. By looking into the eye also with the ophthalmoscope certain characteristic appearances would be found wanting. The enlarged pupils could also easily be reduced in size by eserine, or would reduce themselves in a very few days if the individual were kept under observation."

Dr Forbes gives a useful test for detecting simulated blindness of one eye, a common form of deception among conscripts and recruits. "If a pencil, say, be held about two inches distant from the eyes of a person with natural vision in both eyes, he will have no difficulty in spelling out each letter in every word of a line of small type. If, however, he tries to do the same with one eye closed, the pencil will effectually cover the pupil of the open eye, and several consecutive letters will be lost to view. Hence, if the supposed one-eyed recruit can spell out the letters of each word with a pencil held in front of him, he has in truth performed an impossible feat, and the imposition at once stands revealed."

2. Shamming Deafness

When deafness is feigned it is a very troublesome business for the Investigating Officer, especially when the inquiry is a hurried one which cannot be postponed and there is neither time nor opportunity to call in a medical man. If we suspect the person to be shamming, it is important to let him see at once that we are not taken in. There are several ways of doing this which even an amateur can make use of.

Ave-Lallemant recommends the employment of ushers or attenders to shout the questions in a loud voice into the ears of the deponent, until he gives up pretending. But this is a very irregular procedure; besides, it is not always easy to carry out, and, as a matter of fact, proves nothing, for such shouting is painful even to persons really hard of hearing.

A simple method is to strike the ground with the foot or let some heavy object fall behind the suspected individual. The man really hard of hearing perceives the disturbance, owing to the conductivity of the ground, the chair, his body; he "feels the noise" more or less. On the other hand, the pretender thinks he ought not to hear the noise, hence the former turns, the latter remains motionless.

If a person, as frequently happens, pretends to be deaf in one ear, the truth can be discovered with certainty by causing two persons simultaneously to whisper different words in the two ears. If one ear be quite deaf, the person can understand what is whispered in the other ear and can speak it. But if he can hear with both ears, what is whispered on the two sides becomes so confused that he understands nothing and can repeat nothing.

Caspar Liman however, remarks, and rightly, that the best means of detecting a simulated deafness is to observe the features, though this plan serves rather to enlighten the Investigating Officer than to confuse the pretender. But if the Investigating Officer during the inquiry continuously watches the features of the person under examination and notes the impression produced by certain questions or remarks on the supposed deaf man, he will soon see, by a flash in the eyes or a protesting motion of head or hand, that he has been understood. If the Investigating Officer then quietly and firmly explains this, the "deaf" man will generally abandon his now useless attempt.

The same observations apply to deaf-mutes, for deaf-mutes are only persons deaf from birth, who have consequently never learned to talk. If then mutism is feigned, deafness must be feigned also, for it is very rare that one becomes mute after birth, and such cases are still more rarely simulated. It must also be remembered that deaf-mutes hear almost all the noises produced by solid bodies, stamping of feet on the ground, fall of heavy articles, etc.; they therefore turn round while the pretender remains unmoved.

3. Shamming Epilepsy

Epilepsy is simulated not only before a magistrate to avoid an interrogatory or a conviction, but before the military authorities to escape from service. Such simulations belong for the most part to the domain of the medical jurisprudent, but it is frequently important for the Investigating Officer to be able to decide at once whether an attack of epilepsy be real or feigned, for example when about to arrest a person upon a warrant or, as just indicated, when a suspect desires to interrupt an embarrassing examination. If the Investigating Officer discovers the trick at the first glance, he will of course proceed very differently from how he would act if in doubt. Besides, we may have to wait a long time for the medical report, for shammers are generally very careful not to have a fit in presence of the medical man. Even if the latter be summoned speedily, our man will cut his fit short, so that no complete diagnosis of it can be made. As a rule, feigned attacks are good imitations and consequently difficult to detect. The reason doubtless is that no one feigns an epileptic seizure without having often seen one. Unfortunately this terrible malady is so widespread that opportunities for observing it are only too frequent. Much has been written upon the easiest methods of detecting feigned epilepsy, all treatises on Medical Jurisprudence deal with the question, and army surgeons have also published many handbooks treating of this and other feigned disabilities for military service; each one has characteristic symptoms on which he relies, depreciating those of his colleagues, so that on the whole little really reliable remains. We can, however, say:—

1. An attack is always suspicious when it comes on at a critical moment favourable to the individual attacked, at the moment of arrest, during an examination etc. It must not of course be forgotten that extreme emotion, great fright, etc., may bring on a nervous attack in the case of persons really ill.

2. The manner of the fall is important. The individual whose attack is genuine does not select the spot of his fall; he falls without taking any precautions or guarding himself with his hands; thus he is often severely wounded, especially on the face, is he falls forward. The shammer sinks down gently, protecting himself in his fall by stretching out his hands or opening his elbows. Even if he does not act thus and should by chance hurt himself, he cannot completely repress some manifestation of pain, is a contraction of the features etc.

3. The startling but very characteristic cry of the epileptic, so well known and, once heard, so impossible to forget, this unique cry, proceeding from the throat and accompanied by foaming at the mouth "*rauque plutôt qu'aigu*," as the French doctors say, "hoarse rather than shrill," will afford satisfactory proof only in certain cases. If the sick man repeats the cry frequently or continues it for some time he is certainly pretending, but if he cries out only once then the attack is genuine or the imitation perfect. If the cry be absent the attack may yet be genuine, for it is often wanting in the case of well known epileptics.

4. An important symptom and one impossible to imitate is the muscular contraction, those convulsive movements and peculiar tremblings of the muscles in the region of the back and the nape of the neck, what might be called "muscular anarchy" or confusion. Some very strong men, especially expert gymnasts, can produce this contraction in the upper part of the arm, but no one can at will provoke it over the whole body; in the true epileptic this phenomenon occurs spontaneously. The individual who feigns, throws his limbs about on all sides, shakes, trembles, struggles, but the play of the muscles is wanting.

5. Perhaps the most important symptom is the colour of the face, which in the true epileptic first becomes extraordinarily pale and then changes to bluish violet. The person feigning can never produce this paleness artificially, although many men can produce the lividity as often as they wish.

When a person under examination is seized with an attack of epilepsy true or false, it is above all necessary not to lose one's head, for as just stated, fright and emotion may produce a genuine seizure. Such fits therefore do occur from time to time, and in the case of the young Investigating Officer unaccustomed to such shocking sights, deprive him of all presence of mind and prevent calm observation. What he usually does in his otherwise excusable excitement is to run about crying for help, looking for water, throwing himself about, so that when the medical man questions him as to what he has observed, he is incapable of furnishing any information. If a case of epilepsy does occur, the Investigating Officer must, as a rule, deal with it as genuine, affording the sick man such help as is usual in such cases. Care must be taken that the patient does not injure himself by removing from his vicinity all angular objects, he must be allowed fresh air and his tight fitting clothes must be loosened, the attempt must be made to introduce between his teeth some elastic body a cork, a folded linen pad wood, india-rubber so that he may not bite his tongue taking care that this gag does not slip into his mouth and choke him Nothing else can be done have patience and look out for signs of shamming sending at once for the medical man to succour the genuinely afflicted or unmask the hypocrite But this must be remembered that nearly every true epileptic lies, is violent, and bigoted

1 Shamming Paralysis

Dr Forbes points out that physicians themselves are sometimes deceived by cases of sham Paralysis and gives the following details of a particular case

'A man was brought into hospital by a sympathetic policeman He was able to state that being on the top of an omnibus, he suddenly and completely lost all power in his right leg and arm His speech was not much affected nor were any unusual symptoms present Here was a case apparently of paralysis of one side of the body All might have gone well so far as the deception was concerned, had not one of the nurses recollected having seen the same man three weeks before suffering from similar symptoms Now a case of genuine paralysis is never quickly recovered from, and suspicion was aroused In genuine paralysis there are, of course, present various symptoms which affect different parts of the body These symptoms are all in harmony with one another, and more or less interdependent The man was for instance told to put out his tongue It came out quite straight, but in genuine paralysis affecting the right side for instance, the tip of that treacherous organ should distinctly diverge to the left Again, when the sole of the foot on the paralysed side was tickled the man drew up his leg The leg should have remained quite motionless and insensible The treatment was simple in this case The man asserted he had no feeling in the leg It was gently but firmly explained to him that a hot iron passed along the course of the nerve always gave excellent results, and would in the case be quite painless A pretty vigorous electric current was also applied This treatment was so successful that the sufferer there and then decided to walk out and that without assistance "

5 Sham Fainting Fits

To be able to recognise a pretended faint is most important, as the attack rarely lasts until the arrival of a medical man The infallible sign of a genuine faint and one easy to observe is the extreme and sudden paleness, which, just before the attack, spreads not only over the face but also over the mucous membrane, lips, gums etc If this phenomenon be wanting the fit is a sham For the paleness is not the consequence but the cause of the faint, it is nothing but lack of blood in the brain and head that brings on the attack and is indicated by the paleness The eyes remain motionless the pupils are generally strongly dilated, the eye does not move when touched the winking of the eyelid ceases

The awakening from a true fainting fit is very different from the recovery from a feigned one. But special knowledge or at least considerable experience is necessary to discriminate. For the amateur it must suffice to note the profound paleness which no one can produce artificially.

There is a spurious fainting fit occurring almost wholly among women. A shock, anxiety, congestion of blood in the head, anæmia of the brain substance, is followed by a slight giddiness, the brain follows suit, there is light-headedness, imagination, a little comedy in short. It is easiest and pleasantest to shut the eyes and sink down. The sufferer is pitied and a half-way definition is found: the condition is not a real faint but it is not false. Eighteenth-century writers called such attacks "*the vapours.*"

6. *Pretended Insanity*

It frequently happens that a person under examination makes himself out to be a bigger fool than he really is: this is often very advantageous for the accused and some of the witnesses, but for the Investigating Officer it is as troublesome as dangerous. For the guilty man the advantage is twofold; on the one hand he may hope not to be suspected of an offence requiring perhaps a considerable amount of ingenuity for its accomplishment, and on the other hand he manages to be thought unable to understand a simple question, and so gains time for reflection. A similar pretence is perhaps quite as convenient to the witness who, for some reason or other, does not wish to speak the truth: perhaps he wishes to shield the accused, perhaps he is afraid of compromising himself in telling the truth, perhaps he is afraid of contradicting another witness. However wearying and annoying such a pretence may be, an Investigating Officer of ordinary sharpness with a minimum of psychological knowledge will easily discover the trick.

Two methods that lead to the same goal—proof of contradiction—may be adopted. In the one, this contradiction occurs between different statements, some of which are deliberate and cunning, while others are awkward and stupid. In the other, the contradiction is found between the words and the expression in the eyes of the person interrogated.

As to the former method, it will be difficult for the cleverest person, especially in the course of a long examination not to give, at least once, an intelligent answer. The Investigating Officer must know how to entangle a witness, provoke him about the case, lead him on to show himself in his true colours and if he extracts but one answer more intelligent than the rest, he may safely conclude that the man is shamming.

It is the same with the antagonism between look and word, between eye and mouth. No intelligent man has an idiot's eyes, and no idiot has intelligent eyes. The whole physiognomy, the deportment, the gestures, may deceive, the eyes never, and whoever is accustomed to watch the eyes will never be taken in.

It is true that what we call "the expression of the eyes" exists only partially in the eyes themselves, the parts neighbouring on the eye produce the chief effect, and these parts can be transformed at pleasure by means of the corresponding muscles but this forced change cannot last long nor be mistaken for a genuine expression. A comedian of a most intelligent countenance, can often make himself look a thorough ass, but his eyes, despite all his art, will be never truly brutish for more than a few moments.

If then we have the least suspicion that the person we are interrogating is trying to make himself out a fool, we have only persistently to keep our eye on his and however hard he tries to appear stupid and indifferent, he will be unable, especially if he finds himself cornered, to prevent at least one intelligent glance escaping. Remember also that the shammer, when he thinks no one is looking, casts a swift and scrutinising glance on the Investigating Officer to see whether or not he believes him. If the Investigating Officer can catch but one of these glances, he can no longer have any doubt as to his man; if he be certain the man is shamming, he very speedily tells him straight that he is found out. The Investigating Officer will then explain to the suspect why he does not believe him, will impress upon him the consequences of the attitude he has assumed, will continue his examination without bothering about the pretended idiocy, and frame his questions to suit the intelligence he may reasonably conclude the man to possess.

7. Shamming Catalepsy

Catalepsy, which in its extreme form is quite indistinguishable from ordinary death, always demands the intervention not alone of a medical man but of a medical expert in diseases of this nature. We quote two cases, cited by *Dr. Litton Forbes*, to show that even such unusual phenomena may easily come within the sphere of the Investigating Officer.

"A man condemned to death threw himself voluntarily into a cataleptic condition. Strong stimulants, such as ammonia applied to the nostrils, needles inserted into the body, and immersion in cold water, all failed to induce any response. At last alcohol was forcibly administered. This caused partial intoxication, disturbed the mental equilibrium, and so restored consciousness. Another remarkable case is that of a soldier in France whose death had been certified by the regimental surgeons. In due course they proceeded to make a post-mortem examination. The first incision, however, at once restored consciousness, and the now wounded man suddenly sat up, while the medical men rather ignominiously ran away."

Section iv.—Signs and Signals.

By the word *Signs* every scoundrel understands "a secret mode of communication." The great variety of these signs, their multifarious application, and their extended employment render them of the greatest importance. For example a robbery committed appears altogether impossible; only one thief has been seen and caught, but he cannot be made responsible, as, for the commission of the offence the co-operation of several persons was essential, and no connection can be discovered between him and others. Again secret communications in prison may paralyse the greatest efforts of the Investigating Officer, who is unable to unravel these communications if he does not know the secret signs.

The Investigating Officer, especially in the country, must busy himself not only with the isolated cases which may come up before him, but also with everything which happens within his jurisdiction—as to the people wandering there and the ties by which such vagabonds are connected. The minute study of the ways of criminals will, as a rule, enable an Investigating Officer in any special case to advance surely and methodically; after the crime, it is too late to study the ways of scoundrels; that must be done in time of peace.

A Graphic Signs

Graphic Signs are most interesting from every point of view and deserve special study.

At first these signs were only a sort of mark employed by bands of incendiaries for designating houses to be burned or attacked, just as a forest-guard marks trees to be cut down. Thus an arrow with several oblique strokes showed a house to be burned, an arrow with little circles at the end of the oblique strokes showed that the necessary combustibles were already to be found in the house.

Later on there appeared, besides these objective signs, others of a subjective nature, which were merely a kind of coat of arms or crest of the person who bore it. This was the general tendency of the period. Just as the emblazoned bearings of the nobles enabled them to be recognized though concealed beneath their coats of mail, so the house marks designated the owner of the house and everyone dependent on him; masons, carpenters and sculptors had also their emblems serving as distinctive marks of the master workman who had built a house or carved a statue; traders were also distinguished by special marks and the incendiaries made use of their signs to show that such and such a member of the band had been there and would return. These incendiary signs go very far back, certainly to the 15th century at least. At the time of the Reformation they were very common, and it was generally believed that the incendiaries were members of bands sent by the Pope into Germany to annihilate the Lutheran Reformers by fire and sword.

An incendiary sign, dating from that epoch, has been preserved on the wall of a lonely chapel in the midst of the Thuringian Forest (Fig. 6). The first line is the summons, the second the response to the invitation. The former means, "The fourth house from here in the direction of the arrow will be attacked on the night when the moon is next in its fourth quarter." To decipher this line it was not necessary to know how to read books, for anyone could understand it, and anyone who could understand it was welcome. Now all sorts of vagabonds passed that way; they read the invitation and each one who wished to have a share in the job added his mark with black lead, red chalk, a burnt stick or a knife, for every criminal had, and has to this day, a mark known to all his friends. Thus we find in the lower line, a bird, a die, a key, a pot, a chain, five marks of five incendiaries, and the organiser of the crime had only to come and look to be sure of the assistance of these five individuals. We shudder even to-day in thinking of the terrible significance of these marks, apparently so harmless, but few among us know that the tamed offspring of these

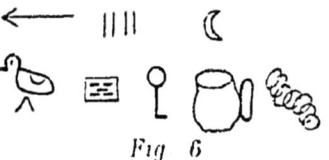

Fig. 6

savage ancestors still exist, and make under our very eyes their marks, which are read and understood

We have only to observe closely chapels, farmhouses crosses, palings, walls, especially in lonely places and at cross-roads, to find signs of criminals in abundance Certainly they do not often nowadays point to murder and incendiarism, but they indicate that such and such a comrade has been at the spot, alone or in company, on a certain date and that on a certain day he has departed in a certain direction The most important indications for these birds of passage are those pointing out the houses where beggars are hospitably received, the most dangerous is the intimation that a robbery is about to be committed in the neighbourhood and that assistance is required A few of these signs may be usefully given here

Ave-Lallemant cites as examples a key with an arrow —mark of the burglar (*Fig* 7)

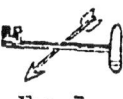

Fig 7

Two crossed swords—mark of the begging student

Fig 8

Cards with an arrow—mark of the wandering card-cheat

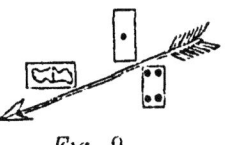

Fig 9

Ave-Lallemant takes *Fig* 10a as the sign of tramps in general, but it is badly copied and ought to represent a heart with three nails, *Fig* 10b This is the ancient distinctive mark of the nail-maker, hence of the nail-maker on the tramp The author was able personally to note this as a sign of a nail-maker who subsequently took to the road

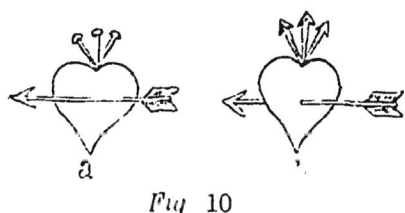

Fig 10

Figure 11 is the mark or sign of the tramp in general, it indicates only direction and date The zeros stand for children, the long strokes for companions, the half-stroke for the wife The date 4-12-'58 The mark sometimes differs in different countries, *e g*, the strokes may be children and the zeros companions or accomplices

The following marks are taken from the author's own collection, formed over a series of years

Figure 12.—A country scene with a fir tree, drawn without lifting the pencil or graver: the very common mark of a famous tramp who had once been a landed proprietor. Such pictures traced with a single stroke are

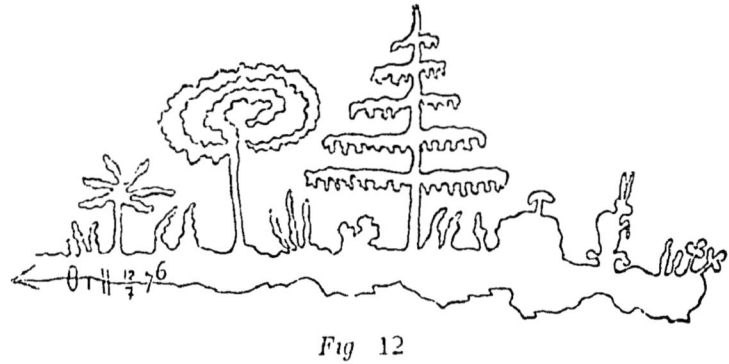

Fig. 12

much favoured by malefactors and bear witness to their great antiquity. They are met with especially during the transition period from the 15th to the 16th century.

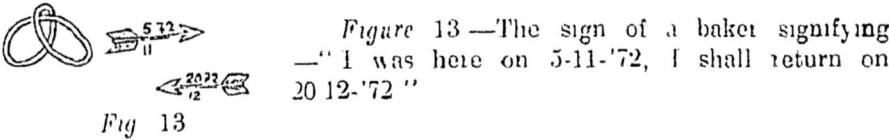

Fig. 13

Figure 13.—The sign of a baker signifying—"I was here on 5-11-'72, I shall return on 20.12-'72."

Figure 14 is one of the most interesting the author has met with.

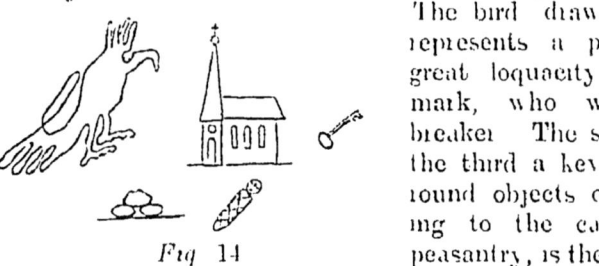

Fig. 14

The bird drawn with a single stroke, represents a parrot, alluding to the great loquacity of the owner of the mark, who was a famous housebreaker. The second sign is a church, the third a key. Below, we see three round objects on a line; this, according to the calendar of the Styrian peasantry, is the emblem of St. Stephen, i.e., three stones placed on the ground, alluding to the martyrdom of the Saint by stoning. They here indicate the date, viz., St. Stephen's Day, 26th December. By the side is an infant in swaddling clothes, this indicates the birth of the Saviour, the date being 25th December. The whole thus means: the owner of the parrot sign intends to break into a church on 26th December. He desires accomplices, and will accordingly be in the neighbourhood of the sign (a lonely chapel in a wood) on 25th December to meet whoever turns up. The police, knowing the importance of the signs, took a copy to the Magistrate, a priest helped to interpret the liturgical emblems, and on Christmas day four dangerous criminals were captured near the chapel in the wood.

Figure 15.—An open book, a broken baton, a human foot, and three dates. The interpretation is unknown.

Besides these signs there are others intended to communicate useful information to other wanderers. This shows clearly the comradeship one might almost call it the organisation existing among these vagabonds, all the members render each other mutual services without even knowing each other, in the hope at some other time of obtaining assistance in return.

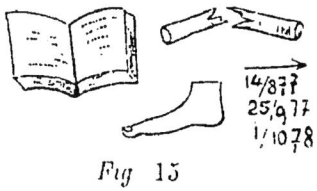
Fig 15

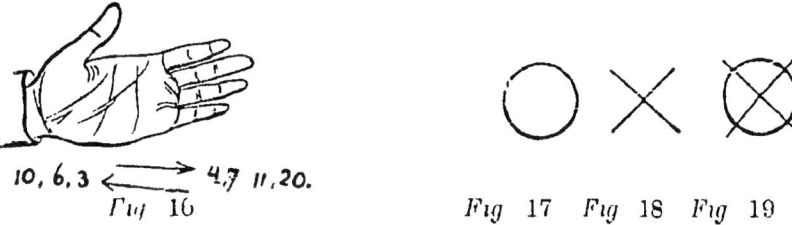

Fig 16   Fig 17 Fig 18 Fig 19

Marks on houses where alms are or are not given

Figure 16 is very common. An open hand signifies that one will find a generous hand, in the 4th, 7th, 11th, and 20th houses to the right, and in the 3rd, 6th, and 10th to the left, it is thus an indication that one may beg successfully at these houses. Sometimes a special mark is put on each house, to show if it is worth while stopping there to ask for alms. The sign is generally very simple: an empty circle, *Fig* 17 shows that here something may be obtained, probably a coin, a cross, *Fig* 18, indicates that nothing can be had, while a combination of the two signs, *Fig* 19, means, "people do give something here, but nothing a tramp wants, *i.e.*, you will only get a piece of bread, a glass of cider, potatoes, an egg, or something else to eat—no money."

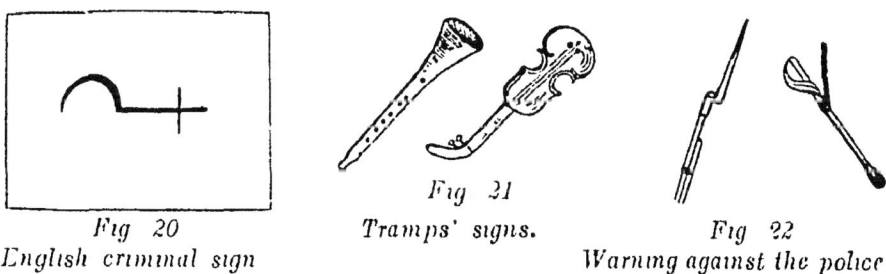

Fig 20
English criminal sign

Fig 21
Tramps' signs.

Fig 22
Warning against the police

English criminals employ similar marks. *Fig* 20 is found in England as well as on the continent and means that stolen goods can be disposed of at the house thus designated. Marks of a violin and flute in their simplest forms, are also very common, *Fig* 21. The violin is a good sign, "people are bountiful", here is an allusion perhaps to the old saying 'the heavens are full of violins." The flute means just the opposite, taken perhaps from the proverb, "you can come here to play the flute"—and no more. In *Figure* 22 are warnings that the police are very active, the signs speak for themselves.

Sometimes also these signs are accompanied by other marks containing a menace or a prophecy, or perhaps also inviting to join in an attack. Some years ago in Eastern Styria a gendarme was found murdered, his body being pierced with innumerable stabs with knives. An inspection of the scene of offence showed that he had sat down by the roadside to fill his pipe,—the tobacco spread out, the pipe half-filled. On account of his conscientious strictness, he was feared and hated by the tramps and gipsies, who had traitorously attacked and murdered him in the manner indicated. A few days after his death there was found on a ruined wall not far from the scene of the crime a rough drawing. It was an easily recognised caricature of a face surmounted by the gendarme's plumed hat, the military moustache was very typical. Round the head four daggers were clearly drawn.

The drawing was certainly not made after the murder for it had been half effaced by rain and no rain had fallen between the day of the crime and the day of the discovery. Here was clearly a threat and call for help; if the discovery had been made in time the officer could have been warned and thus saved his life, at least he would not have taken such a lonely night journey alone. This shows how carefully the places where such signs are likely to be found should be scrutinised and the signs themselves noted.

But the old heraldic signs formerly used by criminals are being gradually supplanted by international written signs, which can be used anywhere. Just as heraldic ornaments and the distinguishing of houses by escutcheons and crests are disappearing, to be replaced by monograms without colour and without meaning, so the old original and interesting marks of criminals are disappearing. Nicknames take the place of the picturesque crest. This is of course due to the great modern spread of reading and writing. Thus inscriptions of the class shown in *Fig. 23* are frequently found

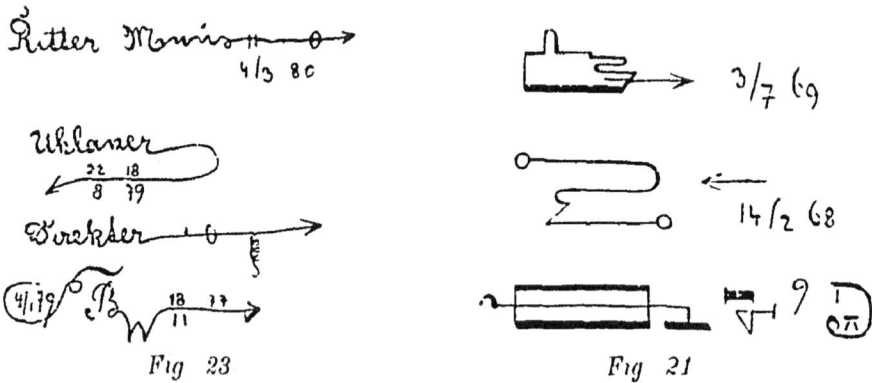

Fig. 23   Fig. 24

In contrast to this modern tendency we may cite criminal marks found in a mountainous and lonely district of Lorraine inhabited by well-to-do peasants, *Fig. 24*. All these were shown to belong to members of the same band, for the marks were all taken from the same book. According to this book, these signs mean: (1) *Dæmonium Mercurii*, (2) *Intelligentia Saturni*, (3) Sign of the guardian angel for Saturday, called *Cassiel*. These marks are found in the "*Pneumatologia occulta et vera*," published at Salamanca. This celebrated book of magic probably came into the hands of a band of rogues, who were so captivated therewith that the magic signs in it awoke from their sleep of centuries to a new life

To this class also belong gipsy signs, which in some way or other indicate their presence in a neighbourhood, not only when they have made an innocent transit, but also when they have committed some crime; in the latter case however, they conceal the signs more carefully or mark them on places difficult to find. The most common mark is a shaded triangle which is supposed to represent a harp; it is generally found on houses where the gipsy has passed the night (Figure 25).

Fig. 25

The gipsy also suspends strips of clothing from a house, a stake, a tree, etc., this is a certain sign that one of the fraternity has passed that way and he has been able for centuries to make the country people believe that these rags are bewitched, producing diseases in the persons touching them, hence no one is bold enough to lay hands on them and they remain there for the information of other gipsies as they come along. As a general rule this sign is found near cross-roads or wherever the gipsy following may be in doubt as to the route taken by the one in advance.

At other times gipsies employ wands twisted together, branches, or even blades of grass or straw, rolled one on the other. They place, for example, by the roadside three stones, one on the top of another, a sign not likely to be noticed by the uninitiated but quite plain to him who knows. Fig. 26

If along the road there should be sand or bare earth or snow, the gipsies make their marks on the ground, which are clear but of course not lasting; as a rule they make three strokes, the middle being the longer and indicating the direction in which they have gone.

Fig. 26

Gipsy signs

The author for a long time believed that these signs were special peculiarities of the gipsies, which they might have brought with them from their Indian home. This is however a mistake, as the German *Schönbach* has shown. In an unprinted sermon (*Leipzig Manuscript*, No. 496), of *Berthold von Regensburg*, who was without doubt the greatest preacher of the Middle Ages, the speaker says:—"The Devil does as the robbers, who put certain signs on the way, so that wanderers think they are on the right way while these signs lead straight to the den of the robbers. Of these signs there are three: Crossed twigs, stones placed together, and connected rods or briers." These are exactly the three last mentioned signs showing the gipsies' road and we must accept it that these signs have for more than five hundred years been widely known and used among the common people though they are now forgotten by these people and remembered only by the conservative gipsies. The latest research on the subject is thus summed up by W. Cooke ("Things Indian," 1906 p. 217)

"The connection between the European gipsies and the East is obvious from philological considerations alone. But the circumstances of their westward migration have long been disputed. On one theory their arrival in Europe, which is recorded for the first time in 1417, was due to the escape of fugitives before the armies of Timur, who reached India in 1398. Another suggestion connects them with a body of Jat minstrels imported from India to Persia by Bahram Gur about A.D. 420, whence they gradually worked their way into Europe. A third theory identifies them with various Indian vagrants of the present day, such as Doms, Bediyas, or Nats. Lastly, Mr. F. H. Groome identifies them with a prehistoric body of wanderers from the East, who brought with them the art of working in bronze. On this view of the case, the modern gipsies may be akin to some of the present vagrant tribes, but the separation occurred at a very early period.

Heinrich Glucksmann declares that gipsies of a certain stock, and particular gipsies of that stock, have special signs (hairs of animals, rags, bits of wood, etc.) as if they were families of tribes. These signs are combined with others in order to give information to stray gipsies. The personal sign, for instance, partly covered with cow dung, gives warning of police; human excrement betokens success and luck; an elder twig—illness; a half-burnt elder-twig with straw—a death; a fir-twig,—an engagement; a willow-twig—a birth; an oak-twig—the return of a traveller, or an arrested comrade; a birchen rod—a capture by the police. Skin or leather cuttings direct a person to hurry to a rendezvous. Holes in the leather betoken a town, when square,—if round, a village. If, for instance, two round, one square, and again one round hole are found in a piece of leather, then the gipsy must pass through two villages and one town in order to reach the next village—the place of meeting. Pig's bristles portend approaching luck, the hairs of dogs danger and insecurity, fragments of glass a dead animal. To understand the somewhat startling science of gipsy fortune-telling and card prophecy, one must also pay attention to the graphical signs which the wanderers draw on the walls of houses, either with a nail or a bit of coal—figures the inhabitants do not notice, as they are scarcely distinguishable from the marks made by time, wind or weather, but which to those who have the necessary knowledge are of extreme importance. According to *Wlislocki*, a cross means that there is nothing to be had, a double cross—rough usage, a circle—liberal treatment, a double circle—unusually benevolent people, two longitudinal lines, and over these two cross-lines—the home of a Magistrate or an Investigating Officer, a double circle and under it two lines—a theft of which gipsies are suspected, a vertical line—the joyful news "Here we have found" (that is "stolen"), a triangle—"Here by cards or fortune-telling money may be made", a circle over the cross urges to a deed of revenge, two serpentine lines show the desire of the woman of the house to have children, two vertical lines bound together by one serpentine line show that the woman will have no more children, two serpentine lines through a circle betoken the death of an old woman, through two circles, the death of an old man, points in a circle show inheritance through death, a serpentine line cutting a triangle—the death of householder, two such lines through the same figure—the death of householder's wife, a serpentine line through two circles—the unfaithfulness of the wife, a circle between two serpentine lines—the unfaithfulness of the husband, a vertical with a horizontal line under it, and under this again a circle—matrimonial designs, etc. It is easy to see that these signs are very useful in fortune-telling and card prophecy, and it is worth while to notice the camaraderie of these people who help one another, expecting in the same way to be helped in turn

All these gipsy signs are certainly met with among other tramps but they prove that the man employing them, if not a gipsy himself, is at least in close touch with gipsies and has become practically one of themselves

These marks of criminals must not be confounded with those of peripatetic grinders, made on the houses where they have received scissors, knives, etc., to sharpen. There is no doubt that their marks closely resemble those of criminals and trace their origin to the times when knife-grinders who were also generally umbrella-menders were wont to wander along the roads in company with tramps of all sorts. When then a grinder has collected during the day a number of knives and scissors, all so much alike, it would be impossible for him to return them to the true owners without a special mark for each house (such as dyers and laundrymen) These marks often furnish a useful *memoria technica*, they are curious and sometimes ancient, but their only importance for us is to distinguish them from true criminal signs. When we are in doubt, we must ask the first grinder we meet, whether perambulating or stationary, for each knows accurately the marks used by other grinders

A curious and somewhat impertinent sign which was at one time believed by the author to be purely local, but is now shown (by *Klausmann* of Berlin) to be very widespread, is that of a human caricature followed by three marks of interrogation. The plain meaning of the sign, wherever it has been discovered, is unmistakable "Where is the thief? Can't you catch him?"

B Hand Signals

Signals or signs made by the hands, as means of communication between malefactors, constitute a complete alphabet, the letters being formed by the different positions of the fingers, sometimes the ordinary well-known deaf-and-dumb alphabet is employed. But this alphabet is not identical in all countries, and though the changes are not in essential constituents, yet they are sufficient to prevent the deaf and dumb of different countries communicating with each other by this means. It is said to be different in the case of criminals who have so altered the alphabet as to make it in a sense international. Be this as it may, the important thing is not so much to understand the alphabet employed, as to realise the fact of its existence, to know that two accomplices can carry on a conversation from the prison windows across a wide courtyard

Another mode of communicating with the hands is to write slowly in the air with the fingers words that a quick observer can easily read

All such modes of communication are specially employed during those "confrontations," or bringing of the parties face to face, which many persons are so enamoured of, but which the present writer considers both insufferable and dangerous. One may confront honest and unsuspected witnesses, a mistake leading to grave consequences may thus often be readily cleared up, and also fresh starting points may thus be obtained which repeated interrogatories could never furnish. But beyond that "confronta tions" have many drawbacks and at most afford an easy way of getting out of a corner by simplifying the rest of the inquiry. Whoever knows with what ease and rapidity two malefactors can come to a thorough understanding by means of their secret alphabet will take care not to let them have such a simple and easy means of communication; at the moment of the confrontation and during the preparation of the record they will perfectly comprehend each other in spite of the strictest supervision.

In the widest sense of the word, these "signals" include every kind of mutual understanding, arrived at by means not comprehended by the uninitiated. These understandings, often leading to serious consequences, are arrived at when prisoners are allowed to communicate with their relations and friends, even under the very eyes of the Investigating Officer. Often the latter will be astonished at the explosive violence with which persons, deemed absolutely incapable of any emotion, throw themselves on each other's necks, weep, cry out, express their feelings in the midst of renewed embraces, until the Investigating Officer thinks this exhibition of grief has lasted long enough and separates the weeping participants. Generally the only object of all this scene is to slip into the possession of the accused a letter, a file, or some other small object or to whisper in his ear hints for his defence or the name of an alibi witness. On the other hand the accused may slip over to the visitor some small object which he has hitherto been able to conceal, or in turn to whisper some words in his ear.

Lee *Lallemant* relates the case of the concubine of a prisoner who passed from her mouth to his a piece of gold, with which he shortly afterwards attempted to bribe the warder. The same writer suggests, and on good grounds, that the infants women bring with them are often dangerous; it is not surprising that the prisoner should spend a long time nursing and caressing his child, but at the same time he takes care to secure all the objects which the infant is made use of to convey.

True, a certain amount of smartness is required to thus give and receive, in spite of the close supervision exercised over prisoners, but those who are dangerous are not precisely the unskilful ones, and all possess more or less the cleverness of the pickpocket.

To prove the adroitness of these gentry, an example may be given to show how readily such exchanges may be effected. A police official one day informed us that he had something interesting to communicate. On going to the lock-up we found a pickpocket who, having just completed a sentence of imprisonment, was about to be handed over to a foreign power. The criminal had been ill and well-cared for by the authorities, and on the eve of his extradition had offered to "show something". This something was then shown. The speciality of our man was to ask for "a light". The prisoner asked one of the company to place an object like a pocket book in the inside pocket of his frock-coat but without buttoning it, then the victim was requested to light a cigar and hand one to the experimenter. The latter, in a natural manner, threw his great coat over his arm and advancing with a polite bow requested a light for his cigar. The person addressed consented, keeping all the time an eye on the book that represented the pocket book. The man took a long time to light his cigar and was very clumsy over the job. The cigar would not catch fire, and the other party had to take two or three strong pulls at his to give more fire and make the lighting easier. At last the cigar burned, the thief made another polite bow and retired, but the book was no longer in the pocket. The hand under the great coat had worked so cleverly that the book was extracted without the slightest contact being felt. It was certainly remarkably clever to distract the attention of a person forewarned by a show of pretended clumsiness. How easy it must be then for criminals of this nature to transfer objects when both parties are active and can warn each other by a glance, a sign, a movement, that there is something to give or to take.

But even the over-prudent Investigating Officer who deems he has avoided all danger by forbidding "embraces, handshakings," etc., cannot prevent these people from communicating with each other by signals, glances, movements of the hands, etc., the communication may be short and swift, but will convey everything essential and compromise the success of the inquiry. A single moment may cause the irrevocable loss of all the trouble taken, all the skill employed.

Among the modes of communication reference may be made to the secret writing of prisoners. Everyone knows that this writing exists, for persons even use "sympathetic" or invisible ink for perfectly inoffensive purposes. These inks are solutions of salts of cobalt, copper, iron, etc., sulphuric acid and water, milk, urine, etc. Some of these are not worth much from the present point of view, as they necessitate the use of chemicals both for writing and for reading what is written. The prisoner under lock and key will not find it easy to find chloride of cobalt or protochloride of iron to write with, nor a solution of gall-nuts to enable him to bring the writing to light. Only substances easily procured are dangerous and important, such are as concerns writing coming into prisons, all inks that become visible by heating, rubbing with burnt paper, ashes, dust, etc., for such agents are easily found in every prison. If, e.g., one writes with a solution of chloride of cobalt, the gentle heat of a stove or of a burning match will make the writing appear, at least for the moment. If the writing be made with a solution of gum arabic, one has only to breathe on the letter and then rub it with ashes or dust, and the written characters stand out quite distinctly. The breath causes the gum on the surface to become sticky, and the dust thus adheres to the gummy characters but not to the paper. The necessary ingredients, especially dust, are found in all prisons.

Particularly dangerous inks are such as can be made to appear and disappear several times; the accused can thus read them over and over again, he can also with this ink make notes of things he does not wish to forget and even carry them about with him. Whenever he wants to refresh his memory he can do so at his ease. Such inks are very numerous, the best, and best known, is that called "Weidman's" ink—one part of linseed oil, eight parts of liquid ammonia, a hundred parts of water. Before writing this ink must be well shaken and the paper moistened, when the writing will be visible but will disappear when dry. Another ink, easy to prepare and consequently much used is the following: copper is dissolved in hydrochloric acid, a little azotate of potassium is added, and the whole diluted with water until the writing obtained is no longer visible. Everytime the paper is heated the writing starts up in dark yellow, completely disappearing when cold.

Great attention should be paid to writings of this kind and it must not be forgotten that such secret intimations are generally found between the lines of documents otherwise perfectly harmless.

Letters coming out of prison are almost always written either with urine or with milk, the writing is easily made clear by heating or rubbing with dust. Such communications generally pass between one prison and another, but are also sent to the outside world. Even when the very natural precaution is adopted of not allowing the prisoner to write except under the supervision of the warder, it may be possible to change the paper for another on which he has previously written with urine, or to scribble without being observed a few words with urine during the formal writing of the letter. The author knows of the case of a female prisoner who, while writing in the office of the superintendent of the jail himself, moistened a small piece of pointed wood with milk from her own bosom, and thus inscribed several lines between those written in ink. There are two expedients to get over these tricks: to heat every letter that enters or leaves a prison or better still to let nothing either come in or go out.

The first method should be always employed, the second should be adopted in all important cases. When a letter arrives addressed to an accused under detention, he should be sent for, the letter should be read to him, several times if he desires it, but should never be handed over to him; the fact of reading should be entered on the record and the letter attached to it. In this there is an additional advantage, no paper enters the prison, and it is well known that the margins and backs of letters are often used for fresh correspondence. When a letter of a person under detention is to be sent out of a prison, the letter should be carefully copied and then compared and signed by the prisoner in presence of the superintendent or the magistrate himself, the original should be attached to the record and the copy posted.

But in spite of every precaution we may be taken in, as the following case will prove. The proprietor of a small piece of forest land was suspected for many years of receiving stolen property and conveying it across the frontier. He was arrested, his wife being allowed to remain at liberty; she was under her husband's orders, could not be suspected of wishing to run away, and had in the house several little children, one being an infant at the breast. The man at his first examination denied everything but expressed a strong desire to speak to his wife. In spite of the distance she was accordingly brought to the courthouse. The unusual insistence of the man appeared suspicious, accordingly an interview was refused, but the prisoner was allowed to send any message he chose to the woman. After a lot of bother he stated that all he wanted to say to his wife was that she should look well after the cattle, as he had done until his arrest, and see that they had plenty of nourishment. This apparently harmless message was accurately communicated to the wife. But doubts remained, and the same day a police constable was sent to see the cattle possessed by the couple. His report was that they possessed three goats and a half-starved horse used for carrying the stolen property across the border. Undoubtedly the Investigating Officer had been humbugged and been made the agent of conveying an ambiguous and disastrous message. The matter remained an enigma for a long time. Later on the Investigating Officer had in confinement a young woman who had grown up among gipsies and had been taught to steal with great skill. A great deal of interest was taken in the girl because it was suspected that she had been stolen when a child, although inquiries as to her origin proved fruitless. She showed her gratitude for the interest taken in her and the kindness shown her by giving a great deal of hitherto unknown information about the manners and customs of the gipsies, and among other matters about their double speech. Asked as to the meaning of the expression "feed the cattle," the girl said it meant locally "deceive the officers of the law and admit nothing." Thus the meaning of the message from husband to wife was ' I have admitted nothing, do not you admit anything on any consideration.' Of course the language of swindlers and thieves is full of ambiguous expressions, most of which are however perfectly well known. Another mode of communication is by means of letters deeply cut in wood. Thus if letters be deeply graven in soft, smooth wood, so that the deeply cut characters form together a word or phrase, and if, above these characters, the wood be scraped with a sharp knife or better still a piece of glass until the writing is no longer visible on the surface, it may be made to reappear by soaking the wood. In fact, the fibres of the wood, where pressure has been exerted to form the letters, remain compressed, although no trace of the compression is visible to the naked eye. If, therefore, the portions of wood thus compressed be soaked in water, they swell and the writing stands out clearly in relief. Any wood may be used, but the finer the grain (as maple or pear) the better the chance of success. Accordingly every morsel of wood coming from outside must be examined, as the handles of brushes, combs and mirrors, or of tools, boxes containing provisions, etc. In one case the writing was on a wooden spoon, and only appeared when the spoon was put in the soup. It was represented that the individual was "so accustomed" to this spoon and no difficulty was therefore raised to his using this "harmless" utensil.

Of another kind of communication the following example may be given. In a big affair twenty-eight persons were arrested, the cells were limited in number and it was quickly seen that the persons under detention communicated with each other in various ways. The superintendent of the prison went on watch himself and observed that from the peephole, or inspection hole, of each cell, left purposely open to render supervision more easy, a hand was protruded as the soldier sentry passed and deposited a small article on the top of his cartridge-pouch hanging on his back. As the soldier passed the next cell another hand appeared, removed the object placed on the cartridge-pouch, and so on thus the soldier guards were the innocent means of communication between the prisoners. As they had no paper, the prisoner used scraps of linen torn from their shirts. The only pencil they had travelled with the letter.

C Signals of Recognition

These are essentially international and enable members of the criminal classes to recognise each other anywhere. Wherever they may be, in a hotel, in a shop, at church, on the railway, in prison, if two members of the criminal classes meet it is important that they should recognise each other at once, so that they may act together or not interfere with each other, or perhaps not try their games on each other; a card cheat, for example, only wastes his time in endeavouring to entrap another cheat. For the Investigating Officer it suffices to know that these signals exist, are known, and understood wherever criminals congregate. If an Investigating Officer ignores this fact, he will be continually meeting strange things he cannot explain. For example a man is accused of having attempted to rob a fellow passenger in a railway carriage. The accused in his defence pretends that it was impossible for him to make such an attempt as a "gentleman" was seated opposite to him who would have seen everything, and besides he would not have dared to steal under the very eyes of the gentleman. The latter had continued his journey to an unknown destination, but could not be an accomplice as he got into the train half-a-day before the accused. One might perhaps believe this story did not one know that a single movement of the hand exchanged between the two was enough to assure them that neither had anything to fear from the other.

Again, in an hotel a swindler sells something false as genuine, pretending to be absolutely honest, so much so that two perfect strangers are greatly taken with the article, declaring they would have bought it, if the dupe had not previously practically completed his purchase. True enough the two men are strangers, but just as truly a single sign enables them to play the game of the cheat.

It is exactly the same with card-sharpers who assemble, especially on market days, in hotels and other places of public resort and immediately assist each other though they may have never met before. They play with each other a harmless game in which now one, now another wins. This works admirably and the people about gain confidence. Or they play at guessing puzzles, and the guesser generally gains although he who has propounded the puzzle declares it insoluble. They play, at first, only for love, but when the spectators get excited and join in they play no longer for love but for the hard-won money of the countryman who suspects nothing and loses everything. Or one plays while an accomplice sits behind his partner and indicates the cards held. In any event this recognition prevents a swindler from wasting his time in trying to dupe another member of the fraternity.

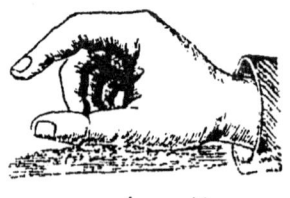
Fig. 27

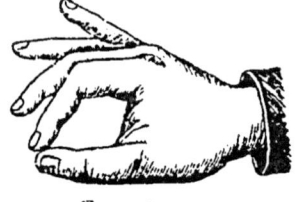
Fig. 28

The signals employed are numerous, among the Roman nations especially, among Italians and French a great number are recognised. Pitre ("Archives de Lombroso," IX., 1888) has collected 18 signals of recognition employed by Italian criminals alone. For our purpose the two here illustrated are the most important, being known by all the scoundrels of the civilised world for centuries. Fig. 27 is most commonly used in the north of Europe, Fig. 28 in the south.

Another signal, of less interest to the Investigating Officer but of great importance to criminals, consists in closing one eye and squinting with the other towards the nose. It is a piece of face play we all know, and often indulge in as a joke, to show some secret understanding. In the life of the swindler the sign is of great importance and often forms the starting point of a more or less prolonged partnership in crime.

It must be remembered that the "friendships" of these gentry do not generally last long. There are many causes leading to the disruption of harmony between them—the division of the spoil, suspicion of treason, difference of views as to the mode of carrying out a scheme, jealousy of the superior cleverness of one, discontent at the clumsiness of the other, etc. Often too they are dispersed as a consequence of the miscarriage of some plot, by imprisonment for different periods of detention, and other accidents. Besides it is not to their interest to remain too long in company, for the forgathering of a number of persons, who enjoy a bad reputation with the authorities is suspicious and attracts an amount of supervision most disagreeable to them. Thus there is a continual changing in criminal partnerships, they unite for one or two schemes, share the danger, the booty, and the secrets, and separate never to meet again. Thus they are always under the necessity of seeking new accomplices and for that only a little address is required. Men pursuing the same aim, whether good or bad, meet and recognise each other easily, we might almost say instinctively. This phenomenon is based to some extent on our knowledge of ourselves. Each of us knows to some extent his own qualities, and easily recognises them in others. An observer will quickly perceive that ardent huntsmen recognise each other as quickly as pederasts, that chess players and men of science will take to each other as quickly as gamblers and tap-room companions, so one sharp will pick out another among hundreds of honest men. A wink of the eye to make sure one is not deceived, a response of recognition—and the same evening they commit a robbery in company, both alike risk their liberty, but each is absolutely sure of the devotion of his new comrade. This is the only explanation of the inconceivable rapidity with which those people make friends who come no one knows whence, and who have hardly arrived before they are found working hand in hand.

We may here recall the report of a police officer upon a big housebreaking, which stated that the author could be no other than a famous operator, who had always a very characteristic plan of operations, were it not that he had been released from a long period of imprisonment only two days before, and could not therefore have had time to recruit the three or four accomplices absolutely necessary for the commission of the offence. Accordingly he let the man slip quietly away, and only later was it proved that he had organised the robbery; one of his accomplices admitted that he had found and enlisted his assistants by this sign.

D Acoustical Signs.

These may be divided into two classes—

1 Calls and cries of warning

"Calls" consist almost exclusively of imitation of the cries of animals especially those that are accustomed to make a noise at night. Naturally persons planning a night attack on a person in a forest or jungle, or a night attack on a house, do not call to each other by name or make any noise that would attract attention. The cry of an animal especially when well imitated is never suspected, and when there is a previous understanding it is as certain a call as the names themselves.

Thus is imitated the crowing of a cock, the pipe of the quail, the croaking of a frog near water, or of a toad, but above all the hooting of the owl. Owls are everywhere, in the forests, in the fields, in the mountains, in the marshes, in isolated spots and close to human dwellings. Early in the evening as well as before dawn the cry of the owl is never suspected, it is even used in broad day by hunters summoning each other to the woods. No animal fears it, white men have a superstitious dread of the hoot of the owl, hearing it they will sooner stop then ears than watch their pockets. According to the distance, the hoot of the small barn-owl (*Strix Scops*) or that of the great night owl (*Strix Noctua*) is used (see Fig 29).

This matter may be important. When the question is whether an attack in a forest or a house-breaking has been committed by one man or by several as accomplices, the witnesses should be asked whether shortly before or after the crime they have not heard the hoot of an owl. If the answer be in the affirmative, it will be a strange coincidence if just at the time and place of the crime an owl should have been hooting. Watchmen of all kinds should also keep their ears open for such sounds.

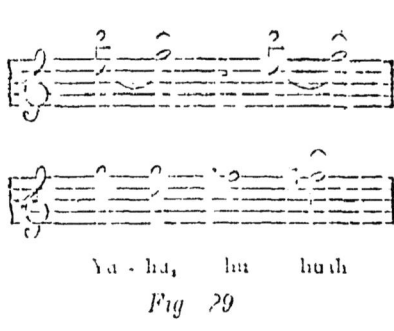

Fig 29

As for cries of warning, all kinds of noises are made use of, as a rule they are heard only when things are going amiss and the only resource left is flight, for this a very distinctive convention is necessary, a whistle, a clapping of the hands, a loud cough is enough as a signal of danger.

2 *Phonetic communication in prison*

This means of communication is more widespread and more dangerous than ordinarily believed. It is generally imagined that it is impossible for criminals to transmit long and precise messages to each other, short communications it is supposed are useless, and not worth wasting time over. Such an opinion shows that a man has never known his own prison, that he has never taken into account the consequences of such correspondence, in short that he is a silly dupe.

Whoever will take the trouble carefully to study prison life, will very quickly learn how things go on, even in the best-managed establishments. Near the doors and the windows, by day and by night, in the cells or at the walking exercise, one hears phrases, words, numbers, inarticulate sounds which prove that noises have been heard, for otherwise the system would not be carried on so methodically. The most extraordinary stories are told as to means of communication employed. One man pretended to be a fool, and uttered nothing but numbers; in the neighbouring gallery another man was wicked enough to mock the poor fool; when the one below had finished bawling out his numbers, the man above commenced his mocking. And so they went on time about. When at last it was discovered that the two were carrying on a conversation, it was too late.

In another prison two very pious Jews were confined who daily chanted Hebrew melodies. But the peculiar thing was that they never sang at the same time so as to interfere with each other; it was only found out later by chance that the pair were communicating by means of their chants and psalms and that they had been able to tell each other everything they wished.

When persons under detention sing in prison, everyone is quite pleased; the prisoners are assumed to have nothing to complain about and they are permitted to sing away to their hearts' content, but no one pays any attention to the meaning of their songs. But if the Investigating Officer would take the trouble to bestir himself, he would be surprised to find that the text, or *motif*, of the songs is some portion of the investigation. Signals, and not unimportant ones, are made by whistling; it is said that by practice persons can thus come to understand each other perfectly. This is quite possible; one has only to consider the wide vogue of the system ' *Hakesen*,' that is, communication by the means of blows struck on an object. In certain countries the practice became so extended and common that completely new buildings had to be erected at great expense. Cells were built with triple walls, and Avé-Lallemant says that once at Weimar clocks were placed in the prison corridors, so that the vibratory sound of the pendulums should interrupt the communications of the prisoners among themselves. The most interesting example is that of the unfortunate *Franz v Spaun* who, towards the end of the 18th century, was confined as a " state prisoner " for ten years at Mukacz and Kufstein. He had discovered that a certain Frenchman (afterwards Duke and Minister) was confined in the next cell and wished to communicate with him. He began by knocking frequently on the wall but always 24 blows at a time, until his neighbour came to understand that the 24 knocks designated the 24 letters of the alphabet. After this response, Spaun commenced knocking once, twice, thrice, etc., until the other understood that these meant a, b, c, etc. Thus in a short time the two could perfectly understand each other and talk freely. The Frenchman was released before Spaun, but did not forget him and later on procured him a pension. It is said that Spaun went to see the Frenchman at Munich and began to knock on the door as of old. " It is either Spaun or the Devil," cried out the Frenchman. Avé-Lallemant declares that at the present time the Morse telegraphic alphabet is in common use in prisons, the dash and a 's being represented by sharp and prolonged knocks.

It is a good plan for superintendents and warders when they hear this knocking to knock back; this will at least interrupt the communication. It should always be done when a new prisoner is brought in; the ultimate result being that intercommunications are thrown into utter confusion.

It is stated that prisoners confined on the same story often communicate in the following way: they lie down flat on their faces on the floor and speak slowly and distinctly along the planks. If one person in the other cell however far away, places his ear to the plank, he can hear perfectly everything said. Of course for this the co-prisoners must have a previous understanding and must also have arranged the hours of the interviews. It is certain that correspondence can be thus carried on, one has only to think of the incredible distances at which one can hear the sound of cannon, the galloping of horses, the tread of men, etc., when the ear is applied to the ground. It can also be tested in practice, by trying it in our own houses between rooms most distant from each other.

E. Marks of Stigmata on the Face

To "stigmatise" is to place a mark on the person of a criminal who has been guilty of treason to his fellows.

Some assert that these stigmata are very rare at the present time, and *Lallemant* avers that he has only seen one man, an old Jew, so marked. This may perhaps be true for the North of Germany, but in Austria and Eastern Europe the thing is common enough, especially among gipsies. The author has frequently had to do with gipsies of both sexes bearing marks which, by their own admission, were those of "stigmatisation."

Not far from the Hungarian frontier is a district infested with gipsies. In the east of this district is a police station. The station-house officer, a middle-aged man, very active and intelligent, had by long experience acquired a most intimate acquaintance with gipsy customs—the way he travels, the route he follows, the neighbourhoods where he steals, how he gets his information, what he steals, how he gets clean away, where he sells his booty, in fact all the special customs of the gipsies were as well known to him as if he had lived with them for years. Of course this station-house officer was equally well known to the gipsies, and so feared by them that he had become practically useless at that station. He was accordingly transferred to another district equally ill-famed for the numerous house-breakings committed by gipsies.

One day a gipsy came to this station-house officer and endeavoured by mysterious cries to enlist his confidence. At last he showed a fresh scar on his cheek, stating that his comrades had unjustly accused him of treason and thus stigmatised him; now out of revenge he desired to become a traitor in real earnest, and offered himself as a spy in the service of the station-house officer. The latter accepted the offer, the gipsy was well informed and worthy of confidence, the station-house officer was apprised of many house-breakings before they took place; if he always arrived too late to catch the robbers, that was not the gipsy's fault, no more was he to blame if he could assist the station-house officer to discover only a small portion of the booty and that of little value. But in time it was observed that, by some strange coincidence, every time the gipsy gave information about a proposed house-breaking, a much more serious one took place several leagues away. In short, the whole thing was discovered to be an imposture. The gipsy, a new Zopyrus, had caused the wound to be inflicted on his cheek, so as to be able to assist his comrades. He always diverted the attention of the authorities to some trifling occurrence, while his confederates thus safely carried out most profitable expeditions in other quarters.

True, on another occasion a member of a band with wide ramifications denounced a most serious crime which was to be committed. Some years later this informer, a woman, was seen with a great scar on her right cheek. We may well suppose that here was cause and effect.

In all cases Investigating Officers are bound to be extremely careful when face to face with persons thus hall-marked. The only rule is, "each case must be treated according to its peculiar circumstances."

CHAPTER VIII

SLANG OF CRIMINALS.

In this chapter the author treats of the slang peculiar to German criminals. To us the study of such slang can be of but little practical utility. We cannot do better than reproduce with additions the list of books given by *Barrere* dealing in some way or other with slang. We expressly recommend the writings of *Rev. J. W. Horsley*, who has had intimate acquaintance with criminals as a prison chaplain. For the rest, as we have stated, each Investigating Officer must study for himself the slang of the criminals with whom he comes in contact. He will find any knowledge thus acquired will be of inestimable service in the elucidation of crime.

Barrere (Albert) — Argot and Slang. London, Whittaker & Co.

Ainsworth (W. Harrison) — Rookwood — Jack Sheppard

Bampfylde-Moore Carew — The History and Curious Adventures of. London

Brewer (Cobham) — Phrase and Fable, Cassell, London 1904

Brome (Richard) — Jovial Crew, or, The Merry Beggars, 1652

Chatto and Windus — The Slang Dictionary, Etymological, Historical, and Anecdotal, London, 1885

Davies (T. Lewis O.) — A Supplementary English Glossary. London, 1881

Dickens (Charles) — Works

Farmer (J. S.) & Henley (W. E.) — A Dictionary of Slang and Colloquial English, 1905, Routledge & Sons

Fielding (Henry) — Amelia — Jonathan Wild

Greenwood (James) — The Seven Curses of London — Dick Temple — Odd People

Harman (Thomas) — Caveat or Warening for Common Cursetors, London, 1568

Hobson-Jobson — A Glossary of Anglo-Indian Colloquial Words and Phrases, and of kindred Terms, London, 1903

Horsley (Rev. J. W.) — Autobiography of a Thief, Macmillan's Magazine, 1879 — Jottings from Jail, 1887

Kingsley (Charles) — Westward Ho' — Two Years Ago

Lytton (Henry Bulwer) — Paul Clifford — Ernest Maltravers

Pascoe (C. E.) — Every-day Life in Our Public Schools, London

Sims (G. R.) — Rogues and Vagabonds

CHAPTER IX

WANDERING TRIBES.

Section i.—General Considerations.

We shall commence with some remarks upon the manner of living of wandering tribes, the author having learned by experience that it is difficult to have relations with so remarkable a people when not sufficiently known, and that the elucidation of a case in which they are involved is very much facilitated by some amount of familiarity with them. The gipsy differs in every respect from the civilised man, however coarse and degraded the latter may be; and all that one has learnt and brought into practice in dealing with other types is of absolutely no utility when one's business is with the gipsy.

The difference which separates the gipsy so entirely from other criminals is as great as the resemblance which gipsies have to one another. Gipsies have remained unchanged since they have lived in civilised countries, and on reading the oldest documents, government orders and reports of cases in which they have been concerned, we cannot help thinking that we must be dealing with the gipsies of our own time. In the course of centuries gipsies have spread throughout all countries, they have remained, until the present day and wherever they are to be found, similar as regards height, build, appearance, language, manners and way of living. *Milosich* reduces all the gipsy dialects of all countries to a single neo-Indian dialect, forming with the Cafri language and the Dardu dialects a single linguistic group. *De Gerandu* says —' between the gipsy of the French departments neighbouring on the Pyrenees and the gipsy of Hungary it is impossible to establish any difference." *Schwicher* says —' almost the same habits, the same virtues, and the same vices, are found among the gipsies of all countries", and *Liebich*, a well-known criminal lawyer, remarks "one real and authentic gipsy is a type of all the rest."

These ideas regarding a resemblance as remarkable as it is difficult to explain, ideas which are shared by all those who have any knowledge of gipsies, are apparently contradicted only by the fact that two gipsies, the one a French gipsy and the other an Indian one hardly understand one another. But the reason is simply this, that on the one hand the French gipsy has mixed with his language as many French words as on the other hand the Indian gipsy has mingled Indian words with his. But if the Indian gipsy were able to write something in his language and if the French gipsy were able to read it, the latter would be sure to understand what his Indian brother had written, and the small number of foreign words would not trouble him very much, and even when gipsies would, owing to modifications in pronunciation not be able to understand one another, it would be found that they nevertheless speak the same language, a language which is the daughter of the root language of India and the European gipsy would none the less be found to be nephew of the Indian. They call themselves Sinte because they assert that they come from Sind, i.e. Ind (Hindustan). Speaking of Romany (the Gipsy language) a learned Slavonian said that he found it interesting to be able to study a Hindu dialect in the heart of Europe (Leland, "English Gipsies," Chapter VIII., p. 109.) This language contains about 5,000 words, the chief of which are corrupt Sanskrit.

Wlislocki, who has lived among the gipsies and knows them perfectly, has characterised them the best:—"Their moral qualities," he says, "are a strange mixture of vanity and vulgarity, of coquetry, seriousness, and light headedness, and an almost complete want of manly judgment and intelligence, accompanied by a perfidious ingenuity and cunning which are the usual complements of a general ignorance; in addition, they have also in their ways and habits an outrageous sycophancy tending to the spoliation of others; they have not the slightest regard for the truth, and sustain the pro and the contra with an affrontery at which they cannot blush—shame being to them entirely unknown. The pain of blows alone can make them pause, and in their sentiments they are even more sensual than they are cruel and vindictive."

To this excellent picture we may perhaps add that Wlislocki was acquainted with the "Kortorar," a wandering Transylvanian tribe, the members of which, if all the descriptions of it are to be believed, are considerably superior to the general run of gipsy. When dealing therefore with gipsies with whom we have business, any praise which may be found hidden away in the passage we have just recited must be greatly diminished, and, while not forgetting the incorrigible laziness, thirst for vengeance, and extreme cruelty common to the ordinary gipsy, we must also mention a trait of character which he possesses in a very high degree, namely an incredible cowardice which passes all limitation. Indeed this fundamental trait of the gipsy is the most important from the point of view of the criminal expert, since not only to judge of the character of a gipsy, his acts, intentions, motives, and his aim in view, but also to know whether a particular act has been committed by gipsies or not, the fact must be continually borne in mind that a gipsy and cowardice are inseparable.

In answer to this we are often reminded of how in 1557 the gipsies defended, on behalf of Francois Perenyi against General Puchheim, the castle of Nagy-Ida (near Kaschau) and there showed proof of bravery. In the first place this is almost the only case that we know of in history of gipsy courage, and, moreover, on this occasion they were sheltered behind walls and intrenchments, and finally, they only defended themselves with the courage of despair in order to save their own lives—which indeed, they ended by losing. Nor can any conclusion be drawn from the fact that gipsies sometimes make good soldiers. Another case has recently cropped up in which some gipsies showed fight on being evicted from some waste land on which they had squatted. But these gipsies, who were known as the Black Patch gipsies, soon gave in, and it appears that only one or two of them, and these women, did anything more than throw a stone.

'It is only after having been a soldier for a long time and become a practised pillager,' says *Captain Sulzer*, of the Austrian Army, a man who had a thorough knowledge of gipsies, ' that the gipsy exposes his breast to the bullets of the enemy with the ordinary courage of the soldier, nor does he seize a wayfarer's purse without first, from the ambush of a thicket, killing him or rendering him incapable of resistance. On more than one occasion I have had experience of this in Transylvania, Wallachia, and Moldavia; I have seen one determined man, a stick in hand, put to flight half a village of gipsies, and in Transylvania there is a proverb to the effect that with a wet rag fifty gipsies may be put to flight."

But there is no need to travel in Wallachia to become convinced of this. Hardly a day passes in which we have not occasion to see how a single policeman or even a gamekeeper, armed merely with a sword, can make short work of a whole band of gipsies. At one period of the author's professional career he had dealings with gipsies extending over a considerable space of time. One day a single policeman brought in a band of more than thirty gipsies, about twenty being men, whom he had arrested on suspicion of theft. They had only one van with them, and the policeman had seized the horse by the bridle. None of them had tried to escape. The jailer related to the author that he had asked them why they had allowed themselves to be arrested by a solitary policeman. "Sir," the eldest of them had replied, ' the policeman had a rifle and in that rifle were seven cartridges.' To the remark that the policeman could not have killed them all, the jailer received the following characteristic reply :—' Oh, no, certainly not all, but at least seven, and none of us was desirous of being one of the seven.' A gipsy,'' says Smith, ' a big, cowardly, hulking fellow and an Englishman had long had a grudge against one another. The Englishman could not get the cowardly gipsy to fight it out. At last the Englishman offered the gipsy half-a-crown and a gallon of beer to let him have one round with him. The gipsy consented to this condition. The money was paid and the beer drunk, after which the gipsy wanted to back out of the bargain. Before the big gipsy would at the last minute undertake to fight the little Englishman, the gipsy stipulated that there was to be " no hitting upon the nose." The Englishman did not like this shuffling, but he agreed to it, and they stripped for the encounter. For a few minutes they sparred about until the gipsy saw his opportunity to hit the Englishman full tilt upon his nose, which he did with a tremendous force sufficient to break it. When the gipsy was asked why he did it, he said, 'I could not help it, my hand slipped.' "

Equally characteristic is the fact that all murders committed by gipsies of which the author has heard have been committed only upon persons asleep or attacked from behind and from an absolutely safe ambush, or killed with the aid of poison. It is certain that a gipsy has never been known to commit a crime where there has been any danger to be faced.

The truth of this is not impeached by the fact that gipsies often make excellent spies. It is particularly interesting to note how a gipsy does not mind being employed in this trade, for the skill he can make use of when engaged in his own work of thieving is thereby proved. *Schwicker* relates how in 1625 Wallenstein was able to congratulate himself on the employment of gipsies as spies. Jean Zapolya, the Hungarian usurper, employed them against Ferdinand of Austria, and the Imperial General Count Basta would have been unable, without the assistance of a gipsy, to have introduced a letter into Bistritz when that town was besieged in 1602. In Upper Hungary seven gipsies and a French engineer named Pierre Durois (who had lived among them for seven years) were made use of in 1676, and with their assistance the King of France was enabled to obtain plans of the principal strategic positions of Germany and Austria. Grellmann remarks, and with reason, that the gipsy lends himself perfectly to spying, because he is so easily attracted by a money prize, and because he is always in needy circumstances, and also because his peculiar ideas of ambition and pride lead him to think that he becomes in this way quite an important personage. It must be remembered that the gipsy has wandered for centuries, and often in difficult circumstances, over countries entirely unknown to him, and has thus acquired a strongly developed bump of locality. He must know what it is to have to seek out a locality with which he is acquainted only by hearsay, and where, e.g., the band is going to commit some theft, that is he must know how to find the shortest and safest way, how to split up the band and bring it together again, to follow with the plunder a different but as safe a road on the return, to find his band suddenly scattered and yet able to pick one another up again in a predetermined spot, all without map or compass, without knowing how to read and without being able to question the inhabitants. And this is what a band of gipsies has to do every day.

In the campaign of 1878, immediately after the taking of Sarajevo, it was necessary to establish communication between the eastern wing and the main body of the Austrian army. One night about two o'clock two hussars rode up to the outposts with despatches for the Commander-in-Chief. They had only been pointed out the direction which they had to follow, and ordered to find the Austrian outposts, who would send them to General Philippovic. The two hussars,—a corporal and a private—left on horseback about nightfall, had to cross a most difficult portion of country, occupied on all sides by the Turks, had on two occasions to take to the water and swim, and yet arrived safe and sound in a very short space of time. The author asked the corporal how he had been able to find his way in a country absolutely unknown to him, and he made the characteristic reply:—" I didn't know, but my comrade there is a gipsy." Thereupon the author looked at the other hussar and noticed by the feeble light of the camp-fire the ruffian like face of the veritable gipsy, who at that moment was ten times more interested in a half smoked cigarette than in the whole countryside. It was learnt later that this gipsy and his corporal successfully effected their return. If you would know how the gipsy finds his way about you have but to ask his brother the "bird of passage" how he finds his way to a far-distant country and returns.

This faculty, which we can hardly realise, must never be lost sight of: when we wish to know whether a particular act has or has not been committed by gipsies, we must remember that they find their way about everywhere, that they never make a mistake in direction, that they see everything and take part in anything. It may be said without too much exaggeration that all is possible to the gipsy and, if it is asked what this word 'all' means, we may say that it embraces cunning in the highest degree, skill, effrontery, astuteness, and greed.

The gipsy must be considered to be the product of his natural character and the life which he has led for centuries—his food, dwelling, combat with the elements, the fact of his having been persecuted like a beast of prey added to the natural intelligence peculiar to man—when compounded together must produce a being in a sense powerless, but to whom, in another sense, nothing is impossible. It must be remembered that, since his appearance in Europe, the gipsy has always been governed in all his pre-occupations and anxieties by the same narrow and limited circle of thoughts: he desires to go freely and without being interfered with wheresoever it is his pleasure to go, he does not desire to rule anyone and he does not desire that anyone should rule him; it is his greatest happiness to be able to abandon himself to his laziness and he consequently seeks to obtain from him who works all that is necessary to satisfy his small number of wants. Honour, country, family, government, nationality, the past and future of his race—ideas which have led every civilised people to the highest rungs of destiny and to the finest actions, are things absolutely unknown to the gipsy; on the other hand we find that he possesses an idleness which passes all bounds, an animal hunger, a sensual love, and a trace of vanity. He has no other resources, and the combination of these factors has naturally no other result than to induce him to obtain by illegal means the goods of others.

If we remember that civilised man has for thousands of years stubbornly consecrated his efforts to the attainment of divers aims and ends of which each man claims for himself an exclusive application, while the gipsies have from time immemorial consecrated their knowledge and their forces to trying to live at the expense of others, we will not be astonished to find that the latter can do many things which would seem impossible to other men; and the fact that they are endowed with almost an equal number of attributes as the civilised man is thus explained.

Section ii.—Their Methods of Stealing.

The most important thing for us, as regards thefts by gipsies, is the extreme skill which they employ. This importance arises especially from the fact that when a theft is committed people who form part of the household, and particularly domestic servants, are often accused, and accused wrongly, of being the authors, simply because it is supposed that it is 'impossible' that an outsider could have had 'sufficient knowledge of the habits of the household' to be able to commit the theft in question, and that the skill and effrontery necessary to get into the house were of a kind "that could not be reasonably attributed to anyone." But in most of these cases gipsies have had 'this skill, effrontery, and gift of observation' which could be attributed to no one. What the servant who has lived for many years in the house, and what the neighbour who has lived for a long time near by, have not noticed, the old gipsy woman who has come begging or fortune-telling has observed in a very few minutes, and with the aid of these revelations such combinations have been made as have enabled the most brazen-faced theft to be carried out. The place where a "mouse cannot have passed" has been passed through by a little gipsy boy as easily as if the door had been opened wide, and where an acrobat could not have gone in spite of all his skill the gipsy can conquer with his hook—that instrument that he never fails to carry. The locksmith is capable of quickly and surely finding the faulty point in a grating, the system of a lock, or the feeble spot in a door hinge, only if he is allowed to observe these objects from all sides; the gipsy needs but a glance or a jerk from outside to know exactly what he ought to do.

Compare the time and the trouble taken by a mason or an architect in measuring and examining a wall before pronouncing an opinion upon its capacities of resistance and solidity of construction, with the hole dug by the gipsy in a wall. The latter has found the thinnest, dampest, and most easily broken spot, where moreover no obstacle is made by furniture inside. At the place chosen by him we will find no stone of large size which he might have to turn, or which might cause him to demolish unnecessarily a larger portion of the wall. He generally attacks that part of the wall which is not so thick as elsewhere owing to the situation of the chimney, and where he has no fear that pieces of tile or of mortar will make a noise in falling. He is able from outside to take his bearings in the house so as to find the wished-for room without having first to open closed doors or pass near the sleeping inhabitants, and, if at times he cannot do otherwise, he knows better than anyone else how to pass near sleeping persons without knocking over the smallest article or making the slightest noise. "It can only have been a ghost," says his victim afterwards, "how can anyone have passed so near my bed, I, who hear everything?" Yes, the gipsy goes and comes like a phantom, noiselessly, one might almost say without existing, desiring evil and doing it.

All that remains to him is his particular and persistent odour which can never deceive one and which one never forgets when one has once smelt it. It resembles, they say, the odour of the negro—which is equally characteristic. Judges who know this odour and have a fairly keen sense of smell perceive, on entering the law courts, that gipsies have been brought there. It seems to stick to the walls. This circumstance can often help to give us information about the presence of gipsies. If gipsies have committed a theft somewhere they have had to stop a certain amount of time and must have touched more than one object, the greater part of the time they have opened boxes, unmade beds, etc., so that the clothes and linen are scattered about pell-mell and have had an opportunity, especially cotton cloths, of becoming impregnated with the odour, which they preserve for some time. If then it happens that a person who knows the odour of gipsies comes along a little time after the passage of the thieves he will be able to say with great certainty whether or not they were gipsies. One cannot give a better idea of the odour of gipsies than by comparing it to a mixture of the smell of fat and the smell of a mouse.

If the skill of the gipsy in penetrating into the interior of the house is remarkable, it is still more admirable to observe the prudence with which he prepares his way of escape and guards against all surprise. Like every other hardened thief the gipsy thinks always of flight, but with his dexterity and promptness he has no need to prepare it so conveniently or in such detail as the ordinary thief; one bar of the window grating bent over to one side, a little opening in the wall, or a half-opened cleft in the door is sufficient in case of need to enable the gipsy to disappear once for all with the agility and the suppleness of a weasel, so that when his victim arrives on the scene of the theft he always believes that the thief has gone a long time, whereas in reality he has only just escaped from under his nose.

The gipsy always guards against surprise by means of sentinels and outposts, who with an incorruptible and indefatigable attention, observe and give warning of everything that happens. They have the sight of the owl and the eye of the fox, enabling them to recognise, even during the night-time, each passer-by long before the latter has perceived the sentinels, and in the silence of their immobility they hear all steps which approach; gipsies are moreover trained to this service from infancy and they are consequently better suited to this task than anyone else. Add to this that the gipsy is hardly ever alone or in company with but a few others; he is much too great a gossip and too fond of society to live in isolation. Nothing is more displeasing to him than to be solitary. Therefore he travels and steals as a member of a large band and each member of the band, man, woman, and child, is a comrade in theft upon whom he can count, so that his sentinels are many and his outposts well recruited. The gipsy sets out to thieve accompanied by his comrades, including women and children; the men help him in the theft itself, the women mount guard and assist him in carrying away the plunder, the children do the same, and are besides obliged to pass between the bars of windows or squeeze through little openings so as to open doors from the other side. It is of the greatest importance for the success of the enterprise that the outposts be well furnished. This is an old principle, which they vigorously observe, for the more numerous the outposts the greater is the security, the greater the security the calmer the thief will be, and the calmer the thief the greater will be the booty. Calmness in carrying out the theft itself is a distinctive trait of the gipsy. After the theft one gathers the impression, which is difficult to get rid of, that the thieves have searched for, chosen, and carried away the stolen articles with the greatest calm and tranquillity. This can only be explained by the great safety in which the gipsy works, for he has as many associates as there are members in the band to which he belongs.

The second precaution always taken by a gipsy is to bar the doors to prevent any surprise from the inside (see *Part II, Chapter XVII, "Theft"*). As soon as he has penetrated into the place which is to be the theatre of his activity he starts by seeing to the doors which lead to the other parts of the house from that in which he is going to operate. Even when he finds a key on the inside he is not content with turning it. He knows too well that the ordinary lock of a door offers but a doubtful guarantee of safety. He therefore proceeds to prop up the door when it opens towards him or to tie it up if it opens away from him. The first operation is very easy (see "Theft" *u s*), the second requires a certain amount of skill, for it is necessary to tie up sufficiently firmly the latch to the bar so as to prevent the wood being split or a knife introduced and the cord cut. For this purpose the gipsy prefers a metal wire to a cord. In all cases the skill which the gipsy shows in tying up doors must be recognised. If it can be said that the operation has been executed promptly, simply, noiselessly, and with much ingenuity, it is for certain the work of a gipsy.

It would be an exaggeration to say that, each time such a discovery is made, gipsies are at the bottom of the case, for one finds often enough that all sorts of vagabonds of forbidding aspect form part of these gipsy bands, living and thieving with them for a time and afterwards having learned from the gipsies their manner of stealing, starting work on their own account. No civilised man, however degraded he may be, can live with the gipsies for long. Their mode of existence is so injurious to the health that the gipsy alone is capable of supporting it. Moreover their habits are so shocking, they are so dirty, so cruel to animals, their food is so disgusting, etc., that in time their manner of living must become quite insupportable to anyone who is not himself a gipsy. Outsiders may also use gipsy methods, but they use them in quite a different way to the real gipsy. It must sometimes have been noticed that whereas the gipsy works with much elegance, the outsider who has learned his methods proceeds very clumsily. We may say that whenever the doors are not barred the authors of the burglary are not gipsies. They never omit to make fast the doors unless they have some reason for not doing so—as when e.g., the doors lead into rooms which have no other doors and whose windows are covered with gratings. Before starting work the gipsy knows the exact situation perfectly.

Another means of recognising whether or not a given crime is the work of gipsies is to compare the qualities necessary for the accomplishment of that crime with those qualities which are well known to belong to gipsies, and to then consider whether a gipsy could have committed the crime in question. In this connection his great cowardice must not be lost sight of. As has already been seen the crime should not be laid to the account of a gipsy when the circumstances show that the criminal has been exposed to some danger, e.g., if in a case of murder he has boldly faced his victim. A theft will never be committed by a gipsy in a house where several men reside from whom resistance may be expected.

If a thief who has been surprised has taken to flight, and made good his escape with incredible skill by following the gutters, eaves, waterspouts, creepers, or leads, etc., he may very well be presumed to be a gipsy; if on the contrary he has made a bold leap, without exactly knowing the height, at the risk of breaking a leg, impaling himself, or doing himself some other injury, he is certainly not a gipsy. It may be remarked that when the gipsy goes thieving he very often has arms in readiness; he takes with him his cudgel and his battle-axe; he even goes to work with an open knife in his mouth to have it ready to hand if he be surprised. If surprise takes place, he tries all means of getting away before having recourse to defence; and in every case he attempts to make off as fast as his legs can carry him. It frequently happens that gipsies when in flight fire upon their pursuers, but only when, thanks to the darkness, they are out of danger and can hide behind a house or a tree and there take aim in comfort.

When they *do* dare, the manner in which they commit a crime is also very significant. The policeman who has been treacherously attacked and killed by gipsies will be found to carry numerous deep wounds—which for the most part must have been inflicted after death. The gipsies have continued to strike, partly to increase their safety by making certain that their victim is quite dead and can do them no harm, and also partly to satisfy their cruel desire to kill, they glory in being able to hack a detested enemy with impunity

A very striking trait in the gipsy is his insatiable and bestial greed To see something desirable and to lay hold of it are with him one and the same thing In those countries which suffer most from gipsies it is known what care ought to be taken of the swine-flesh when gipsies are about during the slaughtering And what we must notice here is that it is not from having learned by the fact of the slaughtering that there is swine-flesh at such and such a place, for no gipsy is unaware that peasants have from time to time swine-flesh but it is entirely the sight of this flesh itself that has incited the gipsy to return and steal it

"We cannot do better," an old gipsy once said "than place a piece of gold on a gipsy's tomb, his hand will grow and shoot from the soil to seize it"

Every peasant knows how dangerous it is to allow anything valuable or which may induce covetousness to be seen when gipsies pass—but how often does it happen that the gipsy sees the peasant? and how rarely it is that the peasant sees him! The gipsy glides like a fox round the house, the village, the temple, or the palace, seeing all and being seen by no one, and only when he has departed with his booty is it supposed that *perhaps* gipsies have been there

The lawyer *Karenil* of *Laibach* has drawn the author's attention to a particularly crafty method of gipsies with regard to horse-stealing He has noticed that gipsies regularly steal horses when a horse-fair will be held within the next day or so in the neighbourhood of the theft The man from whom the horse has been stolen expects to catch the thief and the horse at the fair, and so he neglects to follow the thief and take steps for the recovery of the horse The gipsy counts on this, and calculating that it will be the argument of the man he has despoiled, by the day of the fair he is far away Such incidents truly show the gipsy to be a true psychologist

Section iii.—Child-stealing.

Do gipsies really steal children? Everywhere it is said and believed that they do, but no one has ever seen them do it, stories have been written about gipsy child-stealing which make one creep, but no authentic account of any such case exists It must also be remembered that gipsies are very prolific and in consequence have no need to bring up other people's children—without taking into account the fact that such thefts would expose them to great danger Indeed, thanks to this general widespread belief that gipsies steal children, a strange child perhaps blind or crippled, found in their hands would always awaken people's suspicions and would probably lead to the gipsies being lynched

In the author's opinion the stories of thefts of children bring one back to former times when the gipsies used to be accused of cannibalism and when they were executed by hundreds after having made confessions obtained by torture All that must have been only a product of popular imagination, which fixes everything that is strange and monstrous upon people of peculiar appearance, who cannot be understood and who are predisposed to do evil

There is one particular which may deceive us according to popular belief gipsies steal for preference children who have red hair (*bolo harr meshro*), and, indeed, according to the gipsy golden or red hair is lucky And from this circumstance it may be said that gipsies, who have only black-haired children (except albinos), have only a step to take to procure these "lucky children," and that step is to steal them There is no doubt that gipsies who come begging and telling fortunes as a rule take particular notice of children with red hair and have perhaps even gone so far as to state in terms that this was a quality which carried happiness, and since the belief that gipsies steal children exists, it is permissible to believe that people who have children with red hair have sometimes been greatly upset on account of the gipsies, fearing to see their darlings subsequently abducted, for " do gipsies not steal everything they want ?"

This fear that the child runs a risk of being stolen may, by the mere force of repetition have led people to believe that gipsies have at times really stolen red-haired children does one not see every day fiction thus turned into fact ? As such stories are so often related it can but be expected that they will give birth to the belief that gipsies do carry off red haired children In this case the general opinion of people upon the subject and the superstition which gipsies are known to possess concerning golden hair cannot be a purely fortuitous coincidence, but the one must proceed from the other, and here we have an example of that common fault of logic which has been the cause of many paralogisms and which consists in considering phenomena one of which is not the consequence of the other, as being complementary to one another and having mutual support—*simul cum hoc, ergo propter hoc*

In the only case in which the author has suspected gipsies of having stolen a child, the missing child was indeed a little girl with red hair

Section IV.—Their good points and their Superstitions.

It is unhappily never possible to be sure that a gipsy has any good points at all, his gratitude, for example, is often hypocrisy, though he protests it in such a way that it seems humanly impossible not to believe in it not one single case does the author know of in which a gipsy has shown real gratitude, whereas those in which he has shown black ingratitude do not need seeking for

One day gipsies broke into a large peasant's house and stole everything that it was possible to carry away, so much so that the owners were reduced to the direst straits Everything led to the supposition that the authors of the theft were gipsies On the victims being asked about this they replied that they had not had gipsies in the house for some time and that they had not even had any of them calling at the house—at least to their knowledge They also related to show that it could not have been gipsies, how a little time before they had found in the forest, during a snowstorm, a gipsy woman who was in the pains of child-birth and was incapable of proceeding on her way, and how they had taken pity on her and gone to her assistance The woman was delivered in their house, was ill for a long time, and she and the child were loaded with care and attention, this latter fact being also spoken to by the neighbours. When she was well enough to continue on her way she expressed her gratitude in such a manner that those standing by her could hardly keep back their tears.' On her departure as well as during her illness, she had often assured them that they would find that she at least was not wanting in gratitude and would take care that no gipsy would ever harm this good house.' These people affirmed that it was impossible not to believe her. But the police were less credulous and so obtained as accurate a description as possible of the woman (she was blind of one eye and extraordinarily big), and a short time afterwards caught her, her band and a part of the stolen property. She had shammed at least a part of her illness in order to obtain information as to the disposition of the house, the habits of its inhabitants, and other details; she had even taken impressions of the keys, and the gipsies had thus been enabled to profit by all the information that she had been able to gather.

Nor can we any longer believe in their boasted reverence towards the dead any more than in their pretended gratitude. It is said that the gipsy ceases to lie when he is asked to repeat what he has said, adding thereto the words "*op i mulende*" (by the dead). The author has no experience of this; if it be true that the gipsy dare not lie when he has taken this oath, it is not by reason of 'piety to the dead' but only on account of his ridiculous and childlike fear of ghosts, which is, so to speak, the alpha and omega of all his religious sentiments. It is very characteristic that the word *mulo* means among the gipsies at the same time a corpse, a spectre, and a vampire, so that to a gipsy a dead person and his ghost (which they fear beyond everything) are practically one and the same thing, so that they dare not take to witness insincerely a "*mulo*" or a "*mulende*."

There is another point which the author would like to mention and to which sufficient attention is not paid and that is that the gipsy, who has always some Christian knowledge (we do not say *ideas*), makes practically no difference between *deuel* (god) and *beng* (devil). *Deuel* has nothing in common with the *diabolos, teutel, diable, devil*, but belongs to the Indian family, *deuu*, an idol, in Persian *dei*, an idol, and *dins*, god, and to the root *diu* from whence is derived *dvos, Zeús* and the genitive of Jupiter (Zeuspater), *Iovis*. These two words *Deuel* (god) and *Beng* (devil), mean to the gipsy supernatural powers of good and evil and he does not take the trouble to differentiate between them. For purgatory he says *bengeshero jak* (devil's fire) as well as *deueleshero jak* (God's fire), and things which are far from agreeable to him he calls "divine," for example *deueleshero sno* (God's weather or tempest) or again, he says speaking of an animal which has died, "God has killed him"—an expression which the ordinary person would turn into "He's gone to the devil." See also *Borrow*.

When a people have so few religious notions that they may be said to have practically none at all God does not appear to its members as the Father of the Universe, a good and protecting Almighty, but only as an irritable, hostile, and superior Power; they confound the idea they have of God with that which they have of the Devil and come to believe in spirits and ghosts, which soon take a more important place in their minds than their ideas, confused as they are, of God and the Devil.

The Investigating Officer who has to deal with gipsies and has learned to know this people so different to all others, will not be astonished at this view of them. All that has been done for them in the course of centuries is to hound them from place to place and persecute them. Attempts to civilise them have been for the most part temporary, violent and as much in contradiction as possible with gipsy nature. Nothing more has been done for them. We criminal experts have only to deal with them when they thieve or commit other criminal acts against the public, no one troubles about those crimes of which they are one another's victims. Have we ever intervened when one gipsy has received from another gipsy a cruel beating or mutilation? Who has ever placed his veto upon the numerous cases of procurement of abortion practised amongst the gipsies? Who has protected the honour of their young women—many of whom become mothers when they are still children? Who has avenged a gipsy who has been poisoned by others? Who knows exactly what is that terrible poison of theirs called "dry"? Who has seen a gipsy cared for in hospital? Of what do they die? Where do they go? Where are their graves?

Section v.—Instruments used for Theft, Poisoning, etc.

Asking ourselves what we find remarkable about gipsies (when our profession places us in direct relations with them) we are forced to the conclusion that the results are deceptive. Rarely do we find a gipsy in possession of a housebreaking implement which is really of use, such as other professional thieves are accustomed to carry and regard as their most precious possession. Though working hurriedly, the gipsy is none the less a skilled blacksmith at need, and he is a locksmith by birth, yet in spite of this he makes no instrument of theft, false key, etc. He is too lazy to make them and too timid to carry or keep them. Nor is it in his nature to work with false keys and artificial instruments, he gets into a house by the window or in any other convenient manner, for he has previous and accurate information as to the strength of the locks, and with a knife, twisted nail, etc., can open almirahs with astonishing skill he may be primitive but he is practical and sure.

Gipsies are always found in possession of fishhooks and lines. The hooks are put to various uses according to their size and shape but are hardly ever used for fishing, in which sport the gipsy rarely indulges. The fishhook of the gipsy principally serves to catch with ease and certainty all kinds of birds hens, ducks, geese, and, if need be, even pigeons. The men, and sometimes the women, approach quietly a flock of such birds, not in the immediate neighbourhood of a house, but at a little distance and not under supervision, and throw some bread crumbs to them. These crumbs are said to be impregnated with a substance likely to attract the birds, sometimes said to be chives, sometimes assafœtida, and sometimes crushed aniseed. When they have been baited with this food, larger balls of it are thrown to them and finally one containing the fishhook. This hook is attached (as in fishing) to a silk cast fastened to a strong gut cast or sometimes to a thin metal one, the bird is naturally enough caught on the hook, pulled in, and gets its neck twisted, it is then fastened to a lace already arranged under the gipsy's clothes. The other birds are frightened for the moment but soon come back, and the operation recommences

At times also for geese, artificial bait is used in this case the gipsy uses pieces of green rag or even, in case of need, leaves, fashioned into an artificial frog which easily deceives a goose, a hook is hidden inside the frog, which is then drawn before the flock of geese at the same time being made to jump by means of the line A goose cannot resist this temptation Thus the gipsies procure a dinner and the peasants believe that their birds have been lifted by a fox, they do not suspect the game the gipsies have played upon them

Another use for the fishhook, and a much more dangerous one, is its employment as a throwing weapon Three or four hooks are bound together and set into a leaden ball split open and then reclosed (Fig 30) A single hook may be used but it is much less efficacious than a system of hooks, which becomes attached to an object whichever way it falls (in the same way as does a ship's anchor), the leaden ball is to lend the apparatus the necessary weight to allow of its being accurately thrown As regards the throwing gipsies, especially the children, are remarkably skilful Among all races children amuse themselves by throwing stones, but their particular object in doing so is to throw them as far as possible Not so the young gipsy, he gathers together a heap of stones of about the size of a nut and then chooses a target, such as a fairly large stone, a small plank, or an old cloth, at a distance of from about ten to twenty paces, he then launches his stock of projectiles, never tiring of throwing them at the same target He keeps going for hours and soon acquires such skill at this exercise that he never misses anything larger than one's hand When he has reached this stage he is given a throwing hook and a rag, the latter being placed at a certain distance from him He soon ends by catching it every time The young gipsy throws the hook in all possible and imaginable ways The occupation is very characteristic of the gipsy it gives him a distraction devoid of trouble and offers him the prospect, when his skill has increased, of gathering in valuable spoils The young gipsy comes out of his apprenticeship when he is able to strike and carry off a piece of rag thrown upon the branches of a tree among which he has to cast his hook

Fig 30

The practical utility of this accomplishment is to enable him to carry off linen, clothes, and such-like things, in houses into which it is difficult, not to say impossible, to penetrate In this way he fishes for linen hung up to dry in an enclosed courtyard, entrance to which is difficult or dangerous It is really with astonishing skill that the gipsy fishes in the downstairs rooms through a barred window for the clothes of a peasant who is eating in the next room He even goes so far as to fish clothes hanging from pegs, here he raises them until they are just on the point of falling to the ground and then draws them towards him until they reach his greedy hands

Sometimes the fisher removes articles through the open windows of lofts and granaries, if they be not too high, or again he hides behind a hedge and fishes off the horsecloths from the backs of horses standing waiting for their masters in the road No doubt the latter can, through the window of the inn, see " all the people passing up and down the road ", but as to the gipsy behind the hedge, neither has he seen him nor will he see again his new horsecloth. A great number of those "mysterious" thefts, the authors of which have not been seen and whose approach to the scene of the theft cannot be explained, are thus quite easily accounted for. Gipsies have even, they say, fished hams hung in the chimney for smoking after having hoisted themselves on to the roof, which in such cases is not very high.

Gipsy talismans and medicines are always more or less cabalistic in nature. Various greases and burnt or unburnt hair play an especially important role in the composition of love potions and erotic powders. The author is not aware of the composition of their famous medicine for procuring abortion, which all gipsies are said to know and possess; it seems to be infallible and the only real abortifacient.

The gipsy is generally found in possession of phosphorus and arsenic. This does not indicate that any danger need be expected from them, for the former is exclusively employed as a medicine for animals, whereas the latter only seems to be used for the destruction of rats and mice. Every gipsy willingly engages in this sport and does so the more readily as it is an excellent way of visiting a house and its outhouses in the most minute manner without attracting any suspicion.

When the gipsy wishes to poison someone he uses neither phosphorus nor arsenic nor the like, he uses his infallible "dry" (also called "dri" or "drei") which is unknown to anyone else and is the most terrible of poisons. It is said to be a fine brown powder made with the spores of a mushroom (perhaps the *aspergillus niger*). These spores grow in animal organisms, developing a greenish-yellow shoot of about twelve to fifteen inches in length. This powder is dissolved in lukewarm liquid and the spores, becoming fixed in the mucous membrane, and rapidly developing there, bring on consumption, coughing, often spitting of blood, and death finally ensues after two or three weeks. When the body becomes cold the mushroom also soon dies and disappears so completely that after death no trace of it can be found.

Section vi.—Attitude before the Authorities

When brought before the authorities the gipsy at first conducts himself in a manner which is at the same time savage, prudent, and somewhat groping. Like the Jews and Oriental peoples he is fond of answering all questions with another question so as to gain time for reflection. This is so much a habit with him that he often says when asked his name: "What name can a poor gipsy have?"—if asked his age he replies: "What age can I be?" "How can I tell when I came into the world?" "Who is able to say my age?"—if asked if he has already been punished he replies by a perfect deluge of protest. "Why do you wish me to have been punished?" "Who has said that I have been punished?" "Have you ever seen me in prison?" "Do I look like a man who has been already punished?", then commence his protestations of innocence in the past, the present, and the future. Soon he comes to himself, his modesty disappears, and his effrontery, self-consciousness, and even his pride, come to life in a torrent of words which it is preferable to allow him to give vent to. The author agrees with other Investigating Officers that it is best to allow all great talkers to finish without interruption rather than pull them up, as some advise. It is useless waste of trouble to ask a gipsy to be brief, he will then begin his story all over again and not only will nothing be gained but the time already spent will be wasted. It is excellent on the other hand to write down or to have written down by a clerk everything the gipsy says. He is often discovered in the most flagrant contradictions, often also this procedure bothers him and he commences to express himself more briefly. In all cases his boldness and self-confidence increase visibly as the examination goes on, especially when the Investigating Officer is calm and silent. The gipsy takes this for stupidity and gets bolder. One may perhaps appear to be somewhat convinced by his reasoning, thereupon he lies the harder; suppose one doubts just a little some good action or other or some noble quality which he pretends to possess, he exaggerates it all the more. He should be allowed to work himself up for a while with his own words (a certain dose of frankness may always be expected from even the boldest and the most intelligent) and then, when the moment arrives, his contradictions should be shortly and energetically pointed out to him and the proofs against him brought together.

Rarely can we obtain the real truth from a gipsy, but one quickly notices that his crime may be brought home to him when he loses his boldness and begins to supplicate and complain. The naïveté which induces him to lie all the more, while pretending in the rest of his conduct consciousness of and repentance for his crime, must not be lost sight of. The gipsy does not know the proverb which is otherwise so true:—"the more one recognises that one is wrong the more pig-headed one becomes", and the more he notices that his crime is out and that he is vanquished the quieter he becomes and the more does his confidence and effrontery desert him. But even when the gipsy makes a confession, he does so not without hesitation, the ample use of equivocation and even, if possible, a fresh batch of lies. The author only remembers one single case of receiving a full confession from a gipsy with at the same time important information concerning his accomplices. A man and his wife were suspected of having committed some time previously a crime with which a gipsy had some distant connection. This gipsy, a little while after this first crime, had been convicted of wilful murder and sentenced to imprisonment for life; he had already been imprisoned for several years. During his examination he denied (as also did the couple above mentioned) with imperturbable obstinacy, ever having known the victim or yet the suspected couple; he knew nothing about anything. He made the mistake of relying on the circumstance that some time had elapsed since the crime was committed and did not know that immediately after the crime a searching inquiry had been carried out, the results of which were now before the authorities and enabled them to know exactly how the crime had been committed and reconstitute it even as regards its smallest details. When the gipsy, who was a cunning rascal, found himself to be so grossly mistaken and that everything was known much better even than the authorities actually allowed him to think that it was known, he remained silent for a little while and then began:— "I am a poor devil shut up for the rest of my life. You surely do not wish to hang me for this new business and besides you cannot sentence me to a longer term of imprisonment than imprisonment for life; this couple wishes to throw unjustly the whole blame upon me, I shall tell all." He then related the whole story of the crime the accuracy of which was immediately verified and he added some supplementary information which the author found of great interest from a psychological point of view. The man and the wife were not of the same nationality, the man being a German and the woman a Hungarian. The gipsy said to me — if you do not wish to condemn the innocent unjustly and make the case even more notorious than it is, these two people must be treated on their merits, that is to say the German in one way, and his wife, who is not a German, in another way." Thereupon he began to characterise the German and the Hungarian races with surprising acuteness and clearness. All that he said concerning the German race was not exactly flattering, but all the same he was right. The author was even inclined to abandon in some degree his unfavourable opinions concerning gipsies, if this one had not spoiled all by giving him some advice as to their capture. His instructions were so mean and so diabolically cunning that all the baseness of this infamous race was shown up anew. We tried to make him understand that the authorities could not possibly take the steps he advised, but he looked at us in stupefaction, shrugged his shoulders and was silent.

Section vii.—Their Corporal Characteristics.

As regards the corporal qualities and capabilities of the gipsy they must in no way be judged according to the ordinary standard by which we judge the rest of mankind. This is especially true when the question is whether such and such a thing is "possible or not" to a man. One can in general say that a man has been able to do such or such a thing, but it is not the same with the gipsy, and it is best to believe him capable of anything. This is especially the case when distance is in question, as when it is said — "If the roads are good, and if one knows the way and is unencumbered, one may go there in so much time, if the road is bad and one does not know the way, and is loaded with baggage in so much time." this may very well apply to the average mortal but not to the gipsy. Be the road good or bad, know he it or not, carry he anything with him or go he free, it matters not to him, when necessary he can cover his distances with incomprehensible rapidity, knowing no obstacle but one— the wind. This peculiarity has been often remarked, gipsies cannot bear the wind and are distressed when they have to struggle with it. Another thief steals for preference on stormy nights, not so the gipsy, he hides himself when his enemy howls. If he be obliged to set out in the wind it takes him longer to cover his journey than any other man. If a theft has taken place on a stormy night it may be safely presumed from the outset that the authors of it were not gipsies.

The illnesses and the sufferings of the gipsy ought also to be judged differently to those of other people. Care must be taken not invariably to conclude that illnesses contracted while a gipsy is in prison are mere shamming. Even when the doctor is unable to discover what is the matter the gipsy is none the less often ill, and dangerously ill, just as the hillsman is when he is forced to live in the plains or the dweller in the plains when transported to the hills, and just as is the bird of passage when shut up in a cage. The gipsy has become accustomed for centuries to a life in the open air and cannot support the deprivation of it any more than he can the change of food and clothing, and the imposition of the order and employment consequent to regular life. He falls ill, at first in mind and then in body, and, if his liberty, the sole means of curing him, cannot be given him, he should not be tormented the more by taking him for a sham and treating him as such.

It is important for the Investigating Officer to notice the rapidity with which the wounds of gipsies heal, owing doubtless to their Oriental origin. At least this peculiarity has been remarked among Eastern races. The author has been informed by a German doctor who was attached to the Viceroy of Egypt and was, for a considerable time, head of the Cairo Hospital, that the power of healing among the Arabs for example, is extraordinary. One day a fairly old man fell from the roof of a somewhat low house upon a stockade, in such a way that he was transfixed on three bars which entered the upper part of the thigh and passed out again for about a hand's breadth. And that was not enough, for the unfortunate man had been removed from his position so unskilfully and with so few precautions that the bars considerably enlarged the wounds, and yet the three wounds healed without suppuration or fever. No doubt the climate there was not without its influence, but all the same the wounds of gipsies, both in Europe and in other parts of the world, cure with astonishing rapidity. The gipsy is very sensible to bodily pain and yet he is able to continue his wanderings with severe wounds, and above all it is wonderful what he can support when he is in flight. A gipsy had been run down at a horse mart by a carriage and had been so badly hurt that the doctors of the hospital to which he was carried in an unconscious condition considered that it would be several weeks before he would be well. Probably the conscience of the patient was somewhat troubled, for the third night after the accident, he escaped by the window and disappeared—not forgetting to carry off with him his bed clothes.

If then the question is, whether or not a gipsy, wounded at such and such a moment, has been able, in spite of his wounds, to do such and such a thing, care must be taken to view the matter in a different manner to that in which it would be viewed if he were not a gipsy. In the same way, if the question is, at what time a wound already cicatrised has been received in the case of a gipsy the time must be considerably diminished for, as an experienced surgeon once told the author, ' one sees the wounds of gipsies closing before one's eyes.'

The gipsies and their partisans attribute the promptness of these cures not to bodily constitution but to the medicines they are supposed to employ. Recently a constable wished to arrest an extremely dangerous thief who had lived for a long time among the gipsies. The thief engaged, in an inn, in a fight with firearms with the constable. The constable fell, as to the thief his lower arm was completely shattered by a bullet of the constable. But he was able to take to flight and meeting a lad who had often given him shelter he said to him —" If I can only get to my people (the gipsies), they will soon cure my arm, otherwise I am lost." These words prove the confidence which this man had in the art of healing as practised by the gipsies.

The same may be said of the illnesses to which the gipsy, like other men, is subject, but with this difference, that the former remains in the open air without shelter and is sometimes even obliged to continue his march. There are many gaps in the statistics regarding gipsies but all the same it may be supposed that mortality is no greater among them than among others. We meet among them a surprising number of old men of astonishing freshness and vigour.

In the small number of cases in which the gipsies have illnesses, it would be false to conclude that the theft could not have been committed by a band of gipsies simply because, for example, their children were stricken with the small-pox. Such a circumstance would in no way deter them, a fact which also explains the sudden appearance of contagious illnesses which have been communicated by gipsy beggars and thieves.

Section viii.—Gipsy Proverbs.

We shall end this chapter with a few specimens of proverbs of and concerning gipsies, for, as we have already said, no better aid to knowing a people exists than the proverbs of which it is the author or those which others have applied to it. Above all the Investigating Officer ought to know the people with whom he has to deal.

The following proverbs have been selected from various sources:—

'Better a donkey to carry you than a horse to throw you.—If you keep a secret in your heart no one will ever know it.—Choose neither a wife nor a cloth by the light of the moon.—Do not seek for what you cannot get.—It is not thieving that is shameful but the being caught.—It is easier to steal than to work.—He who holds the ladder is as bad as the thief.—He who loads you with flattery has deceived, or wishes to deceive you.—To wait to be asked to eat is to risk being often hungry.—A happy life makes good friends.—Children tell what they do, men what they think, old men what they have seen.—The fool has his heart on his lips, the wise man has his lips in his heart.' The foregoing are specimens of proverbs of the gipsy's own making. The following are about the gipsy:—'They live like gipsies" (when husband and wife come to blows) —"To be a gipsy."—"You howl like a gipsy."—"The gipsy does not know how to hold the plough" (doesn't work).—"He rides a gipsy horse" (he lies).—"Gipsy trade" i.e., theft.

All that is bad, valueless or deceitful has the epithet 'gipsy' e.g., brass=gipsy gold. Fish full of bones=gipsy carp. Wild grapes which no one can eat=gipsy grapes. Bad wine=gipsy wine etc.

All this shews how the gipsy imposes upon the countryside and is hated for it, detested and harried by everyone, it is by injuring and destroying that he lives out his wretched life. For gipsy signs, See *Chapter III, Section iv*. Gipsy magic and superstition *Chapter X*. See also *Chapter VIII Section vi A and E*

CHAPTER X

SUPERSTITION.

It is curious to notice the effect of superstition, even at this day, upon the criminal classes. Criminals often rely upon the superstitions of others, often also they are slaves to superstition and allow themselves to be led by it to quite inexplicable acts.

Great importance is often attached to a fact or action when one has merely to deal with a piece of superstition or other practice of the kind having no connection with the crime itself. The author has himself seen "soporiferous candles" made of the fat of virgin children and used to see whether anyone is still awake in a house about to be burgled. Many great crimes are only explicable by superstition. If one were to reject these abominable acts as being due to an abnormal state of mind, one would be committing an error; the doer of them is perfectly sane but is wrapped up in a cloud of superstition. Even to-day we meet, not only all those doings of the slaves of the south connected with the belief in vampires, but also those necessitating the use of the blood of innocent children, and, above all, acts connected with what is called the "feast of the heart." At all times it has been believed that the heart of a stillborn child, eaten while yet warm, gives supernatural force and renders the eater invisible, thus aiding him to steal. F. Ch. B. Ave-Lallemant cites numerous cases of this kind, and similar cases have also been reported more recently.

To show how strong superstition still is in Berlin we have but to turn to the many curious requests made to the officials of the Society for the Protection of Animals in that city. A woman went to the depot and asked to buy three drops of blood from a coal-black dog which she affirmed would ward off illness. The dog must not be killed by poisoning but by hanging. Dog's fat is in great demand by the superstitious multitude, for it is asked for almost daily at the institution; it is supposed to be a preservative against phthisis. With a white cat, killed at midnight, a woman expected to discover hidden treasure. That donkeys are "lucky" animals the officials learned every day; these long-eared gentry were only bought to bring luck.

Among Londoners it is a common superstition that a piece of raw steak buried in the garden at dead of night will cause the disappearance of warts from the person. The steak, however, must have been stolen or it will not produce the desired effect. A stolen herring-tail serves the same purpose on the Continent.

To this day in Italy, and especially in Sicily, it is believed that treasure can be unearthed with the assistance of the blood of innocent children. In 1891 on one occasion 24 children, and on another 20 children, were murdered for this object. This superstition travelled to Germany more than a century ago with the Italian "stone-seekers" (half miners, half diggers for hidden treasure). It is to-day firmly believed by Italian stone-masons and builders. On the Continent of Europe there is everywhere a firm belief that the Jews use the blood of Christian children in their ritual.

A universal Indian superstition is that of the "foundation-sacrifice", this probably took its rise in an attempt to propitiate the "earth-deities" of the spot. The sacrifice is considered so indispensable that the superstition is transferred to the English. "Whenever we build a great bridge or harbour mole our engineers are suspected of being on the look-out for victims, and people are careful not to wander abroad at night during the time the foundation is being laid" (Crooke, p. 263, and see Sir E. C. Cox in his Indian detective work, "John Carruthers," Cassell, London).

Cases in which a person attempts with the help of alchemy to become younger are also not unimportant. The means used are nearly always dangerous to life, and when death is caused by them, murder by third persons may easily be wrongly suspected.

A case is reported by M. Friedmann, of Wiesbaden, of two soldiers who agreed that the one should shoot the head off the other. The victim firmly believed that the survivor could with certain words of sorcery charm his head on again and that after the operation the latter would be able to discover hidden treasure. The first half of the experiment was duly performed and apparently without any difficulty, but the sorcerer dismally failed to replace his comrade's head as agreed upon. It was established that he did not intend to kill his friend, but, with his assistance, for them both to discover hidden treasure, nor could he be considered negligent or careless as he did what he did carefully and on purpose, being convinced of the harmlessness of the act. If he was punished for anything it was for mere ignorance and stupidity. This incident actually took place as recently as 1900.

In another direction a knowledge of superstition can explain a previously inexplicable laxity of morals: for instance the almost universal superstition that sexual illnesses can be cured by intercourse with a girl under the age of seven. This is the motive for many rapes.

Section i.—Superstition attaching to Dead Bodies and to Objects abandoned at the Place of the Crime.

Almost every thief carries upon him a magic sentence or formula of immunity, and it often happens that he leaves behind him on the scene of the crime some object which belongs to him, for he believes that in this way his act will pass unperceived, or at least that he will not be suspected.

The mistress of a famous housebreaker had abandoned, one winter's night, her child of ten months old, leaving beside it her own shoes which a shoemaker had just made for her. The shoemaker lived only a few furlongs from the place and therefore was able to point out the criminal. The latter confessed later that she had only abandoned her shoes so as not to be discovered. For the same reason a rough (who had already undergone 18 years' hard labour for murder) had relieved himself near the body of his victim at the scene of the crime. This latter circumstance, it may be said in passing, served, in a roundabout way it is true, to discover the criminal, the doctor of the district noticed that the excrement must have belonged to a man of herculean build, and in fact the murderer was the most robust man the author has ever seen.

In North Germany murderers believe that they will never be discovered if they leave their excrement at the place where they have committed a crime. While the excrement preserves a vestige of warmth the crime itself even cannot be discovered. It is therefore often found carefully covered up with a cloth or a hat in order that it may retain its heat the longer and so put off the discovery of the crime. Some time ago a quantity of excrement was found on the scene of a large burglary in a jeweller's shop in Berlin.

For the same reason a criminal washes his hands or intentionally leaves footprints on the scene of the crime; in these cases he also leaves behind something belonging to him and thus hopes not to be discovered.

In a big burglary case the bloody impression of a man's hand was found upon an almirah, and many conjectures were raised on the matter. It was believed that the criminal was badly wounded, or that there had been two of them and that they had come to blows over the division of the booty. When at last the burglar was discovered it was found that he had inflicted a slight injury upon his own hand and then rubbed it over with the blood in the hope that he would not be discovered if he left behind him his blood and the impression of his hand.

We find, almost without exception, that seeds of *datura* are left at places where gipsies have committed a crime. They are said always to leave a few seeds, but as at times it happens that they are short of them and as they often hide them in out-of-the-way corners, they are frequently not noticed. This peculiarity is little known to other people, and no one else would be likely to use this as a means of diverting suspicion from himself and throwing it upon the gipsies. As for the reason for this habit, an old gipsy once told the author that it was because of the evil spirits who sometimes annoy thieves at their work. He also said that they "throw" this seed at evil spirits, but as the seeds are often hidden and not thrown, the old man was probably telling a lie. At all events it may be presumed to be an act of superstition since they put these seeds to other analogous uses.

The native women of India are supposed to deliver themselves over to their lovers in the very presence of their husbands to whom they have given a decoction of datura. The husband sees all, but it matters little for he can remember nothing. Indian thieves also employ it in the same way as do the gipsies. The connection we find here again between the gipsies and India is noteworthy.

Another common practice of gipsies is to leave at the place of the crime a stick, generally a walking stick. A gipsy informed the author that this was done to prevent the dogs barking.

Section ii.—Superstition attaching to Objects carried on the Person.

We have so far only spoken of superstitious articles which have been found left behind upon the scene of the crime. We must also discuss those found upon thieves themselves which must be considered in the nature of charms; they throw a characteristic light upon their possessors.

One finds, for instance, up in the hills, while searching houses of people accused of poaching, small roots in the shape of a hand which, so say those questioned on the subject, are very efficacious in warding off the illnesses of domestic animals. A cunning poacher has already secreted in the forest his arms and ammunition and all instruments of the trade he follows. He assures us that he has never fired a gun in his life, that he has never tasted goat, and that he would hardly be able to distinguish between a stag and a cow. But even when he has no ammunition, poaching instruments or remains of game in the house, this little root suffices to betray him. It is a little hand of St. John, shaped from the root of a fern dug up on the night of St. John (the summer solstice, 24th June) and which has an important use when the poacher, at the time of the new moon, makes his enchanted bullets which he fires with unerring aim.

It is also very suspicious to find a person in possession of sacramental bread. Either he will perpetrate a crime or he has already done so, for the possession of such is supposed to make "the Magistrate inaccessible to the bearer." It is well to pay attention to such things which most people would consider quite harmless.

Special attention must be paid to those objects which their owners believe to be little capable of awaking suspicion, and which for that reason they do not hide. So also with the spring-root or mandrake. This plant, which was esteemed and so much boasted of in the Middle Ages, is still in our times more believed in and more extensively used than one would suppose. In many places crafty criminals, who to all appearances are well educated, pay a high price for it. When it is pure it is the root of the aluna (*mandragora officinalis*), but the roots of the peony and of the white vine (*pryonica alba et dioica*) are also employed, as well as certain roots of ferns and of the *euphorbia lathyris* and the *allium bulbaris* in case of need. All of these, but especially the first mentioned, when dried and shaped a little with a knife, have the form of a little man, and in the 18th century were supposed to be productive of happiness, riches, love and influence. To-day they are only useful in opening closed locks, or at least in opening them without too much trouble with the help of a picklock and skeleton-key. If one of these aluna or mandrake gentlemen is found upon a suspected individual, we may be sure we have to do with a veritable expert in house-breaking.

Resembling the "soporiferous candles" made of the fat of innocent children, which have already been mentioned, is the "slumber-thumb," used only by gipsies. It is the left thumb of a corpse nine weeks in the grave and disinterred at new moon. Possessed of one of these thumbs, a person may penetrate at night into a house without fear of awaking the people therein. Gipsies of all countries are said to possess a "slumber-thumb", the author has himself never seen one. French thieves, among whom these "theft thumbs" bear the name of *main de gloire*, are to-day no doubt in possession of them. Amongst the objects found on suspected persons and which render them all the more suspect, are proverbs, incantations, and exorcisms. These always point to criminal conduct.

The right hand of a suicide is also made use of in Eastern Europe, especially in Poland and the countries adjacent thereto. The right hand of the corpse of a suicide, nine days in the grave, is taken and dried, and the door of the house in which stolen goods are suspected to be concealed is knocked therewith seven times. If the inhabitants do not wake, it is presumed that the dead person "holds them in sleep." This was exemplified in a recent case reported in many newspapers.

That human fat is used for various erotic objects and for love charms, and that warm human blood effects superhuman cures, especially for epilepsy, is shown every day by numberless newspaper reports and law proceedings. Human fat is kept, in spite of the assurances of apothecaries to the contrary, in the shops of many country apothecaries, and for the same purpose the lard of dogs, bears, badgers, apes, and wolves is taken and preserved. But warm human blood cannot be obtained from an apothecary, that can only be had with the help of the criminal.

An abominable superstition which has not served for robbery, but may have caused many cases of poisoning is the belief that the froth from the mouth of a lately deceased person will cure habitual drunkenness if the froth be mixed with the drink (wine, brandy) that the tippler is in the habit of taking. In the same way it is believed that all that is loathsome and unwholesome can be removed by love potions and love charms. The same and similar superstitious means were used for prolonging life. A careful attention to such things, which are often neglected, can prevent many mistakes; often by such knowledge a strong suspicion will be aroused which will lead to the discovery of a criminal. It is believed for instance that epileptics can be judged by drinking water in which a corpse has been washed, or by masticating rotten coffinwood, and that wounds in middle life can be cured by *adipocere*, i.e. the extraordinary transformation of adipose membrane and muscle of a corpse found in stagnant water or a damp grave.

Written charms and incantations must not be considered to have no existence. The author has come across two, on one occasion on a gipsy half-blood and on the other upon a card cheat of most elegant appearance. That they are so seldom found is no proof whatever that they have practically ceased to exist; they are not found simply because they are not looked for. No doubt they will not be discovered carefully folded and put away in the pocket book of the criminal, but, tattered, filthy, almost repulsive, they are preserved in some hidden pocket or sewn into a hem or collar. The value of these documents, apart from their historical worth, is very great to criminalists. By their means indeed the Investigating Officer can find out one side of the character of his man and be sure that he has to deal with an individual who has to exercise caution, for honest folk have no need of such incantations.

The spells called the "Stick-spells" are not less remarkable from our point of view. They are of several kinds. The spell is uttered and committed to writing when the stick is cut, which is done only at appropriate times and accompanied by particular formalities. It differs according to the use to which the stick is to be put, be it to facilitate a journey or strengthen a cudgel with which defence is to be made against brigands, vagabonds, and dangerous animals of all kinds, in particular against snakes. If these incantations only serve to strengthen and develop the natural qualities of the stick, there are yet others which give it supernatural qualities. They prevent the owner from losing his way, protect him from the Will-o'-the-wisps and other terrible dangers on a journey, and even enable him to strike down an absent person. For each operation a special stick cut for the purpose of the person to be chastised, whose name must be included in the spell, is necessary.

Such a stick has played an important role in establishing the culpability of a woman and brought about her conviction for poisoning. This woman had been imprisoned on purely circumstantial evidence and her prosecution was about to be dropped, for there was no proof forthcoming that she had lived on bad terms with the person whose life had been attempted or that she had ever uttered anything which might lead to the supposition that she hated the victim and desired to be revenged. Before liberating the accused the Investigating Officer made further search at her house, and he found, in a prayer book, an old letter upon which was written a "stick-spell." In this formula the object was indicated by his initials and those of the place where he lived; there was a demand that the stick (which remained to be cut) would strike him *in absentia* "because he loved one other than he ought." The existence of bad terms between the two was thus established and not long after the woman made a complete confession of the crime.

We have also picture-charms and picture-spells which trace their origin to a similar belief in working *in absentia* or from a distance. The possibility of influencing from a distance a person of whom a model in wax etc. has been made, has been accepted from the earliest times. It is necessary however that an objective resemblance be established between the person and the picture. In the wax of which the image is made such things are needed as hair, nail-parings, blood, urine, perspiration, etc., of the person concerned or the wax must be brought into contact with his footwear, clothes, etc. One is reminded of the great significance which the "atzmann" or image made of wax, etc., had in German witch cases, and the *vols* or *voûts* had in the French royal law cases when it was asserted that the lives of kings had been aimed at by such pictures. In Catholic village churches, especially in places of pilgrimage, copies of human and animal figures or single limbs in wax, lead, or silver, are to be found which owe their existence to the belief that by their assistance illnesses can be caused to vanish from men and animals.

Finally we have murder-prayers and murder-masses. The murder-prayer means that with the help of mystical accessories (hair of the person concerned plays an important part) the life of someone is "spirited away." Persons still exist who firmly believe in this and the author has himself met a woman who was convinced that she understood the art. The "murder-mass" is used with the same object; on a certain day, generally the birthday or the name-day of the person who is to die a mass is said for his soul with certain precautions, and a piece of money is given to a priest who has formerly confessed the person to be got rid of. The discovery of such a murder-prayer may possibly give us a starting-point for further investigation in cases where more violent means have been subsequently used.

Numerous and apparently harmless forms of superstition may also be of importance in our work; indeed every superstition that reigns in a particular district has its own influence in investigation. Perhaps an important witness who has received a summons does not appear in Court because she does not wish to make her first appearance in a Law Court on a Friday or other unlucky day. Perhaps the honour and freedom of a man depends on a superstition and the knowledge of it. So not long ago in Vienna, a poor girl was arrested because she had sold a very valuable opal ring. She declared that an unknown person of elegant appearance had given the ring to her in the street. Naturally, nobody believed this, but the lawyer contended that it might be correct, because it occurred to him that the opal is an unlucky stone.' Inquiries proved that a lady of position had inherited the opal ring. Opals bring misfortune, and this can only be avoided by giving the unlucky stone to the first person one meets in the street. This the lady had actually done, and so had caused the girl to be arrested and had thus brought misfortune upon her.

Section iii.—Divination and Fortune-telling by Cards, etc.

A manifestation of superstition, often very disagreeable for the Investigating Officer, and which may lead to error, is the 'discovery' of the criminal by methods of superstition. Whether popular education has made progress or not seems almost indifferent here. In all countries and amongst almost all classes divination, fortune-telling by cards and otherwise, and other magical sciences and superstitions, are believed in. The author has indeed met with such belief in the best society. How many on spilling the salt dare not neglect to throw it over the left shoulder? How many are unhappy all day if they pass someone on the stairs? What trouble there is in the house when a looking-glass is broken or a portrait falls down, what consternation has often been caused by the ticking of a death-watch or the screeching of an owl. So too do people believe in horoscopes, fortune-telling, and lucky and unlucky days and hours for the accomplishment of important pieces of business. How many people there are, and especially women, who have presentiments." Every Investigating Officer has received during his career denunciations accusing with inexplicable certainty a certain person of being the author of a crime. This certainly only grows when the victim, generally a woman, is questioned, although she is not able to allege any particular facts capable of proof. The Investigating Officer finally becomes convinced that the victim cannot or will not give any sure indication, but at the same time has sufficient motives for considering the person named to be the author of the crime. Aided by these indications the investigation is commenced, inquiries are made, and warrants are issued, until the moment arrives when he perceives that he has been misled. He often even discovers that the superstitions communicated to him repose only upon the revelations of some old fortune-teller with regard to some person at first regarded by himself with suspicion. It also sometimes happens on the other hand that the person upon whom his suspicions rest is defended with energy simply because the revelations of some old woman show that person to be innocent.

The author once had to elucidate a big theft case, the victim of which was a young noblewoman all of whose jewels, which were very precious, had been stolen. Everything pointed to the thief being a young man-servant who had just entered her service. The countess defended him with such force and energy as to lead to the belief that very intimate relations existed between them. But the practical effect of her deposition was that the man remained for a long time at liberty and was not arrested till he had already sold a large quantity of the stolen articles. The lady then confessed that a celebrated fortune-teller had assured her that the thief was not one of her servants but an outsider. It finally came out that the diviner was the aunt of the servant, who had recommended this Pythia to his mistress.

The manner in which these predictions are made varies greatly, though the result is nearly always the same. Ordinarily the person who divines is the "magician" or the "seer" to whom must always be shown an object touched by the thief, such as a pocket-book from which he has abstracted money, a bureau into which he has broken or even, in case of need a latch which he must have lifted. Our magician then examines this object with the greatest attention, at the same time carrying on certain mysterious practices and asking all sorts of questions. She then gives her reply, which is naturally very vague: a neighbour, a member of the family, a person of the house, a stranger, or a pretended friend is suggested. Certain other general complementary indications are given and when the victim combines what he or she has heard with his or her own point of view a certain conclusion is come to as to the identity of the author of the crime, an idea which is sufficiently precise to communicate to the authorities and send them off on a false clue, thus doing a great deal of harm.

It is known that such performers often make use of middlemen to obtain information regarding the previous history of the foolish persons who come to them. In many cases, however, the fortune-teller does not require a middleman, for he is a good reader of human nature and is helped by his client's simplicity, who, all unawares, gives him more materials than he requires to produce an impression as a great reader of the past.

Another kind of divination is made with the aid of an instrument which according to *von Wlislocki* ("Concerning Wandering Gipsy Folk"), was formerly employed by the gypsies of Transylvania, but is nowadays very extensively used and finds numerous applications. This apparatus consists of a little box pierced in one side with a small hole to which the eye is applied, a diaphragm being inserted on another side which only allows as much light to penetrate as the owner of the miraculous box thinks proper. Opposite the first-mentioned hole is a mirror inclined in such a way that a person looking through the hole sees reflected an apparatus placed in the box. This apparatus consists of a cylinder, fan, or circular slide, representing several different things, such as an old woman, a young girl, or even the Devil. The magician then asks the person seeking information and wishing to see the thief that has pillaged his or her house to look through the hole. He lets a little light through the diaphragm into the interior of the box and by means of the cylinder, fan or slide, shows what seems to him best fitted to the case in point (for example, the old woman). The portrait shown is obliquely reflected into the mirror which again reflects it at the same angle of reflection into the eye of the observer—who is thunderstruck. It goes without saying that the portrait itself is not a good one, that the lighting is insufficient, that the time is relatively short, and that imagination does the rest. In this way is completed the portrait of a person who has already been suspected by the victim of the theft. She pays well for this revelation and then runs to the authorities, whom she assures that the thief can be only the person whose portrait she has seen in the box. Naturally she does not mention how she has arrived at this discovery—the magician takes care by the use of threats, to prevent her doing so—but she explains the matter (the magician has generally given her the necessary instructions) in such a way that the authorities are obliged, whether they wish it or not, to take some action upon her depositions.

DIVINATION AND FORTUNE TELLING

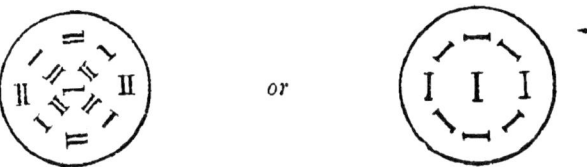

Figs 31 & 32

There exists another apparatus which is very often employed by gipsies, and if the author be rightly informed only by them. It is a large hoop of thin wood (like that used for a drum or a sieve) on which the skin of an animal has been stretched. The wood of the hoop should have been cut in a particular manner, and the skin must be that of an animal stolen at a particular time.* Figures are then made upon the skin, generally 9 or 18, or 7, 14, 21, as in Figs 31 & 32.

To reply to a question the gipsy throws upon the skin as many seeds of dagura as there are figures drawn on the skin and then strikes as many blows with a hammer or a piece of wood upon the frame as there are seeds at the same time pronouncing magic formulæ. These blows make the skin vibrate and the seeds jump. The manner in which the latter group themselves during the blows is of some importance, and their position round the figures, after the last blow, gives the true solution, and it is according to that position that the question is answered. The drum is especially employed for questions of love, and when it is necessary to know whether or not to put into execution a formulated plan and whether the issue will be good, but above all for the discovery of thieves. For this purpose the instrument is of very great importance. Some years ago the author was informed within a few days of a number of thefts. The theft was generally stated to have taken place some time before, in some cases, indeed, a very long time before, and the reason assigned why information of the crime had not been given was simply because no one had been suspected. All these denunciations, as numerous as they were sudden, had this in common, that they stated the names of the criminals without indicating any precise or convincing facts to prove that it was indeed such or such a person who had committed the theft, itself in most cases already forgotten. At last an old peasant woman, from whom a considerable sum of money had been stolen 30 years previously, came and accused her brother, with whom she had lived on excellent terms ever since. He was a man of the highest character rejoicing in the universal esteem of all who knew him, and in fact at the time of the denunciation he was Mayor of his town. Being unable to understand such an accusation the author began to question her very closely and finally learned that a little while before a 'celebrated' old gipsy woman had traversed the country working miracles with her magic drum. People had crowded to her and the good wife who had come to the author had thus learned that the theft had been committed by one of her near relations who at present occupied a 'high position.' As she had no other near relation in a high

---

* This belief that a thing used in certain superstitious practices should be stolen is as widespread as the belief that certain things should be found, begged, acquired by heredity, or made by oneself. This may throw some light upon thefts committed by persons who are otherwise perfectly honest (as in the case already referred to where warts are removed with a piece of stolen steak or the tail of a stolen herring)

station it could be no one but her brother the Mayor. Further investigation showed that all the surprising accusations received were without exception due to the gipsy's magic drum. If the accusations had been less numerous or less surprising, much harm, or at least much useless work, might have been the result.

The " hereditary sieve," which is well known all over Germany, has some analogy to the drum. It is employed in various ways to discover a thief. Beans (stolen if possible) are thrown into it one by one, a name being pronounced as each goes in. If the bean jumps out of the sieve, the owner of the name pronounced is innocent; if the bean remains in the sieve, the person named is the thief. Sometimes also the hereditary sieve is suspended from the edge of an hereditary table by an hereditary key—all these articles having come down from the father or grandfather. Then various persons are named, and when the sieve begins to move the thief is found.

Similar is the still popular "sieve-spin;" here two fingers are inserted in the handles of the blades of a pair of scissors, the points of which are stuck into the wooden ring of the sieve; the operator begins calling out names of suspected persons and at the right name the sieve moves.

The most important role in divination belongs to card-reading. The card-reader has throughout all ages replied to innumerable questions of the heart, commenced many a dispute, and laid many an Investigating Officer by the heels. It is the last case alone that is of interest to us here, and what has already been said concerning the influence of divination applies also. The victim of a theft often runs to a card-reader *before* going to the authorities or at least after but a little while, if justice has not immediately placed its hand upon the guilty person. She, or he, then comes back with very precious data about the author of the crime, to be communicated to the authorities. The latter are deceived, and often allow themselves to follow the false clue pointed out to them, abandoning perhaps a better one which they have already discovered.

But how, it may be asked, is it possible to avoid such unlucky errors? The rule so often recommended to Investigating Officers must here be repeated: always insist upon obtaining the *ratio sciendi*. Let this rule never be neglected and one will find, in nearly every case of this kind, that the person listened to is only resting his statements upon imaginary facts, and it will not unfrequently happen that one will obtain the confession—" it was a card-reader who told me."

It would be useless to give here a complete account of the theory of card-reading; the rules vary greatly according to time and place; every card-reader has perhaps his or her own particular method of arranging the cards and telling their meaning. Yet it is remarkable that the signification of the different cards is everywhere and always the same. Whoever cares to take every opportunity of getting information on this subject will never notice very great differences. The person who asks for the revelation is always the queen of hearts, if a woman—the knave of hearts if a man; the ace of spades signifies hope; the queen of diamonds a bad friend, etc. Only a small number of cards are of importance to us; we give them all because it often suffices to name, off hand, the proper card, in order to unmask the witness in these doubtful cases.

A lady of good education who had been the victim of a theft said to the author one day at the end of the interview in answer to the remark that it would be difficult to convict the thief— "yet I have great hopes." These words provoked his attention and he replied "the seven of Hearts was on top then?" (the seven of hearts signifies good news when it is on top) The lady replied in confusion "Yes, but how did you know it?"

HEARTS — Ace—success in all enterprises. King—an elderly person favourable to the inquirer. Queen or Knave (according to the sex of the inquirer)—herself or himself, his wife or her husband, his or her lover. Ten—happiness in love, health, etc. Nine—success in near enterprises—but "Take care." Eight—concord, peace, happiness, marriage, birth. Seven—good news.

DIAMONDS — Ace—mourning, grief, quarrels, losses. King—an elderly person who is injuring the inquirer without knowing it. Queen—a doubtful and false female friend. Knave—a false and deceitful male friend. Ten—small hope of love or happiness etc. Nine—idle gossiping, evil reputation, suspected by the police. Eight—separation from a person loved. Seven—society of false friends.

CLUBS — Ace—illness, death, prison. King—priest, or lawyer. Queen or Knave—hostile and dangerous persons. Ten—misfortune in all undertakings. Nine—losses to which one is exposed. Eight—loss of honour or goods, theft. Seven—bad news.

SPADES — Ace—hope, a journey. King—a good friend. Queen or Knave—well-disposed persons who bring misfortune by their want of tact, and prattling etc. Ten—according to circumstances means happy marriage or divorce. Nine—great honours in sight. Eight—reconciliation with an enemy. Seven—good society, hotel, conversation.

Section iv.—Treasure-finding, Dreams, and Chiromancy.

We now come to those practices in which superstition is used for the purpose of emptying the pockets of credulous people.

The various methods used in such cases are so numerous that it would be impossible to describe them. One or two of the artifices used may however be briefly stated, to give an idea of how these cheats go to work. For example, we have the bewitching of cattle, the only object of which is to ease the purse of the owner. In treasure-finding or the transformation of valueless articles (generally charcoal or rags) into gold or banknotes, the trick consists in obtaining from the person who is being deceived a loan of some object of value, which is immediately made away with. They demand for example that all the money in the house be placed in a box. The whole is then covered over with charcoal. Of course there is not enough charcoal and while more is being brought the money disappears. The chest or box is sealed up with all sorts of magic rites accompanied with the express recommendation that it is to remain closed and is not to be touched during a considerable lapse of time (seven weeks, ninety-nine days, or until the night of the new moon), then all the coal will be transformed into gold. This is the usual way of proceeding, the details of course varying continually. The search for treasure does not differ much. Usually a stranger turns up in the village inn and, by chance, begins to speak of hidden treasure; if he can judiciously lead the others up to the subject so that they appear to have started it and not he, so much the better. He, for his part, gives out that the thing is theoretically acceptable. They go on talking until one of his hearers lets out that there is also a man in the village who believes in it. The stranger waits until he can gather the name, and if possible the position of this believer in hidden treasure—and such people are to be found everywhere. Some time elapses, and then the accomplice of the stranger appears on the scene. It is the former and not the latter who repairs to the believer and obtains great influence over him, because he, not having been seen by many people in the village, can more easily relate, in a mysterious and detailed manner, a number of facts about his victim. He passes insensibly to the question of treasure-finding. The practised magician then commences with the aid of enchantments of all kinds, to fix upon the place where digging is to commence. He has, of course, examined this place previously and he provokes much astonishment when he is able to say that at a quarter of an hour's walk from the house, and at about a hundred paces from the cross roads, there are two trees and between these two trees there is a little bush. At that spot they must dig. Everything is exactly as he has indicated, they dig and find there an old pot, closed up and very heavy, which the cheat has taken care to place there beforehand. He absolutely forbids the pot to be opened until the specified moment. But in the meantime all the money and silver that can be found must be placed upon the pot, and it must be reburied. The count victim sometimes sells everything he possesses in order to obtain sufficient silver to place on the pot, and the whole is then carefully buried. Of course the thief makes off with the money that very night. When such a case happens, all that the authorities can do is to make it as widely known as possible, so as to prevent the recurrence of such cheating and at the same time bring about the discovery of the cheat. To prepare a note for circulation among the police is not enough, the occurrence must be published in full detail in the press if it is to be made as widely known as possible.

In such cases moreover we must not forget the accomplice. Knowing that for the moment he is doing nothing criminal or even reprehensible in merely talking about treasure-seeking, he often does not take sufficient care to hide himself. He has probably spoken in his own dialect and, for want of another subject to open the conversation, has dilated upon his travels and adventures. He may have described towns and localities or made allusions to his former trade or profession. In a word it may be very easily possible to obtain such *data* as may enable him to be discovered as well as the actual thief who has, in most cases, not come upon the scene until a long time afterwards.

The interpretation of dreams and chiromancy are not so unimportant as might at first thought appear.

The author once had to deal with a case in which a peasant woman had had her hand examined and had been informed that she would one day be poisoned. This idea preoccupied her day and night. She sought out a second fortune-teller, who, unfortunately, told her that she was menaced by a danger coming from her husband. These two predictions were in agreement, she would be poisoned by her husband, with whom she lived on good terms. A long time afterwards this woman was attacked by pains in the stomach of no consequence, but her imagination, emotion, and fear, combined to make her so ill that it was found necessary to call in a doctor.

who diagnosed traces of vegetable poisoning. It is possible that the doctor had not made his inquiries with much skill, and, as he questioned her on the supposition that it was really a case of poisoning, the woman replied "yes," to all the questions put in that sense, and, in consequence, her husband was arrested. It was only after some time when the woman had been removed to the hospital of the nearest city that it was ascertained that she was suffering from gastric hysteria and her husband's innocence was established beyond all doubt. Her state, which was in no way simulated, characteristically improved when the impossibility of her having been poisoned was pointed out to her.

When the Investigating Officer has to deal with a case in which he believes divination to have played a role he is at a great advantage if he is aware of the methods employed. At all events he will very quickly obtain the confidence of the person deceived if he shows him that he also has some knowledge of the subject and does not need to call in a third party to help him. To acquire this knowledge is not difficult. If the interpreter of dreams is to be examined, all that is necessary is to buy (for a few pence) one of his "Egyptian Dream Books," taking care at the same time to find out of what country the accused is a native. These books vary somewhat and the employment of one more than another is a matter to be considered. But when all is said what they contain is very similar.

It is otherwise with chiromancy, which, since Artemidor, Cardanus, Porta v Hagen, Pratorius, Goclenius etc., has not varied in its chief points. This fixity has been considered by Paracelsus to be a proof of its truth; according to him, chiromancy is not a mere chimera and he makes it rest upon "sure and certain foundations." In spite of the widespread practice of chiromancy it is not easy to get accurate information on the subject and one generally has to fall back upon tradition and hearsay, although in recent times there have been numberless pretenders to the art.

The most information on this subject is to be found in Hislop's book, which has served as a guide to the author.

According to him the line A (*Fig* 33) at the wrist denotes riches and honour. If the line B touches the line A, the person will obtain them by marriage or, at least, through a person of the opposite sex. The eminence of the thumb at C when furrowed with little lines signifies illness, misery, an unhappy marriage, and a premature death. If the folds at the joint of the thumb are furrowed that signifies misfortune. Happiness may be hoped for when the line B ends in the line A and when the eminence C is smooth and rounded. When B and D join the greatest happiness may be looked for. If the line E cuts the line D the happiness will be destroyed by envious people. When the line E is missing altogether its absence signifies a long life full of happiness and prosperity and a happy marriage, especially when the eminence under the middle finger is large. When furrowed with little folds,

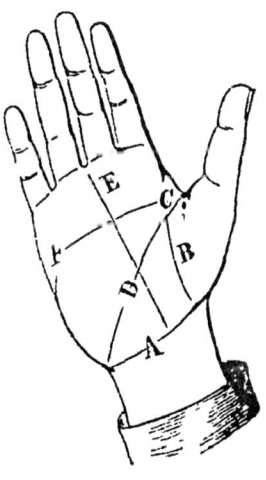

Fig 33

this eminence denotes marriage in the near future. If the line F cuts the lines B and D, one's unhappy lot can only be attributed to oneself, for one is false, avaricious, and mean. If the line F does not come up to the line D or joins it at the line E, the owner of the hand will die a violent death. If the space under F does not contain any folds the death will be by drowning. If, on the contrary, the space is filled with wrinkles, fire will be the cause of death. If the line F reaches the line D and if the fourth and little fingers are covered with wrinkles and folds at the joints, the person in question will live in good health to an advanced age. Thin and long fingers denote much illness, short fat fingers signify health. Happy is the person in whose hand the line A joins the line B and the line B the line D. E should be missing altogether, F should reach to D, and the surface C should be smooth and rounded.

The different beliefs attaching to the fingers, their size and length, white marks on the nails, etc. denote only happiness or misfortune, and do not interest us here. There is still a strange and widespread belief that by means of a drop of blood placed upon a nail one may find out where to find a lost or stolen article. Wlislocki relates that for this purpose the Transylvanian gipsies let three drops of blood from the middle finger of the left hand drop upon the middle nail of the right hand. A youth or virgin girl should then interpret the shapes taken by the drops of blood and say what he sees.

Section v.—Superstitions regarding Oaths.

Here again superstition has not yet disappeared, and it is the more dangerous because many people on taking an oath would conform to the truth if they did not believe that they possessed a means by which they can take a false oath with impunity. And to-day people have still many such means. One can, for instance, take a false oath without fear if one be resting the eyes upon a hoopoe (a holy bird with a hooked bill and cinnamon crest, a peewit will do, it is always lucky in court), if one has upon one's person a bone of one's own dead child, or if one folds the thumb (especially Jews who swear upon the Thorah or Pentateuch). Others are safe when they place the left hand upon the hip or spit before and after taking the oath, or when they place several little stones in the mouth or a gold coin under the tongue. Other methods are to wrench off a trouser button by turning it round while being sworn or to have some mistletoe leaves in one's boot beneath the sole of the foot, or to carry on the person a morsel of sacramental bread &c.

In some parts it is a judicial custom to open the window when a peasant takes an oath. It is thought that then the Devil can come in and fetch away the soul of a false witness, he cannot come in through a closed window.*

A number of other superstitions used in Court have to do with the dead. They are Slavonic by origin, and are widely spread. The cloth with which

---

* The same custom is said to prevail in the Upper Alps, but is otherwise explained. There the Devil does not come in by the door or window, but down the chimney. He gets out best, however, through the window, the panes of which do not hurt him, but so that he may not injure the panes when he takes the soul of the man with him the window is opened for him. Old servants of the Court in the country, to this day do not fail, in certain cases, to throw the window open and so prevent perjury.

the chin of a dead person was bound must be taken into Court when one has to appear there, and so long as the knots in the cloth remain tied, the law cannot harm one. It is equally efficacious to carry in one's boot the cord with which the feet of a dead person were bound so that one's adversary cannot get the better of one; it is also well to wipe one's face before the Judge with a cloth that has belonged to a dead person.

The best thing to do is to inquire of the poor people in the district in which one is working what are the usual superstitious practices to be found there. If one then suspects that a witness is perjuring himself, one may be in a position to find out whether he is carrying some such article of protection.

CHAPTER XI

CONSTRUCTION AND USE OF WEAPONS.

Some knowledge of weapons, especially firearms, their construction, use, and effects will be advantageous to many Investigating Officers. Undoubtedly the best and most complete text-book will not teach much to one who has never in his life handled a gun, and one may be a very distinguished lawyer without knowing how to load a rifle. Thus the best plan will be to get some sportsman or other expert to show and explain the working of a few guns and pistols. Of course, nothing can take the place of early familiarity with firearms, the practical knowledge thus gained being completed by a study of the best recent treatises on the subject. Thus fortified, the Investigating Officer in any given criminal matter will perhaps be able to offer a better opinion than so called experts, such as gunsmiths, who understand well enough how to adjust the different parts of a weapon, or to mend an old gun but who know nothing of ballistics, of the technicalities of shooting, or of the other scientific notions involved.

The following pages, compiled from various works on the subject as well as personal experience, are intended merely as a *vade mecum* to refresh the memory.

Section i.—Firearms.

The Investigating Officer is in a more complicated position than the soldier or the sportsman, the latter are satisfied with acquaintance with weapons of one or at most two or three types, while the former must know all types, of all ages. One has only to look at a collection of arms to comprehend that a criminal act may be committed as easily with a musket of the fifteenth century as with the latest American model. Indeed *accidents* are just as likely to occur with old weapons as with new. Other motives sometimes operate. Thus a servant wishing to commit suicide selected from his master's collection of arms an old matchlock, this weapon having an enormous calibre, appeared to him most likely to ensure rapid death. If his intention had been to kill someone else, he would probably to command success have selected the same instrument.

In all countries however we find old-fashioned guns, what may be called "family weapons," used not only for sport but for protection against robbers and wild beasts. When percussion guns were in vogue the country people still used flint-locks, and when breech-loaders came in percussion guns in turn became unfashionable and therefore cheap, though still perfectly serviceable, and displaced the old flint-locks. It is the same everywhere; the common man who does not wish to spend too much money, especially when the object is not one of prime necessity always buys the fashion that preceded the last. He thus obtains at a low price objects of good quality and quite useful which have been discarded solely because something better, perhaps only more fashionable, has taken their place. It is the same with clothes, tools, machinery, carriages, books and a thousand other things. This fact is by no means unimportant, it will often help us to guess, from the arm found, the station in life of the owner, and conversely, knowing the person suspected, to conclude the nature of the weapon he would be likely to use.

A. General Considerations

As it is extremely improbable that an Investigating Officer will ever have to do with heavy guns or artillery, we confine our remarks to small arms. These are generally guns, rifles, pistols, revolvers and magazine weapons. The constituent parts common to all these arms are: the barrel, the stock, the plate and the accessories. It is according to the differences presented by the three first mentioned that firearms are classified and named.

If the barrel is long and the butt end of the stock transverse to it, so that when fired, the weapon can be placed against the shoulder, it is called a gun or rifle. If the barrel be short and the stock curved down so that the weapon must be held in the hand when fired, it is a pistol or revolver. If the weapon can be loaded only from the muzzle end of the barrel, we call it a muzzle-loader, if on the other hand it is loaded at the plate end we call it a breech-loader.

If the weapon has one or more short barrels loaded separately, it is an ordinary pistol, if, on the other hand, it has only one barrel and a turning cylinder permitting several shots to be fired in succession, it is a revolver. It is clear that in the most important weapon, the gun, the differences in the barrel and in the plate may be innumerable. Speaking generally—

(a) The *barrel* is the metal tube in which the charge is placed ready for firing and in which it is exploded. This tube must compress the gases developed during combustion, and give the missile its proper direction. The barrel is now almost always of steel, formerly we find it constructed of iron, and even bronze, copper, brass and other metals.

(b) The *stock* is that part by which the weapon is held and which supports the barrel. It not only enables us to hold and manipulate the arm, but to it also are fixed the plate, the rings surrounding the barrel, and the other accessories. It is almost always of wood, in small pocket pistols and revolvers it may be of horn, ivory, vulcanite, and even metal.

(c) The *plate* contains or supports the apparatus for the discharge of the weapon. Whatever its shape, its object is by means of a gentle pressure, to produce a violent and sudden blow, causing the ignition of the powder directly or indirectly through a morsel of fulminate.

(d) The *accessories* include all the parts of the weapon besides the three just named, as the sight, the muzzle, the barrel-rings, the bed-plate, the ram-rod, the trigger guard, &c. These accessories vary in importance but must not be wholly neglected. For example, it may be most relevant to an inquiry to know whether a gun be well or badly sighted.

B Different Kinds of Firearms

1 GUNS (INCLUDING RIFLES)

Guns may be classified from several points of view,—single, double or more barrelled—muzzle or breech-loaders—rifles or shot-guns. We shall classify them according to the projectile, the important point for us is to know the *nature of the wound inflicted*, and consequently the nature of the projectile employed.

(a) SHOT-GUNS

Shot includes all projectiles in the form of small balls, loaded into the barrel not singly but in quantities, and not compressed but simply retained by the wad.

While bullets are cast in moulds, shot is obtained by allowing molten lead to fall through a sieve, from a sufficient height, into water. The melted lead in falling takes the form of drops, and enters the water as small round balls. To render the lead more liquid, from ¼ to ½ per cent. of arsenic is generally added, this detail is not unimportant when the shot has remained some time in the human body. Intermediate between bullets and shot come buckshot, here each shot is of the size of a pea and is cast in a mould like a bullet, but in use several are loaded together like ordinary shot.

Shot is generally manufactured according to numbers, each number indicating a special size. The pellets are so small that no person could measure them without delicate scientific apparatus, so they are distinguished by the number of pellets per ounce weight. The following table may be accepted as a fair standard

Table giving the number of shot in one ounce of Newcastle chilled or soft shot

Sizes	SSG	AAA	AA	A	BBB	BB	B	1	2	3	4	5	6	7	8	9	10
Pellets per oz	11	10	18	36	64	76	88	104	122	140	172	218	270	340	450	580	850

There is shot much smaller than this, the size known as 12 contains 1250 pellets per ounce, while D runs up to 2600 pellets. These very small sizes are, however, in practice used only by naturalists shooting small birds so as to avoid injuring the plumage. Buckshot can be distinguished by the circular mark and the remains of the 'jet' of molten metal, caused by the fact that the two halves of the mould do not fit with mathematical accuracy, and the necessity of a small opening for pouring in the liquid. From the difference between shot or buckshot and bullets arises the difference between shot-guns and those carrying bullets, the former allowing of a lighter barrel than the latter. In sporting guns of good damascened steel, the muzzle of the barrel is sometimes as thin as paper, cutting like a razor, while the arm loses nothing in quality and is perfectly safe. If, however, the projectile be forcibly compressed or rammed down into the barrel so as to close hermetically all passage to the gases of combustion until it leaves the barrel; the latter must offer a strong resistance to the expansion of the gas and also probably to the pressure of the bullet; hence the barrel must have an increased thickness. We may, therefore, fire a bullet from a shot-gun, provided that the barrel is sufficiently thick and that the calibre of the bullet is not greater than that of the barrel. But we cannot, of course, fire either so far or with such precision as with a rifle, the gun not being intended for this purpose. So also we may fire shot from every bullet gun, so long as the manipulation of the cartridges (in breech-loaders) presents no difficulties.

With a non-rifled muzzle-loader it is indifferent whether shot or bullet be used. If the barrel be rifled we must be careful not to employ shot, as they destroy the rifling. The pellets rebound with great force from the edges ("lands") of the rifling, leaving there a little lead called "leading," or "metallic fouling." This must be removed by the armorer with a file, which alters the calibre and thus causes much inconvenience. If then shot has been fired from a rifled gun, there must be some special reason—as people do not usually set about destroying their guns just for fun.

These remarks are intended to draw the Investigating Officer's attention to this point: that one can never be too careful in drawing a conclusion or making a guess as to the projectile employed, from the suspected weapon, and, vice versa, from a projectile found to the weapon probably employed. A too hasty conclusion can never be justified, and may lead to grave consequences. There are many reasons why a weapon may have been loaded improperly, that is with projectiles other than those for which it is intended: carelessness, ignorance, chance, the supply of proper projectiles may have run out, or through deliberate intent. Intent again may have different motives, the most important being a desire to mislead as to the character of a weapon employed.

For example, a man wants it to be believed that a bullet has not been fired from a well-ascertained shot-gun, say, the only firearm he is supposed to possess. He secretly gets hold of a rifle, of say six grooves, with this he fires a bullet from a distance into a bank of sand or into the water: the bullet is uninjured, but the traces of the six "lands" of the rifling are distinctly visible. Or if he lives near a rifle-butt he can pick up plenty of bullets that have missed their aim and show no other trace of usage but the marks of the rifling. He then loads this bullet, wrapped up in some moss, into the barrel of a shot-gun; the weapon will not be injured as the bullet does not touch it; he can then fire on a man, and at a short distance or point blank with a deadly aim. When this bullet with its marks of six riflings is found in a corpse, it is unhappily too likely that suspicion will fall not on a shot-gun and consequently not on the guilty man.

Further, let us suppose that shot has been discharged from a rifle. Usually one discharge is enough to produce "leading", but if this leading is so slight that a little cleverness can destroy it with a wad-extractor, then whatever traces may remain are at once destroyed by firing a bullet from the rifle. Further, if this sportsman knows the dodge of enclosing the shot in a small linen bag, which will not tear until it arrives at the muzzle, there will be no "leading" at all.

Therefore, once more, be very careful in drawing conclusions.

Naturally, when we find shot we suppose it has been fired from a shot-gun, and when we find a bullet we conclude that it has been fired from a rifle of corresponding calibre and rifling; but we must never forget that the fact may be quite otherwise, and above all we must not dismiss legitimate suspicions on the sole ground that "the projectile does not fit the gun."

We can now classify *shot-guns* according to the nature of the *barrel* and the *plate*.

a. The Barrel

(1) *The Material of Gun Barrels*

The material of the barrel is important to us from only one point of view, that is, in recognising and describing the material we may be able to discover the owner. It is unlikely that a young peasant should possess a gun with high-class damascened barrels. Minor matters may sometimes come in useful. The *material* of the barrel of a shot-gun is of no importance as to its accuracy of fire, the cohesion of the grains of powder, the range, the liability to misfire, &c. A man may shoot very straight at a long range and with perfect certainty with the most ordinary iron barrel and get exactly opposite results with the best drawn-steel barrel ever made. Of course, we assume that both barrels are in good condition (not twisted, flattened, &c.). As we shall see presently, the charge alone is, from this aspect of importance. Do not then be led away by amateur experts, who will tell you, "this shot was never fired by the famous damascened steel Laminette, the shot would certainly have gone further or remained packed longer", or again, "with a wretched iron gun it is absolutely impossible that in firing from such a long range the shot should not have been scattered"; such statements indicate only an absolute lack of judgment, for the material of the barrel has nothing to do with the accuracy of the firing. Some, indeed, suggest that the form of the inside of the barrel is important, and that for a good gun the bore should be conical, diminishing towards the muzzle, this narrowing, of course, being exactly proportioned. But this statement has never been established by proof. Another matter is the solidity of the barrel, and its safety for the sportsman. It is easy to see that an ordinary iron barrel is much more subject to rust, to twisting or to splitting at the muzzle. Also, and this is important, the more carefully the barrel has been made, the less the danger of its bursting and wounding the person firing. Further, if the original material is good, the weight can be reduced so that good barrels will be thinner than ordinary barrels and consequently lighter in weight and easier to carry.

But all this is not of much importance for criminal investigation, our hints on this point being only to facilitate the understanding of records, reports, descriptions, &c.

The simplest material is iron or steel. Iron, owing to its weight, is employed only for low-class cheap guns. Solid steel is rarely employed for shot-guns as it must be bored, and boring costs money. All the qualities desiderated for a good gun-barrel are to be found in steel manufactured by the Damascus process. Whether for gun-barrels, sword-blades or knives, Damascus steel is invincible. It is produced by the welding together of thin plates of steel and soft iron alternately. If we thus weld together (by hammering on an anvil when hot) *ribbons* of steel and iron we have ribbon Damascene. If threads are used we get ordinary Damascene work, but if the threads of iron and steel are carefully *plaited* before welding, we obtain the highest quality. The price and the resisting power rise in proportion.

In the manufacture of a barrel from Damascus steel the ribbons or threads are rolled round a core of the same calibre as the barrel; they are then hot-hammered until thoroughly welded. The barrel is then polished and engraved with an acid (vinegar or aqua fortis). This attacks the steel more than the iron, so that a design is produced showing the positions of the iron and steel. These designs, assuming many different forms (with which we need not here trouble ourselves), have been imitated in many ways, the result being called "damasceening"—an art not to be confounded, as it often is, with the process of manufacture. Webster, s.v., always a reliable authority, enumerates the following modes of "ornamenting metal" by the process of damasceening

"(1) That in which the design is formed by means of wires laid in so that they project. (2) that produced by engraving the design with deep cut lines, inlaying gold wires, and rubbing them down level. (3) that in which the design is made by small holes which are filled with gold and burnished. (4) that in which gold leaf is laid on a rough etched surface to which it adheres in part (Kuft-work). (5) that in which the design is simply etched upon steel or iron" as in common gun-barrels, "and (6) that in which the pattern or watering is produced by a mixture of silver or other metal with the steel, with which it does not perfectly alloy." We need hardly point out that "damask" as applied to silk, linen, and other stuffs has a similar origin.

We thus obtain a barrel not only thin and light but offering special security to the sportsman. When an iron or steel barrel bursts, it splinters into pieces which scatter themselves far and wide, while a barrel of Damascus steel will tear up, with a greater or less fissure just like a piece of cloth, but will not fly into fragments at least, such an occurrence is extremely rare.

(2) *Number of Barrels*

Single-barrelled shot-guns are not very common, but are still manufactured to be sold to country people at a low price. Old ones, however, are often found inlaid with gold or richly damascened, which the owners would not willingly throw away.

The number of the barrels has no influence on the accuracy of fire, double-barrelled guns are most commonly used nowadays.

Two kinds of guns are important for the Investigating Officer to be acquainted with. They are single-barrelled and not easily recognised at first sight walking-stick guns and guns that take to pieces. They may occasionally be constructed to take a bullet, but are usually shot-guns. Walking-stick guns are often very remarkable. The barrel is made and painted so as to resemble a bamboo, the handle is usually crutch-shaped and contains all the firing apparatus, which may be taken off and carried in the pocket, or even folded up in the handle itself.

The Investigating Officer must keep a sharp look-out for a weapon of this kind during a house search, or in describing the articles found on an accused. Every article bearing any resemblance to a walking-stick gun must be carefully examined; every stick, even the most innocent in appearance must be taken in the hand to test its weight, for a walking-stick gun is always naturally heavier than an ordinary stick of similar appearance. The sound made by a walking-stick gun, even when put down gently on the ground, is characteristically different from that of an ordinary walking-stick, even if the latter be heavily ferruled. There can be no doubt that many crimes are committed with this traitorous weapon. If further it be used with smokeless and noiseless powder, we may believe anything of its powers.

Guns which can be taken to pieces are as important, and in certain cases even more important, than walking-stick guns. These weapons are often constructed with the greatest skill.

When we consider the ingenious mechanism of many of these weapons we can appreciate the remark of an old forest guard, "A clever poacher carries his gun in his waistcoat pocket." Hence we must never allow ourselves to be led away by the assurance of witnesses, that the suspected person "certainly carried no gun," or after a search, "no trace of a gun could be found."

The author recollects a case in which a gamekeeper had been killed by poachers, where the only object found on the search was a piece of a gun-barrel about 5¼ inches long, with the furrow of a screw running through the wall of the barrel. It was concealed in a pot in the kitchen. Although this had naturally attracted attention, no other portions of the weapon were brought to light at that time, although a subsequent and more careful search disclosed them all to be in the house. Pieces were found in a truss of hay, in a horse collar, behind the crucifix, in a crack in a large lump of salt, and in a split in a rafter. The accused believed that his house was continually kept under observation and, therefore, had not dared to seek an out-of-doors hiding-place.

β. Explosive Action

Guns may also differ according to the mode in which the explosive agent is set in action. By this we understand the apparatus by which the gunpowder placed in the gun is ignited. The object is to procure the result with the greatest rapidity, facility, and certainty. We can well understand that it has been a long and weary way from the original system, where the powder in the barrel was set directly on fire by a piece of red-hot carbon or a wick (the matchlock), to our up-to-date breech-loading magazine rifle. Keeping in view the two elements of apparatus of ignition and method of loading, we shall now classify guns as muzzle-loaders and breech-loaders.

(1) *Muzzle-loaders*

In *muzzle-loaders* the charge is introduced by the muzzle of the barrel and poured or rammed into the breech chamber, where the powder is ignited. The *arrangement* is exactly the same as in a cartridge. First comes the powder, then the thick wads by which the powder is firmly rammed home, to prevent, as explained *supra*, the escape of the gases of ignition, then the shot or bullet; in the case of shot a thin wad is added to prevent the pellets falling out.

The Investigating Officer will rarely have to do with a matchlock, but flint-locks are fairly common. In a gun of this class there is on one side of the plate a scooped-out projection (the pan *bassinet*) in which a little powder is placed; a hole pierced through the barrel allows this powder to communicate with that in the barrel. To keep the powder in the pan there is an elbow-shaped cover kept down by a spring, the perpendicular part of which is faced with steel. Opposite this is the hammer, holding a piece of flint. When the hammer falls, the flint strikes the metal, which rises, uncovering the powder, and at the same moment the same stroke produces a spark which ignites the powder in the pan, this in turn igniting that in the barrel.

The flint-lock was an extraordinary advance on the matchlock and other old-fashioned devices, but had its own drawbacks; it often missed fire, the powder in the pan either not igniting or not igniting the charge (" a flash in the pan "). Damp and rain were also great enemies ("keep your powder dry"). If then an Investigating Officer suspects a flint-lock to have been used, he must consider the points just enumerated. For example, was it raining at the time and moment when the shot was fired? There is also an appreciable interval between the firing and the ignition in the barrel, hence a person not accustomed to a flint-lock always fires behind the object aimed at, when the latter is moving.

The flint-lock betrays more readily than any other firearm that it has been recently fired. The smoke of the powder leaves distinct traces in the pan, the channel, and the neighbouring parts, the marks made by the flint on the steel are shining and not oxidised, and the marks on the flint whence small pieces have been chipped off in firing are, when recent, easily recognised. Of course, other things being equal, one can shoot with a flint-lock just as safely and as far as with any other make.

More frequently we come across the percussion gun. This originated in the discovery, towards the end of the eighteenth century, of substances (chlorates, fulminates, etc.) igniting not by a spark but by a blow or shock. It was only a step to place this substance in the pan instead of the powder, and to allow the *hammer* to fall directly upon it, without the intervention of flint or steel. The progress was easy to the "percussion cap," wherein the fulminate is placed in a capsule or cap of copper, fitting on to a projection or "nipple," which takes the place of the pan and on which the hammer falls directly.

This species of gun was long considered absolutely perfect, and such weapons, of the best quality, are still in use in country districts. They would not be employed, except with some special motive, by regular sportsmen, amateur or professional, hence when the question is of a percussion gun of unknown ownership, the first conclusion will be that it belongs to a peasant.

The question, "To whom does this gun belong?" "With what kind of gun was this man killed?" are of frequent importance, and in looking for an answer we must take into account the make of a gun and its accessories. For instance, if a muzzle-loading percussion gun has been used, we must, in making a search, look out for accessories peculiar to this weapon *e.g.*, the small tool used to place the caps quickly and easily upon the nipple, and consequently useless with a breech-loader. Also if we find a ramrod plug, wads, shot-bags, powder-horns, and such like, we know they belong to a muzzle-loader. These accessories are often of a very primitive make. Fig 34 shows an Indian powder flask and shot-bag taken from a Moplah in the outbreak at Manjeri in March, 1896, in which ninety-three Moplahs were killed. If the Investigating Officer knows nothing about firearms, and has to carry out a search of this kind, he should take care to have with him some trustworthy person who does know. Such persons it is true are not rare, and confidence may often—not always—be reposed in them, but we cannot too often repeat, that the Investigating Officer must not wait for the time of trouble to arise, he must, like the soldier, be in time of peace always prepared for war.

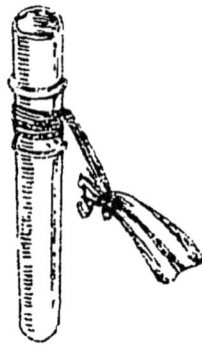

Fig 34

(2) Breech-Loaders

Breech-loading guns are to-day in general use. By this title are designated all firearms in which by a special mechanism, the barrel can be opened and loaded from the rear, that is the end nearest the butt. After introducing the charge, the weapon is closed. Although firearms of this description form the modern model, their invention is by no means recent. Museums show specimens as old as the sixteenth century, many constructed with wonderful ingenuity. It was long before they became popular, mainly on account of the complication, inherent weakness, and difficulty of procuring a hermetic seal, as compared with the "simplicity and strength" of the muzzle-loader. An impetus was, however, given to inventors when rifling came into vogue, on account of the slowness of the process of loading when the bullet had to be forced into the grooves of the rifling. The most important development was the "system *Lefaucheux,*" wherein the barrels are hinged and swing to or from the false breech. In one guise or another this forms the foundation of almost all the modern breech-loading shot-guns. But though *Lefaucheux* brought out his gun in 1832, it was invented 130 years before by an unknown master-armourer, whose work can be seen in the Dresden Museum.

The first military breech loader was the *Needle-gun* invented by *Dreyse* in 1838, adopted by Prussia in 1841 and in use during the war of 1870. The various species of military rifles since invented are legion.

In shot-guns there are three systems of percussion—pin-fire, rim-fire, central-fire. In the pin-fire the original invention of *Lefaucheux* a pin passes through the cartridge perpendicular to the axis fitting into a small recess in the barrel, the hammer falls on the pin, which causes the cap to explode. Rim-fire is practically unknown in common use. Central-fire cartridges introduced by *Lancaster,* are now almost universally employed. Here the cap is in the centre of the cartridge case behind, so that the axis of the cap coincides with that of the cartridge. A small pointed projection on the hammer strikes and explodes the cap.

(b) BULLET-GUNS

Guns of this class generally have a single steel barrel; sometimes they are double-barrelled, and occasionally we find a gun with one barrel smooth for shot and the other rifled for bullets. For us the most important point is the mode of loading, as many muzzle-loading rifles are to be found. It is at times necessary to distinguish between shots fired from a muzzle-loader and from a breech-loader respectively. Here we must remember the way in which muzzle-loaders are charged: the powder is first poured down the barrel; the mouth of the barrel is then covered with a well-greased piece of cloth called a '*patch*' on which the bullet is placed, pressed down, and finally rammed home. Hence only certain projectiles can be used. The long slender bullets of modern small-bores cannot well be treated in this way; round balls or short cylindrical bullets with conoidal ends are generally employed. A round bullet is the almost certain mark of a muzzle-loader. Besides, the bullet almost always bears marks of having been thrust down the barrel, especially when a too small bullet has been used which rebounds from side to side. Of course, such marks must not be confounded with any caused by the bullet in its flight striking a hard object.

Marks are also left by the patch, but this happens on the contrary when the bullet fits very tightly. Hence the patch is compressed between the bullet and the rifling, the result being visible on the bullet. The marks of the rifling (i.e., of the 'lands') are not impressed accurately and are even wanting where the patch has been folded; in looking at such a bullet, uninjured by hitting a hard object, the impression is at once given that it has not been in direct contact with the rifling. A more accurate description is impossible; the effect must be seen, and whoever has with his eyes compared a bullet thus fired from a muzzle-loader with one fired with no intervening envelope from a breech-loader will never forget the difference.

Again, it frequently occurs, if the bullet be of soft lead, i.e., without any alloy of tin, zinc, antimony, &c., that the complete design of the patch is imprinted on the metal. On examining the projectile carefully with a good magnifying glass, we can frequently find such accurate traces of the cloth as to be able to identify the material employed. A poacher was suspected of having killed a gamekeeper. No bullets similar to that found in the body were discovered in his house, but he was in possession of several rags (apparently designed for patches) evidently torn from an old flour sack. The projectile found in the corpse and these rags were subjected to microscopical examination; a sufficient large imprint was found on the bullet, and taking into account the special arrangement of the threads, their thickness, and their number in a given square unit, the experts were able to state that the bullet in question must, when fired, have been wrapped in a patch exactly similar to those found in the poacher's house.

The importance of the patch thus used with a bullet, and of the paper of the wad used with shot, is well recognised by criminal experts. Indeed it can hardly be exaggerated, for they frequently lead to startling conclusions, as when a man wraps up a bullet in a fragment of his mistress's pocket-handkerchief, or uses one of his love-letters as a wad. Hence these must be looked for with great care; but as usual we must not jump too hastily at conclusions, for the criminal may have laid himself out to deceive us and transfer the blame to innocent shoulders. In every case the presence of a patch proves the use of a muzzle-loader—always supposing the patch has not been put there for the express purpose of deceiving the Investigating Officer. But if no patch be found, no conclusion can be drawn, for it may have been destroyed or lost. Besides, when the bullet fits loosely in the barrel, a patch need not be used; the projectile may be wrapped in paper moss, dry leaves, &c.

The constituent parts of a bullet gun—barrel, stock, &c.—are essentially the same as for a shot-gun. The most important variation from our point of view is in the rifling of the barrel. The barrel is naturally thicker than for a shot-gun, the ball having to be more tightly compressed by it. The cavity traversed by the ball is the chamber or calibre, the walls of the chamber are the thickness. If for example the thickness of the barrel be 3 mill., the calibre or diameter across the lands, 10 mill., the total diameter will be 16 mill. (3 + 10 + 3), or .625 inches.

Rifling seems to have been originally introduced merely with the object of diminishing the fouling of the barrel and facilitating cleaning. The powder on burning leaves a black shiny residue, which dries quickly and forms a sort of crust. This crust lessens the calibre of the barrel, rendering the introduction of the bullet more difficult. When there is rifling, this residue gets into the grooves, leaving a free passage to the bullet. Hence the early rifling consisted of straight grooves each exactly parallel to the axis of the barrel. But soon a twisting or spiral direction round the axis was given to the groove. One result of this was to retain the bullet longer in the barrel, whereby resulted more complete combustion of the powder with increased force. But the great advantage was that the spiral imparted to the bullet a rotation or spin round its own axis, which spin was preserved by the bullet on leaving the barrel. Hence, according to the well-known principle of gyroscopic stability, whereby a rotating or spinning body retains its axis of spin, perfectly and simply illustrated by the ordinary humming top, the ball on leaving the barrel preserves its axis of spin and goes straight in its trajectory, "equalising in all directions its tendencies to erratic flight just as the top spins upright on its point until friction and wind-pressure gradually destroy the rotatory spin."

The hollow portions of the rifling are the 'grooves,' the projecting portions between the grooves are the 'lands.' The number of the grooves varies, 3, 4, 5, 6, 7, &c., so also does the form. A common form is that known as "concentric," see the sectional Fig. 35, where the breadth of the groove a b is equal to that of the land c d. Again, the corners may be rounded off, giving the sectional figure as a curved line, as in the Metford system. The depth of the rifling varies; if the grooves are too shallow they do not produce the proper effect—if too deep they are not filled by the lead and the gases of combustion escape. The spiral or twist of the rifling is the "pitch," just as in a screw. The pitch may be measured by the angle made by the groove with a line parallel to the axis of the barrel, or more easily in practice by the length of such a line intercepted between two twists of the same groove, i.e., the distance parallel to the barrel in which the groove

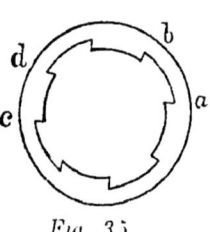

Fig. 35

makes one complete circuit of the barrel, thus in the Martini-Henry there are seven grooves and each makes one turn in 22 inches. As the length of the barrel is 33.2 inches, the rifling makes 1½ turns in the length. If, as we look along the chamber from behind, the spiral starts from the left and rises towards the right, then we have right pitch, i.e. the spiral runs "clockwise" as in an ordinary corkscrew. If it starts from the right and rises to the left, the spiral runs "counter-clock-wise", the famous French *Chassepot* was rifled on this principle. In every case the matter of prime importance for the Investigating Officer, when either a rifle or a projectile comes into his possession, is to examine carefully everything appertaining to the pitch, number, and shape of the rifling for such an examination will enable him at once to draw conclusions as to the projectile or rifle employed, and may later on provide absolute proof, when the missing arm or projectile is discovered.

a Muzzle-loaders

A common problem for an Investigating Officer is to know whether a certain specified gun has a long and accurate range. We have already seen that in shot-guns the quality of the shooting depends only on the charge, if the gun be properly loaded and in good condition one cannot help shooting well (always supposing that one can shoot at all). It is different with bullet guns, with them the first consideration is the construction of the barrel which can generally be easily estimated without even firing off the weapon. If all the little exterior details have been carefully executed, we shall not risk much in concluding that the barrel itself has been carefully constructed. This, indeed, is an *a posteriori* argument, but correct none the less, for the gunsmith would not expend money and labour on the accessories to a rubbishy barrel. Conversely, if the stock be of a common wood, if the sights are badly fixed, the plate rough and unpolished, we may readily guess that the barrel is a poor one also. But a barrel may be first class when it comes from the hands of the gunsmith, and may be ruined by the ignorance of the owner, fouling, age or luck. It should therefore receive at least a cursory inspection. When the weapon is a muzzle-loader, only the end of the barrel can be examined, for one can see through it only if the breech be removed, perhaps there is no gunsmith handy, and besides in a preliminary inquiry nothing must be done which might change or modify the condition of the weapon.

If the Investigating Officer is provided, as he ought to be, with a "barrel reflector" it will be of considerable help to him, if not, he must have recourse to the old device of sergeants and corporals, when troops were still armed with muzzle-loaders. Take a strip of stout white paper about eight inches long and in width slightly less than the diameter of the chamber. Placing the butt of the gun on the ground with the muzzle towards a window, we can slip the paper into the barrel, and, getting the latter at the proper inclination, the light is reflected from the paper against the upper part of the chamber. We can thus see clearly if the grooves are clean or rusty, if they are sharp or show signs of usage, if there be powder crust or particles of lead, in short we can say if the barrel is in a condition for good shooting. Of course in this way we can examine only the upper end of the barrel, but there is no reason why the other parts should be in a different condition. What destroys a rifle barrel is when using it frequently, we neglect to clean it; if the muzzle end be dirty or shows marks of use, the rest will be in the same condition. The barrel of a rifle rarely becomes twisted or warped; through the stock becoming damp the walls are too thick for this kind of deterioration.

We must always take the greatest precautions when a gun connected with any offence falls into our hands. A muzzle-loading rifle generally gives most trouble owing to the difficulty of drawing the charge; while the handling of the accessories of a rifle are more delicate than of a shot-gun. Hence we shall give a few hints on this subject.

First of all it is indispensable to ascertain whether or not the weapon has passed through the hands of strangers since the offence was committed; that is, is it still in the same condition? All the information available on this point must be carefully recorded before proceeding to describe the weapon itself. This description should be accurate and minute, even in the case where someone has touched or handled the arm previously, either for amusement or with an object. And the ordinary rule of conduct must be followed, write a full description before touching the weapon. Only then can it be taken in the hand, and even then we must be careful to do nothing which would permanently alter the condition of the rifle, unless there be some absolute necessity. We can see an Investigating Officer hastily picking up a gun just found, cocking it with an "expert" hand not observing that the exploded cap has fallen among the grass—blowing down the barrel to see if it is unloaded, and finally inserting his little finger in the muzzle to see if the weapon has been recently fired; he has learned a lot, not perhaps altogether without importance, but on the other hand there are a crowd of questions which must remain for ever unanswered owing to his bungling. In every case when a gun is taken in hand for examination, whether because examination cannot be longer deferred or because the critical moment has arrived, all our movements should be slow and deliberate, all details must be recorded and all legal formalities strictly observed. Not only duty and conscience but ordinary good sense tell us this. Quickness may gain time, but will only create difficulties for the future.

Having thus taken up the weapon carefully we complete the description by noting any new detail hitherto overlooked; anything abnormal on the under side may be noted—dew, spots of blood, traces of rust or other dirt etc. Then we cock the gun, being careful to hold the plate over a plane, smooth, clean surface, so as to catch anything that may fall. At the same time we expressly call the attention of all present to what we are doing. In his young days the author attributed to ridiculous and antiquated pedantry the manner in which his venerated chief and teacher was wont to proceed when thus in public examining a gun, but he now finds it the only method. He would commence thus: "I cock this gun which has been discharged; as you see gentlemen, it moves easily and silently to half-cock, it can be pushed a little further and there sticks fast. Meantime I find upon the nipple which is very rusty a copper cap of which the side walls have burst in five irregular pieces. As far as can be seen at the moment, for we shall defer for a little a more minute examination, it appears that a morsel of the cap has flown off. We find besides that the cap is covered with recent verdigris, both on the sides and on the flat top. I request you, gentlemen, to carefully observe and confirm this peculiarity, for we may draw therefrom the conclusion that some time has elapsed since the gun was fired. For if the cap had received its coating of verdigris before firing, the blow of the hammer and the explosion would have caused the disappearance at least of the verdigris on the top of the cap. The experts will be able to calculate for us the time necessary for the formation of this verdigris, but to facilitate their task and render their reply more certain, we shall note that verdigris covers about one third of the upper portion of the cap. As to the sides, we shall say that the largest of the five pieces has verdigris on about one-fourth of its surface and the others on, approximately, one-half. Are we agreed on this point gentlemen? For when the cap leaves our hands to pass into those of the experts everything may change. This point being important, we shall direct attention to the exterior circumstances in which we have found the weapon, for these circumstances may have influenced the formation of verdigris.

We observe then that the granary where the gun was found is not well protected from the rain, as witness the holes in the roof, and further the ammoniacal vapours coming from the stable below have left very significant traces. These are circumstances which, together with the action of the gases of gunpowder and fulminate of mercury set loose by the explosion, are favourable to the formation of verdigris on the cap. We now place the cap on one side wrapped up in paper, sealed and properly ticketed.

" But as it is indispensable to know, whether, when, and with what, a shot has been fired, we examine the barrel. Introduce into the muzzle a piece of twisted paper: it is blackened, hence we conclude the gun has been recently fired. We preserve this piece of paper also. Now we draw the second charge using for the purpose the wad-extractor of the gun itself. Thus we take out a paper-wad, we unfold it carefully and see that it is a piece of a newspaper—which paper we do not yet know, but we find on it intimation of a death bearing a certain date. This also is recorded and preserved. Now we carefully extract the shot, we find small shot and buck-shot mixed. As shot is easily lost, we count it at once: there are x small pellets and y buck-shot. Then comes the second wad, which must be very carefully extracted, as some shot frequently adhere to it. In fact, in unfolding it two small pellets roll out, which we put with the others, correcting the total number. This second wad is also a piece of newspaper —' The Mail ", putting the two pieces together they are seen to come from the same leaf. On the second we find, written in pencil, a sum in addition. The figures are well formed, even elegant, and the handwriting firm: it is that of an educated man. We come now to the powder, which is loosened by the aid of the wad-extractor and poured out on a sheet of paper. Powder grains vary greatly in size, the size here is medium, the grains are angular, the colour dull, there are no white points on the surface, hence it is not damp; the grains are hard, the powder has been well mixed. It does not discolour the paper, and is therefore of a good make. We thus have before us gentlemen, a good powder, in sufficient quantity, and as carefully loaded as can be done with paper wads. "

Proceeding thus we can in a short time obtain everything necessary to enlighten us. Besides we have prepared the way for the experts (for *Experts in Firearms,* see *ante* pp. 155—157). Further, nothing has been destroyed, and the examination can be repeated if necessary. But how many reports do we not see like the following?—"The weapon was handed over to experts to be unloaded; they report that it was loaded with a quantity of shot."

Great care and special skill are necessary in drawing a bullet, well rammed home, from a muzzle-loader. As the bullet has to be bored straight by means of a bullet-extractor, an instrument like a corkscrew, and as it should be injured as little as possible, the best thing is to call in a gunsmith who will of course perform the operation in the presence of the Investigating Officer. But if we must have the ball immediately we can only do the best we can with the implements at hand; but above all we must not draw too soon, that is, before the extractor has got a good grip, for nothing destroys a bullet more. If we have not a proper extractor, we can use an ordinary gimlet, welded by the nearest blacksmith to a long iron handle. If all these expedients fail and we are still determined to have the ball—for example if a shot has been fired from a double-barrelled gun, and we desire to draw conclusions from the second charge as to the first—the gun must be taken to pieces at the breech. This can be done by any gunsmith, almost by any blacksmith; the bullet can then be pushed out with a stick—and undamaged. In taking the gun to pieces care must be observed not to discharge the gun. Further, the end of the stick with which the bullet is pushed out should have a hemispherical depression so as not to flatten the projectile, or at least not to flatten it more than was done by the ramrod in loading, a detail often useful to know.

If we wish to discover the owner of a muzzle-loader it is always a good thing to have it taken to pieces; from a breech-loader, owing to the construction of the weapon, we do not learn much by taking it to pieces. To clean a muzzle-loader properly it must be taken to pieces; then something may be felt or disarranged which may furnish a starting-point for further inquiry. We can also look for the mark of the factory or gunsmith. In taking a gun to pieces, particular attention should be paid to the tube underneath in which the end of the ramrod rests. This is constantly being exposed to the outside world, and foreign matter can be easily deposited in it. The author once found therein a scrap of paper containing several lines of writing; true they turned out to be useless, but another case might bring better luck.

β. Breech-loading Rifles

No class of firearm has undergone greater transformation than the breech-loading rifle. We are unable within our limits to give even a summary of the changes since, say, the Franco-Prussian war of 1870, and for the purpose of this work it is unnecessary.* It may be remarked,

---

* Dr Gross enumerates over 100 different systems besides "*et ceteras*." The description of the military rifles in use to-day in Europe fills 80 pages of the War Office *Text Book of Small Arms.*

however, that old-fashioned guns occasionally come into the hands of innocent purchasers, who buy them cheap without anticipating the impossibility of procuring proper ammunition. When this occurs, any catastrophe may happen.

2. PISTOLS

These weapons are not now much used, being superseded by Revolvers and Magazine Pistols, even for duels and suicides which till recently brought Investigating Officers in contact with them.

3. REVOLVERS

This weapon, in our days the commonest used by criminals, is by no means a new invention, but owing to difficulties of construction and ignition cannot be said to have come into general use until the introduction of the well-known "Colt" in 1835. Since that day revolvers have changed less in construction than any other firearm. To elucidate our remarks we here give an illustration of a "Colt" Revolver ready for firing (Fig. 36).

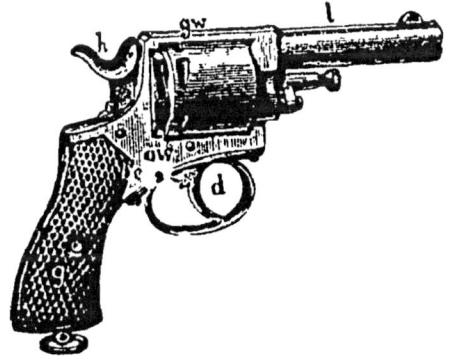

Fig. 36.

At present only two systems, differing little in essentials, are in use—needle-fire and central-fire. The mechanism is the same as for breech-loading guns. The central fire is most in vogue, because it closes the breech more hermetically and is more convenient, the hammer lying behind the cylinder. The many variations introduced to facilitate loading and unloading have no influence on the quality, the precision, or the range of the weapon. Everything depends on the construction of the revolver itself. But as the question, 'What effect can this revolver produce?' is one we have constantly to answer, we shall furnish a few details.

The author has himself heard an otherwise intelligent gunsmith declare as a judicial expert. 'With this revolver I should allow anyone to fire at me at fifteen paces as often as he liked,' because it was an old, small, pinfire weapon. At the same time he declared that another revolver was 'a most dangerous weapon, no matter at what range' only because it was a new central-fire arm of large calibre. The two statements were equally incorrect: a shabby-looking revolver may be a first-class instrument, while another of most formidable aspect may be quite harmless. In fact, with a revolver you may shoot very well with one shot, while with the next the bullet hardly quits the barrel. This is explained by the construction of the weapon.

Every revolver comprises the butt or handle g, the hammer h, the trigger, d, the frame, g u, of which the barrel l forms part, and the revolving chamber, *l* (*Fig* 36) It is a cylindrical piece of steel with five, six, or more chambers arranged concentrically round the central axis, which is pierced and traversed by a spindle (also used as an unloader) passing through the front frame, through the cylinder, and finally entering a recess in the back frame. Thus the cylinder is kept firmly in position. As it revolves, each chamber in succession is brought behind the barrel, through which the bullet from the cartridge passes on pulling the trigger. At the same time the cylinder revolves automatically, and another chamber is brought up to the barrel. The ammunition is, almost without exception, central-fire bullet cartridges.

It is clear from this description that the bullet must, so to speak, jump from the chamber into the barrel, which causes a certain loss of the explosive gas and therefore of power; the amount of this loss will depend on the care and accuracy with which the weapon is constructed. The axis of each chamber when in position should be an exact prolongation of that of the barrel, and the calibres of the two must be exactly the same; in fact, the nearer the two together approach to a single barrel the greater the efficiency. Hence the inefficiency, often the danger, of a cheap revolver.

It is evident that one or more of the chambers may be more "efficient" than the others, hence it is not enough to look at a revolver or even fire a single shot from it, to estimate its real value as a shooting implement; we must also in any given case, endeavour to determine from which chamber the shot has been fired. The usual way is—a revolver is found with one chamber discharged, the others loaded, the intelligent constable who finds it unloads the five barrels for the sake of safety, and removes the empty cartridge for the sake of symmetry, hence the Investigating Officer has a revolver, five loaded cartridges, an empty cartridge case, all carefully preserved. An expert then examines minutely the weapon, and reports that of the six chambers, only four fit the barrel, and could give a good result in shooting. The sole question in the inquiry may be: Does the weapon shoot well or badly? And now no one can tell from which chamber the shot in question was fired. We must therefore ascertain which chamber was used, and in testing the weapon must employ the same chamber. To experiment with the others would be just as if, to test a particular weapon, we used another "very like it."

One consideration must be remembered in appreciating a revolver, that is the ammunition. A manufacturer of sporting cartridges knows that if he turns out rubbish he will lose his customers and his reputation, the sportsman knows a good cartridge from a bad; but the purchaser of a revolver, more often than not, is supremely ignorant. He buys a revolver for fun or to defend himself from robbers or to commit a crime. If, in the first case, the shooting be bad, he puts it down to his own inefficiency or bad luck; in the second case, he is glad he has not hurt his assailant more grievously; in the third, he will take good care not to complain to the manufacturer.

Account must also be taken of the age of the cartridge. If the bullet is firmly fixed in the brass cartridge case, if the cartridge, well greased, has been kept in a dry but not too hot receptacle, the cartridge may remain in good condition for several years, if otherwise, the fulminate will decompose rapidly. This, indeed, may occur even when the cartridge has been well cared for; this is spontaneous decomposition, or gradual decomposition."

Another point is often important: we are sometimes asked if more or less accurate shooting is possible in a bad light, at night, in a dark wood &c. One aid in solving this problem is to know whether the person firing is accustomed to shoot in the American style. We usually fire by pressing the trigger with the *index* or first finger, the American employs the middle or second finger for this purpose, extending the first finger along the barrel (Fig. 37). This permits him to aim approximately, using his finger as a guide. We can aim more easily in this way,

Fig. 37.

when we can only see vaguely or hear persons speaking whom we cannot see. If one tries to shoot thus in the dark, or with the eyes closed on a person speaking, one will see that a very good aim can be taken.

That many strange varieties of country-made revolvers exist in India is certain. In a recent case a number of eye witnesses testified that the accused had shot the deceased several times with a revolver and made off. Their evidence was disinterested, and the case would have been clear had not the investigation disclosed that at least four shots had been fired, in three of these a round bullet being used and in the fourth small shot. The bullets were weighed and expert evidence was given that they could not have been fired from any known revolver. Indeed, a 12-bore gun would have been required to take them. Very grave doubts were therefore cast upon the statements of the witnesses that a revolver was used. On the other side a police officer gave evidence that he had seen a country-made revolver in another district which he thought might be of sufficient calibre to take such a bullet, but that weapon could not be procured. The accused was convicted and sentenced to death, but the point was again raised very strenuously on appeal to the High Court. The appeal was adjourned for a month to enable the Crown to produce a revolver of the required calibre. Every district in the Madras Presidency was circularised, and it was not until the eleventh hour that such a weapon was discovered in a private collection. It was a most extraordinary article. It was a muzzle-loader, having four short barrels welded together. All four were rotated together by hand, bringing a cap under the hammer, and although the calibre was not quite big enough to take the bullet in the case, it was very nearly so. Enough had been demonstrated to prove the existence of such outsize weapons and the conviction was upheld. At the same time a two-barrelled muzzle-loading revolver of large calibre was found, in which the barrels had been bored through one rectangular piece of metal. This case again exemplifies the danger of accepting dogmatic statements from experts of the layman variety (cf. the *Laundry Mark Case*, p. 201).

C Ammunition

Ammunition is not less important, and often more important, than the weapon itself. It is evident that for a long range and great accuracy the gunpowder, other things being equal, should be completely consumed and thus develop all its strength. For this the projectile must be rammed close to the powder so as to retain it in the barrel as long as possible and thus ensure complete combustion. Take a rifle: if the bullet be too small for the barrel the gas escapes all round it without producing any effect, and the bullet itself is hastily expelled from the barrel along with a large quantity of unconsumed powder. But if the bullet fits tightly in the rifling, the gas cannot escape, it produces its full effect, and the powder is completely and uniformly consumed. Take now a shot gun: totally different considerations apply. Here the place of the bullet is taken by the wad (between the powder and the shot). This is true whether the weapon be a breech-loader or muzzle-loader. But the case of the breech-loader need not trouble us, then we use cartridges, and the manufacturer takes care that the wad is all right. It is different with muzzle-loaders. The owner uses as a wad all sorts of things—paper, tow, rags, moss, straw, hay, leather; there are also sold felt wads, well enough made, but commonly used for any calibre of barrel irrespective of fit. In an inquiry, therefore, one of the very first questions to ask is, "What wad was used?"

1 POWDER

Gunpowder has varied little in its constituents since it was first known in Europe about A.D. 1300. It is composed of saltpetre, sulphur, and carbon; it owes its expanding force to the sudden development of gas, containing from 56 to 64% of carbonic acid; it explodes when raised by a sudden blow to a temperature of 250° to 320° C. (482° to 608° F.) and the temperature created at that moment is from 2,500° to 3,600° C. (4,532° to 5,432° F.) These particulars may at times prove useful.

The gases liberated are carbonic acid, azote, carbon oxide, with traces of sulphuric acid, hydrogen carbonates, and nitrate compounds. The residue is composed of sulphate and carbonate of potassium, sulphurate of potassium, and a little unburnt sulphur and carbon. An important point (as when fire has been produced by a train of gunpowder) is that in the open air, a grain of powder can ignite another at a distance of eight to ten times its own diameter.

Good powder can be recognised by the following points:—it has a uniform slate grey colour without white spots, it does not stain, it does not crumble easily between the fingers. Damp has a great influence on gunpowder, so that when desiring to test its effects, we must always register the degree of humidity. Experiments with mortars have shown that, when perfectly dry, powder will project a missile 280 yards, the same powder with 14% of humidity will project it barely 30 yards.

2 THE PROJECTILE

For the sportsman or the soldier this is simple enough, he has to do with his favourite shot or his country's bullet. Far otherwise is it with the

Investigating Officer when a wound or murder is under inquiry, apart from all the legitimate projectiles, he has a host of illegitimate: scraps of lead, pieces of iron, metal buttons, nails, stones, earth, clay, wads of all kinds, and even the ramrod itself. The only thing to be done in such a case is to experiment, experiment, experiment!

With reference to legitimate bullets, the principal point is to consider the effect produced by various makes: e.g., the smashing effect of the bullet of the needle gun or chassepot type compared with the non-stop effect of the modern hard, small calibre bullet. This is dealt with in *Chapter XVI*, in the section dealing with *Wounds by firearms*.

D. Objects hit by a Projectile

It sometimes becomes important to examine not only the object directly aimed at but all the objects which may have been touched by the projectile or projectiles. The quest is often simple enough: suppose one has fired in the open air at a man with shot, it is easy to look for traces of the pellets which have not hit the victim, in any place where there are trees, rocks or buildings. Scratches on trees are easily recognised at once. If the shot has struck the tree directly, the hole of entrance will be contracted. On stones or rocks there are star-like marks, as if made with a lead pencil. Leaves, twigs, ears of corn, etc., should also be examined.

If we know the respective positions of the shooter and the wounded man, the inquiry is much simplified. We take up our position where the former stood, and look in the direction of the latter, we can thus judge the probable extent of the cone of dispersion of the shot, and make our search and take our measurements accordingly. Then, we can establish the force of the shot and deduce the range, charge, etc. We can also thus determine the cone of dispersion, and hence see whether the person hit was in the middle or on the edge of the cone, this is most important when the problem of intention or accident comes in. When it is a question of the position of the person hit—and complainant and accused often give different stories—a comparison of the effects on the wounded man with those produced on the surrounding trees, etc., may often settle the matter.

Further, the projectile found in the body of the victim may be compared with that recovered from neighbouring trees, etc. If all the shot are the same it proves nothing. But if the pellets are mixed, of various sizes, and appear to come from the same discharge, and if the accused possesses shot mixed in the same proportions that will be at least one proof against him.

With bullets it is different. The bullet most frequently is lodged in the body and seldom leaves marks on other objects. But it is otherwise if the bullet has missed its aim, or if after a first unsuccessful shot a second has been fired, in these cases the direction and range of the bullet may lead to important conclusions. Take the following case. A policeman endeavoured to arrest in a solitary inn a man notorious for his feats of house-breaking and horse-stealing. He was apparently going quietly, but suddenly when the constable was off his guard, rushed from the room and fired on the constable from the passage. The latter replied and there was a regular skirmish. The constable fell and the robber fled seriously wounded. The inn-keeper and his servant took refuge in the kitchen at the first alarm, and the subsequent proceedings did not interest them. To reconstitute the scene with absolute accuracy, nothing was needed beyond an examination of the marks left by the bullets: even the nature of the robber's wound could be told: he had evidently opened the door with his bloody right hand and a broken silver finger ring had fallen at the spot. Behind this one of the constable's bullets was imbedded in the wall: clearly the robber had raised his right hand to fire when the hand was hit by a bullet which, breaking the ring and traversing the lower part of the arm, lodged in the wall, where, when found, it was enveloped in morsels of cloth, similar to that of the sleeve of the robber's coat.

Plates of glass pierced by a bullet are frequently objects of careful inquiry, for in many cases of assassination the murderer fires through a window on his victim seated quietly within. Given his choice he will not fire through an open window, the risk of being heard or recognised is so much greater. A plate glass pierced by a bullet should always be carefully preserved. This can easily be accomplished by first pasting on the glass a sheet of strong paper of the same size. The paste may be ordinary flour and warm water. If the glass be much damaged a second person may press with the palms of his hands on the side opposite to that on which the paper is to be applied. If any pieces fall, they should be at once replaced and pasted on. If there are many fragments they must be pieced together like mosaic, a tedious job but worth all the trouble. Care must be taken not to remove any foreign bodies or marks on the glass, as traces of smoke, dirty finger prints, etc., e.g., the criminal in inspecting the interior of the room from outside may have rested his hand on the glass. When the whole is thoroughly dry the plate may be removed from the frame, either by cutting all round with a glazier's diamond or picking out the putty—an easy task.

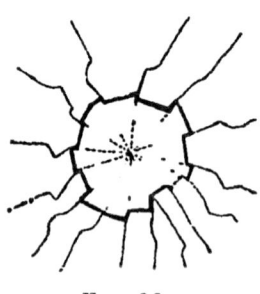

Fig 38

With regard to the hole made by the bullet, we may say generally that the greater the velocity the cleaner the hole. A weak shot from a bad weapon produces almost the same effect as a shot fired close, it crushes the glass without making a clean-cut opening. A feeble shot acts indeed like a stone thrown by the hand, and a shot fired close, splinters up the glass by the force of the explosion of the powder. But when the velocity is high, we may find a clean round hole quite without cracks or starring. If the velocity be medium the result is as shown in Fig 38. Here the bullet on striking has produced the star-like cracks, and then proceeding on has broken off the triangular points of glass between each two cracks.

To ascertain on which side glass has been hit we must look for the tiny splinters, leaving little shell-shaped grooves on the edge of the opening, caused by the ball on leaving the glass, carrying away the last scales (so to speak) which it has touched. The fracture of the glass being as mineralogists term it, conchoidal, the side of the glass where these small fractures are found will be that by which the bullet departs.

These scales or splinters can also show the direction of the shot. If the latter has been at right angles to the plate, the former are arranged pretty evenly round the opening. If the shot be fired at an angle, e.g., from the right, then there will be more splintering on the left and *vice versa*. So accurate is this result, that the acuteness of the angle can be safely calculated from it.[*] Sometimes it is important to decide which of several injuries to a pane of glass occurred first, as when several shots have been fired of which only one has taken effect. An example will best show how this can, under favourable circumstances, be accomplished. A horse galloping through a street cast his shoe with great force against a plate-glass shop window. On the glass could be distinguished three star-like centres with radiating spurs, the distances between them corresponding almost exactly with the distances between the three calkins of the shoe. From this it could be determined in which order the calkins struck the glass.

When a shot is fired at a person through a pane of glass, we have one of the rare cases where, given two points, we can calculate the third. Suppose *Fig. 39*, that a shot has been fired through the window *b* of a house at a person at *a*. If the hole in the glass be *b*, the person firing must have been somewhere in the line *a b c*. It is only then necessary to walk up the slope with a gun at the shoulder, until the muzzle comes in line with *c b a*.

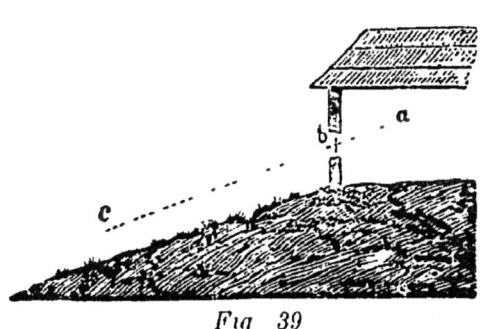

Fig. 39

Section II.—Cutting and Stabbing Weapons.

A. General Considerations

This subject need not be dealt with at any length, for such weapons are well enough known to us all. It will suffice at the most to recall some of the technical nomenclature in order to assist, in his description of a weapon, an Investigating Officer or Magistrate who may have forgotten it. Here also every weapon ought to be given the name generally adopted.

The word "weapon," taken in the broadest acceptation of the word, includes all objects which may, perhaps only momentarily, serve for attack or defence, though not absolutely destined for this employment. For

---

[*] In the criminal museum at Graz are a series of framed window panes, shot through by students with various missiles and under various circumstances. On each is a card recording weapon, missile, charge, direction of aim, distance, angle, direction of wind, etc., so that comparisons can be made with known data.

example, a hammer, a piece of iron pertaining to a carriage or ox yoke, a dull, the use of which is generally quite inoffensive, may very well be termed "formidable" weapons if used for attack. There is one point to which our attention should be drawn: there are certainly many more wounds made with articles of this kind than are produced by real weapons, and it is of greatest importance to thoroughly establish with what instrument a wound has been made, for the nature of the instrument is often the only indication of who the accused is, of his intention, the effect produced by the instrument, and, finally, of the whole manner in which the crime has been carried out. If the wounded person is unable to designate the instrument employed by his assailant, and the witnesses have not seen that instrument, the examination of the wound alone will not permit of the doctor pronouncing a very definite conclusion. If he be prudent and conscientious he will not venture to speak in other than a general way; he will only be able to say, for example, "there is no reason why such and such an instrument may not have been employed." It is to quite other people recourse must be had in order to discover by deduction the nature of the article, and these people are those who, by their position in life and trade, have to deal with tools and implements analogous to the instrument employed. Such persons must therefore be called in. As a rule one has always some general indications, the condition of the wounded man, the place of the crime, the manner of attack, the shape of the wound and the effect produced thereby, the bloodstains, all serve in nearly every case to lessen the circle in which the instrument must be sought. To these must be subsequently added, in order to still further narrow our limits, the depositions of the witnesses and the other results of the inquiry, so that one finally ought to know pretty well in which direction research should be directed.

Let us suppose someone has been wounded: the medical man can only tell us one thing, namely, that the weapon employed must have been blunt, heavy, and not of great size. This is little enough. The *post-mortem* and a minute examination of the part of the skull which has been struck, allow of the supposition that this instrument has been fixed to a handle, for the wound is a glancing one: a stone wrapped in a cloth could not therefore have been employed. Further, the thickness of the skull proves that the blow must have been delivered with violence. It is not improbable, therefore, that the weapon used was a hammer. But what Investigating Officer knows the innumerable kinds of hammer essentially different from another, in use among blacksmiths, joiners, stone-masons, tin-smiths, and other artisans? Perhaps the man best able to furnish the information on this subject is again an intelligent villager, accustomed himself to carry all these articles to be repaired in the artisan's workshop, and consequently having had occasion to see them. The village blacksmith is also a good man to consult. If the wound presents a characteristic aspect, this man will always be able to say that the artisan possesses tools like that seemingly employed in the case in question. Suppose that the edges of the wound are not clean cut, leading to the supposition that it has been made not with a flat but with a convex surface. If we do not ourselves know it, our villager will be able to tell us that such a hammer is employed by cobblers and by tin-smiths. If there be a second wound proceeding from a blunt-edged instrument about two inches long one man will eliminate the tin-smith and only indicate the cobbler whose hammer carries on the opposite side a blunted edge. We will then send for a cobbler and all his hammers and compare the latter with the wound. Of course all cases are not so simple as this imaginary one, but good results may certainly be obtained if one does not recoil before the necessary trouble of interrogating a sufficient number of persons.

It will be very difficult in most cases to exhibit the wound itself; it must therefore be photographed as large and as faithfully as possible, taking the precaution at the same time of getting a medico-legal man to prepare for subsequent use the portion of the skin struck. The photograph, the prepared skin, and the piece of bone will always help a person questioned to give some useful information. A very natural precaution and one often neglected, is to procure an instrument analogous to that with which the wound appears to have been made. Even when a man of the trade, that is to say, one who is in the habit of using instruments of this kind, makes a definite affirmation that, in the case in question, such or such a weapon must have produced the wound, and even when medical jurisprudents pronounce the thing possible, a similar instrument *must be procured and compared with the wound.* One may know an article very well and have often seen it *but it may appear to have quite another aspect when examined with a definite purpose especially when, considering it as the cause, it is compared with the effect produced.*

B. Cutting and stabbing weapons properly so called.

Probably every Investigating Officer has a very good idea of modern European weapons, so that it will not be necessary to do more than give a short definition of some of the most common. Arms which have only an historical interest may be passed over in silence.

1. *Sword-arms.*

Under this heading are comprised all weapons which are carried in a sheath or scabbard and suspended to a belt, and whose length is such that they reach from the hip to or near to the ground.

(*a*) The *sabre* is curved slightly (common sabre) or considerably (Turkish sabre). It has a sharp point and two cutting edges for about a quarter of its length, and has frequently a longitudinal groove, the object of which is to diminish its weight.

(*b*) The *sword* is quite straight and has two cutting edges; it is used for piercing or slashing.

(*c*) The *yataghan* or Afghan sword is a short, nearly straight sabre. It has two cutting edges for a quarter of its length and may be employed as a piercing instrument.

(*d*) The *cutlass* was formerly of the same shape as the sabre. To-day it is more like a hunting knife; it is quite straight and has a simple handle and guard.

2 Arms in the form of a knife

(a) A knife, properly so called, has a back and one cutting edge
(b) A dagger or poignard has no back but two, three or even four cutting edges so that the cross-section of the blade is lozenge-shaped (Fig 10) The edges of a two-edged dagger may in exceptional cases be undulating in shape This peculiarity has no influence on the aspect of a wound

Fig 10

3 Arms in the shape of a lance or spear

It rarely happens in Europe that we come across wounds made by arms in the shape of a lance or spear But such is possible, e g, consequent upon an affray between military and civilians Army lances have almost always heads with four sharp edges and the wounds produced by them correspond in shape thereto

The only other weapon of this description which need be referred to is the bayonet Bayonets used formerly to be straight with four edges This form was replaced by a kind of *yataghan* slightly curved, which was in turn superseded by the modern bayonet, which is short and like a knife Wounds produced by bayonets are fairly frequent and have their own characteristics, which should be known No opportunity should be let slip of examining wounds which one knows to have been produced by a bayonet

1 *Indian Weapons*

The usual weapons employed in crimes committed in India are of an agricultural nature, such as aruvals, kodalies, mamooties, etc, but the warlike hillsmen and the dacoits and robbers of the plains invariably possess spears, battle-axes, and daggers, specially made for the purposes of crime

The Indian mountain tribes usually carry weapons for close quarters According to *Balfour* ("Cyclopædia of India") the *bahbudi* (the strong) is the Afghan knife, for cut or thrust, it is straight-backed, broad near the handle, and fining to a point The *kukri* of the Gurkha has a short handle, and an incurvated, sickle shaped blade widening at the middle, and drawing to a point The *moplah* knife has also a short incurvated blade The Burmese *dah* is a short, straight weapon, hand, for every purpose at home and in battle abroad *Adya katti* is the sword of the Coorg mountaineers For the cutting blow is the *abbassi*, a heavy broad blade, with an outward curve, and suitable for a mounted soldier The *shamsher* or *taluar* has a slight curve and a side-guard The *shah-bakka* has a basket guard The *arangi* is for cut and thrust The *kirch* also is a straight sword The gauntleted *hata* or *saif* is a long weapon used in athletic exhibitions

Balfour states that at present the club form of weapons, the *gur* or mace, the bladed mace, the *tabar* or *battle axe*, are rarely seen, but judging from the number of specimens of these which have found their way to the Madras Criminal Museum we think he must be mistaken

PART III.—CRAFTS SPECIAL TO THE INVESTIGATING OFFICER.

CHAPTER XII

DRAWING AND ALLIED ARTS

Section i.—General Considerations.

Among the numerous things that an Investigating Officer ought to understand and be able to do himself, are certain technical processes which he must learn if he does not desire to be embarrassed at every moment and to throw into a like state those employed under him. Now an Investigating Officer can himself greatly facilitate his task if he has special skill in such matters, and is not obliged to have recourse to lengthy and complicated descriptions of what could be more easily represented by technical means. No one can teach magic, and it is just as difficult to set out shortly how one can become a skilled draughtsman, but some advice can always be given.

In the first place the opinion may be advanced that a man who is very awkward with his hands is as little fitted for the profession of an Investigating Officer as for that of a surgeon mechanician, or microscope operator. A certain manual dexterity is very necessary in this calling. The Investigating Officer has too often to serve himself and use his own hands to be worried with calling in another to help him in every case. Moreover, manual dexterity is constantly accompanied by a certain keenness of glance that is to say, whoever possesses the first of these qualities does not of necessity possess the other, but whoever has a keen eye almost invariably possesses a quick hand, this has been proved by experience and it seems that manual skill and perspicacity may be manifestations of one and the same faculty. Let us add that the Investigating Officer cannot allot and consecrate to such an apprenticeship special periods of time, which he may never be able to find as a rule he will only have at his disposal odd portions of time which he may thus usefully employ and which would otherwise be quite lost. Of the branches of manual skill necessary for the Investigating Officer *drawing* must be placed first.

Section ii.—Drawing.

We do not pretend here to offer a drawing guide to those who do not even know how to hold a pencil. Such men will find the task of Investigating Officer most disheartening. Nor do we address those who have undergone a complete education in drawing and know how to make a sketch at least fairly well. We only wish to come to the aid of those who can draw a little, but who are as yet unacquainted with the art of producing such a plan as is necessary for their work. In this respect the task of the Investigating Officer is limited. He is in no way required, e.g., to represent the scenery of the country around the arena of a riot, over a water channel or in the vicinity of a railway smash. If a scenic representation is requisite in such a case, either photography must be resorted to or a special draughtsman called in. But the Investigating Officer must be able to make a sketch plan of the room of a house, an entire dwelling, the environs of a house, a piece of land of moderate extent, and the like.

Punctilious accuracy of measurement may be laid down as a first general and inviolable rule. No doubt in many cases a plan rapidly sketched at first sight may prove amply sufficient; if well drawn, such sketches will often throw stronger light upon and give more information about the situation than an accurate drawing, in which all the details are scrupulously measured to within a fraction of an inch, but which, as a rule, does not give so good a general idea as the rough sketch itself. The latter is perhaps inaccurate in all its details, but it is taken from a wider point of view and guides the person using it more quickly to the conclusion aimed at by the drawer and without measuring all over again. But it is no easy thing to make such a sketch. A skilled draughtsman, who has no need of our advice, will find no difficulty about it; an inexperienced draughtsman ought, on the contrary, to try to supply by accuracy his lack of skill. No draughtsman should attempt to make a drawing partly from measurements with the tape and partly from distances guessed at sight. This method can have no good result. It has the advantage neither of the picture-effect of a sketch made at sight, nor of the accuracy secured by careful measurement, while possessing all the objections to both processes. With this "mixed" method it often happens that, e.g., the extent of each room is measured and represented with the greatest accuracy, while the articles of furniture are measured and set down only approximately and at sight or after but a hasty measurement. The consequence is that nothing fits in; the last piece of furniture has no space provided for it between the others and the wall, or perhaps the space finally left in the middle of the room is too large or too small, or at least the sketch when finished "does not succeed in conveying an exact impression." Now it is really this "exact impression" which is of the greatest importance. But if it is impossible to understand from the sketch that such and such an event can have taken place, needless doubts spring up, doubts which seem to be perfectly justified but which would never have arisen had the sketch conveyed an "exact impression." If subsequently, after fresh inquiries, new outlines are to be inserted—"the place again is in default"—and all because the drawing is partly accurate and partly guesswork. Accuracy ought therefore to be the primary rule.

The second rule will be:—*try to obtain a general impression of the place to be sketched before actually starting work*. This is often neglected, and the neglect is made apparent by the first glance at the sketch. The work is commenced in a corner and continued as often as not until the paper gives out. Accessories are drawn with accuracy and in the most prominent place, while what is important is neglected or abbreviated. It can be seen that the draughtsman has commenced his work before knowing what he really had to do. It is therefore of the first necessity to start by delimiting the space in question, to note well what is essential and what may be of less importance. The size of the sketch and what it ought to embrace, at what point it should be commenced and how it should be put on the paper, even how the latter will be held when in use so that the result may be as convenient and clear as possible—*all this must be worked out in the head before taking the pencil in hand*.

The third rule is *to ascertain the precise moment at which the sketch should be made*. It should not be taken till the Investigating Officer is in possession of sufficient information as to what should and what should not be included, and it ought to be completed before the examination of the witnesses. If the drawing be made too soon, it causes inconvenience afterwards, and if too late time and trouble are lost without any corresponding gain. For if a witness is heard before the plan is made, it is necessary to say, for example, "at the first window to the right of the entrance which is to the east of the stable," whereas if the sketch has been already prepared it is sufficient to say "near the window F." Such descriptions, costing time and trouble, may be very frequent, making in all no insignificant loss of time. Again, how worrying it is to use a drawing, when it is necessary, in perusing the depositions of the witnesses, to have to study these descriptions at length, only to discover that a door so exhaustively described is really the door P in the sketch, that by the "living room" is meant the room H, and that "the tall tree near the pit" is simply the tree A. Confusion may even be produced by the same object being referred to in different ways in various documents. The Investigating Officer may, *e.g.*, on the day when the scene of the crime was inspected, have designated in his report a certain door as follows :—"the second door on the north-west side of the house, starting from the street"; when, some weeks later, a witness is being examined, the Investigating Officer may have forgotten this designation and writes in the report of the witness's statement "the door leading to the stream nearest the village"; and the reader of these documents will have to make very detailed investigations to discover that the same door is meant in both cases.

It will doubtless happen at times that additions have to be made to the sketch after completion, certain objects, for example, may acquire fresh importance in the light of the examination of witnesses or accused. But that is no inconvenience, the essential thing is that the sketch be finished before the hearing of the subsidiary witnesses. In obeying the foregoing general injunctions the following ancillary rules must be followed:

1. Never forget to record the precise situation according to the points of the compass not only approximately, but with the aid of the compass itself.

2. Do all the measuring yourself, leaving nothing to others.

3. Set down nothing superfluous, that will only produce confusion and difficulty.

4. On principle never postpone anything, *e.g.*, never wait till your return home to copy out your work with more accuracy or fill in certain details from memory. Thus you will not be at the mercy of the good resolutions one generally makes when in a hurry to finish up a day's work. We cannot really observe things unless we are on the spot and can at every moment obtain a fresh impression of them. When we get back home we do not start work again immediately, and when at length we do set about the

business "of completing from memory" our memory fails us, and we do not complete at all, or what is worse, we complete incorrectly.

5. Never mix up the sketch with the text of the report, but, on the contrary, always make it on a separate sheet of paper, which can be kept on one side and compared with the text, for it is a nuisance to have to hunt back.

6. Alphabetical designations ought to be pencilled in on the spot, and the drawing remade at home in ink, or, better still, Chinese ink,[*] the letters without exception being in red ink, thus rendering the whole much clearer.

When the drawing is ready, it is well to protect it from being soiled, wetted, etc., because it will probably often be used, perhaps even in the open air, to be shewn to witnesses and jurymen. The drawing should therefore be dipped, slanting-wise, into a solution consisting of one part of stearine and three parts of collodium. After a quarter of an hour's drying the sketch will be proof against damp or rough usage.

We have already given in *Chapter III., Section* III some hints with regard to the sketch. We shall now deal with the plan properly so called.

A Plan of the Interior of a House

Here the easiest task is to deal with a single room in a house. In doing this the scale must first be settled; as a general rule a metre of actual length may be represented by a centimetre on paper, thus making the proportion 100 to 1. In English measure this will be approximately the same as 8 feet to 1 inch.

One should commence by first drawing one side ab measured in the inside of the room (*Fig. 41*). Then determine whether the angles ab are right angles. This may be easily done by pushing a square table into the corner and noting whether it fits well or not. If the angle be right the perpendiculars ad and bc are erected from a and b. If not, the angles must be determined. The simplest way is to cut a piece of stiff paper to exactly fit the angle, and then draw the angle on the plan by laying the paper angle upon it. Next measure the side cd on the floor and compare it with cd on the paper. If the results do not agree there is some error which must be found out and corrected. When the interior dimensions have been accurately drawn we proceed to the thickness of the walls, which is easily found from the doors and windows. As regards the former, care must be taken to deduct the thickness of any wood facing or projecting joist. To

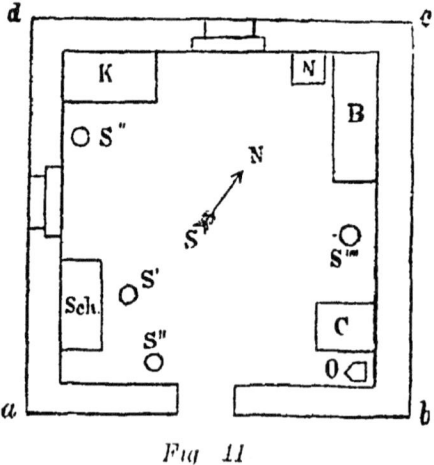

Fig. 41.

---

[*] French Chinese ink is to be recommended. It is an alterable solution used as ink and when dry cannot be effaced. Sketches are often exposed to all sorts of risks such as rain, sneezing, spitting, etc., when e.g. in the hands of the jury. If ink be made with indelible materials the advantage is often very great.

obtain the exact thickness of this facing, take care to measure it from the line where it joins the bare wall. If the measurement of a wall without windows and doors (bc) cannot be taken otherwise we must definitely state that it could not be done. Doors and windows should be drawn as they are usually done in plans. Having indicated the height of the room we pass on to the articles of furniture. These for the sake of clearness should be denoted by the first letter of their names, thus " bed " by B, " stove " by S, " desk " by D, " almirah " by A, " teapoy " by T, and the " chairs " by C′ C″, C‴, etc. In Fig. 41 the letters are the first letters of the German names. There B=bed, C=box, O=stove or fireplace, Sch=writing-desk or table, K=chest of drawers, N=commode S, etc. =chairs.

The drawing should be made one wall after the other. The measurement from the corner a to the edge of the desk is taken, then the desk itself, then from the desk to the window, etc. The measurements should always be verified after each wall is completed by adding the various measures together. For instance, from corner a to the desk, the length of this latter, the space between the desk and the window, the breadth of the window itself, the space between the window and the almirah, and finally the depth of the almirah, should be added together and the sum total compared with the total length of the side of the room. If they do not agree, the measurements must be gone over again until the results are in accord.

B Sketch of Dwelling.

To sketch a flat or floor containing several rooms, and still more a whole house, offers decidedly greater difficulties. The same scale, say 1 to 100, or 1 in. to 8 ft., should if possible be retained. We may first try to procure the plan of the house, which the owner occasionally possesses. If obtained, it should be examined carefully, and if found to be correct, our own plan may be based upon it. But as often as not this resource fails and a new plan must be drawn up. The important point is to choose a convenient working base and to select a happy spot on the plan to start from. When this last is well chosen the rest follows easily. As a general rule fix on the room or passage into which one enters from the principal door.* We should choose, in the house in question (Fig. 42), the lobby I of which the south-east outer wall, judging from outside, ought to consist of the extension of the outer walls of the staircase St and kitchen K. Let us mark on the line ab, in the middle provisionally, the width of the lobby I then, on the south

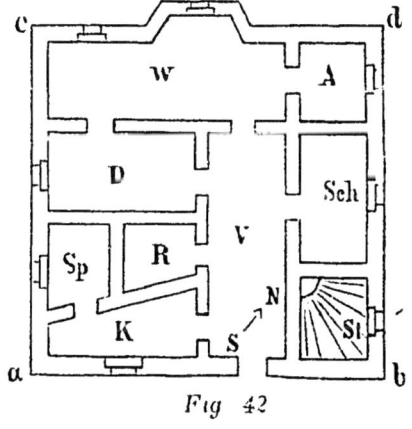

Fig. 42

---

* The fault is often committed of commencing by drawing the room in which the crime has taken place; when this has not a favourable situation it is seldom that an accurate distribution of the rooms can be made.

side, the thickness of the inner wall the depth of the kitchen K, and the thickness of the principal wall ac

Do the same on the east—the thickness of the wall, the depth of the staircase St and the thickness of the wall bd. We have now settled the length of the front of the house. For safety the dimensions may again be taken from outside. If access is possible from without, the lengths ac and bd, may be at once measured and set down. Then returning to the lobby draw its two long sides which will fix the end opposite the front door. It will be seen in room H that the last-mentioned end wall of the lobby is prolonged to meet the side wall ac. Then ed may be measured and drawn. Having finished the measurement of the side to the south-east of the work-room T and the staircase St all the measurements of A, Sch, and St will naturally have been obtained. On the south-west side of the house we note a wall running in an oblique direction. The two sides of the kitchen K towards the south-west and north-east must therefore be measured thus giving the amount of the deviation of the oblique wall. It only now remains to measure the north-west and north-east sides of the pantry Sp, the remaining dimensions of K and of the servants' room D determining themselves.

This is the plan to be generally followed. The important point is to have a fixed base to start from a room measured with accuracy, to think out how all the lengths may be obtained and at the same time how to spare a number of measurings. This was not however possible in old houses full of nooks and corners where no results would be obtained by measuring as above. In such houses the structure of which has been modified and completed at different times, the thickness of the walls often varies in a most surprising way. A wall in one room may be one foot thick and continue into a neighbouring room in a straight line with a thickness of 3 feet or more, with no real reason except that today the mode of construction has changed. Moreover a wall may go on thickening so much that its horizontal section may be quite triangular in form. The author once underwent a painful experience of this fact in connection with a case of prison-breaking. The prison was located in a very old and dilapidated cloister. On passing down a long corridor C (Fig. 13) on one side of which the cells KZ, etc., were situated, one came into the reception room A in which the prisoners' clothes were kept. As may be noticed at the door leading from C to A the wall was of considerable thickness so much so that that entrance (which was closed by a heavy iron door) seemed quite like a tunnel. Naturally everyone supposed that the thickness of the wall continued throughout its whole length until one fine morning several prisoners in the cell adjacent to A pierced the side-wall and made good their escape by the window in A. At the opening made by them the wall was hardly a foot thick and

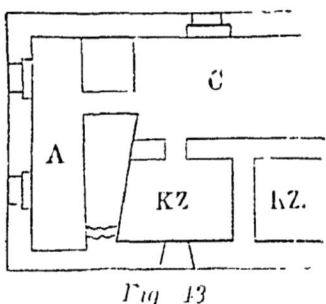

Fig. 13

the work of perforation could not have taken more than an hour. No one knew why the wall had been built in this way. This instance is cited to point out that the making of a sketch often affords an opportunity of discovering such peculiarities, which must be taken into account if the sketch is to be an adequate one.

Having completed the sketch of one storey of a house we may find it necessary to draw those above, and for this the outline of the first sketch may be referred to. It must not be forgotten, however, that the walls of a higher storey are as a rule a brick or two less in thickness and that the rooms are sensibly larger in consequence. Also some of the partition walls may be missing in the higher stories. But if there is an extra one, it will have been noticed already from below, for it will be resting either on a vaulted arch or on an iron girder. In this case new measurements are absolutely necessary.

C Sketch of the Environs of the House.

A sketch of the environs or surroundings of the house may be required either for itself or to indicate the general lie of the house, the detailed plan of the interior being the principal object. In making a sketch of this kind the question of space must be carefully considered. Above all it is necessary to determine what surface the whole should cover (whether a quarter, half, or whole sheet of paper, etc.) and then what extent of it the sketch will cover. The easiest means of arriving at a solution will be to measure approximately the space of which the plan has to be made. At least half of this should be reserved all round for surroundings, so that the space absolutely necessary be properly set out in relation thereto. Suppose one wants to set out the whole sketch on a quarter of a sheet of writing paper, that is to say on a surface about 8 inches by 7 inches. It must first be ascertained what is the extent of the ground to be sketched. Suppose it comprises a garden surrounded by a hedge and containing a dwelling-house, stable, and outhouses. We will take half the breadth of the paper for the length of garden, that is to say 4 inches, in such a way as to have 2 inches margin to the left and right for the surroundings. We now cross the garden lengthways and find it to be 748 paces, and taking each pace to be 32 inches we have in round figures 24,000 inches = 2,000 feet. Now 2,000 feet of ground are represented by 4 inches of paper, so that one-tenth of an inch of paper will equal 50 feet of land, and with a rule measure divided into 10ths of inches an easy scale is obtained. If metrical measures be adopted the whole is immediately simplified. Now if we desire to draw a house of a frontage of say 66 feet 8 inches we know at once it should take up only one-third more than 1/10 inch of the paper. We set down then in the case given below on a reference line ab (fig. 44) the 2,000 feet = 4 inches, we measure the line ac, cd, de, and eb, we take for each 50 feet of actual measurement 1/10th inch, and using the compasses put down on the paper the lengths thus obtained—to measure the angles at c, d, and e would be too difficult. We, therefore, draw at d an auxiliary line perpendicular to ab and measure it as well as ab, and thus without measuring the angles obtain the points c, d, and e

In like manner the dimensions of the house and its dependencies are measured and reduced as well as any ground of real importance as in the above case the garden

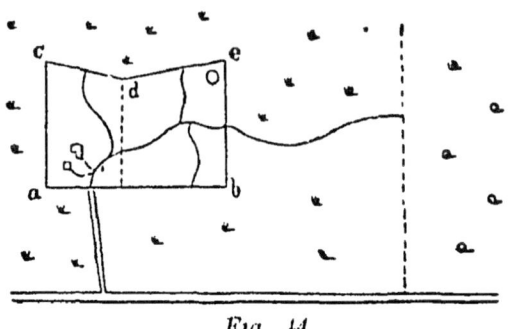
Fig 44

The extent to which paths, sheds, flower beds etc, should be depicted depends upon the various objects in view Everything superfluous must be avoided, but anything which may become important subsequently ought never to be neglected The surroundings should then be put in, i e, the ground all round, so far as is necessary to make the bearings of the house and curtilage clear (see the sketch, Fig 44, which has intentionally been made as simple as possible)

In these drawings use should always be made of the conventional signs adopted in geographical and survey maps. These signs are generally known and understood even by people to whom they have not been specially explained For the most part, indeed, these signs are so significant that they can hardly be misunderstood A sketch made with them gains in clearness and can be more easily grasped It is understood without trouble and proves the work to have been done with accuracy and attention

═══════════	Streets over 15 ft wide
───────────	Streets over 7½ ft wide
─ ─ ─ ─ ─ ─	Streets below 7½ ft
·─·─·─·─·─·	Main road
·──·──·──·─	Narrow carriage road
─ ─ ─ ─ ─ ─	Mule or bullock path
· · · · · ·	Foot path
▬▬▬▬▬▬	Double line railway

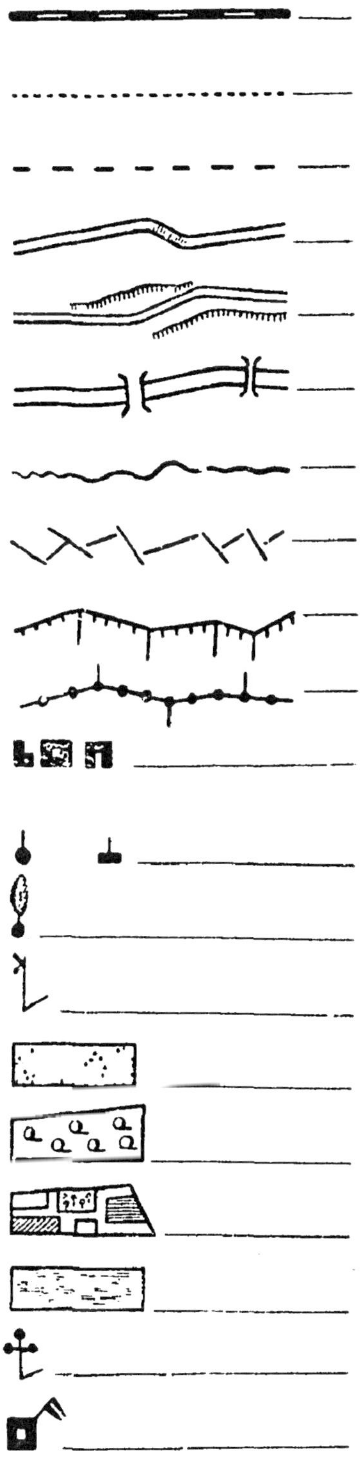

CONVENTIONAL SIGNS

Single line railway

District boundaries

Parish or taluk boundaries

Steep places on the way

Broken ground

Watercourse with bridge (for pathway)

Brook water channel

Hedges or hurdles

Planks

Walls

Dwellings

Boundary stones

Boundary trees

Sign posts

Sandy tracts

Wood, forest jungle

Garden

Swampy ground

Cross

Inn

[symbol]	Monastery, temple, etc.
[symbol]	Church
[symbol]	Cemetery
[symbol]	Water lift
[symbol]	Clay or rubble pit
[symbol]	Single trees
[symbol]	Arable ground, fields
[symbol]	Meadow, maidan, grazing grounds
[symbol]	Vineyards, tea and coffee gardens, etc.
[symbol]	Orchards, topes, etc.
[symbol]	Domestic buildings
[symbol]	Castles or palaces
[symbol]	Chapels
[symbol]	Monument
[symbol]	Wayside shrine
[symbol]	Factory
[symbol]	Quarry
[symbol]	Pool, tank
[symbol]	Spring
[symbol]	Well
[symbol]	Cistern

In tracing these signs attention should be paid to certain details, the lines should be drawn cleanly and clearly, and where there are two (as for main roads, military roads, etc.), as nearly parallel as possible, signs showing various forms of cultivation (fields, forests, etc.) should not be too large and the shadows cast should be marked by horizontal lines. Thus for a wood we make a circle, to the left the outline is clear, to the right there is the outline of a shadow, immediately below we draw a line towards the right, and so on. It is the same for fields, where however, the shadows cast by trees, pillars, or walls, should tend a little upwards.

The work will be considerably facilitated if special drawing pens be used and sheets of paper large enough to allow of the characteristics being comfortably filled in. Besides one will become accustomed in this work to hold the pen in the traditional manner, that is to lean it, not as when one writes in the angle where the thumb and forefinger meet, but on the third joint of the forefinger, counting from the tip. The pen thus runs sensibly parallel to the top and bottom borders of the paper and itself traces the marks indicating shading in their place, that is to say, on the right side of the drawing, this being in accordance with the supposition we have made, namely, that the light is coming from the left.

All these signs should first be drawn large and then smaller and smaller until they are obtained as small as is compatible with the clearness and accuracy of the drawing.

As far as possible the drawing of straight lines by hand should be avoided, it being better to use a ruler. The best drawing appears to be careless and incorrect when the lines are trembling and tortuous.

The sketch may be coloured with chalks or water colours. By using a special colour for each class of object it will be difficult for mistakes to arise.

The following list is in general use and may be taken as a guide.

Light blue—*water*
Carmine—*dwellings*
Light grey—*wood colours*
Burnt sienna—*strata*
Chrome yellow—*roads*
Umber—*fields*

Black—*glaciers*
Dark blue—*vineyards*
Ultramarine green—*hamlets*
Zinc green—*meadows*
Silk green—*gardens*
Olive green—*brambles, bushes*

D. Sketch of a larger Portion of Country

This kind of work, which is the most difficult of all, is fairly frequent. The tracks left by the criminal often lead us far from the scene of the crime; at times it is important to know whether the spot may be seen from a distant point, and what may be seen from that point, and a sketch is the sole means by which a clear idea of the relations between one point of the country and another may be obtained.

In this work we must also look round and make up our minds how much of the country should be included in the sketch. This question is much more difficult to solve in the present case than in the preceding, for the greater extent of land under observation renders the task more complicated and troublesome, and the dealing with, or omission to deal with, some part or other of the country, immediately assumes a great importance. In such cases, therefore, detailed information must be gathered previously by questioning and consulting witnesses and so finding out what it is necessary to take into account. This determined, the extent fixed on should be measured in the simplest way possible, that is, by pacing it. In the simple metrical method the number of paces is multiplied by 8 and the last figure suppressed (1 pace = 80 cms = 32 inches). Suppose the distance paced be 600 paces, multiply by 8 = 4800, suppress the last zero and we obtain 600 paces = 480 metres. In English we multiply by 32 in (one pace) and divide by 36 inches (one yard) i.e., multiply by 8 as before and divide by 9. Thus, $\frac{600 \times 8}{9} = 533$ odd yards. Next measure the paper to be allotted to this extent of ground and try to find a convenient scale between the paper and the ground.

As to the actual work itself the easiest case is when a fairly straight line such as a main road, path, railway, watercourse, hedge, an uninterrupted succession of agricultural boundaries, etc., crosses the length of the surface to be drawn. Such a line, which is not, of course, supposed to be mathematically straight, so facilitates the work that the advice may even be given to displace if need be the natural base of operations a little, if by doing so we are enabled to obtain a base of this kind. This procedure may necessitate, it is true, the inclusion in the sketch of more than is absolutely necessary, but we thereby gain so much in ease and certainty that the extra trouble is not thrown away. If no such straight line can be found—which does not often happen—one must be imagined, making it pass through certain fixed points (a house, isolated tree, boundary stone, etc.), and using it for a working base. This method can always be employed

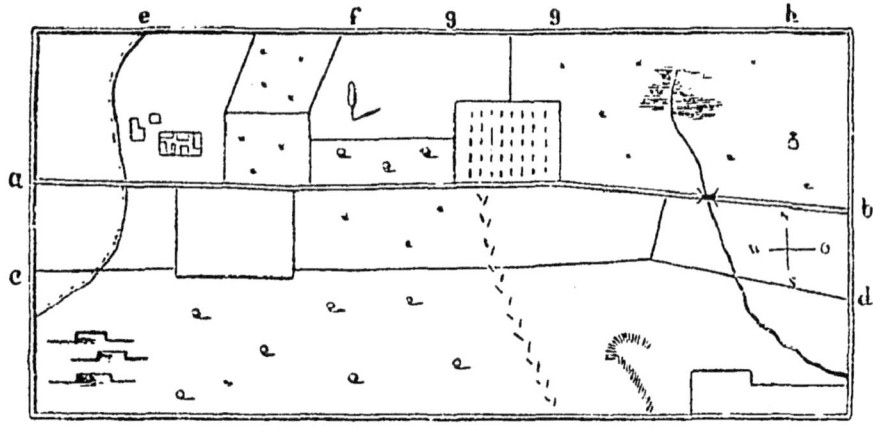

Fig 15

Take then for an example of such work, the sketch *Fig 15*, which is, it is hardly necessary to say, considerably reduced. In reality a figure three times as large would be required to contain everything necessary.

The best case will be where a road *ab* runs across the sketch. In its absence an imaginary line joining the agricultural boundaries *cd*, may be chosen since the boundaries of the fields, of the meadows of the wood, and of the adjoining meadow also form an approximately straight line which may be surveyed and measured. Otherwise the following straight line will have to be imagined—from the house below e to the tree that is visible at a distance below f, then to the edge of the vineyard below $q\,q$ and from there to the shrine below h (the letters are placed outside the sketch so as not to interfere with the clearness of the drawing). Supposing the situation to be such as we have represented first, we commence by drawing the road and determining all the dimensions with reference to it. Beginning at the point a we follow the road towards b, measuring by pacing all the various distances between the points determined by the different lines which cut the road; the results found should be converted to scale and noted down. In the first place the carriage road crosses from right to left, then on the right hand is the boundary of a field, on the left of a meadow, to the right again the boundary between a field and a meadow, to the left the outskirts of a wood and the boundary of a vineyard, to the right a hedge, to the left the boundary of the vineyard, to the right that of a field, and finally a bridge. We measure up to point b, add the various distances, and check the result with the previous measurement of the complete distance from a to b. In the event of these disagreeing new measurements must be taken and errors corrected. Now suppose perpendiculars to be dropped from all the chosen points to the working line (the road), and that these are measured, as also is the distance which separates from a that point where the perpendicular in question strikes the road, i.e., one starts from a counting the paces till arriving at the spot where one supposes that the perpendicular, raised from the point where one is then upon the road, will strike the house (under the point c). This gift of finding the perpendicular is, strange to say, common to almost everyone; very seldom is any mistake made. The length found on the road will be marked on the sketch and the pacing continued up to the side of the house, counting as before and marking the distance. If the counting has been accurate and the ordinates from the house nearly perpendicular to the road, the house will of necessity be located correctly. The other points and hints will be proceeded with in like manner. Each point is determined by two lengths—first on the road, then on the perpendicular or ordinate from the road to the object, on left or right as the case may be.

In certain cases the taking of these measurements may be dispensed with in whole or in part. When one has determined for example, with accuracy the position of the house under c, one can measure directly the neighbouring boundary between the two meadows parallel to the road, by starting from the house and walking parallel to the road and towards the east so as to determine the point where the meadows begin, then size and then the position of the tree "seen in the distance" (under f). Then, turning somewhat to the south measure the short distance to where the wood begins, its extent and, going northwards, the short distance to where the vineyard begins, the size of its eastern side, its length as far as the watercourse, finally from there to the shrine. Of course the guiding line, the road, must not be lost sight of, so as to keep at the proper height. For verification the measurement of the perpendicular joining the last point (shrine) with the road should be taken, so as to make sure that the desired distance has been kept.

Drawings in relief are often of great value, but only skilled artists can produce them and the hints here given are not intended for them.

Section III.—Drawing on Squared Paper.

When the object to be drawn is small and almost or entirely flat, drawing on squared paper is frequently recommended and is very advantageous. This method may be easily employed by anyone who is not hopelessly awkward with his hands, and accurate results may be obtained by its use. It consists in dividing the surface to be drawn into large squares and the paper into small squares, reproducing in these latter everything that may be seen *in natura* in the large squares. No doubt difficulties still exist, but they are minimised to a very large extent.

Suppose that a certain number of drops of blood which have dried upon a plank have to be depicted. The large sketch represents the actual subject-matter and the small one the finished drawing. First examine the portion of the plank to be drawn and its dimensions. This is then delimited by means of a set-square, setting down the lines 1 1' & I I' at right angles. These are then divided into a certain number of equal parts, the more there are of them the more accurate the result will be, parallels are then drawn so as to obtain a certain number of squares of equal size. It is hardly ever possible to draw them straight off with pencil or chalk, &c. as a rule, cotton threads must be employed. When the first division of the periphery is made, nails are driven in at the ends of the lines 1 to E, A' to E' 1 to I, I' to I', using iron nails on a wooden floor, wooden pegs on the ground. If this is not possible four planks may be placed in the form of a square around the space in question, nailing them roughly together or keeping them down with impromptu weights, and driving the nails into them. Then take the first reel of thread to hand and bind the nails together so as to form the corresponding net-work. The ends are then lettered and figured (1 I, &c.) Then a large square like the first is drawn on the paper, containing the same number of squares, lettered and figured in like manner, and in each square of the paper is drawn what is found in the corresponding square of the reality. The operation is surprisingly easy and accurate, and may also be employed for enlargements.

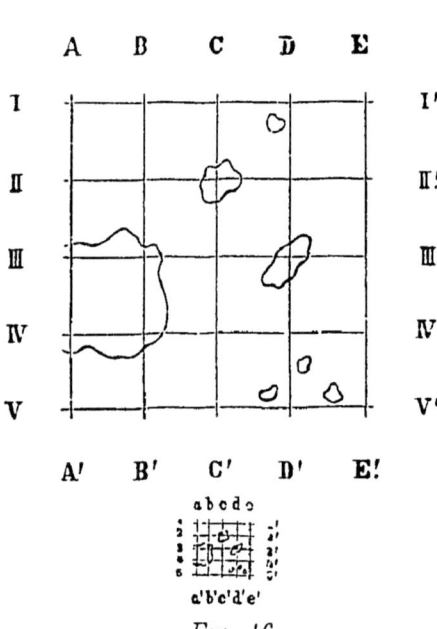

Fig. 46

Whoever has acquired a certain degree of skill, for a totally unskilled person will find it difficult, can for this object use an instrument such as a Pantograph or Mechanograph &c. Whoever procures such an apparatus receives with it the instructions, so details for the use of it are superfluous here. For this purpose the Dikatopter of *Henry Eppers* (Brunswick) can be recommended. By this apparatus the object to be drawn is thrown on the drawing paper between two mirrors, in its natural size or smaller or larger as desired, so that only the outlines need be represented. This apparatus is small and light to carry, and requires for use only moderate skill. In the author's opinion the best of the apparatus for this purpose is the old *Camera lucida* or *obscura*, invented by Wollaston 1809 which shows up clearly and occupies very little space. Every optician has these in stock and teaches their use.

Excellent service is rendered by a net glass which requires little skill and can be had from every optician. It generally consists of a black mirror about 15 cm. long and 9 cm. broad, which reflects the picture essentially smaller. It is enclosed in a light wooden frame with holes, through the holes fine threads are drawn and these divide the surface of the glass into about fifteen squares. If one desires to represent a landscape, trees, buildings, &c., one recedes from the object to be represented until the scene to be drawn is reflected by the mirror. The paper to be used for the drawing is then divided into fifteen squares of the same size, either larger or smaller squares than the squares on the mirror as one thinks fit, and what is shown in each square in the mirror is drawn in each square of the paper. The drawing is very correct, and requires little trouble or skill.

Section iv.—Modelling.

The subject of this section is, to speak accurately, only the modelling of maps in relief, that is to say, modelled sketches reproducing the features of the countryside. Experience teaches that the most accurate and best-made sketch of a countryside has two faults: it is not possible, even when the declivities of heights are indicated and hatching put in, to obtain an exact idea of elevations and depressions and determine what may be seen at various points and what is the relative height of one place to another. Moreover an uneducated man will rarely find his way with a sketch. Even when he assures you that he understands it, you can never be certain that he really does. With a relief map on the contrary, even a peasant will recognise the country, especially when he has been allowed a little time and given a few explanations. He sees with pleasure his house and the neighbouring wood, and the ability to understand comes quickly and easily. The preparation of a model in relief is certainly not an easy matter, yet it requires much less skill and trouble than might be supposed. When the work is done it makes a much greater impression than one would expect, having regard to the trouble expended upon it.

The rough model of a relief map can be made in several ways. The most accurate is obtained by transforming a flat ordnance or survey map directly into a relief map. Every ordnance and survey map is provided with contour lines, *i.e.* curved and irregular lines which join up points of land round a projecting point or hill top, situated at an equal height above sea level. The heights of the different points are moreover indicated in figures. If then we wish to employ contour lines in constructing a relief map, we first determine the part of the ordnance or survey map which has to be made use of. Suppose this to be a rectangular part of the map which would be represented with contour lines (*Fig. 17*). A piece of tracing paper is taken and all the contour lines are traced in their respective situations. The back of the tracing paper is then blackened with pencil, charcoal or the ashes of a piece of burnt newspaper and each contour line is traced on a piece of cardboard, not one within the other but side by side, so that *e.g.* contour lines *a a a*, *b b b*, *c c c*, *d d* stand by themselves.

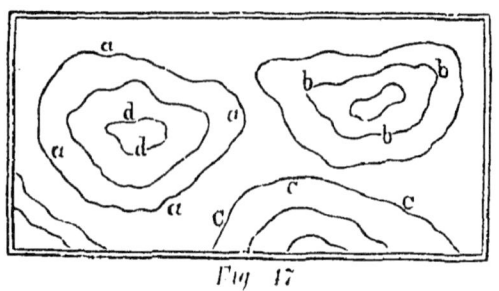
Fig. 17.

All these separate pieces are then cut out with a knife, thus obtaining a separate portion for each contour line. This done, they are placed one upon the other just as they were placed one within the other on the map, and when exactly in place they are gummed together. The heights indicated on the map become real heights, resembling steps. To remedy this last, these steps are rubbed over with a mixture of loam and bran, the bran to prevent cracking, lightly sprinkled with liquid gum. The cutting out of the cardboard is very troublesome; it is therefore preferable to make use of plates of loam made by rolling out a lump of loam with a rolling pin till the desired thickness is obtained. On these plates the different contour lines are traced by piercing them out with a fine needle. It is then easy to cut out the contour plate from the plate of loam. The plates are then placed one upon the other and the steps rubbed over as before with loam and bran. The base of the whole is a plate of potter's clay resting on several sheets of paper. When placed on a plank we have successively a plank, paper, a base of potter's clay, and the various contour lines in their order. The paper is to allow the potter's clay to contract without difficulty while drying, the paper shrinking slightly at this stage. When the potter's clay rests directly on the plank it adheres to it too strongly and splits. Theoretically the thickness of the cardboard or loam is accurately determined. If the map we are working with is to the scale of 1 inch to 2000 yds., a hill 500 yds. in height would only have a height of ¼ inch. This however would not be prominent enough, and as the height is something quite relative and as it is only proposed to indicate the relation of heights to one another we may boldly give each contour line at least ¼ inch of depth *i.e.*, the thickness of strong cardboard.

The method indicated has the fault of being on much too small a scale; it is therefore preferable to represent the relief with much larger dimensions. In this case the extent to be taken is first determined on the map, a rectangular piece of the same size is cut out of a sheet of paper and the latter is then placed on the map so that only the part to be reproduced cannot be seen. The scale of the relief map is thereupon decided *e.g.*, 10 times larger, and the map is drawn in that enlargement on a sheet of paper to serve as a model. On this enlarged model all the heights marked on the map are particularly noted. In rough and hilly country such indications are very numerous. A wooden board of corresponding size is now taken and a sheet of strong paper fixed upon it. The enlarged drawing is placed on this paper and all the points indicating heights are pierced. At each of these points a headless nail is driven in till only as much as will represent the desired height remains above the board. If for example the scale is 1 inch to 2,000 yards then, enlarged by 10, ¼ inch represents 50 yards. It follows that at a point where the height indicated is 350 yards the nail will project 1¾ inches, and where the height indicated is 175 yards it will project ⅞ inch. When all the nails have been driven into the board and their height and position checked, each nail is buried in half moist loam (mixed with bran) till it is just lost sight of. This done, the various heights are levelled with potter's clay referring to the map for guidance, or better still after nature, and the relief map is finished sooner than one would expect. Buildings are represented by quadrangular morsels of the clay of proportionate height. When the whole is dry, any cracks formed in drying are filled up with clay, and if extra clearness is desired the plan may be painted in water colours, fields should be green, roads brown, water blue, and buildings red, see *supra*, Section ii C. The different conventional signs explained above are put in in Chinese ink in the same way as in an ordinary drawing.

For a person who has achieved a certain degree of skill these reliefs are best made either on the spot, or from an accurate survey map. The plan most to be recommended is to make a relief sketch in outline from the map and then proceed to the spot and fill in details from nature.

We do not pretend that the work is quick and easy nor do we advise it to be undertaken in other than important cases where the topography of the scene of the crime plays a considerable part. In all cases where the trouble of making a relief plan has been taken it will be recompensed by success. In many cases it will be possible to have the work done by a specialist. In all large towns modellers, sculptors, figure-makers etc., are to be found to whom this task may be entrusted and who, though they may never have done the like before, will with the indications furnished to them quite understand what they have to do.

Section v.—Moulding and Stereotyping.

These are operations of a technical character which may be employed by anybody and are most useful to fall back upon.

(a) *Moulding* may be resorted to whenever the shape of any article of small size, the original of which for some reason the court cannot have at its disposal is of importance. For instance—the impression of a bullet slight damage to a wall, the form of some article of furniture, a stone, or the like, the teeth or fingernails of a corpse where it has been established that the victim has defended himself by biting and scratching, keyholes, keys, bars of a grating, and a thousand other similar objects.

The material mostly used is wax or gutta-percha softened in hot water, also if need be potter's clay, dough or kneaded crumb of fresh bread. Best of all is the following kneaded mixture given by *Dr. Koller*: 5 parts india-rubber, 1 part sulphur, and 2 parts each magnesia, gilded sulphur of antimony, and coal pitch.

Moulding wax may equally well be used. This is obtained by melting together 10 parts of white wax and two parts of venetian turpentine to a moderate heat, and adding to the mixture little by little some potato-starch kneading the whole till the substance has reached the consistency required for the work in question and the variations of temperature. With the aid of this modelling wax the most accurate and exact models may be easily and conveniently made. Also 3 parts wax, 1 part shellac may be dissolved together, or 1 part wax, 2 part oil and 1 part rye flour mixed with heat. For large representations a mixture of 8 parts cement, 16 parts chalk, 2 parts strong lime water, and 1 part petroleum is excellent, this mixture is very strong and lasting and does not crack.

When use is made of potter's clay, dough or any substance containing water it must be remembered that the moulds obtained shrink in drying. In this case measures should be taken with the compasses and noted for purposes of verification. It is hardly necessary to explain how these moulds should be taken. The wax is slightly heated and pressed upon the object in question. This in no way injures the original and the impression may be carefully examined and compared with the model and the work repeated until the moulding is an entire success.

(b) *Stereotyping.* For larger and flatter objects use may be made of the stereotyping process, an excellent mode of reproduction, much too rarely employed. It especially lends itself to the representation of large and unequal surfaces, which may have acquired importance on account, for instance, of a wound caused to someone who has fallen upon them. These bodies are generally in the nature of stone flags, surfaces of walls, wooden surfaces and such like. Stereotyping may also be employed for more extensive damage, the origin of which is desired to be discovered, or for the reproduction of fairly flat forms which may have attained significance through having brought about accidents, etc.

As regards this operation of stereotyping it will suffice to indicate the process advised by the "Royal and Imperial Austrian Commission for the preservation of Artistic and Historical Monuments" to its correspondents for taking copies of inscriptions engraved on stone. Some not too strong, white unsized printing paper* is taken and moistened with a sponge or piece of cloth dipped in water until it is quite softened and then placed upon the surface to be reproduced. The paper is then pressed in with a not too hard clothes brush till it penetrates all the parts of the surface of which the impression is desired. Should the paper tear in places (which often happens when the original is very rough or has deep cavities) a large sheet of paper, thoroughly moist and with torn (not cut) edges is placed over the tear and beaten down anew with the brush, until a continuous bed of paper well beaten in is obtained. A second sheet of the same paper is then taken and damped, not this time with water, but with thin binder's paste, or a solution of gum arabic or animal gum, a soft brush being used. This is placed over the first paper and beaten in with the brush as before until the 2nd sheet has followed and adhered to the first in the hollow places. If the paper

---

*Printing paper not containing lines is difficult to obtain now days. One must get white blotting paper for smaller things or fine silk paper. Filter paper such as is used by chemists and photographers is well adapted. The modern toilet paper is also applicable being distinguished by considerable toughness. The best cast paper (that which Mommsen applied to stereotype Roman inscriptions was particularly good) is to be obtained from the paper manufactures.

employed be very thin or the second sheet tear like the first, a third must be taken (being damped with starch glue, gum arabic or animal gum as before) placed on the former and beaten in again with the brush. It is a good thing to use thin blotting-paper for the first layer to cover the first cracks and toilet paper for a second layer. Blotting paper is very plastic and unites closely, and toilet-paper produces by its toughness the necessary resistance.

The whole must be allowed to dry and then carefully drawn off. These impressions are almost as exact as plaster casts. They are very light and can be easily rolled up without damaging them. Indeed in many cases they are altogether excellent and quite indispensable. If in a hurry, the drying may be done at a fire or over hot plates. The paper should be quite dry before removal.

When the surface to be dealt with is very large, several sheets of paper are placed side by side, the borders of one overlapping its neighbour by at least two finger-breadths. It is as well not to cut the edges of the paper and if necessary a strip should be torn off, rough borders holding together more firmly. In this case the edges of the sheet forming the second layer should not be placed on the edges of the lower sheets but so that the middle of the second sheet covers the overlapping borders of the lower one.

When the surface to be reproduced is very small, excellent casts may be obtained by following the same process but using cigarette paper. A very light brush must be used and the paper pressed very carefully. Great care should be taken that the second and gummed sheet nowhere overlaps the first, otherwise it will adhere to the surface treated and render separation difficult.

Section VI.—Reproduction of Drawings, Printed matter, etc

There are many contrivances in use nowadays for manifolding, it would however be out of place to describe them here. The nearest type-writing office can always give the fullest particulars of the latest inventions.

Section VII.—Piecing together Torn Paper.

Simple as this kind of work appears yet it no less offers numerous difficulties and is often very awkwardly carried out. An Investigating Officer often receives torn pieces of paper of small size, not infrequently of the utmost importance when pieced together. For this purpose we procure a plate of glass, or better still some tracing cloth of good quality and transparency stretched on a board and fastened with four drawing pins. The pieces of paper are then set out, preferably on a dark back-ground, and we first try to distinguish the back from the front of the paper by noting e.g. whether one side is written on and the other not, or one side is darker than the other. If possible the pieces of paper are all placed the same side up. We then look for those pieces which have two clean-cut sides and which necessarily form the corners of the sheet. On these being found they are placed in their respective places and give us four very useful fixed points. We then look for all the pieces which have only one clean-cut side and divide them into four groups according to whether the cut edge is on top or at the bottom or the left or right sides. This is as a rule not difficult owing to the writing generally found on the paper.

These lateral pieces are placed in position using the corner pieces for guidance and with luck an entire frame is obtained into which the remaining pieces are filled in after some adjustment. This done the pieces are gummed on the plate of glass or the tracing cloth, one after the other in the order in which they lie, commencing at the top left hand corner, care being taken to bring the various edges as close together as possible. While this is being done it must be remembered that the tears are hardly ever perpendicular to the surface of the paper, but are generally directed towards the right on the upper surface of the paper and the left on the lower surface thus forming an oblique surface of separation. In this case the edges must be exactly slipped in one under the other. The pieces should therefore be only partially gummed at first, and only when the piece which has to be slipped under the first is in position should they be finally gummed down. Never gum to a non-transparent place even when there is nothing on the back of the paper, for in some cases the inquiry may turn on the question of why there is nothing on the back.

There is another method which however requires much more pains. In this process we use perfectly clean (by preference distilled) water with which the fragments are carefully moistened before being brought to the right position on a glass plate. They stick with water smoothly and securely to the plate. When this is done, then a second glass plate is laid on the paper of exactly the same size as the glass plate underneath, so that the paper is enclosed between two glass plates. Then follows a thorough drying, the plates not being touched until the water between them is evaporated. Gentle warmth will assist when one goes carefully to work. The plates are then safely and hermetically bound together with pasted slips of soft tough paper.

If the paper in question has been written with copying ink, care must be taken not to moisten the paper. In that case naturally no good copy can be obtained.

When the paper has been submitted to certain processes rendering it illegible, recourse must be had to photography, this never fails to assist us. A sheet of paper was exhibited at the Chicago Exhibition of 1893, the writing on which had been made quite illegible by rubbing and mastication side by side with the photograph of the same sheet. The undecipherable traces left on the paper become perfectly legible in the photograph.

The following case will show how important is the piecing together of torn paper.

One morning a peasant, an old man of considerable means, came before the Investigating Officer and declared that he had been shot the night before. He narrated how he had started from a place called St. and had followed the main road through the village of J. with the object of proceeding to G. While passing before a road-side cross, near a forest, a man advanced and demanded of him his money and watch at the mouth of a revolver.

The peasant had turned away, whereupon the highwayman snatched his watch and at the same time fired. The bullet entered his right ear, the robber made off, and the peasant remained for a considerable time besides the cross in a state of unconsciousness. On coming to his senses he returned to the village of J. to seek the assistance of the doctor of that place

The latter dressed the wound and sent him in a carriage to the hospital. The medical examination revealed a hole produced by a bullet extending from the ear towards the buccal cavity. The peasant having given an exact description of the author of the crime, police were sent out to arrest him and the Investigating Officer went off to the scene of the occurrence.

He was then most astonished to notice that the large pool of blood produced while the peasant lay wounded and unconscious on the ground was situated in the turf behind the cross, which was a large stone one, whereas the road where the attack was said to have taken place passed in front of the cross. This circumstance induced the Investigating Officer, who had no other clue, to repass along the road traversed by the peasant while going to the doctor and take the precaution of being accompanied by a police officer.

Here was found the only clue which might enable some light to be thrown on the concomitant circumstances. When close to J the Investigating Officer noticed some small pieces of torn paper behind a heap of stones. The largest of these pieces bore the words " to live " The paper thus seemed to be important and a search was made for all the pieces of paper. This was by no means easy, the wind having scattered them over a field of stubble. Fortunately the school children turned up on the road and gave willing aid in the search on being promised a kreutzer (2 pies) for each piece of paper. Since the police had arrested two lads on suspicion of the crime and the injured peasant was on his deathbed, it was necessary to establish with all haste what connection, if any, these pieces of paper had with the case. Half a night's work sufficed to arrange and join the pieces on a glass plate. The contents established that the peasant, overwhelmed by a lawsuit he had just lost and being besides in a bad state of health, had made up his mind to do away with himself he bade farewell to his wife, by whom he had had no children, leaving her his property and named as heirs two illegitimate sons. On this writing being shown to him the old peasant made a complete confession, stating that he had fired the shot himself behind the cross, but on coming to his senses had regretted his act and repaired to the doctor at J for assistance. On the way there he had taken care to tear up and throw away the letter of farewell he had previously written which was to take the place of a will. He died shortly after his confession. The reconstructed document not only gave the two lads who had been arrested their liberty but also assured the two sons of the peasant who had never been recognised, a considerable fortune.

In conclusion it may be remarked, that one can save paper in a bad condition if one moistens it with a solution consisting of one part of stearine and three parts of collodium (to be obtained from dealers in photographic articles). Important papers are often much crumpled also, when kept in damp dirty places or found near burial grounds or in water, full of bacteria which soon lead to decay. If such papers are much handed about between lawyers and witnesses, unfolded, smoothed out and folded up again, they soon become unreadable and only an expert can handle them. Treatment makes the paper strong, solid, and proof against bacteria, in short so far as regards ordinary handling almost indestructible.

Section VIII.—Preserving and Deciphering Burnt Paper.

A process somewhat analogous to the preceding but of much greater difficulty and rarely accompanied by success is the reconstruction of burnt paper, or rather to speak strictly "carbonised" paper. It occasionally happens that burnt papers are found during official searches which might, on reconstruction, throw considerable light on the case. The accused, expecting an inquiry, has taken care to burn papers compromising him. It is not however impossible to save some of the writing or printing upon paper which has been burnt. Anyone who has often thrown letters or other papers into the fire and noticed their destruction will remember how the writing or printed character sometimes remains very legible on the carbonised paper. The writing or letters generally stand out in a light grey—almost mouldy colour—or else quite black. In spite of much investigation and experiment we have failed to determine under what conditions this phenomenon takes place, whether a certain quality of paper or writing or printer's ink is requisite to produce the effect, or whether it entirely depends upon the action of a special kind of ink on a special kind of paper, or again whether a certain temperature, air-current, etc., is necessary. Doubtless the most influence is played by the mode of carbonisation, i.e., the temperature and air-current. It is often noticeable that one portion of the same writing is a pale black, another a brilliant black, while yet another part is greyish white.

Let us suppose the Investigating Officer to have discovered while searching a house that the stove contains burnt papers and believes them to have an important bearing upon the inquiry. Often it will be impossible for him to deal with them immediately owing to other work to be attended to. He must therefore secure the stove in some way or other, either by closing and sealing it or else by setting some one to watch it, till he finds time to attend to it. He ought, however, to immediately take away the pipe, that is the part joining the stove to the chimney, and close up the opening with rags, etc. This is necessary, as a strong draught rushes through the stove—especially when it is cold out of doors and warm in the room—which keeps the carbonised paper in the stove in continual motion causing pieces to become detached and fly about. In short the objects are continually subject to a deterioration which must be prevented. The communication between the stove and chimney having been removed the draught of air ceases to exist.

For the work itself a considerable quantity of tracing paper must be procured (as transparent as possible) and fixed with drawing pins on a board. Plates of glass should only be used as a last resort. If they are indispensable, panes of glass broken into more or less small pieces should be employed. Finally, a solution of gum arabic as colourless as possible, is necessary. We now proceed to extract the burnt sheets from the stove, watching them carefully and avoiding any draught.

The best method consists in slipping under each piece of burnt paper, starting with the uppermost, a band of paper of corresponding size, and using some firmness drawing them out one after the other. The tracing paper or pieces of glass should be all ready on a work-table placed near the stove. The tracing paper or glass is then covered with the gum, about as much surface being gummed as the size of the piece of burnt paper. On this bed of gum we now cautiously place the burnt paper and press it down very gently with the finger so that it becomes gummed to the tracing paper or glass; little by little this flattening out process is proceeded with more boldly and with more force until it is finished and the burnt paper is entirely gummed down. Care must be exercised never to touch the gum with the finger before pressing down the smallest portion of burnt paper or entire pieces will be torn from it and quite lost. The greatest difficulty arises from the fact that the burnt paper is not flat but convex and twisted as well as being dry and fragile. On being stretched out it is hollow in many places and stands well away from the gummed surface. When therefore it is flattened out, it breaks up into numerous pieces which fall certainly upon the gummed surface, but not in the right place. The mosaic so obtained presents an unsightly appearance. Here there are large cracks, there the papers overlap, and to read the whole is very difficult. To remedy this inconvenience the carbonised paper must be damped, an operation which happily is generally successful, for the paper is nearly always strongly hygroscopic.

In this connection the author has tried various methods which all have their advantages and their disadvantages. One of these is to soften the different leaves while actually resting on the gummed surface. A sheet of tracing paper or glass of the desired size is gummed over and the carbonised paper placed upon it. Small objects such as little pieces of wood, stones, etc., about three finger-breadths high, are then placed all round the apparatus, and upon them is stretched a piece of cloth several folds in thickness and well damped. The ends of this cloth should come in contact with the top of the table, but should not touch the burnt paper. Both the latter and the gummed surface are therefore in a moist atmosphere. The burnt paper softens and becomes flexible (this unfortunately does not *always* take place), the gum does not dry up, and in half an hour or more the flattening out process is complete and the gumming may be easily accomplished. When in a hurry, if a warm stove is at hand, several gummed sheets covered with burnt paper may be placed in a sieve held above a basin of boiling water, the operation being thus completed more rapidly. But processes in which the burnt paper is softened upon the gummed surface have this great disadvantage, that the edges of the paper twisted and deformed by the carbonisation, become immediately fixed to the tracing paper or glass, so that it is no longer possible to join them completely together or fix them down properly. This method should only be employed when the burnt paper is scarcely distorted at all or when it is possible to place its *convex* surface in contact with the gummed sheet. In this case it will only be resting upon a re-training surface while the raised-up edges when sufficiently softened come to rest in their appropriate places on that surface. When this process is impossible owing to distortions of all kinds in the paper, the burnt paper will have to be softened before being placed on the gummed surface. The softening process will be the same as above, the pieces of paper being placed beneath a wet cloth or in a sieve over boiling water. Then when sufficiently softened flat, and united they are placed upon the gummed sheet. When the paper is sufficiently softened its removal is never an easy matter, for in that state it is so fragile and tears so easily that the operation is but rarely accompanied by success. Another method, in many cases more sure and convenient, consists in placing the several pieces of burnt paper upon the surface of water contained in a fairly large receptacle, such as a wash-hand basin. The basin should be white inside so as to better observe the fragments. When the latter float they may be lifted out upon dry gummed paper and the whole placed upon blotting paper or any inclined surface to dry. The pieces obtained in this way are more legible. Unfortunately the burnt paper does not always float. Frequently, doubtless when there is much baryta in the composition of the paper, it sinks with rapidity and can only be caught up with difficulty—often indeed it cannot be fished up at all. We must in this case try to catch the sinking paper before it has reached the bottom, and to this end the gummed paper is placed under the water so that the burnt paper comes to rest upon it.

There are unfortunately many kinds of paper which when burnt, refuse to become impregnated with water, remaining always friable and stiff in spite of all efforts to damp them. In this case little can be hoped for, for carbon which cannot be softened breaks into little bits when gummed. No doubt it may be softened in oil, but then all the characters, formerly legible, generally disappear. We may add that the skill of hand necessary for this work cannot be obtained without practice, nor can it be supposed that everything will work well when necessity arises; without some preliminary trials—however few they be—no good result can be obtained, and when something of importance is to be preserved, documents of value will certainly be damaged.

When all the pieces of burnt paper in the stove have been collected and gummed so as to leave nothing beyond a few little bits of no importance, we cut up the papers on which they have been gummed, leaving as narrow a border round the burnt paper as is possible, and then begin the troublesome business of reconstruction. The paper is none the less fragile in spite of the gumming and it must be handled with caution. Moreover, nothing can be read except when looking at a certain angle, making the light fall in a particular manner, and, in most cases, only with the aid of a lamp. When some connection is formed between the various pieces, we do not gum them, for a double thickness of tracing paper and gum would render it impossible to read the reverse. The side gummed to the tracing paper is besides nearly always unreadable. We must be content therefore with numbering the different pieces so as to know their order.

Further, it may be remarked that pieces on which nothing can at first be read should not be cast aside, for a chemist may be able to put life into this apparently dead material. If he can do nothing, recourse must be had to photography; professional photography alone can be of service in this connection.

Finally, paper which has been quite recently burnt and which has not been completely consumed may sometimes recommence to burn on coming into open contact with the air. This must not be forgotten or the Investigating Officer may be surprised during the night by a fire breaking out in his desk where everything has been deposited till the morning.

CHAPTER XIII

FOOTPRINTS AND OTHER IMPRESSIONS.

Section 1—Footprints.

A General Notions

Footprints are often of decisive importance but we must know how to observe, preserve, and utilise the impressions in order to be able to get any good out of them. Recourse is rarely had to them for several reasons which it is impossible to pass over in silence. As a rule, footprints are but seldom found where they are wanted. Moreover when they exist they are rarely entire and complete, and for that reason are considered of no value. As regards really clean footprints it seldom happens that they are preserved so as to remain intact, or to inspire certainty that they have some connection with the case. People who have come upon the scene of a crime after it has taken place also leave traces of their feet fouling the important print so that one can no longer tell which is the significant footprint and which the useless one. On the other hand when well-preserved traces do exist the essential thing is to be able to interpret them and to know how to make good use of them. On this science is dumb and has hardly even approached the question.

B How to observe Footprints.

1 Preparatory

The necessity for the Investigating Officer of observing traces of footprints whenever opportunity is offered to him has already been pointed out. In European towns it is a difficult task, for on their pavements, carefully swept as they are, no prints are left and the observations which may be made upon a muddy portion of a road would be too short to give serious results. The country, on the other hand, offers in this connection inexhaustible resources. In the mud, the snow and especially in the fine dust of the main roads what opportunities there are for interesting observations! It is a veritable book, a reading as instructive as it is captivating. It is in the country that our studies must be carried on. Whoever desires to commence the study of footprints upon the scene of the crime will discover practically nothing at all. A footprint is an impression in a sense like all other impressions but in fact very different from them. And in addition it is not always well defined and when it is defined one cannot take it away with one, even if one could, it would be impossible to search the whole town and make experiments with every citizen to see if he is the author of the print. These considerations detract from the value of footprints. One must learn how to see and one cannot learn how to see without practising. What does an outsider see through a microscope? What does a huntsman see in the field and the forest when all seems dead to another? What does the artist see in a picture which is to an unartistic person but an assemblage of coloured figures? What is a confused chaos to a beginner is a world full of life and ideas to the man who knows. A few footprints do not amount to much but to the Investigating Officer they may mean everything: upon them may depend the success of his work—the salvation of an innocent and the conviction of a guilty person. One sees that this microcosm which leaves these prints is not wanting in importance.

Here again the Investigating Officer must unite his observations in a sympathetic whole. It does not suffice to look at large numbers of footprints: by only looking at them no order can be given to his ideas, nothing can be retained, nothing will be grouped, and the utility of what may have been seen will through seeing too much, be nil. To be able to obtain some advantage from these studies one may commence by considering attentively, and by seeing for example on a dusty road, the impressions of the feet of small and big persons, of boots and bare feet, of the footprints of animals, and the wheels of vehicles intermingled confusedly. The beginner will be unable to freely discriminate between them and will have enough trouble in differentiating the footprints of small and big men and those of people with boots and without boots. In time he will notice that the fashions of the shoes or boots are very different, the nails, the heels, the shape of the sole, etc. will present differences. A repeated impression will especially attract his attention by its dimensions and large size. Here he will lose it, there it will appear again and he will greet it with ever increasing interest, the beginner has found a footprint he is now upon "a good track," and will begin to take an interest in the matter. Let us then continue to follow this large footprint. We find an impression of it of particular distinctness. We stop and examine it closely, we can count the nails, observe that some of them are missing, and that the right shoe which has been mended carries on the sole a little bit of leather strongly fastened on. Now it is impossible to lose or confound this footprint. We go on further and we perceive that our friend has all at once left besides the traces of his feet that of a stick. He was no doubt tired and leaned upon his stick which he had up to then been carrying under his arm. In the meantime we note that the mark of the stick is not that of an iron ferrule nor a regular round surface such as a stick in long use would have. The marks are pointed and dug into the ground. We return to the spot where we perceived the trace of the stick for the first time and look around us, and then what do we discover? Beside the road the branch of a thorn bush, of about the thickness of the thumb, has been quite recently cut. Our friend therefore was not carrying the stick under his arm. He cut the stick, rounded it off roughly, and in that way the cleft-shaped impressions were made. Let us follow our man. All at once he has obliquely crossed the road and has then gone backwards and forwards several times. What could have been the reason? The state of things seem to reveal nothing and yet the whole is cleared up—thanks to a prolonged examination. At the border of the road we perceive in the dust the impressions of short foot-steps belonging to a child with bare feet. These footprints come down the road, and it may be noticed that all of a sudden they begin to go backwards and forwards, although the feet do not appear to have turned round, the toes being always pointed forwards. Just at this place a path begins towards a house situated at a little distance from the road. In the dust of this path one sees the trace of a dog which comes and goes. Now it is clear. The child was going along the road. The dog came from the house and began to bark at the child which, too frightened to advance, was forced to give ground. Our friend coming along the road chased the dog with the stick he has just cut and he and the child have then continued on their way in opposite directions.

Let us continue to follow our friend. Here he has met an acquaintance—for his footprint strikes across the road as does that of someone who was coming in the opposite direction. They have spoken together for a long time, for they have often changed their position. One of them has emptied his pipe, for there are ashes on the road, he has relit it, for several freshly struck matches are lying on the ground. Some have been trampled into the dust by the heel of our man. Now, we have some hope of catching him, for the talk with his friend must have taken place not much more than 10 minutes ago. He has used numerous matches to light his pipe. It must therefore be that the strong wind which has been blowing for about 10 minutes was blowing at that time. At length he has continued on the road, but not alone. He is accompanied by the acquaintance with whom he has been talking for so long and who has retraced his steps to go along with him. The pipe has burnt well, and there must have been strong tobacco in it, for the smoker has expectorated beside his footprints on several occasions. The second man is of small stature, for, if we measure exactly, we find that for ten paces of our man his companion takes eleven, and in consequence his legs are sensibly shorter. What has made him decide to turn back? It is easy to guess; at 60 paces we perceive an inn near the road and the footprints lead to it.

We continue on our way to attend to our own business, and several hours later we return by the same road. Long before we near the inn in question we again find the footprints of our friend; we recognise them and are certain of them. Yet they have another aspect. At times they are at the edge of the road, at times in the middle, at times the impressions start away, one from the other, while at times they cross one another; we notice sometimes large strides and at other times small ones. We then make a determination as to time; our friend has remained *a long time* at the inn.

No doubt we do not always have the opportunity of deducing so much from a single print, but it will always be possible, if circumstances are not too unfavourable, to obtain some positive information. It suffices to thoroughly examine the footprint one follows and to engrave in one's memory all the distinctive marks which prevent us losing it, even if it disappear for a little while among others, or under the effect of unfavourable conditions.

Another mode of observation is to select among several footprints which follow or meet one another, those of one particular person and then determine whether they belong to a man or woman, to a tall or short person to a person walking or running, etc., and to thereupon try to catch the person in question and to verify the accuracy of the supposition made. To do this with some certainty nothing better can be recommended than to attentively observe the walk of everyone we meet and who leaves footprints, and then compare the footprint left with the information one may have been able to obtain regarding that person. Redoubled attention will be given to the mark when it discloses certain peculiarities, when it, for example, belongs to a person who takes steps of extraordinary length or shortness, who stamps or shakes, loiters or deviates, to a man who has bow legs (in the form of an O or X) who limps dragging a leg behind or leans upon a stick, etc. When some such thing is noticed one will try to determine if the footprint itself presents any striking peculiarity, and if so, whether the peculiarities in walk can be connected with those in the footprints.

All such observations are only of value if noted down in writing and systematically classified, and, being repeated as often as possible, ranged alongside one another for reciprocal control. It is only when they rise above the suggestions of simple accident, when the series of observations is as extensive as possible, when the same fact often appears accompanied with the same phenomena, that one can really, within the limits imposed upon the judgment of man, speak of cause and effect. When, for example, he has once or twice observed that in certain steps of extraordinary length the outside corner of the heel of the shoe makes a very deep impression in the ground, this may be the effect of chance or of a peculiarity of the person. If this fact is noticed often without finding any exception, it may be presumed that one has discovered a connection of cause and effect, i.e., a rule. And if one finds a *single* impression with the border of the heel print particularly deep, one will say this trace is that of a person who at least at this moment took steps of extraordinary length.

For a science like that of footprints, which is yet in its infancy, the number of experiments can never be considered great enough. No clear ideas can be obtained on the subject until after having collected much material and performed numerous experiments. People interested in the matter may exercise themselves practically in the observations spoken of above by studying artificially made footprints. This is always possible on a suitable surface, fine dust, the half-dried mud of the road, not too deep freshly fallen snow which has not yet begun to melt. Footprints of all kinds can be made: stationary, walking (slow or fast), running, or jumping. Then again walking on a flat surface, uphill or down, burdened and not burdened, tired or fresh, etc. Each footprint thus produced should be studied most minutely and carefully compared with the others to find out what there is in common, note the differences between them, and apply the results obtained to the observation of the footprints of another person.

Most particular attention should be given to the impressions of bare feet, impressions which may be preserved to serve later as an accurate means of comparison. The best method of obtaining these impressions is to produce them on paper. The paper should be fixed to the floor of a room, if possible, with drawing pins. When the paper is not fixed it rises at each step and the impressions do not take on clearly. Then a tin vessel is taken,

12 to 16 inches long and 8 inches wide, in which is placed a piece of cloth felt, or folded linen, a little smaller in size than the vessel. This cloth is then damped with a solution of some finely pulverised colour, as much as possible of an earthy kind, as for example dark ink, burnt sienna, Kassler earth, etc., which may be procured for a few pence in sufficient quantity to make numerous experiments. Ordinary ink or aniline colour dissolves in water and does very well, but it is difficult to get rid of these colours, whereas the powders mentioned disappear immediately on contact with water. This substance then is mixed with water and a little gum arabic, so that the whole becomes of about the thickness of glycerine or oil. The colouring substance is then placed upon the piece of cloth in the vessel so that the cloth is completely impregnated. The vessel is then placed upon the floor. The operator walks, and with bare feet, first on the cloth and then on the paper. Various ways of walking are tried, ordinary walking, standing, running, etc. The foot is not again moistened until the colour has almost completely gone.

It is still better when the sole of the foot is moistened with an alcoholic solution of chloride of iron before being reproduced on the paper. Then the copy is moistened with a solution of ammon. sulf. cyanide 25 parts, alcohol 100 parts, and ether 1000, which gives a very clear copy.

In carrying out this experiment the operator must not neglect to note after each footprint how it has been produced, whether by walking, standing, running, &c., as well as the peculiarities of the person who produced it, as for example whether he be a man of say 30 years old, 5 feet 10 inches in height, strong and healthy, with somewhat small oval-shaped feet. One will also attempt to obtain impressions of the feet of other persons of different ages and different sexes and in different walks of life. Particular attention should be paid to the observation of the footprints of persons whose walk presents certain peculiarities such as swaying, loitering, bow-legged, springing or jumping sort of walk, heavy pace, &c.

Every Investigating Officer ought to have as rich a collection as possible of those impressions which keep well and never get rubbed out. In a real crime he will try to make comparisons with the examples in this collection and in this way will be able to obtain unexpected results.*

2. Observation in an Actual Case

It is natural in criminal cases, especially when they are of great importance and the author of the crime is unknown, that the footprints should be carefully examined. We have already repeatedly said that traces which exist must be carefully guarded from damage and that the subordinate members of the police force and village officers should be given instructions to that effect, for they, in nearly every case, are first to arrive at the scene of the crime. Let us here call attention to a fault which is generally committed. It is commonly only in the immediate neighbourhood of the crime that footprints are looked for, and not further away. It rarely happens that we find on the scene of the crime itself footprints of any utility, either

---
* This collection ought strictly to contain also footprints in plaster and cement, but these are so large and heavy that only people who are special experts in the subject dream of collecting them. Others must wait until we have Criminal Museums in our Law Colleges

through, the criminal having taken the precaution to efface them or on account of their having been trodden upon and rendered invisible by the arrival of other persons.

These reasons no longer exist when we make investigations at some little distance from the scene of action. There nearly always exists somewhere a piece of clean land capable of receiving a footprint; there the criminal has not taken so many precautions as at first and perhaps no one else has yet passed over this spot. No doubt it is much more difficult to establish that a print which is at some distance away has any connection with the crime. But it is not nearly so difficult as is generally supposed.

It is in the nature of things that a criminal does not return by the same road immediately after having accomplished his crime, but on the contrary he makes off in a roundabout direction. If one looks for and finds here a fresh footprint which does not appear to be the continuation of an ordinary walk, it may be supposed to belong to the criminal. It will then be submitted to a most minute study, after we have been assured by the people in the house and by neighbours that none of them have come that way and that they can give no other explanation of the footprint than that it must belong to a person who has been on the scene of the crime before any of them and has been making off in this roundabout manner. If moreover it can be proved that the footprint appears to be that of a person running, another step will be gained, and we will obtain further confirmation if able to determine e.g. that the footprint has been produced by a person who has passed there in the night and without knowing the ground. It may indeed be easily presumed when the individual in question has hit against a stone, fallen into a ditch, rolled over a bank, etc., that he has not passed that way in the daytime.

Other indications often exist, when for example a large number of articles have been carried away from the scene of the crime and the thief has rested on the road, and laid down his burden, or has lost or even thrown away one of the stolen articles. These are certificates of identity of the footprint as certain as can possibly be. Another strong case is that of a single footprint evidently produced by the criminal and found near the spot, resembling other footprints which lead further away. In this last case especially one often neglects, after a footprint has been found, to look for others at a greater distance. But anyone who knows how necessary it is to examine carefully a footprint and studies several of them will not neglect even in this case to look for footprints that may be discovered far away from the scene of action.

Who now is the person who ought to occupy himself with looking for and following footprints? We reply without hesitation, the Investigating Officer. We have far too high an idea of the sphere of the doctor and his functions in all the branches of medical science to think that he can specially occupy himself with the study of footprints. The Investigating Officer has much less to deal with than the Medical Jurisprudent. It is his business to occupy himself with those things which are part of his functions and in consequence he will be called upon to devote attention to the search for, preservation, and valuation of footprints. If his medical expert takes an interest in the matter, the Investigating Officer will accept with pleasure his assistance. For the more eyes used the more things will be discovered

A medical expert who has studied the question is certainly in this connection the most useful specialist the Investigating Officer can have. As the work in connection with footprints is not as a rule of the most simple description and requires time and trouble, the help of a medical man is all the more to be desired since the latter cannot help giving us a better idea of the case. He will then be able to formulate his opinion, which would have been asked for all the same even if he had no help from the footprints, much more easily than if he had remained up to that moment entirely uninformed about them. Only the doctor can decide whether there is room to conclude from the trace of a foot that the owner of that foot has some corporeal infirmity (is a cripple, apoplectic, or paralytic &c.). The Investigating Officer will furnish the materials, will illustrate if need be by loans made from his collections of footprints and traces, and will ask his advice.

But, besides the medical man, the Investigating Officer ought frequently, even in this case, to have recourse to other specialists. If it be a question of booted feet, an intelligent shoemaker can always give useful information. He will be able, no doubt, to say whether the shape of the shoe is common in the neighbourhood or, on the contrary, whence it is likely to come; whether the boot has been repaired and what the repairs are; what class of persons is in the habit of wearing shoes of that kind; whether the wearer uses his shoes in a peculiar manner, wears out more on one toe than on another, and what peculiarities in the bodily build of the wearer experience teaches him are present. A shoemaker who reflects (and the political cobbler has not yet disappeared) can even point out sore places, for he has often had opportunities of observing, thanks to the complaints of his customers and the repairs that he has been obliged to do for them, that there is always a connecting link of cause and effect between the pain and the resistance which determines the wearing away of a special portion of the sole. Thus if one has a sore place or corn on the ball of the big toe, one will naturally tread more heavily on the heel and outer side of the foot so as to relieve the pressure on the part that pains.

The specialist who in this case often renders the best service is the skilful and experienced sportsman. He has made preliminary studies very similar to those which are now occupying our attention. He has often observed the traces of game in order to obtain profit from that knowledge. He sees traces in a spot where another would hardly be able to see a mark. He therefore knows how to determine in what direction the trace continues even when one has only perceived for a moment the impression, feeble and incomplete as it is, of a single footprint, and what is still more valuable, he alone knows how to pick up a lost trace even after it has been interrupted for a considerable distance. The experienced sportsman knows other things as well. He knows exactly the kind of weather there has been each hour for the last few days and what influence the temperature has upon traces. He is also able to say when a particular footprint has been made, and he will not easily confuse with each other footprints which have not been made at the same time. He can thus follow better than anyone else a special footprint in the midst of several others. The sportsman is also accustomed to observe at what speed an animal has travelled; he knows this by what he calls the "glide," or "slide," that is to say the slipping which happens when an animal galloping alights upon damp soil, as is nearly always the case in the forest, and as its feet touch the ground slides forwards to get into a new stride. Deer, roe, and pigs make this mark very distinctly. It is, however, clearly visible only in wet clay. On other soil one sees no traces of it except when accustomed to note it, and this training the sportsman, and the sportsman alone possesses. When we have at our disposal a man of this description, of age and experience, one cannot do better than make use of him. Nothing can possibly replace an assistant of this kind, for he will be able to elucidate many cases which without him would remain unsolvable.

Let us now pass to the different kinds of footprints. In the first place we must determine whether the person who has produced them was bare footed or wore shoes, a matter which is of considerable importance in examining and utilising the print. Those who have occupied themselves with this question are not exactly in agreement. One side, *Zenker* for example, says that it is regrettable that one so seldom finds traces of bare feet, for they furnish the most information. Another, for example *Schauenstein* remarks that the sole of a shoe furnishes, thanks to the nails, repairs, &c., so many signs of identity that it is much more easy to work with foot prints of booted feet than with those of bare feet. The author thinks that the best conclusion would be to say: '*the booted foot gives more clues, the bare foot has more physiognomy*', so that the observer, according to his temperament, may prefer the former or the latter. The scrupulous and accurate observer, trained to take exact measurements and having some taste for mathematics, will prefer the impressions of booted feet. He will carefully take all the measurements of the sole, will count the nails, measure the pieces of leather nailed on to the sole, &c., and will give a perfect image of the general impression, an image which it will be difficult to confuse with others. The other observer, capable of seizing, from a general view and the strength of his memory, a not very distinct impression—able besides to trust instinct for shape and form, by taking into consideration a certain number of signs which it is impossible to express in numbers but which none the less exist with absolute distinctness—such a man will work more readily with traces of bare feet. The measurements in this case give very uncertain results, for the plant of the bare foot leaves always a rounded impression and never presents fixed borders like the sole of the shoe, and in consequence it does not produce a clean impression such as one is able to utilise from the point of view of measurements. We must then look for and describe, so far as possible, striking marks and appearances, with a view to render more accurate measurements which can at best be only approximate. The whole impression alone can elucidate the matter, and it gives in effect, when circumstances are not too unfavourable, a veritable physiognomy, even more precise and more characteristic than that of many a human face.

One may then say with *Masson*, and rightly, that the details of all the impressions of a bare foot are in each particular case so distinctive and so characteristic that it is always possible to differentiate them one from another and recognise again the same impression. This is wholly true only when the impressions in question have been produced under identical conditions. If, for example, one reverts to the process indicated above for producing by means of colouring matter impressions of bare feet, one will be able to convince oneself of the difference in aspect presented by impressions made by the same foot. If the foot has just been well moistened with the colour and is passed over packing paper which has been rolled up as one rolls a carpet, so as to make a continuous path, the first impression is well coloured, while the others become less and less so until quite indistinct. If then the last and the first impression thus produced be compared, one will see how difficult it is to find this famous "characteristic resemblance." The difficulty increases if, in producing the first impression with the sticky colour, one slips the foot a little outwards, while in the production of the others one walks with a firm and confident step. The first footprint gliding and well coloured, and the last firm and poorly coloured present but a hopeless minimum of this "characteristic resemblance."

Similar results are obtained when various colouring matters are chosen (that is to say of different consistency, viscosity and colouring) upon different foundations. The same foot wet with an equal quantity of the same colouring matter gives upon an unplaned and rough plank a very different impression from what it does upon a sheet of smooth and carefully stretched paper.

Masson denies the great importance of pigments (colouring matters) on footprints although all experience teaches the contrary. One should notice when a person steps out of the water and walks on the smooth floor round a swimming bath. The first marks of the quite wet feet are large and full as if made by a flat-footed person. The more the water dries, the smaller and narrower become the marks—this example is as valuable for our work as many a long discussion. It is however, to be noticed that we see, for example in deep, fine dust on the high road, many tracks of flat-footed people. The reason of this is different. If the dust is pretty thick, the foot sinks in so far that the curve of the instep also forms part of the impression where the curve is not pronounced. Then the impression looks as if it had been produced by a flat-footed person. But on closer investigation the deception is discovered, for in the track even the deeply impressed instep appears, while the truly flat-footed person always produces a flat impression, without moulding.

It is easy to understand that the size of the prints may vary considerably. Thus *Masson* has found by measuring different footprints produced by the feet of eight individuals that the variations were—

In length from	9 to 23 Millimetres
In breadth from	0 to 8 ,,
For the width of the narrow portion of the sole from	0 to 5 ,,
For the inclination of the line of the toes from	0 to 21 ,,

These differences occurred not through different forms which the foot may take but when the same ground was chosen to walk upon and the same colouring matter and method of placing the foot down was observed.

To sum up what we have said, we come to the conclusion that the process to be employed for the impressions of booted and bare feet is quite different. For an impression of the former it always suffices for future use to have an exact description of the impression of the sole with the note of the measurements and numbers, care being taken to indicate all dimensions, the number of the nails (not only of those which exist but of those which are missing) in the front part of the sole and in the heel separately, the shape and condition of preservation of the latter, patches if there be any and every other distinctive sign. If the question subsequently arises as to the connection between the sole of which the impression has been found and that of a suspected individual, all that is necessary is to measure and count the whole again. It is quite otherwise with the impression of a bare foot. The impression as a whole, that is to say, its physiognomy, cannot be reproduced by description, by drawing or by photograph. It is besides impossible to fix it for long in the memory, and the comparison of a footprint formerly seen with that belonging to a suspect arrested subsequently when the former is no longer under one's eyes is of no utility and can serve no purpose. We must have the two impressions on the table before us. We must measure and compare them several times before being able to pronounce any opinion about them. And it is even necessary in reproducing the footprint of the person suspected for comparison with the *corpus delicti* to have the latter under one's eyes so that the method of production of the two impressions may take place in as nearly similar circumstances as possible. *Causse*, who has made comparisons of this kind with defibrinated blood, has long ago stated that as much blood must be placed on the sole of the foot on the second occasion as there was when the first footprint was produced. *Schauenstein* thinks that this is easier to say than to do. It seems difficult, but in reality, when the necessary precautions are taken, the experiment is as easy as it is certain. To find the same base will not be difficult, the same wood with identically the same surface, the same flagging, the same paper, etc., can always be found. Nor is there great difficulty in finding out what colouring matter has been employed. If need be, specialists must be asked what was the colouring substance which has produced the first footprint.

All that remains to be done is to determine the quantity of colouring matter used. This can only be done by reproducing a series of footprints. The man who is being experimented upon is described above is made to tread upon a plate washed over and impregnated with the colouring matter, so that the sole of the foot is completely covered, and then he is made to give impressions of his foot, side by side, upon the base in question (without again rubbing the foot in the colouring matter), until the prints are almost unrecognisable. The footprint connected with the crime (we shall in future term this the original footprint) is then compared successively with the footprints that have just been produced, and from among them is chosen that which shows just the same amount of colouring matter as the original. This always and easily succeeds, as the author has demonstrated in numerous cases.

The colouring matter naturally comes off with a regularity which depends on its own nature and the nature of the ground, and, if it comes off in the same way during the experiment, the same thing must have happened when the original was produced. It is therefore *necessary* to find *each time*, by this easy experiment, a footprint resembling the original in *the quantity* of colouring substance, *i.e.*, in the force and precision of the impression. As regards the resemblance of the shape, that is to say the question whether the individual suspected is identical with the author of the original, it is the work of comparison to tell us. What we wish to demonstrate now is the necessity of preserving at all costs all traces of footprints of naked feet, whereas those of booted feet may sometimes be reproduced from accurate measurement and description.

Further on we will point out how to preserve footprints. Footprints should be preserved in the same way as blood marks. See *Chapter XIV*. More often than not they will be found upon planks of wood or stone flags. It is absolutely necessary to remove with the chisel and carry away the portion of the plank in question. In certain cases only, where e.g., only portions of quite small size, such as the impression of a single toe, have been preserved, it will suffice to remove the top layer of wood or detach with the chisel a chip of from ¼ to ⅓ of an inch in thickness carrying the entire impression.

If it is not possible to take the original imprint, a photograph must without fail be taken first and then a drawing made. For this sometimes in order to get good results one must above all things know in what the cement (the binding element) of the trace is soluble i.e., which of various solvents—water, alcohol, turpentine or benzine—should be tried on the edge of an unimportant part of the mark. For instance if it appears that turpentine will be the best solvent moisten a piece of blotting-paper or filter-paper (a little larger than the mark) with turpentine lay it carefully on the mark, and tap with a brush (of course with the point of the brush) until the blotting paper or filter paper adheres completely to the base. The paper is then again sprinkled with turpentine tapped again, and allowed to dry. Finally the paper is slowly raised and with luck is obtained a complete copy, altogether negative, on the paper. Of course the experiment often fails, and for that reason a photograph must be taken before the work is commenced.

The distinguished investigator *Frederick Paul* of Olmutz, whom Criminology has to thank for a number of important experiments, has provided us with a list of clearly distinguishable materials which make copies of hands and feet on smooth flat surfaces. Such materials are, namely, powdered washing blue, powdered iron (which is to be obtained from every chemist) soot, carmine cinnabar, all aniline colours powdered hypermanganate of potassium (protoxide of potash) brimstone of antimony, etc. The tip of the finger for example, is impressed on a glass disc, which is then strewn with one of the before named powders. This brings out the greasy papillary lines distinctly. The same simple method serves to take a hand or a foot impression on a flat surface.

It remains to mention a difference which arises between an impression and a print the former is produced on earth, mud, clay, snow, or other soft mass and is much more frequent. It is relatively rare that one finds the ground composed of a substance on which when walking the sole sticks and leaves marks upon the ground or on anything lying on the ground. These marks may be found when in a murder, etc., pools of blood are formed upon the ground in which the author of the crime has walked or when there are on the floor open vessels filled with coloured liquids which the criminal fails to see and knocks over in the dark as sometimes happens in connection with thefts committed in cellars.

In looking for and appreciating these two kinds of impressions the same procedure must be followed but the method of preservation is different the mark must be detached from the ground-work and the piece itself must be taken away. It is difficult to imagine a case in which this will be impossible or particularly difficult. As has already been said, these marks are only found upon planks and flat surfaces and it is easy to carry away the whole or a portion of these. It rarely happens that one finds in the open air a footprint as distinguished from an impression on the ground, and even when such does exist it is by reason of the roughness and the inequality of the ground which itself will render the footprint absolutely useless. Yet it is not absolutely impossible, seeing that the author of the crime may have touched with his coloured foot a stone abnormally flat or clayey ground particularly level. In such a case the stone or the clod of earth must be taken up. This operation is not without some difficulty, for the upper surface of a bed of clay if raised for example with a shovel is apt to crack. The soil may be neither damp nor soft for then it is an impression and not a mark which one would have. The only thing to be done in such a case is to produce at the spot where the mark is found a firm crust which will not break, and without destroying the mark. This may be done by pouring drop by drop upon the mark and round about it either carpenter's glue (of the consistency used by joiners) or silicate of potassium, that is to say the soluble glass which may be obtained at nearly every grocer's, and by spreading this with a soft brush or a little piece of cotton wool. See *Subsection* E 3 of this Chapter. It goes without saying that care must be taken that the coloured impression does not dissolve in the glue or the silicate. In such a case the spreading must be stopped and the filtration of the liquid awaited. When this is done and the upper surface has become hard, one may with a deep thrust of the spade remove as much of the surface as possible and take it away. The piece thus removed may then be scraped with a knife underneath so as to detach the superabundant clay and only preserve the upper crust containing the impression—thus making it easier to carry about. When the upper bed of clay has been hardened with the silicate, care must be taken that the impression does not deteriorate with time. The acid or potash contained in the silicate gives rise to effervescence in the form of very fine white crystals so that the clay seems to be covered with a white jelly. It often happens that the crystals of white soda rise up from parts of the upper bed of clay. These become detached and fall off, thus deteriorating the corresponding portion of the impression. To avoid losing the impression altogether it must be photographed on returning home so as to preserve it whatever happens. Photography is also a method used on the spot when it is impossible to detach and take away the impression, as for example when it is found upon a rock. Locke has already made trials with photography, but these trials, he himself admits, have not been very successful.

C Origin of the Footprints

(1) SPEED

Every footprint is an incomprehensible problem to an observer when he does not know the elements which have produced it. Each impression is the result of a movement, so that it is useless to speak of an impression produced in the stationary position, for that position almost always follows or precedes walking or running. There would only be a real impression in the stationary position if a person carried by two men were to be placed perpendicularly on clayey ground and lifted up again

All other ordinary impressions or prints, and therefore nearly every one that exists, originates in a movement of walking, running, or jumping it is therefore necessary to pay some attention to these different movements We will take for guide the résumé by Dr Landois in his "Physiology of Man" This work, like nearly all those treating on the question is based upon the labours of the brothers E and H Weber who were the first to describe the mechanism of walking

(a) *Walking*

Let us consider the scheme of two legs (*Fig 48*) in which the thick lines denote the leg with which the walker starts off and the thin lines the leg which follows the movement The little circles designate from top to bottom, the joint of the hip the knee, the ankle joint the ball of the big toe Let us call the leg which moves first A and that which follows behind B

First Position—Position of repose—The two legs seen from the side cover one another the vertical drawn from the centre of gravity of the body passes between the two feet

Second Position—To start the body in the motion of walking displacement of the position of the centre of gravity takes place, and the weight of the body passes to the leg B This is produced by slightly leaning the body to one side on the leg B Two results are thus obtained, the leg A which is to produce the forward movement becomes free Moreover the leg B ought, the moment afterwards to support the whole weight of the body the centre of gravity must therefore fall no longer between the two feet, but at the middle of the sustaining base of the foot B This done, the weight of the body is thrown into the direction of the walk the body and the legs are inclined forwards and the preparations for the first step are complete

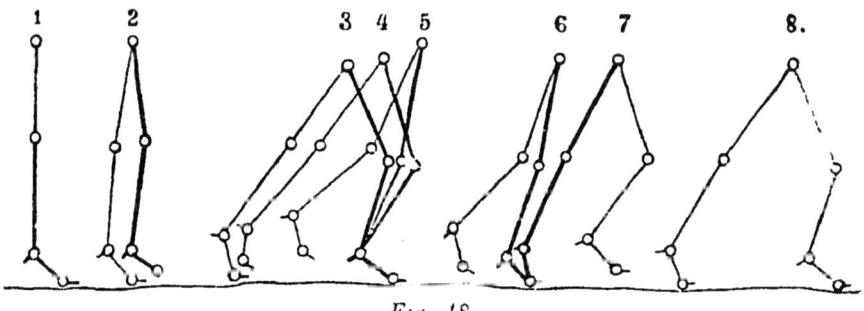

Fig 48

For this there would be no need of a bending of the knee of A if the bone of the leg and the tarsus or ankle bones were at right *angles*, that is to say continued to form the same angle as at the moment of repose or stationary moment But this would have a double disadvantage, on the one hand the muscles which ought to carry the tarsus in this position would be too strained and become fatigued, on the other hand the body would lose the support of the leg A which would greatly complicate the balance The tarsus of A is therefore utilised as long as possible and this is done by rising (physiologists term it "developing") from the ground, not all at once, but according to need that is to say, first the heel, then the anterior portion of the sole of the foot, and finally the toes. But the result is a lengthening of the ankle joint of the foot, i e, the angle of the bone of the leg and of the tarsus will become obtuse and therefore larger. Following this the whole leg from the hip to the points of the toes will become sensibly longer. The point of the toe will then at this movement of A become an obstacle on the ground and must so to speak remain there. To avoid this obstacle, the lengthening of the leg due to the lengthening of the ankle joint of the foot must be compensated somewhere. This compensation can only take place at the knee, which is obliged to bend

Third Position—The leg A is carried forward the sole of the foot, beginning at the heel, is placed on the ground. The knee bends so as to form, relatively speaking, the most acute angle during the whole of the step. At the same time the tarsus of B leaves the ground and the leg B becomes completely stretched. The mechanical scheme shows us that what happens is as follows when A is carried forward the upper part of the body must also lean forward, for it would be a mechanical contradiction to incline the mass of the body in any direction other than that in which the movement is going to be accomplished. The weight of the body ought even to favour this forward movement. When the body is inclined forward and rests in consequence more upon A, the distance between the joint of the hip of A and the place on the ground touched by the tarsus is less than that from the joint of the hip of B to the spot on the ground where the tarsus B rests. But as the two legs are of the same length, and the leg B being stretched out represents in its quality of "*straight line*" the shortest distance between the two extreme points the leg A must make a sort of detour and take up its position by making a broken line, that is to say, by bending the knee. As this bending would become fatiguing to the leg A the other leg must immediately make compensation. The leg B becomes longer by the raising of the tarsus from the ground and at the same time the tarsus of A makes its own upward movement and allows A to stretch out.

Fourth Position—This does not differ essentially from the preceding. The ankle joint of the foot B stretches and the tarsus rises from the ground. To obtain the necessary room for this the knee of A must be pushed forward and then immediately stretched.

Fifth Position—The moment now arrives for the leg B to do what the leg A has already done (*Second Position*), i e, it ought to bend the knee and for the same reason. The leg A now stretches to such an extent that the knee comes more behind than in the preceding position, this is the only backward movement in the whole phenomenon of walking.

Sixth Position—The two legs are brought together. A leans well forward and is nearly stretched out, B continues its forward movement to the

Seventh Position—In this A is completely extended and B makes at the knee the acutest angle during the whole step. A is inclined forward, B being stretched to the ground commencing from the knee and at the

Eighth Position—the third position is again obtained, A becoming B and B becoming A the movement then recommences.

From the preceding analysis we obtain the following results

(a) It is not correct to say as stated in books that walking is merely a falling of the body forwards, protected from an actual tumble by the successive support of the legs. Even an idiot who followed to some extent this system would not walk in such a way as to carry his body forward in order to let it really fall, taking care at the same time to put out his leg to prevent the fall. Every sane person walks by *first* carrying a leg forward and *then* leaning the centre of gravity of the body upon it, in order to be able to continue in the same manner with the other leg. Our diagram proves clearly that this is so, and every experiment with walking demonstrates the same fact. It suffices to try and lean the body forwards and only *afterwards* advance the foot, in order to discover that no one walks in this manner but everyone does exactly the opposite: we first advance the leg and then lean the body.

(b) It is not correct to say that the leg operates like a pendulum, on the other hand a complicated mechanical movement brings it to the front. If the step were but the movement of a pendulum it would be necessary for all the activity of all the hip muscles to be suspended, the leg would so to speak, have to be "paralysed." It is quite impossible to interrupt the tension of these muscles for long; as the diagram shows, it is necessary for a large number of muscular functions to take place at the same instant in order to bring about the displacement of the centre of gravity and the bending of the joints of the knee and the foot. Since so complex a movement is necessary, it would be very difficult to paralyse the leg, there can therefore, be no question of a simple pendulum.

It is easy to convince oneself of this by two experiments. One is to compare the muscular activity produced at the first step, that is when departing from the first or stationary position, with the muscular activity which develops during the course of walking. For the first step it is evidently not a question of oscillation for it is necessary to raise the leg, which up to this time has remained in a vertical position. No difference is noticed between the two activities. The second experiment is to stand upon the left leg only, holding with the right hand, the arm being horizontal, to a door etc., and raise the extended right leg backward and forwards as high as possible "paralysing" it as much as we can and abandoning it to the laws of gravity; it will be found that it scarcely departs from the vertical position. Now if this is so when holding on with the hand and when the muscles are quite inactive, there is much more reason to think that the same thing will happen when all the muscles of the leg are in full activity and this all the more so as when the leg is advanced one aims nearly always at some point which one desires to reach, a result which could not be obtained by mere oscillation. This has nothing in common with the swinging of the arms while walking; the arms really do swing. But there is neither muscular tension nor bending movement and they receive the impulsion which makes them oscillate from the continual displacement of the centre of gravity.

This mechanism of walking furnishes us with the following results in connection with footprints or impressions:

1. Since at each step the centre of gravity first goes over to the leg B upon which the weight is carried, the load must glide from the interior to the exterior edge of the foot. What is shown by very clean footprints is a certain twisting which starts from the inside edge of the foot and

goes towards the ball of the little toe and, in consequence of the thrust to detach the foot from the ground, passes suddenly under the big toe. We feel this immediately when walking barefoot, especially when the sole of the bare foot is rubbed with tallow and then walks on a piece of paper. This twist is, owing to the force of the displacement of the equilibrium and the thrust of the foot, more easily perceived when walking rapidly and when the paces are relatively longer, so that clean footprints alone can permit of any conclusion as to speed being deduced from the fashion of the twist.

2. According to the manner of placing the foot, that is to say, the plant of the foot, commencing with the heel, it must be admitted that the back part of the heel gives the strongest impulsion in walking and ought in consequence to appear much more strongly impressed than the rest of the heel. Hence nearly all men of normal stature use chiefly the exterior and back part of the underneath part of the heel. *Brandt* of Landau has examined and measured a large number of boots and has found that 98% of all the soldiers examined walk in this way, while only 2% press more on the interior surface of the sole and the heel. This is important, for in a case where the last peculiarity is found it would be an almost conclusive sign by reason of its rarity. No doubt it must not be forgotten that M. *de Brandt* has only taken measurements of the boots of soldiers, that is to say, picked men with normal constitutions.

3. As the leg *A* begins to leave the ground while the leg *B* leans forward, the weight of the body hangs for a moment upon the ball of the big toe of the leg *A*, so that the foot digs in, so to speak, at that place. We have then therefore in the footprint two particularly deep spots, the posterior edge of the heel, by reason of the energetic thrust of this edge into the soil, and the ball of the big toe, by reason of the pressure which the body exercises upon it. As there exists for the rest of the sole of the foot no cause for any deeper impression the imprint ought to be in the form of an arch with a sort of elbow near the top as in *Fig. 49* (vertical dimensions exaggerated). The consequence is that the foot which has produced a print, for example in clay, would no longer enter, after the drying of the clay, exactly into the footprint, but on the other hand will remain a little raised up in the front part, if the weight be rested on the back portion, and *vice versâ* if the weight be thrown on the front.

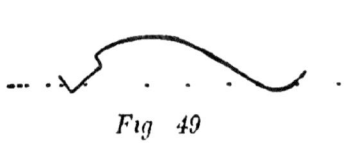
Fig. 49

4. Since the leg on leaving the ground exercises pressure through the ball of the big toe and that toe itself, this portion of the sole of the foot is that which produces on the ground and in the footprint the greatest displacement, so that in every footprint the inside portion of the front part of the foot presents an impression of the whole surface of contact from the moment when the foot was put down until the moment when it was lifted up. This part of the foot therefore appears larger in the footprint than it really is, and one would be tempted to believe that the whole of the anterior part of the foot should appear larger in the footprint than it is in reality. But it is not so, for at the moment of the displacement in question the exterior portion of the front of the foot is already on the point

of being raised up. In other terms the exterior edge of the front of the foot does not remain where it is first placed. It glides a little outwardly and only at that point produces the deepest impression, a circumstance which must not be forgotten when the foot or the shoe or boot is compared with the footprint.

5. The foot B at each pace at the last moment before leaving the soil gives a thrust in order to supply the leg with the spring required to carry it forward. This is particularly necessary in quick walking, in order to obtain stronger propulsion and when the ground is smooth and slippery in order to prevent sliding back. We find this characteristic among the footprints of people who are tall and strong or who carry burdens. As regards the former, because they walk more energetically than others and thus give a more energetic thrust, and as regards the latter because the leg carries a heavier load and ought in consequence to give a more violent thrust in order to give a better spring forwards. The consequence of this thrust is that the anterior edge of the sole (it is most distinct with booted feet) makes a deeper cut into the ground. If then the ground is firm enough to receive only strong impressions, two marks alone, in the form of an arch will be distinguished, the posterior edge of the heel Fig 50 and the anterior edge of the sole, the former as a notch or groove, the second by the thrust, so that one can only perceive two marks and the whole footprint must be completed by dots.

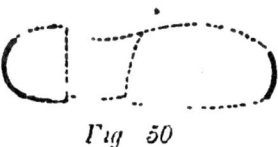

Fig 50

These marks are very frequent but often remain unnoticed by people who do not know what to make of them and do not take them to be footprints at all.

Doubtless one is not very far advanced when one has only discovered two marks of this kind, the more so as one has still to commence to prove that these marks form part of a footprint. But if one succeeds in obtaining these marks, the length of the foot is secured and one can make certain that the footprint comes from a person who walks quickly or carries a burden. Other circumstances will tell us which of these presumptions is accurate. The mark will come from a tall person if the distance between the two marks is considerable, that is to say, if the foot was large or if the distance from this point to the next one is great, that is to say, if the steps are long and consequently the legs are long. If the foot is long as well as the legs, one can presume with almost perfect certainty that the person was tall. The carrying of a burden may be recognised by a special disposition of the foot. But when one cannot come to the conclusion that the person was tall or that any burden was carried, one may conclude that he walked fast. No doubt a tall person or a person who carries a burden may walk fast, therefore we must always be careful to observe the "backward scrape," a peculiarity which is only produced by a person who, walking rapidly, gives with the leg B, or at least with the point of the foot of that leg, a strong thrust in order to obtain the impulse necessary to rapid walking. We can therefore always conclude that a person has walked quickly, on finding this "backward scrape," however slight the trace may be, and it is especially noticeable when new shoes have been worn, the soles of which are not yet worn down at the edges.

6. Distinctive marks are produced in sand, dirt and thick mud according to the manner of walking. The heel has at one and the same time a movement from above downwards and another from back to front, thus pushing before it the yielding soil. The heel also gives way a little at the spot where it was first thrust, that is to say, where it first touched the ground, so that the deepest impression of the heel is produced a little in front of the place where it was in reality made. The substance in the cavity thus formed yields, owing to its mobility, but in other directions than that into which it has been pressed by the heel, which, as we have said, gives a push downwards and forwards. This matter therefore is pushed forwards. But at the same moment the pressure of the anterior portion of the foot comes into play; this bears the load of the body, now inclining forward, but does not remain on the unstable foundation where it has first landed. It slips backwards, pushing with the same movement of recoil the displaced matter backwards. A footprint or impression of this kind will thus show two deep impressions—of the heel and of the balls of the toes and matter heaped up between these two, sand, slime, etc.—that pushed forward by the heel and that pushed backwards by the balls of the toes. The two deep impressions will correspond with the real distance between the heel and the ball, but will, owing to the slipping of the heel forwards and of the ball of the toes backwards, be nearer one another than in reality, that is, the footprint will be sensibly smaller than the foot which has produced it.

7. Tired, aged, infirm, or awkward persons are too feeble or unskilful to bend the leg B sufficiently at the knee, that is to say, to raise it up so that the anterior portion of the foot leaves the ground. If the ground be covered with sand, light snow, etc., the footprint of the leg B dragged along the ground will leave upon the snow, sand, etc., a trace more or less broken on one side the right-hand footprints and on the other the left-hand footprints. If one of these dragged impressions be found, one may deduce therefrom some of the peculiarities just mentioned. The sand, snow, &c. must not be too deep, for in this case the raising up of the foot to a sufficient height fatigues even robust persons who would also leave dragging impressions behind them.

These deductions give us two results; they may be formulated in a purely theoretical manner; although they may also be verified practically, it suffices not to lose sight of the scheme of *Fig. 18* and all the conclusions we have been able to draw therefrom. Many other deductions may then be made from this scheme by asking, in no matter what case, if a point still doubtful can be theoretically deduced therefrom. This will be a method of control for all the observations we think that we have made, so that we will never be in doubt, whether we have to deal with law or chance, when what we believe we have seen is verified by theory.

Another result flowing from these conclusions is that the deductions made are only relative; they can never be expressed by precited data and have only comparative value. It is impossible to give measurements or fixed sizes for the numerous factors—the size, the weight and the other corporeal singularities of the individual walking, his burden, his gait, and the variable nature of the soil—differ in every case and may be combined in so many diverse ways that it is absolutely impossible to give precise indications on this matter. Nothing else then remains to be done than to point out what the Investigating Officer ought to examine with particular attention. When he has found his bearings he will easily carry out the necessary verifications. But he ought never to neglect to do so, for he has only this means of discovering errors of observation and the falsity of his conclusions.

In the majority of cases these verifications offer no difficulty, for we have all the material necessary for the purpose—compact soil and a man able to move. Suppose, for example, that the Investigating Officer has found, in the muddy soil of the forest, a footprint which he supposes to have been made by a tall man walking quickly. He will find out on the same path a place presenting as far as possible the same conditions as the spot on which he discovered the original footprint. On this spot he will make a tall person walk rapidly and submit his footprints to a close scrutiny and that from two points of view. He will try to discover in the experimental footprint the distinctive signs of the original footprint from which he concluded that it was made by " a tall person walking quickly." This established, he will compare in the second place the experimental footprint with the foot of his subject; that is to say, he will take from both accurate measurements for the purposes of comparison. These measurements once obtained in one case he will try a second, third, and fourth experimental step, each time taking the measurements of the foot (or of the shoe) and of the footprint. In this way he will obtain absolutely accurate correspondences; for example, length of the shoe and the footprint equal; the extreme breadth of the footprint x millimetres greater than that of the shoe; the impression of the heel y millimetres narrower than the heel itself, etc. Having made a sufficient number of experiments and noted that the resemblances have remained fairly constant, he will be able to conclude boldly that the resemblances between the original footprint and the shoe which has produced it correspond to those which have been found between the experimental footprint and the experimental shoe, and he will be able to pass to the determination of the different measurements of the shoe or foot of the person who has produced the original footprint, taking this latter as the point of departure for his calculations. This is no doubt troublesome work, but it is the only way to furnish accurate indications and obtain really satisfactory results. If one has but one indistinct footprint and no clue therefrom, another must be searched for.

Suppose the Investigating Officer has only one of those quasi-footprints such as we have mentioned in sub-section No. 6 above; footprints in sand, composed of two depressions and in the middle a heap of sand. He knows theoretically that the foot which has produced this print is larger than the footprint itself; from the distance between the footprints he can deduce the length of the legs, and in consequence the height of the person who has produced the footprint. The Investigating Officer will also be able (see *post*) to discover whether the maker of the footprint has run or merely walked, whether his toes turn in or out, whether or not he was carrying a burden, in a word a sufficient number of points of departure to enable him to go on with his experiments. Following the result of his conclusions he will select a person to walk under conditions identical with those thus assumed, upon a similar base, modifying the data until the moment when the artificial footprint most resembles the original footprint. He must then proceed with several experiments of verification under the same conditions, and if the results remain constant he will be able, in spite of the likeness of the footprint, to suppose, for example, that he was a short person pointing his foot outwards, walking slowly and without carrying a heavy burden. Notes will naturally be taken with much care and precision of the dimensions of the sole of the foot of the subject experimented with, in order to conclude later as to whether the original footprint can have been produced by a particular foot. It is impossible to say more on this question, but these several indications all have their own importance and the results obtained will always be worth the trouble expended on experiments of this kind.

(b) Running

Running is essentially distinct from walking, in that here we have a movement where the feet are both in the air. Let us represent to ourselves the picture of a man whose speed is continuously accelerating, and we will note that the thrust which he gives with the leg B is more and more violent (see page 341, para 5) and that in consequence the interior edge of the sole makes a deeper and deeper cut. The steps always succeed one another more rapidly, the leg B receives, thanks to the stronger impulse, more and more way, and places itself further in advance, that is to say, the steps become longer. The length of the step is limited, partly by the length of the leg, partly by the tension of the muscles which would become fatigued if the step had always the longest possible length. Let us consider a person taking long strides, Fig. 51. We note that the joint of the pelvis or hip joint a descends till it reaches a position much lower than in ordinary walking, that is to say than the point a'. The hip joint and with it the whole body will therefore rise up at each step to a height equal to that which separates the point a from the point a'. When this distance is very considerable, that is to say when the legs are stretched very straight and the step has an exaggerated

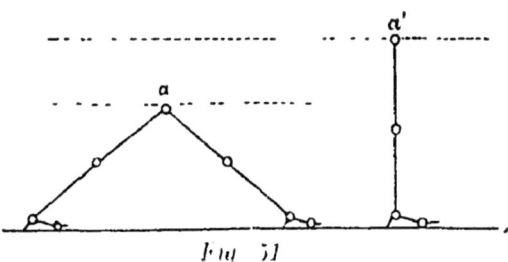

Fig. 51

length, this rising up of the body becomes in time very fatiguing, and not only is no strength and therefore speed gained by making too long strides, but that which is expended in raising up the body is lost. When one feels that the rapidity of the steps cannot be increased with advantage, and that their length will only produce more fatigue, the leg B is placed upon the ground more firmly in order to produce greater rapidity, so much impulse is produced that the body receives a push forward and the leg A does not fall at the spot where it would have fallen naturally, but comes down at a distance further in front proportionate to the force of the impulsion. *This distance is the gain obtained in running over the most rapid walking*, the more violent the impulse, the longer the body rests in the air, and the longer it rests in the air, the further it goes forward according to the laws of motion, and the foot comes to the ground again a proportionate space in advance. But this activity is not uniform, a fact which is of great importance with respect to the origin of footprints. The footprint differs according to the method of running, a fact again explained to us by the mechanism of walking and running. The leg A ought, for the reasons cited above (*second position*), to bend at the joint of the knee but ought to stretch again before being placed on the ground. This is necessary, on the one hand better to sustain the body which is leaning forwards, and, on the other hand, to gain more space, for the more the leg is lengthened at the knee the further in advance the foot comes to the ground. But this extension of the knee requires precisely the same amount of time which the leg takes to go forwards. To this must be added in running the extra time during which the body under the influence of the impulsion of the leg B is being impelled forwards. Then the more violent the impulsion the longer the duration of the impulse forwards and the longer the leg A takes to straighten out and gain space.

As regards the tarsus or ankle joint, it is bound to the leg by tendons and muscles in such a way that one maintains the other without constraint, forming a right angle, and, as *Fig. 52* proves, the leg must, when not stretched out, touch the ground at the ball of the big toe, and when stretched out at the heel.

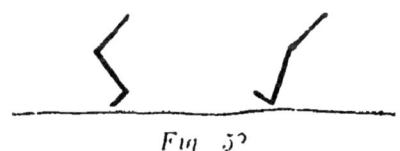

Fig. 52

Therefore, if the thrust is feeble the carry forward is short, the stride is small, and the foot comes to the ground on the ball of the toes; if the thrust is great the carry forward is long, the stride is more considerable, and the foot comes to the ground upon the heel. In the former case, that of the gymnastic step, the running is slow and the footprint shows but a feeble thrust of B, a fairly strong impression of the ball of A, and an impression of a feebler nature of the heel of A. In the second case the running is rapid and the footprint reveals a violent thrust of B, a fairly feeble impression of the ball of the toe of A, and a very strong impression of the heel of A. One may then conclude from the length of the step, the force of the impression of the anterior edge of the sole, and from the depth of the impression of the ball of the toe, compared with the depth of the impression of the heel, that there has been running, and also whether that running has been rapid or slow.

It must be admitted that other views have been put forward. *Schauenstein* for example says: "In running the impression of the heel is deeper than that of the ball of the toe," and *Zenker* says: "The runner always alights upon the heel." The author believes that the theoretical considerations just discussed and which every person in running may at any moment verify by practice, show that the statements of *Schauenstein* and *Zenker* only apply to rapid running. What has just been said has its practical application as is proved by what every gymnastic teacher tells his scholars. He gives them the following advice:—"In long distance running place first the ball of the big toe and in speed running the heel." This is not the way he actually puts it, for in reality he generally says: 'In a long distance race one must run slowly, in a sprint one must run as quickly as possible.'" Alighting on the ball of the toe is, indeed, only the result of the slowness of the running just as alighting on the heel is the result of the rapidity of the running. But to render the matter more comprehensible, they are in the habit of indicating not the cause but the effect.

(2) The "trace" itself

The word "trace" is used to express two distinct notions: firstly, it means the whole series of continued impressions or the "trail" or spoor, and secondly, it means each separate footprint. The first of these meanings is that given to the word by sportsmen, who speak of straight, hesitating, dragging, or crossing trails—expressions which naturally indicate connection between the various impressions of the foot; the second notion is that usually attaching to the word, viz., "the mark of a foot." In considering the first notion we arrive at the "walking image," and in considering the second at the "image of the foot."

(a) The walking image

We understand by this the whole series of impressions left by a person walking upon soil capable of receiving them.

H. Mayer was the first to split up the image of walking into its different lines. If we pick out the lines most important to our subject we find—

(α) The line of direction

That is to say, the line indicating the direction in which the pedestrian is advancing $a\ a$, $a'\ a'$, $a''\ a''$ (Fig 53)

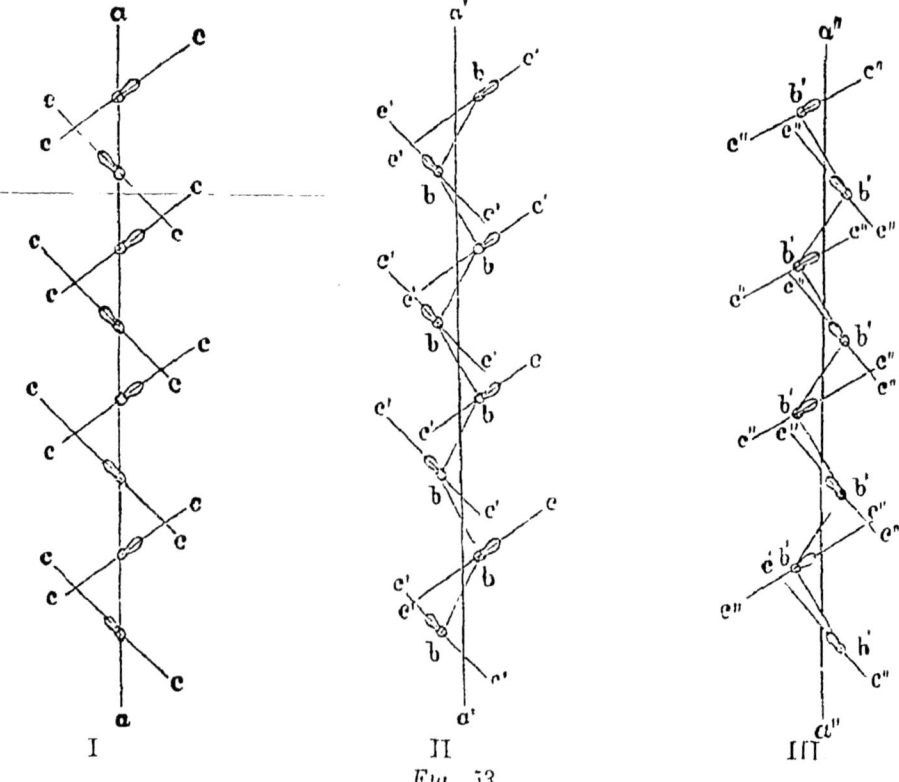

Fig 53

(β) *The line of march*

That is to say, the line uniting the centre of the heels of the various footprints. A person with a normal walk places the feet exactly one before the other, in which case the directing line is identical with the line of march. In *Fig. 53. I.*, the line *a a* represents both the directing line and the line of march. If the heels of the pedestrian do not touch the directing line but the right foot remains on the right and the left foot on the left of it, the line of march is a broken line (*b b* in *Fig. 53. II.*), and the walk is spreadeagled, loose, and awkward. Since, geometrically, the line joining two points is greater when it is broken than when it is straight, it follows that the distance to be covered must be greater when the line of march is broken than when it is straight. Moreover, a certain locomotive energy is employed to produce the right and left movement which must be subtracted from the force which produces the forward movement; on the other hand the surface touched and occupied by the feet in the case of II. is much greater than in the case of I. The base on which the pedestrian rests is therefore greater and gives more security, and we ought to conclude that the walk indicated in II. is that of persons who, for the sake of security, refrain from walking rapidly. This manner of walking is that of sailors, who get it by habit, aged and obese persons, women who are enceinte, and finally all who, owing to some illness or other, cannot easily put one leg before the other, and get out of the difficulty by waddling along, *e.g.*, people with hernia, gout, etc.

The converse of this picture is produced when the right foot crosses to the left and the left to the right of the directing line. In this case also a broken line is the result, *b′ b′* (*Fig. 53, III.*), which differs from the line of march II. in that in the former each footprint is inside the angle of the broken line and in the latter outside it. This "crossed" trail is rare and is peculiar to loiterers, phlegmatic and drunken persons, who sway from side to side when walking.

(γ) *The line of the foot*

So we term the straight line forming the longitudinal axis of the sole of the foot, with reference to the directing line, *Fig. 53, c c, c′ c′, c″ c″*. The angle formed by the line of direction and the line of the foot is called the angle of the foot. It expresses what we call walking with the toes of the foot turned in or out. To characterise a person it is necessary to know if he points his toes inwards or outwards so that it is important to clear up this question when footprints are discovered. But precise facts concerning the angle of the foot can only be obtained when we have before us a whole series of footprints. In case of need a few conclusions may be hazarded when we have at least two or three footprints to work with. We may state as follows about the angle of the foot. We have naturally our feet much turned in, for new-born children have the ankles crossed, so that, if they could stand up upon their legs, the toes of the right foot would incline towards the left and those of the left foot towards the right.

It is remarkable that in many books the same thing is stated to take place with grown-up people who have been suspended by the top part of the body and whose legs have been left swinging freely. It is said that in this position the feet are also crossed the ankles and not the legs, that is to say, the sole of the right foot rests on the ankle of the left foot, the heels being turned outwards and the toes inwards. The author has made this experiment with several persons and has had it performed by two gymnastic instructors with nearly a hundred of their pupils who were not told what it was all about, not one crossed the feet when suspended, e g from rings which allowed the body to hang freely. They all kept their feet either straight or turned slightly outwards, and, curiously enough, one of the feet was almost always more turned out than the other.

It may, therefore, be said that man, doubtless in consequence of the position of the fœtus in the body of the mother, has at first a tendency to cross the feet which disappears under the influence of normal circumstances and ought no longer to be considered natural. As regards the position of the feet in after life it depends upon diverse circumstances. Here natural dispositions must certainly be placed in the forefront. Also the whole structure of the legs, the shape of the joints and especially the joints of the pelvis, influence the position of the feet. It may be noted as to persons who turn out one foot more than another, that this is very common with females and especially with young girls who are not yet entirely developed. They state that they experience difficulty and even pain in the hip-joints when they try to turn outwards to an extent equivalent to the other, the foot which they usually point inwards.

The structure of the foot is of the same importance and we see, e g , persons with flat feet constantly walking with their feet much turned out because the weakness of the tendons renders this position more comfortable than another. It may also be said that habit goes for much in the formation of the angle of the foot. This refers both to voluntary habit which consists in making every effort to acquire a good style of walking with the feet turned out as children are always told to do, and also to habit resulting from the force of circumstances.

The angle of the foot is none the less of importance in forward walking The structure of the knee joint and the ankle joint is such that they bend comfortably only in one direction. If these joints bend at the same time the toes, heel, and knee rest in the same vertical plane, or in other words, if the knee and ankle have been bent naturally a perpendicular dropped from the knee to the ground will pass through the toes and not to the left or right of them. In walking, a bending of these two joints takes place, and, in accordance with their structure, the whole body takes a direction perpendicular to the axis of these joints and preserves this direction when in movement. The body will therefore receive at each step an impulsion in the direction indicated by the longitudinal axis of the sole of the foot touching the ground thus if the feet be straight, the movement will be forward if the feet be turned outwards the movement will be to the right and the left see Fig 54

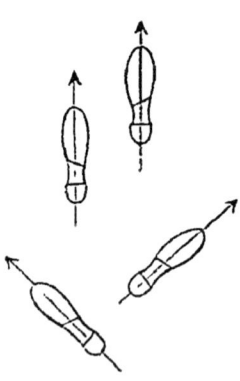
Fig 54

Now in walking, the only object is to *advance* in the direction in which we desire to go, hence the propulsion or forward push given by the foot will have its *maximum* value, i.e. will carry us farthest forward when the feet are straight, in this case the directions of the advance and the propulsion are identical. But when the feet are turned outwards or inwards, a portion of this propulsive force is wasted in carrying the body to the left or right of the path, while the remainder alone becomes effective in carrying the body forward. The more the foot is turned outwards— that is, the greater the angle between the line of the foot and the line of march—the greater the waste of propulsive force. Stated scientifically, only the component of the force resolved along the line of march is effective, the component at right angles thereto is wasted. One can, therefore, tell at a distance of a person whose feet cannot be seen, whether he or she be walking with the feet straight or turned out, for the bodies of those who walk in the latter fashion make a movement at each step to the right or left in the direction of the longitudinal axis of the sole of the foot. This movement only retards progress, and no one who places the feet straight need make it. One advances less rapidly when turning out the toes, every-one feels this instinctively. Thus people who work and have neither time nor energy to waste, who have in fact to get on, put down their feet straight, while a person who has plenty of time before him, who can arrive a little later at his destination, who considers walking to be an exercise for the body and walks for that purpose, and to whom the extra energy expended in going to the right and to the left does not matter, turns his feet outwards. Besides, this style is considered to be the most beautiful. We thus come to an important conclusion. Straight footprints generally belong to members of the working classes, those turned outwards to individuals of a better class. We say "generally," for this is only an "indication" and not an absolute certainty.

It may in general be laid down that the angle of the foot remains almost constant for the same person, so that we may conclude with fair certainty that a footprint turned outwards is that of an individual who habitually walks turning the foot outwards at a corresponding angle. But many circumstances may influence walking. The simple fact of thinking or speaking about it is sufficient to make a person place his foot otherwise than he usually does. To this may be added all manner of exterior influences: the wearer of tight or unaccustomed shoes, will not remain faithful to his natural angle, but will put down his foot so as to avoid as much as possible the discomfort of the shoe. A man ascending or descending smooth or slippery ground will keep his feet straight even when he is in the habit of turning them outwards, for in this way he is opposed to the direction of slipping and less in danger of falling. People who carry heavy burdens have other motives for walking with straight feet. Every oscillation of the centre of gravity must be disagreeable if not dangerous to them, for, in carrying burdens, the centre of gravity is raised and may easily fall outside the polygon of sustentation, carrying the bearer with it in its fall. Moreover, the bearer of a burden is not in a condition to easily correct at will the oscillation produced by the displacement of the leg, for his legs are by reason of their load less mobile and less obedient. He will, consequently, endeavour by all the means in his power to avoid this oscillation to left and right and will not point out his toes. When, therefore, we discover that a trail has suddenly altered as regards the angle of the foot, if there be no other possible explanation, we may presume that the person leaving the footprints was burdened and has laid the burden down. If, for example, the footprints of the thief when he has arrived at the house turn outwards, and when he has gone away are straight, it is very probable that he has carried a heavy burden. If a person's footprints turn inwards and then outwards, it is because he has laid down his burden or handed it over to someone else, etc.

There is yet another reason why people who are enceinte or obese walk with the toes turned out. As has already been said above in speaking of the line of march (*Fig. 53, II.*) these persons have a walk which is spread-eagled, loose, and awkward, in fact they waddle. They oscillate with their line of march broken to the right and to the left, and when they accentuate this movement by turning the toes outwards, there is produced what already existed in the tendency of their walking, then walking with the toes out can only favour their mode of progression. It is very remarkable that everyone, even those who walk with the toes turned outwards, places the feet straighter when walking barefoot, running or walking upon the toes. The first of these peculiarities is difficult to explain. The reason no doubt is that the outside edge of the sole of the foot is much less sensitive than the inside edge. In walking with the toes turned out the interior edge of the foot touches the ground more firmly, whereas, if the feet are kept straight the walking is effectuated almost entirely upon the outside border. Therefore, when the foot is not protected by a boot or shoe, one instinctively walks upon the least sensitive part. The fact that in running, or walking upon the toes the feet do not point outwards is no doubt explained by the fact that in this case the heels are more raised and rub against one another, which is avoided by keeping the feet straight and thus the heels more apart. In running we must also take into account the peculiarity mentioned above, namely, that walking with the feet turned out does not favour the forward movement. As in running quick progression is the aim in view, we instinctively choose that position of the feet most favourable in this respect.

Footprints turning inwards betray crossed or twisted legs, their origin being abnormal it follows that they are rare. The body is obliged to follow the sole of the foot which is placed on the ground and the result is that the body makes a very pronounced movement to one side, a movement which is both peculiar and characteristic but difficult to describe. Persons afflicted with *scoliose*, that is to say, who have a deviation of the vertebral column, owing to unequal weighting on the pelvis, should have unequal angles of the foot. But as a general rule they at length accustom themselves to place the lines of their feet symmetrically, so that inequalities in those angles are only found after very accurate measurement.

(b) The length of the step.

This is the distance of one footprint from the next, measured from the middle of the heel of the one to the middle of the heel of the other. This distance depends upon the height of the person, the rapidity of the walk, and also upon habit. *Drs. Beely & Kirchhoff* maintain that the force of the big toe also exercises an important influence upon the length of pace, and *Totsch* makes it depend upon the mobility of the big toe. As a general rule it may be said that, of two equally agile men the taller has the longer step, and it may be presumed that, of two parallel trails, the footprint occurring more frequently in the same distance belongs to the shorter person, and that occurring less frequently to the taller person — presuming the two have walked together at the same speed. This supposition is corroborated when the longest interval between the footprints corresponds with the largest feet. It will never, of course, be absolutely certain since, as has been stated, other circumstances must sometimes be taken into account. Old people, invalids, people afflicted with hernia and other infirmities of the lower part of the stomach, take short steps although of tall stature. Moreover people who are in the habit of walking with precaution, habitually take short steps for long steps would lead them into uncertainty or, so to speak, the invisible. It is for this reason sportsmen sometimes take short steps, for long ones might easily cause them to walk upon dried leaves or branches, which it is often indispensable to avoid. Long steps are met with among soldiers who have been for years in the army, surveyors, and especially railway employés. These latter are often obliged to walk upon the permanent way and they prefer to walk upon the sleepers, which are not as a rule quite covered with ballast rather than upon the ballast itself. But as the distance which separates these sleepers everywhere exceeds the length of the ordinary pace, they get into the habit of taking extraordinarily long steps.

For a person walking at the same speed, the length of pace, as a rule, remains the same. If differences exist in normally constituted persons they are due to outside circumstances; the walker wishes, for example, to avoid a stone or puddle, etc.,* or perhaps he has looked back while walking and so shortened his step.

The length of pace varies from 50 to 100 cms. (20 to 40 in.), the average length may be taken, for the slow walk of people out for a stroll, 70 cms. (28 in.), for the average pace of business men 80 cms. (32 in.), for an accelerated pace like that of messengers 90 cms. (36 in.). To take longer steps is not economical and it may be presumed at the outset that a pace of a hundred cms. (40 in.) is only attained in running. A running pace of two metres (6½ feet) is rarely met with.

In the higher technical schools of Karlsruhe (Baden) and of Hanover important experiments have been made in later years upon the length of the steps of adults. The following observations have been made. Different persons were set to walk along a road, covering distances from 200 to 300 metres (220 to 330 yards). The shortest pace measured 67 cms. (say 26 in.) the longest 97 cms. (39 in.). A pace of 78 cms. (31 in.) was the most frequent. Paces of more than 87 cms. (34 in.) and less than 76 cms. (30 in.) were rare. The mean of all these observations gave 80 cms. (32 in.) as the length of a pace. One may therefore in measuring a road calculate the distance with sufficient accuracy by counting the paces. We also know the ground covered by the German infantry at a fixed pace of 80 cms. (formerly 75 cms.) by reason of 112 paces (formerly 108) going to the minute.† The pace diminishes with age. A man of 40 years old hardly

---

* This may be important in determining whether the person in question has passed the spot only after a shower of rain.
† This is approximately 100 yards a minute.

takes any other pace than that of about 30 inches while a man of the same height but 30 years of age takes paces of from 32 to 33 inches.

If these irregularities in pace are not due to exterior circumstances, as a rule easily discovered, we may conclude that they are due to something abnormal about the person walking. If, for instance, it is found that the length of the pace is unequal, that is to say, that the paces of the right leg followed by the left leg are equal to one another, but smaller than those of the left leg followed by the right leg, which latter are also equal to one another, it may be presumed that the person walking limps, either habitually or by accident due to some wound to the foot. The healthy leg makes the longest pace and the leg which is feeble, short, or wounded, the shortest, for it has to be humoured. To know which leg limps *the longest pace* has to be sought from the whole system of walking: the footprint in front of this pace comes from the sound foot, the one behind from the bad foot. As a general rule one will also find in this case a difference between the right and left footprints. If the foot be deformed a difference in the impressions results. If the leg is unhealthy, the impressions of the two feet are similar in shape but they none the less differ by reason of the manner in which they are produced: the anterior portion of the foot or the posterior portion, the inside or the outside, etc., leaves an impression different to that of the other foot. In this case it is for the medical man to decide, if he can, what has caused the phenomenon. The Investigating Officer ought to observe and note that the footprints present differences. The cause of the difference it is the business of medical jurisprudents to establish.

Yet other differences may be present. As has been said, in lameness the step of the diseased foot is shorter than that of the sound foot, but the distances between the impressions of the right foot on one side and the left foot on the other remain equal. We have also seen above that in bandy-legged and cross-legged persons the line of march is broken, but the joining lines which pass through the centre of the right heels and those which pass through the centre of the left heels are none the less straight. But if the distances between each of the impressions of the right foot and each of the impressions of the left foot are different, and if the lines joining the right heels and those joining the left heels form an irregular zig-zag, it is because the central organ of the apparatus of locomotion is defective and the footprint belongs without doubt to one who suffers from brain or spine disease: he is a paralytic, inebriate, giddy, or badly wounded person. Such footprints ought of course to be attentively examined, and it is best either to show them to the medical man *in naturâ* or else measure them with the greatest accuracy and remove them. The explanations of the medical man will then be listened to and in many cases he will even be able to tell under what influence the brain has acted; whether the footprints belong to a chronic invalid, a drunkard, or a wounded person, etc.

Other kinds of walking

Besides ordinary walking we have also special kinds of walking which may in favourable circumstances be easily determined and which often furnish important information affecting the elucidation of a case. It is for example easy to recognise a stoppage, for the hind foot is then drawn forward and forms a second impression beside the other. It may even be guessed approximately whether the stoppage has been short or prolonged for in the latter case frequent goings and comings and changes of the stationary position will be observed while in the former case the regular alternation of the steps to the right and the left is interrupted by two footprints beside one another and then the walker starts off again usually with the foot with which he has taken the last step. It is equally easy to tell if there has been a literal jump, stepping aside, slow walking, or several steps made running, and numerous other similar variations from ordinary walking. These should never be allowed to pass unperceived and they must always be carefully noted down, for their importance, which may be considerable, often does not make itself manifest till later.

A person may have been forced to walk backwards or may have done so with the intention of causing confusion. The proof of a fact of this kind has always its own importance for persons never try to deceive others without serious reasons. If one knows that the walking backwards was done intentionally by the walker, the reason for his doing so must be found and, this once ascertained, the whole history of the case, the motive for the act, or some other important fact will be laid bare. The footprints will nearly always tell us whether a person has really been walking backwards. In backward walking the steps are shorter, for our muscles are not accustomed to this kind of locomotion, the directing line is, for the same reason and also because we do not know where we are going, hesitating and uncertain, the impressions present besides a quite distinctive digging of the toe, when the individual in question is forced to take relatively long paces, for to do so he must commence by planting the point of the sole in the ground and then drawing or pushing the foot. If the Investigating Officer suspects that an individual walking backwards has produced a suspicious footprint, he should himself do the same thing upon similar ground, taking backward paces of the same length and then comparing the impressions, it is hardly possible to make a mistake.

It sometimes happens that simulated or dissimulated footprints are found. These are produced when a criminal attempts to indicate a false direction and the length of the road he has to traverse hardly allows him to walk backwards—when, for example, a case of murder is sought to be passed off as one of suicide, or a case of suicide as one of murder (e.g., with persons who have insured their lives). In the first case there will be noticed the footprints of but *one man*, while in the latter there will appear the footprints of *several*, although in reality the facts are quite the contrary. This is done by tying to the feet shoes placed the wrong way round, but an attentive examination nearly always permits the discovery of this. The author of the crime always commits in such a case the fault of choosing soil upon which the footprints may be cleanly impressed and have a good appearance, so that they will not fail to attract the attention and induce the desired interpretation. But when the footprints are clean they are easy to study and one soon discovers that they are unnatural and have not the same appearance as other footprints. It is difficult to explain, but one will immediately recognise from an examination of the footprint that the weight producing it has had something abnormal about it. Here again experiment will clear up everything. The Investigating Officer will make trial alongside the suspicious footprints with shoes of the same size, but worn naturally, and he will immediately notice the difference between the true and the false. Moreover, in all cases of this kind, if the operation has not been performed with care, the impression of the strap used to tie the shoe on backward, and which passes as a rule round the foot a little in front of the heel, will be discovered.

The criminal may also have intended to cast suspicion upon another person, especially if he foresees in advance that suspicion will fall upon himself. In this case also he produces clear footprints which, so to speak, leap to the eyes, either by wearing shoes which differ essentially from his own and which he subsequently destroys, or by tying to his feet the shoes of another person. The former system is employed by those who have small feet and wish to produce large footprints, the latter by those who have large feet and wish to produce small footprints. A tall man who fastens to his feet the shoes of a woman may very well cause it to be believed that the criminal is a woman, and, *per contra*, a woman who puts on the large shoes of a man that it was a man who committed the crime. One may often in this way, as has been proved by numerous experiments, produce footprints which deceive perfectly.

The discovery of such trickery is difficult but not impossible. An excellent method will be to compare the size of the impression with that of the step. The criminal, who is generally in an agitated state of mind, easily forgets that, as a general rule, big feet have long legs, and in consequence make long paces, whereas little dainty feet make short paces. If this false proportion be discovered, suspicion will take shape and the investigation be continued in this direction. If the suspicion be well founded, some irregularities will soon come to light: the line of march becomes unsteady, the step seems hesitating and uncertain, and when the shoes are too big, dragging and heavy, and this is clearly seen from the impressions. When a little shoe has been arranged under a large one, not only the impression of the strap which fixes it may be perceived, but often also, and especially when the subsoil is deep (mud, snow, etc.), that of certain parts of the large foot overlapping the small shoe. However difficult it may be to establish this proof, it is worth the trouble of the attempt. Indeed, by procuring conclusive proof of the falsification of footprints the criminal is more or less surely designated, and on the other hand the innocence of individuals suspected owing to the false impression is not slow to see the light of day. Footprints fabricated in this way are met with only in novels.

(b) The image of the foot

In accurately representing the manner in which a footprint is produced, the procedure above described must be followed, that is to say, we must colour the sole of our own bare foot by placing it on a mixture of some colouring matter, water and gum arabic, and then walk upon paper stretched on the ground. Careful examination of footprints produced in this way will inform us not only about the real image of the bare foot but also about the impression and the mark of the foot, bare or booted. If, after having *once* coloured the sole of the foot, the operator walks several times upon the paper so that, for example, three images of the foot having different intensities of colour may be compared, he will notice

THE IMAGE OF THE FOOT

at once that each particular impression presents in itself an infinity of tints, although the sole of the foot has been covered all over with a uniform coating of colour. The reason is that, on the one hand, the sole of the foot is not a united and flat surface, but on the contrary is unequally modelled, and in the second place the pressure exerted by the body upon that surface is very unequal and shifts upon the surface weighted during the movement of the body.

If now we consider the manner in which the colouring matter behaves during walking, that is, the colouring matter pressed between the paper and the sole of the foot, it will be seen that the damp and slippery matter has yielded at those places where it has been most pressed, in other words, that the sole of the foot at the place where it is most weighted comes on to the paper and drives back the colouring matter. It is then those places where the colouring matter is thus most compressed that will be the clearest, and the lighter the weight exerted on a part of the sole the deeper will be the image produced at that place. Let us consider now the images of *one and the same foot once coloured and impressed three times while walking*. We at once note that less and less colouring matter remains for use and that, as has been stated, each isolated impression shows a different coloration owing to the difference in pressure. One cannot well see on a single impression where and how the pressure is exercised, the whole three must be examined. We will consider them successively. See *Fig* 55 I, II, III.

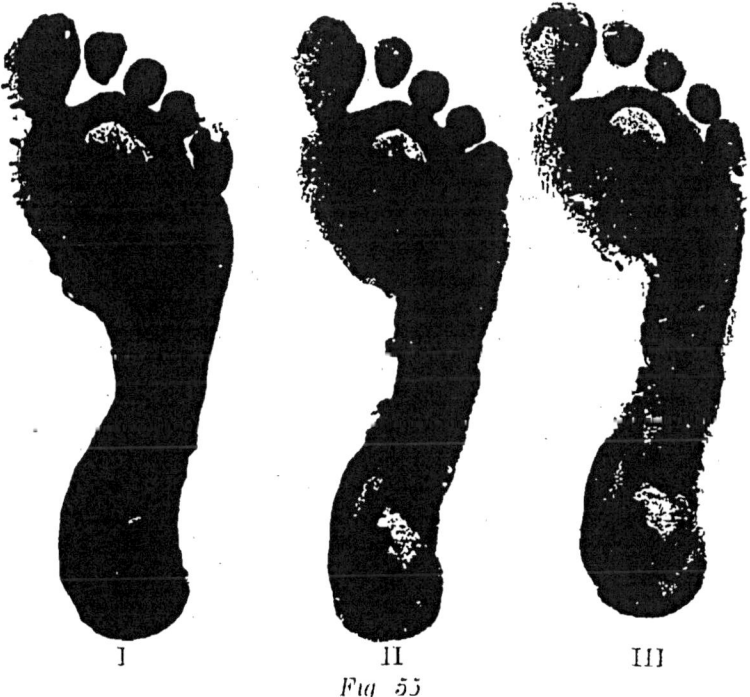

I II III
Fig 55

Impression I.—The lightest place and in consequence the most heavily weighted is that situated between the two eminences of the big and the little toes, underneath the three other toes. The next lightest place is near the heel, towards the outside edge of the sole of the foot. It is like the first clearly circumscribed and at its inside border, exactly below the prolongation of the thigh bone perpendicular to the foot, there is a particularly clear place. The body then principally rests upon these two spots, behind the three middle toes and in front of the edge of the heel. The next lightest places are the inside border of the big toe, continuing towards the inside border of its eminence, then the outside border of the eminence of the big toe, and the middles of the toes themselves, in particular of the big and the little toe. One or more of these places thus serve to form an auxiliary or third support for the body which would not find a stable base on the two most important points just mentioned. Everyone is not in agreement about this, but we believe that the illustrations speak for themselves.

Impression II.—The principal mass of the colour remains upon *Impression I*. What was superfluous has gone and we now obtain a good result from which it may be clearly seen what parts of the sole of the foot chiefly bear the weight of the body. We distinguish on this impression (the effect cannot be seen so distinctly upon our reduced reproduction as upon the original impression) two kinds of colouring perfectly separate and distinct, the one dark and regular as if made with a small paint brush, the other having lines more finely and more irregularly drawn, exactly as if one had taken some printer's ink or other thick colouring matter upon the point of the finger and then pressed it firmly down; in fact it is a *footprint* in the same sense as a finger-print. The former places are those more feebly charged, the latter more strongly; for the latter imprint is produced when the foot is taken away after strong pressure. The places most charged (mentioned in I.) have hardly any more colouring matter left, and the paper presents almost its natural appearance. Among the parts feebly charged there are: the exterior edge of the big toe, the entire edge of the other toes, as far as the place where, by virtue of the convex shape of the toes, a lesser charge commences. Next, a clearly delimited line, running obliquely under the toes, as far as the place most charged referred to above; then the whole of the interior edge of the sole of the foot as far as the heel and the furthest back portion of the posterior part of the heel. At the same time we see from the manner in which the colouring matter has yielded and the formation of the little so called veins, that the general direction of the pressure has been from the exterior towards the interior, then from the heel forwards, and from the front portion backwards on to the ball of the big toe, that is to say the foot has been placed down commencing with the heel and has pushed forward the colouring matter situated at the back. The exterior edge of the sole of the foot has touched the ground almost at the same time and has chased the colouring matter inwards, while the ball of the big toe on leaving the ground has repulsed backwards the colouring matter beneath it.

Impression III.—The last of these three impressions only points out more distinctly what is already noticeable in *Impression II.* It is easily seen what a heavy weight rests on the parts situated towards the forepart of the heel and the ball of the big toe, since the paper remains almost as free from colour as the interior edge of the big toe. Here the colouring substance has already been driven away. The direction in which it has been pushed back is clearly indicated by the projecting veins, and it is at length possible to understand the effect of this species of bridge between the heavily-weighted place in front of one side of the ball and the neighbouring part of the toes on the other side, since the little veins are beginning to show. This bridge serves to join together the place heavily weighted and the toes, since it is not heavily weighted, it allows the foot to pass at each propulsion from the ball on to the toes without propelling the whole weight forwards.

The lessons to be drawn from these deductions are self-evident; it is only when one understands how a footprint is produced, that is to say, the mechanical procedure, visible at each step under normal conditions, that one can understand and utilise different footprints or series of footprints produced under either normal or abnormal conditions, without being obliged to designate at every moment a footprint as being "quite enigmatical and non-utilisable." It is naturally impossible for us to discover every imaginable case. Suffice it to say that when one is acquainted with the process of walking one also knows if there has been an obstacle and if so, the nature of that obstacle in the crystallization if we may be permitted to use the expression of the footprint, if the line of walk has undergone an intentional or unintentional deviation, if slips should be attributed to the nature of the ground or a jump which has been misjudged, whether a burden has been carried or whether dissimulation has been practised, and slowness or sudden rapidity produced etc. The question of the method of production is of particular importance when we have to deal with an impression so defective that we cannot tell whether it is merely a feature of the ground or a footprint. In this examination the order in which the different parts of the sole of the foot touch the ground and which is the portion most heavily, and the portion most lightly, weighted, should never be lost sight of. In this way the smallest inequalities in the ground and the faintest impressions will be dealt with, and it will be easy to establish whether one is in the presence of a partial impression of a foot or only of an accidental inequality in the ground. It will even be possible in many cases to reconstitute an entire footprint from one of these faint inequalities. This is especially important when a series of impressions passes along favourable ground, then on to a soil so hard or so soft that one no longer perceives more than small parts of the impression, and when it is necessary to continue to follow defective traces such as these until they again become more distinct. It is always indispensable in such a case to pay attention to the mode of production of the impressions, for upon that all our work hangs.

D Measurements to be taken.

We would first call attention to certain details connected with the manner in which footprints should be measured and compared. Much prudence must here be exercised and nothing undertaken which shows no chance of success. On the one hand the foot itself varies considerably e.g., it is much smaller in cold weather or after a long rest than during hot weather or after a long march; on the other hand it is difficult to measure, inasmuch as it is not a regular body and must be measured differently according to the parts dealt with.

Zenker says that the foot in repose differs half a centimetre and upwards from the foot in activity owing to the weight upon it. This may very well be in theory, but the author has found it impossible of verification. An ordinary shoemaker's measure is evidently of little value here since absolute accuracy is necessary and 5 mill. is a very little thing, hardly the thickness of a medium sized goose quill, and as the dimensions of the foot can only be measured by dropping perpendiculars. If this latter operation is not absolutely exact, if the square employed presses on the foot more or less strongly, or if it accidentally touches a fresh spot, a difference of more than a half centimetre may result.

It is the same with the comparison of footprints in the walking and the stationary position. It is frequently stated as by *Beely & Kirchhoff*, that a footprint produced in walking is smaller than one produced when the foot is simply placed upon paper. The author has never been able to verify this in spite of numerous experiments, on the contrary the footprints produced in walking often appear much larger than those produced in the stationary position. The quantity of colouring matter, the nature of the ground and its surface, united or unequal as it may be, the manner of posing the foot etc. are all different factors, and it is in them that the causes of the more or less considerable differences in the dimensions of a footprint are to be found.

Now everything that applies to the foot in general also applies to its various parts, especially to the toes. *Masson* says, for example, that the impression of the four little toes of the foot in the stationary position is round, in walking slightly oblong; that the impression of the big toe in the stationary position is like that shown in *Fig. 56*, I, and in walking like that shown in *Fig. 56* II. All this is certainly inaccurate. We do not doubt that *Masson* really saw what he tells us. But if he had repeated the experiment twenty times em-

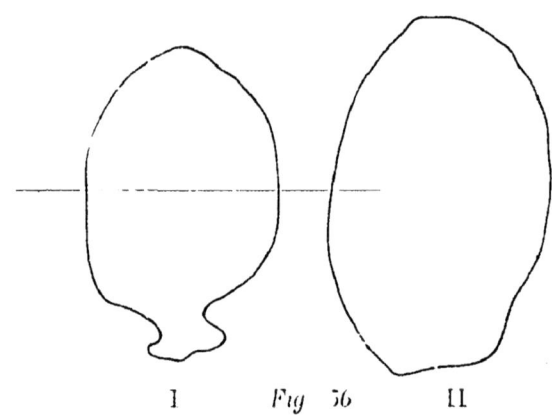

Fig 56   I   II

ploying each time more or less colour on different surfaces and with different individuals, he would have seen that the impressions of the toes of the foot are often round in walking and somewhat oblong in the stationary position, and that the shapes I and II of the big toe are to be found indifferently in the stationary position and in walking. The impression of the big toe depends upon its shape, for the weight varies precisely with that shape. The shape called "antique," where the big toe is shorter than the second toe is often met with, not only in statues, but in children and persons who go barefoot. But this is not a rule, and one often sees persons who go barefoot having the big toe longer than the second. On the other hand we meet other persons who never go barefoot whose big toe is quite classical in shape. This may be observed especially among women wearing very tight-fitting shoes which yet give easily and yet are quite simple. The same may be said of the direction of the big toe. Its longitudinal axis should correspond with the longitudinal axis of the sole of the foot. It generally however forms an obtuse angle with the exterior edge of the foot, so that the big toe seems pressed against the other toes. Badly fitting footwear is generally the cause. Yet this formation is also to be found among persons who work barefoot in soft ground. It must not be forgotten, moreover, that people who go barefoot in summer often wear during the rest of the year boots which do not fit them and injure the feet.

In comparing the impressions with one another, it is important to place the foot or boot in question, anointed with a quantity of the colouring matter approximately equal to that of the original, upon the same surface as the latter, and then to draw one's conclusions from the impression as a whole, in general and in particular, and to measure only where perfectly certain and sure starting points are to be found.

It is the same with the impressions of booted feet. We have already seen (Fig. 19) that in certain cases the curve of the sole in the impression is quite different from what it is in the boot itself. Other important modifications are also to be met with when the foot has slipped backwards or forwards or to the right or to the left, thus producing unfortunate disfigurations.

Often it is easy to perceive slipping but sometimes the reverse is the case. It may happen that the foot has slipped not only backwards or forwards but also to the side, unfortunately, one of the two surfaces of slipping may not be distinct and may pass unperceived and thus easily conduce to error. Suppose for example the forward slipping to be very visible and the slipping to the left side to be indistinct. The longitudinal axis need not be measured as it would give no guarantee, and it would be a mistake to measure minutely the dimensions of breadth and consider them as accurate, for they would of necessity also lead to erroneous conclusions. One cannot then examine with too much attention the question of whether slipping has or has not taken place, and when the nature of the ground causes us to admit the possibility of the former alternative, it must never be lost to view.

If in the case of bare feet it is the whole impression, or as we have called it the physiognomy, which ought to be chiefly regarded, with booted feet it is the details which are important, the nails, the edges, patches, etc., these must always be observed with the greatest accuracy. Not only their number and shape must be accurately determined, but also the distances between them must be indicated with care, for these distances do not vary even in the case of slipping. The nails and the soles may in cases of this kind lead not only to valuable conclusions but also to the most fatal errors, when their number is not the same in the impression and the original. It may happen, for example, that one of the nails of the shoe has come against an almost invisible stone or other resisting object on the ground and cannot therefore leave any mark in the impression. In this case it would be a false conclusion to presume that at the moment when the impression was produced a nail was missing at the part of the sole in question. Moreover, a nail may have been lost or replaced after the production of the impression, so that in the former case we would find in the sole a nail less in the latter a nail more. The same applies to patches which have been added or lost. In a word there a number of important points which may arise in the future and which require those minute examinations to be carried out at the time.

It is often difficult to estimate whether a nail is new or not. In many cases the microscopist will aid the Investigating Officer by examining the head of the nail in comparison with other nails to find out its stage of use, its point, the amount of rust, etc. In urgent cases the Investigating Officer should never neglect at least to examine for himself with a magnifying glass the heads of the nails and to take the advice of an intelligent shoe-maker.

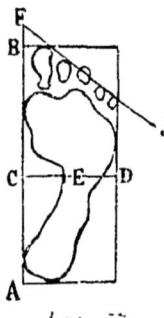

Fig. 57.

There remains yet to speak of *the manner* of taking measurements, when one wishes to compare the original impression with that of a suspected individual. Masson suggests the mode indicated in Fig. 57. The tracing of the lines of this figure is not complicated. A B denotes the total length of the foot, C D its greatest breadth measured perpendicularly to A B, C E the depth of the bend of the sole, the angle C F I the slant of the toes. However good this process may appear in theory, it is only of practical value when we have an intact original impression and when in producing the artificial impression, exactly as much colouring matter is employed as has been in the original. If the original is not preserved absolutely intact it may frequently happen that one can only trace one or other or even neither of the lines A B C D. The length of the line C F depends not only upon the curve of the foot but also upon the quantity of the colouring matter. The author has made numerous experiments in this regard and believes that that the simplest and the best method is to trace upon each of the impressions to be compared two lines perpendicular to one another, lines which will constitute the starting point of all measurements.

Suppose an original but incomplete footprint is to be compared with that of a suspected individual. They would first be both accurately drawn by tracing them on tracing paper, in order not to damage the originals. We will then look on the incomplete original footprint for two points as far from one another as possible but which have been clearly determined upon the artificial footprint, for example in Fig. 58 the interior edge of the heel at the place where the curve is most pronounced. We thus obtain the lines $a b$ and $a' b'$. We then look for a second fixed point from which a perpendicular is dropped upon $a b$. This point is chosen so that the second perpendicular should, as far as possible, extend into the footprint, here, for example the exterior edge of the little toe, $c d$ $c' d'$. We thus have two co-ordinate lines whose

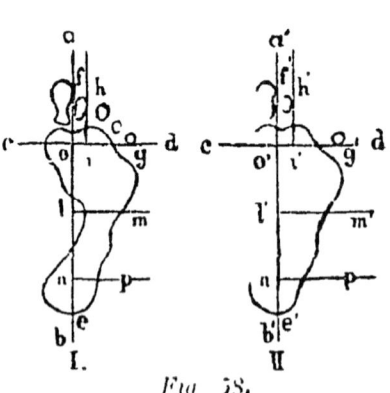

Fig. 58.

intersection gives us the point o from which every measurement and comparison may be made. We now measure and compare all the points to be found upon the two co-ordinates $o\ e$, $o'\ e'$, $o\ f$, $o'\ f'$, $o\ g$, $o'\ g'$. To fix the position by any other point it suffices to measure two lines, one, the perpendicular from the point in question to the line $a\ b$ or $c\ d$, the other the distance from the point of intersection thus obtained to the point o (i.e. the *abscissa* between the foot of the perpendicular and the origin).

It follows, a perpendicular dropped from the exterior edge of the impression of the second toe upon $c\ d$ will reach $c\ d$ at i. Let us call the point on the second toe h, we are able to compare $o\ i$ with $o'\ i'$, and $i\ h$ with $i'\ h'$. Or inversely if a length (or *abscissa*) of 3 cms is drawn from c and o' in the direction of d and d', and a perpendicular raised from this latter point, the distance $i\ h$ will be the same as the distance $i'\ h'$ 5 cms. The latter or inverse process is followed when we wish to compare curved lines with one another. We measure starting from o and o', two lengths of 5 cms, in the direction b and b', and designate the points thus obtained by $l\ n$, $l'\ n'$. From these points perpendiculars are raised upon $a\ b$ and $a'\ b'$ and lines $l\ m$, $l'\ m'$ and $n\ p$, $n'\ p'$ measured. If these lines are equal to one another, one can be certain that the deviation of the interior edge of the sole is the same in both footprints. This procedure is continued until all the important points are measured, the more there are the better. The method seems more difficult to the reader than it really is in practice. It suffices to try it once to recognise its simplicity.

This method will only exceptionally be employed for footprints, e.g., when the impression is not deep and its curves do not prevent the tracing of straight lines. It goes without saying that the auxiliary lines will not be traced upon the footprint itself but upon the plaster cast, upon which it is easy to draw and which at the same time is a material object like a foot or shoe.

If the impression of a booted foot is in question the reproduction on the tracing paper will be directly compared with the boot or shoe of the individual suspected. But if it is a bare foot one will not naturally compare the reproduction on tracing paper of the original footprint with the bare foot of the individual, who would not be able to keep it sufficiently still and from which it would be impossible to draw any conclusion. In this case the individual should be made to walk upon some substance analogous to that upon which the original impression has been made, that is to say, a new footprint for verification will be obtained, of which a reproduction will be immediately taken on tracing paper. The two reproductions on tracing paper may be then compared.

As a rule there will be no need, when dealing with booted feet, to draw auxiliary lines for more marked peculiarities will be here met with than the mere vague curves of a bare foot. With a pair of compasses or a measure the distances between the nails should be taken, also the distance from the outside corner of the front part of the sole to the front corner of the inside of the heel, or the length of the right side of the heel, etc., and the measurements found should then be compared. The original impression and the object of comparison may present small differences in measurements which will not invalidate our conclusion, but, beyond that, it must not be forgotten that certain phenomena of drying and other modifications of shape take place, occasionally producing surprising differences. It is thus, for example, that an impression made from potter's clay may contract as much as four-fifths of an inch when the clay becomes dry and the particular nature of the soil allows of its drawing together, there being no obstacle on the surface. This is not very common, for the clay, adhering to the base on which it rests, cannot shrink throughout its whole extent and is obliged to split. The total width of the parallel splits indicates how much the clay has contracted in drying. The consequence of this shrinking is naturally that one has to deal with dimensions which are quite untrustworthy. The distance between the various nails may be regular *in natura*, e.g. one cm. In drying, the clay undergoes in its various molecules a stronger and stronger tension until it breaks at the place which offers the least resistance; after this it contracts more and more on each side of the split, the breadth of which increases with the drying. The latter process finished the distance between the various nails which at first was 10 mm. will have been reduced to about 8 mm. But if a split 5 mm. broad passes between two nails, the distance separating them will not fall from 10 mm. to 8, but will increase to 13 mm. This phenomenon sometimes affects proportions more than one would believe possible especially when dealing with badly impressed footprints, and also where the clay happens to split across the nail. Thus, if the split crosses the heel in the direction of its length, two nails more will be found than appear upon the original.

It would be a mistake to suppose that the phenomena of drying always take place in a uniform manner and that, e.g., the percentage will be the same at the toe as at the heel. Several factors must here be taken into account. The thickness of the bed of clay, the admixture of stones, grass, straw, pieces of wood, etc.; also one portion of the footprint may remain fresher than the other owing to trickling water, and inversely one part may be more shaded than the other during the heat of the day. The most remarkable phenomena of drying take place when the ground on which the footprint is impressed has been successively dry and damp. We do not of course allude here to rain, which would destroy the footprint altogether, but to humidity coming from the air, fog, etc. Especially during the fine days at the end of autumn, in the night and in the morning heavy mists occur which moisten and extend the footprint, during the day a summer-like heat prevails, under the action of which the footprint dries up and shrinks. Let these changes of temperature continue for several days and very unequal contractions result, so that one cannot be too prudent in taking the measurements of the footprint. In such cases it is absolutely necessary to question specialists, such as a doctor who makes a hobby of physics, or else a professor of physics himself, and not to forget, if he is unable to observe the object for himself, to give him the most circumstantial details upon the whole matter. Among those things to be noted will be the nature of the soil, the conditions of dew and shade, the time which has probably elapsed between the discovery of the footprint and the moment it was made, the temperature and the weather during that interval, all other influences to which it has been submitted, the method of reproduction etc. When a specialist possesses all these data he will be able to say with what force the drying has acted, where its action has been strongest or feeblest, and what influence the cracks have had, etc., in a word he will be able to reconstitute the footprint as it ought to appear without the effects of the drying action. Similar modifications will be found in dealing with snow when the upper surface has been successively thawed and refrozen. Snow footprints have often remarkable appearances. When they have been produced during a moderate degree of cold, the snow is pressed under the sole and specially under the heel, so that at the first drop in temperature that follows it freezes and becomes ice. If the snow then melts, these morsels of ice disappear less quickly and we find small pieces of ice bearing the shape of parts of the sole and heel, which remain until long after the rest of the snow has disappeared.

But not only the impression itself may vary, that which has produced it may become also larger or smaller. A foot in repose is, as has been already stated, shorter than a foot warmed by walking and swollen by the heat and the blood, the latter having a downward tendency; a dry sole is shorter than a damp one, be the humidity due to a wet road or in fine weather, to perspiration from the foot. The advice of a specialist will here also be very important.

E. Reproduction of Footprints

1. GENERAL

We trust it is unnecessary at this stage to repeat that all important impressions must be reproduced. One can hardly imagine an Investigating Officer so indifferent or so inexperienced as to experiment with the original footprint itself. It is however a fact that such persons exist, so that we cannot too strongly point out the danger of damaging an impression. Such damage may render it useless for the future, or a deterioration may be produced leading to the loss of one of the most important proofs in a criminal inquiry. To do so voluntarily would be unpardonable and it rarely happens that the decision which has to be made by the Investigating Officer is so pressing as to compel him to handle the footprint itself, before being able to reproduce it. If speed is so necessary, such a rapid examination must be made as will in no way cause damage to the footprint, e.g., the nails will be counted, distances measured with the compasses, etc.

Moreover the footprints which seem important should be covered with a large box and guarded by a trustworthy man. And here we may say that a trustworthy man does not solely mean a man who cannot be bribed. He is a man who will *carry out his orders*, and not allow himself to be wheedled by a newspaper reporter, or anyone else, into removing the cover and submitting his treasure to the attentions of an eager crowd. The Investigating Officer will then attend to the rest of his investigation and can return to the reproduction of the footprint when he has time. If a comparison is to be made, on no account try to fit the foot of the suspected individual into the footprint so as to destroy it entirely, as was done by our friend mentioned above. In such a case the suspected individual may be made to give an impression of his foot *beside* the original impression for convenience of comparison, although with any acuteness the suspect can produce almost any impression he likes.

But even in making the reproduction we must not act without precaution. We must always remember, especially when we have but a single footprint at our disposition, that, in spite of great skill and much care, an accident may always happen to destroy the whole impression. The Investigating Officer will then have nothing at all, neither footprint nor reproduction, and it goes without saying that at no price must the risk of such an eventuality be run. He will therefore at first do everything possible to obtain a representation of the footprint before touching it, that is to say it will be described, drawn, exactly measured, and the measurements noted down. After having carefully done this and having avoided touching or deteriorating the impression, he may think about preserving it for subsequent comparison. How to do so is far from an easy question.

2. Various methods

The most radical method is certainly to carry away the original impression. *Hodann* advises doing this by placing round the footprint an iron coffin as large and as deep as possible (but where shall we find it?) embedded deeply in the ground. The soil is then dug all round the coffin with a spade so that the footprint enclosed in the coffin rests upon a little mound isolated from the rest of the neighbouring ground. The mound is then dug away to as great a depth as possible underneath the footprint. The latter may thus with precaution be raised up, placed in a box, and carried away. *Hodann* himself says that his procedure is certain but complicated. *Schauenstein* replies, and rightly, that it is not so complicated, but that the impression thus obtained has no great value, as desiccation modifies its dimensions and shape, and as also it is liable to crack and split, etc.; for ourselves we believe that this method is good for nothing, for the footprint suffers too much during the transportation to which it is in most cases exposed. If the ground where it happens to be is dry, *Hodann*'s process is not practicable at all, for the whole thing breaks up into little pieces; if on the contrary the ground be damp, the transportation is no longer possible. On one occasion the author, after a case of train wrecking, discovered a footprint belonging without doubt to the author of the crime and planted by him at the moment when he had jumped over the railway fence. It had been drawn, described, measured, reproduced in plaster, and as the case was an important one and as the operation was easy, the author resolved to remove the footprint by following *Hodann*'s method. The piece of ground was placed in its box upon a railway trolly. It seemed that these conditions of transport were the most favourable possible, for the trolly could be moved carefully and a thick bed of straw had been placed under the box. In spite of all precautions the piece of soil with the footprint arrived in such a state that it was difficult to recognise the place where the footprint had been. The joltings and shakings of the relatively short journey—the distance in between two succeeding railway stations—had been sufficient to level the mass of earth in an absolutely regular manner. In carriage on an ordinary road the same result would have been produced much more rapidly, so that this process can only be recommended in the cases in which the footprint ought to be preserved at the locality itself. We might in certain circumstances utilise it by employing one of the methods of fixture to be discussed later.

Another process also recommended by *Hodann* is to obtain a reproduction with the aid of a mixture of equal parts of plaster, cement and sand. This mixture is spread upon the footprint, covering it to the height of about an inch and surrounding it for about three fingers' breadth. A damp cloth is then spread over the whole and watered with a watering can until the mass is thoroughly wet. The reproductions thus obtained have a certain solidity, but they none the less are always so friable that pieces may be detached with the finger even after several days. This process has besides numerous inconveniences; the watering for example produces an inundation most disadvantageous as regards neighbouring footprints; it is besides difficult to know if and when the mixture is damp enough. Again, if the footprint is upon damp ground not yet dry at the moment of operation, the composition never becomes dry, which is of course very inconvenient in many cases.

Hugoulin indicates a process which would seem to offer great advantages. He suggests the placing on the footprint of a grill whereon a sheet of tin is placed, a little larger in size than the footprint. Upon this live coals are deposited so as to heat the entire impression. The grill, tin, and coals are then lifted up and as much finely pulverised stearic acid is spread upon the footprint as the heated soil upon which the impression lies can absorb. As soon as the surrounding substance cools, the stearic acid solidifies and it is then only a question of skill in separating this crust of stearine from the surrounding substance. When the operation succeeds, a neat and clean shape is obtained, having the advantage of representing the footprint itself and not a mould of it.

The disadvantages of this method are first the difficulty of procuring the necessary materials, and secondly the excessive care with which the stearic acid must be introduced and the print lifted up. Stearic acid can be procured in some places, since it will suffice if need be to reduce to powder a stearine wax taper. But it is impossible to obtain fine enough wax by purely mechanical methods. The pulverisation has to be made by a process of dissolution and precipitation by placing the powdered taper in alcohol and when dissolution has taken place, adding cold water thereto until the stearine swims on the surface in extremely fine flakes. The liquid is then poured off and the stearine powder dried upon blotting paper. Theoretically a fine substance is thus obtained. But in reality the whole condenses while drying so that we only obtain a crusty substance, no finer than the stearine scraped with a knife. It is difficult to prepare on the spot and to carry it with one is almost as embarrassing. Finally we must not forget that a footprint in earth or clay considerably changes in shape and in an irregular manner owing to the suddenness of the desiccation by heat, so that the stearine impression obtained will no longer claim any degree of precision.

There is one case where this process may be recommended as being the only practicable, and that is when the footprint has been produced in sand, dust or the like. In this case the heat does not alter the dimensions of the footprint; the powdered stearine may be spread without disarranging the grains of sand, and when the stearine is allowed to cool, it is easy to detach the shape produced from the sand. The author is inclined to follow the advice of *Sonnenschein* who recommends not to commence by heating the footprint and then spreading the stearine powder thereon, but on the contrary to follow the inverse process. A large quantity of stearine powder is spread upon the footprint by scraping above it a stearine taper with a knife. A hot iron is then held over the footprint until the stearine is melted and has penetrated into the sand. At the places where the quantity of stearine was insufficient a little more is scraped and the heating continued. The footprint may then after solidification be easily lifted up without any damage. Any operation on sand with cement is naturally impossible for it would completely destroy the impression, sand having no consistency. The stearine method is therefore the only one practicable.

Jaumes has modified *Hugoulin's* method by employing stearine acid only at the fixing of the footprint. He follows *Hugoulin's* process exactly but he fills the stearine crust with *plaster of paris* before lifting it up. This method has the same inconveniences as the preceding, there is still the difficulty of procuring the necessary materials, counterbalanced only by a somewhat less fragility in the product obtained.

Hugoulin advises in certain cases the employment of moulds of glue especially for footprints in snow. The joiner's glue is melted, taking care however to make it a little thicker than usual. It is then allowed to cool until it begins to congeal, and is then poured into the footprint. It is best to leave the glue until a coating has formed on it. This is pierced and the glue beneath is allowed to run out. It soon hardens into a jelly-like mass easily separable from the print; it will be quite hard in 10-12 hours. If the favourable moment during the cooling of the glue is seized excellent reproductions are obtained, even in the snow; indeed, the cold of the snow absorbs the heat of the glue sufficiently quickly to allow the latter to harden before the snow melts. It is also possible to operate upon damp clay, damp earth, or mud. When the footprint is dry it must be greased, otherwise the glue mould could not be detached. The advantages of this method are its simplicity and the facility with which the materials can be procured, for joiner's glue is to be found everywhere. A relatively small amount of glue is necessary, it requires scarcely any time to heat and turn out, operations which anyone knows how to perform. But glue moulds have also their bad points. They are not very accurate. It happens, *e.g.*, that not very distinct impressions of nails are not reproduced and that the mould obtained shrinks, twists, and strains sensibly in drying. Moreover a mould of this kind may during very hot weather become unrecognisable in a few hours. It is necessary in consequence to cover it with a cloth which does not touch it and must be kept continually wet so as to enable a plaster reproduction to be made as soon as possible. When one has only glue at one's disposal, it may always be used, and indeed for footprints in snow no other method exists. It is a good thing before spreading the melted glue to stretch small pieces of thin string over the footprint in such a way as almost to touch the bottom. As the ends of the string will project on both sides of the footprint, when the glue is poured out we can easily seize them and raise the mould when cold with their assistance. This precaution is unnecessary for footprints in snow where the moulds are deserted by their melting environment.

Hofmann recommends the employment of plaster or pulverised cement and then follows *Hodann's* process. The author has made numerous experiments and can recommend cement only in cases of absolute necessity. As it is impossible always to carry several pounds of cement about with one, we have to fall back upon common country cement, which is nearly always useless. Specialists say " Good cement is very good, bad cement is very bad " Indeed moulds in bad cement are valueless. Even those in good cement are not always very clean, and they harden with difficulty on damp ground even after a considerable time. Often in favourable conditions the cement hardens but slowly, and if there be the slightest trace of clay, the mortal enemy of cement, in the sand or water one is obliged to add thereto, the mould obtained is often fit only to be thrown away.

We do not understand how anyone can recommend a mixture of cement and plaster, since the action of plaster upon cement is always unfavourable *Bruno Keil* ("Treatise on Technical Chemistry " *Muspratt*) says that even two per cent of plaster is injurious to cement and that the presence of plaster however insignificant, always retards the solidification of the cement If obliged to employ cement to fill up a footprint, it is best to take 2 parts by volume of cement one of sand (deprived of all clay), and one half part of pure water. With *dry* sand, mix first the cement and the sand if the sand be damp, mix first the cement and the water then add thereto the sand and pour out the mixture upon the footprint (*Bruno Keil*) The cement increases in volume in the proportion of 100 to 118, so that the resulting cast is materially larger than the footprint itself If we have no sand free from clay and no time to wash the sand then we take only cement with half as much water. It is difficult to prepare these moulds during frosty weather, for the water freezes before the cement has hardened and the mould does not solidify The *Tonindustrie-Zeitung* recommends in working with cement during a frost to dissolve in the water as much salt as it will absorb This is theoretically accurate for a solution of salt freezes with difficulty but we have on several occasions made the experiment and obtained nothing but a sandy and crumbling mass unfit for any service

To sum up what has been said we conclude that all the methods already mentioned ought only to be applied exceptionally and in particular cases Moreover we can nearly always have recourse to the process recommended by *Krahmer*, a very old process which employs plaster of paris Wax is also quite as good, and, in many cases, preferable

3 METHODS RECOMMENDED

On the other hand we can easily procure plaster of paris anywhere, and, on the other use relatively little, so that its carriage is not onerous, at least when footprints are expected to be found Good plaster, as used by sculptors, should be obtained and kept as dry as possible It should be preserved for preference in bottles closed with a cork and wax, and filled as full as possible in order to prevent air remaining within Before filling the bottles the plaster should be dried in the sun and care be taken that only perfectly dry bottles are employed

When it is desired to fill a mould, that is, in the present case, a footprint, the mould should be carefully prepared for the purpose First any small stones, pieces of earth, etc. which may have fallen should be detached with precaution and any water which may have collected be removed with a rag or piece of blotting paper.

If it is possible to solidify somewhat the walls of the footprint it will greatly aid the rest of the work. The best agent for this purpose is a solution of shellac in alcohol. If handy, obtain ordinary joiner's varnish, the basis of which is nothing but shellac and alcohol. To apply this solution use for preference a hairdresser's scent spray, but in the absence of such the solution may be spread with precaution upon the footprint with a camel's hair brush or morsel of cotton-wool. This operation must be proceeded with cautiously, for a drop of the solution resting for example in the impression of a nail of a shoe would entirely fill it and render it invisible on the cast. This process only serves, as has been said, to further solidify the footprint and is in no way indispensable.

The next important matter is to devise some method of raising the cast, in other words, of greasing the footprint. We do not advise the employment of oil which would not remain on the surface but filtrate through into the ground without producing the desired effect. Any greasy body may be recommended having the consistency of an ointment or pommade, such as melted pork or beef fat, melted butter, a mixture of oil and hot tallow or any ointment. With this the footprint is rubbed, care being taken to see that there nowhere remains any mass of grease likely to produce incomprehensible and bothersome marks in the cast.

Footprints in the sand or on a damp substance are the only exceptions here. As has been pointed out above, casts cannot be taken of a footprint in the sand except with stearic acid, and footprints on damp substances would be damaged by the touch of a camel's hair brush, the marks of which would be found upon the reproduction even when the greatest precaution may have been taken. For these substances there is besides no need of greasing, as the author has proved by numerous experiments. When the plaster has solidified in a footprint on wet clay, slime etc., the cast comes away as easily as if the footprint had been oiled. If, in spite of all, the operation does not succeed, the plaster cast must be raised along with the footprint by means of a crowbar introduced underneath them. The whole must then be placed on the table and the earth surrounding the reproduction carefully taken away, picked away, so to speak, from the cast. In this case the cast is naturally not white but the same colour as the substance in which the footprint has been made, and moreover some small pieces of earth will still adhere to it. They may be removed without any danger by washing the cast with a wetted brush, so that finally a clean footprint is obtained.

As to the dilution of the plaster of paris there is but one thing to remember. If the water be poured upon the powdered plaster it forms into a mass of pasty clots which will not penetrate into all the intricacies of the footprint. These clots would require to be broken up, an operation requiring so much time that the plaster would commence to set before it was completed. To remedy this inconvenience a vase should be used, half filled with water, into which spoonfuls of the powdered plaster are poured or, better still, passed through a sieve, so that the surface of the water is equally and several times

Fig 59

powdered over. This is continued until a little eminence forms just rising above the level of the water, see *Fig. 59*. At this stage no more plaster is poured in, and the mixture of water and plaster is rapidly stirred.

The result is a homogeneous soup without lumps or clots, which is poured on to the footprint. The operation must be performed rapidly in order that the plaster may not harden. But too great quickness must be avoided, or the layers of the soup in forming upon one another would produce air bubbles and the corresponding spot upon the footprint would remain empty. The best method is for one person to pour the plaster of paris slowly into the footprint while another spreads it carefully with a spoon as it falls without touching the footprint, and thus assisting it to penetrate into all parts.

During this operation, at the moment when the ground is covered with a bed of plaster of about one centimetre's thickness, small pieces of prepared wood should be placed, by a third person if possible, upon the plaster, after which the remainder is poured out. If the footprint be very deep, we may when these sticks have been covered with about one centimetre of plaster, further superimpose yet more pieces of stick, *Fig. 60*. These pieces of wood are intended to form a skeleton inside the plaster cast and thus to give it more solidity. The plaster may be also stiffened in another way. Besides the pieces of wood twisted string may be placed, giving both solidity and stiffness. It should be remembered that the wood, as also the string, should be soaked beforehand in water so as to be thoroughly wet through. Without this precaution the wood and the string would absorb water from the plaster of paris, swell, and cause the whole to split. It is also advisable in this case, to allow certain of these ribbons to project, thus enabling the mould to be seized and lifted up, when the right moment has come.

Fig. 60

As regards the period of the operation, it will be found that good plaster thickens in a few minutes and becomes fairly set after about ten minutes. The mould may then be lifted up. The fact that good plaster sets so quickly and develops a certain quantity of heat has the further advantage of not hindering the work even during a hard frost. Only when the cold is extremely severe will it be advisable to light a small fire on the side whence comes the wind, in order to raise the temperature during the time necessary for the plaster to set. When the cast has been lifted it must be examined to see how far it corresponds with the footprint, and in the report the faults, omissions, etc., which have been produced will be most minutely noted down. Little pieces of earth, etc., sticking to the cast may be removed as explained above by means of a wetted brush.

The increase in volume of plaster is compared to cement, relatively small and does not surpass on the average one per cent., so that a piece one metre in length would measure after expansion 101 centimetres, with a human footprint of 27 cms. in length, a fair average for a male, the reproduction in plaster will be 2.5 mms. longer ($\frac{1}{10}$ inch). For smaller distances, as from one nail to the next, the breadth of the heel etc., the co-efficient of expansion is so insignificant that it may be altogether neglected. The operation will be particularly successful when one is able to use, in preparing the plaster of paris, water which has just been boiled but allowed to become cold. It contains hardly any air and prevents the formation of air-bubbles in the plaster. These bubbles may arise at important places and cause much trouble. It is therefore always necessary to guard against them.

When it is desired that the plaster should harden slowly, for example, when the work requires great precaution or when some obstacle or other prevents the semi-liquid mass being easily poured out, the end may be attained by mixing marsh-mallow root with the plaster. With 50 parts of plaster are mixed 1 to 4 parts of this root finely powdered, more or less according to the degree of retardation desired, and for the rest the procedure is as before. Thanks to this the plaster will only completely harden after about 12 hours, whether one will always have marsh-mallow root handy, is another question.

It may perhaps also be necessary to render a plaster cast more permanent e.g., when it is desired to send it away, or when it is feared that it will deteriorate in the hands of the jury, etc. Plaster casts are indeed very fragile, but thanks to silicic acid they may be rendered as hard as stone. *Professor M. Dennstedt* describes a process which consists in plunging the plaster reproduction into a solution containing 15 per cent of silicic acid and leaving it there until thoroughly impregnated. It is then placed in a moderately warm spot, and the operation repeated several times. The reproduction is next dried at a temperature not exceeding 104° F (10° C), and then steeped in a solution, saturated when hot, of barium water at a temperature of 140° to 158° F (60° to 70° C), it is then sprinkled with tepid water, and allowed to dry in a gentle heat. A most simple method consists in steeping the cast in a solution of 1 part of alum and 5 parts of hot water and leaving it there for from 15 to 30 minutes.

If the plaster of paris used by sculptors cannot be procured, common plaster, such as is frequently employed by farmers as manure, will be obtainable. It is easily transformed into modelling plaster if care be taken to cook it. In doing so the procedure is the same as in roasting coffee, the plaster is deposited in a receptacle placed over a fire and continually revolved. The time this operation should last depends entirely on the quality and age of the plaster. We proceed tentatively, a little of the plaster is taken on the point of a knife mixed with a few drops of water, and the result awaited.

We consider that the value of wax is equal to or even superior to that of the best plaster. It is nearly always easily procured, every country grocer stocking it. The wax is melted and allowed to cool till it begins to darken, it is then poured upon the footprint. It matters little whether the latter is in wet clay or in dry earth, wax may always be employed except in snow, sand, dust, or the like. Much skill is unnecessary, the mould is easily raised as soon as the cooling has finished, and is clean and distinct. But it must not be forgotten that it is sensibly smaller than the original.

The same result may be obtained at a low temperature and on damp footprints with ordinary suet, which may be procured at any butcher's shop. Much precaution must be used on raising the mould. A piece of earth must be detached therewith at the same time and made to fall on the ground by pressing on the edges until the suet be separated. It goes without saying that a plaster reproduction of this fragile object must be taken as soon as possible.

Pitch and resin are also useful especially in certain woody districts where they abound. These are heated over a gentle fire and poured slowly into the impression.

When none of these materials are obtainable, recourse must be had to cement, which is rarely to be found in good quality, but which, however, is procurable almost everywhere. It is employed as stated above.

In case of need, but only when the footprint is very hard and very solid, good reproductions are obtainable by kneading clay, easily procurable in a quarry, at a potter's, or elsewhere till it has the consistency of a paste and pressing it in little pieces on the footprint; this is continued until the latter is completely filled and covered with a small mound of clay. If the footprint has been well greased the clay is easily raised, and if the necessary care be taken the lifting up may be carried out without danger. The cast should be slightly baked at once.

In the same way any paste of flour and water or of dough may be used. This has the advantage that it may be spread no thicker than the breadth of the thumb, thus making it easier to raise. The impressions, when pressure has been properly effected, are very accurate. Their only fault is that they do not exactly represent the undulations of the footprint. The paste contracts too easily owing to its leathery consistency, but as we have said the distances and the reliefs are easily recorded.

To summarise what has been said we must employ —
   (1) for footprints in the snow *joiner's glue*;
   (2) for footprints in sand, dust, flour, etc. *stearine*;
   (3) for other footprints *plaster*, or *wax*, or in case of need—*cement, fat* or *suet, clay, paste*, or *bread-crumb*.

Section II.—Other Impressions.

We mean by " other impressions " all marks and imprints produced, in some way or other, in a soft substance. It is unnecessary to say that every impression of this description may be of great importance and ought not to be neglected. To observe, examine, and refer to them in the report is not sufficient; they must also be described and reproduced. They are often as important as, and perhaps more important than, the footprint of the criminal himself. In many cases the observation and reproduction of such a trace present great difficulties, but this in no way absolves the Investigating Officer from the obligation he is under to examine it in the most thorough manner.

Suppose for example that the criminal has been walking with a stick the impression of which can afford us important information, may even, when sharply moulded, establish identification. When one reads in a report of a "medium-sized stick" with an "iron ferrule" we do not advance very far for the words "medium-sized" and "iron ferrule" are expressions altogether vague. But when the impression is accurately moulded and one has subsequently a chance of comparing the plaster reproduction with the walking-stick of the suspected person, it is possible to lay a proof of identity before the jury, which has as much value as that of two footprints. We may also gather from the depth of the imprint whether the holder of the stick has leaned heavily upon it or not, i.e., whether he was tired, aged, infirm, or burdened. Care will be taken to establish whether the stick was carried in the right or left hand. If the latter, we may suppose that the person was left-handed or carried his stick in the left hand because of pain in the foot, both matters of importance as regards identification.

Let us suppose that the individual in question carries his walking-stick in his right hand. In a slow sauntering walk he will place it on the ground every second step near the toe of the right foot. If he is going quickly and is really making use of his cane to accelerate his speed he places it at the fore part of each impression of the left foot. In this class must also be placed tired, aged, or infirm persons who, even when walking slowly, really make use of a stick to help them on their way. There are exceptions to this rule, though in the great majority of cases it holds good, as anyone may convince himself by observation and experiment.

The marks of horses may also be important. The most difficult thing in this connection is to distinguish the four impressions which go together. Those who are not well up in horses should refer to specialists. It is easy to distinguish between the fore-hoof and the hind-hoof from the position. It is nearly always a matter of difficulty to recognize from its appearance alone, the fore-hoof or hind-hoof. As a rule the fore-hoof is rounder and more confined, whilst the rear-hoof is more elongated and more open. The size and shape of the shoes, the number of the nails and the distance from one another etc. are often so characteristic that their impressions may very well serve to establish identification. To determine the speed of the animal, the position and the relative distance of the nails from one another must be measured so that the specialist is able to give the necessary advice. The reproduction of the impressions is performed in the same manner as for human footprints. It is hardly necessary to add that in certain cases other foot impressions, as for instance those of a dog, may also be of great importance.

The marks made by carriages are not without value. Therefrom can be seen the breadth of the wheel, the distance between the right and left wheels, the manner in which the coachman has driven the carriage, the deflections to right and left he has been forced to make, what use he has made of his brake, where he has turned, etc. Wheel impressions are also of importance from the point of view of the direction followed by the carriage, for the ground is often so hard that no trace of the horse can be found but only of the wheels, especially when the vehicle is heavily loaded. If the ground over which the vehicle passes is strongly compressed by the wheel, compact masses of dust, earth, mud, snow, etc. are detached from the track which are visible in the form shown in *Fig. 61*. These are due partly to portions adhering to the wheel of the carriage and partly to the continuous crushing and pushing forward. In the illustration the result is greatly exaggerated, but it is

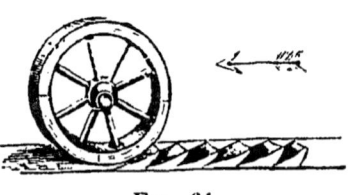

Fig. 61

quite sufficient to observe it with a moving vehicle especially one heavily laden. Once seen never forgotten.

As to other marks, as of bullets, shot, stones thrown, blows, crushings by vehicles, discoloration on weapons and implements employed etc., they will be discussed in their proper places. In every case it is evident that such marks must be looked for, described, and, if possible, moulded. The manner in which this latter operation should be carried out depends upon each particular instance. They may be moulded with plaster, clay, bread paste, putty, wax, gutta-percha, etc., according to their shape and size, and in certain circumstances they may be traced. The universal rule is always to reproduce them, for we never know if we will not subsequently desire to recall the exact form of an impression of this kind.

Neither must we forget, when opportunity offers, to mould anything which may give rise to an impression, e.g., the front teeth of a corpse, a key, or other instruments and objects, we may not have them to hand when wanted.

Finally we have certain marks on the human body such as callosities or hard places and cicatrices. In any given case they may be of supreme value in establishing the identity of a corpse or of a prisoner who has given an assumed name or whose name is unknown. *Felix Hement* has called attention to these marks in an excellently illustrated article ("La Photographie Judiciaire") in which he shows that as a rule, they are not very distinct or visible on the body itself, whereas they come out clearly in the photograph (see pp. 212-213 where many examples of this kind are cited).

CHAPTER XIV

TRACES OF BLOOD.

Section 1.—Search for Traces of Blood.

What the expert can tell us and what the Investigating Officer should ask him regarding blood-stains have already been mentioned above (see p 129) we will now speak of what the Investigating Officer ought to do, either by himself or better still with the assistance and under the superintendence of medical men, in order to facilitate the work of the expert and obtain therefrom as much profit as possible

Here we shall specially deal with cases where the Investigating Officer has arrived on the scene of the crime unaccompanied by a medical man, either because he has had no time to summon one, or because he has considered one unnecessary There are many cases, especially in the country, where 'medical jurisprudents," who assist Investigating Officers, are, perhaps, excellent general practitioners, but who are not really as well up in this class of work as they ought to be from a judicial point of view In all such cases the Investigating Officer has only himself to rely upon, and ought to do his very best to conduct the case alone But here again the work of the Investigating Officer who wishes to acquit himself conscientiously of his task commences long before the real judicial case begins The person who generally arrives first on the scene of the crime is an inhabitant of the house, a neighbour, a village officer, or some other person, and we cannot conceive the amount of harm they can do with respect to traces of blood

Schauenstein, a talented medical jurisprudent has laid special stress, and in severe terms, upon the curiosity of intruders, and the awkwardness of the local police, who efface and destroy traces of the highest value for the elucidation of a case Times without number it happens that they make new traces by walking in already existing pools of blood and then tramping all over the place, so that subsequently no one can tell whether the traces of blood have any connection with the crime or have been made afterwards by chance or owing to awkwardness and carelessness

In large cities the police being promptly on the spot can generally prevent such accidents, and to this end the Commissioner of Police should issue the necessary instructions to the force. In the country this is no simple matter, but in compensation it is easier to hold the crowd in hand. No other resource is possible than to profit by all opportunities which may offer of instructing the local police and village authorities in the best method of procedure. The latter, on their part, will exercise a satisfactory influence on the populace, and, as a matter of fact, most of us know that country people are better informed as regards these matters than the denizens of towns. The inhabitants of country villages seem to know perfectly well that where there is no hope of saving the life of a victim of a crime, everything ought to be left *in statu quo* until the arrival of the authorities. For example in England people have in one particular this principle firmly ingrained in them, namely, that when a man has been found hanging, he should be left to hang. In such a case they think it inadvisable or even illegal to cut the body down until the police have arrived upon the scene. A well-known London coroner recently stated that it was certain that many a life had been lost owing to this practice. No doubt if the victim is really dead when found the police may be aided by finding him still hanging. But such cases are almost invariably cases of suicide where it is not really so important to leave things undisturbed. But people do not always act thus in other cases than hanging.

The principle which should always be kept in mind is the following: request the local police to tell the populace to leave, as much as possible, everything in the same state as it was at the moment of the discovery of the crime; for their part the local police should watch carefully, even when they have been called at first to the scene of the crime, that nothing be disarranged, effaced or picked up before the person who will conduct the inquiry arrives on the spot, to which we assume he has been summoned with all possible expedition. To illustrate the importance of this the following case is most instructive. A woman was discovered brutally murdered in the open. The woman's friends were prepared to swear to the identity of three individuals whom they alleged they saw running away from the scene of the crime. The local police, knowing that a magistrate was in the neighbourhood, carefully left the scene of the crime undisturbed, at the same time arresting the three accused men. When the magistrate arrived on the spot he proceeded with the utmost care to make an inspection of it. He discovered near the corpse in a pool of bloody mud some small beads which were found to belong to a necklace worn by the woman and broken in the struggle. He proceeded to collect the beads and in doing so, he discovered a tiny piece of raw flesh attached to a piece of nail, which on examination was pronounced to belong to a man or a woman, it could not be definitely said which. There was little doubt, according to the medical evidence, that it had been bitten off by the woman from the finger of her assailant during her desperate struggle for life. On examining the three accused persons the fingers of all of them were found to be intact. This led to further inquiries being made, when it came out that a man with whom the woman was alleged to have been intimate had fled the village. He was subsequently brought back from a neighbouring district and on examining his fingers the tip of one of them was found to be missing. He was tried along with the other three accused and convicted of the murder, while they were acquitted. Had the scene of this offence been disturbed, the end of the finger might never have been found, three innocent men might have been convicted, and the real criminal might have escaped.

If, however, it is absolutely necessary to approach the *corpus delicti*, the police must be instructed that the first thing to be done is to safeguard with the greatest precautions the traces of blood upon the ground by covering them over, e.g., with pots, baskets, or boxes. If the blood-stains be too large they must be covered over with a species of bridge made by placing pieces of wood or bricks on each side upon which a plank rests; it is, of course, not enough merely to guard the largest and most visible traces; the small ones also should be seen to, for in spite of their apparent insignificance they are often the most important. It is not necessary to guard stains of blood on walls, furniture, etc.; it is sufficient to prevent their being touched in any way. The protecting circle cannot be sufficiently enlarged, for at the outset no one knows in what direction blood traces must be looked for or how far they may extend. In all cases the following rule can be laid down:—"The greater the surface guarded the better."

If the crime has been committed in a house the place of its commission must be isolated as much as possible; if it has been committed in the open, it is necessary to trace as large a circle as we can around the spot and to isolate it completely.

When the Investigating Officer arrives on the scene of the crime his first business ought to be to make sure that neither he himself nor his men efface the blood upon the ground. He will do well to obtain information before repairing to the actual spot, regarding the places where blood has been found and the steps which have been taken to safeguard them, etc. Moreover, he should be informed about any persons who may have been at the place before the crime has become known. If such exist, he must question them minutely in order to find out the precise spot where they have been, so as to ascertain whether they may have perchance walked in the already existing traces of blood. Finally, it only remains to recommend the Investigating Officer on arriving at the scene of the crime itself to attend to the traces of blood first and foremost, unless there may be particular circumstances connected with the crime which imperiously demand otherwise. Thus the Investigating Officer will be much freer in his movements, for he will no longer be afraid of destroying at every step some mark of blood.

It is especially necessary to remind the reader that blood stains are not always of the dark red colour of popular imagination, and this variation depends upon their age, the substance upon which they are found, the temperature, etc., which make them assume all imaginable tints: reddish brown, greenish brown, light olive green, light rose. Sometimes they are almost colourless (*Liman*), so that they may be taken for anything else but blood. The author remembers having seen, upon a multicoloured tapestry, splashes of blood having the most peculiar tints; the various colours of the tapestry had acted differently upon the blood-stains. Here they had been dissolved in the blood there the blood had been altered by them, and yet in spite of their difference in colour the stains fitted together so exactly that it was impossible to doubt their authenticity but if they had been separate, only a very few of them would have been recognisable. To establish the identity of traces of blood it is therefore much better to be too scrupulous than the reverse, if a stain is not blood a microscope will say so and no great harm will have been done,—but it is not the same thing if certain blood-stains remain unnoticed and unrecognised as such.

It is to be remarked that blood-stains fade rapidly in the sun. A piece of linen dipped in blood and laid in the sun keeps its colour longer underneath, while on the top it very soon becomes grey.

Traces of blood, found upon the scene of a crime, are never without importance they must therefore (1) be looked for (2) described, and (3) detached and removed, or else drawings taken of them. Searches for blood often present great difficulties. On the scene of the crime the thing to do first is to ask where is it *possible* to find traces of blood? that is to say, where is the blood which has flowed from the wound in different directions? and finally where has the author of the crime possibly left traces behind him? This question answered, we begin to search step by step, always taking care to obliterate nothing. When uncertain whether a stain is blood we must consider whether or not it is possible for it to be blood taking into consideration the apparent or presumed manner in which the crime has been committed. We shall first therefore look at the place where the wounded person has last been, or where the murdered man was found then at the place where he has been or may have been after having received his wound, and finally at the spot where the aggressor may have been after the perpetration of his crime.

This search is not always easy, few difficulties arise with regard to stains upon floors or walls but it is not the same thing with regard to blood-stains upon articles found in rooms, for their multiple shape, defective lighting and the colour of the furniture etc, prevents their being noticed. On furniture of polished wood (which is generally reddish brown) traces of blood can only be seen with difficulty. In such a case one will always do well to make use of, even during the day-time, an artificial light for preference a candle first because every corner may thus be submitted to a uniform light, which is impossible when the room is only lit by the side light of a window, and also because one will search more carefully, examining one by one surfaces of small size. On the other hand the dried blood has generally an appearance of varnish, so that it can only be seen if the source of light changes position. Finally, with the help of artificial light it is easy to see, as *Olivier, Billon Liman*, and others have remarked, stains of a reddish brown colour on a dark background, which can only be perceived with difficulty by daylight, especially when they are small and few and far between. In an important case, in spite of the most thorough search on a cellar ladder no traces of blood were discovered. When the ladder was photographed by magnesium light blood marks were discovered on one of the steps and could be seen with perfect clearness. The step was then detached and removed for examination.

It being as a rule important to know whether a wounded person especially if now dead, has been able to do certain acts after the blow and before succumbing, and on the other hand, whether the criminal has himself been either wounded or stained with the blood of his victim, and has done any act after his crime, e.g., searched for booty, particular attention must be paid to those places which do not at first strike the eye, but which are often found stained with blood, for example the lower edge of drawers which have no handles to open them, or which may be opened without the assistance of handles; again in most cases, the author of the crime stains the wood forming the bottom of the drawer, when rummaging it for money or valuables. It is curious that almost every time a criminal has blood upon his hands he leaves traces thereof underneath the edge of the top of the table (at a part a in Fig. 62). Indeed one often sees common people cleaning their dirty hands under the table in this way, and so it is done by habit after crime.

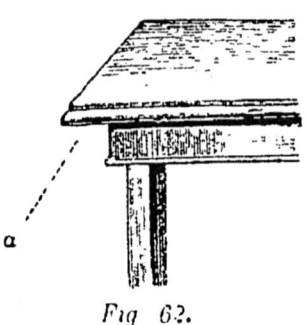

Fig. 62.

The following case shows in what out-of-the-way places traces of blood may be found. An old woman had been killed and robbed. The author of the crime had apparently given himself a wound in some way or other, from which the blood came drop by drop. When the place was inspected this fact could be easily certified to, for, beside the front door (a glass door with curtains) which gave straight on to the street, there were several groups of blood drops which could certainly not have come from the murdered woman. The likely supposition was that the murderer had after the crime gone several times to the door in question and peeped through the curtain to ascertain whether the coast was clear for his escape; each time he had thus approached the door drops of blood had fallen from his hand and formed the groups above mentioned. But the room had another entrance on to the courtyard, and thence along a corridor into the street. Quite close to this latter door (to the left on going out) was a fairly long table covered with a light cloth which fell nearly to the ground. On searching for other traces this cloth was lifted up, when, *under* the cloth towards the back part of the table and on the ground, was found a drop of blood. No one could explain the presence of this drop of blood, at a spot which, as we have stated, was hidden by the portion of the cloth which fell from the table like a curtain. It was noticed however by the merest chance that on opening the door near the table a draught was each time produced, which blew the hanging part of the light table-cloth under the table so that the place where the drop of blood was found could be seen. It was therefore beyond all doubt that the murderer had opened the door with his right hand, that the cloth had been displaced by the wind, and that from his left hand a drop of blood had fallen which was hidden from view as soon as the cloth had attained its original position. This blood-stain thus brought about the discovery of this important point, that the author of the crime was wounded in the *left hand*.

Liman cites a case which shows the importance of searching for traces of this description. A warder of a Berlin prison had been found murdered in his bed, the murderer was a prisoner on remand, who affirmed that in attempting to escape he had been surprised by the warder in a corridor, and had been maltreated by him to such an extent that he had been obliged to kill him in self-defence he had then, he continued carried him to his bed A careful examination brought about the discovery on the wood of the head of the bed, of a little trail of blood containing a particle of brain matter, it was therefore certain that the warder had been assassinated in his bed and not in the corridor consequently the whole story of the defence broke down A similar case is that commonly called the "*Spicer case*" where the accused declared that his wife's injuries were caused by falling downstairs The number, shape, and direction of the drops, often minute established not only the fact that the case was one of murder, but also the position of the parties the direction of the blows, and their nature

The importance of traces of blood, especially of those met with on corpses is also demonstrated by another case which, from the numerous and interesting difficulties it presented, is very well known to Austrian criminalists as the "*Krumpendorf murder*" The corpse was found covered with numerous wounds and a mass of blood-stains to which, as often happens, no importance was attached, for "it is natural for a corpse bearing numerous wounds to be covered with blood It was not till later, after the *post-mortem* that it was noticed that the shirt of the murdered man (he was wearing no under-shirt at the time of the crime) showed, near the shoulder a very characteristic stain of blood, which seemed to be caked upon the cloth After a series of examinations and comparisons it was concluded that this stain could only have been made by the murderer, who, after having placed his knee in a pool of blood, knelt upon the shoulder of his victim The mark of the cloth was clearly seen impressed in blood upon the shirt, thus giving a clue to the author of the crime, thanks to which it was possible, when a suspected individual was subsequently arrested, to establish with absolute certainty the identity of the texture of the cloth of his trousers, which had in the meantime been washed, and the bloody impression left upon the shirt of the murdered person This was the strongest piece of evidence against the murderer

If an accused person is to be searched for traces of blood one cannot make the search too minute In one case the accused had two small blood drops on the back of his coat, between the shoulder-blades It was presumed and afterwards confessed by the accused, that the hatchet with which he had committed the murder had been immediately after the deed carried by him on his shoulder with the blade upwards Thus, the two drops of blood had trickled off the hatchet and fallen on his coat This case calls to mind one that *Taylor* often cited in which on the back of the left hand of an alleged suicide the bloody impression of another left hand could be distinguished

If there is a possibility that the suspected person carries traces of blood on the soles of his feet, we must make sure about it, even if some time has elapsed and the accused person has travelled some distance We must take off the boots or if the suspect is barefoot, his feet must be carefully washed, and the water must be kept for the examination of an expert How cautious one must be about drawing conclusions concerning the non-existence of marks of blood is shown by the case cited by *Taylor* in which the murderer had made himself entirely naked so that his clothes might show no marks of blood. With this may be compared the case described by *Imschl* where in favour of the accused was the circumstance that soon after the deed no one could find traces of blood on him, although the murder had caused great loss of blood. This circumstance could only be explained by the fact that the murderer had, until the day of the crime, been seen only in a very long overcoat which from the time of the deed disappeared. Evidently the accused had worn the coat during the perpetration of the murder, and had then washed his hands and face and done away with the blood-sprinkled overcoat.

It is much more difficult to discover and protect traces of blood in the open air than under cover. Besides the fear of obliterating or treading on them, we have also the anxiety of protecting them from the effects of weather and temperature. Rain and dew combine for their destruction and the wind and sun dry them up so thoroughly that they cake and become detached from their bases. If the Investigating Officer has time to deal with them at once he has nothing to fear, provided there is no rain. But if his attention has to be directed elsewhere and night or bad weather supervene so that the Investigating Officer has to postpone their examination till later, he must protect them as well as he can. It is often insufficient to cover them with pots and pans, etc., for the rainwater may flow underneath the covering. In such cases pieces of board, sheets of tin, or slips of glass, must be planted in the ground at the places threatened, to form a sort of rampart against the filtration of the water. Once those traces which have been discovered at the first glance are sufficiently protected, others, smaller or more hidden, must be searched for, which may be found upon grass, the trunks of trees, stones, or the ground. Such are often of great value and inform us at least whether the wounded person has arrived bleeding at the place where he has been discovered, whether he has been dragged there, whether the perpetrator of the crime has tried to get rid of the blood upon him, whether the soles of his shoes were stained with blood, and many other often very important points.

It is especially difficult to determine the presence of blood which has fallen on ground containing absolutely no vegetation and which has become dried up thereon because its colour in such conditions alters greatly according to the composition of the soil and the blood may be unrecognisable. In such a difficulty the author has on two occasions had recourse, and with success, not to a medical man, but to an experienced sportsman. The sportsman is accustomed to find and follow the traces of blood of the animal wounded by him and he is able to say with certainty "this is or is not blood."

On another occasion a dog was successfully employed. Upon a road running through fields, the dead body of a young and unknown man was found covered with serious wounds. The corpse was extraordinarily pale, the individual must therefore have lost a large quantity of blood, and, as the pool of blood found there was insignificant, it was presumed that the victim had been wounded somewhere else and had lost there, and upon the way traversed by him to reach the place of discovery, sufficient blood to cause his death and indeed the whole of the way covered by the wounded man was marked with drops of blood more or less apart. These drops of blood led to a forest away from the road, where it was possible to follow them, though with much trouble. It was there concluded that the man had turned round and round in large circles. It appeared therefore that he had covered this road the night before and that he had wandered about not knowing what he was doing owing to the loss of blood. In spite of all the efforts of the persons investigating the matter they could not discover the blood traces denoting the starting point of these circles, that is to say, the place whence the victim had come. An excellent bloodhound was sent for, which commenced by twice going round the circle, but finally found its bearings and following up the trail arrived at a farm where a large pool of blood was discovered carefully covered up with earth. The inquiry revealed that the person found dead had attempted to commit a theft in the neighbourhood of this house, but had been discovered and maltreated by the farmer's son; he had lain for a considerable time where the pool of blood was found and had then tried to drag himself away. In another case a bloodhound discovered a piece of straw to which some brain matter was adhering. It was concluded that at this spot the body of the murdered person had been taken from a cart and in fact the corpse was found buried close at hand.

In searching for traces of blood the Investigating Officer will do well to make use of a good magnifying glass, with which he will find it easy to rapidly examine a large surface but on the other hand he will of course and in the most absolute manner, avoid touching the blood with damp fingers or on his own authority submitting it to any chemical reagent whatsoever.

The only reagent to be recommended to the layman as successful for blood is the tincture of guaiac, as shown by *Dragendorf*. But even that should be resorted to only when the matter is extremely pressing, for instance if an arrest depends on it and the opinion of a medical expert cannot be speedily obtained. It may also be safely used when there are several stains so that the loss of one is of no importance.

Dragendorf describes the process as follows. Cut out the suspected stain and lay it in a small clean vessel such as a chemist's measuring glass, moisten it with distilled water, and wait for a time. Then lay on it a piece of thin, colourless, filter-paper of the same size and press this firmly on to the stuff with a glass rod. After about 30 minutes take up the paper and with a clean glass rod lay on it some oil or spirits of turpentine and an equal quantity of freshly prepared tincture of guaiac.

If no blue colouring appears, it is *not* blood. If the blue colouring does appear the suspicion as to blood is justified, although it may be some other substance. Such a test, however, though not absolute, is most useful in cases of doubt and emergency.

Frequently it is of importance to know whether the person from whom the blood has dropped was, at the time when the drop fell, standing still

382 TRACES OF BLOOD

or moving, and in the latter case in which direction and how fast. For this purpose we may experiment with the blood of animals or with a coloured substance of the same liquidity as fresh blood. We shall be able to establish first that each drop which falls from a tolerable height on a surface not too rough, produces a splash. If we let the drops fall on a sheet of paper with a steady hand, the globular drop flattens to an approximately circular disc, round which the splashes are pretty evenly distributed (Fig 63 a). Next we lay on the floor a large sheet of paper, fill a glass tube, open at top and bottom, and about 20 cm (8 in) long, with animal blood, closing the tube with the finger. We then walk past the sheet of paper opening the glass tube sufficiently to allow a drop to fall on the paper. If we now compare this drop (Fig 63 b) with the other, we find two differences, the form of the new drop is not circular, but elongated, and the splashes are not distributed evenly round it, but are to be found only on one side. If we repeat the experiment until we are certain of its accuracy we shall find, as a rule, that the extension of the drop lies in the direction of our movement, and further, the splashes are now found only in the same direction, that is, the splashes point in the direction whither the person from whom the blood dropped was at the moment proceeding. If we now in making the experiment alter our pace, we find that the faster the movement the longer the spot or blot. This is explained by the spherical shape of the falling drop, which, when it strikes the paper, continues its forward movement. In the same way, the faster the motion the more are the splashes prolonged in the same direction. But this rule has an exception. If a person has a wound on the hand, and swings the hand while walking rapidly, the drop left by the backward swing will then show the splashes in the opposite direction, the hand having a backward movement. Mistakes will not however easily come about in this way. No person will form a conclusion on a single drop, but if several, say a row of drops, are observed then all of them will certainly not have come from the backward swing of the hand, and we shall thus be nearly always able to establish with certainty the direction of the walker. Experiments may be easily made at first with ink. Anyone who desires to minutely study the effect of drops coming from a moving object on a stationary one, or vice versa has only to observe the forms of raindrops on a railway carriage window.

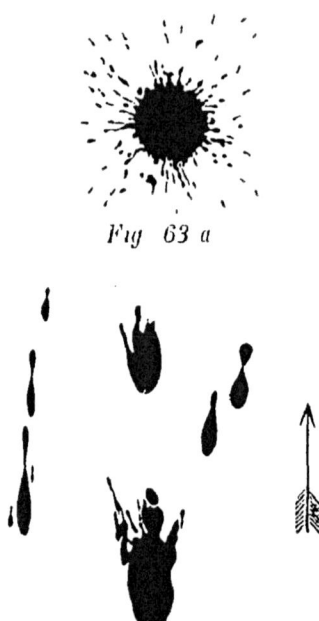

Fig 63 a

Fig 63 b

Section ii.—How to register and describe Traces of Blood.

The Investigating Officer will only start this work when he has undertaken and completed his general description of the locality. If the blood-stains are few in quantity or if they are only of secondary importance they

REGISTRATION OF BLOOD MARKS

may be indicated and described upon the main sketch (see *Chaps III* and *XII*) But if they are undoubtedly of great importance and particularly if they are very numerous and scattered in all directions, it is expressly recommended that they be specially drawn upon a second sketch, traced from the first against a window, indicating the furniture, etc., thereon summarily, but without designation by letters. In most cases these two sketches will not alone suffice, other sketches will have to be added thereto, reproducing the details of these traces of blood, which it will then be possible to draw not only with perfect accuracy but according to a scientific scheme. In proceeding thus it is much more easy to read and compare the sketches, thereby facilitating the work, for the inconvenience of having too many things on one piece of paper is obviated.

To more easily explain to the beginner this work, far from complicated though it be, we give an example as well as its explanation.

L Corpse of murdered person
K Pier table
S to S'''' Chairs
N Night table
B Bed
T', T" Tables
Sch Chest of Drawers
O Stove
F', F" Windows
Th', Th" Doors

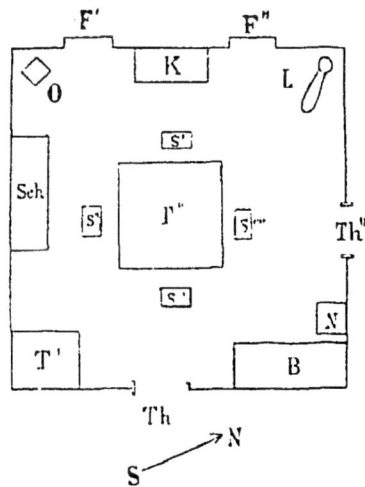

A General aspect of the situation, Fig 64 a *

a Extended pool of blood
ß Blood rubbed on the top part of the table
γ Blood rubbed on the stove
δ Splashes of blood on the stove
ε, ε' Drops of blood on the ground

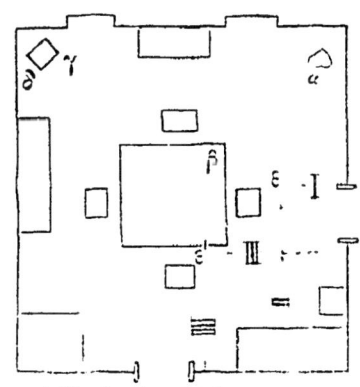

B Sketch showing the situation of traces of blood, Fig. 64 b.

---

* The initial letters of the German equivalents are here used, this and the following blocks having been prepared for the German edition. Of course English Investigating Officers will employ the initial letters of the equivalent English words i e for L, K, S, N, B, T, Sch, O, F, Th use C, P, Ch, N, B, T, Dr, S, W, D

C. Details of α (Fig 65).

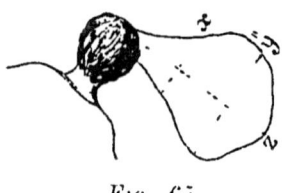

Fig 65

Head and back of corpse with pool of blood commencing at the head. This pool of blood is reproduced in approximately the same dimensions as the body. Length of the three dotted lines.

in the direction of x =   Cm
    ,,   ,,   y =   Cm
    ,,   ,,   z =   Cm

D. Details of β (Fig 66).

Fig 66

The top of the table B seen from below, with three marks of blood, probably made by the pressure of three fingers of a heavy left hand.

E. Details of γ (Fig 67)

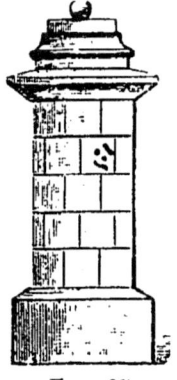

Fig 67

Four drops of blood which have spurted on to the back part of an earthenware stove at a height of 187 cm. δ is an isolated round drop of blood, 179 cms from the ground and 107.5 cms from the corner situated behind the stove, the distance being measured horizontally.

ε and ε' are drops of blood which have been projected on to the ground at an angle of about 40°.

The lines drawn on the walls, here represented by dotted lines on the floor, are line I = 106 cms, line II = 197 cms which fixes ε, line III = 82 cms, line IV = 221 cms, which fixes ε'.

From these model sketches we can see how simple are the means required to give an absolutely clear image of the situation, and nothing then remains to be done but to describe the objects more accurately, reproducing them in their natural size and detaching if necessary the actual blood-stains themselves.

In the case with which we are dealing all these operations must be undertaken. The pool of blood is of special importance in a case where it is not known whether the person killed has lost blood *only* at that spot, if, for example he has been brought to the place where found. It is evident that a medical man will be able to at once inform us on this point, for the rest it suffices to indicate the principal dimensions of the pool. Note that *in every case*, in view of subsequent verification the lines delimiting the dimensions should be drawn at right angles to one another; thus here the principal axis is drawn first in the direction of z and the other lines y and x are drawn perpendicular to z. As to the splashes of blood β they should be preserved without more ado by taking off the top of the table and keeping it as a "material object" for the trial. For further safety these traces of blood will be sketched and described. As to the other drops of blood γ, it will be scarcely possible to proceed thus; there is no other means but to take a sheet of tracing paper, place it over the brick or stone and patiently trace the drops one by one. Any person can perform this task even if he has never had a drawing lesson in his life; getting someone to hold down the tracing paper, he has only to set to work with good will and success is certain. But it must never be forgotten that this work should on no account be commenced, however inoffensive it may appear, until the traces of blood have been carefully described. The misfortune may happen in tracing one of the blood-stains that the base on which it rests breaks, so that we have neither the drawing nor the description. The safest plan to follow is, first describe, next sketch, and lastly reproduce from nature.

As regards the drops of blood δ, ϵ, ϵ', it will be sufficient to describe and take the necessary measurements, and if they present any peculiarity, as for instance, splashes sideways, they should also be drawn in natural size and in some cases they must be removed. Even when fortunate enough to be able to photograph the traces of blood, the duty of describing and sketching them must never be dispensed with. They must be described, because every image without an explanation is lifeless, and they must be sketched because a photograph, in spite of its accuracy, does not always produce the desired impression. A photograph produces everything, and the points to which the attention is desired to be drawn are often less visible and less to the front of everything else than they ought to be. A photograph is, in such cases, very desirable, but it should never be permitted to replace the hand sketch. As for blood-stains of larger size, which, for some reason or other, cannot be traced or drawn by hand, they must be copied if possible with the assistance of squared paper (see *Chapter XII Section iii*)

Section iii.—How to detach Traces of Blood.

All the traces of blood having been described, measured, and sketched they can now be detached as they are, *in situ* if this be possible, and if their form and aspect seem sufficiently important to have some bearing upon the conduct of inquiry. But as every trace of blood may turn out to be important, so the following rule must be laid down: remove *in situ* everything which it is possible so to remove. The procedure differs according to the substance upon which the blood is deposited. We shall here study the more important cases.

The best, safest, and at the same time the simplest method is naturally to carry away the article itself, as was done for example, with the top of the table mentioned above. This may also be done in other cases, for example, with clothes, small articles of office furniture, paper, books, etc., also window frames, doors, pieces of wall-paper etc., finally in the open air, when not too large, stones, branches and twigs of trees, which may be cut off and taken away. Moreover glass and growing corn stained with blood may easily be removed. A good pair of scissors or a sharp sickle is taken and the plant cut down level with the ground, the object is then placed in a box if need be between two sheets of paper, where it is fixed in some convenient way (see *infra*).

In removing plants stained with blood, it is essential in the majority of cases to preserve their freshness as long as possible, for in drying, they shrink, and the drops of blood, drying more quickly, often become detached from the plant, not leaving the slightest trace of their presence. To preserve the freshness of the plant the stem is cut obliquely with a sharp knife, and is then plunged rapidly into a mixture of water and glycerine or into lime water, the former is generally easily found, the latter almost always. Through the absorption of this fluid the flowers become blackish and faded. But, though weak and limp, they remain moist, as the glycerine does not evaporate like water. To transport the plant, the liquid in question is placed in a small bottle and the stem inserted through a hole in the cork. It will of course, have to be carried in the hand.

When the object is such that it cannot be taken away the blood must be removed along with a portion of the surface on which it rests, or may be detached, with or without injury to the surface. When traces of blood are found upon wood it will nearly always be possible to raise a part of the wood. Such would be done in the case of the blood-stains *e* and *e'* on the scheme constructed above, they are upon the floor and, as in all cases of this kind, must be raised and taken away. To perform this work a tradesman is necessary, either a joiner, turner, carpenter, barrel-maker, or any other worker in wood. Among the peasantry, plenty of persons sufficiently skilled are to be found who practically make the whole furniture of their dwellings. Such people are perhaps the most useful assistants, for they know how to lay their hands to anything. Suppose, for example, there are several drops of blood not covering a very large expanse of floor touching only one or two planks, in such a case the simplest method is to cut out the planks above and below the blood with a cold chisel. It is sometimes better to use a horizontal saw instead of the chisel as by an accidental rebound of the latter the marks may be injured. In this way the object may be obtained *in naturâ*. While this work is progressing great care must be taken to protect the blood-stains and prevent them from being damaged by the splinters and shavings which fly about. On the pieces of wood when cut out their cardinal direction is indicated by an arrow and the letters N and S to denote the points of the compass. In this way no doubt will arise regarding their situation with respect to the principal sketch. These indications must never be forgotten, even on very small pieces of wood, for these may, in spite of their great importance, prove quite valueless if their true position be unknown. When it is not possible to raise the plank or beam throughout its whole depth, or when the drops of blood are far apart only the upper part of the wood is detached. A sharp chisel is dug into the wood above or below the blood in the direction of the grain, care being taken to insert the steel obliquely, at an angle of about 45°, until it is firmly fixed. The same operation is performed on the other side of the blood, and finally the handle of the chisel is pressed downwards thus pressing up a sufficiently thick splinter of wood, if the latter be too thin it may twist and the drop of blood run the risk of peeling off and falling When dealing with hard wood (beech, oak, the wood of fruit trees, etc) two cuts are generally insufficient the chisel must then be dug in all round the blood-stain on the sides of a square by which method instead of a splinter of wood a sort of quadrangular pyramid will be obtained, the large base of which carries the blood The same procedure will be followed when the blood rests upon a wooden partition, a beam, or the branch of a tree There is no difficulty in raising the bark of a tree, but when it is thin like that of the birch or pear, etc, we must be careful that the drop of blood does not become detached from the bark which as we have indicated above, may shrivel up The same methods will again be followed for furniture which cannot be removed in entirety, the more so as it is almost always easy to detach with a saw that portion of the article of furniture which is desired to be preserved If the furniture be veneered, the veneering is removed by cutting all round the place in question with a sharp knife and detaching it from the soft wood underneath In this latter case the surface is smooth and polished and the blood does not hold to it firmly great precaution must therefore be exercised in performing the operation If the splash of blood be important, and the surface so smooth that the former may probably fall off, it should be protected This is best done by covering a piece of fine transparent paper—cigarette paper is very good—with an absolutely clean solution of gum, and laying it on the surface so as to cover the drop We must then get to work before the paper dries otherwise the whole, paper and blood, might drop off

To detach traces of blood from a wall its surface must be submitted to a preliminary inspection If it has been several times whitewashed it is best to attempt to raise the thin sheets of dried whitewash, but if the wall has never been whitewashed, or but once, it is necessary to raise at the same time a portion of the mortar To find out the correct method to follow, it is only necessary to scrape with a knife at some place or other near the stain If one can detach several thin and solid leaves the first mentioned method is the correct one, if not, that is to say, if one comes directly to the stone and mortar, the second will be best But we must not lose sight of the fact that the operation may be unsuccessful so that, and it cannot be repeated too often, the blood must first have been described and sketched The operation of detaching blood-stains from a wall is as follows a piece of transparent tracing-paper, which every Investigating Officer should carry with him (see *Chapter II*) or a piece of fairly strong glass of suitable size is gummed over the blood Pure gum arabic should be used which, provided it has been mentioned by the Investigating Officer, will trouble neither the chemist nor the microscopist who may have to subsequently examine the object To detach the whole more easily when the proper time comes the upper edge of the tracing-paper is entirely gummed down, thus rendering it easier to seize if glass be employed, a ribbon of strong paper or, by preference, a band of cloth should be placed under its upper edge leaving the ends jutting out for convenience in removing the glass The tracing-paper or the glass plate is then pressed firmly and cautiously against the wall, being careful to lean a pole slanting against it as its weight might cause it to slip After this, it is only necessary to wait until the gum is quite dry, which takes a considerable time. For this reason this work should be done at once, so that while the gum is drying we may proceed to another branch of the investigation.

To ascertain the precise moment when these plates are dry, trials must be made at places on the neighbouring wall; several pieces of tracing-paper or glass should therefore be gummed to the wall in the same way as over the blood; this work necessitates little trouble and time and prevents mistakes. When it may be presumed that all is dry, an attempt is made to detach one of these trial plates; if the operation is successful we may proceed to the proper plate, but if it comes to grief we wait a little and then experiment with another trial plate, and continue so doing until it is certain that the *corpus delicti* may be detached without danger. If the surface *i e*, the wall, has been several times whitewashed it is desirable to obtain the latest coat of whitewash, or at least several of these coats, which will not be difficult, for they do not hold solidly to the wall, but the precaution must be taken to detach the plate or the tracing-paper slowly and commencing from the top, inserting a sharp knife between the plate and the wall. In this way a certain number of layers of lime-wash will be obtained, then the blood stain, and finally the tracing-paper or glass covering the whole. To better, and more completely, protect the arrangement it will be well to gum on the back of it (i e, on the surface of separation) a piece of thin wood or a piece of cardboard or cloth.

But if the wall has not been several times whitewashed the operation is not so easy. It is then necessary, using a chisel or knife, to detach a layer of mortar in order to obtain at least a sort of plate. When the mortar is fine and not very friable the matter is easy, but if it is coarse and contains little lime, the work is rather troublesome and we must proceed as with *hard wood* (see *supra*). The operator places his hand upon the plate which might become detached and fall suddenly, then another person picks out the mortar all round the plate and raises the portion of wall with a chisel; this portion will naturally be much greater than is required. In proceeding thus it is hardly possible not to be successful; in all such cases it is the only method of bringing the work to a satisfactory conclusion, and no better method is known even for detaching old mural paintings.

When traces of blood have fallen on the ground and are of some importance, the clod of earth must be detached with a knife or spade and preserved in a vessel to prevent either desiccation or the jars of transportation destroying its form in any way. If the earth be damp the vessel ought to be impermeable; if on the contrary the soil be friable (dust, sand, cinders etc.), we must endeavour to obtain a certain amount of cohesion and thus prevent it from breaking up and losing its shape. Specialists frequently remark in this connection that one must be careful not to carry away with the earth certain animals, particularly worms. This is no doubt quite correct, since such animals feed upon the organic substances of the earth. An earth-worm would absorb for example the portion of the ground impregnated with the blood, which latter it would digest, evacuating the inorganic substances, so that in a short time there would be nothing in the box but the earth and the worm, the blood having disappeared. If it were only a question of protecting the blood it would be very easy to get rid of these animals, for example by heating the clod of earth, sprinkling tanning-water or a decoction of tobacco or other disagreeable liquids upon it. But the chemist and the microscopist would object, and rightly, to all such methods, so that we can recommend but one plan and that a purely mechanical one. Before raising the clod of earth in question, the ground all round the blood is struck twenty or thirty times with a strong pole or a large stone, etc. This striking is excessively disagreeable to worms, which, if they are within the space in question, immediately come to the surface.

As to metallic objects bearing blood-stains, such as bolts, keys, locks, door hinges, etc., the best thing to do is to carry them bodily away. If this be impossible, the procedure depends upon whether the object is smooth or not. If there be roughness an attempt will be made to detach the blood-stain (after having, of course, described and drawn it) as above indicated for stains on walls with this difference however that a plate of glass can never be used, but always tracing-paper; a piece of tracing-paper will be gummed over the stain with gum-arabic and detached before the gum is quite dried. In the majority of cases the stain will thus be obtained in its entirety. If any of it be left behind it will be cautiously scraped off, placed in a clean piece of paper, and preserved. From perfectly smooth surfaces (glass-discs, glazed Dutch tiles, very flat polished wood or metal, etc.), one can remove traces of blood by laying on them filter paper, moist but not soaked through, and pressing the filter-paper down firmly. After a time the two can be cautiously removed together.

On the other hand it is absolutely necessary to protect the back of the plate thus obtained. The best method consists in taking a sheet of ordinary glass of sufficient size, covering it with gum-arabic and pressing it upon that side of the tracing-paper upon which the blood stain rests; the latter, enclosed between the glass and the paper is completely safeguarded and may be seen directly through the glass. The self-same methods will be followed when traces of blood are deposited upon other very smooth objects which it is impossible to remove, such as large pier glasses, large smooth stones, slabs of marble, stoves with smooth surfaces, as found in our scheme, Fig 67. In all such cases an attempt must be made to detach the blood and safeguard it in the manner indicated. It goes without saying that the gum must not be allowed to become quite dry; the tracing-paper must be detached when the gum begins to offer a certain resistance.

If the surface be rough, for example, rusted iron, a large undressed stone, etc., nothing else can be done but carefully to scrape off the blood, collecting it in a piece of paper held underneath and firmly pressed against the surface of the object. The paper ought always to be very smooth letter paper, for the blood gets crushed on a rough paper, breaks up, and ends by becoming lost. The best paper would be the glazed paper in which druggists retail their fine powders, such as aniline dyes, etc. It is extremely smooth and retains absolutely no particle of the powder, but yet we must discountenance the employment of this paper for it is not always glazed simply by hot rolling but with the help of various ingredients which may subsequently gravely compromise the work of the chemist.

In desperate cases we must invent some device. The author had at one time to handle a blood-stain on a rock of very hard gneiss. The hardness and the structure of the stone would not permit of blasting, scraping was also impossible owing to the great roughness of the surface. The face of the rock on which the stain lay sloped a little, so a ridge was made round the drop of blood from the wax of a small candle from the outfit case (*Fig 1, p* 101), then some clean water was dropped on the stain. In half-an-hour the drop was softened and loosened. It was then rubbed with a clean piece of wood and the mixture sucked up with filter-paper. The soaked filter-paper was put in a small clean glass, kept damp by a few drops of water and given to experts with an exact description of the circumstances, together with the wax ridge, the piece of wood, the unused filter-papers, and a sample of the water used. The experts at once detected blood. Whenever blood has thus to be scraped the work must be done as quickly as possible. Thus *Caspar Liman* praises an Investigating Officer who, discovering immediately after a crime, a blood-stain upon the thumb-nail of the suspected criminal, scraped it off carefully and preserved it. It would have been still better, if he had gummed with concentrated solution of gum arabic a strip of tracing-paper over the blood and thus detached it, one can readily test with what ease a blood-stain can be removed from a nail in this manner; and if the individual suspected allowed his nail to be scraped he would be no more opposed to the other process.

But the Investigating Officer ought always to ask, and the question is an important one, if, in certain cases, it would not be better not to expose traces of blood to the dangers which always accompany the operation of detaching them, and whether he ought not to postpone the operation until the inquiry has thrown more light on the whole case. Of course there need be no hesitation when the blood is found in places where it is exposed to the influences of the atmosphere, or may be exposed to damp or the contact of persons, that is to say, when it is in the open air or in places which for some reason cannot be isolated, but if it is in a closed space capable of being completely and surely shut up, and kept thus for some time, it is certainly better to leave it alone. If on the contrary it is impossible completely to protect it, as will be the case in many circumstances, no risk must be run, it must be removed and taken away.

As for every *corpus delicti*, so here it is particularly important that the description should be made at once, and as accurately as possible. Moreover we must clearly state as regards each trace of blood what was the fate of the victim, under what conditions the body, if any, was found, whether damp, dry, warm, cold, etc and if it has been moved by others, or could have been moved. These data may be of the utmost importance for experts. Particularly important are many circumstances which must be accurately reported to the expert, as, for example that the blood discovered had been repeatedly frozen and again thawed, whereby the blood corpuscles might be disturbed. Again, if the blood marks had been subjected to ammoniacal vapours, as of a sewer or latrine, whereby the blood corpuscles are deprived of hemoglobin and loosened. In the same way *over-heating* is worth mentioning. *Liman* relates that blood marks on a coat could not be loosened because they had been ironed over by a tailor.

Section IV.—Search for traces of blood which there has been an attempt to remove.

We must now say a few words concerning the search for blood there has been an attempt to get rid of; such search is by no means an easy matter, as criminals employ herein remarkable skill and cunning. Fortunately they often happen to forget just the essential thing, so that there is always a weak point, and not only a weak point, but, so far as concerns the criminal, a most grave error. To discover this point often constitutes the entire work of the criminalist; having found it, everything else is easy.

First let us deal with the body of the criminal himself; we will find only suspicious traces of important *indicia* upon him when he is examined within a short time of the commission of the crime. A person whose hands have been stained with blood, invariably washes them, and it is a most suspicious circumstance when a person of the lower classes presents absolutely clean hands, especially on a working day. This peculiarity ought always to cause us, if there exist other incriminating circumstances, to submit the individual's hands to a minute examination. Even upon hands carefully washed, traces of blood may, with a good magnifying glass, often be found either under the nails, or upon or under the skin where the nails are embedded in the fingers. In such a case one will naturally attempt to detach and preserve these little particles of blood, with the assistance of a knife or other pointed instrument. Of course the suspected individual may not submit to this treatment, but in practice the matter resolves itself into this, that, if the individual permits the removal of blood (an operation which ought if possible to be performed by a medical man), one is certain of obtaining it; whereas if he refuses, the fact is mentioned in the report of the investigation and the hands of the accused are examined in the presence of the medical man, the Investigating Officer's clerks or assistants, and two or more independent witnesses; the accused cannot oppose this examination; by doing so he would make the case look very black against him, for his refusal would amount to a tacit admission that there is indeed blood there.

More important still than the examination of the hands, is the examination of the face and hair of the criminal, who as a rule does not think of there being blood upon these parts of his body; he therefore does not wash them or at least does so only very superficially. Here again recourse to the magnifying glass must not be neglected, for careful and intimate examination. It goes without saying that this work legitimately appertains to the medical jurisprudent but it generally happens that the Investigating Officer comes in contact with the accused before he can have a medical man at his disposition; he will often be required therefore to undertake this work himself. In doing so he will not be acting contrary to the law, for he will not be doing the work of the specialist but simply collecting the materials of his inquiry, which is his essential business.

As regards clothes, linen, footwear, etc., they should first be examined superficially to determine whether an attempt to wash them has been made, always a suspicious circumstance. The accused is frequently satisfied with scraping off the kind of crust formed by the dried blood which however always leaves a stain not difficult to recognise. The washing is often done very carefully but is confined to those clothes which directly strike the eye, the boots, the inside of the pockets, clothes of dark colour, or dark stains not easily noticed, are forgotten.

Thus the author had on one occasion to examine a peasant who had washed his clothes, much stained with blood, in the most careful and skilful manner, but had forgotten his boots. These boots, old, frequently wet through, hardly ever brushed, had taken on a reddish brown hue, so that the numerous drops of blood with which they were stained were invisible at some distance; this person had not thought of taking off and carefully examining his boots, but had kept them on his feet, and being able to see them only at a distance, had not perceived the stains which were the same colour as the leather.

In this class of cases it is of the greatest interest to know whether the washing has been done with cold water or with hot. It is easy to get rid of blood, especially fresh blood, by washing in cold water, whereas hot water fixes the colouring matter, making it almost impossible to remove. Women know this better than men, for they have often to get rid of the blood of menstruation staining their linen; they therefore rarely commit the fault of washing out blood in hot water, which men regularly do in the hope of better success. Just the contrary happens: the blood-stains will remain visible, we do not say at the exact spot they were at first, but at least in what may be called the *cartilage*, i.e. in that part of the material surrounding the stain properly so called, whence the blood has spread in consequence of the washing.

If the material be washed in cold water and with sufficient skill to prevent anything being seen in the neighbourhood of the stain, it is not impossible that the colouring matter may be deposited by the water in the adjacent hems and seams and remain upon the sewing cotton and in the folds of the cloth. For this it is of course necessary that only the stain and its immediate neighbourhood should have been washed; but if the hems and seams have been wetted at the same time as the stain there is always the possibility of finding therein particles of blood. In such a case we therefore recommend the investigator not to be content with a mere examination of the suspected parts properly so called, but also to unstitch the hems and seams in order the more carefully to observe them. *Fig.* 68 represents the left corner of the front part of a man's waistcoat showing the opening of the pocket. The smallest circle is the stain of blood properly so called, the larger represent the 'cartilage' mentioned above. In the case in point we should examine first the cartilage, then the hem *a b c*, and finally the hem of the pocket *d e*.

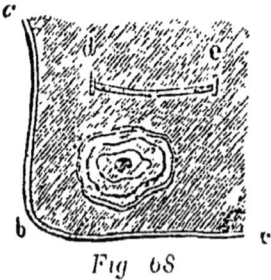

Fig. 68

The same procedure will be followed in examining instruments or tools which are supposed to have been washed: the blade and easily visible portions of a knife, for instance, may appear to be perfectly clean, whereas the covered places often contain in large quantity stains of blood deposited there either directly or brought there by the water in which the knife has been washed. Before placing an instrument on one side as perfectly clean and therefore not to be regarded with suspicion and referred to the examination of experts, it must be taken to pieces and the hidden places examined. Thus the wooden haft or handle of a hatchet must be withdrawn from the iron blade in which it is fixed in order to examine the outside of the form and the interior of the latter; at the same time it is necessary to observe any cracks to be found in the wood. As regards pocket knives, and even knives with fixed blades, the rivets must be removed for the purpose of inspecting, separately and in detail, the various parts. Of equal importance are the cracks and splits in walking-sticks and cudgels and the incrustations on metal tools of all kinds, be they artificial or naturally produced by rust.

These operations must, in view of their importance, necessarily be performed by experts, or at all events in their presence. Of course there are exceptional cases where the Investigating Officer is obliged to act himself; but in order to shield himself from every breath of suspicion, he must proceed with the very greatest prudence and the most scrupulous propriety, taking care to call in respectable witnesses, not merely as a matter of form but for the purpose of calling their attention in the most express manner and continuously throughout the proceedings, to every detail and every striking particular connected therewith. Nor must he neglect to describe with the utmost minuteness in his report all that has been done to delineate every object having any possible bearing upon the case and to obtain the signatures of the witnesses and of members of the panchayat to the completed report. Although the Investigating Officer must be permitted in many instances a certain latitude of choice, a certain allowance of judgment, yet in the majority of cases it is not for him, especially if he be in the subordinate ranks of the service, to decide what may not be of subsequent utility. Even the shrewdest mind and most acute intellect cannot always foresee the march of events.

Frequently enough attempts are made to get rid of blood deposited in the open air or in premises etc.; in such a case it is always necessary first to establish with certainty that this attempt has been made. This certainty may obtain the same value as the discovery of blood itself, for in many inquiries, it suffices to know that there *has* been blood and *where* it has been. The shape, size, and the number of the stains found on a particular spot may be of secondary importance. If, therefore, the Investigating Officer is in a position to establish that there have been stains of blood, and that an attempt to obliterate them has been made, he must proceed as if they really existed, describing, measuring, and sketching the places that have been washed, scraped, or planed down. Even in detaching traces where an attempt has been made to get rid of the stains, he must proceed as if the stains really existed, for some may have passed unperceived or, being more deeply impregnated, have remained visible in spite of all efforts to remove them. These efforts themselves may furnish us with characteristic indications: it is possible to deduce from the manner in which a portion of wall has been removed, the spot where the largest part of the drop of blood has lain, the general bearing of the stains, the direction of the small splashes, and the instrument with which the wall has been scraped, etc.

As regards wood *e.g.* a beam, a wooden partition and especially a floor, which has been washed, we must not despair of still being able to find traces of blood, especially if hot water has been used as mentioned above. A floor, if not new, has often deep cracks and straight splits into which blood frequently finds its way, unperceived by the criminal. The space separating two planks also absorbs the water used in the washing at the same time as the blood, without the person washing taking the slightest heed. As in such a case the blood must be in very small quantities it will be best to remove the whole of the wood in question. For polished wood floors, special attention must be paid to the matters found between and under the different planks: dust, sand, tobacco ash, rubbish and a thousand other substances. All this may have soaked up blood or water mixed with blood, and may be of importance. It should therefore be collected and preserved, along with all debris of stones and other materials underneath the floor. It is just in these cases that it is necessary to accurately describe the spot where such an object has been discovered, for we generally have to deal with very small quantities, so that it is all the more important to know whence they come.

Suppose it is necessary to remove with a chisel two pieces of wood from two adjacent planks. Before beginning an arrow should be drawn across the two pieces of wood, with a pencil having no peculiar chemical properties such as might interfere with chemical examination, the actual position of the object (*Fig. 69*) will be designated by the points of the compass—N S.; it will then never be difficult to determine the actual position of the two planks. Everything will then be wrapped and preserved in different pieces of paper ticketed as follows: 1 and 2, the two planks; 3, 4 and 5, contents of the cracks, a a', b b', c c'; 6, 7, 8, debris beneath the cracks a a', b b', c c'.

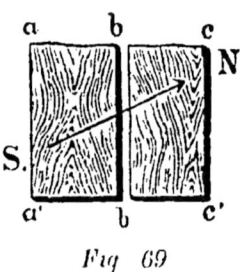

Fig. 69

If anything particular be found, for example a little ball which may consist of dried blood mixed with dust, it must be placed by itself and labelled as follows: 9, found in the crack c c', at a distance of 14 inches from c' in the direction of c, near the surface.

If for some unusual reason or other, it is impossible to raise and remove the plank, the cracks separating the plank must be cleaned as far as possible with a bent iron wire or any other suitable instrument, carefully preserving everything discovered. Fragments of wood, of the same length as the stains suspected to have been washed, must also be cut off from the two planks forming the crack in the floor; finally the floor is scraped until perfectly white, and everything removed therefrom carefully preserved. It would also be advisable, in such a case, to carry away the instruments used in the work (bent iron wire, knife, scraper) in order, if need be, to hold them at the disposition of the court, for here we have the objection which must always be expected that the instruments may have been stained with blood, either at the time of the operation owing to a slight wound, or previously, and that the fact of blood having been found by the experts proves nothing. If such objection be made, the instruments used need only be produced.

An expert may soak the blood-stains with dilute sulphuric acid, subsequently washing them with a solution of soda.

Stains that have been whitewashed over or mixed with broken earth will be easily recognised. In such cases we must proceed as if they have not been touched.

Section v.—Finger-prints in Blood.

Finally there are certain traces of blood of particular importance, namely impressions made by a hand or several fingers coloured with blood or by certain portions of the sole of the foot. Finger-prints have been dealt with at considerable length in *Chapter V., Section x.*, and footprints have been most exhaustively discussed in *Chapter XIII.*; we shall not therefore, repeat what has been already stated, presuming that the reader has already studied the subjects there. Several points, however, fall more properly under the heading "blood," which we shall deal with here.

We all know how often finger-prints are found in wounding and murder cases; we have seen them for ourselves, and in 50 per cent of criminal cases in which blood has been spilt, impressions thereof exist although the criminal, of course, has had no intention of " leaving impressions behind him." It is not difficult to understand the reason. From numerous murder cases, and even the confessions of criminals, we learn that these latter have an idea that it is easy to kill a person; they believe it to be a much easier job than it really is; they imagine that a single blow of a knife or club will suffice to despatch the victim. Either in the excitement of the moment the blow is too feeble, or else it does not touch a vital spot, or it may be that, speaking in a general way, death does not take place instantaneously, but it generally happens that the victim although thought to be mortally wounded is still able momentarily to place the criminal in danger; the former may cry out, take to flight, or place himself on the defensive.

Thus are explained those horrible struggles the details of which clearly appear upon the dissecting table, and from which we learn that the murderer, while only intending to deliver a single blow at his victim, has continued to strike long after his work is fully accomplished. In this case it is almost inevitable that the criminal gets blood upon the hand with which he has seized his victim, some instrument, or other object. It frequently happens that, immediately after the crime, the criminal in his search for valuables, groping in the darkness, opening and shutting doors and windows, seizing jugs to wash himself leaves behind on all kinds of articles the impressions of his hands and his several fingers. Let us add that blood lends itself admirably to the production of neat and distinct impressions; thanks to its greasy nature it spreads rapidly on the warm hand, and as it is also very sticky, it attaches readily to any object impressed, so that after the second contact there remains just enough blood to produce a perfectly clear impression.

It is therefore, easy to explain the relative frequency of the presence of these impressions; they must be always sought after and registered. The most difficult part is the search for them, for they are as a rule small, made up of fine lines, are less easy to see than even the smallest drops of blood, and finally are frequently only to be found in out-of-the-way places.

It is true that these impressions are of no value from the present point of view when deposited upon a rough surface or when the hand or fingers have been simply wiped upon, for instance cloths, unplaned wood, rough metal, or those parts of the body covered with hair, etc. Cut and visible impressions will be found on those parts of the body of the victim which are smooth and hairless, as the forehead, cheeks, the bald head, the inside of the hand, etc. To preserve them we can recommend but one method, namely to have the part of the skin in question carefully prepared by a specialist and the blood mark photographed, before the skin has become shrivelled and dried up.*

Impressions are also to be found upon instruments used by the criminal e.g., on the handle of a hoe, the handle of a knife, on a crowbar and on agricultural implements; also upon smooth wood, such as household utensils in soft or hard wood, or metal plates or on windows or flat stones.

Particular attention must be paid to certain portions of furniture. The underneath part of a table top (Fig. 62), drawers at the places where they are laid hold of to be drawn out, also to papers which the criminal has handled while searching for money, etc. Of equal importance are covers of books which have interested him. The traces having been found and described, it is above all necessary to establish with the assistance of medical experts from what portion of the body they proceed. This point it is frequently impossible to decide until after continuous trials and minute study, which may, however, sometimes be carried out on the spot; the impression may come from the forefingers of the left hand, the palm of the right hand, left foot, etc. This point elucidated, the work becomes easier, and the most urgent thing next to be done is to *establish whether these impressions do not perhaps proceed from the victim of the crime himself*. It may be that on being wounded he has placed his hand to the wound and then upon some article or other or even his own person. Have we not often found in the hand of a murdered person tufts of hair, which he has torn out from his own head in the midst of his agitation and semi-consciousness? He may thus seize part of his body firmly with his own hand and thus produce an impression.

We may compare this with a well known case where the left hand of a murdered man showed a clear impression of a left hand—which could not have been his own. The importance of this question is beyond doubt, yet we deem it not inadvisable to elucidate it by reference to a criminal case which created a great stir at the time.

Not many years ago a celebrated professor was found dead beside his bed. He carried several wounds on the forehead and left temple, these wounds were bleeding profusely and seemed to have caused his death, especially as the deceased was an old gentleman, unable to defend himself against such bodily attacks. This in itself was strange, but suspicion was doubled when it was observed that a drawer of the office table in the room, at some distance from the bed, was open and the clear impressions of three blood-stained fingers were perceived upon a newspaper on the table. This newspaper was resting near the far corner of the table. The staircase leading

---

* It has already been mentioned (*page* 180) that photographs of papillary lines should be taken in a very strong lateral light, shadows augmenting the relief.

to the deceased's bedroom gave on to a large ante-room, whence the rooms occupied by his family were reached his room, which served both as study and bedroom, being, however, situated quite apart from the rest. He had chosen this isolated room so as to be able to work, go to bed, and get up at will, so that neither the family nor the servants had the least suspicion of what was happening on the night of his death. The murder theory immediately took shape, being supported by the suspicious position of the deceased beside the bed, the wounds upon his head, his excellent state of health the night before, and the open door, all leading to the same conclusion. Moreover, some very zealous friends of the professor had immediately noticed that some important manuscripts and chemical preparations were missing from the study, besides, in spite of all plausible explanations, there was always the bloody hand of the murderer on the paper, its significance was far too clear to admit of the idea of a natural death. On top of all this some unhappy creature took it into his head to link up a series of the most insignificant facts and forge a story which spread throughout the town, growing from day to day, and, just as the horrible is always most readily believed so a large number of people in the town were soon convinced that the old gentleman had been murdered and robbed by his own son. And the public found these suspicions all the more overwhelming, for the son was a man of calm and learning, rejoicing in the general esteem.

The magisterial inquiry, most carefully conducted, resulted as follows. The old gentleman had been attacked during the night with heart failure, a complaint he frequently suffered from, full of solicitude for his household as was his custom, not desiring to trouble the sleep of anyone, he left his bed to search for some medicine in the drawer of his table. Arriving there he had been attacked with another spasm and had fallen to the ground, wounding himself on the corner of the table. This was the cause of the wound in the temple, the corner of the table corresponding exactly thereto. The old gentleman had then placed his hand to the wound and tried to get up with the assistance of the table, this was the origin of the blood upon the newspaper. At last he managed to get back to his bed, where he was the victim of a renewed attack which caused him to fall a second time, striking his head upon the foot of the bed, the carving upon which also exactly corresponded to the wound he had then received. Finally he had dragged himself as far as the bed-flounce, where he had succumbed to general failure of the heart's action.

In spite of the irrefutable results of this inquiry, much time elapsed before the public abandoned its unfortunate pre-conceived opinion and did justice to the son of the dead man so cruelly wounded in his honour. With what ease and rapidity would not the whole of this troublesome case have been cleared up if the theories regarding finger-prints had been brought to bear and the papillary lines of the fingers of the deceased compared with the "hand of the murderer," which in public opinion was the strongest piece of proof!

Let us now, taking into consideration the consequences of this most instructive case, obtain some profit therefrom. We must, before everything, on every occasion where blood impressions are found, procure for subsequent comparison the finger prints of the victim. If doctors are able to tell us with certainty from what part of the body the impressions discovered proceed, it is but natural to take *first and foremost* the corresponding impressions upon the corpse. But this is not enough, for later other traces may happen to be discovered belonging to the other parts of the body. There is therefore nothing else to be done but to take the impressions of all portions of the hand of the corpse, and if he is barefoot, also of the soles of the feet bearing the lines in question, an operation which indeed requires but little time.

It may happen that out in the country the printer's ink advised for the taking of these impressions (see p. 193) is not to hand. This, however, is not the only article which may be used. We have already mentioned lamp-black, advised by *Galton*. But both printer's ink and lamp black are not the most appropriate in all cases. Any oil colour may be used spread out on a metal or glass plate, upon which the part of the body in question is pressed and then several times upon paper, quietly and firmly, until a successful imprint is obtained. Sometimes it suffices to press the finger, dried or slightly greased, upon a very polished surface, e.g., glass, porcelain, or metal, on which is then sprinkled some flour, powdered colouring matter or fine dust, taking care to blow away any that does not stick. In the same way any colouring matter soluble in water, may be used as ink or black coffee, etc.—the finger is damped therewith and pressed upon white paper. In case of need even colouring matter may be dispensed with. According to an experiment made by *Gross Jun.*, it is only necessary to rest the finger on a plate of hot glass for a moment. When for instance the funnel of a lighted lamp is seized between the thumb and the fore-finger, and the fingers rapidly withdrawn, too quickly for a burn to take place, very good finger-prints are left upon the glass. These being due to the fatty matter secreted by the skin melting on the hot glass, the image obtained will soon be destroyed if still exposed to the heat, the lamp must therefore be at once extinguished and the funnel allowed to cool. Of course any hot plate may be employed in this way. We have seen (p. 193) that Messrs *Henry* and *Farndale* have gone still further and have been able to preserve clear impressions of the fingers of criminals left while committing their criminal acts upon bottles and tumblers and even boxes. A drinking-glass which has been seized by a burglar has but to be microscopically examined, if impressions cannot be discovered with the naked eye, and if finger-prints are found, on being treated with hydrofluoric acid, they will stand out quite plain.

In many cases all these methods are impracticable, especially in the case of a corpse: here the best thing to do is to select some plastic material and press it upon the fingers. In this way excellent imprints may be obtained with ordinary paste, heated wax, with fresh kneaded bread-crumb, clay, moistened earth, plaster just becoming hard, very fine tin foil or, and perhaps best, the paste used by engravers. The paste is manipulated till a uniform surface is obtained, upon which the fingers are firmly pressed without pushing to one side or to the other; clear impressions are thus produced which may be examined by a magnifying glass. It is hardly necessary to add that the different impressions taken from a corpse must be ticketed with most scrupulous accuracy, or most vexatious confusion may arise.

Finger-prints having been found on the scene of the crime and impressions of the fingers of the person killed taken, the next most pressing thing is to establish by means of experts whether these impressions do not proceed from the victim himself. If they do, they are of no value beyond informing us of what the wounded man did just before his death. But if the impressions do not correspond with the papillary lines on the fingers of the wounded man, it is a natural supposition that they proceed from the author of the crime. And in such a case they may be of value in two ways; firstly they serve to prove the innocence or guilt of a person under arrest, and secondly they may bring about the discovery of the actual criminal. As an instance of this latter we refer our readers to what is known as the Mask Murders fully reported on p. 194. In order to assist rapid and accurate comparison it is best to photograph the original impression of the bloody finger and enlarge it photographically three or four times. If then it is desired to compare these impressions with those of an individual, the matter is perfectly simple; the fingers of the suspect are inspected through a magnifying glass and compared with the enlarged finger-print.

To take a case: the bloody imprint of the thumb of a left hand (according to experts) is found on the scene of a crime and it is established that the lines on the left thumb of the suspected criminal are identical with those found. Presume moreover that the remaining facts are very strong against the individual in question and that he is charged and brought for trial. The similarity between the impressions constitutes an overwhelming piece of evidence against the accused and, as this similarity is difficult to demonstrate with small reproductions, the finger-print found on the scene of the crime must be photographed and enlarged as much as possible. Naturally the enlargement must not be so large as to confuse the lines, retouching being absolutely debarred, as such would completely spoil the argument. The impression of the left thumb of the accused is then taken, if possible with some drops of bullock blood in order to obtain a similar shade, and on the same background as the original, e.g., on paper, wood, iron, glass, etc. This impression is also photographed and enlarged in the same proportion as the other, so that in both cases the conditions are alike. If then the impression found on the scene of the crime really proceeds from the accused person, the two enlarged photographs on being compared will present so striking a resemblance that no one, not even a man least acquainted with this sort of thing, would doubt their identity.

It must also be remarked that papillary lines may be produced not only with blood, but also with all other colouring matters imaginable into which the hand of the criminal has been plunged. In certain circumstances they may even be produced without colour, as when the criminal places his fingers, etc., on a smooth surface such as glass. Let the reader try for himself, that is, press his fingers firmly upon the window pane and note with what distinctness the papillary lines appear.

For private enlargements the Investigating Officer may conveniently use a good projection apparatus.*

---

* The author used for many years and with much satisfaction in the Graz Criminal Museum the apparatus called "Ala" made by J. Moll, Tuchlauben 9, Vienna.

Section vi.—Preservation of Blood Marks.

The next question for consideration in dealing with blood-stains is the precautions to be taken for their preservation so that they may come into the hands of the experts as intact as possible and in a state of integrity which cannot be questioned. All who understand the significance of the expression 'to work with accuracy,' understand that the work of the expert will be much surer, more valuable and at the same time easier when the *corpus delicti* is handed over to him in all its integrity. Unhappily experience teaches us that too often the greatest amount of imprudence is committed with respect to this. To take an example, one day a handkerchief stained with what appeared to be blood was found in the possession of a suspected individual, the handkerchief was a blue one and in consequence the stains were not easily noticed. This person declared that the handkerchief did not belong to him and that a stranger, who was no doubt the criminal, had made him a present of it on the road. Now the Investigating Officer to whom this suspect was brought had the unhappy idea of handing the handkerchief to a policeman with orders to show it to people in the neighbourhood and ask them if they knew to whom it belonged. Here then is our policeman, tramping the whole countryside with the handkerchief and its suspicious stains, showing it in every residence, visiting every public-house and accosting every passer-by, and finally returning with the reply, which might have been expected, that no one knew the handkerchief. But in what a condition were now the stains of blood! Instead of the shining and thick crusts as before, there were only insignificant marks, the last traces of the blood absorbed by the cloth. And with what amount of certainty could it subsequently be stated that they were really original blood-stains? How could it be proved that they might not be of quite recent date, that they did not proceed from the policeman himself, who might have been bleeding at the nose or, without knowing it, from a slight wound in the hand.

Here is another example which clearly shows the necessity of proceeding with caution in such a case. It is an example borrowed from *Schauenstein*, the well known chemist who used regularly to cite it in his lectures. This case, interesting from more than one aspect, has already been discussed from another point of view in the first chapter of this book. One morning on the bank of a river running through a town a coat was found in fairly good condition, made of brown cloth resembling felt, much in use in hilly districts. The coat was handed to a police sergeant but as it was much blood-stained it was transferred over to the authorities. There had been up to that time no report of any occurrence on the previous night near the spot where the coat was found. *Professor Schauenstein* was consulted as a matter of precaution. After a very few hours *Schauenstein* waited on the Investigating Officer and made the following statement: the owner of this coat is no longer alive. Here is the explanation of this surprising declaration. *Schauenstein* had found in the half-dried stream of blood which extended from the collar to the right-hand pocket of the coat one of the small bones of the tympanum known as the "stapedial bone" which is situated deep down in the interior of the skull. Now a person with a wound so severe as to cause a loss of blood capable of detaching the stapedial bone could not live for any length of time and must have been at that moment most certainly dead. It was therefore apparent that this was a case of homicide, probably a murder, and subsequent investigations proved that the coat belonged to a cattle merchant who had in fact been assassinated the night before. The corpse was found under the snow only during the following spring. If all the necessary precautions had not been taken nothing would have been easier than to have lost the little bone, which was sticking quite loosely to the coat. It would very likely have been presumed that the blood was the consequence of some insignificant affray, no particular research would have been made, and when in the spring the corpse was discovered, no doubt the connection between it and the coat found might have been noted, but it would have been then too late to prove that the death was indeed due to violence.

We may in this connection mention the well known case cited by *Taylor*, in which a certain razor was identified as the instrument used by a murderer, through finding thereon, in the dried-up blood, a shred of cotton, identical with the material of the night-cap, which had been cut through, of the murdered man.

We shall now briefly pass in review the manner of preserving various articles bearing blood-stains. First and foremost we must not lose sight of two general principles: avoid all confusion, and pack solidly. The first principle means that the object must be denoted both inside and out by words, figures, or letters, and that plenty of packing material must be employed such as paper boxes, etc. The second injunction is satisfied by fixing each article so that it cannot move, but without damaging the blood thereon. Blood-stained clothes will only be packed in trunks, care being taken to fix them so that the blood marks are uppermost; holes are pierced in the trunk through which are passed cords with which the clothes are securely tied, being very careful the meanwhile not to damage the blood in any way. Blood-stains upon paper do not require particular attention, especially when they are quite dry and do not form thick crusts: it is best to place them between two sheets of paper and put them away in a note-book or among the papers belonging to the case. Often, indeed, we come across papers bearing blood-stains perfectly intact among documents exposed for many years to all manner of uses. If the marks are upon small pieces of wood or splinters or upon shreds of cloth, in short upon any small or light article, boxes of corresponding size must be obtained, the articles placed at the bottom, and fixed thereto with string passed through the box and fastened outside. More difficult is the packing of large and heavy articles such as spades, hoes, hatchets, axes, hammers, bars of iron, heavy sticks, etc., all these objects ought to be packed with much care, for they may fall and all the blood be knocked off.

When we consider the importance of blood marks and when we remember the ease with which they disappear on being shaken or rubbed, we are involuntarily seized with a slight shiver on reading a report ending as follows: "Finally material object No. 1 difficult to handle owing to its great weight, was intrusted to the Municipal Authorities for transportation to the police station." But the "Municipal Authorities" mean the Mayor or the Chairman of the Municipality, who hands it over to a servant, who in turn consigns it to some carter who happens to be on his way to town. Thus it is that the iron bar or whatever it is, arrived at its destination unpacked and unprotected, perhaps in the midst of a cartload of oxen or pigs, just slaughtered then it is handed over to the expert. What a ridiculous spectacle it is to see the expert proceeding conscientiously and minutely, following all the rules of his science and his art, to the examination of an article which has been treated with so much negligence. He measures it, weighs it, examines it in the most scrupulous manner for traces of blood, some of which have been knocked off by the shaking of the cart, while others have only come into existence since the article started on its journey. Action of this description is in the first place to make a fool of the expert, and, further, shows a marked want of professional conscientiousness. Such an easy and graceful attitude in the conduct of an investigation may have the most unjust consequences, for it is the *corpus delicti* that will perhaps establish the guilt or innocence of a person.

It is evident that in packing neither trouble, time, nor money may be spared, the interest of the case also demands this. It is indispensable that the boxes requisite for this manner of packing be procured, then the article is fixed to the bottom of the box, already pierced with holes in several places through which cords are passed holding the article so firmly that no shock can detach it, see *Fig. 70*, which represents the method of fixing a hatchet to the bottom of a box. It is hardly necessary to state that the cords should neither touch nor rub the blood-stains.

Fig. 70

If there be blood-stains on both sides of the hatchet it cannot be laid down as depicted, in such a case the article must be placed upon pads or cushions of paper fixed on the wood with nails so that the hatchet reposes with nothing to touch the blood-stains. It is only in case of absolute necessity, namely, when the article is too big to enter a box, that it will have to be transported without packing, but in such a case the blood stains must be safeguarded in a very special manner. Suppose that we have some blood-stains at the point *a* (*Fig. 71*) on a long pole which for some reason or other cannot be cut, we attach blocks of wood above and below the blood with strong cords and surround the whole with little strips of wood and stout paper, so that the stains are quite free,

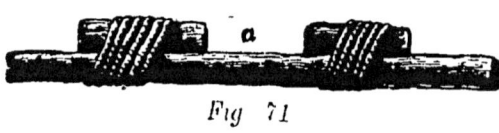

Fig. 71

though being perfectly preserved from all external deterioration. For small objects such as shavings, scrapings from bloodstained walls, etc., these are preserved, as already indicated, in paper (good, smooth letter paper) folded into little packets. The first packet is wrapped in a second to prevent any particles being lost in transit to the hands of the expert. It is also very important that traces of blood, pus, sperm, or other organic matter, be sent to the expert as soon as possible, every day's delay can only compromise the obtaining of a definite result, especially when the stains happen to be upon rusty iron.

CHAPTER XV

CIPHERS AND OTHER SECRET WRITINGS.

Section i.—General Considerations.

Every person who is endowed with patience and a natural aptitude and is favoured by luck may be able to decipher secret correspondence of the simpler kind. It will doubtless be difficult to distinguish complicated cipher writing from simple cipher writing, but it may be added that this difficulty is purely subjective. To a person wanting in quickness and practice the most simple of cryptograms will present the greatest difficulties, while a good cipher-reader attached to the Foreign Office or War Office will be able to read very complicated ciphers promptly and correctly.

Secret writings are met with in judicial inquiries much more frequently than one would imagine, but they must be sought for. If one takes the trouble to check the papers, notes, letters, and chits of the accused and to search in the pockets, seams, and folds of his clothes a mass of communications may be brought to light which on close inspection may turn out to be a cipher correspondence. More than one letter seemingly *devoid of sense*, more than one *involved* remark, and more than one *insignificant* scrawl, to which at the outset no importance could be attached, may turn out to be nothing else than cipher writing. The inquiry, when a secret correspondence is found, will immediately take quite another complexion, at least it may possibly become much more important than before the discovery. Possibly the effect of packets of cipher letters found on the accused is absolutely nil, but this is an eventuality never to be admitted at the outset, the correct supposition is the contrary one, namely, that if a cipher writing is found the matter is vastly more important than it seemed to be. If a recently arrested thief, who has stolen perhaps only a silver watch, is found in possession of cipher communications, the Investigating Officer may at least suppose that he has to do with a criminal of refinement, a band of thieves, etc.

The following principle should never be departed from,—everything in cipher must be deciphered, or at least an attempt to do so must be made. How to proceed is quite another matter. At first sight a simple cannot possibly be distinguished from a complicated cipher. Some cryptograms seem at the first glance to be very complicated (when, e.g., the vowel cipher has been employed and nothing but a long string of vowels can be seen), and yet are very easy to read. Again some appear to be perfectly simple (made for instance according to the transposition of letters system) whereas the most skilful cipher-reader is unable to decipher them. The Investigating Officer will have no other course but to himself unravel all ciphers that fall into his hands. For this purpose the following hints may be of use to him or if he has more ambition and feels that he has the necessary amount of skill he may obtain one or more of those books which deal separately with the subject of secret writing. Dr. John Ludu von Kluber's Cryptography, though no doubt very old, can render great assistance. It forms the basis of all subsequent works on the subject and contains a list of previous writers.

According to all the books, one can learn to read the most complicated and difficult cipher if one is only endowed with stubborn perseverance and a certain natural talent in this direction. But there is no doubt that without a little luck nothing can be accomplished. A mere chance may enlighten what several days' work has failed to make clear. This piece of luck must be lain in wait for and exploited when it comes. It is the same in all branches of an Investigating Officer's work; when a satisfactory result is obtained it seems to be to his 'luck' that it is due, but in reality through his skill and patience alone he had the 'luck' to observe the favourable moment and to seize it. In addition the Investigating Officer who would decipher secret writings must have his heart in his work, perseverance, never-failing interest, an observation that allows nothing to escape, and the gifts of combination and deduction. These are indeed general qualities which every Investigating Officer ought to possess. One might almost say that every man who is of the stuff out of which Investigating Officers are made is capable of reading ciphers.

In large towns the Investigating Officer may have the luck to come into contact with recognised experts for the explanation of ciphers, such are retired military men who have held high staff appointments, diplomatists, and mathematicians. Such persons have generally dealt with similar questions in the course of their career and continue to take so keen an interest in them as will lead them to use their special knowledge for the good of the public. But only exceptionally can competent persons of this kind be made use of; in most cases the Investigating Officer will have to rely upon himself. Besides it must not be forgotten that in this connection the Investigating Officer's position is very much easier than that of the diplomatist or military man. The former has to decipher messages of the first importance and the later to make sense of a cipher captured from the enemy. Neither as a rule can say what is the language of the writing, who are the people in correspondence with one another, what the writing ought to be about etc. One thing done they know, namely, that it is a communication made with the greatest art and with the minutest care—and this knowledge is not calculated to facilitate their task. Of course they may have come into possession of the key, but in this case the 'art of deciphering' in the sense we attach to these words will not come into play.

In the majority of cases the task of the Investigating Officer will be much easier. With few exceptions the suspected person to whom the communication is addressed or the one from whom it emanates is in a safe place, the Investigating Officer consequently knows if only approximately, the degree of education of the individual and in what language he has thought or written, can make suppositions about the nature of the manuscript, can gather from the status of the accused the degree of accuracy to be expected in the spelling—this last is most important—and finally, judging by his intelligence, can come to a conclusion as to the kind of secret writing selected, for a tolerable amount of intelligence is required to understand and employ certain of the more complicated kinds of cipher. To throw light on this point the inquiry must be taken up anew for this very purpose and from the beginning—as must always be done whenever a particular point has to be cleared up which has not been dreamed of previously. The attention is entirely concentrated on the information one is in search of at the moment; when one is under the impression that he knows every word figuring in the course of the inquiry he is correct only to a certain extent, they are indeed known in a general way, and those special points which have been the particular object of the inquiry are remembered, but certainly something new will be discovered when the whole is gone through again and the investigation directed towards another end. If therefore in the course of an inquiry a cipher writing is discovered the whole record must be once more perused and the attention devoted to everything that may throw light on *this particular point*. This having been done, all papers belonging to the accused or having any bearing upon the inquiry in general must be re-read. This revision must be carried out even when one thinks he knows the whole case by heart. Then all the clothes, pockets, seams, inside linings, etc., must be examined in the minutest manner as well as every article connected with the inquiry, taking care to place on one side and register all written or printed matter, whether letters, syllables, words, phrases, figures, or peculiar strokes or characters, etc. Above all letters, notes, and chits should be submitted to the most minute and thoughtful examination. They may furnish not only an indication about the subject of the cipher documents, but also give a direct starting point for deciphering the entire writing. The method of proceeding in deciphering a former communication may be discovered. Perhaps a word may be underlined, or another which seems to have no reason for being where it is (e. g., in the middle of a phrase) may turn out to be the key-word unlocking the secret manuscript. Without this key-word the writing cannot be deciphered and possibly the writer has noted it down somewhere for safety's sake and called attention to it by underlining it, etc.; frequently also the word or the cipher key, the stencil or the secret alphabet, etc., as the case may be, be written in a sympathetic ink, i.e., ink words written with which are legible only when treated chemically, or exposed to heat, etc. The paper is carried upon the person of the correspondent and the writing made to reappear as often as desired. For this reason paper must be examined even where there is no writing at all to be seen and care must be taken to ascertain whether secret interpolations are not to be found hidden between the lines in letters covered with ordinary writing.

Figure 22 (p. 106) is a specimen rather of a picture writing than of secret writing, but which may be easily mistaken for the latter. Though it was connected with a civil action it is of none the less interest from our point of view. In a suit dealing with a difference in accounts an aged peasant produced an old calendar containing the signs depicted. According to the explanation of the man, who could neither read nor write but knew how to play the game of tarot, a species of whist, and in consequence understood the Roman numerals, he had marked out with signs the debts contracted with his opponent and read them as given under the illustration.

Suppose such a writing is found upon a dangerous criminal, the first idea would be that it was a quite undecipherable secret writing, but when the Investigating Officer knows that some of these writings are perfectly simple he will be able to read them as easily as any ordinary script.

It sometimes happens that certain facts obtained quite by chance are of great importance; an accused who was the bearer of an extensive secret correspondence possessed a watch on the inner cover of which the maker's number, 27491, was engraved. The cipher writing resisted all attempts to decipher it. Finally 'luck' guessed that the accused might have used the cipher called *Count Gronfeld's* cipher (otherwise *General Trochu's* cipher) and had chosen 27491 for the key number, as a convenient number for him to verify without having to make any suspicious note of it. This is exactly what he had done, and with the help of the number of the watch the whole correspondence was easily read. It may also happen that a small pocket

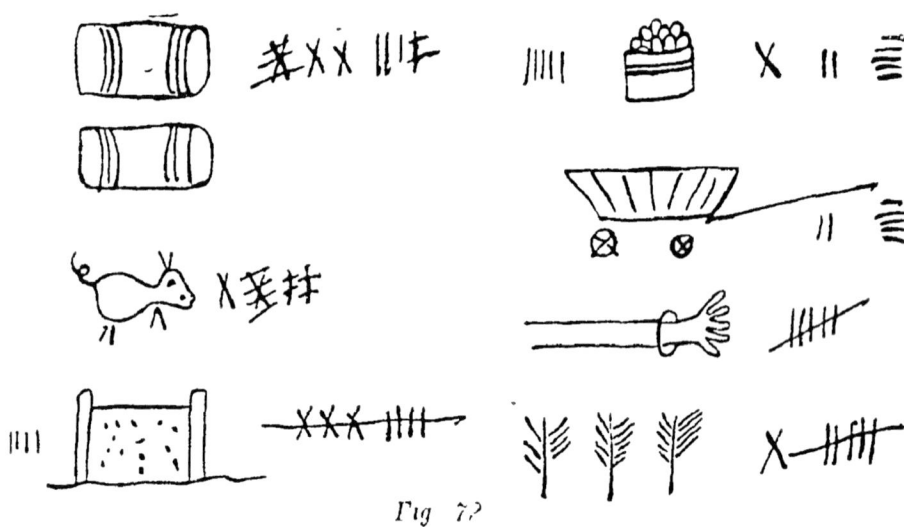

Fig 72

2 barrels of wine for	34 florins		Paid 11 florins	leaving 23 florins
1 pig	,, 22	,,	,, 12 ,	,, 10 ,
4 lots of fire-wood	, 34	,,	,, all	, nothing
5 baskets of potatoes	12 ,	50 k	,, nothing	12 fl 50 k
Hire of a cart	2	,, 50 ,	, nothing	,, 2 fl 50 k
A hand loan	5	,	,, all	nothing
3 trees	15	,	,, 5 florins	10 florins

dictionary is found among the belongings of the accused, which will indicate if printed in double columns, that the word-system (see *post*) has been employed. Again it may be supposed that the criminal has upon him doubtless well concealed, a stencil of paper or thin white metal enabling him to read writing made with the assistance of its duplicate. In short the Investigating Officer must remember, now as always, that even the most cunning of criminals will commit "the fatal blunder" that is his undoing, so well known and so often commented upon. Here the "blunder" is to carry on the person the key, be it a word, number, book, or stencil, to the cipher itself. In so doing the criminal believes himself to be in complete safety, for he does not dream of his possible arrest. In short by submitting everything connected with the inquiry and the cipher correspondence to a minute and profound examination and combining the acquired results in a thousand different ways, the Investigating Officer may perhaps succeed in *forcing* his luck, finding the necessary starting point, and even discovering the solution of the whole problem.

Section II.—Various kinds of Ciphers

Among the many systems of secret writing in use those only have been chosen for description that are capable of being deciphered by an average Investigating Officer either on account of the simplicity of the system adopted or because the Investigating Officer has in some way succeeded in finding a clue or key to the enigma, for this key alone is useless if he does not know how to use it. Indeed in many cases it is impossible to recognise the system unless very familiar with that particular variety. For instance when a cipher word is found among a person's papers or some strange book in his possession, it may be at once assumed that the discovery, if only its use be known, may furnish the solution of the whole secret writing. No attempt is made here to deal with writing very difficult to decipher—even with the help of the key. In the following pages little that is new will be found—at least as regards the essential parts of the subject; it is sufficient to reproduce what may be read in the many and voluminous works on the subject. The old authority *Kluber*, mentioned above, has been mainly consulted, as well as the modern work of *Pleissner von Wastnowitz*.

In all secret writings we find as a rule certain conventional signs which have a general signification.

(α) *Non-values*, i.e., signs having no importance and signifying nothing, the sole object of which is to lead the decipherer astray. It is arranged for example that all the vowels, every third letter, all numbers divisible by six, and so on, do not count. In writing with the stencil this arrangement is useless, for only those letters or words count that can be seen through the openings of the stencil, while the non-values are added after the message has been written, in the portions covered by the stencil.

(β) *Signs of antiphasis*, indicating that the phrase which follows should be understood in a contrary sense to its real signification, i.e., "a friend" equals "an enemy."

108 CIPHERS

(γ) *Signs of 'cancellation'* signifying that the whole communication does not count and has no other aim than to mislead the reader. Such communications are very frequent and their object is to throw the Investigating Officer off the scent and give him a mistaken idea of the meaning of the correspondence.

(δ) *Signs of change of system* indicating that use is being made of a new key or table, that the writing is in another language or that after that sign the cipher must be read from right to left, etc. We now proceed to describe a few selected systems.

A. Numerical ciphers

1. The simplest method consists in replacing letters of the alphabet, ordinary words and common phrases by one or several fixed numbers. In the latter case the numbers are employed indifferently.

2. Almost as simple is where the letters are expressed by two combined numbers; these numbers are previously divided into groups and the groups numbered.—*e.g.*

c g l p t v	a e i n r w	b f k o s z	d h m q x	u y
1	3	7	4	8

Every letter is thus represented by the figure indicating the place the letter occupies in its group (c a b d u are 1, p n o q are 4) together with the number of the group in which it stands, *e.g.* g = 21, k = 37, etc., "to-day" would be expressed in the following manner:—

51, 47, 11, 13, 64.

3. We may mention here the cipher said to have been invented by *Mirabeau*. The letters of the alphabet are divided into five groups, each group bearing an order number, *e.g.*

1	2	3	4	5
m c s o k	r i n v t	h b s e q	g f c z u	p j y d w
1 2 3 4 5	1 2 3 4 5	1 2 3 4 5	1 2 3 4 5	1 2 3 4 5

Each letter is now represented by a fraction, the numerator formed by the group number and the denominator by the figure denoting the position of the letter in the group. Since there is no number above five, the figures 6 to 9 and 0 are employed as *non-values* to make up double fractions and ring the changes on anyone trying to decipher the message. The word "thence" might be expressed as follows:—

Without non-values $\quad \frac{3}{3}\ \frac{2}{2}\ \frac{5}{4}\ \frac{3}{4}\ \frac{2}{3}\ \frac{1}{4}\ \frac{5}{4}$

With non-values $\quad \frac{83}{37}\ \frac{25}{62}\ \frac{50}{27}\ \frac{93}{48}\ \frac{29}{37}\ \frac{40}{39}\ \frac{36}{64}$

B Alphabetical ciphers

1. The simplest cipher of this kind, called Julius Cæsar's cipher, consists, like the numerical ciphers, in the simple transposition of the letters of the alphabet, e.g. $a = f$, $q = z$, etc. Though not very safe, this method is frequently employed to-day—so much so indeed that every Investigating Officer must come across it some time or other. It is evident that this device may be rendered more difficult to decipher by neglecting to separate the letters from one another, joining them altogether irrespective of words, mixing in non-values, or employing like the *Abbot Tritheim of Wurzburg* (1462 to 1516) from 10 to 25 letters of the alphabet one after the other in a definite order. Sometimes for instance the first word, line, or phrase is written in the first alphabet, and the second word, line, or phrase in the second alphabet, thus rendering the solution much more difficult.

2. A cipher very often employed is a vowel cipher in which the accompanying key is used. It is self-evident that the order of the letters may be changed at will. Each letter is expressed by two vowels, which are found in the key as follows

	a	e	i	o	u
u	d	e	r	b	i
o	q	w	a	p	h
i	l	z	k	y	s
e	m	f	v	o	c
a	x	n	u	g	t

The first of the two is at the extremity of the same horizontal line and the second is at the top of the same vertical line as those in which stand the letter to be understood, thus a becomes oi, f becomes ie, g becomes ao, and the message "start" will be written as follows:—

   iu ua oi ui au

This seems quite senseless enough, but it may be made more puzzling by adding consonants as non-values and making up words therewith. We might then obtain, e.g. the following message:—

   "Still much call upon him luck ill such fun"

Several other arrangements can be made with this table.

This cryptogram will at first sight appear to have been written with the assistance of a system of words and will be extremely difficult to decipher.

3. The extension of this system gives us the multiplication cipher, also called the square cipher, the undecipherable cipher, or the Russian cipher. It is said to have been invented by a diplomatist named *Blaise de Vigenère* in 1589. It is most extensively used, offers the greatest possible security, is easy to work, and only necessitates the possession of the appended table

	1	2	3	4	5	6	7	8	9	10	11	12	13	14	15	16	17	18	19	20	21	22	23	24	25
1	a	b	c	d	e	f	g	h	i	k	l	m	n	o	p	q	r	s	t	u	v	w	x	y	z
2	b	c	d	e	f	g	h	i	k	l	m	n	o	p	q	r	s	t	u	v	w	x	y	z	a
3	c	d	e	f	g	h	i	k	l	m	n	o	p	q	r	s	t	u	v	w	x	y	z	a	b
4	d	e	f	g	h	i	k	l	m	n	o	p	q	r	s	t	u	v	w	x	y	z	a	b	c
5	e	f	g	h	i	k	l	m	n	o	p	q	r	s	t	u	v	w	x	y	z	a	b	c	d
6	f	g	h	i	k	l	m	n	o	p	q	r	s	t	u	v	w	x	y	z	a	b	c	d	e
7	g	h	i	k	l	m	n	o	p	q	r	s	t	u	v	w	x	y	z	a	b	c	d	e	f
8	h	i	k	l	m	n	o	p	q	r	s	t	u	v	w	x	y	z	a	b	c	d	e	f	g
9	i	k	l	m	n	o	p	q	r	s	t	u	v	w	x	y	z	a	b	c	d	e	f	g	h
10	k	l	m	n	o	p	q	r	s	t	u	v	w	x	y	z	a	b	c	d	e	f	g	h	i
11	l	m	n	o	p	q	r	s	t	u	v	w	x	y	z	a	b	c	d	e	f	g	h	i	k
12	m	n	o	p	q	r	s	t	u	v	w	x	y	z	a	b	c	d	e	f	g	h	i	k	l
13	n	o	p	q	r	s	t	u	v	w	x	y	z	a	b	c	d	e	f	g	h	i	k	l	m
14	o	p	q	r	s	t	u	v	w	x	y	z	a	b	c	d	e	f	g	h	i	k	l	m	n
15	p	q	r	s	t	u	v	w	x	y	z	a	b	c	d	e	f	g	h	i	k	l	m	n	o
16	q	r	s	t	u	v	w	x	y	z	a	b	c	d	e	f	g	h	i	k	l	m	n	o	p
17	r	s	t	u	v	w	x	y	z	a	b	c	d	e	f	g	h	i	k	l	m	n	o	p	q
18	s	t	u	v	w	x	y	z	a	b	c	d	e	f	g	h	i	k	l	m	n	o	p	q	r
19	t	u	v	w	x	y	z	a	b	c	d	e	f	g	h	i	k	l	m	n	o	p	q	r	s
20	u	v	w	x	y	z	a	b	c	d	e	f	g	h	i	k	l	m	n	o	p	q	r	s	t
21	v	w	x	y	z	a	b	c	d	e	f	g	h	i	k	l	m	n	o	p	q	r	s	t	u
22	w	x	y	z	a	b	c	d	e	f	g	h	i	k	l	m	n	o	p	q	r	s	t	u	v
23	x	y	z	a	b	c	d	e	f	g	h	i	k	l	m	n	o	p	q	r	s	t	u	v	w
24	y	z	a	b	c	d	e	f	g	h	i	k	l	m	n	o	p	q	r	s	t	u	v	w	x
25	z	a	b	c	d	e	f	g	h	i	k	l	m	n	o	p	q	r	s	t	u	v	w	x	y

If necessary this table can be recomposed from memory; its employment presupposes the existence of a key-word. Let us suppose the key-word to be "london" and the message to be sent "start quickly." We commence by writing the message with the letters spaced so that each letter of the message corresponds with a letter of the key-word. When the letters of the latter are used up the word is begun over again thus —

    s t a r t   q u i c k l y
    l o n d o   n l o n d o n

We look for the first letter of the message s in the first horizontal line of the table on p. 410, and the first letter of the key-word l in the first vertical line of the table, and, starting from the letter s, we descend the perpendicular line till we meet the horizontal line, followed from l, at e. This is the first letter of the cipher. In the same manner we take the second letters of the message and the key-word, t and o respectively, and following the appropriate lines as before we obtain q, and so on till the message is exhausted, when we obtain the following cryptogram —

    e q n u g c c u p n y l

To read this message we recommence by placing the key-word under the cryptogram thus —

    e q n u g c c u p n y l
    l o n d o n l o n d o n

then look for the first letter of the key-word in the first vertical line to the left of the table, then follow it till we find the first letter in the cipher, e, and then ascend vertically to the top horizontal line where we find s, which is the first letter of the actual message. And so on with all the remaining letters.

Using the same table, numbers may also be employed. Taking the same example as before, the first letter of the key-word, l, corresponds with the number 11 just beside it, and the first letter of the message, s, with the number 18 just above it. Then instead of taking the letter e as formerly we take the sum of these two numbers, that is 29. The method is used much less frequently with numbers than with letters. The latter are nearly always used by fairly intelligent persons. Chance alone can be counted upon to elucidate cryptograms of this description, for in no cipher does chance play so great a part. The Investigating Officer may have the luck to find among certain papers belonging to the correspondents the cipher table, which may have endless variations or he may discover the key-word. It will sometimes be possible by taking into account the character, social condition, and connections of a person, to guess the key-word. Generally it is a proper name, and by making trials with names which have some connection with the individual the right word is often hit upon. We may try the native town of the cipher writer, the country of his birth, the chief river of the country, the name of the town or country last visited by him, and the names of men who may have some notoriety or celebrity at the time or who have some importance as regards his position or trade, e.g., purely local public men or persons well-known in his particular walk of life. Rarely does a man of education, and hardly ever a man of no education, abandon the choice of the key-word to chance—laziness, natural indifference, and the attraction influenced over us by matters which we already know, all come into play and induce us in such cases to choose words with which we are familiar rather than indifferent or meaningless ones. The Investigating Officer has now an opportunity of exercising his faculties of combination and deduction. Materials will rarely be wanting and success will not often fail to crown his efforts.

4. The cipher writing of *Napoleon I* is based on an analogous method, and is connected with a system invented by *G. della Porta* in 1510. Here again a key-word is necessary. The table alphabet is formed as below. Omitting *j* and *z* there are 24 letters. These are first arranged in their natural order in two lines with the marginal symbol AB. The next alphabet is arranged also in two lines, but the last letter *y* of the second line is transposed to the beginning of that line, leaving *x* as its last letter, the marginal symbol being CD. In the third alphabet *y* comes to the head of the second line, reading x y n o p q r etc.—symbol EF, and so on through G H, I K, L M, etc. In this way it is clear that 12 alphabets can be formed.

```
      ( a b c d e f g h i k l m
A B  (
      ( n o p q r s t u v w x y

      ( a b c d e f g h i k l m
C D  (
      ( y n o p q r s t u v w x

      ( a b c d e f g h i k l m
E F  (
      ( x y n o p q r s t u v w
```

Now suppose the key-word is B E D. Here we employ the three alphabets given above, A B, E F, C D. The key-word is arranged under the sentence to be ciphered, as previously described, and any letter, say *s*, coming above B will in the cipher become *f* and *vice versa*. Thus suppose the message to be sent is the words "nothing new," we obtain the following cryptogram:—

```
n o t h i n g  n e w
B E D B E D B  E D B
a d h u t b t  e q k
```

In alphabet B, n corresponds to *a*; in alphabet E, o corresponds to *d*; in D, t corresponds to *h*, and so on.

5. *Count Gronfeld's*, also called *General Trochu's*, cipher is notable for its simplicity. All that is required is a key-number and an alphabet agreed upon by the two correspondents, who must also know whether any letters, is *j* or *z*, are excluded. Suppose the key-number is 519 and the alphabet is the following:—a b c d e f g h i k l m n o p q r s t u v w x y z and that the message to be sent is — "all goes well," we commence by

spacing the letters of the message and writing the key-number underneath them as many times as is necessary

```
    a l l   g o e s   w e l l
    5 1 9   5 1 9 5   1 9 5 1
    f m u   m p o x   x o q m
```

Each letter of the message is then replaced by the letter in the alphabet which stands in the position relative to the former expressed by the number placed under the letter of the message. Thus the first letter in the message is 'a,' under which we find the number 5; we must therefore count off in the alphabet 5 letters from a and obtain the first letter of the cryptogram, *f*; the second letter is 'l,' under which is the number 1, the second letter of the cryptogram will therefore be *m*; the third letter is also 'l,' but the number under it being 9 it is now represented by *u*, and so on. This message is most difficult to decipher unless the key-number is known; but as has been already remarked it often happens in such cases either that the number is a common one, as 365 or the current year, or that, if non-suggestive, it will be discovered noted down among the papers of the two correspondents. Once in possession of this number we write it under the cipher and, aided by these numbers and the fixed alphabet, we obtain each letter by counting backwards; thus instead of *f* we take the fifth letter before it, namely, a; and of *m* the letter before it, namely l, etc.

C. Syllable and word ciphers

(a) *Syllables.* The syllabic system consists in inserting in a letter various syllables having a signification of their own apart from the letter. It is for instance settled beforehand that only the first syllable of the third word in every line, odd or even, counts. The method when well carried out is extremely safe, but it is none the less rare, being very difficult of application, the style of the letter being generally unnatural and suspicious.

(β) *Words. Heidel's method.* The letter is composed of two parts consisting either of the letter proper and a postscript or else of two distinct paragraphs (of course no third paragraph must be present in the letter). The words of the message to be sent are inserted in the first paragraph in their proper order. The second contains the key, e.g., each word in the latter which begins with a *t* indicates by the number of its order the place in the first paragraph of each word which is to count. Suppose it is wished to communicate the following words:—" I will come to you place to-morrow." The letter may be written as follows:—

I have not yet heard whether Thompson *will come* but shall send my servant this evening *to* ask him. If *you* promised letter arrives in time we shall be able to visit the *place* together. I should like to settle the business before the day after *to-morrow*.

" *The* idea is a good one but *the time* is short. As soon as I see Thompson we shall certainly *take* steps at once. I suppose it is quite an impossibility for you *to* accompany us on our visit? I shall let you know Monday or *Tuesday.*"

In the second paragraph the words 1, 8 9, 17, 21, 31, and 47 each begin with a *t* thus indicating that in the first paragraph only the words 1, 8, 9, 17 21, 34 and 47 are to be taken into account. For short communications the system is good enough but is easily betrayed by a forced and unnatural style

2 The *book* system is somewhat complicated but gives great security, always assuming the book is not found. The two correspondents are each in possession of a copy of the same book (same edition) and agree that each letter of the message will be represented by three numbers, the first denoting the page of the book, the second the line of the page, and the third the letter of the line to be used. Suppose the letter *g* is to be ciphered. Let us suppose *g* is the 17th letter of the third line of page four. The letter *g* will then be expressed by the three numbers 4, 3, 17. When the book used is unknown the message cannot be deciphered but as in such cases possession of the book is indispensable, the Investigating Officer will probably discover some book among the belongings of the individual in question and will be careful not to lose sight of it; if he subsequently comes upon a suspected cipher he will at all events first try to elucidate it with the assistance of the book.

3 The *lexicon* cipher presupposes the existence of a similar dictionary in the possession of each correspondent, the pages of which are printed in double columns. In writing a letter each word is looked up in the dictionary and, instead of the word found, the word in the same line of the same page but in the neighbouring column is taken. When this method is employed, the Investigating Officer generally discovers the dictionary—all that is needed to read the cipher. If the dictionary cannot be found and one is convinced in spite of everything that this system has been used, it may be worth while to attempt the solution by examining a dozen or more recognised dictionaries. When the two correspondents are known, we can sometimes tell beforehand where the books have probably been procured for it must not be forgotten that they can hardly have employed dictionaries used by them for a number of years, for no two people possess two old dictionaries absolutely alike. As the last condition is essential they must have been specially bought for the purpose, and the Investigating Officer will hardly fail to obtain them in some way or other.

4 The book system proper is the most perfect of cipher methods. A special dictionary is used in which all words, writing, signs, and numbers are represented by groups of letters or numbers. As a special precaution in important messages a key-number may be added to or subtracted from the cipher numbers. In commerce, a code published by the International Telegraph Office at Berne is employed. In it the words to be ciphered are not expressed by groups of numbers but by other words borrowed from the best known languages of civilisation.

D The Stencil or Blackline cipher

Here the cipher is written and read either by placing a stencil over the paper, or a ruled paper, such as the blacklines used for teaching writing under it the lines being visible through the paper written on. Its use can be easily detected, for in the first case the writing is not exactly straight while in the second we observe the transparency of the paper. The Investigating Officer will be unable to read the cipher unless he can lay his hand on the stencil or the ruled paper. They must be searched for among the belongings of the correspondents. Being small they will probably be carefully concealed, and the stencil may have been rolled or crumpled up.

E. Miscellaneous ciphers

(α) *Angle-writing.*—School children often make use of this method. The letters are grouped 2 by 2, one being dotted and the other not. The method is clear from the diagrams; suffice it to say that a non-dotted letter is represented by its appropriate angle with no dot, while a dotted letter has a dot in the angle.

This cipher is naturally not difficult to read, being based on a very simple system of transposition. On account of its simplicity it is much used by criminals.

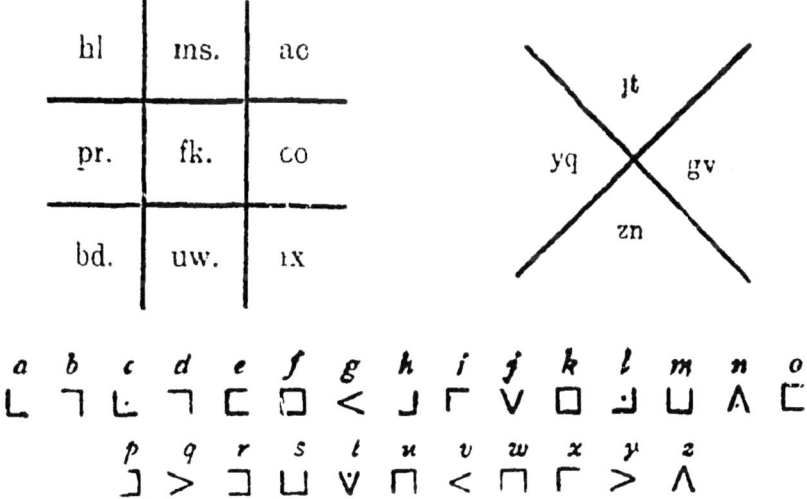

(β) *Thread-writing.*—Each correspondent is in possession of a stick divided into 26 equal parts and in the spaces thus obtained the letters of the alphabet are inscribed in an agreed order. "Writing" is carried on by measuring distances on the stick with a white thread, starting from the end of the stick to the first letter of the message and there marking the thread with ink, then measuring from the first to the second letter, and marking the thread again, and so on to the end of the message; the thread is then rolled up and conveyed to the correspondent, who has only to measure it on his stick in order to read the message. The latter can if necessary dispense with the stick by drawing its counterpart on the table, floor, or wall, provided that the distances are fixed and easy to reproduce, e.g., the diameter of a coin, the length of a match, the breadth of the thumb, etc. In this way correspondence may be easily exchanged with prisoners for it is not easy to hinder the introduction into the cells of a thread which may, e.g., be holding a garment or the dressing of a wound together. The Investigating Officer must therefore be on the look-out.

In the two preceding cases the series of letters is fixed in an order easy of recollection, e.g., from z to a, or by altering the letters in some such way as follows:—

a c, b d, e g, f h, i k, j l, etc.

(γ) *Foot-rule cipher.*—A line divided into quarters of an inch, millimetres etc. is drawn on a long band or strip, a table, wall, floor, etc. and in every second, third, fourth of these divisions we place a letter of the alphabet. When writing with an ordinary yard measure we measure off the distance from the beginning of the line to the first letter of the message. The number of quarter inches obtained (say 17) denotes the first letter of the message. The distance between the first and the second letter is then taken (say 6) and the number of quarter inches denotes the second letter in the message, and so on, the whole message being formed exclusively of figures. Care must however, be taken to distinguish the numbers obtained by measuring from left to right from those taken from right to left. Suppose the customary order of the letters of the alphabet has been retained and the message begins with the word "Albert." It is evident that to go from A to l we must first measure from left to right, then from l to b from right to left, and from b to e from left to right again. The numbers furnished by the measurement from right to left need not be specially marked, the others may be underlined, written in red ink, or marked with a point, etc. But this indicates at once that we have to deal with a special kind of cipher. The author had never seen this cipher described, when one day the governor of a prison discovered and handed to him a letter composed of figures which was supposed to have been exchanged between two international thieves then under arrest. When the two men were immediately searched, a strip of paper was found on each of them. It was straight and thin and divided into centimetres, it was immediately supposed that these strips were connected with the secret message, and it was not till after considerable trouble and patience that the author was able to discover the system employed, a system which is certainly not wanting in originality.

(δ) *Puncture-system.*—This writing is also easy to introduce surreptitiously into prison. Each letter is represented by a number and the numbers are ranked together in a manner easy of recollection.

A sheet of paper covered with writing or printed characters is taken, e.g., an old and dirty piece of newspaper used for wrapping up something, which may be easily introduced into the cells. Suppose the alphabet to be the following:—

a b c d e f g h i k l m n o p q r s t u v w x y z
1 2 3 4 5 6 7 8 9 10 11 12 13 14 15 16 17 18 19 20 21 22 23 24 25

and that the message to be sent is "no," n is represented by the number 13, the writer therefore counts up to the thirteenth letter on the paper starting from the beginning, and pierces it with a needle. The next letter o is represented by the number 15, we therefore count on from the letter last pierced, n, till the fifteenth next letter is reached and pierced in like manner. It is certain that many a piece of news or information is passed into the prisons in this manner. It must not be forgotten that instead of being pierced the letters may be marked with sympathetic ink, using, for instance milk, so that the message may be read on heating the newspaper.

(ε) *Playing-card cipher.*—A pack of cards is arranged in a known order, care being taken to note the top and bottom card of the pack. The pack should be quite new, or at least the edges should be newly cut. The pack is then held tightly together and the message written, generally in figures, on the side of it. The pack is then well shuffled and forwarded to the correspondent, who places it in the pre-arranged order, presses the pack, and reads the message.

Another way is to write a letter on each card of the pack in a pre-arranged order, and read the message by re-arranging them again in the same order.

(ζ) *Count Vergennes' method.*—It is said that at the end of the eighteenth century the French Foreign Minister made use of a special method of corresponding with his foreign diplomatic agents when a letter of introduction was handed to persons going from Paris to foreign countries and *vice versa*. A traveller requesting such a letter would receive a paper which carried certain ornamentation on the borders furnishing information regarding the bearer of the letter, or it might be conveyed by the manner of writing or printing, words underlined, and the numbering of the letter. They could tell immediately from such a missive who its bearer was, what were his aptitudes, whether he was a safe man or a suspect, whether rich, poor, intelligent, a fool, married or single, the reason for his journey, who were his relatives, etc. It is not improbable that this refined method of correspondence is still in use among a certain class.

It is related that the Russian and Polish Jews used to correspond with one another in the following way when the postage of letters was still very expensive. The recipient would take the un-stamped letter, examine the envelope all over, and then refuse to pay the postage or receive it, but he had learnt all he had wished to know from the shape, colour, and size of the envelope, from the special writing of the address, and from the manner in which the letter was sealed. It may be presumed that our prisoners correspond in like manner with their friends outside and often under the nose of the Investigating Officer himself when he hands them letters addressed to them which have been examined and found to be "quite harmless."

(θ) *The Scytal Cipher* of the Lacedemonians, derived, according to Plutarch, from *skutalē*, staff. When the Spartan ephors wished to forward their orders to their commanders abroad they wound slantwise a narrow slip of parchment upon a *skutalē* so that the edges met close together, and the message was then added so that the centre of the line of writing was on the edges of the parchment. The receiver had a similar staff, and wound the paper upon it, and so alone could the contents be read. This system is also known to sharpers.

Section iii.—Suggestions as to Deciphering Secret Writing.

It may be asserted "no fixed rules for the deciphering of secret writing exist." By the word "rule" we must understand "principles permitting of the solution of a cipher."

The rules to be observed are as follows: —

(a) Carefully transcribe the cryptogram, or, better still, trace it on a window or through some tracing-paper.

(b) Make a list of all the signs to be found in the message counting them and classing them in their order of frequency.

The order of frequency of letters and the commonest words in English is as follows: —

Letters —e t (well ahead), then, a o n i, r s h d l c u n m f y g p b, v k, x q j z

Double letters —ee oo ff ll ss

Words of one letter —a, I and O

Words of two letters —of, to, in, it, is, be, he, by, or, as, at, an, so

Words of three letters —the, and, for, are, but, all, not

Words of four letters —that, with, from, have, this, they

(c) Search for the vowels in the short words. These are more easily found and furnish more certain starting-points than the consonants.

(d) Write each letter as discovered under its corresponding cipher sign and if in doubt add a mark of interrogation.

5. It is absolutely necessary to pay attention to every article a criminal has tried to make away with; the police should therefore be especially recommended never to consider as insignificant any scrap of paper, wood, cloth, or the like thrown away by an accused on his arrest. It is the rule that a criminal who is in possession of a cipher letter or a cipher key will try to rid himself thereof either immediately on his arrest or as soon after as possible, and even when the constable notices this the accused will easily persuade him that the discarded object is "of no significance," especially when the former is unaware of its importance, and yet such an object "of no significance," e.g., a piece of newspaper, a length of thread, or a piece of paper with holes cut therein may after all be the pivot of the whole inquiry.

PART IV.—PARTICULAR OFFENCES.

CHAPTER XVI

BODILY INJURIES AND POISONING.

Section i.—General.

In indicating here the most important points to be kept in view in the examination of injuries to the body, it is not intended to intrude upon the particular province of the medical man, but merely to give such brief hints to the Investigating Officer, be he magistrate, policeman, or lawyer, as may preserve him from making serious blunders when at the first moment before the arrival of the medical man he finds himself obliged to form a provisional opinion

The position of the Investigating Officer in such matters is somewhat delicate He must know how to manage the affair himself, when no medical man is at hand, but at the same time should not go a step further than the situation demands He must direct the work of the medical man and see that it fits into the general plan of the inquiry, but on the other hand he must show all respect to the special knowledge of the scientist He must accept his statements with confidence, but should also, by skilfully directed questions, lead him to the special point demanded by the object of the inquiry To accomplish this task successfully, to be able to discuss scientifically different cases with the medical man without wearying his patience by useless questions and irrelevant suggestions, the Investigating Officer should possess a fair amount of medical knowledge, more at least than is usually expected from a man of ordinary education Such knowledge indeed the intelligent medical jurisprudent expects the lawyer to possess, so that the latter may assist the former and render his labours fruitful He desires to be able to discuss matters scientifically, for he knows only too well that conversation in which neither party understands the other renders all collaboration impossible

It must be confessed that while there exist many books on medical jurisprudence, they have been written neither by nor for the lawyer, the medical man, with the very best intentions can never place himself at the exact point of view of the lawyer who has no medical education, he does not know in what the Investigating Officer is deficient, in particular he does not know the requirements of that officer when no medical man is available

The following remarks are accordingly made solely from the legal point of view, *they are not mere extracts from books of medical jurisprudence, they attempt to answer questions commonly arising in practice which must be answered before the arrival of the medical man* Instances of difficulties occurring from one cause or another will also be cited

Section ii.—Wounds by Blunt Instruments.

These injuries are the most frequent and among the instruments employed may be mentioned the fist smooth stones, sticks, poles, clubs, hammers and, in India the handles or backs of mamooties laths male bamboos, rice-pounders, and ox-yokes also many household objects, as brass vessels, etc In fact the number of objects that may be used for striking or beating is unlimited, and the knowledge of what instrument has been employed is often of first importance in procuring the identification of the assailant One sometimes comes across the most unlikely weapons

In mountainous and other districts where the inhabitants are often endowed with exceptional strength and exceptional brutality, strange things sometimes happen One day a woodcutter in the midst of a quarrel seized a large piece of wood over nine feet long part of a tree which he had just cut down and holding it in front of him like a ram rushed on his assailants, inflicting no fewer than five serious wounds (fracture of ribs, fracture of collar bone, dislocation of hip joint, etc) In a quarrel in a tavern a young man of gigantic height seized the heavy top of he inn table and brandishing it in the air brought it down on the heads of the young men who were fighting with him, inflicting a dozen grave wounds on the skull With wounds made by blunt striking instruments we must class other injuries, somewhat difficult to distinguish from those just mentioned. Such are wounds following a fall upon a collision with, or a push against, some hard substance, and also wounds caused from large moving masses, as in railway accidents, boiler explosions, accidents in factories, etc

As to all these kinds of injuries we note the following points —

1 It is not always possible to decide from the nature of the wound itself what kind of instrument was used, indeed the wound sometimes presents appearances pointing to a cutting or stabbing instrument as the cause

(a) Although not strictly in this class there are cases which must not be neglected, where an instrument to all appearance perfectly blunt yet has some sharp or pointed projection, more or less visible, such as a fence stake with a nail not very readily observed, or a small sharp splinter on a branch of wood In one case, a farm servant had received on the forehead a wound so deep and accompanied by such brain injuries that it was believed to have been caused by a blow from a hatchet or a sword The inquest, however, disclosed that he had received a blow from a carriage cross-bar, which had a splinter over an inch in length This splinter stood out at right angles to the hard beech bar, and was so firmly fixed that it could when gliding over the skin produce a wound being all the appearance of a slash or cut In cases of this kind it must be remembered that the portion of the instrument which gave the wound its special character may be easily lost, the nail may drop out the splinter of wood may be broken off and this is the more likely as the guilty person does not usually exercise special care in laying down the instrument he has used, on the contrary, in alarm at the result of his onslaught, he generally throws the weapon violently from him. One should never therefore summarily lay aside instruments which at first sight appear to have no connection with the crime, but on the contrary examine them most minutely for the purpose indicated.

(b) Instruments really blunt may in certain cases inflict long wounds with clean-cut edges, especially on those parts of the body (as the skull) where the skin is stretched tightly over the bone. In the case just mentioned one of the young men who was struck by the table-top had a deep wound right across the skull, the skin being completely rent. The same result may happen from a blow on the front of the leg, and once, on a person on whom a heavy mass had fallen, there was found a clean cut in the integuments of the abdominal wall. *Hofmann* has laid down that wounds caused by a cutting instrument are always wedge-shaped at the base, while the base of the wound caused by a blunt instrument is crushed or bruised; but the latest surgical authorities declare that it is often difficult and sometimes quite impossible to draw any distinction. It may be said that if the bottom of the wound shows signs of crushing or bruising, the inference that the instrument employed was blunt may be drawn; but in the other case where the bottom is wedge-shaped no inference can be safely drawn one way or the other. In ordinary riots where the combatants are armed only with sticks, there are frequently head wounds bearing all the appearance of incised wounds, from which the inference is sought to be drawn that axes or knives have been used, and the accused are consequently charged solely on this hypothesis, with the serious offence of rioting armed with deadly weapons.

2. Effusion of blood proves little in itself as to the force of the blow. The amount of blood varies with the form of the instrument, the part of the body struck, and even with the individual. It is well known that the same instrument, used with the same force, may produce from an adult but slight bleeding, while causing considerable effusion from an infant or in old man.

3. If the direction of the striking instrument has been perpendicular to the part struck, the surface of separation of the wound appears cut, bruised, or crushed, while if the instrument has glanced on one side, the wound is ragged or torn.

4. If the blow has caused rupture of an internal organ it is almost always fatal. Yet the wounded person may live for some time, for example, with a rupture of the liver from five to eleven days—with a fracture of the base of the skull, three to twelve days—with a rupture of the intestine, ten hours.

In one case a man had been thrown from the top of a balcony or verandah, but there was no external wound. Four days after he died, and his death was attributed to a stroke of apoplexy. A *post-mortem* disclosed a rupture of the liver nearly two inches in length.

5. When considerable force is exerted, as in the case of a fall from a height crushing under a heavy weight, etc., serious internal injuries may be caused without the slightest external mark. Even when there is no internal rupture, death may follow from shock.

In a case of robbery a workman begged an old peasant who was passing to take him along in his carriage on the pretence that he was ill, and the peasant agreed. As they were going along the old man fell asleep whereupon the workman seized him, threw him out of the vehicle, went off at a gallop and sold the horse and carriage in a distant village. Some time afterwards the peasant was found dead at the very spot where he had been thrown out. Apparently he had fallen on his head, without losing his hat of hard felt which saved him from any external wound. The *post-mortem* discovered no injury, not an organ was damaged. As, however, it was impossible to attribute the death to a stroke of apoplexy, it was necessarily the result of shock, and so the medical men, taking all the circumstances into consideration, recorded as their opinion, " that the man must have been thrown from the carriage " though at that time nothing more was known than that the peasant had, the previous evening, quitted a neighbouring tavern; the whole truth subsequently came out, the accused confessed, and every detail was verified.

6. In public-house brawls, attacks of robbers etc., fractures of the base of the skull often happen. It is now established that *Wall's* theory that the direction of the blow can be established from the aspect of the wound is correct.

Section III.—Wounds made by a Sharp Instrument.

In this category are included instruments for cutting and stabbing, frequently the different blows are combined—a blow with the point and sharp edge, a blow with the handle and the edge, and it is precisely in such a case that it is important for the Investigating Officer to form an idea of the instrument that has caused the wound, before the arrival of the medical man. Generally the shape of the wound, its dimensions, and its situation, will afford some information on this point although it is true that it will be difficult for the layman and even for the medical man to distinguish blows by some instruments, although very different from each other. It is easy to confound a blow from a hatchet with one from a knife, or a blow from a piece of wood with sharp angular sides with that made by a sword. Above all the examination should be prolonged and patient, care being taken to place the wounded person in the position in which the blow was received. If one concludes that a certain instrument has been used, the whole scene must be reconstituted in the mind and its possibility verified. If doubt remains, one passes on to another instrument, a new hypothesis is formed and tested, and so on by a process of elimination until the real instrument has been found. This is a very simple method and gives even to an outsider a good idea of the whole affair especially if the inquiry be conducted calmly and carefully.

1. Among the wounds produced by cutting weapons some at least can almost always be referred with certainty to an easily determined instrument. Thus wounds made by broken glass (which frequently occur in tavern brawls) are arched and somewhat shell-shaped, like the broken outline of the glass itself. Straight cuts due to broken glass are rarely observed. Again, wounds inflicted by sickles and scythes never show a straight line but a broken zig-zag line. This is because sickles and scythes are not sharpened in the same way as knives. Knives are sharpened to a

straight edge, while scythes and sickles are thinned out by hammering on an anvil with a steel hammer they are hammered until thin enough to cut but there still remains a slight serration, so that the wounds produced by them are irregular and very characteristic A wound of this nature once seen can never be confused with another Wounds inflicted by axes, or axe heads, with convex edges on long shafts are often, especially if well aimed, straight and clean cuts

2 In wounds caused by cutting instruments the form of the wound rarely corresponds to the true form of the weapon This frequently causes serious mistakes Often an instrument is neglected, solely because it does not correspond exactly with the wound Further, it is of very little use to compare with any instrument wounds which are either swollen or cicatrised and healing indeed the process of healing which commences from the moment the wound has been inflicted, rapidly transforms the wound so that it is hardly possible to recognise the primitive form Even some perfectly fresh wounds and those in which healing is impossible owing to the death of the victim correspond but imperfectly with the instrument The wound lengthens out when it runs along the muscle on the contrary when it runs across the muscle it contracts It is evident that the edges of a gaping wound must be drawn together before measuring its length for the edges of a gaping wound are two curved or bow-shaped lines, which are straightened by bringing the two edges together It is only after this operation that measurements can be taken, if taken before they will be too short

In few cases will the length of a stabbing wound made by a knife correspond with the size of the instrument, unless it be withdrawn from the body exactly as it has been inserted What most frequently happens is that the opening made at the moment of penetration will be lengthened by the act of withdrawing the weapon Stabbing wounds made by a knife have another important peculiarity which frequently passes unobserved They almost always present the form of a slit having two pointed extremities, so much so that one is tempted to believe that the wound has been inflicted by a dagger, an instrument with two cutting edges To verify this experiment may be made on a soft body—clay, dough, wood, tanned skin, etc , if a vigorous blow be given with a pocket knife (i e , a knife with one cutting edge and a blunt back) to such a substance the wound will undoubtedly be *wedge-shaped* But these substances are not the human skin, and the experiment by no means proves that a similar result will follow a blow on the human body Examine the point of any knife, we see that this point presents two cutting edges for a distance of at least ⅜ inch Beyond that, one of the edges commences to thicken so as to form gradually the back of the knife If then one sticks the knife into soft wood, for example, to the depth of ⅜ inch, the cut will have the form of a slit with two pointed ends, but, if one proceeds to force the knife further in the back will straighten out one of the points into a line, the wound will definitely assume the shape of a wedge When the knife is withdrawn, this shape of the wound remains for the wood is not sufficiently elastic to resume its original form, that is a cut pointed at each end

But it is very different with the human skin, which is extremely elastic When the point of the knife penetrates into the body to the depth of half an inch more or less, it forms at first a wound with a sharp or pointed angle at each end, as the knife proceeds further in, the end in contact with the cutting side of the knife naturally remains sharp and pointed, but the other end which is in contact with the back of the knife remains so also. This is because the back of the knife does not give its shape to the skin, but only causes further separation *so that the skin continues to be torn in the original direction and still forms a sharp and pointed angle*. Medical authorities call this property of the skin its "fissibility" or tendency to "split", and point out that it is prone to take different directions according to the different parts of the body. The skin thus possesses the same property as some other substances, that namely of continuing to split or tear in the original direction even under the action of a blunt body. The same phenomenon is observed in tearing cotton cloth or paper which has been folded. If the uncut leaves of a book be cut with the back of a knife or a round pencil the result is seen in a simple form.

Thus when a wound has each end sharp and pointed, it must not be concluded that the wound has been inflicted by a dagger or other double-edged instrument, more frequently the wound has been caused by a knife with a round or square back.

Another peculiarity must be taken into account. Frequently the wound is somewhat narrower than the instrument employed. This is a very important point, often leading to the exclusion from the hypothesis of some instrument which all the time was the weapon really employed. Hofmann, who is believed to have first pointed out this interesting peculiarity, explains it thus. A case of this kind can only occur when the point of the weapon is slightly blunted, when such a point touches the skin it depresses the latter in the form of a cone, a simple experiment showing this is to apply the point of a slightly blunt lead pencil to the skin, say between the thumb and the first finger. When this depression has become somewhat extensive, the continued pressure causes the instrument to penetrate below the surface. But in consequence of this depression, the skin, which is extremely elastic, is much dilated, and when the pressure ceases and the knife is withdrawn from the wound, the skin contracts again, the result being that the exterior wound opening is narrower than the knife. The maximum difference between the size of the wound and that of the knife may be according to *Hofmann* ⅛ to ¼ inch, a quantity not to be neglected.

3. Another important error may arise with reference to the number of blows struck by the knife, often one might think there have been several, while in reality there has been only one. This will occur when the blow has been struck on a part of the body where the skin is folded back on itself, as on the necks of old and thin persons. On stretching the skin, one sees several cuts connected together in the form of the letter Z, or even completely separated one from the other. In the same way, if a knife be struck into a piece of cloth folded or rolled up there will be several cuts.

In one case a young peasant had his ear completely mutilated by a terrible wound. It appeared as if the ear had been transpierced by a number of blows by a knife starting from the ear hole and going upwards to the top of the lobe. The medical man at once declared that there had been only one blow struck. Owing to the folds of the skin and the peculiar anatomical construction of the ear, the knife with a single blow caused a wound showing six strips of flesh, so that an outsider would have imagined that there had been as many separate wounds inflicted.

4. If it is of importance to know in what direction the blow of a knife has been delivered it should be remembered that a medical man can seldom give precise information on the point by simply inspecting the wound; hence all the accessory circumstances must be examined and recorded with the closest attention; for instance the position of the corpse, the shape of the wound, the number of traces (however slight) of effusions of blood, as well as where they are found, the position of the clothes, and, if the hypothesis of suicide cannot be safely put on one side, the position of the hand, whether open or shut, etc.

5. Wounds caused by a sharp instrument may prove mortal though there be no trace of hemorrhage. They may consequently pass absolutely unperceived. Of these the most important are wounds made by bayonets or other weapons of a similar shape. Every war furnishes an opportunity for observing a number of such wounds. The most remarkable are wounds caused by a bayonet with four cutting edges, as in *Fig. 73*, the wound produced is in the shape of a cross, the length being greater than the width, generally without hemorrhage, even if death ensues from the wound. One must therefore in all suspicious cases search with minute care for marks left on the body by weapons of the bayonet class, which are numerous.

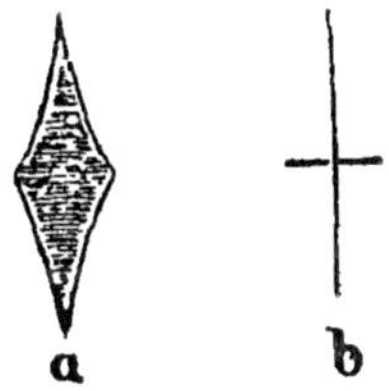

Fig. 73

In one case a person had been killed by a blow from a gimlet in the abdomen, but the wound was not perceived by the examining doctor. His oversight was excusable, for the wound could hardly be seen from the outside, although on examining the body and holding a *post-mortem*, it was clearly exposed.

Again, it is very difficult even for experts to estimate the depth of such wounds. The officer who makes the first investigation frequently reports, " a small wound, insignificant and superficial, having no possible connection with the death of the individual," while in reality the wound is both deep and mortal. This difficulty of ascertaining the depth of a wound caused by a cutting instrument arises for the most part from the fact that the wound closes upon itself owing to the contraction of the muscles underlying the skin and the first cellular tissue. The problem is still more difficult when the wounded person has turned at the moment of receiving the wound; the parts are then twisted, when they regain their previous position the twisting disappears and the different layers of pierced flesh are superimposed differently from before, they have been displaced and no longer correspond. Each layer pierced is closed by an unperforated portion. Thus one must act with extreme caution when one hears of an "unimportant blow with a knife" in a case of suspicious death.

When the knife penetrates into one of the cavities of the body, e.g., the pleural cavity, the depth of the wound can as a rule be ascertained only on a *post-mortem* examination. The contrary is equally true. Some knife wounds present a horrible aspect and yet are not mortal or even dangerous. This is notably the case with wounds of the head. A skull in *Professor Hyrtl's* collection bears in a cicatrised wound a knife blade one inch in length. The individual died of an illness having no connection with the wound many years after the knife had been stuck in his head. The following case can be vouched for as authentic. One man had in a quarrel stuck his knife into the head of another man, M, just where the hair commences to grow on the forehead. The knife was so firmly fixed that none of the persons present could pull it out. M went to the blacksmith, who tried his utmost to extract the knife with his largest pincers but to no purpose. M then repaired to a medical man, three-quarters of an hour's walk, who at last succeeded in pulling out the knife with the help of a crow-bar. Fifteen days later, M appeared in Court to testify that he was quite well and completely restored to health.

Again an old shoemaker in a fit of frenzy drove five nails each about two inches long into his head, and yet he left the hospital perfectly cured. Many similar instances might be cited. We cannot often enough repeat the words of the celebrated surgeon *Liston*:—'Every wound affecting the head, however slight it may be, runs the risk of becoming grave; while however grave such a wound may appear to be, hope should never be abandoned."

Great care must be exercised in valuing the often too dogmatic statements of medical witnesses in cases of wounds. The more senior men are generally much more cautious in their statements than the subordinates, but even the former sometimes make statements that go too far, especially if they have been engaged as experts and received a fee for their evidence. In India a great many cases turn upon the question as to how long a person could have lived or what actions could have been performed by him after having received a given wound or wounds. On one and the same day, the editor recently appeared for the Crown in the appeals in two cases, the first of attempted murder and the second of murder. In the first, the accused had driven through the middle of the frontal bone of his victim the blade of a sharp knife. The knife had entered up to the very hilt. Indeed, no less than 1½ inches of blade had penetrated the brain. His relatives, bystanders, even the accused himself tried to pull it out, but without success. The man was taken home and later sent across country to hospital. He remained perfectly conscious throughout. On arrival at the hospital the assistant surgeon tried to withdraw the knife, but desisted for a time and sent for a magistrate who recorded a dying declaration. Then about midnight, after half an-hour's hard work, the assistant surgeon worked out the knife and disinfected the wound. The man made a perfect recovery and gave evidence against his assailant. In the second case, the right pulmonary artery had been severed by a severe stab. The deceased was said to have run a distance of about 200 yards before he fell dead, and it was said that this was impossible after such a wound. The Court, while acquitting the accused on other grounds, declared that no definite conclusion could be come to in such a case as to how far a man could go. I feel certain that in the first case many a medical man would dogmatically state that such a blow must have been fatal, and that no man could live for over twelve hours with 4½ inches of the blade of a big knife embedded in the middle of his brain.

6. Very sharp knives do not always produce clean cuts, in fact a knife, however sharp it may be, the point of which touches any part of the body, can produce only a slashed and irregular wound if its blade, instead of being guided in the direction of the wound, is held obliquely thereto. If then, Fig. 74, the knife takes the direction a b the wound would be clean cut; if on the other hand it takes the direction c d the wound will be slashed. Wounds made not with the point but with the edge of the knife are never very deep.

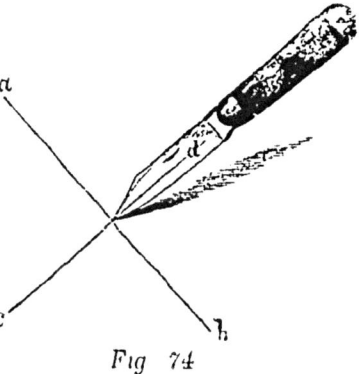

Fig 74

7. Scratches are often very important, especially when they arise from the resistance of the victim to an attack. When both individuals are available—the scratcher and the scratched—the nails of the scratcher must be at once examined to see if there is any relation between the nails and the scratches observed. This examination must evidently be made at once, as the nails may be cut, pared etc. The dirt under the nails (see p 114) often affords strong evidence and should be examined by specialists. This must always be done when there is reason to suppose that a person assassinated has attempted to defend himself by scratching his assailant—a case by no means rare, women especially in despair have recourse to this means, when they have not been rendered defenceless at the outset. The dirt under the nails of the corpse should be collected by means of a piece of wood or paper folded several times, a knife should never be employed, as it may scrape scales from the skin and so lead to serious mistakes. Microscopic examination of this dirt will show if it contains traces of skin or blood, in which case the assailant should bear marks of scratching. On the contrary if the corpse bear marks of scratches and the dirt under the nails of a suspected person contains traces of skin and blood, some relation between the accused and the scratches on the corpse may be inferred.

8. One cannot be too careful in examining weapons put forward as the supposed instrument of crime, it is a strange fact, often observed, that a guilty person, while otherwise making a full confession, brings forward a weapon very different from that actually employed. An error of this kind may be the starting point for grave blunders.

The Graz Criminal Museum contains a skull the roof of which is damaged by many dents, given with a heavy shovel. On the corpse only a cut 3 centimetres long was to be seen, which looked as if it had been caused by a sharp knife, and at first a youth was arrested whose pocket-knife showed traces of what was supposed to be blood. So also in wounds to bones, the fissure and instrument do not always agree. The Graz

Criminal Museum possesses a piece of skull with the knife that produced the wound. The wound is almost rectangular, only a little longer than the breadth of the knife, but three times wider than the thickness of the blade. One would have imagined that the wound was caused by a wide two-bevelled chisel or some similar implement.

Section IV.—Wounds caused by Fire-arms.

In *Chapter VI* we have summarised the technical details likely to prove useful to Investigating Officers in dealing with fire-arms. In treating of wounds caused by the discharge of a fire-arm, the following points have to be considered:—

(*a*) The projectile or projectiles
(*b*) The wad, the patch, and the cartridge case
(*c*) The explosive gases
(*d*) Grains of powder unconsumed
(*e*) The flame of the powder
(*f*) The smoke

The production and even the existence of the effects caused by these various factors depend on the nature of the arm, the charge, and the distance at which the shot is fired, not to mention other accessory conditions, such as the action of the wind, the angle of incidence, etc. Obviously the results may be combinations of different elements, so that the same result may arise from different causes. Thus an arm of inferior quality with a heavy charge of powder may at the same distance produce the same effect as a superior arm with a smaller charge, or a first class arm with a heavy charge may produce the same result as an inferior arm with a smaller charge fired from a shorter distance. In general the best effects so far as accuracy and range are concerned are produced by breech-loading rifles especially with modern bullets of small calibre, then come shot guns, and finally revolvers. Here again it is clear that the make of the arm is of great importance. Our remarks will for the most part have reference to fire-arms of medium quality.

For the following details reliance is placed chiefly on the excellent work of *Hofmann*.

The orifice of the wound is large, mangled, with flesh torn away, when the shot has been fired point-blank or the weapon is of first class quality. This is explained by the fact that in such cases the gases developed by the powder penetrate directly into the opening made by the projectile, expanding under the skin, which is torn and in part blown away. This happens especially when the part of the body struck is near a bone, the gas cannot then penetrate far into the flesh and is, so to speak, driven out again. A further proof of the shot having been fired point-blank is that the hair or garments around the orifice are burned or singed, which is due to the heat of the flame of the powder. The presence of a sort of dry border around the orifice of entry of the bullet does not prove absolutely that the shot has been fired at close quarters. This border, though much narrower, is met with also in shots fired from a great distance, and may be due to the shock of the projectile; but if the wound is blackened by the smoke of the powder and if grains of powder have penetrated the skin it is certain that the shot has been fired point-blank. The presence of these grains of powder in the skin is of greater importance than usually recognised, as it is possible from them to draw conclusions as to the construction of the weapon. Remember that the firing of the powder takes place from behind forwards; all attempts to set fire to the powder in front have failed. From the time that a small quantity of the powder is set fire to, the impulsive force is developed, and eventually the portion of the powder not yet consumed is drawn out of the barrel along with the projectile.

If the powder is very inflammable, if the barrel is very long, or if it be rifled so that the bullet is compelled to turn relatively very slowly, the powder has time to be completely consumed. But in the contrary case—powder burning slowly, short barrel, and no rifling—the powder is not entirely consumed, a portion remains intact which is drawn out with the lead, with sufficient force, if the range be short, to penetrate under the skin. It is impossible to efface the black mark caused by the grains of powder, while marks made by the smoke are easily obliterated.

If then grains of powder are found imbedded in the skin, it may be safely concluded that the shot has been fired from a very short distance and with a weapon preventing the complete combustion of the powder. So far nothing further can be stated with confidence, but the Investigating Officer should note minutely the number of grains and how they are scattered, e.g., three grains on the jaw at such and such distances from each other, ten on the forehead, four on the temple. If the grains are on a flat surface, as the breast or the back, the best and easiest method is to mark on a sheet of paper the positions of the grains and the distances in the natural size.

If subsequently the weapon be discovered, experts can in any particular case give important information. If there be several unknown quantities, for instance if the range and the strength of charge be unknown, experts can naturally say little. But if the range be known and there is anything to lead to a conclusion as to the strength of the charge, then experts can give very precise information; by experiment with the weapon in question it can be verified whether it is capable of discharging against a fixed target an equal quantity of grains of powder.

Again, the depth to which the grains of powder penetrate varies between 1/32 and 3/32 inch (1 to 2 millimetres). These grains will be found buried in the object by the discharge of a large American revolver at the distance of one yard, but not at five feet; for a saloon pistol the distance may be seven feet, and for guns and rifles even further, according to the experiments made by *Hofmann* upon dead bodies. Other experiments, however, show that the combustion of the powder is, owing to the length of the barrel, more complete in guns than in pistols and revolvers; thus while the grains are thrown as far, they are more nearly consumed and the penetration is no greater than for the other weapons.

As for other effects, a shot from a pistol will set fire to paper at a distance of 20 inches, revolvers (of 9 millimetres=about 3/8 of an inch calibre) will singe the hair at a distance of 10 or 15 centimetres (4 to 6 inches), and blacken the object up to 1½ feet.

The following points should be noted:—

1. Gun-shot wounds (using the phrase gun-shot to describe com-

pendiously all wounds caused by the discharge of a fire-arm) are distinguished from wounds made by a knife or dagger by the channel of the wound. For the latter the channel is contracted as the wound goes deeper while for the former the channel expands the further the projectile penetrates. But wounds from a fire-arm and from a sharp weapon are not often confounded.

2. Shot discharged at short range may produce a wound similar to that made by a bullet, because the shot on quitting the barrel remains packed, separating only later to form what is called the cone of dispersion, for this phenomenon, like others of the same nature, is often influenced by many accidental and unforeseen facts. This distance may be from four to six feet and even more, it being difficult to calculate it with precision; in modern choke-bore shot-guns the distance is much greater, the object being, of course, to concentrate the shot and so cause greater destruction among a number of birds flying close together.

This dispersion of shot differs with, and has no co-relation to, the quality of each arm. Sometimes the pellets remain massed for a considerable distance, but, when they separate, spread more widely than when fired from other arms where they separate immediately on leaving the barrel; but in all cases the cone of dispersion remains the same. This packing or cohesion of the shot depends on, besides their size and number, the strength of the charge and the quality of the two wads. The size of these last and the force with which they are rammed into the barrel or cartridge are of enormous influence. Experience shows that the relation between the weight of the powder and the number of shot is of great importance, with the same arm and wads absolutely alike very different results are obtained, depending on the relation between the shot and the powder. It is a well-ascertained fact that when the pellets are enclosed in a small cotton bag slipped into the barrel, as is the habit of poachers, they remain packed; the same result happens when the shot is mixed with about an equal quantity of sawdust. Thus nothing very precise can be asserted as to the cause of this packing of shot, and great care must, therefore, be taken in forming too precipitate conclusions, as to, e.g., the distance from which a shot has been fired, when the only factors one has are the wound itself and some projectiles found by chance. But even when the weapon itself can be experimented with, conclusive results cannot be arrived at, for the weight of the powder and shot must be known. Further there are always unknown factors of primary importance, as, for instance, the position of the charge, the force with which the wads have been rammed home, and a crowd of other secondary matters. Experiments can easily be made on the cone of dispersion. Let screens of paper be placed parallel, one behind the other, at distances of ten paces between each. Let the first be fired at so that the shot pierce successively the screens (as many as liked may be used). Then by examining the screens the scattering of the shot can be easily seen. Using a first class muzzle-loading gun, which permits the charge to be more easily regulated than a breech-loader, with the same weighed weight of powder and the same counted number of shot, with similar wads rammed home with equal strength, with the same wind, etc., all the conditions being as nearly as possible identical in the various experiments, in spite of every precaution the results were absolutely different, or at least so different as to prevent any practical conclusions of legal value being deduced from them

3 The edges of the orifice made by the projectiles are not always turned inwards (inverted) as is commonly supposed, frequently there is so much tearing and mangling that there cannot be said to be either inversion or eversion. Often the edges are raised up by the fat beneath or bloated through advancing decomposition

4 Bullets properly so called (i e, cylindrical with a rounded conoidal end) often make peculiar openings, not at all resembling those usually made by a shot from a fire-arm. Sometimes they are triangular, appearing to have been made by a lancet, not rarely they resemble a knife thrust

5 While there is little satisfactory authority as to wounds caused by the wind of a passing ball yet serious effects may be produced by the explosive gases from a blank shot, i e, without projectile. 1 *Beck* examined forty suicides whose skulls were smashed into innumerable morsels, who yet had fired blank. Naturally in such cases the muzzle of the barrel must be placed directly under the chin or in the mouth. It is not therefore, impossible that a murder may be committed in this way, and all the more likely as it lends itself easily to the suspicion of suicide, it is a fair supposition that a person asleep stupefied or bound, may thus be killed by a blank charge fired point-blank

6 Although appearing impossible wounds due to a fire-arm may be confounded with wounds due to a cutting instrument. This mistake is in particular easily made in portions of the body where bones are found directly under the skin. The following case was reported in 1893. A man was found apparently killed by a blow from a knife in the nape of the neck. The judicial *post-mortem* confirmed this supposition. The individual it was believed, had received in the nape a blow from a knife, which not being very deep was not thought mortal. By mere chance suspicion was aroused that the man had been killed by a shot from a fire-arm, exhumation of the body and a new *post-mortem* confirmed this suspicion, for a revolver bullet was found lodged between two vertebrae of the neck

7 Another difficult question which frequently arises is whether death from gun-shot is due to suicide, accident, or murder. Here medical knowledge and the *post-mortem* itself are of less value than an attentive, minute, and exhaustive examination of the attendant circumstances. Frequently, too, the Investigating Officer has to come to a decision before the arrival of the medical men and before the *post-mortem* as to whether the presumption of murder exists, necessitating a judicial inquiry, or whether the case is so clearly one of suicide or accident as to warrant the abandonment of further proceedings

Few general rules can be laid down for this purpose. The exterior circumstances are generally the most important—the position of the corpse and the weapon, the personality of the dead person, and analogous matters. Here above all it is necessary not to lose one's head and not to attribute any decisive signification to isolated facts and suppositions wanting in a solid foundation. On the one hand it must not be forgotten that persons who attempt their own lives have frequently the most odd and eccentric notions, so that from facts not clearly established murder cannot be presumed. Even the place of the wound proves nothing, cases have been recorded where persons have fired at the stomach, dying only after horrible suffering.* Again it may happen that the shot goes astray, owing to too heavy a charge, and the projectile goes elsewhere than the spot aimed at, the lungs, for example, instead of the heart. On the other hand it must be remembered that it is often very easy so to arrange matters as to make a murder pass for a suicide or accident, especially at a superficial view, and even after a more minute examination. The situation and position of the body may have been arranged artificially after the fatal wound, and false letters may be written in which the victim bids a touching adieu to the world. A very important and in fact almost certain proof of suicide is the manner in which the corpse retains the weapon in its clenched fist. Many experiments on persons just dead, by pressing objects into their hands, have proved that they cannot retain such objects with the convulsive grasp of a person holding the object in his hand during life and in the death agony. The last point must not be overlooked, for it is possible a very refined murderer may place a weapon in the hand of a dying victim.

Another important and rather frequent circumstance is when the weapon bursts. This generally happens when a suicide determined not to fail in his design, overloads the arm, which a murderer would think quite unnecessary. Further a fire-arm pressed too closely against the body is especially if of a poor quality, likely to burst owing to the inability of the explosive gases to escape. The murderer would rarely require thus to press the fire-arm against the body, and even if he did, the victim would always shrink back sufficiently to produce between himself and the fire arm a space by which the gases could escape.

On the other hand, the presence of the weapon is for the most part quite indifferent; it is common to find no weapon beside persons who have undoubtedly committed suicide. This is generally attributed to the theft of the weapon by those arriving first on the scene, the weapon used by a suicide being usually supposed to produce superstitious effects. The following is a most instructive case. Early one morning the authorities were informed that the corpse of a murdered man had been found. At the spot indicated, in the middle of a bridge crossing a rather deep stream, the body was found of a grain merchant, A M , supposed to be a well-to-do man, face downwards with a gun-shot wound behind the ear. The bullet after passing through the brain had lodged in the frontal bone above the left eye. His pocket-book was missing and the seam of the inside pocket in which it was usually carried was ripped up, as if the pocket-book had been rapidly and violently snatched out. His watch and chain were also missing, of the latter the ring attaching it to the waistcoat button was alone left. A policeman stated that A M had been seen the evening before in a spirit shop where he drank with moderation and left about 10 30 p m , stating that he was about to return home. To reach his house he had to pass over the bridge where he was found dead. In the spirit shop there was at the same time as A M , an unknown, wretched-looking man, who throughout the evening drank but a single glass of spirits and left shortly

---

* It seldom happens, however, that a suicide takes place through a shot through the eye, although this is a sure means of death. Obviously the destruction of the eye is distasteful to a suicide. If a corpse is found having been shot in the head through the eye, it is to be concluded, until the contrary is proved, that it is not a case of suicide.

after A M. The latter had several times taken out his pocket-book, which appeared well filled, though no one could say whether he had any money or how much. The supposition was therefore natural that the unknown had followed A M, murdered him on the bridge, and robbed him: he was accordingly searched for, arrested and brought to the spot. He denied all knowledge of the crime and said he had passed the night in a barn which however he could not point out to the police. Just when the inquiry was concluding and the corpse was about to be removed after the *post-mortem*, the Investigating Officer observed quite by chance that on the decayed wooden parapet of the bridge almost opposite the spot where the corpse lay, there was a small but perfectly fresh injury which appeared to have been caused by the violent blow on the upper edge of the parapet of a hard and angular body. He immediately suspected that this injury had some connection with the murder; examination with a magnifying glass showed nothing important, but it was impossible to avoid the impression that here the murderer had thrown something into the water and thus damaged the parapet. Accordingly the Investigating Officer determined to drag the bed of the stream below the bridge, when almost immediately there was picked up a strong cord about 11 feet long with a large stone at one end and at the other a discharged pistol, the barrel of which fitted exactly the bullet extracted from the head of A M. The case was thus evidently one of suicide, A M had hung the stone over the parapet of the bridge and discharged the pistol behind his ear. The moment he fired he let go the pistol, which the weight of the stone dragged over the parapet into the water, but the pistol had struck violently against the parapet in passing over and so caused the injury observed. Experiment showed the trick to be quite easy and that the parapet was damaged every time. Subsequent inquiries disclosed that the pistol actually belonged to A M, that his affairs were hopelessly involved, and that he had just effected an insurance on his life for the benefit of his family for a large sum. As the company did not pay in cases of suicide, A M had adopted this means to conceal the suicide and lead to the belief that he had been murdered

8 Another important point, not to be forgotten, is this it is not uncommon to find large gun-shot wounds, while the dress covering them is not in the slightest degree injured. Dr Bernard v Beck writes thus "During the campaigns of 1848 and 1849 as well as in duels with pistols, I have observed this phenomenon, especially with spherical projectiles. Once I found a deep wound in the arm with fracture of the humerus without any corresponding hole in either the cloak or tunic. Another time I found a wound in the forearm while neither the chemise nor flannel vest was pierced. I have twice seen the projectile bury itself close to the iliac bone without injuring the linen and several times have found wounds in the region, and even in the joints, of the foot without injury to the boot." Dr Richter also has remarked that it frequently happens that the shirt or the soft upper leather of a boot is driven by the projectile into the wound without being pierced. If then a companion of the wounded man himself drags out the garment, he pulls out at the same time the projectile, which therefore cannot be found in the wound. The same author states that a doctor, on the battlefield searched in the brain of a wounded man for a ball which all the time was sticking in the trimming of his cap, yet the

ball had hit the cap hard enough to break the soldier's skull. Knotz relates an analogous case, in which a woman received a violent horn thrust from an ox. The skin arranged itself like the finger of a glove round the horn, but yet the abdominal muscles were torn. These surprising observations may elucidate more than one insoluble case and prevent serious errors, but they also teach those who arrive first on the scene of a crime either to leave everything exactly as it has been found or, if it is absolutely necessary to move anything, to make the most accurate report to the medical man of everything that has been done, however insignificant it may appear to the outsider. If they do not, the ablest medical man may lose all his trouble.

9. *Wounds by rifles.*—It should first be noted that modern arms of precision produce very characteristic wounds, but the phenomena of these are not identical for all distances, great differences being produced according to the range.

Roughly speaking we may distinguish four zones or ranges:—

I. The first extends to about 500 yards. Here the projectile crushes the cellular tissue, reducing it to atoms and destroying its cohesion, over an extensive surface.

II. The second zone approximately from 500 to 1200 yards, is that of "clean" wounds. The bullet makes a clean passage through the fleshy parts and a hole of its own calibre in flat or spongy bones.

III. At the third range, from 1200 to 1800 yards, the bullet breaks and tears the part touched and causes much destruction, the bones are broken in a thousand morsels, the fleshy parts are mangled, and the orifice of exit by which the bullet leaves the body presents the appearance of a crater seven or eight times the size of the orifice of the entry.

IV. Beyond this range the bullet begins to lose its force, although its killing power may extend up to 4500 yards. The bullet wounds the fleshy parts, shocks, splits, or goes round a bone, and at last produces only contusions. The explosive effect of some non-explosive projectiles has been explained in various ways. That most generally accepted is that the effect is due to hydraulic pressure, by which the incompressible liquids with which the organs and vessels are filled transmit the shock in all directions and thus produce an extremely powerful radiating effect.

The following observations may be made:—

(*a*) The orifice made by the bullet in entering the body is generally small, and may, when the range is very short and the elasticity of the skin comes into play, as in the belly, be less than $\frac{1}{5}$ inch in diameter. The opening is either a well-marked tear in the form of a star, or perfectly round, with very clean-cut edges as if struck with a punch. If the shot has been fired point-blank, as in the case of suicides, the skin round the orifice is burned and blackened, often in an irregular manner. For shots fired at a distance of one to ten yards the orifice is surrounded by a blackish circle less than $\frac{1}{4}$ inch wide, which is not due to burning but to the terrible crushing of the tissues. *This coloration may also be produced at the orifice of exit.*

(*b*) In the first half of the zone, *i.e.*, up to about 250 yards the diameter of the orifice of entrance varies from $\frac{1}{4}$ to $\frac{1}{3}$ inch and for greater distances, may extend to $\frac{1}{2}$ an inch, a diameter rarely surpassed. If the projectile does not strike the body at right angles, the orifice of entry is lengthened or even forms a channel on the surface, and the edges and hair are burned more deeply in the flesh than with round orifices. When the bullet produces an explosive effect, the orifice of entry is often filled with splinters of bone buried therein, or presents strips of flesh hanging outwards.

(c) The diameter of the orifice of exit varies from ½ inch to 1¼ inch. In the latter case the opening generally contains splinters of bone, and damage is also sometimes caused by the steel envelope of the bullet which may become detached. If the fragments of bone and morsels of muscle are thrown beyond the orifice of exit, the range was probably under 100 yards, and if a projectile, which retains its shape, quits the body at a spot where the skin is stretched tightly over a bone, as on the skull, the orifice is firm and tense and so much resembles the orifice of entry as to be easily mistaken for it. In these rare but important cases the orifice of exit is less than that of entry, and such insignificant orifices often lead to the assumption that the wound is of little importance; careful examination alone discloses the severe internal injuries.

(d) If the projectile encounters little resistance, as in the intestines the orifices of entry and exit are generally small, and the projectile is not misshapen.

(e) If the projectile strikes a hard bone, and so gets misshapen, or the steel envelope gets turned up, the orifice of exit will necessarily show traces of the same.

While these results remain true for ordinary rifles, it must be noted that practical experience, particularly in the Anglo-Boer and Russo-Japanese wars, has rather upset the old theories as to the killing and stopping powers of high-velocity projectiles.

The official "Text Book of Small Arms" gives some idea of the principles on which the wounding power of a bullet depends.

"Up to the advent of the modern small-bore rifle below ·320 inch calibre, with its hard-coated bullet, there were no serious complaints of want of stopping power, but, on the subject of the wounding power of small-bore bullets the greatest diversity of opinion has been expressed. This appears to be due to several causes, the chief of which is the fact that the wounding power varies enormously in proportion to the striking velocity and to the resistance the bullet meets with. Most of the experimental work in connection with this subject has been carried out against dead horses or dead men as targets; a correct conclusion cannot be drawn from such experiments, as it is found from experience in South Africa and elsewhere that the small-bore bullet does less damage on living creatures than the experiments would lead one to expect. The following extract from Surgeon-Colonel R. F. Stevenson's work 'Wounds in War,' emphasises this point. 'It is now apparent that conclusions drawn from experiments made on dead animals or men are not borne out by what is observed when living men are wounded by small-bore projectiles. Whether this is because dead animal tissue is harder or more resistant, the fats having solidified, and the liquids being greatly diminished in quantity, or from some other cause, is not just now quite certain, but it is steadily becoming more and more evident that the appalling destruction produced in dead animals and cadavers by small projectiles, tried in any of the ways above referred to,* is not experienced when men are hit by them under the ordinary conditions. In considering the wounding power of bullets, it is advisable to divide the subject into two parts:—

1st. The wounding power at ranges where the bullet may produce explosive effects.

2nd. The wounding power at longer ranges.

The explosive effect observed in some wounds is due to a cylindro-conoidal bullet, travelling at a high rate of speed, striking a hard bone or meeting with great resistance, in its passage through an object. The many splinters into which the bone is broken are driven forward by the bullet with great velocity, and themselves act as secondary missiles, producing great destruction in the neighbouring tissues, and make an enormous exit wound such as would lead one to suppose that the bullet itself had exploded. The effect has occasionally been observed where soft parts only have been traversed, but such cases are very exceptional. With rifles of the Martini-Henry class such wounds might be produced up to 150 or 200 yards, and on account of the leaden bullet setting up and becoming deformed on striking the bone, the explosive effect might be even more severe than that produced by the modern small bore. On account of the higher velocity of the modern rifles explosive effect may occur up to 300 or 350 yards.

When soft parts are struck, bullets of the Martini-Henry type crush through the tissues, causing more laceration and shock than the small-bore bullet with his higher velocity, which cuts through the flesh more cleanly, making a wound which often heals in a very short time.

"At the longer ranges, from 350 to 800 yards, the small-bore bullet and the 450 produce bone fractures of about the same gravity. From 800 to 1,200 yards the fractures produced by the small bore are the less severe of the two. At ranges over 1,200 yards, the small bore, on account of its retaining its velocity better, causes greater destruction in striking bones than the larger bullet.

"At the longer ranges soft parts are more lacerated by the large bore bullet; the latter may also complicate the wound by remaining in it. In experiments with the Mauser rifle bullet of .311 inch diameter it was found that the bullet never lodged in the tissues of the body at ranges up to 1,500 yards.

Taking the surgical results of the South African War as a whole, it appears that although terrible wounds have been caused by explosive effect, the small arm wounds have generally been more successfully treated than in the days of plain lead bullets. It is more common nowadays to hear of cures being effected when the abdomen or brain has been perforated than in the days of the .45 bore. Although this satisfactory state of things must be partly attributed to the advance of scientific and surgical knowledge, and also to the increased range at which modern battles are fought,

---

* The ways referred to consisted in either firing with the full service charge at the various ranges at which it was desired to test the wounding power of the bullet, or in firing at a short range with a reduced charge that gives the bullet the same velocity it would have at the longer range at which the experimentalist desired to ascertain its effect.

still the small-bore hard-coated bullet must be given its share of the credit in bringing about this humane result."

Section v.—Marks on the Bodies of Persons Strangled or Hanged.

All the questions connected with this subject may be summed up in one: was such and such a death by hanging a murder? Was the person assassinated before being hung? It is a fair presumption that a considerable proportion of so-called suicidal deaths by hanging are really caused by another hand. Of course in such cases the murderer will not select a mode of death leaving too distinct traces. One would not hang up, under pretence of suicide, a person killed by a gun-shot wound or with a fractured skull, but this is frequently done in cases of poisoning, strangling, or even killing by means of a fine and long stabbing instrument. Recently a servant in an anatomical laboratory at Cracow was condemned for having killed his wife by driving into her heart a long needle. The case was as follows: knowing the exact position of the heart the murderer thrust in the needle, and prevented any bleeding by pressing his finger over the wound, then he hung up the body so as to simulate suicide, which was all the easier as the left breast of the woman being extremely developed and pendent concealed the minute wound. If he had not boasted about it one day when drunk the crime would probably have never been discovered.

We constantly read in the daily papers of "mysterious cases of hanging without any apparent motive", but how rare it is to read that in such a case an inquiry has been instituted, to see if it was not a case of poisoning. Many of these victims again have been strangled, a surer and less dangerous method, as the proof of murder is much more difficult. A person may be rendered almost instantaneously unconscious or even killed by pressure on the carotid arteries and the vagus nerve. Everyone knows how easily unconsciousness is produced, in a few seconds, by placing the palms of the hands on the cheeks near the ears and pressing strongly with either thumb on the corresponding carotid arteries. The pressure on the arteries prevents the flow of blood to the brain. Unconsciousness follows and finally death. The same result ensues when one throws from behind round the neck of the victim a cord, a cloth, or, like the thugs, a silk handkerchief, and drags it forcibly towards one. The victim cannot defend himself or cry out or make any noise; he dies quickly, bearing no other marks save those of strangulation. If then the body be hung up, care being taken to place the cord approximately over the marks of strangulation it will be almost impossible to prove that death was not due to hanging. A long line of medical jurisprudents has established that marks of strangulation inflicted on a living person are hardly if at all to be distinguished from those produced on a corpse, especially if death be very recent.

Moreover the characteristic symptoms of death by hanging are also those of death by strangulation: the bluish discoloration of the face, the froth of the mouth, the protrusion of the tongue, the erection of the penis, the increased secretion of mucus in the sexual organs of the female, and many other so-called infallible signs. These signs may be absent in deaths of this nature and may be found in cases of death by other means. It must not be too precipitately concluded that a third person has intervened, for there are many instances of suicides having attempted death in various ways before having recourse to the rope, it is not uncommon to find on the bodies of suicides by hanging marks of ineffective gun-shot wounds. In one case an old woman after inflicting several severe wounds in the region of the heart stopped the hemorrhage, carefully washed away the traces of blood, and then hung herself. In another case an old man first gave himself several severe blows on the head with a hammer. Accordingly the Investigating Officer in the case of one of these doubtful suicides must above everything seriously weigh all the exterior circumstances of the affair. To begin with, he will read any farewell writing that may have been left by the supposed suicide, without however deeming it a conclusive proof, and if possible will compare the handwriting with an authentic manuscript of the deceased. If it be impossible to do that on the spot, he can at least see if the handwriting, orthography and style of the document correspond with the education and culture of the deceased. If the document disclose any motive for suicide and it be easy to verify whether such motive be well founded, as for instance, financial embarrassment, family troubles, bodily suffering, the suicide will appear less suspicious, but if no motive be disclosed or only such vague motives as disgust of life or fear of some unknown disaster, suspicion will be increased. It will be the same if the terms of the document are such as to suggest some sudden mental disturbance not existing beforehand.

The Investigating Officer must not forget to verify whether or not the paper, ink, and pen with which the document is written belong to the deceased. If they do, still that will not be a *proof* of suicide for the murderer may have been able to write the false letter on the spot, after the perpetration of the crime, but if there cannot be found among the possessions of the deceased paper similar to that of the document and if the latter has been certainly written with another ink than those possessed by the deceased, the affair becomes very suspicious. It must be remembered that carefully disguised crimes of this nature rarely occur among very poor people whose ordinary motives are robbery, succession to property, jealousy, revenge, but such ingeniously contrived crimes are, so to say, the *privilege* of the better classes. One rarely finds in European countries such pretended suicides among the peasants on the thrashing-floor or in the open air but in the bed-chamber or work room of the deceased where it is possible to proceed to investigate on the spot and find the paper, ink, and pen. It may be established if there has been any robbery, if the deceased left a heir, anyone in short who would profit by the death.

The next step will be examine the instrument of strangulation and the mode of its employment. It must be determined if the cord, ribbon, strap, shawl, cloth, etc., employed is the property of the deceased, if third parties had easy access thereto, and above all, whether the instrument of crime has been carefully chosen with a view to its special purpose. It cannot, of course, be denied that intending suicides frequently have recourse to instruments badly adapted to their object (as braces, weak cords, etc.) but this almost always happens when either they have no other means handy or act with such precipitation as to render a careful choice impossible. This is notably the case with insane persons. But as a rule the suicide proceeds to choose his instrument with the greatest care and minuteness, he takes precautions that it is strong and safe, that the knot runs easily and rapidly, and above all, strange as it may appear, that the material coming in contact with his body should not hurt the skin. It is for this reason that the suicide so often selects cloths, shawls, thick and soft ropes etc., very rarely is iron wire used. In one case only, to the knowledge of the author, was a chain used for hanging and that was not a case of suicide. A woman passed a chain round the neck of her husband when dead drunk, threw the free end over a beam, and so suspended and strangled the unfortunate man. When she found suspicion rest on her, she hanged herself in turn, but selected for the purpose a soft handkerchief. In every case the Investigating Officer must be careful to describe with exactness the instrument, whence it comes, its nature and size, and the mode in which it has been used, so that if at a later date suspicion should be aroused, he possesses a basis for further investigations.

It must be remarked again that the best means of observing important details is to write down with scrupulous exactitude the description of how everything is found on the spot. So long as one only looks on the scene, it is impossible, whatever be the care, time, and attention bestowed, to detect all the details, and especially to note various incongruities; but these strike us at once when we set ourselves to describe the picture on paper as exactly and clearly as possible. This point can never be sufficiently impressed on the young Investigating Officer. It has frequently happened that important circumstances have been overlooked, which, as the dictation of the report was proceeded with, were noticed and threw a flood of light on the affair. Naturally to obtain this result one must proceed slowly and methodically.

It is easy to understand that one takes note of contradictions, omissions, improbabilities when one reasons from the general to the particular, from cause to effect, from preceding events to succeeding, from intention to action. Artists readily appreciate this when they recollect that defects in a drawing are most easily and surely detected when it is looked at in a mirror. So here, the exact description of the surroundings is, so to speak, the mirror in which all "defects of the situation" are reflected. But *the "defects of the situation" are just those contradictions, those improbabilities, which occur when one desires to represent the situation as something quite different from what it really is, and this with the very best intentions and in the purest belief that one has worked with all the forethought, craft, and consideration imaginable*.

But this is not always the procedure, especially in great crimes; there, with hardly an exception, the Investigating Officer can discover the "grand blunder," which the most experienced and crafty criminal rarely fails to commit. Take an illustrative case. The scene was the room where a man was supposed to have hung himself; the Investigating Officer was sent for before the corpse was cut down; absolutely trustworthy evidence showed that nothing had been changed or disturbed. The body was hanging in the middle of the room from the bracket of a chandelier, the feet about 18 inches from the ground and absolutely isolated from a chair or any other object. As far as seats were concerned there were in the room, which was the office room of the deceased, only an office chair, two sofas and an ordinary chair. The office chair was as usual at the desk, the sofas in a corner beside a smoking-table and the ordinary chair was beside the office chair, covered with books and papers. At first the Investigating Officer observed nothing extraordinary, but dictating his report, the idea suddenly struck him. "But how did the man hang himself?" It happens often enough that persons attempting suicide by hanging remain standing upright while passing the cord round their neck and then let themselves fall forward. See illustrations in *Taylor's* "Medical Jurisprudence," Vol. II. The body is then found in an inclining position, often on its knees, and sometimes almost lying down, but if the feet are separated from the floor, the victim must have attached the cord to a nail, a bracket, top of a door, etc., while standing on a chair, stool, box, etc., then passed the noose round the neck and leaped from the support, or kicked it away with his feet, and if the feet do not touch the ground and there be no chair or other support near, the only conclusion is that another hand did the deed. So it turned out to be in this case. There was neither suicide nor murder. The old man, who was an invalid, has been placed by his relations in charge of two servants, who went out one night to a ball without permission. On that very night the old man had a stroke of apoplexy, dying alone and uncared-for. To escape being taxed with their neglect the two servants, a footman and a cook, resolved to pretend that the old man had committed suicide; with the help of a long dusting brush they attached the rope to the chandelier, the footman lifted up the body and the cook put the rope round the neck. The only thing they forgot, in their hurry to rob their master's safe, was to put a chair beside the corpse.

Above all things it is to be remembered that every complicated situation does not point to murder. Some years ago the wife of a peasant in Galicia was found dead in a well. On the corpse being pulled out, the magistrate noticed on the neck of the corpse clear marks of strangulation. It was concluded that the peasant had strangled his wife and thrown her into the well, whereupon the man was arrested. Only after some time had passed by was the true cause of the marks discovered. The people who had pulled the corpse out of the well had been clever enough to put a noose round the neck and so drag it up. The woman had without doubt in a fit of melancholy thrown herself into the water.

Section vi.—Bodies found in the Water.

When a corpse is discovered in the water various kinds of guilty acts suggest themselves. There may be simply negligence, when, for example a child is a victim of an accident for want of being looked after, or a person falls from a bridge badly protected. On the other hand a person may have been wounded and then thrown into the water, living or already dead, and lastly the water itself is sometimes employed as the agent of death. A person may be simply thrown into the water, or he may be plunged under the water and held there until he has lost consciousness, or till he is dead. This is the usual method when it is intended to represent a suicide. Questions of this kind present the greatest difficulties.

There are no rules indicating the course to follow in such cases, all the more that there is generally wanting one important starting point which we possess for the other kinds of death, namely, the position of the corpse after the crime. For even when the person has been drowned in still water and left there by the murderer the corpse through eddies in the water, currents of air and even animals living in the water, undergoes such changes that there can be hardly any question of the "situation remaining intact." Besides, people who find a body in the water do not generally leave it there, they are always anxious to bring it to life again. When a body is found on the ground it is easy to see if it has received a gun-shot wound in the head or a stab in the neck. One has only to touch it to see if it is cold or if the heart has ceased to beat; the merest amateur can conclude that the person is dead without in the slightest degree altering the position of the corpse, and the Investigating Officer can then find it in its primitive position. It is very different for a body found in the water: the wounds, the stoppage of the heart, the coldness of the body, can rarely be ascertained if the corpse be not taken out of the water; when that is done the coldness of the body is attributed to the effect of the water, the wounds slight or supposed to be slight, are assumed to be accidental—and the consequence is that people frequently try to bring again to life corpses which already show symptoms of advanced decomposition. It follows that on the arrival of the Investigating Officer the corpse is almost always found in a place of safety, and the Investigating Officer has to describe it as he finds it. This description may be of importance afterwards, and should never be neglected when suicide is not absolutely certain. The wounds on the body, disarrangement of the clothes, appearance of the hands, mud or sand found under the nails should all be ascertained and described.

In forming a conclusion on suicide or accidental death one must not be too hasty and let oneself be led into a careless acceptance of any theory. Particularly dangerous in this direction is a decided conclusion on the existence or absence of clothes. Thus, for example, a man was poisoned in his home and died in bed. He was afterwards fully dressed by the prisoner and his confederates, with fur cap and winter coat and thrown into a part of the river free from ice, so that the conclusion was that the dead man had fallen into the water.

In the same way it is related in a newspaper that a young man was suffocated, then dressed in swimming drawers, and thrown into the water, so that the conclusion might be arrived at that the misfortune had happened while bathing.

On the other hand the wounds that the unfortunate one suffers living as well as dead on jumping into the water, grating on stones, etc., and striking against objects, are often put down to murder, and the impression of a shirt-collar or a cravat on the swollen neck of a body that has been in foul water has been taken for strangulation.

It is so common as to be considered an almost certain test of suicide that a Hindu woman before throwing herself into the water draws her cloth tightly between the legs and fastens it firmly at the waist, so as to prevent any indecent exposure of the person on discovery of her body. The same feeling renders it most improbable that a woman committing suicide in the manner suggested in the next paragraph would divest herself of her clothing.

One, however, should never be too ready to jump at the conclusion of suicide or accident. The following case is instructive on several grounds

One day there was found in a stream the corpse of a young peasant woman, perfectly naked. The season was the height of summer and everyone at first took it for granted that the young girl had been drowned while bathing. A *post-mortem* however disclosed that she was four months enceinte, when it was at once as rapidly concluded by the crowd that this was a motive for suicide. But the corpse bore on the back and the buttocks curious parallel marks of a deep red colour, presenting all the characteristics of scratches made on a person during life, which showed that the deceased must have passed over some object bearing sharp points fixed at equal distances from each other, and that it had passed over this object while still in life. Exact measurements as well as a drawing of these scratches were taken, burial was delayed in case new comparisons might be necessary, and the borders of the stream were followed in the direction whence the body had floated. Observing attentively the stream and everything found in it, there was at last discovered a piece torn from a garment, sticking on the root of a tree covered by the water. Other pieces were found attached to prominent objects. Meantime a policeman had established the identity of the deceased, and brought the mother before the Investigating Officer. It was then easy to determine that the fragments discovered belonged to the clothing of the young girl, that she was certainly not naked when she entered the water but that her garments were torn from her body by the strong current of the stream and the stumps of trees, etc., which were very numerous. She was not in the habit of wearing shoes.* After having followed slowly and carefully the borders of the stream and fished up nearly the whole of the remains of her garments, the Investigating Officer came to the dwelling of the young woman, about fifteen hundred yards from the bank, without having discovered the obstacle which had produced the wounds covering the body. Meanwhile, it was ascertained from the mother that her daughter had a lover who was employed in a tan-mill, situated a little further up the stream. It was therefore presumed that the deed had not been committed beyond the mill, and indeed there was discovered just below it, a big wooden rake which was jammed across the mill-race, this rake carried teeth sticking out several inches from the transverse axis, the latter being submerged in the water. The distances between these teeth were then measured and they corresponded exactly with the scratches on the back of the deceased. It was therefore no longer doubtful that she had fallen into the water above this rake, but at a very little distance above,— for the appearance of the scratches clearly showed that she was still alive when she passed over this apparatus. A little above this was the mill where the lover who without doubt was the father of her child lived. It was proved that two days before he had sent for the girl to come to him and that from that moment she had never been seen alive. On the other hand the young man could not be found in the mill, he had disappeared as soon as he learned that the body had been discovered. There remained no longer any doubt that it was he who had thrown the young woman into

---

* To say that footgear is the only thing a corpse does not lose easily through the action of water is inadequate.—the author has never been able to believe it is ever lost. Bodies often make horrible journeys especially in swiftly flowing mountain streams over boulders and trunks of trees, and thereby occasionally lose whole limbs. But if the feet are kept intact and if the corpse has on boots or shoes, not mere sandals, these are never lost, the foot swells, the leather shrinks, and so the footgear 'fits uncommonly tight.'

the water, not wishing to have the unborn infant fathered on him and intending to marry some other girl.

Frequently there are other accidental circumstances which enable us to ascertain with precision, as in the case just related, the exact spot where the person has been thrown into the water; such are injuries or objects attached to the body which could come only from one definite place; other peculiarities can be discovered only by the most minute investigations and ingenious theories. Thus there is the case of a corpse found in the water, whose clothes bore traces of oil which could come only from the parapet of a bridge about a league up the river, which was being newly painted. This single circumstance was sufficient to lead to the arrest of the murderer.

The following is an interesting case, though it failed to lead to any satisfactory result. A bailiff of the court, so it was supposed, had been inveigled into a sham interview near a mill-channel, when someone in revenge for some official act had thrown him into the water. The only thing to be done was to determine the exact spot where the crime had been committed. The canal led to a paper-mill where a night watchman had seen the corpse floating on the water; the watchman's duty was to call the time every quarter of an hour, and he was standing near a passage window looking at the water, waiting for the clock to strike 10.45 p.m. Thus he came to observe the corpse, and helped in its recovery. It was thus clear that the corpse arrived at the paper-mill at 10.45 p.m. The watch of the victim had stopped at 10.30 p.m. Two expert watchmakers were then called in, and made a long series of interesting experiments. One of them, when asked off-hand, said that a good watch, i.e., one hermetically enclosed in a case in good order, would go for hours without stopping. The other said it would go only for a very short time unless the case were rendered specially impermeable by india-rubber or leather washers. Different watches were then taken, old works being placed in the cases, and were submerged in water; they all stopped in a few seconds, except two—an English chronometer and a country watch—both of which kept going for 12 to 15 minutes. The latter had a double case made like a demi-hunter. The winding up key had been greased and so was impermeable. Finally the watch of the dead man was cleaned, oiled, and set going; when submerged in water it also stopped in a few seconds. It was thus certain that the person had fallen into the water just before 10.30 p.m., and that the body had been floating for a quarter of an hour when it reached the mill. The drowned man, it may be observed, had only very light summer clothes, which could not prevent or delay the penetration of the water. Next a big sack was filled with hay and sand, of a volume and weight corresponding to that of the human body. This sack was allowed to float in the canal for a quarter of an hour, an experiment all the more conclusive from the fact that the banks of the canal were straight and lined with wood, so that neither the body nor the sack could be caught and delayed by roots or shallows. The distance thus covered was then measured from the spot where the body was seen, and that point fixed on as the place where it had been thrown into the water. At this exact spot indeed nothing was found to excite suspicion, but a very short distance farther up the grass on the edge of the water was found trampled down with every sign of a struggle having taken place. Further, on careful search at the spot a button was found, which was missing from the coat on the body of the corpse. It thus appeared clear that the person had been deliberately thrown into the water, but the culprit was never discovered.

On general grounds the following points should be noticed in the case of corpses found in the water:

1. The supposed external signs of death by drowning are very deceptive, and, if they prove anything, prove only that the body has been a longer or shorter time in the water. But for a body to remain in the water and the person to be drowned, are two totally different things.

2. Again, the lowering of the temperature supposed to be observed on the corpses of drowned persons proves nothing. Every substance acquires after a certain time the temperature of the surrounding medium, and a human body which has been long enough in the water takes the temperature of that water, so if, as frequently happens in warm weather, the water is colder than the air, the body will also be colder than the air; and on the contrary, if a person were drowned in warm water which retained its temperature, the body would also remain warm even after several days in the water.

3. As to the extreme paleness which is said to be a characteristic sign of drowning, it has certainly been occasionally noted by experts, but most frequently it is non-existent. Also it is often found in corpses where death has been caused from quite different causes. Hence this proves nothing.

4. It is the same with what is commonly called 'goose skin' (adipocere) which is frequently found on the bodies of drowned persons, but also quite commonly in death from other causes, especially where death has been sudden.

5. The maceration of the skin—the signs being bluish colour, thickening, and corrugation, of the hands, the feet, and even the knees and elbows—is almost always present on corpses which have remained a sufficiently long time in the water, and proves nothing more than this, a fact which except in the rarest cases can always be readily ascertained. If the point be whether or not a corpse has remained a long time in the water, the fact can evidently be proved by such maceration, though it is impossible to state precisely the period of submersion.

On this point some curious observations were made by the author during the Bosnian Campaign of 1878. In the first weeks of August, in which period most of the battles with the Turks took place, during the day the heat was tropical, while every evening, almost without exception, there was a violent storm lasting all night. As forced marches had to be made during the day and the night had to be passed in the open air without shelter, the soldiers remained sodden with moisture for about a fortnight—during the day from perspiration, during the night from rain. The result was a severe maceration of the hands, feet, knees, elbows, and also round the hips, but that around the body was most marked, as the belt was very heavy—the men carrying a bayonet and two heavy cartridge pouches, and the officers sword, revolver, and sabretache. This maceration, which was very painful, formed a constant subject of conversation and was found to vary without any apparent cause, some suffering in an acute form, others not at all. The conditions were the same for all, and it was found that the difference did not result from the greater or less fleshiness of the individuals, nor from their colour fair or dark the only conclusion possible was that it was due to some peculiar and hitherto unknown character of the skin. An exaggerated value must not therefore be attached to the presence or absence of this sign on a corpse found in the water and too positive conclusions must not be drawn therefrom

6 Perhaps the strongest piece of evidence is the great contraction of the penis, or in the case of a woman of the breast-nipples. When this is found it must be admitted that the person has entered the water while yet alive or perhaps immediately after death

7 A withered umbilical cord, which the water cannot soften leads to the conclusion that the body of the infant has been exposed to the air several days before being placed in the water, in water or damp earth the umbilical cord decays but does not dry up

Section vii.—Injuries to Corpses.

That a body after death is exposed to injuries is often the case. Of little interest to us, however, are instances where the ill-treatment of a corpse has been caused through so-called corpse-robbery, superstition, (Vampires, Werewolfs, etc.) *post-mortem* rape, or the taking away of parts of the corpse for study or scientific purposes

Two classes of incidents may however be referred to as important

1 Injury to a corpse by taking away certain portions. Up to date the details of about ten cases have been published, in all of which the murderer sacrificed his victim without any demonstrable reason. A part of the body or the clothes have been taken away, or scattered around or hung up, and any reason given for the murder is obviously untrue. All that can be said at present about these remarkable and important cases is that they have to do with some superstitious motive of a highly-developed psychopathic individual

It must be remembered (as indeed we have seen, *Chapter X.*) that superstition in varied forms is still very widely and deeply spread among the common people. The normal person will accept a superstitious precedent only when the way it is arrived at is easy or not forbidden, as killing an animal, eating part of it, carrying a portion of it about with one, etc. If however the result can only be arrived at by criminal means, it is a different matter. Thus, for example, the normal superstitious person believes a man can fly or become invisible by eating the heart of a child, that he gains power in a Court of Law by carrying with him there the bones of a murdered person but his fear of punishment prevents him procuring these means by a criminal act. But if compulsion arises, externally through great need or danger, or internally through illness, then the idea becomes too powerful, all bars are burst through, and the necessary crime is committed. These cases are important and occur oftener than is thought. A conclusion as to murder through psychopathic superstition may be arrived at when no motive for the crime can be detected, and when it is proved objectively that a part of the body or piece of clothing has been scattered about or taken away.

2 Not interesting from a psychological point of view, but practically

important, are injuries caused otherwise than by criminals. Injuries inflicted on a corpse by animals, as gnawing by ants or woodlice, and portions of the corpse torn away by foxes or dogs etc., could not readily be imitated. It has happened that a corpse lying in the open air, for instance in a wood, has been shot by a sportsman taking it for some wild animal. This may easily happen with the corpse of a suicide, or of a person who has died suddenly and alone in a wood, and lain there for some time. If such are found with shot-wounds, doubt can arise as to the cause of death.

Section viii.—Poisoning.

Here, more than elsewhere, we appear to be dragging the Investigating Officer beyond his limits and launching him on a perilous quest, but nevertheless many cases arise where it is of the greatest importance for him to have at least some general knowledge of the different poisons and the effects produced by them, especially when he is obliged, without medical assistance, to make a domiciliary search in a poisoning case. The Investigating Officer may suddenly suspect poison and be compelled to act without waiting for expert aid. For the examination of witnesses, moreover, he will find it useful to have some knowledge, however slight, of poisonous bodies. he cannot have an expert to sit with him and advise him; either in such a predicament the Investigating Officer would have to consult with the expert before every question and after every answer, or the expert would himself put the questions and so take the control of the inquiry out of the hands of the officer. Apart from the impracticability of such a proceeding, the presence of medical experts at the examination of witnesses—often many in number—would be both embarrassing and costly.

It must not be imagined that in poison cases occurring in practice a start can always be made from the supposition that A has killed B with the poison X, which is luckily found in A's house. Such a case would be easily decided, it will be sufficient to establish the identity of the poison found in the stomach of the poisoned person, with that which A possessed, and to be sure that the symptoms of B's illness correspond to those ordinarily produced by the poison X. Under such conditions all doubts are removed. But it is not always so easy as that. Suppose for example, that all that is known is that B has died under suspicious circumstances, that a *post-mortem* examination excludes the idea of a natural death and shows symptoms of poisoning, although the doctors cannot on the spur of the moment state the exact nature of the poison, and further that A is suspected as the only person who could have poisoned B. A search in the house of A will probably have no result, for the non-possession of a poison in such a case shows that it has been used, and consequently cannot be found again. Hence the Investigating Officer endeavours to prove by the depositions of witnesses that A was formerly in the possession of such a poison.

We know that it is even when possible, troublesome and difficult to establish poisoning by chemical analysis or microscopic examination. The task of the expert is therefore much shortened when the statements of the witnesses give some indication of the inquiry that ought to be made, as for example, if it is possible to affirm that the suspected individual had been known to possess a certain definite poison. But when the Investigating

Officer wishes to question the witnesses about minerals and plants of which they may not even know the name, then, if he wishes to lead them in the right lines, he ought at least himself to know their external appearance. Of course he can get the necessary information from the expert, but, to be useful, such information should be full and complete, and even then there will always be something wanting, for an expert can never seize all the details which come out in the course of an inquiry. It is therefore far easier for an Investigating Officer once for all to know something about toxicology, something about natural history, and especially about the more important poisonous substances. He should examine the poisonous plants of his country, either fresh or dried; he should observe the mineral poisons under their different forms, and he must do this not once but often, at regular intervals, for such details very easily slip out of the memory and a mistake of this kind may lead to very serious consequences. It should be added that it is absolutely essential for him to know the different denominations of the different poisons in different countries. Poisonous plants in particular bear everywhere different names and many of them have often even in the same district several denominations; besides it is important to have information on the effects which, rightly or wrongly, are attributed to poisonous bodies in the district in question. Popular beliefs are often very characteristic, and may, combined with other information, largely contribute to clear up poisoning mysteries.

Thus in certain districts of Thuringia it is believed that the repeated drinking of a decoction of hemlock produces no symptom of poisoning, but that the individual to whom it has been administered is destined to certain death with all the symptoms of consumption; so that in any specific case if the suspected guilty person has told the witnesses that the deceased certainly died of consumption, while there are no other grounds for suspecting that disease, that alone would be a reason for suspecting him of the crime of poisoning. A similar case occurred in Bohemia. A man had poisoned with dried poisonous mushrooms the whole of a family of peasants. Among the victims was a daughter of the criminal, who was a servant in the family. This circumstance was adduced in favour of the accused, but served only to corroborate the suspicion against him when it was found that, in the part of the country from which the accused came, it was a universally believed opinion that poisonous mushrooms were perfectly harmless to young women.

Besides such scientific knowledge the Investigating Officer ought to have at least an approximate idea of the effects of poisons, but this he can only acquire by careful study of some first class manual of toxicology. Here only the most striking points can be noticed.

1. All cases of death are suspicious which follow a sickness of which the cause is unknown, presenting symptoms not agreeing with the usual symptoms of a natural illness. Undoubtedly such an indication is very vague and still further loses in value when it is remembered that the classic symptoms of poisoning such as vomiting, diarrhœa, giddiness, etc., do not necessarily accompany all poisons, and that on the other hand the sudden appearance of these symptoms does not conclusively indicate a case of poisoning. It is exactly the people who are circumspect, and therefore the most dangerous, who know how to make use of a slow and

creeping poison producing only a sickness marked by long-continued weakness without any of these alarming symptoms

2. An Investigating Officer should never neglect an opportunity of being present at a chemical analysis made by experts—for example, in endeavouring to establish the presence of arsenic in the stomach. Not until he has seen this done will he realise the difficulty and trouble he is giving them. He will also at the same time learn for future guidance what may reasonably be demanded of them and what are the limits of their knowledge. He will also learn that one cannot search for the poison, so to say, in the dark. Amateurs and even lawyers are often found who imagine that to establish the presence of a poison by chemical analysis one can proceed as if one were looking for a lost ring in a bag of flour, where you might also happen to find a pocket-knife, a watch, or any other object that is contained in it. The chemist can, in general, direct his investigations to one single poison or group of poisons alone, and if it is necessary to extend them to another poison or group, special investigation must be made for the purpose. If, for instance, a chemist after a careful and conscientious examination finds no trace of arsenic, that does not prove that the object examined does not contain ten other poisons, and particularly organic poisons. In a case of poisoning therefore, even more than in cases of another nature, the Investigating Officer should endeavour to be in close communication with the experts, to communicate every information he has on the matter, and to endeavour if possible to have a conference between the medical men who treated the deceased, those who made the *post-mortem*, and the chemical examiner, so as to decide in what direction inquiries should be made, whether it is necessary to call in the aid of microscopists or botanists, whether any particular portions of the body should be preserved for further examination, and lastly if, in view of the statements of the witnesses or other indications, it appears necessary to start fresh inquiries. As a general rule, such conferences should always be arranged; they frequently give important results and they ease the conscience of the Investigating Officer. He has the consolation of having done everything it was humanly possible for him to do.

3. When the least suspicion of poisoning exists conformably to instructions the stomach and its contents should be removed by the nearest available medical man, and preserved for the purpose of putting them at the disposal of the Court and the chemical examiner. Then one should scrutinise on the spot and with the aid of the medical man and the assistance of a good magnifying glass, and without avoidable disturbance, the stomach and intestines, etc., to see if any plants, or fragments of plants, suspicious foreign bodies, etc., are to be seen. If there are, they should then be examined, to see if they are poisonous. Organic bodies in favourable circumstances offer little resistance to decomposition and always become very difficult to detect after a few days, but if the medical men remove the stomach at the moment of the *post-mortem* and put it in water, or in alcohol, or dry it for the purpose of preservation they will perhaps have preserved the most important object in the whole inquiry.

4. For the interrogation of witnesses before the examination of the corpse the following characteristic signs should be noticed, which if not altogether conclusive at least justify suspicions of poisoning.

(a) In general poisoning and particularly arsenical poisoning may be suspected when there are found vomiting, violent thirst, sensation of burning in the throat, pains in the stomach, diarrhoea, and cramp in the calves of the legs, or some of these symptoms. Many believe that the perspiration and respiration of persons poisoned by arsenic have an odour of garlic, like that disengaged when arsenic is sprinkled on burning charcoal but it appears that this odour is found only in cases of chronic poisoning. Arsenic is largely used as an antidote to fevers of all kinds, as an aphrodisiac, in cases of rheumatism, gout and syphilis, and externally for skin diseases such as itch and eczema. It is also employed for many industrial purposes, as in curing skins and gold-working, and preserving roofs, floors, and walls of buildings from the ravages of vermin and particularly white ants. For the latter purpose it is commonly mixed with tar and brushed into cracks and holes. The arsenious oxide or common white arsenic is that most commonly used for all these purposes—for homicidal employment, it is frequently mixed with coarse sugar and made up into a sweetmeat. It is sold either as a white powder or as a solid white mass resembling enamel in the latter form it must, of course, be pounded before use. Traces of pounding should therefore be looked for. Red arsenic or realgar, and yellow arsenic or orpiment, are also occasionally employed generally mixed with a proportion of white arsenic.

(b) In poisoning by *phosphorus* there is pain in the stomach, vomiting, feeble pulse and collapse in chronic cases there may be yellowing of the skin, and slight bleeding from nose, mouth, and bowels. The phosphorus for poisoning is ordinarily obtained from the ends of matches and the phosphorus from sixteen matches has been found sufficient to poison an adult.

(c) In homicidal and suicidal cases, *mercury poisoning* mostly takes the acute form. The agent is chiefly corrosive sublimate, or mercuric chloride—a white crystalline mass or crystalline powder. The most striking symptoms are those of irritant poisons generally, as a rule they come on more quickly than in the case of arsenic. Moreover while arsenic is almost tasteless, corrosive sublimate has a metallic taste.

(d) *Opium*, as already pointed out is the favourite medium of suicidal poisoning, and can generally be at once detected by the characteristic odour. Opium both in its solid form and as a decoction is so universally used, especially as a febrifuge that no Investigating Officer needs any description of it.

(e) *Strychnine* causes death by convulsions and immediately renders the corpse rigid, a rigidity which sometimes remains for weeks.

(f) *Datura*, the poison of the thugs, is still used mainly to facilitate robbery, and that chiefly in the Western districts of India where traditions, even memories, of these daring depredators still exist. It has been pointed out that as datura is popularly supposed not to be poisonous to death, the fatal result is due to the overdose necessary to put the robber on the safe side. The datura seeds—whole or broken up—are commonly mixed with sweetmeats or food, and whole seeds or fragments may consequently be found in the stomach or the remains of the meal.

Great care must be taken not to confuse the *datura* seed with that of the *Capsicum* or *Chili*. The seed of the *tomato* may also be mistaken for *datura*, but is in less common use. Chevers notes the following superficial distinctions

The one great distinguishing feature above all others is the form and shape of the embryo. If one of each of the seeds be divided by cutting parallel with the flattened sides, the embryo of the capsicum will be found curved like the figure 6, while the end of the curve in the *datura* is "twisted" or re-curved not towards the down-stroke of the 6 but away from it, or towards the right hand. There are however many minor differences of great importance, when taken together; these may be contrasted thus:—

Seeds of the Common or White Datura	*Seeds of the Common Capsicum*
1. Almost kidney-shaped but one end much smaller than the other	1. Kidney shaped
2. Outline angular	2. Outline rounded
3. Size, rather more than a quarter of an inch long, and rather less in width	3. A little shorter and wider than the *Datura*
4. Colour greenish-brown when fresh, changing to yellow when dry	4. Yellow
5. Attached to the placenta by large white fleshy mass, which separates easily, leaving a deep furrow along half the length of the concave border of the seed	5. Attached to the placenta by a thin cord from a prominence on the concave border of the seed
6. Surface scabrous, almost reticulate, except on the two compressed sides, where it has become almost glaucous from pressure of the neighbouring seeds	6. Uniformly scabrous, the sides being equally rough with the borders
7. Convex border thick and bulged with a longitudinal depression between the bulgings caused by the compression of the two sides	7. Convex border thickened but uniformly rounded
8. When divided into two, by cutting with a knife placed in the furrow on the convex border, the testa is seen irregular and angular in outline, the embryo is seen lying *curved* and *twisted* in a fleshy albumen	8. When similarly divided the testa is more uniform in outline, the embryo is seen lying in a fleshy albumen, *curved*, but not twisted or re-curved

The taste of *capsicum* is pungent, while that of the *datura* is insipid. The most distinctive external symptoms of datura poisoning are giddiness, followed by drowsiness and muttering delirium, picking at imaginary objects, sometimes wild and excited behaviour, but always wide dilation of the pupils of the eyes, while internally the brain is congested, and so also frequently are the lining of the mucous membrane of the stomach and intestines.

(g) *Aconite* (*Aconitum ferox*) though a long way behind arsenic and opium is the third favourite poison in Bengal. Aconite is one of those poisons of which the alkaloid, if discovered in the body, may be hastily mistaken for the cadaveric alkaloids of ptomaine poisoning. For practical purposes the only test available is the physiological, i.e., by taste and it is stated by the authorities that no other alkaloid has yet been discovered with the characteristic results of tasting this alkaloid, namely, tingling of the lips and tongue followed by numbness. The root is the most active, it closely resembles horse-radish root, and as *Chevers* points out is sold very cheap in India. The symptoms resemble those caused by many of the ptomaines. We find irritation of the stomach with vomiting, the membrane after death being of a highly inflamed red colour. There is great muscular weakness with dilation of the pupil of the eye. Aconite is largely consumed medicinally for fever, cholera and rheumatism. It is also a favourite medium for poisoning arrows, and also in war for poisoning wells and tanks and other sources of drinking water.

(*h*) *Carbolic acid* and *Phenyl*, the most commonly used disinfectant of the present day, is a very ready instrument of poisoning. The skin where touched by the acid becomes white and the urine is coloured red or green. The odour of phenyl is known all over the world and is very readily recognised. It is also remarkable that the taste of phenyl is not so disagreeable as one would think. Introduced in a small quantity into the mouth it has a particularly piquant flavour, recalling rather a strong and sweet liquor—which explains perhaps the frequency of its use in cases of poisoning.

(*i*) *Prussic acid* and all its combinations are recognised by the strong odour of bitter almonds, this odour can sometimes be distinctly felt in the room in which the corpse is found.

(*k*) *Atropine* and all the forms of *belladonna* strongly dilate the pupil of the eye, sometimes this dilation is so great that the membrane of the iris is reduced to a very narrow circular ring, besides the person poisoned will complain of this dilation which produces a very disagreeable effect on the eye.

(*l*) *Nicotine* is recognised by the well-known odour of tobacco juice. The general symptoms of nicotine poisoning resemble those of datura.

(*m*) *Santonine* is commonly used for extirpating worms, and as infants are extremely sensitive to this medicament, its absorption is at times followed by sudden death. In poisoning by santonine, the urine is yellowish green.

The use of other poisons such as sulphuric acid, oxalic acid, etc., is not so frequent as to necessitate more than a passing reference here.

5. In cases of poisoning by organic substances generally, the medium cannot, as explained above, be readily detected by chemical or microscopical analysis, but the absorption of organic substances has been frequently noted to produce brain affections, sometimes rising to furious delirium. Such substances are cantharides, henbane, hemlock, datura, belladonna, digitalis, absinthe, opium, hashish and poisonous mushrooms.

The effects of *henbane* or *hyoscyamus*, sometimes called *Koh-i-bhang* or mountain hemp, applied externally or internally, should be noted. *Alzett-Neum* describes how an old lady used poultices of henbane leaves for some disorder; two old servants, who had prepared the poultices, began to quarrel during the evening without any apparent motive, soon they came to blows and finally the old lady herself joined in the affray with the greatest animation. This illustrates a common remark that persons under the effect of henbane poisoning are very fond of quarrelling and beating each other. It is also stated that decoctions of this plant produce violent accessions of rage, and even that the ancient Germans drank it before going to battle to give them courage. The Commissioner of Sind in 1894 (*Lyon*) reports that the Baluchis smoke it exactly like *ganja*. " But it is very powerful and makes them positively mad. Under its influence they strip themselves naked and dance about like lunatics."

Among organic substances, cantharides, datura, and some others are strong erotics.

6. In poisoning by *Sulphuric ether* and *Chloroform*, in the case of women, phenomena similar to those resulting from copulation are sometimes produced, hence medical men have occasionally been falsely accused of having taken advantage of women, while under the influence of narcotic sleep.

7. *Pounded glass* is not infrequently, perhaps less frequently now than formerly, used both homicidally and suicidally. It is not a poison, though popularly believed to be so, but a mechanical irritant, and the more finely it is pounded the less likely it is to do harm to the victim. Hence there is some compensation in its use for homicidal purposes, for the poisoner, to avoid detection as soon as the food is taken into the mouth, is careful to pound it as finely as possible, and thus diminishes the risk to his prey.

8. *Cocaine*. The unauthorised sale of this costly drug has become alarmingly common of late. It is conveyed in all kinds of hiding places. It is sometimes dyed brown and sold as snuff. Occasionally it occupies the middle of a cigarette or is pasted between two playing cards in a new pack. (For details of this traffic see *Goodwin*, " Sidelights on Criminal Matters," Hutchinson & Co., 1920.)

9. In concluding this section, a primitive method for ascertaining the presence of arsenic may be described, arsenic poisoning is so frequent that the Investigating Officer constantly finds himself under the necessity of deciding, even at the moment of the *post-mortem*, whether the case be one of murder or not, and consequently if he should take further action in the inquiry. For example, the *post-mortem* proves the existence on the mucous membrane of the stomach of small red spots or lines containing small white or yellow grains, the natural conclusion is that the substance is arsenic, but such suspicion is not sufficient for the arrest of anyone on so grave a charge as poisoning. Recourse should then be had to the following simple experiment, so simple that it should never be omitted. Take a glass test-tube closed at one end (which the Investigating Officer should always have with him), remove from the mucous membrane one of these white or yellow grains, being careful to leave sufficient for the purposes of the chemical examiner, dry it with very clean blotting paper or cigarette paper, and place it in the tube, heat carefully, holding the tube in an inclined position over a candle or spirit lamp. If the grain be arsenic, it will be vapourised, the vapour will be condensed and will be deposited on the cold portion of the tube as a white or yellow patch. This does not indeed absolutely prove that the grain is arsenic, but the probability is so great that the persons supposed to be guilty may be arrested without hesitation. Of course all this should be carefully recorded and the test-tube preserved intact.

The following table from Lucas Forensic Chemistry (1921 Arnold) summarizes the results of the chemical analysis in some notorious cases of poisoning

Nature of Poison	Amount found	Case	Date
Aconitine		Dr Lamson	1882
Antimony	0.5 grain antimony. Strychnine also suspected but none found	Dr Palmer	1856
Antimony	Victim (a) More than 2.55 grains as metallic antimony, also more than 3 grains of mercury as metallic mercury. Victim (b) More than 0.68 grain as metallic antimony	Dr. Pritchard	1865
Antimony	Victim (a). 20.12 grains calculated as tartar emetic. Victim (b) 29.12 grains calculated as tartar emetic. Victim (c) 3.83 grains calculated as tartar emetic	G Chapman	1903
Arsenic	More than 87.9 grains as arsenic trioxide	Madeleine Smith	1857
Arsenic	From 0.01 to 0.05 grain as arsenic trioxide in various organs	Mrs Maybrick	1889
Arsenic	From $\frac{1}{500}$ mgm to $\frac{1}{10}$ mgm as metallic arsenic in various organs, total arsenic calculated as trioxide in whole body 2.01 grains	The Seddons	1912
Hyoscine	2.7 grains	H H Crippen	1910
Opium	No poison in body, opium on a sheet and bed gown	E M Chantrelle	1878

Section ix.—Abortion.

Cases of abortion or supposed abortion must inevitably come for final report to the hands of the medical expert, but here as in other directions the Investigating Officer must possess such elementary knowledge as will enable him to grasp the situation when he arrives first on the scene and collect and preserve for the expert everything of a suspicious character. The external condition of the patient, the expelled matter, and any suspicious mineral or vegetable debris lying about, should all be scrutinised with the most assiduous care.

At the same time great caution must be used. In the first place miscarriage may be perfectly natural or caused by accidental violence. Disease in the mother, mental shock, or even a predisposition towards miscarriage, may be the cause. Again, exceptionally violent exercise, a blow or fall, or even tight-lacing, may produce the same effect. Again the matter expelled may not be an embryo at all—a blood-clot, a tumour, or other internal growth may be naturally extruded. In the latter case any suspicious matter will of course be carefully preserved for future examination. Further, the Investigating Officer must remember that many abortifacients, and especially the minerals, as arsenic and mercurial compounds, are employed as poisons and medicines; and therefore their mere discovery in a dwelling is no conclusive proof of abortion, though combined with other circumstances it may go far as corroborative evidence.

CHAPTER XVII

THEFT

Section i.—General Considerations.

Between comparatively inoffensive thieves and the international burglar, who is a man of refinement and whose object is rolls of bank notes or boxes of jewels reposing in safes guaranteed proof against burglary, which safes are situated in shops perfectly lighted and always watched, there is not such a very great difference. If the Investigating Officer would take the trouble to thoroughly investigate thefts of small importance instead of merely going through the usual and absolutely indispensable routine, if he would attempt to completely clear them up, he would not be slow to obtain self-instruction and be very soon able to bring the most important cases to a satisfactory conclusion.

In the same way as the thief educates himself by thefts of small importance so the Investigating Officer should by then means familiarise himself with the manner in which the thief conceives and executes his thefts so that when occasion arises he may know how to deal with more important thefts.

It is not rare to hear it said: "All watches are stolen in the same way" in a general sense this is true but anyone who studies the motives for the theft, the preparations which have been made for its accomplishment, the precautions which have been taken to hinder its discovery, the employment of the subject matter of the theft, and the consequences of the crime, will not be slow to perceive, that, among a thousand cases of theft there are not two alike, that facts which seem quite identical are really very different from one another, and that each case presents an interest of its own. The Investigating Officer who has attentively and minutely made a point of studying minor thefts, will start upon the study of important cases with just as much ardour and from their outside aspect at least will not fail to disentangle them. While treating in the following pages of some particular points concerning thefts and different varieties of theft we have not endeavoured to reduce these crimes to a single system, or even to indicate to people how to guarantee themselves against thieves, we simply desire to give certain indications to the Investigating Officer as to what he should ask a witness or the victim of the theft, and upon important points what should be the object of his attention. He will doubtless find here many things he knows already, but we have thought it as well to touch upon certain details for the benefit of those who for one reason or other are still unaware of them.

Section 11.—Thieves' Scouts and Spies.

Commencing with the facts preceding the theft the most important matter concerns thieves' scouts and spies. Without going so far as Ave-Lallemant, who sees a spy in every intruder entering a house, we may yet say that strictly all *may* in fact be so. All sorts of persons in various capacities may make their business but an excuse for exploring localities. Such are pedlars, beggars, cripples, infirm persons, the blind man who can see but is led about by a child, the child who weepingly relates the miserable circumstances of its parents, the bold youth who asks, with malicious smile, a stranger stopping at an hotel whether his sister's female cousin may come to see him, the timorous young girl who asks for his linen to wash and mend so as to enable her to support her old mother and her brothers and sisters, the commission agent who tenders his assistance, and the commissionaire who offers his services, the respectable old lady who changes a bank note at a money-changer's, the commercial traveller who unpacks his samples, the unfortunate orphaned daughter of an officer who comes for advice to a profligate, and many others. This preliminary investigation is made from different points of view. It is first necessary to know the topography of the place, make sure of its situation, get to know the neighbourhood and decide whether the doors and windows shut and open favourably for the carrying out of the theft, a view of the premises must then be obtained by daylight so that the thief may be able to find his bearings in the dark or by a dim light; next the places of entry and departure, the number of persons necessary for the actual commission of the theft or to keep watch inside or outside must be decided; particular attention has to be paid to the closing of doors, windows, and almirahs— not forgetting the key itself. An expert thief can not only judge the quality of a lock by taking a rapid glance at the key, but he can remember besides the size and shape of that key as well as a dozen others, and this so accurately that when the moment for action arrives he will only have to carry with him a very small number of skeleton keys, thus finding the right one without much noise and without injuring the lock.

The most arduous point and consequently the most important in every such exploration is the study of the ways of the victims both in their public and private life. The first difficulty is to collect information as to the connection existing between these persons and outside; particulars must be obtained as to the number of persons in the house, how many servants there are, whether people sleep in the house and where or at what o'clock they go home, whether they sit up talking and drinking, whether they are armed or are in communication with one another or outside (bells, telegraphs, and telephones). It is evident that a thief who has been but once inside a house cannot learn such things, but if several persons belonging to the same band of thieves visit the house, for the same person never goes twice, if they watch the goings and comings from the house and the time of lighting up and putting out the lights from some neighbouring point of vantage; if in an important crime one of the male members of the band makes the acquaintance of one of the female servants or *vice versâ* a female member with a man-servant—the thieves may obtain information upon many points, and if they know how to put two and two together they are soon *au courant* with all they require to know.

It is more difficult for them to find out the details of the private life of the inhabitants of the house, details of a psychological nature which, however, the expert thief considers to be most important. He seeks to know whether the master of the house, his family, and other persons, are orderly, whether they regularly and scrupulously shut up the house, whether they put the keys in a safe place, whether they live freely or economically, whether the people of the house are on good terms, whether or not they are intelligent folk, he will try to find out the character of the servants and whether the men of the house are timid or brave, all such details concerning the character and manner of living of the inmates are of the greatest importance. A thousand points are useful, such as whether the master gambles, or the mistress has a guilty liaison, whether the daughter is a flirt, or the son short of money—the love affairs of the footman and the cook, the date the master receives his salary or dividends, what he gives his wife for the housekeeping, and how much pocket-money the children receive.

It must not be supposed that this information is only sought for in important thefts of rare occurrence, an individual who desires to be taken for a particularly skilled thief—and this is the ambition of them all—practises the minutest researches in minor thefts, where indeed as in all things preparatory study is necessary. It must be admitted that too little attention is paid to preparations precedent to thefts of no great importance, it being supposed that the thief has merely entered the house, seized the first thing he could lay his hand on, and decamped. But even for insignificant thefts criminals make preparations of all kinds. And this is proved by the fact that while an enormous number of such thefts take place but a relatively small proportion are detected. This would not be so if the plans had not been carefully laid and all the necessary information most minutely obtained. It is just these preparations, these apparently inoffensive explorations, which, in the hands of an experienced and dogged detective, may bring about the discovery of the criminals.

When a theft of some importance has been committed it is the custom to start by first questioning the victim of it, then other persons, who all affirm that the objects have in fact disappeared and that so far it has been impossible to find them; next the objects are described in a special circular, the police authorities being requested to make "active search", and here the whole matter ends. The thief not having left his calling-card, what more indeed can be done? Such is the habitual formula of consolation. But the facts are quite overlooked that the culprit cannot have acted on the spur of the moment and that long preparations have been necessary which can themselves become points of departure for further investigation. Here again we take exception to the opinion of those who consider that the Investigating Officer must not make researches "which are the duty of the police" or that such work is beneath *his dignity*. The duty of the Investigating Officer is to throw light upon the case and it would indeed be assigning to himself a role unworthy of his position if, abandoning the whole of the work to the police, he leaves to himself only the business of coming in afterwards, when they have made everything ready for him, to complete those formalities connected with the accused and the witnesses, etc, specially prescribed by law to be his particular duty. Even when the criminal is unknown, the Investigating Officer should go through with and terminate his inquiry just as if an accused had been already brought before him he should make all necessary investigations and assure himself of the whole story of the theft so as to have every proof ready against the day when the thief may be discovered and arrested. Moreover the great experience and high intelligence of the Investigating Officer should give an impulse to the whole course of the inquiry and guide it in the right direction the complete case will then be presented to the court as it ought to be to ensure a fully satisfactory trial

Moreover an Investigating Officer when questioning the victim of the theft and the people of the house should spare no trouble to elicit every scrap of information about all details having any connection whatever with the preparations made by the thief, he should ask about people who, recently or even at a distant date, may have visited the house, and concerning all the parts of it they may have been able to observe, such as—the rooms from which things have been taken, the places where the thief has got in and out, and even the spot from where the above mentioned persons have been observed. In most cases a negative answer will be the result for these visitors, if they have had any approach to cleverness, will have endeavoured to prevent drawing anyone's attention, and seeing that the theft has succeeded their end in view has been attained

The Investigating Officer has therefore no other resource but to question the witness, however intelligent he may be, just as if he were questioning a child has he seen a beggar, a commissionaire, a peon, a commercial traveller hawker, or any other stranger going into the house or has he seen people who come seeking situations in his employ, or observed children or young girls who have come into his house under some pretext or other, etc, then he must pass to the personal relations of the master of the house, of his family, and of his servants, in order to help to clear up the matter. This cannot be gone through without the commission of some indiscretion, more than once must delicate points be touched upon, points difficult to approach but which nevertheless must be elucidated in the interests of the case. But we may say that, taking them altogether, these delicate questions are not so difficult to deal with as is generally believed the Investigating Officer often only decides with repugnance and hesitation to put certain questions and he is perfectly astonished to hear in what a simple and natural way he is answered This is because in the office of the Investigating Officer people speak quite differently to the way they do at other times, and—when the Investigating Officer knows how to be precise and when the person questioned is aware that it is nothing but his keen interest in the case that makes the Investigating Officer speak as he does that his questions are really necessary for the elucidation of the matter and that he wishes to know how to put together bit by bit the information that he receives in order to furnish a logical whole—the witness speaks with the best grace in the world and even with a considerable amount of frankness

Having in this way found, after prolonged and troublesome research, a certain number of persons who may have some connection with the facts in question, the first precaution to be taken is to note them down carefully and then reduce as much as possible their number; to do so there is no other way than first to eliminate all the persons who do not appear suspicious; this elimination ought to be made with the greatest circumspection, the statement of the individual questioned should never be alone relied upon, for the best spy is exactly that person who can put on the most innocent air in the world. Only those persons, therefore, should be eliminated whose innocence is absolutely incontestable and the certainty of this innocence must be due to the private analysis of the Investigating Officer as well as other circumstances of a trustworthy character.

The Investigating Officer must then try to find out whether there is not a certain analogy in the behaviour of all those persons who have been noticed. This is an essential point. It must not be forgotten that in crimes of some importance one person is not sufficient to obtain all the necessary information; the first only explores the lie of the land in a general way, he seeks a good opportunity, and on the same day he turns up as a beggar, a commercial traveller, or canvasser in a number of houses, and chooses such or such a one among them as the theatre of his exploits; but this first person does not minutely examine the locality for he does not know whether he will not find something better later on; it is just a voyage of exploration, and as the same person, as we have already said, never comes twice to the same place, a second person is sent who endeavours to fix all the details and obtain all important information. It may be that this spy has neither the time nor the opportunity to study everything, and that many points at first sight insignificant assume in the course of the subsequent planning some further importance which makes it indispensable to know more about them. In this case a third, a fourth, or even a tenth individual is sent, till the whole scheme is made as clear as possible.

It is, therefore, easy to understand that the methods of such persons present certain points of resemblance, points which will evidently not escape an experienced Investigating Officer, who has to deal with an accomplished fact but which would not strike an outsider—especially before that fact was accomplished. The witness ought, therefore, to be asked if he has not noticed, while observing the suspected individual, any glances, any constant effort to arrive at such and such a place, any desire to remain in the house after the pretended object of the visit was definitely obtained or had encountered failure, or certain questions or peculiar turns of expression, etc. Often people are seen to arrive in a house one after the other who seem to have a certain resemblance in their dialect, attitude, costume or some other mark of appearance, or are distinguished by their importunity or humility, who lower and hide their faces to prevent their being seen and looked at, and who in a word betray in some way or other that they belong, so to speak, to the '*same family*'.

It is easy to understand that such inquiries are difficult, and this the more so because scouts never as a rule address the same person twice, they ask to see sometimes this person and sometimes that, to-day exploring one part of the house, to-morrow another, in such a way that their goings and comings do not draw suspicion towards them. The Investigating Officer will only obtain a satisfactory result by questioning all the people in the house and combining their answers. It is true that even when this result is arrived at, that is to say, when it has been settled and established that various suspicious persons have tried to approach the house, he is hardly at the end of his work; suppose he knows, e.g., that under various dissimilar pretexts one man, two women, and one child have been seen in the house, then if at least an approximate description of these people can be procured the police will be able to find out without great difficulty whether a family of this kind and number has been observed near the scene of the theft and at what spot it may be found. In all cases this band must be suspected of having taken part in the theft in question and a starting point will be obtained for further investigation.

It is always very difficult to find the beginning of the thread when but a single person, or at most two, have been employed on the business of exploration, for rarely in such a case can sufficient matter for their identification be obtained; but of this we may be sure, that those thefts where but one scout has been sent out either are very insignificant, or among those who have taken part in the theft there will be at least one person who has exact knowledge of the locality and the personal relations—such as is possessed by dismissed servants. In this case it is quite superfluous for the thieves to undertake a fresh investigation, especially where no great space of time has elapsed since the servant was dismissed; a rapid examination is then sufficient to make sure whether any change has taken place. And here the Investigating Officer obtains a fresh clue which greatly lightens his task, for the thieves will send the person who knows the place and can therefore most easily and rapidly carry out this work of verification. What generally happens is as follows:—an old servant comes to his old master and asks his assistance in a matter that will take some time. When they have parted on fairly good terms, he generally pretends to have lost his certificate of character, to which he attaches great value and asks for a duplicate; or he requests a letter of recommendation to a new place or advice, information, or sometimes even assistance; but in all cases he will have sufficient time to make sure that everything remains as it was before, or on the contrary to notice and remember any changes that may have taken place.

If the presence of some such old employé comes out in the course of the inquiry he or she may very well be suspected of the theft in preference to anyone else, but a too natural precipitation must be guarded against and before taking extreme measures it will be as well to watch carefully. If however the enquiry points to no such scout, if it is certain that no previous exploration has taken place, and if on the other hand the theft is one which could not be carried out without a previous investigation, there can be no doubt that among the participators in the theft must be a person who is *au courant* with the habits of those in the house either through having served in it or in some other way. One must doubtless be sufficiently circumspect to decide the question whether there has really been such an incident as that described, for on the one hand it may have taken place so far back that the victim forgets it or omits to mention it, judging the date to be too remote, and on the other hand it may have been carried out with such precaution and so naturally that it has passed unperceived and no mention is made of it, in spite of all the perspicacity exercised by the Investigating Officer in his interrogation.

Section III.—Other Preparations for the Theft.

The emissary sent by the thieves is not content with merely obtaining information; the scope of his work is not settled for him in advance; he ought on the contrary, without drawing attention to himself, to do all that he possibly can to render the operation more easy. Thus when leaving the house, he will as if by mistake go the wrong way, instead of going out by the principal entrance he will make in the direction of the back door or a side verandah, there to open a bolt, lift up a latch, push a box in front to make a step, make note of a passage-way, and in short take stock of a number of details, almost imperceptible and apparently insignificant but upon which will perhaps depend the ultimate success of the undertaking, he will not miss a chance of stealing a key, or taking an impression of one, or at least copying the key-hole. Let us then distrust all those strange persons who have always something to do near doors and in places where keys are hung up.

In the country, part of the business of the scout is to poison the watch-dog, he is therefore always furnished with some prepared substance for that purpose. It is but exceptionally that one hears of watch-dogs who refuse to accept anything from strangers, and there are very few dogs who will refuse to be tempted by the bait of some dainty. One has only to glance through the narratives of important burglaries committed in the seventeenth and eighteenth centuries to find, stereotyped one might say, the mention of the fact that so many days before the theft the faithful and brave watch-dog, who would certainly have hindered the theft if he had been still alive, had unexpectedly, accidentally, or inexplicably, died. It is related in "the Official list of thefts in churches, and burglaries accompanied by murder committed by a band of Jewish thieves," that these rascals, before committing their crimes used to poison the watch-dogs with *nux vomica*. Lipps Tullian, the prince of all burglars of all time, gives the following good advice:—"Keep a little watch-dog *inside* your house, a dog outside the house is no obstacle to an accomplished house-breaker." Now the poisoning of a dog furnishes us with all kinds of clues, if the theft has not yet taken place and the poisoning cannot with probability be attributed to some other person (such as a disagreeable neighbour, or a sportsman when the dog is one given to poaching) we may expect a burglary in the near future. In this case, as well as when the theft has been actually committed, after the poisoning of a dog, the Investigating Officer must turn all his attention towards persons who have been seen to occupy themselves with the dog; these are often, if not always, those people who seem to be the least offensive in the world: an old woman who kindly offers a piece of her dry bread to the dog when it barks at her approach, or a child who plays with the dog and runs away crying because "the naughty doggie had taken its slice of bread and butter"; in such a case one has a chance of laying one's hand upon at least one member of the band of burglars and the inquiry has some chance of being brought to a successful conclusion. The important thing in most inquiries is to find a tiny clue in the inextricable chaos of events. Once this is laid hold of we need no longer despair of disentangling the problem.

A very original procedure with regard to dogs consists in the employment of bitches; no dog can resist a bitch in heat; even a dog that has been castrated will nearly always follow a bitch in heat. It is always possible to prevent a dog being poisoned by never letting it out without a muzzle, care being taken to submit it to this torture *without interruption*, but against a bitch in heat there is no remedy at all, unless one keeps a dog so old as to be insensible to such things—but then such a dog is quite useless for anything. The bitch, whose period of heat must naturally be awaited, can only be made use of during the actual night of the theft; it is led in a leash and *with* the wind to the house where the dog to be incited is to be found. As soon as the latter scents the bitch he becomes harmless and tries to get near her, if he is at large he goes at a run and the person leading the bitch makes a half turn and goes off in the opposite direction to the house; the dog quietly follows the bitch and her master, who can when far enough away seize him and tie him up or kill him. If the dog is not free but tied up he will not bark at the approach of the bitch but will permit its leader, who must naturally advance with the utmost precaution, to come up to him without making a noise; this result attained the dog will be left with the bitch until the burglary has been committed, or if possible the dog will be unchained and enticed away with the help of the bitch and thus rendered inoffensive.

It is therefore not a surprising fact that wandering tribes have so often *bitches* with them; doubtless, as is affirmed by sportsmen, bitches are more attached to their masters, and are more docile and more easily managed; they do not so often go off by themselves but remain not far from the house, are much more equable in temper and regular in their habits, but all this is not a sufficient explanation why vagabonds are almost exclusively accompanied by bitches; it must therefore be presumed that they are used, as we have pointed out, to lure away watch-dogs, and it is difficult to understand why bitches are so rarely used in the country to guard the houses. The inconvenience caused by their having puppies is largely compensated by their usefulness as watch-dogs.

If then a burglary has taken place and it is concluded that the dog has been drawn far away from the house in this manner, it is above all necessary to take stock of those wandering people who are in possession of a bitch and have been seen in the vicinity of the place of the crime. It should moreover be remarked that the same result is often obtained without actually bringing the bitch to the spot; these people sometimes content themselves with rubbing their shoes, trousers, and clothes against the sexual parts of the bitch in heat, and this produces much the same effect on the dog as the bitch would herself; the dog will not bark at the approach of a person giving off this odour and will follow him wherever he wishes. The scout often has recourse to this expedient in order the more easily to approach and explore the house and observe it at greater length without being betrayed by the barking of the dog and so discovered by the inmates. When the Investigating Officer learns from a witness, naturally, after long questioning on the subject, that, a short time before the theft, he noticed a beggar on whose approach a usually vigilant dog has not barked but has run like mad to meet him, caressed and jumped up upon him, and been loath to leave him, he knows of at least one person who has taken part in the theft. Especially is this means used by horse-stealers who thereby are able to pacify the most ferocious dogs.

A quite up-to-date device employed in large cities is to decoy away from his house or shop the person to be robbed, or even his whole family, by an anonymous or pseudonymous writing. Whether the communication be the request for an important consultation, or for a tender rendezvous or free passes for the theatre depends on the person to be deceived. In any case the Investigating Officer will be careful in examining the document, as it shows an intimacy with the private circumstances and habits of the person addressed, and allows inferences to be drawn concerning the identity of the writer.

Section iv.—Thieves' Equipment.*

In the execution of his often hazardous schemes the thief requires all sorts of tools. It is easily understood that this is an important matter for the Investigating Officer, for the discovery of such tools often constitutes overwhelming proof against the person in whose possession they are found; no doubt a person who is arrested with the skeleton keys pincers, and files about him will at once make a bad impression upon us, but it is rare to lay hands on such implements, for every thief of any experience at all takes care to get rid of such compromising articles, when he has no immediate use for them, but on the other hand there are many things necessary and even indispensable to a thief which he does not fear to carry with him, the more so in that they seem quite inoffensive and their use and importance is rarely known to outsiders.

Speaking generally we may say that all articles found upon a suspected person, the use of which does not appear clear, ought to be considered suspicious. It is, therefore, impossible to give a list of compromising articles and we must content ourselves with saying that those things which appear to be the most inoffensive may be the most dangerous when it is impossible to determine their necessity and natural usage. In this way light slippers or short thick stockings found in a person's house indicate that their owner is a thief who operates in hotels and who slips furtively about houses; in winter he finds it too cold to walk barefoot or in ordinary socks. Long thin rods or large quantities of bird-lime betray the thief whose speciality is money deposited in charity boxes in churches and elsewhere !† A piece of black cloth can be for no other object than to render the thief unrecognisable by masking his face. Only recently two London experts who broke into a house and murdered an old couple for the sake of

---

* See also Chapter IX (Wandering Tribes) and Chapter X (Superstition).
† This was known as long ago as the 14th and 15th Century and is carried on much in the same way to-day. In the Graz Criminal Museum are several instruments of this kind in which instead of pieces of whale bone, splinters of reed were employed hidden in a bamboo used as a walking-stick and to the eye harmless looking enough. Walking sticks which appear to be tipped with a piece of black metal, really wax or resin, are also to be suspected, for with them small articles exposed for sale in an open window may easily be removed. Sometimes these sticks are made to lengthen out like a fishing rod or the leg of a patent camera stand, thus rendering them all the more dangerous.

a few shillings were convicted mainly on the evidence of some old pieces of black stocking. One of the victims had been able, before death, to state that the thieves had their faces partially covered with black cloth, and on a search being made one of the masks was discovered under the murdered couple's bed. Similar pieces of cloth were found in the house of the accused men and this practically secured their conviction. Every burglar or house thief is furnished with a piece of tallow, stearine, or candle to enable him, if need be, to find his way about in the dark places of a strange house. Again, the thief who foresees that he will have to break windows without making a noise, will take care to be provided with some adhesive substance, e.g. cobbler's wax, waxcloth, gum, etc. spread on paper or cloth, which he affixes to the window to be broken into.* The pieces of glass then stick to the adhesive cloth or paper, and the thief thus avoids the noise that would otherwise be made by their fall. Often a strong fish hook attached to a thread is discovered. This is used for throwing through open windows on a level with the ground to catch clothes, chains attached to watches, etc., which are then drawn out without difficulty. (See *Chapter IX., Wandering Tribes.*) Equally suspicious are long sack-like pockets, carried more particularly by market thieves to hide stolen merchandise. Almost any object may be compromising; thus a signet ring furnished with little knives proves that the owner uses the latter to cut open pockets of garments from the outside and abstract pocket-books; odd gloves, especially if stuffed up, betray the railway, bus, and tram thief who wishes to conceal his own hands which are occupied in stealing. A pickpocket with an entirely false arm was recently arrested in a London 'bus. The papers found upon a suspected person are also very important, it cannot be too often repeated that such papers should be submitted to a minute examination, it often happens that the smallest piece of paper saves endless trouble, all addresses should also be noted, they often enable us to find out the names of accomplices, receivers, or even prospective victims of the thief. Finally we may mention lists of the markets or race meetings which generally denote market thieves or card cheats.

Section V.—Accomplices.

Important thefts, such as burglaries accompanied by sneaking entrances or carried out by armed burglars, etc., are nearly always committed with the help of people who keep watch or mount guard; this is only natural and these watchers often furnish a point of departure for further investigation. Whoever commits a theft does an act compromising in itself, he must, therefore, take the utmost caution not to be seen, and as a matter of fact he is very rarely observed if his watchers are good ones; but the watcher himself has nothing reprehensible about his appearance, he will no doubt try if possible, not to be seen by passers-by, but without directing all his efforts to this point; indeed he will often not hide at all but intentionally attract attention to himself; he will even pick some quarrel so as to get himself arrested for drunkenness or resisting the police in order that he may give the comrade for whom he is keeping watch a chance of carrying out the theft

---

* Much in use is the well known fly paper called 'Tangle Foot' which may be purchased all over the world.

comfortably and quietly. Such procedure is often met with and leads to mishaps as vexing as they are comical.

Since a novice is not usually chosen for mounting guard it may be easily understood that he will not remain motionless at his post of observation, nor will he march up and down like a sentinel; he will seem to be coming out of a drink-shop or bazaar, or going to or coming from a rendezvous; he whistles, hums, sings, stumbles about in walking, leans with his hat over his eye and discourses to himself against some house or lamp post, or he lies down in the middle of the road in the attitude of a man who is dead drunk; but as often as not, on the approach of a person of suspicious mien he wakens to his work and takes care to be in an easy position to get a sight of the newcomer, so as to find out whether he is dangerous and whether in consequence the alarm must be given.

This warning is of two classes: if the thief is merely to be invited to be careful, use is made of a whistle, a smacking of the tongue, an unsuspicious cry, such as "Hullo Tom!" or "Mary Ann, open the door!" or "Bill, father'd, are you coming?" etc., or else of a cry indicating that all is lost and the best to be done is to take to immediate flight.

The attitude of the watcher towards an intruder depends, partly upon the circumstances in which the theft is committed, and partly upon his discretion and presence of mind; above all he must have a practised eye so as to be able to recognise at a glance the relative importance of individuals coming to interfere; neither the merry-making tradesman, nor the student going home gaily singing, will be judged worthy of any attention; it will be enough to make their presence known in some way or other; if he observes other people coming who at the time have no suspicion, but who may become suspicious on seeing a light or hearing a noise as they are passing near the scene of the crime, he will warn his companions by a prearranged signal (a whistle, smacking of the tongue, etc.), to interrupt their work for a moment, to make no noise, and to extinguish the light, till the danger is passed; a second conventional signal will inform them of the moment when the coast is again clear.

When the person living in a house where a theft is going on comes back home in the nick of time, or when a neighbour or watchman comes along, and yet the danger is not quite great enough to give the signal for a general and sudden stampede, not only must warning be given, but also enough time must be gained to allow those working inside the house to hide, or even to slip away with the booty already collected. The watcher outside must, for this purpose, hinder intruders from advancing, and, at the same time, make enough noise to drown that necessarily caused by his companions during their flight; he will himself accost the person who has come along or else will manage to be accosted by him; he will ask the way, or the name of an hotel still open, or the time; he will request a light for his cigar, or will beg for help to get up, pretending that he has fallen and hurt his foot; sometimes he will relate in a loud voice and with many details that he has a paralysed arm and has need of someone to help him on with his overcoat, remarking how chilly the night has suddenly become. Taking up another line he will draw the attention of the passer-by to something abnormal: he has heard a cry for help or groans; he has seen a glare in the sky, or the hooligans who infest the neighbourhood, or he has even met a mad dog; but all this in a direction calculated to make the stranger look or walk away from the spot where his companions are carrying on their work. If he has courage and finds a suitable piece of waste land, he will play the drunkard, will give the passers-by the benefit of a lecture under three heads, will launch into politics and criticism, will quarrel with those who, for amusement, take up the argument, then he will make it up with his adversaries and finish by offering them his friendship. And when this "rum cuss," for this is what he is in the eyes of passers-by, has at length taken himself off, his companions have also disappeared—with the booty.

The author remembers how, as a student, he was going home one night with some of his companions, when the party was accosted by an old man who on some pretext entered into conversation. He prophesied the approaching end of the world and proceeded to prove it from the prophet Jonah. After a long talk the parties separated in a friendly way. Meanwhile, about two hundred yards distant from where the conversation took place the Freemasons' Lodge of the town was broken into, and not only all the "working tools" stolen, but also the new tiled roofing, much to the satisfaction of all the good Catholics of the place.

The cleverest watcher is without doubt one sharp enough to induce others to accost him: he looks about on the ground and declares to the sympathetic person who questions him, that he has lost a coin, his watch or some other article, and when the newcomer helps in the search, relates to him, not only everything concerning that loss, but the whole history of his life into the bargain. Another lies stretched upon the ground groaning so lamentably that the passer-by cannot help asking him the reason for his doing so, then amid continual cries of pain he tells how he is suffering from a broken leg, strangulated hernia, or colic, until our compassionate soul goes off to find a doctor, who naturally fails to discover the invalid. One day the proprietor of a house where a theft was going on, returned home unexpectedly, all at once the accomplice, who was watching near the front door and who had not heard the return of the master of the house in time, the latter wearing rubber soled shoes, began to ring the bell like a madman. The master of the house asked our friend what he wanted and the latter replied that his wife had just been suddenly attacked with the pains of childbirth, that she was suffering terribly and that he had come to fetch the midwife who lived there, he was answered that there was no midwife in that house, that there never had been one and that there never would be one, but our men refused to listen and continued to babble and bewail his fate, till the master of the house offered to conduct him to the dwelling of the nearest midwife, the offer was accepted with a thousand thanks and they both went off in haste to find her, and when the master of the house got back home, bathed in perspiration, he was just in time to catch sight of the last of the thieves escaping from the house, loaded with much rich booty.

Above all the approach of the police must be hindered, but as it is not always easy to draw them into a conversation under some stupid pretext or ask some useless information from them, there is no other resource for the watcher than to attract the attention of the police to his own strange behaviour. If possible, he will do so in a way which exposes himself to no danger, he will pretend some illness or make some important communication, etc., if this experiment does not succeed or if the danger is very menacing, there is nothing else for him to do but to get himself arrested. Without doubt he will take care that this does not cost him too dear; he will, therefore, for preference pretend to be drunk; he will stumble about, sing, cry out, bang up against the policeman, in short he will do everything he possibly can to get himself arrested, and to make this arrest as prolonged as possible he will try not to walk, will lie down, protest his innocence, ask pardon, but he will take good care to do no more than is absolutely necessary, that is to say, he will not go so far as to assault the policeman, for this would only have the effect of aggravating the offence and increasing the punishment. When he gets far enough away from the scene of the theft his behaviour will get sensibly better, and when nearing the station-house or the police court his drunkenness will have so far disappeared that there will be no longer any reason for keeping him in custody, and if, on the way, his custodians have found him to be "a decent sort of chap" and see that they have not got hold of an old offender or suspected person, they may let him go with a severe warning, cautioning him not to behave like that again.

If the pretended drunkenness does not succeed, either because the police take no notice of it or it will take up too much time, the watcher is obliged to have recourse to a misdemeanour which will bring about his prompt and certain arrest, the offences practised will be those generally committed by vagabonds when they desire to procure "board and lodgings" for the winter, e.g., insulting the police, disturbing public worship, or any crimes rapidly committed, and needing no preparation. The police may therefore safely not trouble about those small offences committed in words such as insulting the police, the Courts, or the powers that be, especially if the words have not been heard by other people and it is impossible to discover the reason for their commission at the particular moment. If this reason is difficult to discover it is because it has been carefully and intentionally hidden, and the police constable would do well not readily to fall in with the wishes of the offender and assist him to fulfil the service with which he is charged, he will then notice a hastiness on the part of the individual in question to commit some more serious offence, which will thus betray his desire to be arrested; the prudence of the constable thus warned must then be redoubled, and he will have every facility, while consenting to the desire of the criminal to be arrested, to keep his eyes open so as to find out what it is that the latter wishes to hide. In India such accomplices have a ready refuge in "a night case"—a bait which no Indian policeman can avoid swallowing with avidity.

The following anecdote told of Count Sandor, a person well known for his jokes and eccentricities, proves how easy it is to get oneself arrested. About the year 1830 the Count made a bet with the Chief of Police of Vienna that he would get himself arrested without having done anything in the least reprehensible. He disguised himself as a vagabond and drank in a disreputable drinking-shop a glass of brandy which he paid for with a genuine thousand gulden note; ten minutes afterwards he was arrested. But if Count Sandor succeeded in being arrested without having committed anything reprehensible the expert swindler will succeed much more easily, as it costs him little when necessary to commit a real offence if the success of the coup is worth it

The lesson to be drawn from the preceding considerations is therefore as follows: the police should not lose sight of the fact that the suspicious behaviour of a man *may* always have some connection with a guilty act which is being committed, and that this is all the more likely when the person in question, inoffensive as he seems to be, cries out on the approach of a policeman on his beat or any outsider; he must, therefore, pay particular attention to what is going on. Doubtless, in many cases, it will be impossible to prevent the watcher from carrying out his design, especially when he sees the police first, and yet, even in this case, it would be a fault to be no longer anxious. Suppose that an individual who is lying on the ground, whistles on the approach of the police, so as to inform his companion that there is danger, of course the effect of the alarm cannot be prevented, but if, as is usual in large towns, two constables make the beat together, one of them can occupy himself with the person who has just whistled while the other will try to find out as far as he can whither the whistle was directed and whom it was meant for, in short, discover the place where the theft is being committed and take the necessary steps. If the policeman is *alone* it will nearly always be better to prefer the certain to the uncertain and make sure at all events of the suspected individual, then he can call for reinforcements to look after his capture while he himself goes off to discover the main case. In many instances a noise is sufficient to make criminals seek for safety, it is better, therefore, at once to look after the individual arrested and the case will soon be cleared up. The sprained ankle will soon get well, the drunkenness will be found to be quite a pretence, no papers of identification will be found on our friend, and after an attentive examination he will be recognised as an old offender. One individual of the band being in custody, the search for the others will be simplified to a great extent.

The role of watcher is best filled by a woman, particularly a girl of fourteen or fifteen years old. A woman is more patient, more attentive, more cunning, and more reflecting than a man, she can count less upon bodily strength, quickness of flight, and personal courage, all of which qualities she is obliged to replace by an indefatigable attention, a straining of all her senses, and an ability to take advantage of all circumstances—qualities which naturally obtain for her this position. A woman is less suspected than a man, she excites compassion and needs assistance and protection; every man feels himself forced in spite of himself to offer assistance to a woman whom he meets alone in the middle of the night. Moreover a woman can make use of a number of situations in which she has a chance of invoking someone's assistance, situations which, thanks to her sex, she alone has at her disposition, she is more easily exhausted by fatigue, has more frequent fits of feebleness, and is more often in need of help than men; she can be turned out of doors by her husband, can be overtaken by the pains of childbirth, may be obliged to wander without a situation and without shelter, and she may be exposed to all the tortures of hunger, and in addition she has at her disposal the whole domain of sex. A woman, alone and in the middle of the night, especially if she is young and as often as not, in the darkness of the night, pretty, will nearly always succeed in stopping a passer-by, and if he does not accost her, she will know very well how to speak to him and make him stop. Nothing is more natural than to ask him a question, make a request, or utter a complaint in his presence; nothing is easier than to get him to stop, if not altogether to turn him from what he is about, and if the woman pretends to be ill, unhappy, hungry, etc., there is no one brutal enough to quietly continue on his way.

We have said that it is the young girl who succeeds best in this task. She will generally be met with crying discreetly; she is questioned with sympathy, and the little one then tells with sobs how she has been turned out of doors by her cruel stepmother and does not know where to take refuge; she will not go home where she has been so maltreated for anything in the world; this very day she had been beaten so hard that her body is all bruises; naively, she pulls up her sleeve to show the bruises—which however do not exist; she has them also on her legs, and childlike, she lifts up her little dress to just below her knee to show the marks of the blows. All this can but excite the interest of the compassionate man; he has seen no bruises but he has noticed a nice, white arm and a well-rounded leg, and then the little one babbles so prettily; she is almost willing to accept the hospitality her new protector offers her for the night, but all at once she changes her mind, for she has heard a slight whistle which informs her that the theft is successfully carried out; she decides to look for a friend, and, presto! she is gone. We all know the sort of stories, which are indeed more numerous than we suppose, for people who meet with such adventures are hardly ever willing to relate them.

A rather amusing story may be told in this connection. Two students on arriving home in the middle of the night had just opened the front door and entered the lobby when they heard the most dreadful groaning coming from the back garden; they at once ran to the spot from whence came the cries and perceived a woman on the ground, seemingly suffering from the pains of childbirth. Without leaving the students time to inquire how she had got over the high hedge which surrounded the garden, she entreated them to lay hold of her arms and hands, adding that she had need of nothing else and was well aware of what it was, etc. After a few moments she declared that it was time to find, as quickly as possible, some woman in the house; hardly had the two students got up, when three men rushed out of the door, the woman was also on her feet, and all four, bolting across the garden, disappeared through a hole previously made in the hedge. The amazed students were soon able to find out that the first floor, whose tenant was in the country, had been broken into and stripped.

To keep guard in the interior of a house is the most difficult part of a watcher's business. He must have self-possession and presence of mind to be able to justify his being in the house or even, when it is divided into flats, inside a particular flat. The most incredible examples of effrontery are met with on the one hand, and of credulity on the other. A case may be mentioned where the actors were gipsies. A well-to-do peasant having carefully shut up his house had gone to work in the fields; on returning home to fetch something he found, to his great astonishment the front door open and a gipsy woman in the corridor who, on sight of him, began to blow him up for having left the house open, she added that she had visited the stables and found an animal very ill indeed. The peasant made in amazement for the stables, and at the same time a gipsy escaped from one of the rooms and through the corridor, whence he made off along with the woman carrying away the peasant's money and watch. Of course there was nothing the matter with the animal. Even in presence of the police the position of a woman watcher is much easier. It may be too much to say that women try to seduce them with their advances—that is exceedingly rare—but it is none the less true that a policeman, as much as any man, generally shows more regard and compassion to a woman than to a member of the male sex. Without wishing to blame them, yet we must never tire of pointing out to them by examples that a woman is as a rule a more cunning scoundrel than a man, and in the present connection it would be as well to suspect every woman whatever her age, whom one meets alone in the middle of the night. Genuine cases of women suddenly overtaken with the pains of childbirth or illness, or who have been turned out of doors at midnight by an unsupportable husband or stepmother, or for some other reason are exceedingly rare, and in such cases the utmost prudence is necessary.

The position of the commissioner of police and the magistrate is quite different to that of the policeman on his beat. The latter can only discover the watcher when the theft has not yet been completed, for once all is over the watcher is no longer at his post. The police constable infers from the discovery of a watcher that a theft is going to be committed in the vicinity about the same time—a theft of which he as yet knows nothing, it is very rare on the other hand that an individual is brought before the commissioner of police or a magistrate for watching, or whose arrest is a certain indication of an as yet unknown theft. Usually the crime is reported and no one knows whether anyone has come across a watcher in the neighbourhood of the scene of offence, but if the question is not looked into, it may happen that the watcher for the entire band of thieves is lying at the police station for 'drunkenness' while the inspectors and Investigating Officers are deliberating over a bold burglary and lamenting the absence of the least trace of a clue to the criminals.

It goes without saying that in a big burglary other important investigations should not be dispensed with on the pretext of looking for the watcher and this refers particularly to the inspection of the scene of the crime, yet an Investigating Officer is never so short of men as to be unable at once to allot one of them exclusively to search for the watcher. The latter always exists when the theft is one of any importance, and if it has taken place in a town or other frequented locality, the watching cannot be done without the watcher being seen by several persons, the essential thing, therefore, is first to find out the persons who have seen him. The most difficult case is where those persons who have seen or even accosted him are members of the police force, who are ashamed to confess that they have had the principal criminal under their hands. In this case it is the business of the superiors to let their subordinates understand that they have committed no fault in not arresting the watcher in question, if the latter is very skilful he knows how to pretend to be quite inoffensive, and it is not possible to arrest or even watch closely every person, merely because he or she is found in the street at a late hour of the night, but even if the watcher has been awkward, or his appearance so suspicious that the police ought to have been and were able to arrest him, and have refrained from doing so because duped by him, the best remedy, as in all cases without exception is to own up to the mistake which has been committed. This avowal will be all the easier since the fault will generally be quite pardonable, for the watcher usually carries out his task with the greatest address, and the only fault of the policeman in not having unmasked a person so little calculated to arouse suspicion is, that he has not acted with the *most particular* prudence and the greatest *presence of mind*.

But when a police functionary has the confidence of his subordinates and when the latter are aware that the fault is not an unpardonable one, it sometimes happens that he learns from the constables of his division that they have perceived such and such a person in the neighbourhood of the burglary on such and such a pretext. In the light of such information the suspected individual must be arrested and a practised police constable, who has seen and perhaps accosted the man or woman is generally able to describe him accurately, or he will at least foresee the possibility of discovering a reliable clue.

But if no constable has seen anything abnormal it is necessary to find out—and as quickly as possible—whether a passer by has observed any one. This passer-by need not of necessity be an habitué of the immediate neighbourhood in which the theft has been committed—he may have come from a distance, it is therefore indispensable that the circle of investigation be enlarged as much as possible—especially when an important theft is in question.

In this, as in all analogous investigations, the Investigating Officer must proceed with much circumspection so as to avoid scaring people, who often imagine they are going to be made partly responsible for the offence. the main cause of the difficulty in finding persons capable of giving information about a theft is that, having an idea that they have not done their duty, they prefer remaining in the background to coming forward and making important statements. In the present case they probably do not wish to appear to have been duped by the thieves, or perhaps they imagine this fact alone has rendered them criminally liable or it may be that they are too ashamed of having conversed with the woman on the watch to say anything about it—yet *another* reason why a woman watcher is more dangerous than a man.

So far we have only considered watchers employed in cases of burglary or sneak-thefts (i.e., secret introductions into houses) we shall now say something about those met with in other branches of the profession. Besides their rôle of watcher they have often another mission as well, namely to screen and divert attention from the actual thief, in short to facilitate him in his work by all the means in their power. Let us here repeat that there is no graver error than to try, while in the midst of difficult investigations, to reach one's goal right off and immediately lay hold of the criminal, one rarely succeeds at the start, and it is generally by a detour that we obtain our first results which then enable us to march straight ahead. No doubt this depends on the manner in which the theft is committed the actual thief tries to remain as little in the foreground as possible, while the assistants and watchers can and ought often to expose themselves for his sake. Hence we question the victim of a pickpocket to try and find whether he has not noticed any individual brushing against him in a peculiar way or touching him, or whose general bearing has been suspicious; the answers to our questions are generally negative and, if we are contented with these first answers, we have hardly any chance of laying hands on the pickpocket; the attention of the victim must therefore be directed towards all persons who have been strolling near him, have accosted him, asked for some information, requested a light for a cigar or who have rendered him any kind of service; these confederates may have drawn the victim's attention to some object or other such as one of the beauties of nature (a rainbow or sunset), or a remarkable picture in a gallery, or perhaps some comical or dangerous situation in which third parties are mixed up. They may have seized him all of a sudden and drawn him to one side to prevent him from being run over by a carriage or overturned by a man with a bundle; if duty they may have sympathetically brushed him down; they have asked him whether he has not lost his handkerchief or something else, has not taken someone else's umbrella by mistake, or forgotten his stick. All such questions are put with the object of assisting the thief to touch and examine the person questioned, or else cause the latter to examine his own person, thus drawing his attention to that part of his body touched and rendering him incapable of feeling any other contact effected soon after. This requires some explanation. The human body has a general sensibility, and a sensation already localised is easily confounded with another analogous sensation effected on another part of the body, though, as a sensation, the latter has hardly any independent existence—presuming this second sensation is not vigorous enough to annihilate the effect of the first. This psycho-physiological peculiarity, besides being remarkable in itself, will explain more than one case of pocket-picking which might otherwise appear impossible. These statements may be proved by an experiment which requires certain preparations. Two persons A and B plot to carry out the following on a third party, X. A all of a sudden gives X a blow with the elbow on X's *right* side, excusing it by making some such explanation as "Look," "Stop" etc. Soon after B will in his turn give X a blow with his elbow, but on X's *left* side and with less force than A. The most difficult part of the experiment is to discover the exact moment when B should strike: he will strike too soon if X's attention is not sufficiently fixed on the point indicated by the blow and cry of A, and he will strike too late if X has had time to recover from the blow and cry of A; to strike with profit B must seize the exact moment when the sensation caused by A has reached its culmination. If the experiment is successfully carried out, X, when questioned as to what he has felt, will be sure to answer that he felt the blow and heard the cry of A and that he immediately afterwards felt a new sensation of *that* blow but harder or more prolonged; as to the blow given by B he has not noticed it as such. The effect of the blow given by B does not therefore produce an independent effect but becomes added to the effect of the blow given by A, although the former was given on the left side and the latter on the right side of the body. In practice the experiment is verified by the following example.

One afternoon a gentleman had his inside coat and his overcoat slit open and his pocket-book containing a large sum abstracted from the breast pocket of the former, he had not felt the slightest contact and yet to make the slit, which was in the shape of a cross, the operator however skilful and circumspect he might have been must have exercised fairly considerable pressure. Moreover to get the pocket-book out, it must have been pulled with some force, for the slit was not sufficiently large to enable the pocket-book to drop out of itself. Added to this, that the gentleman had noticed nothing extraordinary, had been in no crowd, nor been run up against or elbowed about, in short nothing suspicious whatever had happened to him. At last after many questions he began impatiently to remark that he had seen something but it had absolutely nothing to do with the theft in question. He then stated that an old gentleman, exceedingly well dressed, who happened to be following him had remarked to him with the utmost politeness, that he had stepped in some filth, the old gentleman added that he had been following him for a considerable time and had noticed an unsupportable odour and this would be very disagreeable if our victim intended to pay any visit. The latter thanked the old gentleman and stopped to look at the sole of one of his shoes, then, finding nothing, he raised the other leg to examine his other shoe. At this moment the old gentleman seized him firmly by the arm and exclaimed laughingly: "It is not easy to stand on one leg, you were nearly over just now, but I see you have nothing on that boot either it must have been myself who has stepped in something and I have been laying it on your back—or rather under your feet!" The old gentleman laughed most heartily at this "amusing episode" and that very evening was arrested as an accomplice of the pickpocket. It was proved later on that the real thief had in shutting up the coat naturally taken advantage of the moment when the "old gentleman" had seized his victim by the arm on the pretence of preventing him from losing his balance and falling.

The procedure of the pickpocket's accomplice depends on the circumstances under which he "operates," and what chiefly characterises pocket-picking is that it is always, or nearly always, committed with the aid of a comrade. It is best to admit that a pickpocket rarely steals by himself, in most cases he is seconded by one or more helpers, either men or women. The railway thief has nearly always a woman with him. In Europe if he be a high-class operator he travels first class and in express trains or he may appear to be a respectable old countryman who travels third or fourth class with the country folk, in both cases he will generally be accompanied by a woman who will occupy the victim with her looks, talk, or something even still more intimate. The procedure is nearly always the same. The most difficult part is the choice of a victim, the latter ought to be well-to-do, not too intelligent, and not insensible to "a bit of fun." The pocket-book must be a fat one, and visible in the left inside pocket, and with respect to this, every pickpocket who wishes to live by his trade possesses an excellent eye. It is a mistake to suppose the railway thief only travels at night, all detectives are aware that these kinds of theft take place as often by day as by night, for an expert pickpocket is not afraid of the light and he knows that travellers look after their valuables more carefully at night than in the daytime. It goes without saying that the thief and the woman who goes with him do not appear to know one another, one of them gets into the carriage first and looks about for the information mentioned above. If there is nothing tempting, he gets out again, but if business can be done he makes a sign to the accomplice to follow. It is generally the man who gets in first, for it is easier for him to do the necessary exploring, to walk on the platform, look into the carriages, and get in and out of them if necessary. In the daytime they will do their best to be alone in the carriage with their victim; it might on the other hand a number of passengers does not worry them, for railway carriages are generally badly lit and the thieves trust to most of the passengers dropping off to sleep.

As to the order in which the travellers sit, the real thief must at any price be beside the victim, and the confederate who has to occupy the victim's attention must be opposite him. The thief takes part in the conversation for some time and then drops off to sleep—but he takes care to lose sight of nothing that is going on; he nearly always has a sham hand on the side next his victim, this false hand is joined to the real hand on the other side and rests upon the knees, while the real working hand is hidden under the large folds of his cape or cloak and is ready to thrust out at the side at any moment. When the victim is engaged in animated conversation with his *vis-à-vis*, the true hand of the thief begins to move; if this movement is awkward and is perceived by the victim, he is soon reassured on seeing the clasped hand of his neighbour who is beginning to snore. The theft once committed, one of the two gets out at the next station, and the one who gets out first is always the person carrying the purse or pocket-book; this is hardly ever the thief himself, for the latter endeavours as soon as the theft is completed to skilfully pass the pocket-book to his confederate, who of course is quite harmless in everyone's eyes. Indeed if the theft is discovered before the pickpockets have got away, the actual thief willingly allows himself to be searched, and his confederate is exempt from any suspicion; for how can people who are seated face to face and talking steal from one another? As a rule the second cut purse gets out at the same station and nearly always under the pretext that the first has forgotten something which ought certainly to be given him. Naturally the train starts before he comes back.

When dealing with one of these railway carriage thefts the following points should be borne in mind, especially during the examination of the person robbed and the witnesses.

As a rule the former makes no mention of the thief's helper, unless the helper was a man; when the helper was a woman she is never mentioned; either he does not like to talk about a woman whose acquaintance he has struck up in a railway carriage, or he does not think it worth mentioning "as she did not know the person suspected," or "appeared to be so natural," or "she was so well bred that it is quite impossible to suspect her of the theft."

Another way to recognise these people is that one of the two never tells his destination, for indeed he cannot get out before the theft has been committed; it is more often the actual thief who says where he is bound for—generally a fairly long journey—for he only follows the companion to whom he has passed the spoil under the excuse of giving him something he has forgotten. When the fact of the theft has been promptly discovered, it is often possible to catch the thieves by keeping watch at the two neighbouring stations, on each side of that it which they have got out; they never entrain again at the same place, but go on foot to the nearest station up or down the line, whence they take a train back again, or perhaps in the same direction as formerly in order to make use of the rest of their tickets.

Train thieves carry little or no luggage; in the first place they have no need for any, and then their movements are freer when looking for their carriage, changing their compartment or place, and getting in and out of the train, etc. If the victim has some little acquaintance with and is a good observer of mankind and things, he will not have much trouble in noticing that these people seem suspicious. If they are in a carriage with country people they give themselves the airs of decent peasants, but their hands are in no way spoiled by work, their shoes are not those generally used in the country, and their knowledge as regards agriculture seems to be at fault; if they have set up to be extremely elegant it is still more easy to unmask them, for there is always one place where their elegance is threadbare. Everything which comes first before the eyes is of course irreproachable: overcoat, waistcoat, watch-chain, cuffs, tie, etc., but the shirt, which is almost entirely hidden and only appears by chance, is of a doubtful whiteness; the stockings which have come into view of a sudden leave something to be desired; it is the same with the boots; and what the clothes do not betray the hands tell. No doubt, a person who can observe well enough to draw such conclusions has not much need of an Investigating Officer and the latter cannot teach him very much. The only useful thing to be done is for the intelligent Investigating Officer to question the intelligent observer with precision, so that the latter will communicate those observations which, without the questions of the former, he might omit to mention.

A curious role is that of the confederate of the thief who sneaks into the rooms of hotels when the traveller is asleep or absent. If the thief be caught in the act he asks a skilful question in order to be taken for a person who has come there on business or has been summoned for some good reason or other; perhaps he is a hairdresser, a cobbler, a chiropodist or it may be a dressmaker, midwife, etc. Now if the individual who has come across the thief seems satisfied by the question or representation, the latter goes off slowly and with excuses; but if he persists in his suspicions, speaks boldly and so on, the confederate cries out suddenly in the corridor:—"Hallo! there, it is not there you ought to go, but to room No. 60 and so."

When a theft is not to be committed at hazard but from a determinate individual who it is known in advance intends to stop in such and such an hotel, the confederate of the thief will also take up his lodgings in the same hotel, and, if possible, on the same landing; he will then not only be in a position to find out all necessary information, but also if need be to effectively help the thief in some such manner as we have indicated. The role of the confederate of a pickpocket is very difficult when the latter operates in the street and the bazaars; he must know how to gather together a crowd, by drawing the attention of people to some object or other or in offering himself as an object of curiosity for the passers-by; he will pretend to be ill, to have a fit of epilepsy, to be drunk, to be an idiot, or a madman; he will pretend to have been the victim of a sudden theft, or he will trump up a quarrel with someone. When the crowd has been got together it is easy to commit the theft, or at all events easier than in ordinary circumstances. At the same time the confederate will lure the individual whom they have decided to rob by relating or showing or giving him something, or by warning him of some danger. If the thief has to beware of the watchfulness of third persons, of public officials, companions of the victim, or even the general public, the confederate will have to be his screen, that is to say, he will have to divert the attention of such persons, or put himself in such evidence as will effectually cover the operations of the thief. As regards this, the auxiliaries of the thief are at times capable of master-strokes; they seem to have the power to as it were double themselves, or, at least, make themselves appear to be twice as big as they really are.

An amazing and pathetic story was recently told to a London magistrate. A decently dressed man, describing himself as a tailor, was charged with attempting to pick pockets. The detective said that the prisoner had been seen leading a blind girl about 14 years old from the pavement towards an electric tram car around which there was a crowd of people. The prisoner was seen to "tap" the dress pockets of two ladies and then return with the girl to the pavement. He kept the man and the girl under observation for about half an hour, during which he saw them mingle amongst the crowd around a dozen or more tram cars. At last as an elderly lady went towards a car the prisoner ran after her pulling the blind girl with him. Partly under cover of the girl he lifted up the lady's cloak and put his hand in her pocket, but, looking behind him and seeing the sergeant, pushed the blind girl into a tram car and jumped in after her. The officer followed and arrested them. The prisoner protested that he was a respectable man. But at the station the girl said that she knew her brother to be a pickpocket, adding that she did not know what he was doing that evening. Two skeleton keys were found upon him.

The confederate must be particularly skilled in receiving the stolen article; there are naturally a thousand different processes; the article stolen passes from the hands of one into the hands of the other either quite simply or with a skill allied to conjuring; or the confederate, following a settled plan, rubs up against the thief who thrusts the stolen articles into his pocket, or the thief drops the article to the ground, or better still lets it glide down beside his body, when it is nimbly picked up by the confederate. In this respect the Hungarian pickpockets are astonishingly skilful; they go over the frontier to visit a market, commit their thefts, and return back quietly into their own country laden with booty. One of these thieves used to wear at the end of his shoe a short pointed needle which he thrust rapidly into the pocket-book let fall by his colleague and then bending his knee, he would raise up his leg underneath his long cloak and cleverly seize the pocket-book with his hand. A woman was skilful enough to withdraw at the right moment her foot from her shoe and seize the pocket-book with her bare toes; then she would lift up her foot under her dress and, with a skill which would have done credit to a circus, drop the pocket-book into a bag attached low down in the inside of her under petticoat, then she again thrust her foot into her shoe, the whole business being executed without the slightest help from the hands. Still cleverer was a young girl who wore stockings with the ends cut off, to enable her toes, which were as mobile as fingers, to protrude; she used skilfully to seize the pocket-book slipped down through his or her clothes by the real thief, and would then fold her leg, raising her foot so as to place the pocket-book between her thighs, where she held it by a strong pressure, which did not however prevent her from walking rapidly and without effort; she only came to a standstill on finding a favourable opportunity of withdrawing the pocket-book from its hiding place. For a long time, the actual thief, a female, had been observed and suspected in the markets, and arrested on more than one occasion, but there was no proof against her, no stolen articles being found in her possession. She used to arrive at the market from one side while her companion came from another, and when the woman was seized, the young girl, whom no one suspected, was already far away with the booty. The latter was only arrested thanks to a clever police constable who had often seen the woman in the market and set himself to watch the persons constantly close to her; he noticed that the girl, while generally remaining some distance away, never lost sight of her and even went up to her at a prearranged signal; finally he succeeded in observing a stolen purse slipped on to the ground by the woman which was immediately picked up by the girl in the manner described.

The task of the auxiliary of the shop thief is quite analogous to that of his comrade the pickpocket's assistant. Thefts in shops and similar places such as open bazaars and markets, etc., are much rarer nowadays than formerly. The number of thefts in markets has probably diminished because the owners of stalls and shops keep better watch and there are more police about than in the old days. As regards shops, there are generally more employés than formerly, which helps the watching of customers. When all the attendants in a well-frequented shop consisted of the master and an apprentice they had too much to do serving their customers to be able to keep a look-out for thieves. The introduction of cashiers' desks has also contributed to make the life of the shop thief a hard one. The desk is usually placed at the back of the shop and a little on one side, so that the thief must turn his back to the cashier when facing the server and is consequently always in fear of being observed from behind. In shops containing such desks there are far fewer complaints of theft, but when they do take place, the thief is always accompanied by his confederate to distract the attention of the cashier, screen the theft, and take charge of the stolen articles.

The most frequent and most important thefts are those committed in jewellers' shops. There are always two thieves, one coming in a little later than the other. It can be easily understood how the shopkeeper, alone in the shop with a customer difficult to please, loses his head when he sees a second customer come in, who appears to be impatient and seems as if he would make good purchases. One sees a jeweller who is not perfectly at home in his business and hardly a man of routine become quite nervous in such a case; he runs from one customer to the other, then back again to the first, bangs his boxes and cases about, pushing them here and there, and does everything rather than properly guard his valuables. It goes without saying that the first customer has taken care before the arrival of the second, to mix up the articles, taking them out of their boxes and cases, placing them in a heap, and in short doing everything to prevent their being efficaciously watched. Then when the second is already very impatient, he ends by selecting his jewels and has them addressed to his hotel where naturally he will pay for them on delivery, at the same time he does not forget to steal all he can. Hardly is he outside when the second customer starts his work, that is to say, he keeps the jeweller out of breath so as to give him no time to immediately check and arrange his jewels and so discover whether he has lost anything and what. If need be a third arrives while the second is still in the shop, and during all this time the thief gets the stolen articles safely away.

The time-worn methods of thefts from jewellers are well enough known —how a sickly, coughing purchaser drops his handkerchief on the jewels displayed, in order to remove one, how another lays a visiting-card with sticky stuff on the back upon a diamond, how a lady throws into the hat of a beggar who comes into the shop a coin, and with it some stolen rings, how Mr T buys, the salesman or commissionaire accompanies him to the door of his house, and has the door shut in his face—these are things that are always to be read in the newspapers. How many thefts of jewels are effected is illustrated by a story which *Griffiths* heard at a great London jeweller's shop. He had, partly for amusement, a large brilliant lying apparently free, but in reality protected by an unbreakable, immovable, and practically invisible glass plate. The jeweller assured Griffiths that it was incredible how many attempts were made to remove this jewel "lying about" and often in the most wily manner. A much favoured method is for a thief to appear in a shop and place a lump of wax or some sticky stuff underneath the projecting glass counter cases. He then asks to see many things, fixes his attention on something small but very valuable, catches it at the right moment, and places it on the wax, which cannot be seen from any part of the shop. If the shopman misses the jewel the thief allows himself to be searched, if followed in the street, he is quite sure that it is not on him. A few days later an accomplice comes to the shop and takes the ring or other valuable away, unnoticed and without danger.

The first thing to be done is to throw light on the concomitant circumstances of this category of thefts. It often happens that the victim of the theft has absolutely no idea which of the customers has robbed him before their arrival his stock was intact, and after their departure many things were missing. In such a case the fault is often committed of suspecting all but believing that only one is guilty. Hesitation and uncertainty is the result, suspicion is thrown upon all but only one can be arrested. Another idea, equally bad, is to allow the victim to nominate one of the two or three customers as the presumed thief, because he seemed perhaps to be more awkward, or because he was not so well dressed, or because he discovered the loss of a jewel after his departure, and to be led into the mistake of tracking that person alone, though he has already got clean away or at all events is no longer in possession of the stolen article.

In such cases the important thing is always to find out what has taken place before and after the theft. When the victim has related the story of what he believes he has seen and has suspicions as regards some particular person the Investigating Officer is often contented with taking the exact description of that person and noticing the reason for which he has been suspected, while the essential thing is to find out from the victim who was in the shop before the suspected individual, what he did and what was his mien, then who came in after the suspected individual or at the same time. In this way a faithful picture of the whole case will be obtained and precise information regarding the way the theft has been carried out and persons of whose participation in the theft there can be no doubt.

Section vi.—The Theft Itself.

As regards the theft itself a report must be drawn up as to the state of the premises, and if an Investigating Officer desires, with some chance of success, to carry through the inquiry as it ought to be carried through he should see the state of the premises as soon as possible after the commission of the offence. Unfortunately this inspection is often neglected for reasons of convenience or economy, or if made, is carried out by lower-grade police officials who are contented with a summary description of the spot where the thief has broken in, the article stolen and the place where he had made good his escape, and as a rule the conclusion of the whole report is as follows:— "No trace whatever can be found of the thief."

But, more often than not, this is incorrect, for in nearly every case the thief has left the most important trace of his passage, namely, *the manner in which he has committed the theft*. Every thief has in fact a characteristic style or *modus operandi* which he rarely departs from, and which he is incapable of completely getting rid of; at times this distinctive feature is so visible and so striking that even the novice can spot it without difficulty, but on the one hand the novice does not know how to group, differentiate, or utilise what he has observed, and on the other hand, the particular character of the procedure is not always so easy to recognise. Only a practised, intelligent, and fervent observer is capable of distinguishing those traits often delicate but always identical, which characterise the theft, and draw important conclusions therefrom.

We have often heard tell that in such and such a district numerous burglaries have taken place, greatly troubling the population, or that a legion of pickpockets is infesting certain fairs, and, because in both cases "any clue to the thief is missing," nothing whatever is done, neither a report as to the state of the locality is made nor even the victims of the pickpockets examined; only the most indispensable formalities are gone through and there the matter ends.

Naturally, it cannot be supposed that the thief will be always captured even if a minute and intelligent examination of the scene of the crime be made in every case, but better results might be hoped for and the continual turning up of the same facts avoided if we resolved always to make the necessary inquiries even in thefts of minor importance.

Above all the Investigating Officer must learn to recognise, by studying previous cases of theft, the procedure of certain known thieves, and a kind of register should be kept at least in those districts in which they generally carry on their operations. With the help of such a compilation it may be established whether or not a certain crime is characteristic of the usual methods of such and such a band, and if it is, the Investigating Officer will know how to proceed with the case. Secondly, quite a series of crimes of which the authors are unknown may be attributed to one and the same person, the expert noting a common and permanent character about them all. Finally, it often happens that a thief, who has been caught red-handed in some theft of minor importance, is soon released after undergoing a short term of imprisonment; but if all the thefts recently committed in the district were carefully examined from the point of view of their method of execution, the same procedure may perhaps be found as that practised in the case for which our thief has been arrested, and he may be rendered responsible for all those crimes which bear the same character.

Keeping to the broad lines of thefts in general, it is natural to commence with what are called "specialists"—and nearly all thieves are specialists nowadays. Their speciality is due to various causes, but is based on principles of general significance. In the first place, it is birth and upbringing that assigns each criminal his own particular line: he who is by nature self-possessed, becomes a burglar; he who is quick with his hands, becomes a pickpocket; he who has audacity and effrontery, ceretes himself in houses. "The coward thief must also live," it has been said, and this explains why a member of a band of criminals whose speciality is burglary leaves his comrades to become a bazaar thief. But once a thief has become habituated to work in a certain manner—for everything requires study and practice—he sticks to it and learns no other. Competition produces analogous effects. When there are already many thieves whose speciality is to sneak into houses, a newcomer will find it difficult to earn his bread, for thieves of the same class object to new competition and watch with jealous care that no outsider intrudes within their domain. The most lucrative, but at the same time the most dangerous, branches are practised by the sharpest and most courageous. Others must be content with inferior methods, and if one among them be still young or less clever than his companions and yet possesses certain gifts, he will have to choose some branch which has as yet been scarcely exploited in the district or is indeed quite a new one. If he is a success, he goes on till he works it so extensively and so well that he has elevated it to the rank of a speciality. Chance also plays a large rôle in this connection, especially as regards individuals who, once honest, have become thieves by chance. The procedure that chance has presented to them they preserve as if there were no other way of carrying out a theft, and except in particular circumstances they do not lightly quit that path on which they have once set out.

In this connection *Lieut.-Col. Sir Henry Smith, K.C.B., ex-Commissioner, City of London Police*, states:— "Criminals, if they will pardon me for saying so, show a strange want of originality. The streets of London have thousands of pickpockets; they began to pick pockets, and they continue to pick pockets. The omnibus thief remains the omnibus thief, and the stealer of milk-cans steals milk-cans and nothing else. The stealer of dogs might surely diversify his programme by occasionally stealing a cat, but no, the feline race concerns him not; with a pocketful of liver, rendered additionally attractive by an admixture of aniseed, he prowls about annexing everything canine from the lordly St Bernard to the pitiful pug. With strange stupidity they frequent the same line of omnibuses, return to the same streets, and, till Nemesis overtakes them, steal the same articles. In the higher walks of the profession these peculiarities are still more striking. The bank robber and the forger are fascinated by their own style of business. They never have an idea in their heads beyond bank robbery and forgery. The coiner is always severely dealt with, but whoever saw him take to a less dangerous pursuit? The ruffian who robs with violence, uniformly knocks his victim down as the slaughterer pole-axes an ox, the good old-fashioned "stand and deliver" would in the vast majority of cases be quite sufficient, entailing possibly only six weeks or two months instead of five years or ten. The murderer, should he escape capital punishment, immediately on the expiry of his sentence commits another desperate crime and again puts his neck in jeopardy. Women have less scope for the exercise of their talents and have fewer openings to choose from—baby-farming and decoying their younger sisters to ruin being the most common, and with a good *clientèle* far the most lucrative."

Although the words of Sir Henry Smith are no doubt very true in a general sense they cannot be accepted without some qualification. Experience shows that no thief confines himself absolutely to his particular speciality, the inveterate forcer of doors, breaker of window bars, and crowbar expert will have no qualms about pocketing a gold watch that can be easily stolen, but as a rule the specialist will not depart from his speciality unless he is influenced by chance and necessity.

This speciality is of several kinds, it may refer to the particular kind of theft such as burglary, pocket picking, sneak thefts, etc., or it may denote the particular way in which, for some reason or other, a theft is usually carried out *e.g.*, in a theft of money the thief may be in the habit of leaving part of the money behind to make belief that it is a domestic theft, or it may be his custom to enter at the attics and lay hold of one of the hand-bags generally put away there, he will hide the stolen articles in this and calmly go off with it in his hand, or he turns up as a workman sent by his master, and goes off with anything he may find in the hall or he comes to read the gas-meter or perhaps his speciality is to conceal himself near houses in the country to try to find out where the farm people hide their keys when they go to the fields or it may be he steals only soiled linen hung out to dry, or brass bolts and locks, or mats in the entrance to houses, etc.

Here some particular practices must be noted which, although they have no connection with the actual theft, may help in discovering and convicting the thief. At the bottom of all the methods there seems to be a trace of superstition, the thief having noticed that his enterprise is successful whenever he proceeds in a certain way. Thus a very clever jewel-thief was in the habit of asking, in the jewellers' shops where he intended to commit a theft for an emerald necklace. A pickpocket of most irreproachable appearance invariably gave his profession in the hotels in which he stayed when travelling about in the interests of his calling, as that of a traveller in Java wine. A poacher belonging to Upper Styria, who for many years committed misdeeds of all kinds and whose name was surrounded with a circle of legends never showed himself in his audacious expeditions without an old "black silk hat" on his head, decorated with a peasant's plume two feet long, his face was also always blackened. A band of burglars, greatly feared on the confines of Hungary, was in the habit of leaving behind a rosary wherever a burglary had been committed. At the commencement of the nineteenth century a great number of thefts were committed in London in the following manner—the thief, with the greatest possible impudence, used to open with skeleton keys the houses of people who were absent (generally for the summer holidays), and clear out all the money and other objects of value he could find. No lock was too complicated for him, he opened and closed them without damaging them and apparently without the slightest difficulty. Apart from the astonishing boldness of the thief he had another remarkable peculiarity, he left behind in all the houses he ransacked a strange perfume, of great strength and persisting for months, it was always the same and could be recognised by no one, the accounts tell us of the terror inspired among people who noticed this "thieves' smell" on their return home, for it signified a great loss, this mysterious individual was never discovered, but it is more and more curious that this penetrating odour, known to all the London Police as "thieves' smell," never betrayed the criminal, either in the street or in any other place whatsoever.

We must also consider in this connection, and it is perhaps the most important point in discovering a thief, certain tricks of the hand, knacks, or technical manipulations peculiar to individual thieves. These knacks are innumerable in quantity and can only be discovered and grouped by attentive and detailed study. It may be noticed, for instance, that in a certain district the watch dog has been poisoned before each burglary and also that in every case the same poison has been used, or it is observed that the burglars always effect an entry by the ground floor window in such a way that it must be supposed that they have already succeeded in somehow opening the window during the daytime and shutting it again to all appearance, thus enabling them to get in easily and noiselessly during the following night, or it may be found that a particular method is always followed in forcing padlocks, filing window bars or opening locks with the object of diverting the attention of the person who is being robbed.

The fact of being the only possessor of an instrument is also a very distinctive sign. In England there formerly existed a sole individual, who employed, in cutting open the pockets of greatcoats, a signet ring provided with little knives set on springs and perfectly hidden—an instrument now quite common among thieves. In the same way certain instruments used in breaking open safes "guaranteed burglar-proof" are first the property of but a single burglar, and are a great source of profit to him, until the day when others are able to obtain the same instrument and enrich themselves in like manner.

To gather in and utilise these particulars in a given case is partly the business of the detective police and partly of the Investigating Officer, every representative of authority must watch, and, if necessary, communicate his personal observations and deductions to the Investigating Officer, whenever the latter has been unable to repair to the scene of the theft on his own account. It is in noticing such particulars that the greatest difficulty lies,

A C I

for this a broad and extensive view is necessary which does not become absorbed in some particular point for only he who has learned to dismiss from notice trifles of no importance is able to appreciate details of real value, points of no significance and no precise character should be rapidly observed in passing and a full stop be made only at essentials. An unskilled observer will examine attentively hundreds of broken padlocks and forced drawers and will find them all either entirely alike or else absolutely different from one another, according to his manner of looking at them an intelligent observer, on the contrary, will also find them all alike or all different, but he will further notice one or more common points of resemblance in a great number of them, and he will know how with more or less rapidity, to arrange all such points into different groups each bearing a mark indicating one and the same origin. This done, these points or peculiarities must be utilised, that is to say, they must in turn be grouped, for this it is necessary to have two categories, according to whether the particular observed belongs to a known person or not. We must then note as regards the thief whose speciality is known, the particular process he has used, and register the cases where this process has been noticed. In this connection the *person* of the thief himself must be taken as a point of departure. But, if the thief is unknown, care must be taken to mark those particulars which strike us in various thefts, they are then grouped according to their *nature*, i.e., their *particular character* is noted, and they are then added to the list of all other thefts bearing the same character. When a new theft occurs showing a particular feature we first look through our *personal* list and try to establish whether it can be attributed to a known thief; if it can, attention must, in the first place, be directed to that thief and if the observance of the particular sign is accurate the thief will be found. But, if it is impossible to attribute the particular sign or feature which has been discovered to a known thief, we shall try to find out whether there is not an analogous precedent, and if it is determined that similar thefts have previously been met with, the authors of which have remained unknown, there is nothing else to be done but to register this new case in the same list as these others presenting the same character; if subsequently we have the luck to discover the author, either of one of these old thefts, or of a new one belonging to the same category, a mistake will hardly ever be made in rendering the person arrested responsible for all thefts bearing the same characteristic signs

The importance and usefulness of this process are of the highest order; it may seem at first somewhat futile and difficult to turn to practical use, but whoever has tried it soon perceives that the trouble given is largely compensated by the results obtained. It may also be noted that this kind of research work is interesting and adds variety to the monotony of our daily work

A. Burglary and Housebreaking.

1 GENERAL

In the following pages it is not intended to set out at length all kinds of thefts accompanied by breaking in or out, which have been so well studied by *Hut, Thiele, Ive-Lallemant*, and others, nor do we pretend to set out entirely new ideas, but simply to bring together facts known to all criminal investigators and abstract therefrom those points which are worthy of notice in inquiries relating to burglaries and housebreaking. In Europe the Investigating Officer nowadays hardly ever has to do with a real case of "breaking," committed openly upon an inhabited house, and where the thief is stopped neither by the noise that he makes nor the resistance with which he is opposed. *Phin* and his like used to seize farms by assault, breaking in the doors with trunks of trees, exchanging gun-shots with the inhabitants, beating back in a lively skirmish any neighbours who came to the help of the persons attacked; now, indeed, it is doubtful whether an Investigating Officer, even in the country of the Carpathians—one of the most savage districts in Europe—has ever seen farms attacked in such a way. Many persons must have wondered while walking through thinly populated districts why these kinds of assault do not happen oftener; everywhere there are lonely hamlets inhabited by wealthy peasants, whose houses are often so far away from each other that even rifle-shots would not be heard by the nearest neighbour; the master of the house goes off to the cattle market and the farm labourers go courting the girls, perhaps a league away. A band of "merry men" combined and resolute, would not have much difficulty in stripping the house, the more so as it would be easy for one of them to mount guard, so as to decoy away or stop approaching police patrols by some pretext or other. In short it is not at all impossible that the Investigating Officer may even in our days have to deal with such cases.

Cases of breaking into uninhabited houses or houses inhabited by sleeping or harmless persons are frequent; we have both cases of breaking from the exterior, and breaking from the interior. By breaking from the interior we mean such breaking as the breaking of a closed cistern loft which is inside the building and into which the thief has secretly introduced himself by means of a ladder, or in some other way. The legal distinction in English law between housebreaking and burglary need not trouble us here, suffice it to say that, generally speaking, burglary is feloniously breaking into or out of a dwelling-house during the night while housebreaking is feloniously breaking into any house or outhouse during the day as well as the night.

In each case of housebreaking it will be essential carefully to establish the condition of the locality, and first of all examine all traces which the thief or thieves have left behind. And let us remember that no details must ever be considered too insignificant, or unworthy of the trouble of examination. Naturally, footprints must be observed to see whether they are made by the criminals or by others. If it is certain or probable that they are made by the former, they must be guarded as much as possible without wasting too much time over them, unless of course, they are exposed to deterioration as, for instance footprints in the snow, etc. would be, or where they constitute presumptions of a grave character against an individual who is already suspected for other reasons. Next we obtain any other information such footprints can furnish us; from what direction have the thieves come, where have they got in, at what place have they got out, and—where have they posted their sentinels? This last must on no account be forgotten. If this work is carried out with care a mass of important points may, with a little luck, be at once established, such as, *e.g.*, the number of thieves and the number of sentinels, their sex, age and even their origin—for the class of shoe permits us to draw conclusions as to whether a person hails from the town or the country. Doubtless, these conclusions must not be drawn too hastily, for it often happens that certain persons wear, either by chance or on purpose, shoes which have nothing in common with their position in life.

Not until this has been completed do we pass to the next important point, namely, the place of attack. This is often characteristic of the whole case. Above all it must be established whether the point of attack has been chosen with care and skill, having regard to the interior arrangement of the house, to the carrying out of the theft, as well as to other analogous circumstances. This is a matter which cannot be sufficiently studied, for it will tell us if the thief was acquainted with the habits of the family and the arrangements of the house, thus rendering possible the elimination of a whole class of possible thieves. In a general way this is not difficult to do, and is always possible, no doubt it must not be forgotten that certain particulars of a house are easily guessed or can be picked up on a very rapid scrutiny. Thus the flats of new town houses and also peasants' houses in the country, at least in certain districts, are constructed upon the same plan, so that a large number of particulars may be known without the slightest observation having been made inside the house in question. The Investigating Officer will quickly find out—thanks to a little experience and attention—whether the thief really knew the exact arrangement of the house, or has taken his bearings approximately with the help of some indicator, or was only able to observe and make a guess from outside, or has set to work with no information whatever. The consequences of these conclusions follow at once; when it is certain that the thief has only had an approximate knowledge of the locality, it is necessary to establish, by questions *ad hoc*, if anyone has been seen who has possibly been watching or if the presence of any people having a suspicious aspect has been noticed roaming round the house seemingly to observe its character and position. No doubt it sometimes happens, though very exceptionally, that the thieves operate on astonishingly little previous information. For example burglars who enter and strip uninhabited villas near large towns during the summer holidays, only seek to make sure that the villa is really not inhabited; all they do is to push a dead leaf into the keyhole and if next day it is still there, the villa is an empty one, and that evening a pantechnicon van turns up, upon which, the doors of the villa having been broken open, the thieves load everything that can be taken away; if a passer-by stops they request him to help them to carry some heavy piece of furniture, they speculate, and with reason, upon the laziness of the onlooker, who generally goes off, and they are relieved of a bothersome witness.

It must therefore, be settled whether the theft has been committed with skill and planning, or without such, or indeed, simply because occasion offered. The last point, as a rule, is not difficult to recognise and whoever has seen half a dozen burglaries can soon tell whether a theft has been committed with art or has been hurried over. The most significant thing to note with respect to this is a certain consciousness on the part of the thief of the end to be attained. An experienced thief avoids all useless work, he knows how precious time is, he knows how dangerous it is to remain with no object in a place, he is careful to make no more noise than is absolutely necessary, he husbands, and does not vainly exhaust his forces. If he has become a thief, it is nearly always because he was too lazy to work and worry himself, and these traits of character are manifested in all that he does. When it is noticed, for example, that the thief has first tried to break a window, *i.e.*, that he has filed several bars or tried to tear away the grating, and has finally abandoned that window to try another one, it can be immediately, and with absolute certainty, presumed that it is not the work of one who has grown grey in the profession. The latter takes care to thoroughly examine his object and to this end possesses all the requisite information. He distinguishes hard and good iron from that which is bad and soft, he recognises the quality of a door and the way its panels are set into the frame, he knows what is good or what is bad about the lock, the hinges, and the bolts. he can tell whether the bars of a window are buried deep in the stone and whether a wall may be pierced and he can tell at first sight whether he himself or his boy will be able to get through a hole which already exists, or squeeze in between two bars, and once he has recognised the weak point of a place and has decided to attack that point, to file here, and to cut there, he sticks to that place and does not give up the work once commenced. Perhaps he may be forced to completely renounce his burglary and be obliged to leave the work half done, but he will never try to break in at another place, only the inexperienced thief, the botcher, will attempt such extra work, the thief who is a past-master in his art will never do so. It seems almost that a point of honour or perhaps even of superstition forbids him to give up what he has begun for the purpose of starting upon another task.

It is somewhat curious that the thief often makes use, while breaking in, of some article brought from the house itself or even from a neighbouring house, at first sight one is tempted to believe that this is the procedure of a dilettante or of a person who is merely a thief by chance, it is difficult to get rid of the idea that some person or other of not very strict principles has happened to pass that way and has noticed a ladder and made use of it quite by chance to get into the nearest house. But this is not as a rule the case and such procedure ought really to lead us to suppose that the thief is a professional one, such a thief objects to walk long distances carrying some heavy object which is bothersome to himself, renders him suspicious in the eyes of passers-by, and moreover hinders his flight after the theft, the professional thief also takes good care not to have in his house instruments the use of which cannot be explained and which may cast suspicion upon him.

In this connection one often hears of the 'accidental theft,' that is to say, where the thief chooses as the theatre of his exploits a house in the neighbourhood of which he finds an instrument fitted to his purpose and easy to carry. when, therefore after a case of housebreaking an instrument of this kind *borrowed* in the neighbourhood has been found, it is necessary in every instance to turn the whole of one's attention upon that instrument. Before all, the instrument must be properly identified, then its situation before the theft, how it came to be there and whence it could be seen etc., and lastly we must try to find out how long it remained in that place, this last detail is of some importance, because if the instrument has really only been carried there on the eve of the theft, e.g., in a coach house giving on to the road, the theft must have been committed quite accidentally by some one passing down the road; but if the article has been there for some time the first hypothesis is the likelier, namely, that the thief had every hope of finding the object in question still there when he wanted to make use of it.

Another point to establish is whether any intruder has been seen busying himself with the article, looking at it attentively, or taking it in his hands; this procedure happens more often than one would think. In one case the thief himself, and not a more or less stupid auxiliary, entered into conversation with a peasant some little time before the theft and asked him whether a jack which he pointed out was always in the open stable, whether it did not rust lying there, whether it would not be stolen, whether people did not take it to make use of without his permission; and, when he was assured that it was always there and it was never touched, the implement was subsequently made use of to prize open the bars of the windows of a house situated some distance away from that of the owner of the instrument.

Since an implement found near by may be made use of, since a strange one may be left on the scene of the crime, or since there may be no trace of an instrument at all, the Investigating Officer must do everything he can to try and find out how and with what the breaking-in has taken place. Natural though this point appears to be and important as it seems at first, it is none the less true that he often neglects to clear it up; it is also important in that it enables us to find out the particular procedure of the thief; we may perhaps recognise therefrom the characteristic manner in which a burglar goes to work; a new procedure may perhaps be discovered, and later, when we come across it again, we will remember to have seen it before.

We often discover moreover a technical process, common to quite a category of workers; we recognise the hand and skill of a carpenter, a joiner, a stone dresser, or a turner, etc.; a skill which is often appropriated to the end sought after, but which is often not so, and which is turned to some other use; we remark a particular way of attack, of working, or of fixing an object, work which while seeming to respond to the aim in view yet denotes a certain knack; we get the impression—this procedure shows the skill of a workman but he is out of place here. The explanation is very simple; the accused has been in the habit in his trade, industry, or ordinary occupation, of working in a manner particular to his class, and when the day arrives when he must make use of his knowledge to commit a burglary he employs no doubt the same procedure. But this last point may be of some importance; it is, therefore, advised that, in all cases where one of these characteristic methods has been noticed, experts should be examined one after the other until one is found who can give the information desired. Generally speaking the circle of workmen to be questioned will not be extremely large; first it must be determined whether the advice of a worker in metal or in wood is required; this done, it may be settled in the former case whether a blacksmith, locksmith, or founder, and in the latter, whether a joiner, turner, cooper, or carpenter should be sent for; generally the case will only require two or three different specialists who may be found almost anywhere. Experience teaches that in this respect the ordinary workmen of the country are worth more than the skilled artisans of the towns: the latter are usually specialists who do not attack all kinds of work; they employ all sorts of instruments, machinery and other auxiliaries, often even with the assistance of workmen under them, but the country workman is obliged to tackle everything that is brought to him, he himself does the whole of the job or a greater part of it, using old and ordinary methods; he is, therefore, better fitted to reply to the questions put to him, he knows the usual way they work in his trade, and can say more readily than his comrade in the towns what idea the criminal had and what special knowledge he possessed.

It must also be remarked that in this class of work recourse to experts should be had much more frequently than is usual; the men chosen by the Investigating Officer to be his experts, necessarily men of intelligence of whom he can make use when need be, will learn something new every time they are called in to examine and make a report; they will fill up the gaps in their technical education, and as time goes on will be better able to enter into the spirit of the Investigating Officer's ideas; the latter will thus gradually bring together a regular staff of experts who, in the various cases that crop up, will place their best services at his disposal.

Moreover the experts will also lend their help in the subsequent investigations, for the thief is not contented with employing violence in order to get into houses but also employs it in order to break open safes and other closed receptacles. Here again we can clearly see the professional habits of the criminal; anyone who has lost the key of an almirah and been obliged to have it opened by force must have learned that one has only to observe the workman summoned for the purpose in order to note the difference between the various methods, according to the trade to which he belongs. The locksmith will attack the lock itself, the joiner the wood of which the almirah or table is constructed; the locksmith will open the lock with a master key or, if that does not do, he will smash it; the joiner will try to raise the top of the table or the lid of the cash box without touching the lock, or perhaps he will turn his efforts to the joinings of the planks or try to pull out the nails which hold the hinges to the doors; in short, each workman works in his own way and, when a workman of one class has done a job, the specialist can immediately say what that class is.

It is therefore necessary carefully to inspect, describe, and if possible draw and take mouldings of all the damage done by the thief to doors, windows or any other object. The trouble of doing so must not be shirked, for if such information, obtained with so much difficulty, cannot be made use of at the moment it may come in handy in some other case of perhaps considerable importance. For example:—a theft had been committed in the house of an old widow, who was not very rich; the thief had got into the house with the help of false keys, had broken open a box disguised as a seat, and taken therefrom a small sum of money. There was no clue to the criminal. The theft having been brought to the notice of the authorities, the Investigating Officer went with a policeman to examine the scene of the offence, but with very small result. The box opened like a trunk, that is to say, by lifting up the lid, the lock was an old and rusty one and did not offer much resistance, the wood was also old and worm-eaten and in consequence sufficiently soft to receive the impression of the instrument which had been used to force off the lid, it was easy to ascertain that the thief had thrust in his instrument, which must have been a kind of cold chisel, quite near the lock, between the upper edge of the front of the box and the lid, and had exercised on the handle end of the chisel a downward pressure, the iron was pressed into the front of the box at one place and the sharp end leant against the inside of the lid. An attentive examination of the impression made by the chisel in the top edge of the front of the box showed that the tool was not the same breadth over all its length but narrower towards the sharp end—as screwdrivers generally are, it was also noticed that in the inside of the lid, where the sharp part of the chisel had rested, one of the corners of the sharp edge was broken, for the mark was not straight but terminated at one end with a broken line the picture of the instrument used could from this be easily reconstructed it was known that the sharp edge was incomplete, a corner being wanting that it was now 38 mm in breadth while before the accident the breadth was 44 mm. It was also known that the chisel was 54 mm broad at a distance of 99 mm from its sharp end. All these measurements were accurately set out in the official report but it was impossible to discover the thief and the papers were pigeonholed.

Some time afterwards a big burglary was committed at a rich corn merchant's in the same neighbourhood and a large sum of money stolen; the most minute inquiry gave no positive result, but shortly a rumour got into circulation that a man well respected in the neighbourhood was the guilty party, he was supposed to have been seen hanging about the neighbourhood of the house where the burglary was committed, and he was said to be in a troubled condition of mind ever since no *conclusive* proof could be given of his guilt little by little the rumour gathered shape and substance, but the authorities abstained from making an inquiry with respect to it, for, as we have said, the man was perfectly irreproachable and was well esteemed by all, nothing would permit of his being made responsible. The case was about to be forgotten, when, quite by chance, the policeman who had assisted at the examination of the scene of the first theft visited the individual whom rumour publicly accused of the second, he had to talk to him about quite another matter and was on the point of leaving, when he perceived in the hall some tools, he continued his conversation a few minutes longer, at the same time observing the tools in question, among them was a large and strong screwdriver, the sharp end of which was incomplete—a corner was missing the policeman carried off this tool on some excuse or other and a few minutes later the Investigating Officer and himself were measuring the screwdriver and comparing the measurements with those indicated in the old case they were exactly the same to a fraction of an inch. This "respected" gentleman was very miserly, he kept no servant, and inquiries among the local tradesmen made it clear that the present owner of the tool had bought it long before the date of the theft committed in the house of the old widow, our gentleman was therefore proceeded against on the charge of the first theft, and there being nothing now against such a course, he was also accused of the second, in the end he confessed to the theft in this way all the charges brought home to the perpetrator were due to the attentive examination *in loco* of the circumstances of a theft of absolutely no importance

But not only must the damage done by the actual breaking be established, but also all traces, however insignificant, left behind by the thief must be observed with the greatest attention everything the thief has abandoned on the scene of the theft may be of interest, a garment, a tool, a bit of paper All these objects should not only be noted in the usual way but they must be examined, described, and compared without losing sight of the fact that the accused may have placed them there to put the police off the scent

It is moreover, important to establish what measures have been taken by the thief to prevent surprise, it may generally be noticed that every thief has particular practices which, as we have already explained, have an importance of their own with regard to other thefts committed subsequently For instance one burglar used to stop all the clocks in the rooms in which he worked perhaps he was very nervous and could not bear the ticking or perhaps he feared that the noise would prevent him hearing the steps of an intruder It is a fact that in our own homes we hear neither the ticking nor even the striking of our clocks while in other houses this often inconveniences us, it is therefore natural that a thief may be influenced by the ticking of a clock in a room in which he is working When later on the thief in question was captured he was called to answer for all the thefts of recent date in which the clocks had been stopped, but curiously, he was not the author of all the thefts committed under these conditions and it must be concluded that there were more than one of these "nervous" thieves

One important characteristic of a thief and a method of distinguishing whether he be a novice or an old offender, is the manner in which he covers his retreat "It is easier to get in than to get out" say all thieves, or "one can always dispense with getting in, never with getting out"—once you are in you *must* get out As a general rule a thief of cunning will not rely for his flight entirely upon the opening by which he entered, he will take care to reserve a door, a window, or some other exit for escape should his presence be discovered, he will also secure every inside entrance to the room where he is carrying on his depredations, so as not to be disagreeably surprised by the master of the house In this respect the methods of the gipsies are very significant gipsies belong to the class of criminals who obtain information, with the greatest precaution and the greatest accuracy, before committing their thefts, besides their nomadic life and habits of mendicity greatly facilitate their operations in this direction Moreover a gipsy is not obliged to thieve in any particular house he can do it in the next house or further off still, he hunts about, begging, telling fortunes, mending pots and pans, etc, until he finds the place that suits him best He generally chooses, in a peasant's house, and it is such houses he attacks ninety-nine times out of a hundred, a room where no one sleeps, but where there are almirahs full of clothes, linen, and other materials, and where money and other precious objects are shut up, such rooms are to be met with in every rural district and also in large country houses, among the latter the gipsy chooses if possible a corner room on the ground floor, with two windows facing in *different* directions, the number of interior doors being of no importance to him; he starts by tearing out the iron bars from both windows, so as to make sure of a free passage on both sides: he counts, and rightly, upon the fact that if discovered it will not be on both sides at once; the people of the house or even outsiders will come in the direction of one window or the other, and he will either hear of their approach in the room itself or be warned by his confederate on the watch, and will easily escape by the window which is not threatened.

To prevent surprise from the inside, gipsies practise another method which is quite peculiar to themselves; it is necessary for them to shut at all price the inside doors of the room in which they are committing their theft. First the gipsy ascertains whether the key is on the inside of the lock or whether the door is furnished with a bolt: in the latter case he slowly and gently pushes the bolt; if the key is on the inside he turns it with precaution till he can draw it out, then he plunges it into some oil which he carries with him and then locks the door, the oil thus preventing the key from grating. If there be neither key nor bolt he has recourse to another method of closing the door. For doors opening towards the outside he takes the following precautions:—he places transversely across the door-frame a strong piece of wood which he ties to the latch as securely as possible. It is then impossible to open the door, or at least to open it sufficiently to allow anyone to get in (*Fig. 75*). But if the door opens towards the inside, he fixes it by a piece of wood placed slantingwise against the door, one of the ends of the piece of wood leans against the latch and the other rests upon the ground where it is held by a strong gimlet driven into the floor, preventing the wood from slipping. A door closed in this manner cannot, as a rule, be opened easily.

Fig 75

Such methods nearly always denote that the thieves are gipsies and we cannot explain why other thieves so rarely employ them, for they are very practical and an excellent guarantee against surprise. See *Chapter IX*, *Section II*.

As a rule other housebreakers are content with locking or bolting the doors, where this is possible; but if there is neither key nor bolt they place large articles against the door such as lumps of wood, poles, tools, chairs and the tops of tables, which fall upon the person wishing to enter. The noise they make in falling, the injuries they may bring about, and the obstacles they place in the way of the intruder, give the thief the necessary time to take to flight.

2. ENTERING BY THE WINDOW

We have now to treat of the methods of entering a house by force. In the first place we must consider the window bars, which are the point of attack usually preferred by housebreakers. This is because a door, as a rule, is more solid and offers more resistance than a badly constructed window grating, moreover people imagine that windows furnished with iron bars are perfectly secured and in consequence the thief is very well aware that having raised these bars, his work is over. He naturally chooses the easiest way to overcome them, that is to say, he will first try to slip through; if he himself cannot succeed, perhaps his boy may be able to manage and once in the house he will simply open the door, bolted from the inside, and let his companion in. If it is impossible to open the door from the inside, this simple way of getting into the house will be far too difficult for flight and the boy will perhaps be caught in a trap, but if they can succeed in opening the door, they certainly prefer to make their first entry by slipping between the bars.

Speaking generally, a man can pass wherever his head plus the thickness of his extended arm can pass (Fig. 76) at least if the formation of his body is not abnormal such as a particularly small head, very large shoulders, or a very bulging chest. But as regards ordinary window bars it may be said that every individual whose head alone can get through is able to squeeze between them, for there is always room enough for his arm. Window bars 5¼ inches or more apart are quite useless, for there are plenty of people whose heads (including their ears) are no more than 5¼ inches in diameter. And as there are many (generally children) whose heads are still smaller (often 5¼ inches), the distance between the bars ought never to exceed 4¾ inches. This detail is also important from the point of view of the culpability of a certain class of people, for often the residents in the house and the servants are accused of having committed a theft for the sole reason that it is deemed impossible that anyone could have passed between the window bars, if however, the bars are fixed more than 4¾ inches apart, it can always be said that an entrance may have been effected from outside.

Fig 76

If it is impossible to squeeze between the bars, the entire grating of the window must be removed, the way to do so will depend, for the "accidental" thief, on the means at his disposal, whereas the experienced criminal will choose his instrument with regard to the difficulties to be surmounted. He will commence by attentively examining the grating which, thanks to his skill he will do in a few moments, he will then be guided in his procedure by the weak point of the grating. if it is solid and very thick and well fixed into its frame, the thief will decide to only partially remove it, if he finds in it some fault furnishing a suitable point of attack

Fig 77

Several of these faults are indicated in Fig. 77. In the first bar the rivet hole where the two bars cross and join is too large, and the vertical bar is weak enough at that point to allow of two cuts being made, one on the right and one on the left in order to sever it completely in two. The second bar gets narrow at the bottom at the point where it is embedded in the stone, this happens fairly often especially when the grating is an old one, and is produced by the damp which descends to the base of the bars this occurs most often when the window casing above has become rotten and allows the rain to get through and run down the bars, and thus maintain a dampness of the part of the wall where the bar is fixed. It also frequently is found when the wall round the window is of stone, some of which is particularly hydroscopic, that is to say, contains saltpetre, at this part of the wall it is always damp, and if a bar of iron be placed there it quickly rusts. The third bar presents a defective soldering in the iron; in order to solder two pieces of iron which have been warmed and softened, the same method is followed as in uniting two pieces of wax warmed in the hand, but the iron is beaten with a hammer while the wax is only pressed with the hand. If therefore the soldering is not carefully done, the iron not being hot enough or the hammering not strong enough, the joining of the two pieces of iron is not complete and by breaking a bar of iron thus soldered the work is considerably simplified, as it suffices to separate the parts soldered—the rest coming away by itself.

When the thief discovers such a fault he will not think of taking the trouble to remove the whole grating. He will be contented with cutting through the bars at the feeble spots and folding them over at the fixed point, that is to say, they are folded back until they are in a position perpendicular to the grating, the middle bar being bent upwards, the two others downwards, and once a part of a bar is raised or lowered an opening is formed by which anyone can get in. Formerly, when window bars used to be cut with big files or with watch springs made into saws, a difficult piece of work, this operation used to be considered quite a masterpiece of burglary. Nowadays the first criminal one comes across, perhaps hardly grown-up, can do it, he has only to buy a few English files and some good fretsaws. After that all that is required is to have patience to oil the instrument continually, and to prevent any noise by enveloping the iron in cloth, tow or, better still cotton wool, the iron however thick it be, if it is not of very excellent quality, will soon be cut in two. If the grating has no weak point but is not well fixed in the frame, neither file nor saw is employed, but an attempt is made to remove it entirely. Different processes are resorted to for this purpose: the best known is to take a strong and long crowbar which is passed under the cross-bar and rested, as near as possible to the point of attack, upon a support such as two pieces of wood placed crossways, or even on a single block of wood, a lever is thus obtained on the end of which one of the thieves sits so as to exercise sufficient pressure, and if the arm of the lever between the grill and the point of support is sufficiently short in proportion to that between the point of support and the power, a considerable force is obtained which even a solidly constructed grating is unable to resist.

The author has himself made experiments in this way upon the gratings of the windows of a house in process of demolition; he employed the method just described as well as that of the jack which will be dealt with later on. The operation was found to be astonishingly easy. If besides, it is done slowly and with precaution the noise which results is insignificant and is even reduced to a mere light cracking. It is only when the bars are, though well embedded in the stone, yet not very firmly fixed to the wall, that small pieces of stone or brick become detached and fall with some noise upon the ground. One of the thieves is then obliged to keep always near the window, to look out for these morsels, stop the work of his comrade operating the end of the lever, and carefully pick up the debris with his hand or some tool.

Another method of forming a passage through window bars is to employ the jack we have spoken of above. The criminal has recourse to a jack when he knows that one (generally called a "coffee-mill") may be found in the neighbourhood, or when he supposes that this instrument will save him the trouble of having to remove the entire grating. Indeed, he can find lateral points of support for the jack in the bars themselves, which will then be forced apart from one another, thus forming a sufficient space for him to get through (Fig. 78). The parts of the grating which yield so as to give the bars the necessary extension in bending, vary according to the construction of the grating; sometimes it is the iron itself which stretches, sometimes the rivets which start, or sometimes the bars give way at the top and the bottom, or it may be that the horizontal bars work out of the masonry, or several of these effects or even all of them may happen in combination, but the operation nearly always meets with marvellous success. If the

Fig. 78

thief has to give up the idea of thus widening the space between the bars, either because he cannot find convenient points of support or because such a narrow opening appears too dangerous in the event of his having to take to flight, he will remove the whole grating. As a rule the jack will not be high enough to reach from the ground to the lowest cross-bar, but the thief will remedy this inconvenience by placing it on a stone or block of wood, or by leaning it upon a long beam which he will rest against some fixed point, such as the foot of a building opposite, or in the angle which a tree makes with the ground or, more simply, in a hole dug to no very great depth in the hard soil; he will thus obtain, so to speak, an extension of the jack. The only difficulty consists in keeping the jack and the beam exactly in the same plane, that is to say, to prevent them coming away at the place where the jack rests on the beam, the result being to throw the whole out of gear. The difficulty is generally got over by fixing underneath the point where the jack and the long beam touch another beam to support them, and tying the whole together with thin ropes or chains (Fig. 79); moreover if care be taken to guide the beam with the hand, raising it and lowering it to avoid any displacement at the junction of the jack and the beam, then the jack may be counted upon to work properly, and after the operation the

Fig. 79

thief has but to get rid of the whole paraphernalia and leave the peasant who is his victim, and very often other persons as well, completely amazed and unable to explain how on earth the grating was torn away.

Besides the grating there are other obstacles to be overcome in order to get in by a window. In the first place there are, if the windows are folding ones, the flaps or shutters, persiennes or jamals, which are sometimes in front of and sometimes behind the grating, or even in exceptional cases on both sides of it. Here again there are different processes which depend nearly always on the particular construction of the window; those presenting the least difficulty are outside shutters, opening outwards, for then the hinges are fixed on the outside and are easily accessible. The hinges in country houses are notoriously so weak that they can often be detached with the aid of an ordinary pocket-knife. Once the hinges of the two folding doors are taken away it is easy to separate the latter, except where the system of bolting is particularly complicated. But if the hinges offer considerable resistance or it is found impossible to remove them, or if the window opens towards the inside, then the attack is directed towards the window itself. The thief must naturally find out beforehand the system of fastening, and as a general rule, he is informed on this point long before the theft; if the bolts are ordinary ones or any other fastening not particularly complicated is used, it is relatively speaking easy to open them; for this purpose a large hole is drilled with a gimlet at a suitable distance from the window-fastening, an iron wire is passed through this hole, grappled to the bolt, and the window opens; this is not very difficult, for the thief can follow the direction taken by the iron wire by looking through the window. But in the event of difficulties presenting themselves or the manner of fastening not lending itself to the employment of iron wires, there is nothing else for him to do but to break the glass, when the fastening will be easily reached.

We have often heard it said that thieves sometimes cut out the window panes; the author has never seen this done and does not believe that a thief would bother with such work even if he has been apprenticed to a skilled glazier. Indeed, to cut out a window from its frame the glass must first be cut with a diamond and then knocked on the whole line where the diamond has passed until the glass becomes detached and falls, but the thief will never make up his mind to create a noise by rapping the glass, and if in a case of theft, we were to see a pane of glass cut in this manner, we should consider at first that the theft was a sham one. Indeed the piece of glass may have been cut out at leisure and replaced and then made to fall at the opportune moment, to make believe that a theft has been committed from outside.

Occasionally a pane of glass is removed by detaching the putty which holds it to the frame, especially is this the case when the glass has just been put in and the putty is still soft, or on the other hand, when the putty is already old and has become friable and easily broken, through being exposed to the heat of the sun. Putty is composed of chalk and linseed oil, which, in time, oxidises and becomes incapable of resisting the effects of temperature so that little is left of the chalk but a solid substance of an earthy and friable nature, nothing then remains but pieces of putty dry, prism-shaped, having no force of cohesion, which can be easily and noiselessly removed with a knife or chisel. But, as we have stated, it is rare to find the putty quite soft or completely dried up, and as a fairly long time is necessary to remove it, the thief is generally satisfied with breaking the glass.

Thieves usually perform this last operation in a marvellously skilful manner. The noise of the falling pieces of glass must of course be taken into account; it is therefore necessary to prevent them from falling, and for this purpose they are stuck or gummed: a kind of plaster comprised of a piece of cloth of the size of the pane of glass and spread with a substance of a cohesive nature, such as birdlime, black pitch, grafting putty, wax mixed with turpentine or even with soot, or simply clay, or clay mixed with dung or half-liquid pitch, etc., is spread over the whole window. When this is done, some soft object is stretched over the surface so as to smother the noise ensuing when the glass is shattered: for this a garment, towel, sometimes also grass, hay, or moss, etc., is used. When all these precautions have been taken, the middle of the glass is slowly pressed with increasing force till at last it smashes. As a rule the noise made is insignificant: the sound of the breaking glass is deadened by the pad, and the fragments remain attached to the plaster. If in spite of all noise cannot be avoided, the thief stops work to make sure that it has not been heard; if all is quiet in the house he can continue his operation and remove the plaster.

Omitting special notice of the window shutters, for what we shall say concerning doors will also be applicable to them: the thief will pay attention to all the objects which are usually placed inside the room, such as bottles, vases, flower-pots, and other articles, which common folk especially are in the habit of placing on the inside window-sill; still the thief even takes care as a rule to exactly ascertain the existence and position of these objects beforehand for on opening the window he may cause them to fall and thus lose all the trouble which he has taken; if he has made certain of the presence of these disagreeable articles there is nothing else for him to do but to try and reach them, pull them out through the broken window and throw them away. If he cannot reach them all he may have to break another pane of glass or perhaps give up the attempted theft altogether. The curtains and blinds which are generally seen in country inns and other places are also very disagreeable to the thief, for he cannot open a window noiselessly on which one of them is hanging, as they are generally made of stiff and well-dressed material. In this case he has to break a pane of glass near the cord of the blind or curtain so as to draw it up. If the window frame is narrow he may perhaps be able to reach the cord by passing his arm through the half opened window as far as possible, and if he fears the noise, he will sometimes cut off the blind crossways with scissors or a sharp knife.

It is worthy of note that spring roller blinds are very distasteful to thieves as when such a blind is down the window cannot be opened without noise and an instrument must be introduced to release the catch of the blind or cut the cord. Care must also be taken to prevent the blind springing up quickly and causing a noise. One method is to cut the blind across the top but then the top part of the window must be lowered first, which is not always so easy. A thief as a rule avoids a window with a roller blind.

3. ENTERING BY THE DOOR

Breaking open doors and shutters is extensively practiced, the differences between and the combinations of the methods used are very considerable so that the subject can only be dealt with quite generally. As a rule doors are fastened in a more or less complicated manner and they present two points of attack for the consideration of the thief, namely the surface and material of the door and the mode in which it is secured

(a) Attacking the door itself

There are many other modes of breaking open a door than battering it in with the trunk of a tree, a heavy beam or a crowbar used like a ram. There are numerous ways of opening it without making a noise or attracting attention. The method most like those we have just been considering is to raise up the door by introducing a lever or wedge between the frame and the threshold; one of the parts of the door is bound to yield, the part depending upon its construction; if the force used is only sufficiently great either the lock, staple, hinges, or the whole door will give way. No doubt this cannot be done without noise and proves the criminal to be either extraordinarily audacious or sufficiently acquainted with the situation to know that the noise will not attract anyone's attention; he is aware that the house is untenanted, or that the residents are too far away from where he is working, or that he knows them to be fearful folk who will not budge in spite of, or because of, the noise.

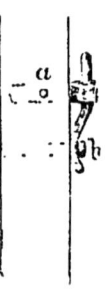

Fig 80

If the thief cannot raise the whole door in this energetic manner he attacks a part or parts of it. He chooses the hinges for preference, if they are accessible from outside, that is to say if the door opens outwards. In towns and populous places doors hardly ever open outwards for they are situated on the pavement and would encroach on someone else's ground. But in the country they open outwards much more frequently than is convenient and the hinges are in consequence also fixed on the outside, and if these hinges are not fixed as shown in Fig 80 they may be removed almost noiselessly by the first blockhead who comes along; to fix them properly it is necessary that the arm of the hinge be fixed to the doorpost at point a while the support of the hinge is strongly bolted at b by a screw passing right through the doorpost from one side to the other.

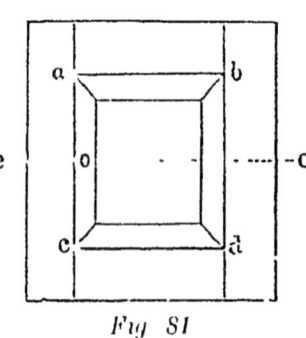

Fig 81

If the thief cannot succeed in taking off the hinges he will attack the wood of the door (or shutter) and in this connection the manner in which doors are made, i.e., with panels greatly helps him. Such doors have certainly their advantages; they look well and there is little probability that the wood of which they are made will split or decay, but on the other hand they seem to be constructed for the very purpose of housebreaking; their manner of construction excludes any chance of solidity (Fig 81). They are made by slipping the panels, the edges of which are thinned down, into grooves in the four boards which form the frame. If then we take a section of the door from c to c (Fig 82), we can see that all

panel doors are particularly thin between the frame and the panel itself,
ie, at o o. We can all notice this on our
own doors. It may be seen that the wood
can be easily pierced at o with a knife, the
blade of which is inserted in the direction
of the grain of the wood. The two oppo-

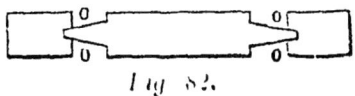

Fig 82.

site sides of the panel can then be easily cut, slitting the wood gently, it is
naturally more difficult to slit it against the grain since a saw cannot be used
for fear of the noise, a gimlet is here resorted to and little holes pierced side
by side in the wood, the spaces between them
being subsequently cut away with the knife. In
Fig 83 lines a a' and b b' are cut with the knife,
lines a b and a' b' with the gimlet. Having thus
cut round the panel the thief can remove it and
get in through the opening obtained, the weakness of such doors has been frequently noticed,
especially in village inns, where people have been
known to push out in a drunken quarrel, the
panel of a door by a mere pressure of the back,
a kick, or a knock with the head.

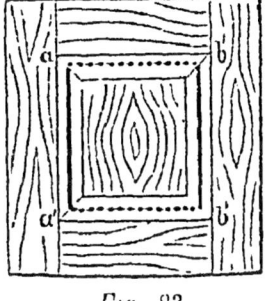

Fig 83

At other times the thief attacks the cross-
bolts which are fixed in various ways and, all things considered, render
excellent service. Naturally they are useless unless the door itself is a good
one. A door furnished with a cross-bolt cannot be lifted from its hinges or
opened by a master-key, but if its construction be light it will offer no more
resistance to either a gimlet or a knife than any door without bolts at all. In
addition the bolt must be fixed securely, not so that it may be pushed from
one side to the other. Let us consider one of these systems of shutting up
doors or windows. In the country the door is provided with a wooden bar
of more or less strength which generally rests in a lateral hole in the wall
and is slipped through two rings or guides and into a hole in the wall
opposite the first mentioned wall. For window shutters the fastening is
made with a cross-bar which turns on a nail strongly driven in and hangs
in a vertical position during the daytime. In India this method is also
commonly used for doors: to fasten the shutter or door the bar is turned
round the nail and fitted into a staple or hook in the opposite wall. To be
of any use it is not sufficient for the door or shutters to be of solid construction, the must also be well fixed, if not all that is necessary
to render the bolt quite useless is to make a small hole in the door, this
hole must of course be made in the proper place and be a little larger than
the lever that is to be used. It should be pierced just behind the bolt, and
the lever—such as a thin bar of iron with a pointed end—should be placed
with its arm or handle away from and its point towards the latch edge of
the door. The point of the lever is then dug into the bar or bolt and levered
backwards and forwards, thus pushing the bar back little by little, no
doubt it only moves a fraction of an inch at a time but if the operation
is kept up the bar will be withdrawn and leave the door free to open. The
same method is used for the bolt or bar which turns on a pivot, the hole
is again made exactly behind the bar and the same lever used, but instead
of pushing the bar horizontally, a circular and upward movement is em-

ployed till it comes out of the staple or hook. This process is of course impossible where the bar is fixed by some means or other, as e.g. by a pin passed through the hook or staple, above the bolt and terminating in a hole in the door frame.

All these methods are generally interesting from the point of view of the police. As regards the Investigating Officer, they are very important, for whenever a breaking-in has been effected in this way, he may presume that the thief has been in the locality before and ascertained that there was a bolt, how it was fixed, and whether or not it was furnished with a safety-catch, etc.; a thief who does not know all this is also ignorant of the method of making the hole and of how to use it when made. Of course, we do not mean to say that he would have to take measurements of the place where the bolt is fixed; it is enough for him to look for certain indications which can be seen both inside and out, and to which he will direct his attention. Suppose he notices, for instance, that the bolt of the door is about a finger's breadth above the key-hole, he has but to draw a horizontal line to fix the whole position of the bolt; or at the window he may remark the pivot rail, which in all probability runs right through the bar from back to front and ought consequently to be seen from outside, but the bolt when shut is horizontal and thus it is easy to find its position throughout its whole length.

Fig. 84.

In many cases, as when the bolts are small iron ones or the thief decides to attack the lock, or some reason or other renders it convenient to insert the hand inside the door, a larger opening has to be made. The method mentioned above for removing a door panel is generally followed, but the gimlet holes will be made in a circle and then joined up with the aid of a thin knife, thus obtaining a continuous circular section which will come away and allow the hand or piece of bent wire or other instrument to be inserted. In Fig. 84 the holes are shown drilled and the joining lines cut.

That locks may be opened, bolts withdrawn, and safety catches manipulated in this way may be readily understood, but what often appear incomprehensible are the smallness of the hole and the distance from it at which the thief can operate inside. It seems all the more remarkable when we remember that he can see nothing of the field of operations from outside and cannot trust to his sense of touch, as it is with a wire and not with his hands that he works.

Openings made with a gimlet or drill in this way furnish the Investigating Officer in every case with rich material for deduction; the place itself where the hole is made permits him to form an idea as to what the thief knew concerning the interior arrangement of the door. Upon examining this opening a conclusion can be formed either that the thief had absolutely no knowledge of the interior aspect of the door, or that he had an approximate idea of it, founded upon a rapid observation, or that he had an exact and complete knowledge of the situation such as only an old servant friend, or even as has happened former occupier of the house must have had. If the opening does not appear a success the question must be asked what reason the thief could have had for making it in that way rather than in some other manner. The examination of this question, based as it is upon all the circumstances however small, gives at times most interesting results, for it may be discovered for example that the accused must have seen the inside of the door but only from a very special point of view which has given him a false idea. Certain researches, if properly conducted, may perhaps be able to put us on the track of persons who must necessarily have considered the situation from that point of view. Finally the impression may be obtained from this inspection that the accused's only knowledge comes from outside sources, such as descriptions and rough sketches, and he has thus obtained a false idea of the state of things, a discovery which will give the Investigating Officer a fresh point of departure for new investigations.

In such cases it is above all important to have the scene of offence attentively examined by experts, for the work of the thief will nearly always present some characteristic signs. It may perhaps be established what kind of instruments have been used by the thief, whether the criminal is a workman of a special class, what trade he belongs to, whether he had enough time for his work, whether he used a light, whether he employed considerable force, whether he proceeded with skill or originality, and knew how to profit by certain advantages as for example to avoid nails or other non parts—in short, it will perhaps be possible to discover a certain number of particular circumstances capable of characterising the thief and bringing about his subsequent arrest. This result appears to be more unreal than it is in fact, for it must not be forgotten that these are not isolated points which have been determined but are very frequently corroborated by other determined points, noticed by some person or other who has been called in to give information and thus become more definite in form.

Care must of course be taken not to heedlessly express any opinion which has been formed, or which one may have thought it possible to form, nor to communicate it on the spot to people present, who will perhaps believe themselves obliged to agree with Mr Investigating Officer, and immediately start about making a number of more or less inexact observations, solely in order to be agreeable. We all know how often we have been led into error by such people animated by the best intentions in the world, but we also know that if in such a case we observe the state of the locality with attention, take the advice of experts, and hold ourselves in reserve before communicating to the witnesses the results acquired, if we then gather with care the opinions of the latter, and if we combine the information thus obtained success can hardly be missed.

We may here cite a case where the thief had made such an opening as we have been discussing, the case is interesting from more than one point of view, and at the same time the opening made was a larger one than the author ever met with before, it was not however made in the door. A coachman of the name of Cr—, after many long years of work, had saved a fairly round sum and hoped to live quietly upon it in his old age. He was a bachelor of a distrustful nature, and his distrust increased when he learnt that about the same time as he was retiring from his business one of his old fellow-coachmen had just been the victim of a mysterious theft and had been despoiled of all his fortune. He rented, on the down-stairs floor, a room which had only one door; he got the two windows fitted with bars and shutters and the door with all kinds of bolts and locks, he bought a revolver, and at last thought he was safe. As for his money, he placed it in the savings-bank; in the day-time he carried his bank-book in the pocket of his coat and at night he placed his coat beside his bed, still leaving the book in the pocket. Now Cr—— was still in possession of an old carriage, a relic of his old business, stabled in the same house in which he lived. One fine morning, he was awakened by an individual who said that he had come to see the carriage with a view to purchase. Suspicious by nature, Cr—— hurried out to show the carriage to the unknown purchaser, and finally both repaired to a neighbouring job master to borrow a couple of horses to be attached to the old carriage, for the purchaser insisted upon trying it. Cr—— and the purchaser drove about during the first part of the morning; the latter was satisfied and promised to return in the afternoon with his money to pay for the carriage and horses to take it away. But hardly had he gone off than Cr—— discovered that instead of his savings-bank book his pocket contained another one, similar to his own but which showed a balance of only a single gulden. He went off to the savings-bank where he learnt that the whole of the deposit had been withdrawn about an hour before by some unknown person. Naturally the buyer of the carriage did not turn up in the afternoon and there was no manner of doubt that his story of a purchase and the trying of the carriage was only a feint for the purpose of keeping Cr—— occupied and hindering him from discovering the loss of his bank book, and at the same time giving the confederate of the "purchaser" the necessary interval. At the outset it was supposed to be a case of pocket-picking skilfully carried out by the purchaser himself who, it was supposed, must have removed the book from Cr——'s pocket during the examination of the carriage or during the trial drive and then skilfully slipped or thrown it to a confederate.

But an attentive examination of Cr——'s room gave other results. Under and towards the back of his bed, and in consequence invisible even to a person at some distance from the bed, a nearly square hole of fairly large size, having a diameter of about 16 ins., had been made in the floor. Following the process above indicated, a large number of little holes had been bored beside one another and then joined up with a knife, so that two floor boards were each found to be cut in two places rendering their removal perfectly easy. The floor consisted of parallel beams about one yard distant from one another upon which were fixed strong planks which formed the floor of the room as well as the ceiling of the basement (Fig. 85 represents the ceiling seen from below). Underneath was a cellar used for storing vegetables which some unknown woman had hired, under a false name, about two weeks before the theft

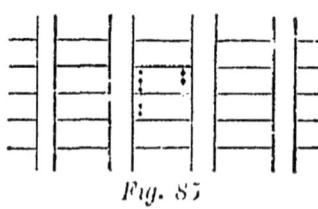

Fig. 85

and where she had deposited some vegetables of practically no value. The thief must have hidden on several occasions in the cellar, which was all the more easy as there were never many people in the courtyard, and then during the daytime when he heard C⸺ go out, have started making the holes; he doubtless worked noiselessly and cautiously, for the room next to C⸺'s was occupied by a tailor who was at home all day. When the hole was made the thief slipped one evening under C⸺'s bed knowing him to be sound asleep and took hold of his coat and changed the bank book in the pocket for another one, the false book was to serve to tranquillise C⸺ in case he looked to see whether his treasure was still in the pocket of his coat; as regards this point the thief's speculations were correct. He had then withdrawn in the same way, and had taken the precaution of rendering the perforated place as difficult as possible to recognise; he had indeed placed a screw in the lower part of each piece of wood, the screw carrying a large fixed ring serving as a handle to open or shut the trap; and before replacing the two pieces of wood after having committed the theft, he had smeared their edges with wet clay which on being pressed, when the section was replaced, squeezed out and hid the cut surface. The thief hoped in this way that if by chance they looked under the bed—where it was fairly dark—the clay would be taken for dust and the manner in which the theft had been carried out would not be discovered. The lower part of the section was also easy to hide for there it was only necessary to pass the finger over the clay which was squeezed out in order to make believe that there was only a dirt stain there.

As the description of the woman who had hired the cellar was known, as well as that of the self-styled purchaser of the carriage, the thief was discovered and in the end confessed to having committed the crime in the circumstances indicated. What is still more interesting as regards this theft from a psychological point of view is that the thief pretended that he had buried the money, on several occasions he was on the point of indicating the place where it was buried, but yet never did so; he died in prison and this large sum of money (16,900 florins) was probably lost in the ground.

(b) Attacking the lock

Ever since locks have existed people have attempted to open them either by force or by using false keys, and as the locksmith's art has progressed so has that of housebreakers made corresponding progress—when necessary these gentlemen can rank as artists.

But if the locksmith's skill is such that it can only be attained as regards its highest flight by but a few even among themselves, e.g., as regards the manufacture of safes, the thief has to replace the professional skill which is not in his possession with craft and cunning. Let us take an example, when a safe, guaranteed fire and burglar proof, is sold, three similar keys are handed to the purchaser, the first he himself carries, the second is enclosed in the safe itself, whereas the third is intrusted to an intimate friend or confidential servant, but it is certainly not the manufacturer himself who makes these three keys but one of his workmen, and, whatever confidence we have in the latter, we cannot help supposing that there may be a dishonest one among them, what hinders him from making a fourth key like the others and keeping it for himself? And when he is in possession of a certain number of these keys it will not be difficult for him to find out, from packers and servants employed in the factory, to whom these safes have been sold and whither they have been sent and, when he knows who are the purchasers of the safes of which he has keys in reserve, he will only have to obtain access to the house, as a servant if possible, or as a workman upon some job, such as a chimney-sweep, water-pipe man, gasman etc., or if he does not succeed in entering the house in this way, he goes courting the cook or the nurse in short, he will be able to get at the safe "guaranteed against burglary," and will know how to make use of his key to open it. We therefore advise that two safes be bought from different manufacturers, a small and a large one and that they be placed one inside the other, in which case a fourth key will be useless.

But as often is not it is by strength and skill that the lock is forced. Let us first deal with padlocks, false keys are used much more rarely for padlocks than for fixed locks or locks screwed into doors, for force can be much more easily used with a padlock. In this case the thief has only to profit by the unheard-of thoughtlessness of most people. It may often be noticed that the peak or peg ($a\ b$ in Fig. 86) is simply let into the wood without the two parts of the end at b being stretched away from one another or twisted round, it is ridiculous to attach to such a peg a heavy padlock which serves for hardly anything else than to allow a thief to get a good hold of the peg and pull it out. It often happens also that the hasp c of the padlock is strong and massive and cannot be worked with a file, while the ring a of the peg is so weak that the thief need not even have recourse to a file but can cut it in two with pincers but if the peg is well fixed, if the stems are stretched apart and bent round, and if the iron of which it is made is strong, the thief tries to wrench the padlock off, and now the desires of the thief seem to have been foreseen, especially in the case of the padlocks called "American," which are quite round and have a very high hasp. The work and manufacture of these padlocks are doubtless excellent, for the tumblers of the locks are made by a permutation machine and it rarely happens that two keys are exactly alike, but these padlocks have the inconvenience of possessing an exceedingly long hasp, so that between the ring of the peg and the lock itself, that is to say, the inside of the hasp c, there is a large empty space into which it is easy to insert a bar of iron, it is then only necessary to twist the bar of iron and the padlock is broken. While on the subject we may also draw attention to another weak point in these padlocks they are composed of two cylindrical capsules, one being set into the other, and it is in the space inside that the lock system is situated. But the capsules are frequently not riveted but simply joined at the edges, which are made to overlap one another. In such a case it is sufficient to knock all round the edges with a piece of wood, until the capsules become detached from one another. This done, the mechanism is

Fig. 86

disclosed and the lock easily opened. In all cases the method employed should be well noted, for it will generally betray the kind of thief and the way in which he works, and will tell us whether or not he was well informed.

As regards locks fixed or screwed into wood much cannot be said. We all know how the ordinary lock of a door or almirah is constructed, and even if some of us did not know it, the sketch and the description which might be given would not be of very much assistance. The Investigating Officer who is ignorant of the construction of a lock is advised to get the first locksmith he comes across to minutely explain the working of a lock taken to pieces, for without some such knowledge he will find himself, at his first burglary, in much embarrassment and will meet with insurmountable difficulties. The locksmith will also be able to show and explain to him the various false keys and skeleton keys. *Fig. 87* shows a complete set of the different sorts of pick-locks, skeleton keys, etc., that are usually found in the possession of a versatile burglar. For ordinary use he finds the tools shown in the drawing all he requires. But in practice the Investigating Officer must never forget that the fact that a thief has not a complete set of skeleton keys does not prove that he is not a housebreaker and has not been in the habit of forcing doors.

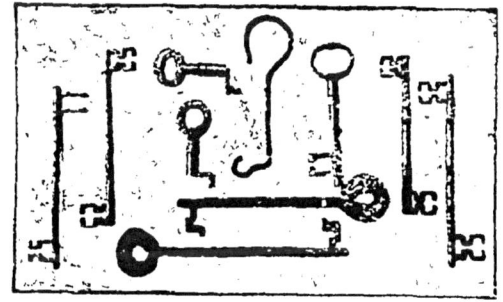

Fig. 87.

Indeed the skilful and experienced thief, whom outsiders never represent without a bunch of false keys, is content with much simpler means, a bent nail, a piece of iron wire, and a knife; the heads of the profession even pretend to be able to open strong locks with a piece of wood and a length of thread. When a thief wishes to obtain the highest regard of one of his comrades he says ' he can open locks by blowing on them,' that is to say, with the simplest of means and in an extraordinarily short space of time (*Ave-Lallemant*). On the other hand, it must be confessed that a bunch of false keys and implements of a fine and delicate nature are often found in the home of a professional criminal; one set was as ingenious as elegant, it seemed no imaginable case had been unforeseen; the instruments were of the finest steel, the handles were of copper and of the most delicate workmanship, the screws were microscopic, and the whole was enclosed in a velvet case.

Something similar is shown in *Fig. 88*, which displays the working tools of a notorious London burglar. Such bags are commonly used by these people, for lawyers, doctors, and others carry similar ones, so that their possession is by no means remarkable. Two things remain to be pointed out. If the thief succeeds in getting near the lock to be opened, he makes first a wax copy of the key-hole, then buys in the first ironmonger's shop a common, suitable rough key of malleable iron, and files it until it fits the key-hole. Then the key is blackened with soot, carefully introduced into the lock, and lightly turned, so that the compartments of the lock are impressed on the sooted key-bits. Then the final act is rapidly accomplished. When however, the question is whether a lock shall be opened with a master-key, then a man gains admission and examines the inside of the lock. This is covered with a dark layer of rust, thick oil, and dust, which are wanting only where the keys rub against the wards. When a master-key has been used traces of it are almost always found, bright fresh scratches and cracks, which do not occur when the ordinary key is used.

As for modern locks, which are often of fine construction, such as those of Chubb, Bramah, Newell, Ade, Hobbs, Fenby, Wertheim, Yale, Kromer-Schlosser, and all other locks of such kind, their mechanism is so complicated and so difficult to understand that it is useless to give a description

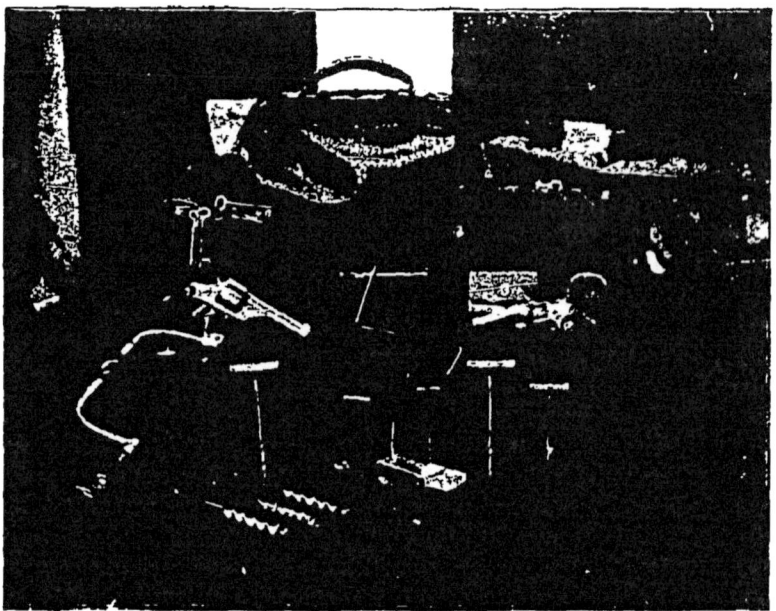

Fig. 88

of them, inasmuch as outsiders will be obliged in spite of all to call in the assistance of experts when necessary, for without them he will be incapable of obtaining any results whatever. What the executioner of London said in his memoirs should be remembered — 'There is not a single lock in the world which cannot be easily opened, but the more complicated a lock is the greater is the mystification'. And indeed it is very true that to open a complicated lock it is not always necessary to make use of very complicated instruments. It is asserted that the best of locks may be opened with a certain number of needles skilfully disposed and even by the vigorous jet from the nozzle of a pipe placed to the key-hole. The most approved method is to introduce into the key-hole fine moist thread, by means of a piece of wire until it is nearly filled up, and all the tumblers are covered. Then a piece of wood in the shape of a chisel is pressed on the thread and the tumblers are pushed back. If this does not succeed, the thread is pulled out, and the same manipulation is tried a second or even a tenth time.

In many cases the thief does not attack the lock itself but some other part of the safe. If the bottom of the safe be screwed to the floor and the top jut out a little, this is a help to the thief; he takes his jack, places it against the top, works the screw, and the safe rarely resists. At times it also happens that the manufacturers of safes are absolutely wanting in conscience. The following fact, which comes from a reliable source, is a proof of this. The owner of a safe, guaranteed against burglary, had mislaid his keys; he sent for a skilled locksmith. The latter did not take the trouble even to look at the locks but started to carefully scrape the varnish at the edge of the back of the safe; he soon brought to light a number of screws, which he took out, and then pulled out the back; the heads of the screws were only smeared over with some substance and then covered with varnish. But it is not always so easy to open a safe and, when necessary, burglars are equipped with the most perfect outfit.

Lately, the public press took considerable interest in implements used in breaking open safes on the occasion of an exhibition of these instruments organised by the Polytechnic Society of Berlin, and connected with a conference concerning electric apparatus designed to protect property. In one of the reports of this exhibition it was stated that a burglar who wishes to make a serious attack upon a safe guaranteed against fire and burglary ought not only to possess great bodily strength and technical skill but must also be in a certain sense, a "man of considerable capital" for the instruments which he requires must be of careful workmanship and represent in consequence a fairly considerable capital. The days when the thief used to pierce a hole with an ordinary centrebit and then make it larger with a cutter are gone. Nowadays housebreakers' implements take up little room and can be easily carried in a small handbag. The most important instrument is a folding lever, with which considerable force may be applied. But in the meantime the manufacture of safes has not remained stationary. In the first place, it was necessary to construct safes offering no hold to pincers or grapnels, hence they are cast in one single piece of metal; it was then attempted to make them proof against gimlet and file by using plates of steel, but as steel is not very elastic a blow of a hammer is sufficient to break it; so then manufacturers combined plates of steel with plates of ordinary iron in order to render such blows harmless, but thieves in their turn made corresponding progress. The skilled thief is furnished with an oxyhydrogen gas lamp with which in from 10 to 15 minutes he can pierce a hole large enough to allow the passage of his whole body; it is true that heavy safes offer considerably more resistance and necessitate several hours' work. Be that as it may, the necessity having been recognised of finding other measures of safety, recourse has been had to electricity. A Munich manufacturer has made an electric apparatus of safety-bells, upon the principle of the contact of wires; these are enclosed in the safe itself, the wires passing through holes, which unhappily are the most vulnerable points. An engineer named Berg has devised another method; he places his apparatus upon the safe itself and establishes communication with bells installed in the watchman's room. The advantage of this consists in the impossibility, even to a clever electrician, of preventing the apparatus working, for as soon as the slightest movement is given to the safe, so soon as a flame is brought to bear upon the electric wires which encircle it, or as soon as the current is interrupted in any other manner whatsoever, the bells begin to ring and the presence of the thief is betrayed.

American apparatus depend on the mobility of mercury. In the safe is a shell filled with mercury, in which is dipped one wire of an electro-magnetic ringing-apparatus, while the other wire hangs just above the surface of the mercury. If the safe is now touched, pushed, shoved, bored into, or otherwise manipulated, then the level of the mercury alters, the second wire comes in contact with it, and the sounding apparatus becomes immediately active. The wires must be led through the back of the safe direct into the wall and thence carried to the watchman's room. In addition to the actual cutting of alarm wires, an arrangement of levers connected to an ordinary working current gives a sure protection. As soon as the thief alters such an arrangement in any way, destroys the battery, or breaks the conductor the alarm at once starts so that the burglar by the very attempt to render the alarm arrangement ineffective betrays himself.

Fig 89

The principal tool is still the familiar crowbar, and it is true that in many complicated burglaries, especially where the burglars have been frightened away, a crowbar is left behind. A glance at *Fig 89* shows remarkable similarity among crowbars. Hence it is not strange that burglars when alarmed, leave behind the heavy and not easily identified crowbar and take away with them only the small tools.

Besides crowbars, we can distinguish between two different systems of burglary implements. One system is not intended to force the whole safe but only to make a hole large enough to reach inside and withdraw the contents. For this purpose the so-called shutter-cutters are used, the lower one being for small and the upper for large holes (*Fig 90*). First a quite small hole must be made with a drill in the side or back of the safe. If the lower cutter is used, then the middle drill of the trifurcated end is inserted in the hole, the head of the cutter is pressed to the breast, and the handle is

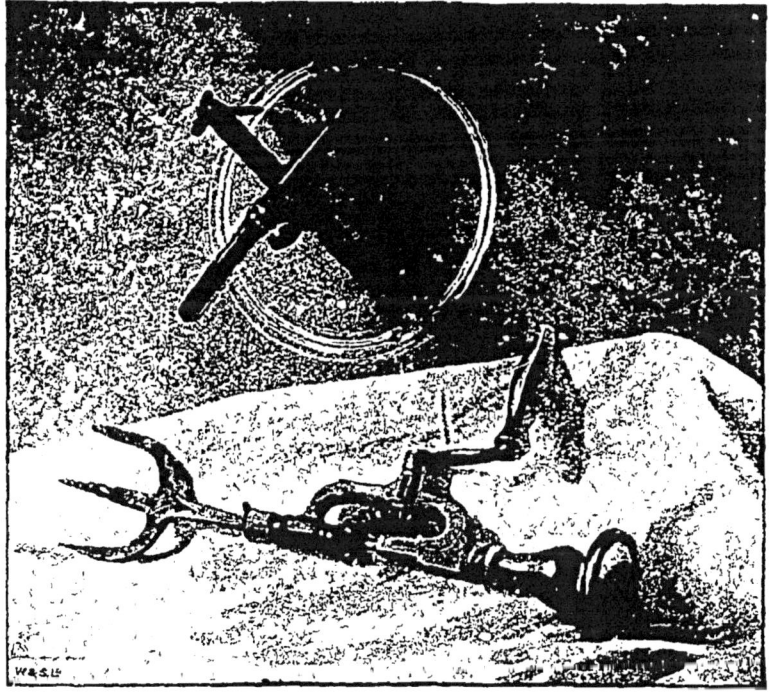

Fig 90

turned with the right hand. The two other prongs of the trifurcated end are sharp chisels that bite further and further into the steel plate and at last cut a circular piece out of it. If the upper cutter is used, the central borer is brought into the drilled bore-hole and the long handle is turned until the two end chisels have cut out a circular piece.

In the second system leverage is used. Here also a small hole is first bored with a drill and this is made larger by the centrebit a in *Fig. 91*, with which the various bits f can also be used. The file c lends a helping hand and projecting edges are removed by the rasp d. When the hole is sufficiently large, the implement b with its steel jaws is brought into use to

308   THEFT

seize and bend the edge of the plate at the hole. The length of this implement ensures an almost irresistible leverage, and thus it is easy to rip open

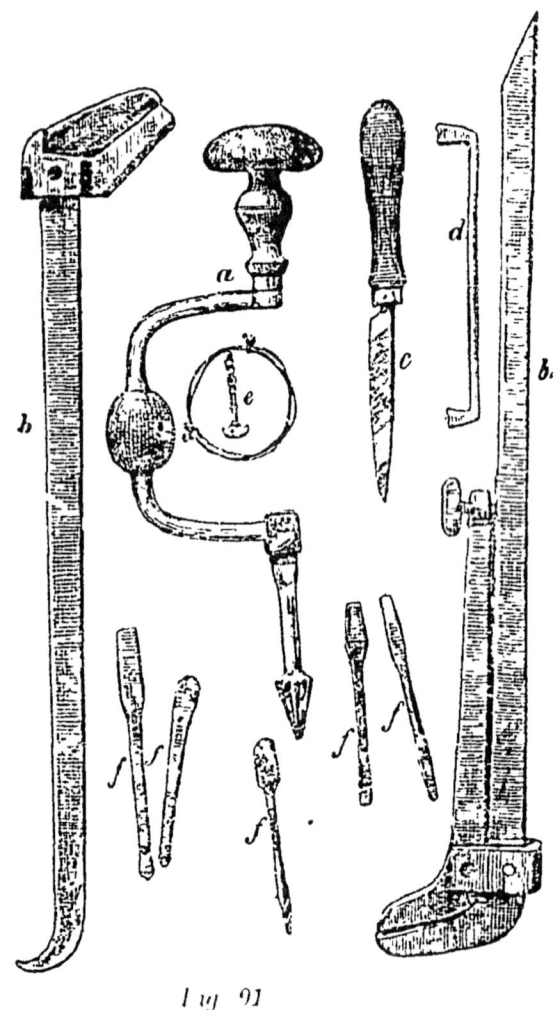

Fig. 91

the whole side of a steel safe. Fig. 92 shows the result of such work for
which a burglar in Hamburg had no more than one hour. An experienced
burglar once said: "Never mind how secure the lock may be, a safe can be
opened like a sardine tin."*

Safes have recently been constructed of 30 mm. plates of which the
steel is so treated by a special process that the outside is as brittle as glass
and the inside as tough as iron. The outside cannot be bored and the inside
cannot be destroyed by blows. Naturally even such plates cannot withstand
explosives.

---

* The above description shows the danger of the keyhole, consequently the modern
technique of safes turns on making keyholes smaller and more secure.

Fig 92

1. ENTERING IN OTHER WAYS

Cases in which the thief enters neither by the door, nor by the window nor by a hole made in the door or the floor, but on the other hand through the roof, as by descending the attic ladder or climbing down the water-pipe leading from the cisterns, are it is true somewhat rare though without being so rare as is supposed. We lay stress upon this way of getting into a house, for, if the thief is a little skilful he leaves no trace of his passage, no one paying attention to an attic or watercloset or bathroom door found open in the morning, and besides the recognition of this method is important, as serving to explain a theft which for want of other indications may be laid to the account of the unfortunate domestics. Of the many false accusations concerning thefts the greater number are laid against servants we have all known many cases where articles asserted to have been taken by servants have been found again or stolen by other persons. This is a fact which is easily explained; an article of value disappears, the servant knows the place where it usually is, he has not been long in service in the house, and it is not known what confidence may be placed in him; besides, the mind of the victim of the theft cannot understand how any other thief could have got into the room. It must therefore be the servant who has stolen the article, and, if the Investigating Officer is not more intelligent than the complainant, suspicion will continue to rest upon him or her; hence, if the thief has been clever enough to leave no striking trace of his passage, one can understand without difficulty the regrettable error that may be committed to the prejudice of an innocent person.

If then a theft remains unexplained, in the sense that the way in which the thief has entered the house is unknown, and suspicion falls upon servants of irreproachable conduct, the question must be asked, whether the thief could not have entered by the roof or the water-pipes. In a well-known criminal novel the plot is worked out on the hypothesis that a person who had been a chimney-sweep descended into the house through a large old-fashioned chimney, and got away by the same channel after having committed a big theft. Though told in a novel, the method is not impossible and it is astonishing that it is not met with more frequently. A clever and audacious Madras burglar, now spending the evening of his days in the Andamans, always entered by the top of the house. He operated on the biggest mansions, the ground-floor verandahs and doors of which were always well guarded by armies of peons and watchmen; he always worked single-handed and never carried an implement of any kind. Being a man of great agility, he easily reached the top story, by means of the outside bathroom stairs so common in Madras, rainwater-pipes, parapets, etc. Here, the coolest part, were generally the bedrooms of the Dorai and Mem Sahib, windows all open, jewellery thrown off after a ball and toilet ornaments lying about. These rooms despoiled, he coolly worked his way downstairs, picking up any trifles as he went, until he reached the ground floor, where he opened a door and made off. Any noise at this stage did not matter as the startled servants always rushed *into* the house to catch the thief, who meanwhile was making his way out of the compound as noiselessly as a cat. He was generally detected through his stupid dealing with the booty.

Breaking into houses through the outer walls, though still most common with the mud structures of India, is less seldom resorted to in Europe, probably because walls are more solidly built now than formerly. Much more frequently we find the thief working through walls or ceilings from one house to another, the operating house being an empty one or rented temporarily for the occasion. If a wall has to be broken through, the job is comparatively easy; it is, however, a work of art to break through a ceiling. This is done either from the next house, or from a loft in which the thief has concealed himself. First, a sufficiently large piece, say about 20 in square, of the floor is sawn through the boards, or the boards are cut out, and then, with great care, a hole about the size of a fist is worked between the beams and through this hole the plaster of the ceiling is carefully examined. Then an umbrella is fastened by its handle to a cord, dropped through the whole, and opened with the help of some previously arranged device. The most recent invention, whereby on pressing a small knob in the handle the umbrella opens automatically, is well adapted for this purpose. Then the small hole is slowly enlarged and the falling material is caught in the open umbrella, and so all dangerous noise is avoided. When the opening is large enough, the thief descends with the help of a rope. Most large thefts in banks and jewellers' shops are nowadays executed in this way.

The most detailed accounts of ultimately successful roof and ceiling breaking are those of the *Chevalier de Seingalt* in his historic description of his escape, after eighteen months' confinement from *Les Plombs*, the famous prison of the Doges at Venice. His ingenuity, audacity, and caution have never been excelled by the cleverest modern housebreaker.

B. Pocket-Picking.

To treat fully of pocket-picking would only consist of collecting together a considerable number of anecdotes, given by all biographers of thieves, and extracts from every imaginable newspaper. This would certainly be very good reading but not particularly instructive to the Investigating Officer. Everyone knows the majority of the tricks of these scamps, but to be acquainted with every device of this class of thief is a pretention impossible to realise, for of all the methods employed we know only those which chance, clumsiness, or the confusion of a thief has unveiled to us. Most of these clever thefts remain the secret of the operators themselves, and many more will be invented and carried out in the future. Once a method is known and has been given publicity, the experienced thief employs it no longer, but abandons it to the tiros of his art and thinks out a new one. And there is no doubt that a new one he will find, for the ranks of pickpockets include the most ingenious of men and the most intelligent of criminals. He who possesses neither manual dexterity, agility, presence of mind, keenness of glance, nor knowledge of men, will never make a pickpocket, for all these qualities are necessary in the profession, but if he does possess them, the most astounding acts may be expected from him. The pickpocket who is a past-master of his art makes it a point of honour to show off his skill to his colleagues, the public, and the authorities, and always to give them ' something new,' which we know nothing of to-day and very likely will know nothing of in the future.

When we peruse the exploits of celebrated pickpockets of all ages and all countries, we become convinced that they employ a new trick only a limited number of times and abandon it immediately on its becoming known. No doubt the *general* procedure remains always the same: the thief wears a distinguished and inoffensive appearance, observes his victim attentively, and tries to find out which pocket contains his money—generally by looking through a shop window where his prey is changing a banknote. Then he must seize the right moment, post a confederate in a favourable place, assure himself of having free access to the pocket, and at last draw out the coveted article with the hand, which he *always* transforms into a kind of scissors.

Scissors making," according to Ari-Lallemant, is either to stretch out the whole hand and form the scissors by keeping the first and second fingers together on one side and the third and fourth on the other side as in Fig. 93a, or by stretching out the first and second fingers only and doubling the thumb and the third and fourth back into the palm of the hand, Fig. 93b. The hand is introduced into the pocket, the back of the hand being turned towards the victim and kept away from his body as much as possible in order to avoid any contact therewith. When the ends of the finger forming the blades of the scissors have reached the purse, they are opened so as to bring it between them; the difficult point is to seize the object with the scissors between the first phalanges, for the further the hand is thrust in the more dangerous the operation becomes, owing to the progressive enlargement of the hand. Yet the article must not be withdrawn too soon for the purse may escape from the ends of the fingers, the operation come to grief, and the theft be discovered. It is the last stage that requires the most practice, but it enables the thief to seize a heavy purse with his fingertips as firmly as we can hold a piece of paper. It is for this reason that an old pickpocket advises a youngster to go in for pocket-picking only if he has long and tapering hands, and principally if the first and middle fingers are nearly of the same length, for then the extremities of these two fingers, having a delicate touch and being protected by the nails, may be brought into contact with one another without it being necessary to bend the middle finger. At least this is what a Budapest pickpocket once told the author, and he also asserted that an individual who did not possess these qualities could never become a "first class pickpocket," his hands must be like those of "an accoucheur or a pianist," he must always keep them in good condition, preserve them from rough work, and constantly rub them with fat, glycerine, vaseline, lanoline or other grease. It is therefore recommended that the hands of an accused pickpocket be inspected—especially when the theft has been carried out with unusual skill, it will nearly always be noticed that these gentry—like cardsharpers (see Chapter XLIII.)—have extraordinarily fine, straight, and delicate hands and very long fingers. The other qualities of a pickpocket mentioned above should also be attended to; he is nearly always distinguishable by his free demeanour, nimbleness, and keenness of glance—unless indeed he pretends to look foolish and awkward. Moreover on the streets a pickpocket is noticeable from frequently carrying a plaid to hide his arm and hand at work.

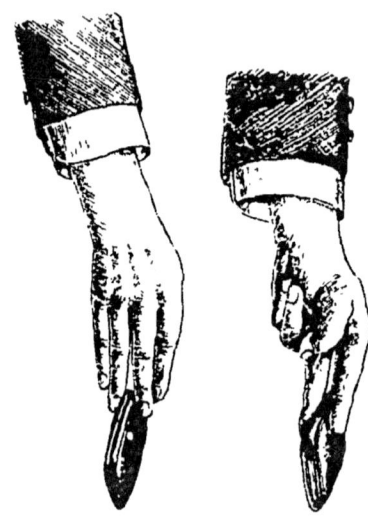

Fig. 93a.   Fig. 93b.

For subsequent investigations the Investigating Officer will do well to deal with everything that accompanies a case of pocket-picking; such as an cut pockets, look for little knives in a signet ring or bracelet, cut watch-chains, small but strong pincers, hidden in a pocket-knife, false hands placed on the knee, which the thief manipulates with his real hand, or artificial mosquito stings which incite the victim to hunt the mosquito or other insect while the thief carries out his work. An individual is also worthy of suspicion if he acts awkwardly in taking a light from another person, or if he bumps against him, or brushes him down, or draws his attention to something or other, or has recourse to similar artifices. But all this will not go for much if the Investigating Officer imagines that this kind of manoeuvre necessarily accompanies every case of pocket-picking. The best thing for him to do is first to consider everything, however unbelievable, as possible, to have the facts related in every detail and without tiring, including all that has preceded and followed the occurrence, and then try to discover the connection of each point of the story—however insignificant it may be—with the theft itself and verify it from that point of view, and finally study minutely the person suspected and try to discover of what he is capable. Here again the relation between the accused and the incriminating facts is of great importance. As to the question of confederates, what we have already said must be remembered, that as a general rule all thieves, from the bazaar pickpocket to the expert railway thief, work with an auxiliary; only the retired thief who is a past master of his art works alone and does not share his profits with another.

The Investigating Officer will find it most useful to get a conjuror to show him the principal tricks of his art, and, in particular, the manner of changing and forcing cards. What the prestidigitator knows so also does the pickpocket, and if we remember the marvellous things the former can do we will the better understand what is within the compass of the latter. The conjuror will be able to teach him the most important point of his art, namely, to know how to seize the psychological moment: he draws the attention of the public to some more or less isolated object, such as a flying bird, a gunshot, a hat confided to another, and during this time he does what he wants to do—and the pickpocket acts in exactly the same manner.

C. Sneak Thefts

The greatest number of articles are probably stolen by sneak thefts. Good preparation, sang-froid, the faculty of seizing the propitious moment are necessary, as well as presence of mind, to allow a good excuse to be found rapidly and naturally in the event of surprise. Among sneak thieves specialists may often be found, who by habit, inclination, or the recollection of the success attending their first theft, invariably operate in the same manner. Thus one individual never stole except from the attics, an occupation he found most lucrative. In all his expeditions he employed the same method; he preferred fine summer afternoons when people are generally out of doors; he would in flats go quietly up the stairs, carrying nothing but a bunch of false keys, and if stopped would ask for someone named X. Otherwise he went right up to the attic door, quickly and skilfully opened it, and putting it on the latch to make believe it was shut would lean his stick against it in the inside, so that if anyone opened the door it would fall and warn him of the danger. He then examined the articles which are often most imprudently kept in the attics, such as linen, winter-clothes in summer, books, plate, etc. He then chose a bag, bags being usually placed in the attics in towns, filled it with the best he could find, and came whistling downstairs as slowly as possible. This is the usual procedure of people who sneak into houses; they pretend to be commissionaires, street porters, cleaners of clothes, message boys, or beggars; sometimes the sneak is a well-dressed gentleman, a foreigner who speaks the language badly, a servant looking for a place, a nurse, a shopgirl, a midwife, or a well-dressed lady; in short he appears under every imaginable guise. They open either the first door they come to or a door explored previously; if they meet anyone, they ask a question suitable to the character they represent; and if they see no one and find something to steal, they steal.

If the thief works hotels he generally obtains some situation of a temporary character in them so as to become acquainted with the habits of the house, take impressions of the keys or become familiar with other difficulties; he then turns up later on, either as a servant with a letter in his hand or as the well-dressed visitor of someone staying in the hotel; passes people he meets quickly or haughtily, opens with his master-key a locked-up room in an empty corridor, and takes everything he can lay his hands on. If he comes in the morning while the traveller is still asleep, he pretends to be a commissionaire, clothes cleaner, chiropodist, hairdresser, etc., enters softly and *never forgets to say "good morning" in a low voice* so as to appear harmless if the sleeper wakes up: in this way he reaches the bed-table, takes the watch and purse generally lying there, and goes off as he comes. These two classes of thieves have often caused much misfortune in the sense that the thefts committed by them have frequently been imputed to domestics, for the simple reason that they could be explained in no other way.

Thieves who work in shops hardly ever sneak into any but small shops which at certain times, such as mid-day, are not well watched, the proprietor being in the back-shop getting his dinner. They open the door, if there happens to be one, as quietly as possible, pushing back the bell with a stick, lay hold of the till or in default of something of value from the stock, and disappear as softly as they have come.

Among this class are to be found some with such remarkable skill and audacity that the thefts they commit appear, at first sight, impossible. We may mention some of the acts of a certain criminal to show that the Investigating Officer should never be misled by anything into saying that a thing is "impossible." The person in question was a Jewish sailor who had thrown over his occupation and now roamed about the docks, where he had lived high for a time and then fallen into the lowest depths of misery. One day he undertook a journey on foot from Trieste to Hamburg —to see the world as he said—and was arrested on the way on the charge of having killed a man by suddenly compressing the carotid arteries with his thumbs, thus bringing about unconsciousness and death. This individual, who was named M.W., had the most sinister face the author ever met with in his career. The suspicions against him were not weak but it was impossible to collect sufficient proof to convict him. During the inquiry, two of his fellow-prisoners who thought themselves grown grey in crime, began to find their companion too compromising, denounced M.W. as the author of a series of crimes which they asserted that he had committed in a number of seaports and always by the same method of sneaking into houses

M W related to his companions that he first of all tried to find out when a respectable family was going to pass the evening away from home at a ball reception concert, etc. On the given day he used to sneak into the house before the doors were shut and hide either in the house itself or in some chosen spot in the courtyard, and there await the return of the family and their retirement to bed. M W speculated on the fact that the people of the house, owing to their fatigue, would sleep soundly and would neglect to lock away the jewels they had worn during the evening, which would be left lying about on the tables for the rest of the night. He then started to open the doors of the bedrooms, which are generally closed by turning the key on the inside and leaving it in the lock. Now as skeleton keys cannot be employed while there is a key in the lock, the key must first be removed. To do this he used a small pair of steel tweezers of fine and special shape and construction or tongs like small curling-tongs with grooved steel arms, which he introduced from outside into the key-hole and with which he attempted to fix a very fine steel wire round the end of the key. This done he seized the head of the key with the pincers and turned it until the key-bit came opposite the key-hole. he had then only to push the key towards the inside and, holding it by the wire, let it fall gently to the ground. If he failed to fix the steel wire, he had to push the key out and run the risk of the noise disturbing the people inside.* The door once opened, M W entered in his stocking-soles and, lighted by a small lantern with a dark-red glass, searched all the occupied rooms, he asserted that the red light prevented the sleepers from waking. He was thus able to steal everything of value and he said he always got a rich haul. It almost makes one uncomfortable to think of this thief with his red light gathering up in haste valuables deposited by the people of the house then sleeping beside him and perhaps determined to use violence should one of the sleepers happen to wake up. This story was at first taken for one of those old robber tales with which prisoners try to beguile the time and impose upon one another. But the inquiry brought out that M W had been at least on one occasion convicted for a theft convicted in the very way he had described to his fellow-prisoners. It was impossible to find out the number of thefts for which he had escaped punishment, and it cannot but be thought that these latter must have been imputed to the servants in many cases, for no one could imagine so strange a manner of thieving. It may be presumed that M W detached the steel wire from the key on leaving the flat and replaced the key in the key-hole, so that there remained no other trace of the presence of the thief than the unturned key

---

* Some burglars carry a collection of small cylindrical steel tubes of different calibres. These serve the double purpose of gripping the head of the key to be turned and pushing it outwards when turned.

In hotels provided with verandahs the hotel thief sometimes ties one end of a rope to the verandah of his window and lets himself down to the verandah below. Arriving there he fastens the other end of the rope to the lower verandah and proceeds to burgle the room on that floor. He afterwards re-ascends to his own verandah and unties his end of the rope and lets it fall to the ground. The other end remains tied to the lower verandah and suggests that the room has been burgled from the ground (Goodwin "Sidelights on Criminal Matters" Hutchinson & Co 1923)

—a detail which might very well pass unnoticed in the morning before the discovery of the theft.

D. Thefts in Bazaars and Shops

This subject has been treated to some extent in the section dealing with thieves' accomplices. Little remains to be said. All know how thieves steal from bazaars, and as regards shops, stealing from them is a much more difficult matter than formerly. The essential thing in such cases is to immediately search the house of the suspected person as well as the houses of persons who have recently visited there. This often brings to light regular depots for stolen property, a result often of great value. No doubt it is difficult to find out to whom these goods belong and when the thefts are from grain merchants it is quite impossible. One day when a big bazaar thief was captured, the authorities had the bright idea of holding an exhibition of the recovered property; it was held in the Sessions Court, which happened not to be in use, and a list was published in the papers. Many tradespeople visited the Court and nearly all the stolen property was identified.

E. Domestic Thefts

For many reasons domestic thefts are the most delicate of all thefts. As already stated on several occasions, among numerous false charges the most frequent are, without contradiction, those brought against domestics, and we Investigating Officers must try to make amends for old sins thus committed by others. We do not say that servants do not thieve, and indeed the proceeds of domestic thefts represent quite a fortune if we take into account everything that servants supposed to be "most honest" make away with, such as small sums of money, food, cigars, articles of cutlery, pieces of cloth, and a great number of other trifling articles, but all that does not cause very great prejudice to a master, and it is really impossible to abolish this "ancient custom." Our single aim will be to try and repress these grave thefts to which all obliged to employ servants are exposed.

The denunciation of a theft committed by a servant, and the preliminary investigations of the police are generally of a very summary nature; such and such an object has disappeared, and it is certain from the circumstances of place and time that the theft cannot have been committed by an outsider, the servant has not been very long in her place, she makes a bold denial, her boxes are searched without giving any result, but she has had every opportunity of placing the stolen articles in safety, so she is arrested and placed in the cells. The case seems quite simple, but just because the only property of the poor young girl—her liberty and her honour—is in question, the most rigorous prudence must be used.

As often is not the question is not asked as to whether the article is mislaid or lost, or whether the theft does not belong to those delicate cases where the criminals are no other than the children or wife of the victim; nor is it asked whether or not, after all, the theft could not have been committed by an outsider; and finally the Investigating Officer does not worry to find out whether or not the servant has had up to that time an irreproachable character. Because she has only recently entered into service that is no reason for saying that she must be guilty and, because she does the marketing and runs errands and thus has an opportunity of placing the stolen articles in security, that is in itself no sufficient reason for bringing any charge against her. There is, therefore properly speaking no reason to suspect her and in spite of this her arrest has taken place. And even if there has been some reason for suspicion, let us say the typical reason in such a case, that is to say the discovery in the servant's trunk of the stolen article or some article which does not appear to belong to her, action must not be taken too precipitately, for it only too often happens that other servants slip stolen objects into the trunks of their comrades through vengeance, jealousy, or envy.

In a well-remembered case a nursery-governess of a wealthy family thus threw suspicion on the housemaid. The governess was a young person of innocent and inoffensive demeanour and irreproachable behaviour. But she had a lover whom she suspected all of a sudden of not being indifferent to the charms of the housemaid, in whose room their secret rendezvous used to take place. She therefore stole from her mistress some jewels which she found not put away and hid them in the bottom of the housemaid's trunk, she had then with extreme skill and without any suspicious insistance, awakened the suspicions of her mistress, who at length, searched the servant's trunk and there found the stolen articles. It was not till long afterwards that the truth came out by the merest chance. We may add that this innocent creature when arrested later for theft and slander was found to have syphilis.

The surest method in a domestic theft is, as before, to check as minutely as possible all the circumstances in which it has been committed. The antecedents of the servant must be verified with as much care as the amount of the savings that he possessed on entering into service, his expenses should be controlled step by step, flirting among girls and drinking among men produce here much the same result. The passions are satisfied much more often with stolen money than with money earned with difficulty, and here such expenditure forms in many cases more overwhelming proof than other so-called irrefutable conclusions. A love affair is graver for men servants than for female servants—at least when the latter are not old or ugly and the man is young and handsome, for the lover has to spend money upon his girl and his wages are rarely sufficient. We have already cited the old proverb known among peasantry :—"When the farmhand steals the wheat he buys new slippers for his lass", attention must also be paid in such cases to the "expenditure" of the lass as well as to that of the servant who is accused.

It must also be investigated whether the accused servant supports one or more illegitimate children, a servant's wages hardly suffice for her own expenses, and if she has in addition to pay board and lodging for her offspring the necessity for thieving is, so to speak, thrust upon her. It is a fact proved by experience that a cook who has an illegitimate child unknown to her master, regularly steals the tea and sugar, in rations small, it is true but daily, to help the person who is bringing the child up and keep her quiet while awaiting the arrears of payment. In such a case the times of absence of the servant should always be checked. They take place with astonishing regularity. They are usually for no purpose but to send the stolen articles to their destination. These pickings may be insignificant but end by mounting up to a considerable total. If a servant is suspected of stealing the house linen, the soiled linen must be taken into account. Some ladies have been quite comical when they have assured the author that they had absolutely no idea how their linen could have disappeared; "I counted," says a lady, "the sheets when I gave them to the washerman: he gave me back the same number. I put the same number into the wardrobe. I took therefrom every week the number necessary for the usual changes: the account was always accurate, everything was in the best order, and yet here I am with so many sheets short"; no doubt,—but the soiled linen was counted only when it was given to the wash and the servant had only to steal it from the dirty-clothes basket. Again it is quite incomprehensible how so many mistresses arrange their linen cupboard like a sanctuary and yet consider the soiled linen as it, so to speak, of no value. It is thrown, without counting or watching, into an unlocked box or basket and kept there, often for some time, either in an ante-room or up in the attic, as if it were another thing altogether from the clean linen. The servants profit by this negligence and hardly ever steal any but dirty linen. If the mistress of the house does not keep count and overlooks this point, the Investigation Officer should never forget it.

In such a case it often happens that the Investigating Officer is obliged to check the knowledge of the mistress of the house of the farmer or of the tradesman and to draw his conclusions from the result of these observations. *A servant* only steals when he notices a detective watchfulness or insufficient knowledge which he can *exploit*, and if the Investigating Officer can establish such defects he has found at least the facts which have occasioned the theft or have rendered it possible. If the owner of the horse does not know what food a horse needs to look as he ought and do his work, it is not astonishing if the stable-man steals from his master when he discovers his ignorance, and if the mistress of the house does not worry about the amount of flour necessary for the preparation of the pastry, she must not be astonished if the cook profits by her negligence, but the Investigating Officer ought to know all this and take it into account.

It is not an uncommon device of outside thieves to leave some part of the stolen property hidden in the house to cast suspicion upon the servants. Last year the editor had his watch and purse stolen from his bedside while he slept. Next day the empty purse and wrist-watch case were accidentally discovered under an old screen. In this case it would have been wrong to presume that the theft was committed by some one in the house, for this device of burglars is well established.

F. Thefts through Superstition

In the elucidation of crime the question of motive must never be lost sight of and this rule is peculiarly important in the consideration of thefts through superstition. In the first place it does not do at once to declare a theft from purely superstitious motives to be a crime. No doubt the thief is a big fool but at the same time he may be acting in the utmost good faith, a perfectly honest man. At all events the influence of superstition may be so great as to allow of his offence being considered purely a technical one. A good deal of discrimination is requisite in such cases. The old proverbs, "Stolen bread tastes the best" and "The neighbour's grass makes the cow give the best milk," though acknowledging the dishonesty of the statements contained therein, yet savour a good deal of superstition, and if it could be proved that the bread or the grass was appropriated because of the proverbs, the heinousness of the thefts would most certainly be mitigated. But a great many thefts take place *purely* through superstition and may be looked for in circles where crime does not usually exist. We have pointed out elsewhere that weapons used to commit suicide are often stolen for superstitious reasons, and in Catholic countries many a church has been broken into to obtain some Holy emblem deposited therein. The majority of such thefts, however, are connected with love-charms and the healing of illnesses. All over Germany it is believed that much stolen material is to be found in buildings standing on insecure or dangerous ground. According to *Wuttke* girls carry stolen wood when consulting a fortune-teller.

Warts are driven away with the help of stolen steak or herring (see p. 261). Stolen grass makes a horse strong and healthy. Stolen manure improves the manure from one's own stable when mixed therewith. Bands torn from the sacks in a mill will cure sprains. Many similar superstitions are well known to us, but they are kept secret, so that if in a certain case, no motive whatever can be suggested, we must not lose sight of superstition and pronounce the case inexplicable.

CHAPTER XVIII

CHEATING AND FRAUD.

Section 1.—General Considerations.

If lawyers find a certain difficulty in understanding the nature of fraud because it is by no means easy to fix the exact line of demarcation between civil wrongs and criminal wrongs, the Investigating Officer finds quite as great a difficulty in carrying on his investigations into them, all the more that a great many frauds demand a mass of special technical knowledge. For such knowledge there are frequently no experts and, even when there are, their detailed report is of no good, for to compare the depositions, to understand every side of the question, the Investigating Officer ought to be himself an expert, and to catch at once the signification of every expression if he wishes himself to put new questions. Although the number of different kinds of fraud is very considerable, we can in the following pages deal with only a few of them. On the one hand we cannot enter in detail into all the knowledge necessary to the Investigating Officer to unravel the procedure of frauds. On the other hand we can hardly give any other counsel than this, " Instruct yourself in this branch of human knowledge also." For, if one man has deceived another in the delivery to him of cloth, glass, iron, wood, grain, the Investigating Officer himself ought to know all about matters pertaining to cloth, glass, iron, wood, or grain, and if it is a complicated business concerning a railway, the Stock Exchange, or an inquiry in which special details have to be taken into account, it is the duty of the Investigating Officer conscientiously to instruct himself in these different branches of knowledge. In grouping the various classes of fraud of which we intend to speak, we have started from different points of view and have by preference dealt in the greatest detail with those concerning which little has as yet been published, e.g., the falsification of stamps or seals, and those on which much has been written but in a form not suited to the wants of the Investigating Officer, e.g., frauds in horse dealing. We do little more than mention those classes, the particular study of which presupposes special knowledge previously acquired, and the complete explanation of which can in any particular case be given to the Investigating Officer by his experts, e.g., frauds concerning antiquities and objects of art or again those on which sufficient information can be found in books e.g., tricks with cards, in all other cases we cannot do better, as we have already said, than advise the Investigating Officer to seize every opportunity of instructing himself practically on all such questions. A day will come when he can put to profitable use the knowledge thus acquired.

Section ii.—Falsification of Documents.

A Falsification of documents in general

Falsification of documents presents a wide field of activity for different experts and notably for the Investigating Officer. Many of the documents falsified are false passports, receipts for payments, passes for cattle or forest produce, etc, and, however small the importance of such papers may appear to be, they deserve the closest attention in the interests of public security, for they are such as enable the State to exercise its right of supervision, and which at the same time, afford an opportunity to the Investigating Officer, with the help of the false document, to discover a criminal for whom he has been looking. The most important cases are falsifications of wills, falsifications, partial or complete, of acknowledgments of debts or other documents which are due, not to the bungling hand of the tramp or even of the vulgar professional forger, but to the refined art of the expert. A not uncommon case is to forge in whole an official document which is placed in some public record, either as a new document or in substitution of the genuine one, or the genuine document on the record is altered then application is made for a public copy of the document, the copy, of course represents the false document and may be used for many purposes without exciting suspicion. All such cases demand not only the most minute and continuous study on the part of the Investigating Officer but also the knowledge of a whole series of experts. Recourse must be had to experts in handwriting, to chemists, to paper manufacturers, to botanists, to photographers but the Investigating Officer will be helped most of all by his own energy, his perspicacity, his gift of combination, his patience, and above all, by constantly keeping in mind that " great blunder " (*grosse betise*) which is almost inevitable in the greatest crimes and which the most expert forger rarely fails to commit. The author has seen a most important document which had been manufactured with supreme skill, it was really a work of art,—paper, writing, text, form, everything had been chosen by the hand of a master—and yet, incredible though it be, the forger spoke in the text of his ' late Majesty Francis," although the document was dated two years before the death of that Emperor. The forger, at the time of executing the false document, had been in the habit of hearing talk of the ' late Emperor Francis,' this habit led him to put the word ' late " in the document, and this piece of stupidity led to the discovery of the fraud Wills, in his " Principles of Circumstantial Evidence," relates a similar case. A certain Alexander Humphreys attempted in the High Court of Justiciary, Edinburgh, in the year 1839, to procure large sums of money, relying upon ancient documents. These documents were marvellously counterfeited but it was discovered that one of them, dated December 7, 1639, had been signed by the Chancellor Archbishop Spottiswood, who had died on November 26, 1639. The forger, who had consulted the list of Chancellors only knew that Lord Loudon, the successor of Spottiswood, had not entered on his functions until 1641 and thought that Spottiswood had been Chancellor up to that time, he was ignorant that between the two there had been an exceptional interregnum of two years. In an important letter which was the basis of a big suit, the date 18-12-1881 had been altered into 18-11-1881; the forger had overlooked, however, that in the document the 31st of the month was referred to, which was in keeping with December but not with November.

A common blunder of this kind is when misspellings are found in the document which would not be likely to be made by the executant. A celebrated example of this occurred in America during the Presidential campaign of 1880, in which a letter was published advocating the importation of Chinese cheap labour and purporting to be written by Mr Garfield, who was subsequently elected President. Apart from certain peculiarities in the handwriting the letter was at once detected and denounced as a forgery through three instances of bad spelling which General Garfield could never have committed; the words were "economy," "companys," "ohgeously."

What we have stated shows how important it is to examine from every point of view the text of a suspected document, for the inconsistencies, the tricks of style, the anachronisms, the transposition of persons and events constitute of themselves certain proofs. We may here recall certain forgeries and their discovery, which will not of course occur under the same form to the Investigating Officer, but which, apart from their general interest, will show what trifles must be taken into account and what methods should be employed *mutatis mutandis*, in modern cases. One of the most scientifically interesting forgeries was that by Wenzel Hanka, without any lucrative object, of the manuscript known by the name of *Koemgmhofer Handschrift*. He had manufactured with infinite trouble and undoubted ability poems in the old Bohemian Slav tongue, with the intention of endowing his country with a poetical treasure similar to that of other ancient nations. These Slav poems were so successful that for many years they struck the whole world with astonishment and admiration and even gave to Goethe the first idea of one of his songs, and yet all these poems are to-day recognised as forgeries. The colour employed in the design of one of the initial letters of the text could not resist minute criticism of the exterior form of the document, for the chemist found in the letters supposed to be drawn about the year 1300 *prussian blue* which was discovered only at the commencement of the eighteenth century by Diesbach. This discovery was confirmed by the results of a critical examination of the matter, which showed that the linguistic form, the notions of law and other conceptions in various branches of knowledge, corresponded to the point of view of the year 1820 and following years—a point of view which even to-day is past and recognised as inexact. But if in the supposed poem of 1300 the linguistic forms, the social references, etc., are represented according to the ideas of 1820, and if it is also proved that the forms and the real social manners of 1300 were very different from what we find in the manuscript, the latter cannot be authentic. For example, in one of the poems there is mention of drums which it has been shown were unknown at that period. Finally, after the death of Hanka all the instruments of fraud were found in his library, not only all the books and treatises calculated to assist him in his work but also innumerable specimens of handwriting, which showed clearly how Hanka had, little by little, prepared himself to write his collection of poems

From this case we may learn

1 How important the help of a chemist frequently is, although he may be the very last person we should think of having recourse to, one is almost tempted to say that our inquiries are frequently rendered successful only by good luck In the preceding case no one certainly had the slightest idea of looking for prussian blue, but it was found by pure chance A student of the History of Art, desiring to know what paints were used in Bohemia in the thirteenth and fourteenth centuries, caused a chemical analysis to be made of all the colours found in the manuscript, and curiously enough discovered prussian blue

2 The results of the criticism of the matter of the document such as were obtained in the *Koeniginhofer Handschrift* can also be obtained in the most modern fabricated documents Just as in that manuscript mention is made of drums which at that time did not exist, so in a false will mention was made of the name and date of birth of an infant who was not in existence at the date of the will

3 The examination of Hanka's library shows how important it is to make in all cases domiciliary searches We neglect too easily the making of new searches once we are in possession of the false document itself, and we lower the value of what remains to be proved by exaggerating the value of that which is already established Too much importance cannot be attached to this point when one has found a valuable piece of evidence one is apt to give it an exaggerated significance and to neglect the collection of other pieces of evidence which later on may be of great value, if the fact which has been established turns out to be of less consequence than was thought The objects found in the library of Hanka were not searched for intentionally *ad hoc*, for it was only by chance that they were found when his goods were sold by auction after his death many controversies would have been spared if they had been looked for at the time, a proceeding always easy in a criminal investigation by domiciliary perquisition

We may mention also the interesting way in which the discovery was made of the falsification of the manuscript of the songs called *Wiener Schlummerlieder*, which in 1859 Feifalik entrusted to the care of Professor Zappert The microscope showed that the spots of grease on the parchment, which were the proofs of its antiquity and consequently of its authenticity, were to be found *under* the writing Another blunder almost comical in its nature was committed by a celebrated forger, the Greek *Simonides*, who did not recognise the nature of an eye hole in the parchment, a blunder which hardly explicable in a cheat of his ability, led to the discovery of the forgery Owing to the great value which parchment possessed in those days, people made use even of the morsels of skin which were incomplete, as, for instance, the skin of the head in which naturally were the holes where the eyes should be Now, Simonides had amongst his parchments a leaf with such a hole in it, which he used like the others, as we have said, he mistook the nature of this hole and wished to pass it off as a subsequent deterioration in the manuscript, so as to give it a greater appearance of authenticity. At the place in question there came the word "inmadverted," there he wrote the first letters of the word before the hole and the last letters after it, so that it looked as if the middle of the word had disappeared through the wearing away of the parchment after the writing. This would have been altogether impossible if the manuscript had been authentic, for it was easy to establish with absolute certainty by means of anatomy and microscopical examination that it was an eye-hole and nothing else. If then it was a hole of this kind it must have existed in the parchment always, and, if the document had been really written at the time indicated, that is to say, if it had been authentic, the writer would have either written round the hole or jumped over it; in any case, he would certainly not have wished people to think that the hole was made later on; the forger alone, who had not recognised the true nature of the hole, could have acted in the manner shown by the document.

An equal piece of stupidity was committed about the year 1830 by a forger, who fabricated a document pretending to date from the fourth century, A.D. The parchment of this document had really been gnawed by mice, making a hole in it. On the first page of the writing the forger recognised the existence of the hole and continued the word on the other side of it, but when he came to the second page he forgot this and left out a part of the word, just as Simonides did. Thus, there had been a hole when he wrote the first page and none when he wrote the second: a good enough proof that the document was false. In a recent case in Southern India a pro-note, put in as having been made, stamped, and dated in 1900, bore a stamp with the King's head which stamp did not, of course, exist in that year. *See* Experts in Handwriting (*see* p. 158).

B. Examination of False Documents

When the scrutiny of the contents of the document gives no result or only insufficient proof, we must have recourse to a critical examination of its exterior form. Most frequently the expert alone is capable of this task, he only knowing the various processes to be employed. But here again it may often be necessary that the Investigating Officer, far away from the help of experts, should rapidly form his own opinion on the matter and come to the conclusion whether there has been a forgery or not. In this case he must either put his own hand to the work or have recourse to experts having no speciality in this direction, such as doctors and apothecaries. In such a predicament the first principle which must be religiously obeyed is to do nothing which could injure, much less destroy, the document; in certain cases it may perhaps be permissible to make experiments on an unimportant corner of the suspected writing, or even to destroy a very small portion; but such experiments should be made only under the most exceptional circumstances and in every case of the kind two precautions must be taken. First, a certified copy of the writing must be taken before anything whatever is changed, and if possible it should be taken by photography. Next, an exact statement must be made in the report of what has been done, so that the expert who will study it later on, as well as every magistrate before whom at a subsequent stage it may come, will know the changes which the document has undergone. The most harmless process, specially recommended in all suspected cases, is to examine the writing with the best magnifying glass available, and this examination should not be directed only to the suspected portion but should extend to the whole document, which will thus be verified by the magnifying glass word for word, when one is thus accustomed to notice with care the non-suspected portions and the general aspect presented by the different types of writing, one is able on coming to the examination of the suspected portion to recognise the least difference, however insignificant, much more easily than if one has begun by an examination of the doubtful passage.

When this examination is concluded, the work is all gone over again, but this time placing the writing over the glass pane of a window, so as to observe by transmitted light what has already been seen by reflected light. A large percentage of forgeries cannot withstand such a scrutiny if the magnifying glass be good and the process be conducted with due care and attention. Of course, if it is a question of the employment of different inks, the magnifying glass will not be enough, resort must be had to the microscope. With a high magnifying power the ink marks which, a moment ago, appeared identical, almost always, when they are made by different inks, present striking differences in colour and lustre.

Another examination which cannot in the slightest degree harm the original and at the same time gives admirable results, is by means of photography. Erasures by scraping, washing with *aqua fortis*, the use of different inks, many things which the eye of man cannot perceive more often than not stand out clearly under the photographic test. A comparison between the original and its photographic reproduction often reveals more than the longest and most expensive chemical analysis. Yet in many cases this analysis cannot be avoided.

In another process the document is photographed and a number of prints taken from the negative each on a thin transparent film. These films are laid one upon the other and pressed together so that the sum of the indistinct characters on each forms a copy which may easily be read.

Photographic enlargements may also be employed with considerable success; indeed enlargements to 3600 times have been obtained, no doubt this is somewhat costly but at the same time it is very effective.

If all this does not avail, then the chemist must be brought in. Naturally in many cases he cannot be dispensed with.

For such reasons and also to furnish the Investigating Officer with an idea of what he may expect to get from his experts, we give a summary of what has been written on this subject by *Sonnenschein-Classen* and other experts, information for the most part scattered about in numberless special articles in scientific Reviews and Proceedings.

In the first place, one must be able to distinguish paper of old manufacture on the surface of which is spread a thin layer of animal size, from modern machine-made paper, which is after a fashion sized throughout its whole substance. Pine resin is dissolved in soda and precipitated by alum, the acids of the resin are deposited with the alumina of the alum in a soapy mass; generally burnt starch is added, and the whole mixed with the paper paste. These elements, then, have to be taken into account when we come to test the paper with reagents, as well as other constituents, such as added colouring matter, which for white or blue paper was formerly cobalt or prussian blue, but it is now almost exclusively ultramarine.

It follows that erasures by scraping on paper sized only on the surface remove this coating of size, while on paper sized throughout, they make the surface rough or wrinkled. As it is difficult to write on such a surface, the forger must render it smooth again. This may be done mechanically by polishing the paper with a hard and close-grained substance such as an ivory paper-knife or the thumb nail, or by pouring or spreading on it various substances. For this a solution of gum, of gelatine, of resin in alcohol, of starch or of powdered sandarac, i.e., the resin of the sandarac tree, the old-fashioned 'pounce' of the scriveners, may be used. But all these preparations when applied to the paper can be easily detected by the naked eye, and still more clearly by the magnifying glass, for the portion of the paper which has been polished or to which one of these substances has been applied, always presents a different appearance to the rest of the surface; this is specially visible at the borders between the portions artificially prepared and those remaining untouched.

If the difference cannot be perceived optically, it will generally be sufficient to place one drop of pure water on the suspected portion, and another on that beyond suspicion. If the former portion has really been doctored or tampered with, the drops of water will behave quite differently; the modes in which they will be absorbed or run about will be notably distinct. To make more certain, or if it is desired to know what specific substance has been employed to whitewash the paper, recourse must be had to chemical reagents. Iodine turns animal glue brown and vegetable starch blue, gum arabic is dissolved by water and precipitated by alcohol, the resins in general are dissolved by alcohol, and if a drop of the solution be placed in water, the latter becomes cloudy and milky.

If old traces of ink with an iron base can no longer be distinguished, either by the naked eye or by the magnifying glass, they can occasionally be made to reappear by washing the paper with a solution of tannin. The salt of iron contained in the ink, while remaining invisible, has the property of penetrating more deeply into the paper than the writing itself. In this case, when the ink with an iron base has faded away, we can spread on the paper sulphide of ammonia. This forms a sulphide of iron, and the writing may become legible.

Recently it has been recommended to wash over the erased portions with a 1/10 normal solution of nitrate of silver, and to place them for a short time in the direct sunlight, by means of which the characters come out clearly. Finger-prints may also be brought out in this way. This process should only be performed by experts.

Besides erasure by scraping, a crowd of chemical products are employed to make writing disappear, some of which give excellent results, not only does the original writing disappear but it is often possible even to write on the same place. No doubt each ink must be treated in its own fashion and, if we would know the means employed by the forger to cause the writing to vanish we must follow the same path as he has done. For this purpose we must ascertain the constituents of the ink; that known, no chemist will be at a loss what to do.

The most important chemical products used to obliterate ink marks are:

1. Oxalic acid; this is mixed with a little water, applied with a fine brush, and afterwards washed off.

2. A mixture of equal parts of carbonate of zinc, common salt, and rock alum; this is boiled for half an hour in white wine in a perfectly clean vessel and applied with a fine brush.

3. A mixture of equal parts of saltpetre and sulphuric acid dissolved by heat and applied as before.*

4. Any alkali mixed with finely powdered sulphur; this is enclosed in a small bag of very fine material, and the writing rubbed therewith.

5. A solution of muriate of tin in double its quantity of water, applied with a brush and followed by a washing with pure water.

6. Hypochlorite of soda and chlorine may be employed in the same manner.

All these substances which contain an acid, are dangerous for the forger, they immediately decompose ultramarine and produce a yellow spot. Further it is easy to verify the employment of acids, by touching the place in question with a piece of moist blue litmus paper, which wherever there is a trace of acid, will turn red. If the acid has to all appearance effaced the writing, it can be made to reappear by careful painting with ammonia dissolved in water, it may at times be necessary to apply a solution of tannin immediately after the ammonia. Instead of these a solution of ferrocyanide of potassium may be employed, but this must not be done to any spot on which ammonia has already been spread.

As to different inks the following points may be noted.

Chinese ink is nothing but very fine carbon and is therefore difficult, if not impossible, to remove by means of chemical reagents. But if Chinese ink be not of the first quality the writing or design on the paper may be removed by placing the paper, face downwards, on an empty pot, and directing, as long as may be necessary, a jet of boiling water on the back of the sheet.

Ink made of logwood becomes red under the action of acids, it is difficult to efface, but the processes (2) and (4) above are often efficacious.

Ink made of gallnuts dissolves and disappears under the action of acids diluted in water. This writing can generally be made to reappear,

---

* This mixture, which is frequently recommended destroys, as *Dr Dennstdt* of Hamburg has pointed out not only the ink but also the paper. It should, therefore, when used for ink only, be diluted with water.

more or less vividly by the application of ammonia. Chlorine and hypochlorite of soda causes these two last inks to disappear, and it is then practically impossible to make them reappear.

"Alizarine" ink is composed of a solution of indigo mixed with gallnut ink, which contains ferrous oxide. Under the action of acids dissolved in water, the gallnut ink disappears leaving the blue indigo, which can only be effaced by chlorine or hypochlorite of soda.

Modern aniline inks (usually aniline violet or soluble nigrosine, i.e., coal-tar black) have a special place of their own. Not very fast and easily altered though aniline colours be, yet they can in the case of inks be readily fixed. When fresh they can often be made to vanish by simply washing the writing with water and alcohol, especially if a light hand and blunt pen have been employed. A heavy hand and a sharp-pointed pen cause the ink to penetrate beneath the surface into the body of the paper, whence it is difficult to extract it. Generally after the lapse of some time aniline becomes so firmly fixed that it is difficult to remove.

If the forger has sufficient time at his disposal he has only to expose the document written with aniline ink to the sunlight, which will completely efface the writing. Some years ago an official order written with aniline ink was stuck up on a public notice board exposed to the sun. Soon afterwards the whole order had disappeared and there remained on the paper no trace except the signature of the official, which had been written with a different ink. It must not, therefore, be forgotten that, in a document written with aniline ink, the failure of the chemical test proves nothing, as it is impossible to detect the action of the sun's rays.

The colour, generally violet, of modern rubber stamps is easily effaced by oxalic acid dissolved in water, or by superoxide of hydrogen, the former injures the paper only when used carelessly, the latter never does.

Even when inks identical in composition have been employed, the falsification can in certain cases be chemically demonstrated. This arises from the fact that the older the writing the more it penetrates into the fibres of the paper, and the more insoluble it becomes owing to dryness and the more complete oxidation of the contained iron. Hence greater resistance is offered to the action of the acids dissolved in water than in the case of more recent writing. If then we desire to test whether two specimens of writing on the same paper are of different dates—of course the difference must not be too slight—we must necessarily sacrifice at least one line of each of the two writings. Two are chosen as nearly as possible of equal strength and conveniently close to one another. They are damped with the acid solution, and the time each takes to fade or disappear is observed, watch in hand. If the difference is sufficiently great, the more recent writing will disappear first.

If writing has become illegible through being written over or obliterated and it is desired to reconstitute the original text, the nature of the first ink employed must be determined as well as that of the second used to strike out the original. If the inks are of different compositions, we employ a reagent which attacks the traces of ink attempted to be erased or obliterated, if the same ink has been used in both cases and any time has elapsed between the first writing and the making of the obliterating marks this process is useless. In the latter case we must with extreme care and precaution apply some substance which will remove the top ink and seize the moment when the obliterating mark has, as far as possible, disappeared while the primitive text has been hardly touched. This result is best obtained either by the action of the vapour of the substance employed, or by soaking in it a small piece of cloth which is applied exclusively to the desired spot. In desperate cases, as for instance when the writing has been soaked in ink, the only resource is photography in a particular light and with special precautions. Naturally only specialists of the first rank can successfully carry through this operation, for the difficulties are always great.

The work is proportionately easier when we have to remove an ink writing superimposed on a lead-pencil writing beneath. The characters traced in lead strongly resist chemical action, so that there is little danger of the lead-pencil marks or design being damaged when the ink writing is chemically treated. It is mechanical action which has to be guarded against, for washing with the brush risks the effacement of the pencil marks.

If two writings are superimposed, and it is desired to know which is the older, one must almost always have recourse to the microscope. Sometimes the crossing of the writing is considerable, as when an acceptance and signature are written across a bill of exchange—a very common case; at other times the interference is slight, as when the lines are one above the other and parallel, so that the top and bottom loops only interfere with each other. Thus the tops of the f's and l's may be mixed up with the bottom loops of the y's and g's. The fact is that every ink, on leaving the pen, deposits on the paper a minute mass, which when dry remains on the spot touched in the form of a solid body, and this can be clearly detected under the microscope. If the two lines cross, the microscope shows us the upper and later one lying like a scale upon the lower one, so that it is often thus possible to distinguish between the older and the more recent writing.

Iodine plays an important part in the discovery of written forgeries. G. Bruylants has remarked that dry paper under the action of vapour of iodine comports itself differently from paper that has been damped and redried. The portions which have been damped assume a violet colour, while those that have not been tampered with become yellow or brown.

If the marks of lead pencil be rubbed out with bread crumbs, the portions of paper affected assume, under the action of vapour of iodine, a yellowish-brown or a brownish-violet tinge, in every case, however, of a deeper colour than that of the paper which has not been touched. When the paper is damped the portions effaced stand out sharply defined against the groundwork, which remains pure blue. Portions erased by bread crumbs and treated with iodine have a uniform colour, but those effaced by gum show a tint of a darker colour. Vapour of iodine also discloses marks or depressions made in the paper by means of a blunt object, as a rod of glass, ivory paper cutter, or even the thumb nail—such marks stand out clearly of a stronger colour. By this process we can render visible on the back of the paper pencil-writing which has been effaced, reading it by means of a mirror.

For the examination of inks for legal purposes and especially to determine their nature and the differences between them, *Robertson* and *Hofmann*, the chemists, have prepared a very useful comparative table.

This table will not only facilitate the task of the professional chemist but will enable the Investigating Officer in country districts to undertake, in *urgent cases*, the chemical examination of a document suspected by the medical jurisprudent or pharmacist. But we repeat that such investigation irreparably destroys a portion of the document.

The process is carried out by filling several quill pens with the reagents indicated, making strokes across the letters and numbers to be examined, and observing the changes of colour produced where the ink and the reagent meet.

The chief reagents given by the authors named are:—

1. Solution of 3 per cent. of oxalic acid in water
2. Do. of 10 ,, of citric acid in water
3. Do. of 2 ,, of chloride of potassium in water
4. Solution of one part of chloride of tin with one part of hydrochloric acid in 10 parts of water
5. Solution of 15 per cent. of sulphuric acid
6. Do. of 10 ,, of hydrochloric acid
7. Do. of 20 ,, of nitric acid
8. Saturated solution of anhydrous sulphuric acid in water
9. Solution of 4 per cent. chloride of gold in water
10. Do. of one part of ferrocyanide of potassium with one part of hydrochloric acid in 10 parts of water
11. Solution of one part of thiosulphate of sodium with one part of ammonia and 10 parts of water
12. Solution of 4 per cent. of sodium hydrate in water

With reference to the examination of the exterior form of a document, it is well to commence by observing the nature, the composition, and the exterior appearance of the paper. The chemical constituents and outward form of the paper, its watermark, grease-spots, etc., may often at the very outset reveal the whole nature of the affair. In such a case the paper must be sent to specialists (paper manufacturers, microscopists, or chemists), who should be told all the circumstances and requested to throw any light they can thereon. It is never useless to have recourse to them.

Reagents	Gallnut Ink with Iron	Logwood Ink with Chromate of Potassium	Logwood Ink with Sulphate of Copper	Nigrosine Ink	Vanadium Ink	Resorcin Ink
Oxalic Acid	Disappears	Violet	Orange yellow	No change	Grows pale and smudges slightly	Bright red
Citric Acid	Fades	Do	Do	Dark blue smudges	Fades and smudges	Disappears
Hydrochloric Acid (muriatic)	Disappears but leaves yellow tinge	Purple red	Blood red	Hardly changes	Fades and smudges slightly	Bright rose
Sulphuric Acid	Disappears	Red	Purple red	No change	Fades slightly	Do
Nitric Acid	Do	Do	Do	Smudges slightly	Do	Do
Chloride of Tin	Do	Do	Enschen red	No change	Do	Disappears
Sulphurous Acid	Fades	Grey violet	Red	Do	Fades slightly and smudges	Fades
Chloride of Gold	Fades slightly	Reddish brown	Brown	Do	No change	Brown, smudges
Thiosulphate of Sodium and Ammonia	Dark red	No change	Dark blue	Dark violet smudges	Smudges widely	Brown
Ferrocyanide of Potassium and Hydrochloric Acid	Blue	Red	Tile red	No change	No change	Rose
Hydrate of Sodium	Dark red	Brown	Dark red smudges	Dirty brown, smudges	Dirty brown smudges	No change
Chlorine	Disappears	Disappears	Disappears leaving a yellow tinge	No change	No change	Brown

Section iii.—Counterfeiting Seals, Stamps, and Coins.

A Counterfeiting Employment Stamps

The forgery of seals of all descriptions is so extensive as to deserve special study. Most commonly the seals forged are those of local authorities whose duty it is to attest the certificates given by employers to their workmen and also, for criminal purposes, to imitate the seals and stamps used in public offices and large works such as railways, mines, etc. The author has collected a considerable number of seals and stamps, about one hundred in all, lodged in the Graz Criminal Museum, found on the persons of various criminals at the time of their arrest, and by a comparison of these it is possible to obtain an idea of the way in which they are made and employed. This collection of seals affords more than one useful hint. What strikes one first is the international character of this class of forgery, the stamps although collected in a comparatively small magisterial area, nevertheless bear the names of officials of all countries. It appears even as if the forger prefers the most distant countries, hoping that inquiries made there will be more difficult; for the same object he generally chooses names well known everywhere, so that he can always pretend, if the answer is unfavourable, that the letter has not been sent to the real place bearing the same name. One finds also stamps such as the following, "Muller, Manufacturer of Hardware, St Jean," or " of Newville," etc. Of course these stamps, the manufacture of which requires a great deal of trouble are not intended to be used only once, on the contrary they afford for those who possess them a very considerable income. A tramp who possesses several or even one of these seals and who can write a fairly good hand, gains much more in this way than by simple begging. At the same time he does not neglect, meeting either by agreement or by chance an individual who has not possessed for a long time a certificate of work, true or false, skilfully to draw the conversation to the hardships of life, the want of work, the police, and such disagreeable memories this soon unties the tongue of the other man. When the intimacy has become greater, the tramp tells what he is up to, and soon after his comrade is in possession of a certificate of work, fortified by a seal and a stamp. Of course the giving of this certificate is well paid for, and it is this payment, as well as the danger to which their industry exposes them, that leads the forgers to conceal so carefully their precious stock-in-trade. Generally they hide them in the back or the collar of their coat, in the lining of their boots, or in the hem at the bottom of their trousers. We even find now and then such seals possessing on the edge loops, for the purpose of being sewn on.

Nothing is more easy than to procure ink for the stamps, very thick black ink, carriage grease, boot polish, or even the real colour of the stamp in the shape of aniline violet, coal tar, tannin, black, diluted in glycerine and water, may all be used. The tramp with the real stamp colour in his possession invariably conceals it in a small boot polish tin, of which the label is carefully preserved so as to prevent suspicion; we have often been surprised to find in the collection of curiosities of a tramp whose boots, red with age, could not have been blacked for months, a box bearing the inscription "real brilliant boot polish, free from oil of vitriol." If one had only looked a little closer, the boot polish would have been found to be nothing else but stamp ink, and one or more cleverly constructed seals would have been found on his person.

When it is remembered that the author's collection of seals and stamps is but of recent date, that the district whence it has been collected is very restricted, and that in spite of all about one hundred have been obtained, one can form some idea of the vast number of false seals in circulation and the still greater number of false certificates, for with each seal several certificates can be manufactured which daily pass through the hands of the public, and, to credulous eyes, appear authentic documents. A sentiment of shame, however disagreeable, ought to overwhelm us at the thought of the epithets these vagabonds must in their inmost thoughts bestow on us when we return them their books "found in order," when there is not perhaps a single authentic attestation in the whole of them. Such a state of things should by every means be put a stop to, for the danger is certainly greater than is generally supposed.

False certificates and stamps or seals are the great support of that cancer of society, vagabonds and tramps, for nothing helps them more than being able to obtain, with ease and safety, proof that they are really working men. The true tramp, who becomes so only from his hatred of work and love of idleness, remains a tramp pure and simple, only until necessity compels him to be a criminal, and thus everything that helps the manufacture of tramps goes to make a true school for criminals. Besides, false certificates do not only help the wayfarer in escaping the penalties of being a tramp or vagabond, but assist him directly in the commission of crime. They help—and have helped only too often—to obtain a man a situation which he applies for only with the object of committing some crime, and which is given him on the strength of "characters" testifying that he has previously occupied a similar position and has "given satisfaction."

Further, false certificates are useful, and perhaps most frequently employed, to prove an *alibi* for the person in whose possession they are found. When a *bonâ fide* criminal has committed a crime and has succeeded for a time in escaping from the researches of the local police, his first business is to procure a workman's certificate covering the dangerous period, which naturally names localities far enough away from the scene of the crime. If he is arrested on suspicion, he boldly presents his certificates, and many Magistrates are foolish enough to accept them as gospel. As for the Investigating Officer, his duty is to subject the documents to rigorous examination, and whenever his suspicions are aroused, to make inquiries of the establishment or household where the individual is supposed to have worked, no matter how long it may be necessary to keep the latter under remand.

Suspicion is always based on strong grounds. The first and most important is that we have to deal with a true tramp, incapable of deserving a certificate testifying that he is a "faithful, hardworking, and honest workman." Now one can always recognise a *tramp*, when one has had under observation a considerable number of genuine specimens, paying special attention to their appearance and behaviour. The way they present themselves, their gait, their external aspect, *their hands showing no traces of hand work*, all the indescribable but characteristic atmosphere that envelopes the brotherhood, give them a demeanour so precise and so striking that it is impossible to confound the true tramp with the poor devil who, owing to bad times, has been really long out of work. Once suspicion has become certainty and one is convinced that a real vagabond is caught, the first thing is to search him to see if perchance he has any stamps or seals concealed on his person, and next to make inquiries at all the places mentioned in his character-books so as to verify the authenticity of his certificates.

Suspicion also attaches to certificates in which the employments are very dissimilar and the places at which the work has been done are far apart. This means that the vagabond cannot choose a certificate for any particular work or at any particular place; he has to be content with what the forger who helps him is able to supply him with, i.e., with what is engraved on the seal possessed by that person; it results that the same individual appears to have worked " most satisfactorily " in January as a butcher in the north, in February as a miner 100 miles away in the south, in March as a post maker in some other place and in April he is back again in the north employed as an iron worker. It doubtless often happens that a workman is obliged, especially in hard times, to work at a number of different trades which are, so to speak, strange to him, but yet there is a certain co-relation between these various trades, and moreover it is indispensable that the places where the pretended workman has stayed have a sort of connection with one another and, when considered connectedly, form an itinerary in some shape or other.

The simplest means of laying bare this fraud is to make a list of all the places mentioned, with the time the workman says he was at each, and then to trace out his movements on the map; this route will generally be only a series of detours and zig-zags. The man is then made to relate the whole of his journey by heart. If he has really made it, he is able to relate it; if he has not done so, he is never able to do so; this we can affirm from long experience. This method requires but about half-an-hour's work, gives absolutely no trouble, and often brings the vagabond to confess, when he sees that the matter is going to be gone into seriously, and that he is likely to be kept in custody a considerable time while a correspondence is carried on, which in the end is bound to bring about his conviction.

The fact that the seal is badly or defectively made or even mistakes in lettering (such as a letter being turned the wrong way, e.g., Ν for N, or Ƨ for S) is not sufficient proof of falsification, for many false seals are much better made than the seals of many provincial municipalities. A seal is always awkward when there is only the name of a small municipality without other precise designation. A distinction must here be drawn. When the Mayor of Little Pedlington orders a new municipal seal, he does not order the engraver to add the name of the county, for he supposes that everybody knows Little Pedlington. So if a municipal seal of a town with a rare name contains nothing else but that name, that is no reason for suspecting its authenticity. It is different, however, if the name of the place is a common one. The Mayor of Newport is well aware of the trouble caused by the confusion in the post and otherwise of his Newport with other Newports, and he knows that the higher authorities require a more particular description of his Newport. When therefore, he has a new seal engraved, he takes care to add thereto, if not the name of the kingdom or country, at least some characteristic designation as, *e. g.*, "Newport, Monmouthshire," or "Newport, Isle of Wight," etc. Such a seal may be considered a genuine one, but it may be considered counterfeit when it has only the word "Newport," —the more so if the owner of the certificate does not know which Newport.

The falsification of a certificate is recognisable as well by the writing as by the spelling. It often happens that the signature of the employer is in the same handwriting as that of the legislation of the authorities, or that one of them being forged arouses suspicion. Nothing is commoner than for a master-workman who countersigns a certificate as the Mayor of the Town to write with a heavy hand and make mistakes in spelling, but it would be very suspicious if the chief clerk of a big business or an important municipality signed in such a manner. Spelling mistakes are especially common in forged certificates of large establishments, probably because their stamps have the preference owing to their "pompous" and for that reason more convincing aspect. If therefore we find that a stamp about as long as one's finger which reads, *e. a.*, "Office of the Secretary to the Amalgamated Societies of Calico Printers of Great Britain and Ireland," is placed below a badly-written and badly-spelt certificate signed by the "General Manager" and countersigned by the "Joint Cashier," the whole document is false, however well the stamp may be counterfeited.

The immediate detection of false employment certificates is greatly facilitated by what are called "Beggar-stamps," in use in many places and affixed to the last page of the character-books of people who have received help on their journey. These stamps usually carry an arrangement for changing the date and, as a rule, are made of rubber. They are very cheap and have ordinarily a date and inscription as follows:—"Assisted at X the 19 ." These character-books have as a rule, many such impressions and when the owner forges a certificate of having worked for a certain time at a certain place it often happens that there is a stamp under the same date in his book. The consequence is that he was working at X at the very same time he was begging at Y. It is a fact within the experience of the author that the falsity of a certificate has on several occasions been detected in this way.

If we consider for a moment the fabrication of false seals, we will find that they constitute from all points of view an extremely varied series. As regards their origin we find them in all Continental countries and we often find seals of other countries in our own. In Germany, for instance French and Russian seals are common, the latter probably are preferred because few persons are capable of reading the Russian characters and those who can are unable, as a rule, to find out the names of the authorities to be written to. But the largest number of seals are, as we have already stated, without mention of a country, the counterfeiter having been careful to omit any description capable of determining the situation of the place in question. As regards the authorities from whom the seals emanate they are naturally those whose business it is to give certificates of work, such as Municipalities, the Police Department, Sheriffs Offices, Collectors' Offices, etc. It is only exceptionally that we find the seals of Law Courts which are, as a rule, placed on certificates attesting that an individual has been employed in a

Court, as Copying Clerk, Peon or in some other such capacity. Besides these official seals must be mentioned the stamps of various associations, trusts, and other big concerns such as factories, mines, foundries, agricultural associations, companies, etc.

The materials of which the type or letterpress of false seals are made are also very diverse. Those least often found are metals, from which it may be supposed that forgers are rarely engravers by trade, for the latter would find no difficulty in fashioning the metal; we find on the contrary that the counterfeiters avoid metals as much as possible. Relatively speaking, lead is the most frequently employed, care being taken to add thereto a certain quantity of zinc or tin to render it more durable. Wood is commoner than metal, in particular lime-wood, ivy wood, box-wood, and sometimes also lighter woods which are easier to cut; but the material most frequently employed is steatite (french chalk such as used by tailors) which on account of its softness is easily cut. Forgers may doubtless object to it on account of its great friability, for strong pressure easily breaks the letters. A material largely employed for making false seals is common slate. Its frequent employment in the construction of school slates and in the roofing of houses places it at everyone's disposal, and its consistency, though soft enough to enable it to be worked with ease, is at the same time sufficiently hard to prevent the letters being spoiled by strong pressure. The grain of the stone is uniform and faultless, a very important factor. The portion on which the seals are engraved may be made very thin, thus enabling large numbers of them to be conveniently hidden away. The manner of their manufacture is extremely primitive, at least when the work is done by people who are self-taught in the art of engraving.

The author has in his collection two seals cut in slate which were seized in an unfinished condition upon two tramps, from which it is easy to see, especially with the aid of a magnifying glass, how the forger has set to work. These can be examined with greater ease, for in each case the engraving tool used was also found upon the person of the tramp. This tool consists of an ordinary sewing needle, the eye of which is embedded in the longitudinal section of a small piece of wood about the size of a pencil, which forms the handle of the instrument. The examination of other false seals seems to indicate that it is always this instrument which is used by seal forgers, for it is easy to determine that the sunk portions of all the plaques are scraped with a needle. The way in which these seals are made appears to be as follows:—the necessary divisions, such as those base lines which are curved in shape, are first of all traced with the compasses, which besides the engraving tool is the only instrument employed, then the isolated letters, ornamentations, figures, etc., are drawn in and little by little the whole of the space between the letters, etc., is scraped out. The needle no doubt detaches but very small particles of stone at a time, but then there is no fear that such a delicate instrument will detach too large a portion and damage one of the letters. Experiments made by the author have convinced him that, given sufficient patience in learning, this work may be executed rapidly and easily. It is said that prisoners practise it to pass away the time in prison where a needle and piece of slate may easily be introduced.

Nor is it only people moving about on the highway who handle false seals. The daily papers reported a short time ago the case of a rich man, a master butcher in Berlin, who had obtained a duplicate of the stamps of the inspector of butcher's meat, and stamped the goods himself. When one remembers that the examination of every pig in the cattle yard cost a mark, and that the man sold each week on an average 200 pigs to the butchers' shops and the butchers' market—it will be seen that his fraudulent gain, letting only one-half of his pigs be examined, was about 400 marks a month.

It remains to speak of the means by which this dangerous trade can be fought. The best remedy certainly consists in not being too credulous, in having no fear of taking trouble, and in making the most minute investigation on every occasion when the least suspicion arises of the authenticity of a document. Another excellent expedient is to publish every known case of counterfeiting of this description in the papers and police gazettes. As each false seal is used more than once, and as a large number of books contain it, all attestations made with the same seal are of necessity false when a single one of them is false. Once it has been proved, e.g., that the seal of the 'Corporation of X' has been falsified, the papers should be informed of the fact with a description of the false seal. Information such as the following should be sent by the Investigating Officer:—'Fabricated—the seal of the X Corporation, the fabrication is oval shaped 1½ inch long, 1⅜ inch broad, well made.' If the municipality whose name appears on the seal really exists, an impression of the genuine seal should first be obtained and a description of it added to the announcement. In the above case for instance we should add:—'The real seal besides bears such and such an inscription, and is quite round.''

If care be taken to make this publication in every case and if it is sufficiently well circulated, in a short time not only will all the impressions made with this seal be discovered, but opportunities will at the same time be given to unmask a mass of other false seals and stamps. The character-book of a workman containing one manifestly false attestation most often contains several others. An honest workman is ashamed to make use of a false certificate even when perchance he has been for some time out of work; it is the professional vagabond who usually has recourse to such expedients and such a person is never content with a single false attestation. After some time he wants another, so that generally when a false certificate has been discovered in his book one will do well to distrust all the others in it. If verified from the point of view of their genuineness some fresh falsification will probably be found, which, when published, in its turn will seldom fail to bring about further revelations, so that a single discovery will multiply in a sort of geometrical progression. Such disclosures will only produce their proper effect if each case is punished with the severity deserved by such practices, the dangers of which cannot be exaggerated.

The painstaking book of *Franz Hurmann* gives substantial assistance in the identification of false seals, for in it we find alphabetically arranged the facsimiles of a great number of official seals belonging to all sorts of authorities. If we have a suspicion about a seal, we have simply to make a comparison to obtain a rapid proof of genuineness or falseness. Naturally such a book must be always kept up to date, every new seal struck being inserted from time to time.

But the most radical means of preventing such falsifications is outside the sphere of an Investigating Officer and will only be mentioned here to round off the subject. It consists in public offices seeing that their seals and stamps are really good and difficult to imitate. Anyone who has seen a number of seals cannot deny that not only the greater number of the seals of the smaller municipalities but also those of more important bodies are so miserably executed that one would think they have come out of the hands of a botcher. On the other hand the majority of false seals are so well made that they would serve as models for the former. Doubtless the result would be of little value if the authorities are content with the mere order that "all offices should have artistic seals" for the execution of such an order could not be properly checked.

The only reform possible would be for the State to monopolise, so to speak, the production of seals, making them itself and sending them direct to the authorities requiring them. They might then be put upon the same footing as coin with the same penalties for counterfeiting.

Whoever has had an opportunity of seeing a large number of false seals, document stamps, or banknotes, etc., must know that a clever forger finds practically no difficulty in imitating artistically decorated letters with ornamentation and interlacing lines, etc. But there are certain things he is never able to copy, for instance human figures and in particular, the face and hands. This especially applies to banknotes, everything is admirably done with the exception of the faces and hands of the persons or allegorical figures, etc, which are so badly executed that the work of the forger is immediately recognisable. If the seals are made by the State they should contain such figures. The seals should be made as large as possible for there is always room enough on an office table, and if the impression covers part of the writing on a document no harm is done—rather the reverse. The larger the seal the more artistical it may be made and in consequence the more difficult to imitate.

That which under no circumstances ought to be any longer tolerated is the use of the present universal india-rubber stamp or seal which can be used only with aniline colours. If we bring an india-rubber stamp in conjunction with oil colours the india-rubber becomes sticky and smudgy, and is spoilt in a short time, as oil relaxes the india-rubber. The impressions made by such stamps are easily copied. Press a fresh and well-inked stamp upon an elastic, thick, half-damp substance, as, e.g., an apple cut in two, half of a potato, the white of a hard-boiled egg, half-dry glue, etc., one obtains a clean negative copy of the seal, which is particularly good when one has previously damped the substance slightly with spirit. If one now prints the negative copy, from the white of egg, apple, etc, on damped paper, one obtains a faultless reproduction of the true print of the seal, and there is said to be no means of proving its spuriousness. A second and a third copy may be taken, although fainter. How dangerous, however, is this simple yet widely-known means of reproducing seals, need not be pointed out. There remains no alternative but to banish the india-rubber seal from all offices and return to the old brass seal with oil colours.

B. Seals on Letters, etc.

From the time gummed envelopes were introduced letters have seldom been sealed,* and 'black cabinets' have long since ceased to be useful. Notwithstanding, the opening of sealed letters, especially slightly-sealed letters containing money or something of value, has in no way ceased. The capital of the letter thief is consequently considerable, and as a rule he is only detected when the circumstances of the forgery are known and consequently can be examined into. The commonest method of breaking a seal of lac and renewing it is to use gypsum or plaster of paris. A rim of wax is carefully made round the seal and a pulp of the best, freshly-burnt plaster of paris poured on the carefully oiled seal. When the plaster has set the negative is slowly raised, the seal is broken, and is afterwards renewed from the greased mould. The first impression is generally successful, but it is usually impossible to make a second impression, because, as a rule, small pieces of plaster stick to the hot sealing-wax, so that the impression is spoilt. However the forger only requires one impression. Finally the little pieces of plaster which have stuck must be carefully removed. Under the magnifying glass these are generally found and betray the process employed.

The manipulation is easier when, instead of plaster of paris, kneaded fresh breadcrumb is used. The paste is pressed firmly on, and the seal taken up and dried with heat. We can easily obtain one impression in this way but it is not as sharp as the original.

Chemically, or with the microscope, traces of breadcrumb can be found attached to the seal. If the seal is not well washed the chemist can discover the use of breadcrumb with iodine.

In the Black Cabinet of Louis XIV., the process was to place the letter with the seal upwards on an anvil, and on the seal a small lead plate was laid. Then with a hammer a sharp blow was given, which smashed the sealing-wax into a thousand fragments, but before doing so impressed the seal on the lead plate. The lead plate could be used as a matrix as often as was desired. Such forgeries can be recognised in the impression, as the lead plate makes a mark round the seal on the paper of the envelope.

In this direction it is interesting, and also in our case instructive, to learn how forgeries were done in ancient days. Buoncompagni the Florentine, relates that an Italian abbot used to make seals, papal bulls, etc., of a peculiar, closely-knitted substance which he called *cinerutium*. Joh. V. Schellendorf, a famous forger of the fourteenth century, used sulphur paste. Frequently impressions were cut in a peculiar style, and Innocent III gave special instructions in which he indicated the methods of forging the Papistical seal. The ordinary method with wax seals was to cut them off with a thin, hot knife and stick them on again. Genuine adhering double seals fastened to a false document were cut in two with a horsehair moistened with turpentine and then riveted together again.

---

* On that account it is worth knowing that the use of a light, soluble ink is the surest means of preventing the unauthorised opening of letters. We close the flap part of the envelope, let it dry and write slantingly on the gummed part of the flap the name of the sender with a flowing ink, such as aniline. If any unauthorised person desires to open the letter, the gummed part of the envelope must be wetted, when the writing will smudge.

C. Coining

No useful purpose could be served by describing in detail the methods of coiners. Indeed to do so would be opposed to public policy. The Investigating Officer must try to find out the origin of false coin on the market and if he succeeds he may light upon the coiner himself and the possession of coining articles will suffice to bring about his conviction. If any such articles are found with him they will form very strong evidence of the owner's walk in life.

Section iv.—Horse Frauds.

A. General

Probably no frauds are so common as those connected with horse-dealing and there are none which less frequently come to light. Perhaps this latter fact is the principal cause of the former, for nothing so much encourages crime as the slackness with which justice follows it. Add to this that it is relatively easy to cheat in horse-dealing and that it is also difficult subsequently to prove that a defect discovered after a sale existed before it or, if it did, that the seller knew of it. Besides, the majority of people who require and buy horses think themselves connoisseurs and for that reason never willingly admit that they have allowed themselves to be duped. But the principal reason why frauds regarding the quality of horses are so rarely denounced lies in the fact that the denunciation generally comes to nothing, so that the victims of the frauds lose their time and trouble, reap only unpleasantness, and end by being laughed at. We can easily understand the reason. The successful cheat is very cunning and very knowing, for this reason alone he is difficult to confute. On the other hand the Investigating Officer comprehends perhaps only one case in a hundred, and experts on horse frauds are few and far between.

The Veterinary Surgeon is able to point out the faults and illnesses of an animal, but he probably knows no more than the man in the street what the seller has done to hide up these faults and pass off upon a buyer an old hack as an expensive horse. Cavalry officers, whose large experience enables them to give much information, are seldom available as experts and can only act as such in a private sort of way, and the person who really knows and would be capable of furnishing useful and precise enlightenment, such as the cunning dealer or jobber, takes good care not to inform the court of the tricks he has so often employed and hopes often to employ again. To consult with him and ask him how the business has been done and how his colleague has taken in the unwitting buyer, would be too much to demand.

As then we no longer desire to allow people to be deceived under our eyes and to send them away with the shameful confession that we are too ignorant and powerless to bring about the conviction of the cheat there remains nothing for the Investigating Officer to do but to set to work himself to acquire at least enough knowledge to be able to question witnesses in an appropriate manner and to prepare materials which may be utilised by the expert who is called in. The fraud is intimately bound up with all the circumstances in which the sale has been made, it is then as to these circumstances that information must be obtained from the victim, first, attention should be paid to the methods employed to deceive him for had he known them beforehand he would not have allowed himself to be deceived

It goes without saying that the reading of a few books or, with more reason, a few lines is insufficient to make one an expert in horseflesh and capable of standing up to individuals practised in the art of deceiving, but the author believes it to be possible to give in this respect sufficient information to the Investigating Officer to enable him to question the victim in a fit manner If the Investigating Officer has sufficient force of will to seize opportunities of obtaining information from one who really knows about the nature, structure, qualities, defects, and illnesses of a horse and to familiarise himself with the most important names of the various parts of its body, there will be room to hope that he will not be so feeble and helpless when he has to do with a not too complicated case of horse-coping

In the following pages the author has made a resumé of the most important points gathered by him from the best treatises on the subject, in particular those of *Wilhelm Baumeister* (Dr *A Rueff*), Major *von Tenneker* and *Dr Lentin* (" The Secrets of the Jewish Horse-dealer, Abraham Mortgens," etc), and also from communications made to him during a number of years by those in the know

First it may be said that real tricks, understood only by people in the trade, are not very numerous and can nearly always be discovered if the eyes are kept open The processes employed by the horse-dealer as a general rule differ little from those employed in ordinary life by the merchant who sells some object or other, and one will not be far wrong in affirming *that the skilful horse-dealer who is able to extract a good price for a valueless article owes his success more to his knowledge of men than to his knowledge of horses* He observes his man, studies his character, intentions, and knowledge, receives him with politeness or rudeness as he thinks fit, flatters him when necessary, and ends up by selling a horse for an enormous sum and in the midst of a torrent of words, without having employed the least little trick specially appertaining to the horse itself

When the Emperor Joseph II forbade gipsies, by a decree (October 9, 1783), which had been already in force in Sweden since 1727 to deal in horses, he expressly declared that this prohibition was in no way induced by disgraceful methods employed to set off their horses to advantage but by the damage which they caused to people buying horses from them by deceiving them with talk, oaths, and protestations If then methods are employed which are based upon general habits and peculiarities of disposition, there will be evidently no need for experts in horseflesh, and it will be no longer possible to speak of criminal fraud a he does not ordinarily come within reach of the arm of the law, a he only becomes cheating when it is accompanied with an act intended to lead people into error or serves to exploit an already existing situation

B. Special Methods Employed

Passing now to the special methods employed by horse-dealers, we have on the one hand those which are on the border line between dishonesty and criminal fraud, and on the other those which exploit in an illicit manner an existing situation, and finally those which are really fraudulent, to these must be added methods in which recourse to a third party is necessary.

Speaking generally it cannot be said whether any one of the methods cited should in itself be regarded as criminal. When the seller does not draw the attention of the buyer to an apparent defect in his merchandise, if he brings forward the article brushed up and in its most favourable aspect, if he knows how to show it off in such a manner that its bad points remain in the shade while the good ones are prominently displayed, if he does not cross the purchaser by contradicting him but rather always gives him in the right and tries to put him in good humour by flattering him—these may not be perfectly honest methods but they are certainly not criminal, for the maxim of the law is *caveat emptor*—' let the buyer look after himself.'

Even if, by some artifice or other, he for the moment brings out some quality which does not really exist or if for an instant he masks a grave defect which does exist, so that it cannot be seen in spite of a certain amount of examination, still it cannot be said that a crime has been committed, for after all, it must be presumed that the buyer of a horse has sufficient knowledge for the purpose. *vigilantibus non dormientibus lex subvenit.* Each case then must always be treated separately on its own merits, all that has taken place being considered including the knowledge the seller has of the buyer, what the former has promised the latter, what methods he has employed, in what manner the animal has been shown off, what questions the buyer has asked, how the different dodges have been worked together, what was the nature of the hidden fault or the artificially produced quality, and finally what is the connection between that fault or that quality and the true value of the animal.

There will be fraud when a dangerous sickness has been passed over in silence or hidden by means of artifice, but there will not be when for example a defect of colour in a good horse, for which the buyer has paid a reasonable price, had been hidden up. The buyer will perhaps allege that he would not have bought the horse if he had known of the defect in colour, but if he has got a good animal at a reasonable price what does it matter? We do not wish to make out that an Investigating Officer should awkwardly encroach upon the domain of the veterinary surgeon, it is for the latter to make all technical examinations, but it is for the former to know what the injured individual should be asked and what ought to be brought forward to furnish the expert with material for his work. Thus the Investigating Officer should have sufficient special knowledge to be able to explain to the individual who thinks himself cheated that the dealer has only employed methods which, to say the least, are not expressly forbidden by the law. Thus instructed the Investigating Officer will spare himself and others much trouble and annoyance.

(1) THE HORSE IS SHOWN UNDER THE MOST FAVOURABLE CONDITIONS

Everyone who deals in horses or has one for sale is forced to arrange his stable so that the animals show up to the best advantage. The dealer takes special care to have a well ventilated, well lit, and well fitted-up stable. The horses are arranged according to colour so as to produce an agreeable impression; they wear white belly-bands and halters are placed upon a slope higher in front than behind, when one enters the stable the horse is excited by the noise of the whip, the clacking of the tongue, or in some other way so that he starts forward and pricks up his ears, thus putting on an alert, quick, and wakeful appearance. When the buyer approaches a horse the dealer immediately seizes its head, holds it up, and forces the horse backwards so that the animal assumes the most advantageous position and appears straight-backed, lengthy, and animated; at the same time the dealer tries to mask certain faults—too high withers, too lofty an after-carriage, feet badly planted; in short, the horse makes at first sight a relatively good impression, and this is the impression that lasts. The opportunity is also taken to hide up striking defects, such as an arched back, at least until the moment when the pool or saddle will hide it; the dealer places his hand on the back of the horse as if to caress it and energetically digs his nail into its croup and, if the defect is not too visible, the horse stretches itself out for a little while and holds itself up straight. Anyhow the buyer imagines that the horse has not really got an arched back and that he is only making a "cat's back," as many horses do when rising and stretching.

If the purchaser consider the horse worthy of closer examination, the dealer brings it if possible into a courtyard where the walls set it off to the best advantage by being newly whitewashed. It is placed with the bad side to the wall. If the buyer shows signs of going nearer, the horse is passed to the other side but in such a way as to have its good side still to the fore, the bad side is only shown rapidly in passing when the horse crosses the yard. Advantage is moreover taken of the moment when the bad side is exhibited to make the horse rear so that the buyer has no time to notice the defect in question. If the buyer expressly asks to see the other side the horse is turned before him in the form of the figure eight, and placed against the opposite wall. If the head was first towards the north it now points towards the south, but the buyer in the middle of the yard is still facing the same side; he generally imagines he is looking at the other side for the head of the horse is facing the other way. This can be vouched for from personal experience.

In all positions taken up by the horse the attempt is made to place it so that its hind feet are higher than its fore feet. This position gives it a fiery and lively appearance and has the advantage of completely hiding the faults of the hind legs such as stiffness, giving at the knee, etc. The weight of the body is thus brought on to the buttocks, the hind feet are thrown out to the rear and stiff, while the joints are tensely stretched and motionless.

This is the time when the dealer will have an opportunity of making any little corrections in the horse's height; as a rule he will try to make it appear taller than it really is, tall horses being more sought after than small. Sometimes however he wishes it to look smaller, as when the buyer desires a small beast for some reason or other, but especially when he is selling a pair and of course wishes them to be of equal height, for this he will try to make the smaller one appear taller and the taller one smaller till they seem about the same height. One method employed is to stand the horse so that it appears longer and taller—this it is true can only make a difference of a fraction of an inch; a better result is obtained by presenting the horse with or without shoes or calkins, another fraction of an inch is gained or lost by walking the horse on hard ground or sand (in which latter it sinks considerably). All these artifices in combination produce their effect even before the measuring of the horse is begun. In this operation the most difference is obtained according as the horse is measured straight up and down or slantingly on the withers or by the side of them, as the tape is held slack or tight or brought in the form of an arc over the fleshy parts of the shoulders, or is held straight up and down. No doubt the buyer assists at all these operations, perhaps even measures with his own tape for his own satisfaction, and yet the dealer in the midst of an avalanche of words succeeds in juggling away considerable inequalities.

The horse having been measured it is next bitted, it is a first principle of a horse-dealer never to use trappings which require much time to put on, for then the buyer would have an opportunity to leisurely examine the animal and make discoveries. The trappings should be simple, fit loosely, and be always in the best order, so that they may easily go over the horse's head. The employment of any article manifestly used to mask a defect is avoided. A martingale, the object of which is to prevent the horse from plunging, is never used, nor a mirror-bit to prevent the horse putting out its tongue, nor a sharp bit when the horse is hard-mouthed. During the few moments the inspection lasts the dealer knows other methods of preventing the horse from plunging, putting out its tongue, or being hard mouthed he uses the whip, the spur, the thigh. Later the purchaser can do what he likes, but at present must not know that a martingale, mirror-bit, or sharp bit is absolutely necessary. On the other hand, when advisable, very large harness is used, with a hoisting strap, wither-bands, back-girth, and a breeching, to hide thinness, white marks, bare places, or suchlike defects, or, speaking generally, to make the horse appear more vigorous than it really is. If the buyer asks why this harness is chosen, he is told it is the latest kind, that it fits better, or that horses prefer it.

If the horse has an oriental appearance, it is set out in Hungarian harness, decorated with plaits and fringes, half moons, shells, bells, etc., which, added to the slightly oriental manner in which it holds its head and tail, gives it almost the appearance of an Arab. The hussar saddle, sometimes employed, is of some use, for it completely hides up a mule- or carpback. This saddle is moreover placed as far back as possible, a horse cannot stand this for long, but it puts up with it during the short time the inspection lasts. A saddle placed thus gives a better appearance, and more liberty of movement.

The same applies to walking the horse without shoes, this may be done with no harm for a short time on the sand or peat of a riding school — the horse will look very different on a hard road, heavily shod. If possible the horse is ridden with no saddle, but merely a horse-cloth. We all know how well a circus horse looks with its horse-cloth of a loud colour bordered with gold and ornamented with gewgaws, the dealer knows this and takes advantage of it. A horse, too, goes much more lightly and willingly under a soft covering than under a hard saddle, again to throw a horse-cloth over a horse is the matter of an instant, while to put on a saddle takes a fairly long time, thus giving the purchaser an opportunity to study and criticise the animal.

The time being now come to exercise the animal the same methods are employed as when it was shown in repose, the rider constantly moves the horse about before the buyer so as to show only the good side, the defects being kept well " on the other side ", if e g, the horse is weaker on the right side than on the left, the jumping and exercising is done with the left side to the onlooker, and when the horse is going forward it is always the right side to which the spur is applied If the horse shies readily the owner is well aware which eye is defective, for horses often shy only to one side In this case, care is taken that the horse sees dangerous objects only on the side on which it is least likely to shy What is most to be feared in this respect is the buyer himself who to test the horse's quietness jumps about and makes a noise when it passes, brandishing his stick or waving his handkerchief with a good rider the horse will not mind, and the purchaser will subsequently be astonished that an animal, so well behaved on being bought, takes fright at a sparrow and throws its rider

If the horse has a good fore-carriage, but a bad rear-carriage, it is ridden forwards, i e, jumping and prancing are carefully avoided in the contrary case it is just these exercises which are practised for in them the horse may still cut a good figure in spite of its front legs, trembling and knocked up, on the other hand trotting and walking the horse are avoided, for faults in the front legs would immediately be detected whereas at a gallop only an expert could perceive them The same may be said of horses which founder and have spavins, before the inspection they are trotted to warm them up and are then shown off at full gallop, which always looks well and in no way hurts the animal

As regards horses possessing every imaginable good quality but showing when walking certain faults, such as uncertain pace, defective walk feeble loins, etc, while being at the same time of good colour, elegant shape and fine appearance, great care is taken to show them in repose They dazzle by their grand aspect and the buyer finds pleasure merely in looking at them, the dealer lets loose a flood of words and walks his client twenty times round the animal, till the buyer thinks he has seen it sufficiently and either does not have it walked about at all or, when it is walked about, is still so captivated with its grand appearance that he does not notice its wretched gait Later on, when he has had his fill of the beauty of the beast and wishes it to do some work, he comes and demands the services of the police

Broken-winded horses are never shown after they have eaten, when their stomachs are filled and their lungs are oppressed Horses which have vertigo are not taken in the sun, or made to wear a tightly girthed saddle or a strait collar Slight illnesses of this kind are not noticed at all when the horse is kept in the shade and loosely harnessed

(2) Utilization of certain physiological circumstances

Methods of this kind can no more be considered to fall within the arm of the law than the preceding, yet they may become illegal, when, joined to other expedients, they conspire together to constitute a true fraud The manner in which a dealer attempts to deceive a purchaser about the colour of a horse is based upon physiological principles White mat harness transforms the unequal tint of a black horse into a colour beyond reproach, black harness together with a blue horse-cloth makes a white horse, whose colour leaves something to be desired, as white as milk, a whitewashed wall in the background sets off the colour of no matter what horse, and in the sun, a light bay horse when rubbed with a little grease is transformed into a beautiful golden chestnut.

The same with a horse's stature, for, when showing in harness, one must make up for what has been lost in measuring. A horse that is too tall will be shown bare back or attached to a very big carriage, while a horse that is too small will be given a high saddle or harnessed to a very low chaise. When two horses of different heights are harnessed together, the smaller is placed on the left and the larger on the right. This makes the difference in size hardly perceptible; on the other hand if they are placed in the inverse position the difference appears twice as great. No one knows why this is so, but all drivers are aware of the fact, and everyone who wishes to sell a pair of horses of unequal height takes advantage of this peculiarity. It may be added that the horse's toilet also produces a considerable effect from this point of view; the harness ought to be plentiful and bright-coloured, the impression produced by the largeness of the two sets of similar harness causes the disappearance of the small difference in the size of the two horses. The effect is still greater, when, by means of bearing reins and curbs, it is contrived that the heads and the tails of both are levelled up; this also is a great help in hiding other defects.

Horses in harness are always driven in a figure of eight, under the pretext of showing the buyer everything; it goes without saying that the dealer is not a bad driver, his business is to show off the horse in the most favourable aspect. If the driver is really skilful his equipage will never look better than when being turned in a figure of eight; this has the further advantage to the dealer of preventing the buyer from spotting and remembering the defects of the horse. It is particularly difficult to recognise a defect in one of eight legs in movement. Indeed it is difficult to distinguish the lame leg of a single horse, when seeing the same side of the animal, it must therefore be much more difficult when there are two horses of which we see a different side at each movement. It is then impossible to say whether one of the horses walks badly, does not place its feet correctly upon the ground, or even slightly limps. The fact that it is difficult to recognise a certain defect when two horses are seen together is often exploited to pass off a bad horse along with one which is better. The dealer knows how to place and praise up the good horse, that it "covers" the bad one or, at least, masks its faults; indeed our senses when under the influence of an impression which strikes them forcibly lose a correct perception of smaller matters and do not perceive them distinctly.

(3) UTILIZATION OF CERTAIN PSYCHOLOGICAL CIRCUMSTANCES

Here is the sphere of that eloquence, perspicacity, and skill by which the dealer exploits the feeble side of the character of the buyer. People say:—"of a thousand words said by a horse-dealer one only is to be believed and of that one but the half." *De Tennecker* says:—'To pass off as good qualities in the eyes of the buyer a horse's greatest faults is the characteristic of a consummate horse-dealer.' He knows at least how to take away all weight from its faults; the age of the horse he wishes to sell is always "the best age," its colour is always "the most fashionable," even when the horse is a grey, marked in the most irregular manner; its stumbling gait is always "safest," even when it is quite insupportable to ride; the horse which shies at everything is "very young but extremely spirited"—doubtless an old hack never shies. If the horse is obviously ill, the dealer pretends that it has been ill but when it is completely well it will look very much better; if it is lame, it is the fault of an awkward farrier who shod it badly yesterday. As for the colour of the horse, on clipping it will be the exact colour the buyer wishes. Everything that is objectionable in the way it holds its head up, its habits, or its pace, is "French and the latest fashion," and even if the animal is a stargazer of the worst possible description, the dealer does not hesitate. "Yes, unfortunately he comes from France where nowadays they make the horses take up all sorts of bad habits, and they are specially fond of this absurd carriage of the head, but if you like you will be able to cure the horse of it in a week."

If the dealer pushes things too far and the buyer becomes distrustful, there are always little dodges for giving oneself the air of "an honest man." The dealer draws the buyer's attention to faults which the beast does not possess. Of course the dealer will never say that the horse is a stumbler, bolter, or rearer, for he would never risk frightening the buyer to that extent. But all of a sudden he will discover a very bad mark on its back which he has never noticed before; of course, it will soon be found out to be simply a dust mark or shadow; or he notices that the two horses seem to be of unequal height, though very well aware that, if measured, there will not be a fraction of an inch between them. These "honest" methods of a dealer by which he draws attention to a defect in his own beast, always gain the confidence of the trusting purchaser.

But talking is not enough, the dealer must act. Thus we can always see in the stable a number of venerable examples which taken together hardly make a good impression, hidden as they are beneath coverings and cloaks as if they were the most precious articles in the world. Naturally there are always plenty of people interested in these veiled horses who anxiously inquire whether they are indeed so delicate; "unhappily," replies the dealer, "all the horses descended from the famous stallion *Kohinoor* are extremely delicate." The buyer, who has never heard speak of this famous ancestor, takes care not to betray his ignorance and commences to interest himself only in *Kohinoor's* descendants. With a thousand precautions the coverings are taken off to obtain a glimpse of the horse; but in the open air it is kept carefully covered up, for this trick is only employed during cold weather, and our man finally buys "a pig in a bag" in the literal sense of the last word.

No doubt the dealer will not act in this way towards all buyers, he must first know the people he has to deal with and his art consists in not at once broaching the business in hand, but in trying to get some knowledge of the customer and discovering what he knows and what he wants. He will then act according to circumstances. Nothing is easier than to pass off the same horse as quiet and gentle or lively and mettlesome, and to exploit these particular qualities. Let us presume that the would-be buyer is a man who is foppish and vain but a poor horseman; he will assure this gentleman that with his knowledge of horsemanship he ought to have a real devil of a horse, that unfortunately he has none at present that will quite suit him, will he in the meantime be content with a white horse which has every good quality but is a thousand times too quiet for him? no doubt, he adds, this is his worst fault but it is largely compensated for by a number of good points. The brilliant horseman asserts that he greatly regrets being obliged to take this "old mule," but he takes it all the same, and if it should turn out not to be quiet and to be full of faults he will always have the consolation of having been taken by the dealer to be "an accomplished horseman."

Speaking generally the dealer is never sparing of praises, and when the buyer begins to examine the horse and attacks it like a midwife the dealer begins by saying "There now, I needn't say a word. You understand better than my old master, God bless him!", and thereupon he chatters all the more and points out the greatest absurdities. If the buyer mounts the horse, he calls out his servants and asks them in a low voice, but so that the horseman can hear everything, to note the seat and attitude of the gentleman so that they may "profit by the lesson." The horseman pays more attention to these praises than to the qualities and defects of the horse, and finally he pays for the praises as well as the horse. But to give at least the appearance of truth to his talk, the dealer takes care to have excellent saddles in reserve, safe and comfortable, even family saddles on which it is easy to sit quietly. The buyer puts all this down to the good qualities of the horse.

But it is, above all, at the time when the horse is being shown off by the dealer or his servants that it is necessary to deceive the buyer. The rider or coachman must be imbued with the idea that his business is not to parade his own skill, or train the horse, but only to show it off in the most favourable way possible. He will, therefore, never do what he wishes but what the horse wishes, while all his art will consist in making it be believed that the horse is doing what he wishes. If, consequently, the beast begins to gallop of its own free will he will immediately help it to gallop, he will let it gallop as long as it likes, and not till it begins to trot will he help it to trot; the essential thing is not to give the buyer time to see whether it was the horse or its rider that first thought about trotting.

If the horse turns into the wall the rider immediately allows it to do so and cries out "See how easy it is to bring him near the wall,—he doesn't mind it a bit." If the horse rears, jumps, or kicks, these are all little tricks of skill executed on purpose by the groom, and the dealer standing by the purchaser says in a tone of reproach "I don't care about my grooms making him jump like that, even the quietest animal may get into bad habits." The buyer subsequently discovers to his dismay that the horse has already got the bad habit.

The dealer pays special attention to experts who accompany the buyer; he is most polite to them and tries to make them forget the real object of their presence by telling stories and, if possible, expressing sentiments of gratitude towards them. In this way he will return a thousand thanks to the veterinary surgeon who accompanies the purchaser for some advice recently given him, he admires his perspicacity, skill, and knowledge, and finds nothing to say about him that is not agreeable. The veterinary surgeon is not insensible to these flatteries, especially before the individuals who have brought him and are paying his fee, and finally the two buyers drive a strange bargain.

(1) FRAUD PROPERLY SO CALLED

We will now speak of all those *manœuvres* practised upon the actual body of the horse either to hide its defects or to give it points. They may, as a rule, be considered criminally fraudulent except when they are only methods of embellishment which increase the beauty and, in consequence, the value of the animal in a manner which lasts or which at least is easy to renew. And here again it is the whole manner in which the sale is carried out, the words pronounced and the promises made, which will guide us in deciding whether there is real fraud within the meaning of the law.

In the following pages we shall discuss "embellishments" as the dealer taken *flagrante delictu* is fond of calling them, which are known to the author. The examination, detection, and appreciation of these embellishments are naturally the business of the expert, but the Investigating Officer should be also cognisant of all the tricks of the horse-dealer.

(a) Frauds relating to the age of the horse

The ordinary way of calculating the age of a horse is by its teeth, and for this attention is paid to the marks, which are depressions in the surface of the incisors between the folds of the enamel, depressions which, during a certain period of the animal's life, are black (carbonised). This carbon is worn away by degrees and when it disappears the best and most valuable period of the horse's life is passed. It is, therefore, not rare for horse-dealers to rejuvenate old horses by artificial marks upon their teeth, burning them with a red-hot iron, or blackening with the help of sulphuric acid or some colouring matter. Inversely a young colt, which is not yet old enough for work is made older by a year by, at the proper time, extracting its first teeth, so that the buyer instead of being prejudiced by the fact that the horse can do no work for a year and must be fed for nothing, knocks up the animal by making it work too soon.

Nor is it rare for them to file a horse's teeth. With age, the gums always recede more and more towards the jaws and make the teeth look longer. "Long teeth old age," says a proverb, and this is an inconvenience which must be remedied by shortening the teeth. It is no doubt not easy to cut the teeth so as to make them correspond as before and conceal the fraud, but it is necessary for the horse-market, especially when frequented by country people, that the teeth be shortened.

The dealer also does his best to prevent the buyer thoroughly examining the mouth and teeth of the horse, to this end he makes it foam by artificial means, *e.g.*, by introducing some soap into its mouth. It is then impossible to see the teeth distinctly under the mass of foam. Another method is to make the horse nervous at the mouth, to this end the mouth is submitted to all sorts of cruelties, so that on being touched it fears fresh sufferings and will not allow its teeth to be seen. Most frequently it suffices to file and burn the teeth to produce a fairly lasting effect, but at the end of a certain time the animal forgets the treatment and it has to be renewed a little while before each auction. The horse-dealer is the more given to these tricks as there are many people who ask nothing better than to have a horse 'quiet as a lamb but fearful of its mouth', for on the one hand when the animal will not allow its mouth to be touched it is but a proof of its keenness and on the other hand the buyer is very satisfied that none of his acquaintances can look into his new horse's mouth to make discoveries disagreeable to him. This fraud regarding the age of a horse is usually accompanied with another regarding the salt-cellars, or round pits above the eyes. These salt-cellars become deeper and deeper with age and when very deep usually betray an advanced age. To remedy this defect an incision is made in the salt-cell u, air is blown in through a small tube, a suture is made and the wound allowed to heal. This seems incredible but the author has been informed of it on several occasions by a trained expert who has himself at least twenty vehicles on the road, he has assured the author that he has himself seen many horses in the market thus "inflated". No doubt the effect of this trick can only last a few days.

(b) Fraud concerning the temperament of the horse

These kinds of frauds are closely connected with the foregoing and have for their object to give an old, lazy, and slow animal a young, fresh, and alert appearance. Here before all comes what is called 'gipsies' fire'. Every countryman knows how the horse brought to market by a gipsy is full of fire and spirit but is the saddest and most miserable of beasts as soon as it finds itself in a new master's stable. The usual method employed by a gipsy is to thrash the horse in the most unmerciful manner and then to mount in the saddle and gallop straight to the market. This bad treatment takes effect and the unfortunate animal remains frightened for at least an hour and has a lively and alert appearance. They also give it large quantities of brandy or better a decoction of datura which excites the sexual functions the most played-out mare then begins to dance and prance, there is no doubt that the effects of this treatment are very grave.

The saddle used by gipsies is different from other saddles, it carries inside (under the pads) fine sharp points, which on being pressed by the knee dig into the body of the horse. The gipsy never ceases to state that he needs neither spurs nor whip to animate the animal.

But the substance which works the greatest miracle is ginger or pepper. Either the dealer himself or by preference the stable-boy is always furnished with some ginger (or pepper) which he furtively introduces into his mouth and chews. At the moment the horse is being presented he takes a little of this paste composed of ginger and saliva, upon the forefinger, and under the pretext of caressing the animal or lifting off its covering he adroitly introduces it into the anus of the animal. The effect is superb, the sorry animal fills out, his depressed rump comes up, his laxness is transformed into keenness, his heaviness into lightness, and the most stupid of animals appears to be intelligent and wakeful, but, more important than all, it holds up its tail. Now this is a primary condition for a horse to look well and lively, a good carriage of the tail makes an ordinary horse into a racehorse. It is to give this fine carriage that a horse's tail is cut or put under rollers, operations which are easily dispensed with, at least to give an effect for a couple of hours, by the introduction of a little ginger into the anus.

If the buyer complains that at the market the horse had a brilliant appearance, an elegant air, a noble step, and a lively temperament, and that it now has a miserable, used up, common-looking and spiritless aspect, all that need be done is to reperform the operation of the ginger and the buyer will be amazed to see his horse become again like what it was at the market. But the employment of ginger may be recognised, for the horse, immediately after the operation, makes constant efforts to dung, and its tail is agitated by a peculiar trembling.

For people who are more easily taken in the dealer even has a false tail in reserve which he joins to the crupper (the piece of leather which passes in a loop over the tail) with hard wax. In this way the horse not only has a beautiful tail, but also carries it well. This can only be done with cart and carriage horses.

Is it fraud to accustom horses to eat antimony or arsenic? The question is a difficult one. It cannot be doubted that such drugs give the animals vivacity, vigour, and strong lungs, they make them lather at the mouth, and produce an extraordinarily brilliant coat, further the skin stretches and fills out and they appear well nourished and plump. But it is said that such horses are soon used up, that they easily succumb to illnesses, that they are unaffected by medicine, and that they soon die when the arsenic is stopped. But is the individual who, by conviction or for other reasons, feeds his horses on arsenic, absolutely forced to inform the buyer of the real cause of the fine qualities of the horse and how it ought to be treated? We are inclined to think that in English law at least the maxim *caveat emptor* would protect the dealer. The American practice of "doping" or dosing a horse just before a race, has been forbidden on the English Turf.

(c) Faking the colour

There are various reasons for colouring horses. Firstly, horse-dealers try to render them unrecognisable even to their true owners. They attain this by rubbing the horse with a preparation of lead, a solution of lunar caustic, nitrate of silver, or pyrogallic acid. Horses with irregular colouring are given a uniform colour. As a rule, people do not like horses with white feet, so the white part must be got rid of by artificial means. This artificial colour does not last at longest more than six months, when the defect will reappear.

In the same way they try to hide up marks of use, i.e., light patches spread over various parts of the body. These patches are never indeed of much importance under the saddle, they are due to its frequent pressure and indicate that the horse has often been compelled to hard and awkward work; the same may be said of marks upon the chest and shoulders due to the pressure of the collar which prove the horse to have often been used for draught work. If fairly large white marks appear upon the sides the cause must be looked for in the use of strong liniments employed for combating some illness of the chest, which makes it prudent to distrust the horse's respiratory organs. The artificial concealment of one of these marks of use gives the horse a much higher market value, especially if the mark indicates some real defect which can hardly be discovered in any other way.

Finally, certain old horses of dark colour have the misfortune to become fleabitten, i.e., white hairs appear in their coats and give them an old appearance even from afar. It is said that these hairs have the peculiarity of taking on colouring matter better than other hair; it suffices to rub them over with soap, ether, or potash, and then to wash them with a decoction of ground walnut-shell; they become black and undistinguishable from the others. If, for some reason or other, this operation cannot be performed and the animal in spite of age is still of some value, the hairs are pulled or cut out one by one. The dealer sometimes even does not go to the trouble of using chemicals, the effect of which lasts but a few months, but water colours are used. A retired cavalry officer informed the author some years back, when spotted horses were the rage, that a foreigner calling himself a Russian sold at a market in Poland a four-in-hand of horses speckled in an extraordinarily regular way, but when next day they were washed down they became whites and bays!

If white marks, white stockings, etc., are produced artificially so that they *remain*, it cannot be regarded as deception.

Rapid and regular casting of the coat is a certain indication of the health of a horse; when a horse does not cast its hair regularly, it is given strong doses of sulphur, antimony, salt or juniper berries. This treatment makes the horse appear to be healthier than it really is, but its health is really worse than before.

Artificial marks are also branded on horses with hot irons. ' As long as iron and fire exist so long will we have horses of all breeds ' say the initiated, and indeed it is astonishing to see with what facility the most derelict jades are purchased simply because the dealer has imprinted on them with a hot iron the mark of a celebrated stud. Certain disagreeable marks, e.g., such as the marks on army horses and casters, unlucky marks, etc., are also said to be obliterated in this way though we cannot explain how this operation is performed. It is also said that new marks are burnt alongside the first and the whole branding is then passed off as that of some stable situated as far away as possible.

(d) Hiding defects

A good and healthy horse should have its mouth ' fresh, ' that is to say, moist and foamy under the bit; if it be not recourse is had to soap, pepper, and especially to chewed tobacco, substances which are skilfully inserted into the horse's mouth for a short time before it is shown off. If it is hard-mouthed, fragments of sharp glass are placed in the corners of the mouth in direct contact with the bit, and the horse obeys the slightest movement of the reins. If it has the villainous fault of crib-biting, its incisors are strongly hammered to make them painful, or a small piece of wood is thrust in between the teeth, rendering them so sensitive that the horse gives up the habit for some time at least.

If the horse be blind of one eye, without the eye being deformed, the defect may be hidden by the forelock of the horse, or by a false forelock affixed to the forehead. It is even said that artificial eyes are sometimes used.

Hanging ears completely disfigure a horse; this defect must be remedied at all costs, so a frontlet is constructed in a special manner with rings of horsehair which surround and keep up the ears; or again an operation is performed, wounds being made in the ears and allowed to cicatrise. The ears then stand up fairly well. No doubt the effect is not lasting, for the cicatrice yields under the weight of the ears and these hang down worse than before. It is even said that false ears are used.

There exists, moreover, a very grave fraud sometimes committed with regard to stallions one of whose testicles has not descended into the testicular pouch. Castration is then only partially possible and an animal with only one testicle preserves all the qualities of a stallion. To hide this defect, a wound is made in that part of the testicular pouch in which the testicle would have been if it had descended from the abdominal cavity in the proper way; the scar of the wound induces the belief that the horse is completely castrated; the masculine appearance of the animal is explained by pretending that it has been cut very late when its character was already developed. Such a horse, sold as a gelding, often causes great mischief for its qualities as a stallion may make themselves manifest when they are not expected. Many examples are known of such stallions after remaining quiet for a fairly long time, all at once breaking out on the approach of a mare in use.

(c) Concealment of illnesses

We have already said that horses are never presented at a time when the presentation would make the discovery of illness easier than at other times (a broken-winded horse is not shown after it has eaten and a horse which gets the staggers is never sent out in the sun). It remains now to speak of methods the aim of which is to conceal illnesses properly so called. Such concealments can hardly be practised between one stable and another, for they pertain to latent defects of a nature to set aside the sale, so the stable would be always responsible; but they take place very frequently in horse marts, where one often picks up cheap a fine horse—plus a fine blemish.

Among practices of this kind the most frequent consists in masking paralysis of the thigh or hoof by means of the whip, spur, or curb. Especially on soft ground (sand or grass) do these defects disappear, at least for long enough to effect the sale of a valueless horse at a high price.

A still more dangerous practice is the anæsthetising of horses. On account of its complicated structure and the accidents to which it is exposed through the ground, work, foolish treatment, shoeing, etc., the hoof of a horse is exposed to a host of painful maladies—often incurable though very slow in action, which in time render the beast unfit for all work. And this inability to work must not be attributed to deformation of the hoof, or its want of supporting power, but to the pain the animal feels each time it puts down its foot. Now as the hoof contains only nerves of sensation and not motor nerves, the nerves are cut above the fetlock-joint and a portion entirely removed, so as to prevent reconnection of the extremities and the disease seems cured, for the horse can walk as before. No doubt the cause of the pain continues but the communication between it and the nerve centres being interrupted the horse does not feel the pain and can use its hoof, but in a short time the disease makes such rapid progress that the horse is good for nothing in spite of the operation. This fraud may be detected by trying with a needle whether the horse is still sensible to pain in the foot (e.g., at the crown); if it cannot feel needle pricks it is most certainly anæsthetised.

Often also the horse's tongue is burnt; no one cares to buy a horse which lets its tongue hang out, for, without considering the ugliness, the habit nearly always indicates some illness of the lungs or brain. To prevent the animal hanging out its tongue, the latter is burnt with a hot iron, and for some time afterwards the horse keeps its tongue in its mouth.

A really dangerous fraud is when the nasal discharge of the horse is suppressed; this is often an indication of the gravest illness. Bad catarrh, the bastard strangles, the strangles, ulceration of the lungs, and even farcy and glanders are often accompanied with nasal discharges. Every outsider even knows this and never buys a horse so afflicted, for if the discharge is not serious but merely some passing ailment, this particular time would not be chosen for selling the horse. To hide up this malady a "bung" of well-compressed cotton-wool is taken and thrust as far up the nostril as possible to prevent the nose from running. No doubt this can only be effective during a short time and if the discharge comes from one nostril only, for a horse breathes only by the nose and not by the mouth and if both nostrils were corked the horse would be suffocated.

When we consider how dangerous these illnesses are and also how contagious (e.g., farcy), we must agree that this fraud is all the more grave in that the illness thus concealed may infect and destroy numberless other horses. Farcy is also contracted by men, especially when in ignorance of the illness they do not take necessary precautions in approaching the horse.

If the glanders, the strangles, etc., are dangerous by reason of the ease with which they spread, the staggers is dangerous in that the animal afflicted with this complaint may, during an attack, wound and damage everything around it, especially when one has no knowledge of the illness, and for that reason has taken no precautions. Horses which get the staggers are particularly unsensitive in those places where horses cannot bear to be touched. Healthy horses make a nervous movement when a finger is placed in their ear and draw back the foot when touched upon the coronet (just above the hoof). Horses which get the staggers remain on the contrary perfectly still.

As these methods are as well known as the danger of the staggers itself, no one neglects before buying a horse to introduce the finger into its ear and tread upon the coronet of its hoof. But, when this sensibility is absent, it is artificially produced by rubbing the ears with very strong ointment. No doubt, this rubbing only renders sensitive the pavilion of the ear, but the animal will not allow it to be touched and the desired end is obtained. To render the coronet sensitive, the dealer has in the back part of the sole of his boot a needle or pointed nail with which he himself verifies the sensibility of the horse's hoof to prevent the buyer taking this trouble. The horse may very well be subject to the staggers but its hoof is not sufficiently insensible not to feel the point of the needle, it will certainly draw back the foot and the purchaser will rest easy.

(5) Employment of Assistants

No horse-dealer, however skilful, can do anything alone; he cannot succeed without the employment of assistants; all his men, from his most intimate confidant to his youngest stable-boy, can render him the greatest services but at the same time can do him the greatest harm. The skilled dealer therefore sacrifices no less time and trouble in training his employés than in training his horses. It is of the utmost importance that the groom should keep the stable spotlessly clean, be always at his post, and be able to do exactly as his master would do himself if he was not occupied with the buyer; on the arrival of the latter the grooms therefore station themselves on each side of the horses he looks at so as to hide the animals' defects. The business of one is to calm the horse that takes fright, of a second to correct the curved spine of another horse, of a third, fourth, and fifth to prevent others from lying down or biting the manger, etc.; a sixth caresses one to prevent it from kicking when the purchaser is passing beside him; and thus the first visit passes off in a most brilliant manner.

For showing off horses either in repose or in movement the dealer has special men; on principle he does not occupy himself with the horse, he "takes on" the buyer, watches and scrutinises him, tells him stories, promises him mountains and marvels. Near the horse is stationed the horse-breaker or some other trusted person. Between this latter and the dealer, there exists a prearranged manner of talking whereby the turn of certain phrases, which to the uninitiated appear the most inoffensive in the world, have a very precise signification. When for example the dealer says "Bring the black horse, as he is," that means,—"This man understands nothing about horses; he will not notice that the horse has spavins; it is unnecessary to heat the beast; bring him out straight away, etc."

The same understanding exists between the breaker-in and the groom who holds the whip; the latter is the intermediary between the dealer and the breaker-in. If, for example, the buyer has expressed a fear that the horse turns into the wall, the dealer lets the man with the whip know this, and the latter immediately communicates it to the breaker-in; it is then the business of these two so to treat the beast that it loses all desire of turning into the wall.

It is also necessary to know whether the commands given by the dealer to the groom riding the horse in the presence of a third party are given seriously or simply as a matter of form, and whether they ought to be obeyed or not. When for example a horse gallops badly and soon gets tired, the dealer will time after time order the groom to gallop; but the latter will not gallop or will only gallop for a few moments and then let the horse trot in spite of all the raging and swearing of his master, who will express to the buyer his great regret at not being able to point out precisely the most beautiful qualities of the horse owing to the stupidity of the groom. "Do not whip the horse so much," Mortgens makes his Jewish dealer say; "let him go as he likes, see how well he goes"; but the stable-boys recommence to whip him, for they know very well the horse will not budge an inch without the whip.

Besides those people the dealer employs constantly in his stable, there are yet others with whom he has relations unknown to the public. These are his touts who for a small reward tell everyone about the dealer and sing his praises, especially if the latter does not often come to town. These touts attend the market, admire the horses, try them, and make offers. On the arrival of other customers the false buyers search their pocket-books and finally find that, much to their regret, they have not enough money with them to buy the fine beast, thus inciting the others to buy. These people pretend to be merchants, rich farmers, country gentlemen, and sometimes even cavalry officers. These touts also serve the dealer by speaking of the high price and the strong demand for horses and in deceiving other dealers, all the while pretending they do not know the particular man for whom they "work."

Horse-dealers have also touts and agents among a class of men which exists in all localities, who through either dilettantism or ennui, busy themselves with horses, and, little by little acquiring the reputation of connoisseurs, their opinion is considered to be authoritative. Every dealer, whether he be established in a place or merely goes there from time to time, knows who these people are and tries to make their acquaintance, if he succeeds in opening relations with one of them—and this is not a difficult matter—he makes every effort to have a talk with him on a favourable day; he speaks at great length about his extensive business, fine horses, and especially his honest methods, and finally sells him, often at a great loss, a really good horse at a very low price. The capital he risks earns good interest, for the buyer thus served cannot do otherwise than sing the praises of the dealer wherever he goes.

A trick employed by all horse-dealers and which may or may not, according to circumstances, be considered fraudulent, is to enter into relations with another dealer living in a distant place and exchange with him horses which neither of them can dispose of. Indeed a horse which is stationed for long in the stable of a dealer is practically unsaleable. Every purchaser imagines that the beast must have something wrong with it or it would have been sold, and so the longer it remains the longer it is likely to remain. All dealers have such horses which, if exchanged, will sell readily enough in a new stable as "newly imported" animals.

A common method of the dealer is to get into relations with the servants of his clients, thus the more easily to deceive their masters. We know how certain people, especially elderly people, ladies, and people who know little about horses, allow themselves to be influenced by their coachmen and follow their advice, simply so as not to be condemned to listen afterwards to their continual complaints and recriminations. To get rid of the horse the dealer therefore seeks to gain over the coachman or groom of a customer,—not often a difficult matter. This procedure throws a flood of light upon many a bad bargain.

It frequently happens that dealers corrupt the servant of a person from whom they wish to buy a horse at an absurdly low price. The servant makes the master believe that the horse is ill and vicious and must be got rid of at any cost. For this purpose the servant inserts little pieces of soap between the teeth of the horse, not to make it foam but to make it lose its appetite, and after a few weeks it grows thin, loses its strength, and appears to be of no value. The horse once bought, the soap is removed, and in a little while the animal completely recovers. In the same way small pieces of needle are buried in the coronet of the hoof, these completely disappear and the horse limps more and more, the reason for its doing so remains undiscovered and, finally, the owner of the horse is very glad to get rid of it at the lowest price then the needle is removed and the horse recovers in a day or two These two methods are not only employed by unfaithful servants, but also by gipsies who sneak into the stables and afterwards turn up to buy the valueless horse, good only for knacking

In conclusion let us mention the method whereby a horse is made to refuse to go when drawing a heavy load up an incline Pointed nails are placed in the inside of the collar well away from the shaft side These nails dig into the horse's skin, whenever it begins to pull vigorously Now if a horse absolutely refuses to go on in spite of thrashing, it is unfit for any service in every country which is not quite flat It goes without saying that its owner seeks to get rid of it at any price

Section v.—Cheating at Games.

A General.

Ever since they have been able to appreciate values, and that is long before the notion of money existed, men have gambled, and as long as men have gambled so long have they cheated Those who have devoted themselves to the industry of cheating, '*chevaliers d'industrie*' have at all times been the same and, it is probable, will always remain the same, intelligent, skilful, too lazy for honest work, too good livers to be able to want, too unconscientious to refrain from taking from others sums the magnitude of which is in proportion to the awkwardness and simplicity of their dupes

The card cheat is called in most of the Continental countries a Greek, a word once commonly used to denote them in England also, but now disappearing in that sense *

The word now commonly used in most English-speaking countries for a card cheat is simply "sharp" This word has been employed in the most complete exposition of their methods published in recent years—*Maskelyne's* "Sharps and Flats", where he uses also the word "flat" to signify the person cheated We shall for brevity use these two words in the same sense throughout this section

It is not always easy to prove that a person is a sharp, it is often very difficult indeed to do so If a witness asserts that he has seen a player make a suspicious movement, that is not much in the way of proof If the accused person has won heavily and often, the case becomes stronger, and if marked cards and certain special pockets in his clothes are found upon him the proof is almost complete, but it will only be fully established by an examination of the antecedents of the individual Rarely is this examination so necessary and rarely must it be pushed so far as when dealing with a

---

* Thackeray uses it in "The Newcomes" "He was in adventurer, a pauper, a black leg a regular Greek"—*Chapter XXXVI* The word has its origin in the cheat Apoulos, a knight of Greek origin, who, towards the close of the reign of *Lewis XIV*, was caught in the very act of cheating at play in the palace of the *Grand Monarque* himself He was sent to the galleys and the nation which gave him birth became from that time a by word for swindler and black leg

sharp. Little regarding his past history will be obtained from the individual himself; he will relate romantic stories to make investigation difficult or even impossible. He proceeds in the same manner as those people who, under false names, pass their lives in prison as "unknowns"; he has served before the mast, travelled, wasted his fortune, been a comedian, circus rider, tamer of animals, could tell a tale of people in high stations if he liked; in short he has recourse to all possible subterfuges not to be obliged to confess that he has been without work for so many years and yet has lived well, and always in the company of fools easy to cheat at cards. If an Investigating Officer succeeds in unmasking the man it will be easy to place him in one of those categories of cheats that every Investigating Officer comes across during his career.

There is the sharp who works among the lower and middle classes. He is as a rule a man who in his youth was good for nothing, clever but incorrigible at school, a regular bad boy, up to all the tricks, living subsequently upon the savings of his old mother and other relations, delighting in performing nice little operations in borrowing, and, finally, becoming the bully of some prostitute. Sometimes, when he is blessed with good looks, he is the paid lover of certain women and even levies blackmail. Balancing thus on the borders of crime he is not slow to enter the society of sharps where he can make an easy income, live well, and, taking it all round, have a pretty good time, if he possesses the manual dexterity required for such a career.

There is the sharp who works among the upper classes. He is nearly always the black sheep of a family, who might have done well but has gone wrong through feebleness of character, laziness and taste for an easy and agreeable existence. The society in which he comes to grief, the success of his knavery, the profits he makes, and the moment of his discovery and conviction are all dependent upon his luck and his skill.

Just as all sharps are like one another in their trade so they resemble one another in appearance. Of course we do not contend that, even with large experience, one can pick out a sharp from a crowd of individuals, or that it is possible to say at once of a suspect whether he is a sharp or not. But whenever we have to deal with the true sharp we will soon notice that he has the same airs, the same manner of presenting himself, the same look, and the same behaviour, as all the other sharps one has ever had occasion to see. Be he a cheat who works among the upper ten, or be he one of those who work in the eating-houses and drink-shops of the lower classes, is of no moment; all have at first a better appearance, are more elegantly clothed, have better manners, and a more confident bearing, than their professed walk in life would lead one to suppose; but at the same time there is something peculiar about them, the stamp of which does not seem quite authentic. In what this thing consists it is difficult to say, but all those who have often had business with such people are not slow to get the impression. They perceive that the individual is not what he pretends to be, that everything about him is fictitious and affected, that he is not perfectly natural, and that he is always hiding something.

Let us further consider two things, the glance and the hands betray the sharp. This glance, *which they all have*, has, especially when they do not think they are being watched, something particularly quick, penetrating, and piercing about it. Short-sighted folk are naturally unfit for the trade of a sharp, but those who have good eyes and whose existence and liberty depend upon their skill in observation and in noticing unobserved everything going on around them, get so accustomed to practising this glance that they cannot prevent themselves doing it even when they are not at the card table but find themselves in a grave situation. A further peculiarity is that all these gentlemen train themselves to see things at a distance or to the right or to the left without being obliged to turn the head—at least sensibly. To do this they bend the head a little, half-close the eyelids to form a species of veil, and roll the eyes on all sides with lightning rapidity, and without anyone sitting in front of them perceiving any strange movement of the head, thus the player has no suspicion that the sharp in front of him sees and observes all that goes on around.

When a sharp has to face the Investigating Officer he knows very well that this time the game is a very serious one and that those gifts by which he has so often succeeded at the card table, namely, prudence, perspicacity, sangfroid, and self-possession, may draw him out of the fire, there is no great difference between the actual situation and that in which he has so often found himself, he, therefore, preserves his ordinary methods and rolls his eyes as usual. It only suffices for the Investigating Officer to notice a single one of these glances to learn with whom he has to deal.

Not less characteristic than the glance are the hands of sharps. Just as the tramp does not possess the horny hands of the honest workman, so the card-sharp has hands extraordinarily well cared-for and manicured. They must be soft, supple, skilful, and most sensitive. The sharp takes great care not to do heavy work which would render the tips of his fingers rough and unsensitive. This delicacy of touch is absolutely necessary to enable him to recognise marked cards. It is said that sharps make their fingers more delicate by treating them with chemicals or even by scraping them. The author does not know whether this is true or not, it is hardly likely, for the resulting scars would render the fingers more insensible than before. But this is certain, that they rub their hands with grease, glycerine, cold cream, and other similar ointments.

B Methods of the Sharp

The manner in which card-sharpers proceed has been described in a thousand books and newspaper articles as well as in special works. An anonymous work exists on the subject, the printer of which is unknown, entitled "The Cheat Betrayed and all his Secrets laid bare." Important information can also be found in "The Card Conjurer," by *C L Hoffmann* (Hamburg 1843), and in *Ire-Lallemant*, already so often referred to. In France a short time after the Revolution, a publication concerning cheating was published called "Diogenes at Paris." Two other French works exist discussing very minutely the ways of sharps firstly, that of the conjurer *Robert Houdin*, and, secondly, that of the late chief of the gaming police of Paris, *M Cavaille*. A most complete work is that of *John Nevil Maskelyne*, called "Sharps and Flats" (London) and also one of the best books from our point of view is that of a certain *Signor Domino*, called "Cards, Card Players, and the Secrets of Card Cheats" (Breslau, 1886),

All Investigating Officers are advised to read these last two books and we intend to make several extracts therefrom to show what a sharp is capable of doing.

In the first place the sharp, like the pickpocket, is able to do all that a conjurer can do, and if the latter executes tricks which we call 'pure sorcery,' it may be very well admitted that the card-sharper also performs many "miracles" of the same kind. The principal trick employed by a card-sharper of this class consists in, at the right moment, that is when he contemplates some manipulation, distracting the attention of the person he is playing with by some dodge. He lets a bird fly, a shot crack or gazes earnestly in front of him. All watch the bird, the shot, or look where the sharper is looking. And during that time the artist can do as he pleases,— nobody takes any notice of him. The aristocratic sharp does not use birds or shoot, but he can make a noise, upset a chair, suddenly yawn loudly, etc.—all are occupied with the noise, and during that time the sharp, also, can do as he pleases. How far this can be carried is shown by a story that has lately been circulating in the newspapers. An elegant Tripolitan had determined to break the bank at Monte Carlo. Here a directly dishonourable manipulation is really impossible, as for such a purpose one would have to corrupt all the officials. That cannot be done, but one of them can be bought over, and this took place. Then a female accomplice came on the scene, an elegant lady who was so clumsy with her rouleaus of money that suddenly about 1,000 louis rolled from the table to the floor.

Everyone was occupied in picking up the money, and by the time the lady had secured all safely, a second deal had taken place: arranged cards, with the help of the raking-in croupier, had been brought on the board, and in the course of the evening the people concerned won an immense sum.

It is difficult to say where cheating goes on most, as a rule it goes on wherever games of chance are played. Above all it must not be believed that cheating is only practised in gaming houses where several confederates bear down upon a single individual for the purpose of robbing him; the real sharp who works alone or with confederates tries to get into society where games of chance are played, and once there he begins to operate. For this he employs, says *Signor Domino*, seven elements namely: faked cards, transferring, false cards, accomplices, the false shuffle, the forced cut, and passing.

(a) '*Faking*' cards consists in making them in various ways: the borders of certain cards, e.g. the picture cards and the aces, are scraped with a sharp knife so that they become rough to the touch while the others remain smooth; at times the cards are pricked with a hot needle dipped in white wax, the wax corks the hole and makes it invisible to the eye but it can be felt with the hand; sometimes the backs of the good cards are rubbed with pumice-stone to make them rough while the others are rubbed with soap to make them more slippery. Another method is to draw on the backs of the cards certain marks which are uniformly coloured and which the sharp at once notices.

In marking cards two principles are employed. Either the cards have each a distinctive mark placed in the same convenient position, or the mark is identical in every case, the indications being given by the position which it occupies. Some systems are based upon a combination of the two principles, but all are developments of either one or the other. When the mark, whatever it may be, is placed at the end of the card it is, of course, necessary to mark both ends.

Some players use cards with bevelled edges, as there are four sides to a card and they may be cut straight or slanting, flat or round, there is no want of combinations. Many other methods of marking cards are employed which we cannot mention here. They will be found exhaustively explained and illustrated in *Maskelyne's* admirable book. These processes can only be employed when the faked cards are already there, or can be substituted for the good ones unseen, otherwise the cards must be marked during the game, which is done with the aid of the finger-nail or of a ring furnished with a little point which easily pricks the cards unknown to anyone.

(b) *Transferring* is an operation which consists either in taking cards away from, or in adding cards to, a pack. Here the whole hand is used, the cards being taken between the ends of the fingers, which are slightly curved, and the palm of the hand. The cards are hidden for an instant on the knee, or in horizontal pockets placed in the cuff of the sleeve or in the back part of the trousers.

(c) *False cards* are those which the sharp carries upon him to substitute for others if opportunity permits; thus the cards which are not marked disappear and those which are marked or arranged in a certain order take their place. For this operation the cheat must have, in addition to these pockets, much skill and boldness. He has also certain single cards in reserve, which he employs if their design is the same as that of the cards the others are playing with.

(d) *Accomplices.* Like all other swindlers the card-sharp has need of accomplices; these latter are especially useful when they do not play themselves; the best confederate is, of course, the master of the house, who walks up and down the card room, but if he is not available any spectator makes a good accomplice. The understanding is brought about, for example, by means of the cigar; the confederate places it in the left corner of the mouth, in the right corner of the mouth, in the middle, he slopes it up, lowers it to the right, etc.; then he can play with his watch chain, emit smoke, and so on; a large number of variations are obtainable in this way by which communications may be made. Another system of signalling sometimes adopted is to indicate the fact of certain cards being held by the position in which the cards are laid upon the table. The person signalling, having looked at his hand, wishes to let his accomplice know that he holds a certain card of importance in the game. Therefore, whilst waiting till the other players have sorted their hands, he closes up his cards for the moment and lays them before him on the table. The manner of their disposition will give the required cue, or as it is called "office." The end of the cards farthest from the operator may be taken to represent a kind of pointer or watch hand, which is set opposite to some particular figure upon an imaginary dial supposed to be drawn upon the table. Several cards can be indicated in this way, and for others additional factors can be introduced. For instance, the cards may be spread somewhat, the top card may project a little to one side or over one end, or the operator may keep his fingers resting upon the cards. In fact, the variety of signals is infinite. From the laying down of a cigar to the taking up of a glass of wine, from the opening of the mouth to the stroking of the chin, every movement, however simple and unsuspicious, can be made the means of cheating at almost any game. A code of signals to indicate every card in the pack, and no more difficult to decipher than the Morse Code in telegraphy, can be arranged by anyone in five minutes. Indeed, the Morse Code itself can be used in connection with what the French sharps call *Le dure musible*, a system of signalling to an accomplice by pressure of the foot under the table. In using this system care must, of course, be taken not to tread on the wrong person's toes.

Other accomplices there are whose duty it is to entice flats into the clutches of the real sharps.

(e) *The false shuffle* is very important to the sharp. The sharp shuffles the cards in such a way as to lead everyone to believe they have been thoroughly shuffled, whereas in reality not one has altered its position. *Maskelyne* explains one method of false shuffling as follows:—

"The pack is taken in two halves, one of which is held in each hand. From the right hand half about half-a-dozen cards are pushed off and placed *beneath* those in the left hand. Then, from the left hand, three cards, say, are pushed off and placed beneath those in the right hand. This process is continued, always putting more cards from right to left than *vice versâ*, until the whole pack appears to have been shuffled into the left hand. This looks exactly like a genuine shuffle. In fact, most persons upon having it explained to them, will say that the cards really *are* shuffled, but it is not so. The effect produced is that of a simple cut."

It will be seen that this method of shuffling neutralises the cut, which is in itself a most important thing to be done. The essential point is to note where the separation of the cards is made in the cut. Where a confederate cuts the thing is simple, otherwise the cut has to be "forced."

(f) *The forced cut* may be accomplished by two processes. The first is to get the cut made in the place the sharp wishes. He relies, and rightly, upon the psychological phenomenon whereby we always do what takes the least trouble. He, therefore, slips into the pack a card which is larger than the others, placing it where he wishes the cards to be cut. If this does not succeed he seizes the cards and bends them in the hand lengthways to make a sort of bridge. In the first case the flat or confederate seizes the pack at the place where the larger card lies, in the second he cuts at the place where the cards begin to bend in opposite directions—and the cut is made as the sharp desires it. If this does not happen, the sharp neutralises the cut by placing the cards exactly as they were before. There are many ways of doing this, one is to pick up the bottom half with the right hand as though he were about to place it upon the other, but instead of so doing, he deliberately puts it into his left hand. Then picking up the top half he adds it to the other in the position it originally occupied. Another very simple method is to cross the hands, picking up the right half of the pack with the left hand, and the left half with the right hand. The two halves are then put together in their former order. The crossing of the hands tends to confuse the eyes and mind of the onlooker, so that he really does not know which hand contains the half that should be placed on top. This can, of course, only be done when playing with people who have not their eyes open and have no suspicion they are playing with sharps.

(g) *Passing.* This consists in drawing false cards from the pack. Less skill than self-possession is required for its accomplishment. The second or third card is got ready, drawn right out of the pack, instead of the first, and laid on the table. It is difficult to say how this is done, but it is hardly ever noticed when the cheat is at all skilled.

Besides card playing, properly so called, another card game, or rather gamble, exists which, in spite of its stupidity, is practised the whole world over, namely, the three card trick. The sharp takes three cards, generally a king and two others, and throws them face upwards upon the table, or, as this game is usually played in the train on the way to the races, upon a travelling rug or newspaper. The sharp then takes the three cards and holds them lengthwise between the thumb and the middle finger, the back of the hand being turned upwards; he then takes one of them in one hand, leaving the other two one above the other in the other hand (say the left hand) with about a finger's breadth of space between them. this done he shows the bottom card he is holding in the left hand, which is the king, and asks the player to remember it well; he then turns the cards again, passes the right hand in which he holds the one card to the left, deposits the card on the table, passes the left hand to the right and makes belief to place the bottom card there, and, returning to the left, seems to place the top card beside the first. Then he slowly changes the places of the three cards while the player keeps his eyes always upon the card first placed to the right. If he gives the latter as being the king he is wrong, for, as a matter of fact, the cheat has not let the lower card but the top card fall when his dupe thought he saw the bottom one go down. However foolish and simple may be this game, there are thousands of people who lose money by it. It is usually played with the help of a confederate who acts the stranger to the sharp and invariably wins, thus inciting others to have a flutter.

A similar game is that called Thimble-rigging, or "Little pea, where art thou?" A pea or some such small object is placed on the table and covered with a thimble or half a walnut shell. Two other thimbles are placed beside it and the pea is rolled from one to the other. The flat has then to guess under which thimble the pea lies, but he never succeeds in doing so, for the pea is simply a little ball of wax which the sharp rapidly picks up with one of his finger-nails. With such gentry it will be well to examine their nails to see whether one of them is particularly long.

A similar trick is sometimes played with an endless chain thrown on a table in many coils, some simple, some complex. The person to be deceived is invited to put his finger within one of the coils on the table and to bet whether his finger will remain free or be taken prisoner on pulling away the chain. This he can never guess, because the sharp catches hold of the chain and pulls it according to the position of the finger, so that he is always in the right. Undoubtedly cleverness is necessary and quick sight to know how the coils will run when pulled; if the sharp knows his business he always wins.

Generally the chain is carried as a watch-chain and incidentally the conversation is brought round to the game, and for want of something better the watch-chain is employed. Sometimes a silk pince-nez cord is used. This is made wet beforehand to run smoother and lie flatter on the table. In this "game" incredibly large sums are sometimes lost, because the thing looks so simple and each person thinks he cannot make a mistake. Of the many variations two are shown. The finger is placed on the table at a' or a'', the sharp pulls the string downwards at b after the bet on "caught" or "not caught" has been made. In 1, Fig 94, the finger is not caught by the string; in B the finger is caught.

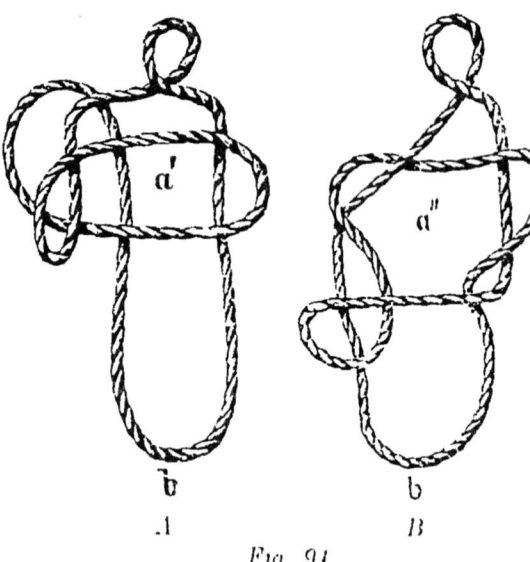

Fig 94

With dice especially there is a great deal of deception, all arising from some peculiarity in the dice that the sharper knows of, but which is not known to the person he means to dupe. With genuine dice it is difficult to deceive. Either some edges of the dice have been ground away, or small bits of lead have been introduced, or the dice are hollow and filled with sand or quicksilver, or short pig-bristles which stick to the table-cloth are introduced into them. In short, with a little practice the sharper can manipulate the dice as he likes. If the dice are seized it is easy to prove what is wrong with them on examination. If the *corpus delicti* is absent, evidence of guilt is hardly possible.

Nowadays dice throwing is dying out and it is unnecessary for us to discuss the varied methods by which they are loaded, manipulated, and thrown. For a complete exposition of the subject we refer the reader to *Maskelyne* (p 229).

To explain all the methods of card and dice manipulation would require a volume to itself, and it is not our intention to go into them fully; all we can do is to give the budding Investigating Officer some idea of what is, and can be done by sharps. If he has to deal with card-sharpers—and some time or other he will come in contact with them—he must make the subject a special object of study, and we cannot do better than refer him to the books we have mentioned.

Section vi.—Frauds relating to Antiquities and Works of Art

Speaking generally, it may be said that the most interesting fraudulent processes are those relating to objects of art and antiquities. The objects in question are in themselves worth the trouble spent upon them, people who fabricate them are hardly ever commonplace people, the sums which change hands in connection with them are often very high, and judicial questions connected with these cases, however interesting they may be, are still for the most part awaiting elucidation. The magnitude and number of these frauds are enormous. The taste for antiquities has in a short time developed immensely, and continues to develop; the majority of objects of incontestable beauty are in hands which will not part with them, the remainder are broken or preserved only in part; the public never ceases to search for curiosities and antiquities, old collectors continue to collect, new collectors start collecting, dealers can no longer comply with the demand, prices are high, the skill of imitators increases, and in consequence when the authentic article cannot be obtained it is made to order. That it is fraud when a false article is sold for an authentic one at a high price there can be no doubt; the difficulty is to know where the fraud begins.

An alteration "repair or embellishment," as people in the trade call it, is not in itself a falsification, and especially with regard to antiquities every falsification is not fraud. One must have spoken on the subject with collectors or be a collector oneself to be convinced that the jurist cannot help being allowed to make some concession in this respect to common opinion. A connoisseur or collector rarely leaves a fine antique in the condition in which he has received it. He cleans it, brings out the colours, alters repairs already made and not in harmony with the rest of the article, gums and glues broken places, and replaces missing parts; in short he tries to repair the object as well as he can to make it appear as valuable as possible. The pride the connoisseur takes in doing up a broken article is considerably greater than that he takes in having spotted, recognised and bought it. Real connoisseurs are nearly always good "renovators," confiding old objects of value to no other hands but their own. Of course they must know how to model, glaze, glue, paint, draw, engrave, cement, solder, and a thousand other similar things.

What beautiful and precious articles we find made out of old rubbish, having no value and no beauty! No doubt for this the "renovator" must be a connoisseur of culture, knowing not only how to give an article shape and colour but also how to do so without changing its style, and restoring it so to speak, instinctively, so that it has absolutely the same appearance as it had when new.

An article thus transformed has evidently gained in value; this cannot be denied, but the question is, has it the same value it would have had if it had never been damaged? and to this question the only reply that can be given is "No!" Ignorant people usually say that an imitation has absolutely the same value as its original if it makes the same impression; if so, an imitation of the celebrated salt cellar Benvenuto Cellini, plus the value of the metal, would be equivalent to the original itself, which no one would dare to suggest. Moreover, a perfectly genuine object has an artistic and historical value which ignorant people cannot understand; but if they would reflect that the history of a people may be read in the articles produced by it—given of course that these form an uninterrupted and authentic series as regards shape, colour, and material—they would be obliged to confess that the great value of an antiquity principally lies in its authenticity. An article which has been renovated may gain in value through being more beautiful, but it loses in value through being less genuine.

But the collector who has renovated an article with much art and care is free to say what he likes about the renovation in question. There are some collectors who are fond of showing what they have done, others on the contrary take care to keep it very dark. The latter course has certain inconveniences, especially as the article may pass into other hands and thus usurp a genuine character; now it is exactly this passing into other hands that is important from our point of view. With the sale of a renovated article, the buyer must be told what is restored and what is genuine, so that he may be able to value the article; if the renovation is passed over in silence there may be fraud. Doubtless, here again good faith may exist. The author has himself dealt with the following case. An article of which there only remained a small genuine portion had been restored that is to say, it was almost entirely new; unfortunately the renovation had not implicitly followed the style of the old piece; the first person into whose hands the article came in this state carefully removed the small genuine piece and substituted therefor a piece in the very same style as the large portion which had been added by his predecessor. Now the second gentleman does not care to sell it, and when he does decide to do so, he may not say that he has repaired it, and, if the repair is found out, he will probably say that he bought the article as genuine whereas as a matter of fact he was himself duped.

The other side of the preceding question has reference to the buyer. Here again large concessions must be made to the customs of the times. People who would not hesitate to inform a shopkeeper that he has given them back too much change or delivered to them merchandise of better value than they have bought, have not the slightest scruple in buying for a song an antiquity of price from some poor devil who has no idea of its value. In this way, a large number of fine collections consisting of the most precious old articles are built up, and no one has ever thought of considering their procedure reprehensible, though they fall under section 197 of the Austrian Penal Code, and section 263 of the German Penal Code. How can a perfectly honest person be or wish to be a curio-hunter?

If prosecutions for frauds relating to works of art and antiquities are relatively rare in some countries, the reason is partly that people who have been made tools of do not like to become the laughing stock of others, preferring rather to keep quiet than lodge a complaint, and also partly that owing to certain technical reasons it is difficult to bring such a prosecution to a successful termination. Fit experts are difficult to find, and Investigating Officers who know something about the matter even more difficult. It is indeed no easy matter to take an interest in a subject which requires deep study and complete detailed information. When he only, so to speak, "swims" on the surface, when he allows himself to drift aimlessly among the depositions of witnesses and the statements of experts, the Investigating Officer is only too happy to wind up such a troublesome case without being obliged to enter very deeply into it. But if he desires to be conscientious and understand what he talks about and has to form an opinion upon, he must take care to attack the subject beforehand, to obtain information from collectors or honest, intelligent, and well-educated curio-dealers and experts and he must also read some special books upon the subject, which are unhappily far from numerous.

In the following pages the author is content to enumerate some of the many articles which are falsified.

A. Prehistoric Objects

These objects are fabricated by the cart-load. The material is cheap, the skill required is very small, and prices are good. The articles made are principally stone weapons (arrow heads, hatchets, hammers) artistic articles (engravings on bone, stones, jewels, etc.), petrified objects, impressions and even antediluvian bones. Many amusing stories are related about the facility with which learned men are taken in by falsification of this kind.

B. Egyptian Antiquities.

For the fabrication of these articles a sort of domestic industry has grown up among the Egyptian peasantry and Arabs, an industry which can hardly meet the demand. Scarabs, idols, mummies of animals (made of glass paste and siliceous clay) are manufactured in enormous quantities and sold at small prices; but in Europe these objects become very dear, though all merchants know their birthplace and sell them as genuine. As regards rolls of papyri, they are unrolled, cut up into strips lengthwise and re-rolled on wooden sticks which are hidden at the ends. Each stick is covered with but a single sheet of papyrus but appears to be a complete roll*; from one roll many others are made, all of them valueless. In this way Rameses, king of Egypt, in a black basalt of Thebes (which was nothing else than Antwerp schist) has been sold for a hundred thousand francs: the manufacture of the Rameses cost the seller 1100 francs. An old Dresden doctor fabricated out of the corpse of a beautiful young girl which he had purchased, the mummy of Queen Nitokris and sold it for its weight in gold; the fraud was only discovered when the mummy began to exude a disagreeable odour.

C. Antique Pottery.

The number of false articles among the vases and small figures we see everywhere nowadays is incalculable. To get an approximate idea one has but to look at the numerous counterfeits collected together in the compartments reserved for the purpose in big collections. And how well made they are! The clay of to-day is the same as that of formerly and the baking is identical, chemistry furnishes us with colours quite as good as those of other days, and we have a sufficiency of models; and in these conditions the real has to be distinguished from the false! The best experts are deceived. Every day, in the most carefully arranged collections, false Tanagra and Myrrhina figures are discovered.

In this connection incredible things occur. Among many cases may be quoted as an example the falsifications of a simple village master mason Michael Kaufmann of Rheinzabern, who for 40 years (1820—1860) deceived

---

* Such scrolls are often to be examined by Röntgen rays, which allow the piece of wood introduced to be clearly recognised. Consequently a roll of pasteboard is now introduced, which under the rays, looks like several layers of papyrus.

many French and German experts. He made Roman ware in immense quantities, plunged the learned in despair with his inscriptions and discredited the Roman art trade with his flying tortoises and other attributes of the Gods, but his falsifications were only discovered after decades when they were brought to a standstill by his making a Minerva with the royal Bavarian padded helmet, and the Roman Emperor, Antonius, with Hessian boots and a full-bottomed wig. But numberless articles from *Michael Kaufmann's* manufactory are still considered genuine in French and German Museums, and the learned controversy over his inscriptions rages still.

At one time old articles of pottery could be distinguished by their great lightness why they are so light we cannot say, but such is the fact. But the falsifier has now succeeded in giving the same lightness to his products by mixing a large quantity of meal, which carbonises in baking, with the potter's clay, but the connoisseur comes along with his magnifying glass and discovers that the articles of pottery thus falsified are, owing to the carbonisation of the meal, much more porous on the surface than the antique. To prevent the connoisseur from discovering this, the falsifier proceeds as follows: before baking, he covers the yet unfinished article, composed as it is of potter's clay and meal, with a thin covering of pure potter's clay wherever the surface is visible, the porosity cannot then be discovered unless the vase be broken and the break examined, but how can this be done? The same procedure is followed in the manufacture of Tanagra figurettes, nowadays so much sought after. Moreover the lightness is increased by fine workmanship, which of course makes them more fragile.

But it is only when dealing with a real connoisseur that it is necessary to use such tricks, for the ordinary commercial, who buys, collects and brings home such articles, all such devices are superfluous; he takes such manufactured articles without hesitation and floods the whole world with them. And as all the falsifications are generally made with the greatest refinement, one can understand the words of one of the greatest experts of the ceramic arts: "For all articles of pottery there is absolutely no sure means of recognition we must trust to the place of origin." Alas, yes, the place of origin! As if there, too, they did not deceive and dupe the world! Whoever wishes nowadays to sell a well-imitated article does not expose it in the shop of a merchant but places it in the ancient garret of some poor widow who swears that it has come down to her from her grandparents, at whose house she played with it, and she finishes by deciding to let it go for an enormous sum. Every day are such stories told and one can hardly help laughing when one sees the happy owner unfolding a certificate given him by the widow certifying that the jug sold to-day (here follows a detailed description of the jug) is a gift made by Count X. to his nurse, the grandmother of the vendor.

D. Glassware

Articles of glass are more easily counterfeited than articles of pottery, for glass changes but little even after a very long time, and even such small changes as tarnishing and iridescence (rainbow-colouring) are easy to produce artificially. Either substances capable of iridescing are introduced into the matter used in the manufacture of the glass or the finished article is treated in a particular manner to obtain the " oldest " glass. Even under natural influences, changes are sometimes produced which, instead of centuries, take but several years; in this way we sometimes find among old stable windows panes much more iridescent than the most beautiful lachrymal urns of ancient Rome. The amount of glass, in imitation of the antique and middle ages, produced from the factories of Isola, Bohemia, and of Belgium, is inconceivable; in the factories themselves it is sold as imitation at a very moderate price, but once it is in the shop of the old art dealer it immediately becomes real old glass.

In the old fortress of Hilgersburg there is a window in the dining hall on which are engraved the following words: "Drinking commenced the 17th May 1519 and was kept up until St Vincent's day and every day all became tight."* This little window has already been replaced many times and for each renewal a collector believes he has the real one.

E. Old Coins and Medals

Coins have been falsified ever since they have existed, and as it is easy to imitate them perfectly it is not so surprising that many intelligent collectors have renounced the pleasure of collecting them, saying that it is impossible to know what one has got.

The counterfeiter knows perfectly well that it is easy to recognise coins made by melting in a mould or covered by electro-plating, so he strikes them from a die. Further, he is not ignorant that in former times there were no steel dies, so he is careful to make his of bronze; in addition to this, he takes the trouble to shake the coins up in a bag and bury them for some time; no one is able to distinguish the real coins from the counterfeit. The sums fraudulently obtained in this way are very considerable.

Particularly dangerous, under certain circumstances, is the at-coinage which often, in an artistic fashion, offers rare coins to collectors. In itself this is very useful, as not every collector can pay the enormous sums of money that are asked for some coins which he desires to have to perfect his collection. The honourable collector says openly which of his coins are imitations. If he dies, the whole collection is perhaps sold, and the genuine coins and imitations go together. In a recent law case, for example, it was proved that to-day so many excellent imitations of the famous *Keutschacher Rubentaler* of 1504, each genuine specimen of which is worth from 1,200 to 1,500 florins, are in circulation that nobody can tell a genuine coin from an imitation.†

---

* Am 17 Mart 1519 hat das Saufen angehebt und biss St Vincenziday gedaurt, und alle Dag am Rausch gehabt.

† This case is very instructive and, if one may say so, very simple. A man obtained possession of a *Keutschacher Rubentaler* and on some plausible pretext was able to get a number of imitations of this thaler made in a well known mint. Then he made impressions of the thaler in tinfoil and sent them to a number of well-known collectors of coins asking if they had a similar coin for sale, as he had a commission to acquire one for 1,100 florins. Naturally all answered in the negative, as only four or five genuine coins of this sort exist. The man waited for some time, then he wrote to the same collectors under another name and offered them a *Keutschacher Reubentaler* at 700 florins. Most of them jumped at the offer with the intention of selling the thaler with a profit of 400 florins to the person who had offered 1,100 florins. The forger did a good business, and so there exist to-day four times as many of these coins as before.

F. Jewellery in precious metals

Such jewels should always be mistrusted, really good articles of this kind are in the possession of rich persons or have passed into the museums and other fine collections; as regards jewels of simple workmanship, they have been melted down or else preserved, so that they cannot be called articles of commerce, if then a really beautiful jewel is found in the shops, it is a jewel manufactured in pieces, being really a genuine article of very simple workmanship which has been covered with ornamentation and flourishes. The verification of the stamp, form, and chemical composition can give no result because all these are genuine and yet it is, perhaps, with this kind of article that falsification is most easily proved. It is, indeed, difficult to manufacture them without a model. No doubt the workman of former days knew how to harmonize with great skill the shape and ornamentation of the article. But the forger, knowing nothing of styles, most often commits blunders. Even when he has excellent models of ornamentation of the period but destined for another shape, he cannot make them harmonize with the jewel. The real connoisseur, who would probably know better how to do it himself, can at once recognize the hand and is at least able to say that the article is not entirely genuine. As regards real models which he requires to copy the forger cannot procure them, he can only look at them and that is not much good to him.

We would hasten to add that the Investigating Officer should here, and in analogous cases, really do something to avoid taking as an expert the first merchant he comes across, he must find a real connoisseur who loves the subject and has an extensive and deep acquaintance with it.

G. Pictures.

Everyone knows that pictures are falsified and that many painters make a trade of it. Numbers of suspicious canvases are sent to the academies and other institutes of art for an opinion as to their genuineness. Here all that is necessary is to remind the Investigating Officer that he ought not to stop his investigations in a case where certain signs seem to plead in favour of genuineness. The Investigating Officer will only too easily find himself being led into calming the complainant and ceasing his investigations if he thinks he is himself an expert and finds no reason for doubting the canvas.

He looks at it from the front, the painting appears really good and old, the tone is gilded and browned, but this tone is not the effect of age, it has been obtained with the help of a daubing of licorice juice, he sees a layer of old dirt but it has been produced artificially with cinders and gum. He turns the picture over, the canvas is quite old and brown, with an old sale mark on it, canvas and mark are equally genuine, but a valueless picture was painted on it and the falsifier has copied a subject of high value over the old and worthless original. The mouldiness is artificial, the signature of the painter is false, the frame comes from another picture and thus, in spite of its genuine appearance, the whole is a forgery. In such a case a precipitate man is always dangerous.

With regard to new pictures it may be said that forgers buy, for preference, in the sales which follow the deaths of well-known painters, half-finished or discarded canvases and sketches, in order to finish them themselves and sell them as genuine. On the other hand it must not be thought that the existence of a copy is a certain proof of its falsity. Very celebrated painters often, nowadays, paint to order, twice or even ten times over, a canvas which has caught on. The first copy goes to Germany, a second to England, a third to America, but it may happen that they all meet in the same country and each owner possesses the original.

Cases as numerous as they are interesting are known in which real experts have been taken in by false pictures, but it seldom happens to an Investigating Officer to have to deal with one of these cases, although examples of this kind of fraud are so frequent.

H. Artistic Engravings

Nowadays these are especially forged by chemical photographic processes, and when the paper is well chosen and coloured with coffee or nicotine and the print is successful, the perfect expert can alone find out the deception. The risk must be very great indeed in the case of engravings which are rarely falsified. Happily the originals are, for the most part, in good hands, so that the forgers find it difficult to get at them, but as we have said above, they attain their end in a roundabout way; art institutes of the first rank publish photo-type copies of the best old engravings and sell them as imitations to people of artistic taste who cannot procure the originals; but when these copies pass to a second or third owner their origin is often passed over in silence and the heliograph begins to circulate as an etching.

I. Enamels

What can be done in this connection is well exemplified in the trial of *Samuel Weininger*, who falsified many precious articles in the famous collection of the *Duc de Modena* (1876—1877). These forgeries were so well executed that, after the case, they fetched a very handsome price.

J. Articles of Earthenware, Stone, and Porcelain.

These are much sought after for collections and decorations, and in consequence are produced in great quantities. The falsification is difficult to detect, for the old manufacturers (such as Doulton) still continue to produce them after their old models and marks. Everything reproduced by unqualified persons bearing real trade marks is manifestly false. Among articles of antiquity which must be considered as false, we class every vessel which is 'discovered' by the buyer. Articles for sale are placed in peasants' houses or in the homes of the lower middle classes, whose business it is to attract the attention of amateurs to them. It is this last operation that is delicate and requires *savoir-faire*. Domestic servants, merchants, and small tradespeople are employed and paid for their complicity, ingenious little advertisements are sent out, etc., the discovery is then made to the amateur and his money is obtained.

In the production of these counterfeits the same procedure is used as for silverware. Indeed, as old baking, glazing, and, generally speaking, old "*timbre*" are not difficult to imitate in earthenware and porcelain, the fabricator buys, for preference, genuine old vases, white or with but little colour in them, especially dishes and plates, these he decorates himself, sometimes with much real art, and then rebakes them. This mixture of the real and the artificial often looks very well and is difficult to distinguish when, as often happens, the artist has done his work with taste.

K Manuscripts, Books, and Bindings

Manuscripts are copied almost to perfection by trained craftsmen thanks to the progress of the industrial arts, the reproduction of the old impression offers little difficulty. Skill and impudence are used in mixing the false with the true. Thus certain genuine parts are often combined with imitated parts by photographic engraving, or various fragments which have had no connection with one another are united together and in a manner so skilful that the forger often ends by not even knowing himself how he built up his work. One of the most ordinary contrivances is to take off the fine bindings from books of inferior value or but little sought after nowadays and adapt them to books which are in demand. Another fraud is to add missing title pages to a book either by printing on blank pages with lettering corresponding more or less to those in the text or by gumming in a new leaf with another title altogether. In this direction the forger can go very far, and whatever may be the skill of connoisseurs in distinguishing each separate letter in the book it often happens that they are not shocked by a title page which jars with the text. Often frontispieces (letters and vignettes) are drawn in with the hand by a chemical process, transferred to zinc, and then reproduced. When the work is well done it is difficult to distinguish the fraudulent from the genuine impression.

Here again care must be taken not to generalise one's suspicions. One knows that the bands enclosing the various forms of a book used often in former days to be made of parchment, and this parchment carries sometimes precious inscriptions. Now, those who go in for collecting and especially book lovers search for these bands and find on them fragments of important documents or old poetry, etc. So to obtain these bands they take to pieces old books and bind them up again. The result is a book which has certainly depreciated in value while all the parts except the binding have remained genuine.

L Furniture and Upholstery

When some years ago old furniture began to be searched out and utilised, it was possible to procure easily and cheaply a complete and genuine installation. But once the fashion became established and everyone wanted to furnish their houses in the ancient style fine old specimens soon became priceless or impossible to discover. As always industry and commerce hastened to find the remedy for the situation. Antiquities and ancient processes were studied, corners and nooks were searched for antique articles, which when found were restored, touched up or imitated, and soon really genuine articles became rarities. These articles are seldom imitated well to-day we have neither the same tools, the same material, the same dyes and stains, nor the same patience. In addition to this the furniture of to-day is made by workmen and not by artists, as are pictures and coins, etc, and in consequence in this branch of imitation, faults so great are committed that it is astonishing to see men of taste allowing themselves to be taken in. Sometimes the process is the least intelligent that could be possibly used: the shopman who has perhaps discovered a really beautiful and genuine settee will take care not to leave it as it is. He will take it to pieces and insert a fragment of it into a certain number of new settees: one has the lid, another a panel, a third another panel, etc. when the article is sold care is always taken to show the genuine portion and the buyer is made to be convinced by all sorts of demonstrations that the whole article is of as good character. This is the lot of nearly every article: the greatest care is taken to spoil the few genuine things which do exist.

Material for imitation can be found on all sides: the destruction of an old house gives worm-eaten wood; the dealer in bric-a-brac provides old genuine locks to which are added a new almirah; one old door-hinge is enough, to copy, make a second and put a door to them. An old piece of used cloth will serve to upholster a brand new chair; two old stove pieces will decorate the doors of an almirah; and two genuine old watch-hands are placed to works and case which have never been used before.

When old material is absolutely not forthcoming, new is made. Wood is prepared by hanging it in the chimney or cooking or maltreating it in other ways; it is then worked up. Sometimes even worm-holes are faked and filled with the excrement of birds. Edges are broken to be repaired. The velvet to be used in upholstering furniture is washed. The interior of almirahs is covered with paper torn out of old books. As regards iron-work, it is rusted in acid, cleaned, and then, if necessary, handed to some countryman to whom the particular person who is looking for old furniture for his home is directed.

But the faults are not difficult to find for an attentive observer, even if he is not an expert. The expert, indeed, scents the falsification from afar. As to the observer, who, without being an expert, has a good eye, he soon notices the want of coherence in the article as a whole. It is precisely this want of coherence which attracts his attention. It is manifest when, e.g., a settee which has already been used as a seat has the lid ornamented with sharp edges,—when an almirah whose exterior is much used is lined inside with paper, which although very old, is yet well preserved and in no way damaged,—when a wardrobe seems to have been much in use and the lock mechanism is in as good condition as if it had just come out of the hands of the locksmith,—and so on. These and other analogous mistakes, which are committed not through ignorance but through want of thought, may be discovered by any person who does reflect a little.

M. Weapons

Weapons are as exposed to falsification as furniture, and these falsifications are recognisable quite as easily as the latter. What is missing in this kind of falsification is the minute, patient, and careful work, applied even to the smallest details. May be an expert will not recognise that a cuirass is false if he only looks at the principal parts; but if he examines the nails, the pads, the thongs, and other details, he will clearly see that the whole cannot be genuine. The rust is produced artificially, as are also the bosses, the marks of usage, and the chasing; but the old rust caused by time bears another aspect to that which is artificial, in the decorations something is wanting, namely the calm and patient care of the workmen of bygone times who used to work slowly and as humour took them. Whoever has seen genuine articles beside the false ones and has come to know their character will almost immediately recognise them.

Speaking generally we may say the expert in antiquities who possesses a certain culture never finds himself in difficulties. If his special branch is furniture, lace, or porcelain, he will not fail also to recognise false weapons although they may require special knowledge. The illiterate expert in antiquities sometimes guesses things by habit, sometimes by instinct. But the statements of such men cannot be implicitly relied upon.

N Miscellaneous.

Besides the above-enumerated objects of importance, everything sought after by collectors is imitated. Old methods are employed in the weaving of cloth, ivory is softened in vinegar for the hands of the carver, and subsequently hardened again in water. The lines of the carving may be a little wrong but that is nothing, the article only appears more genuine. Finally the carvings in ivory are yellowed by smoke and perspiration. Eudel relates that a Jew used to carve in this way pretty little ornaments in ivory which he placed inside the corset of a woman until they became yellow and old. As regards bronzes, production is an accessory question, everyone possesses the material, shapes can be remodelled and easily founded; the difficulty is to produce the *patina* or green incrustation peculiar to old bronze, but that also can be counterfeited so thoroughly that it is often impossible to discover the fraud. Formerly the counterfeited *patina* could be removed with lemon juice, to-day patina is made which will resist all the lemon juice in the world. In the same way they used at one time to recognise bronzes obtained by the electro-metallurgic process by the holes produced by the points of contact of the conducting wires. Nowadays these holes are carefully hidden by corking them with an alloy of nine parts of lead to two of antimony and one of bismuth. This alloy expands on cooling so that no one will be able to see it if the white point is immediately covered over with sufficient patina.

Among instruments of music the violin is the principal one falsified. It used to be thought that the secret of Amati, Stainer, Stradivarius, Guarnari, and other celebrated violin makers resided in the shape and varnish of the instruments and that time had contributed much to augment the value. But shape and varnishing can be imitated, and as to time the wood can be dried. For nowadays no one believes any longer that by usage alone the atoms of wood in the instrument are disposed in a new and more favourable manner. Here again the microscope has done good service and has pointed out that the violin makers of other days used only to employ wood grown in a certain way and of which the rings were superimposed in a particular manner; this kind of wood is rare but it still exists and whoever finds it has but to well dry it in order to be able to make "old" violins.

What else is falsified? The answer is everything that one buys: watches, locks, keys, lace, pewter dishes, cameos, playing cards, fans, articles of wax, cut gems, objects of daily use, children's toys, postage stamps, may all be falsified more or less easily, put on the market and sold. And to be frank we must admit that all this does not do honour to justice, seeing that this shameless trade remaining almost entirely unpunished, seriously injures the public morality. If all this is allowed, why can one not do this or that?" Indeed, it is difficult to say why every fraud which is easy to discover is punished severely, while, on the other hand, grave frauds which have grown into a trade are left unpunished, unless it be that in the latter proof is difficult and dependent on special knowledge. People do not worry and make a fuss. It cannot be said not to be regrettable because it is often the case of an individual who seems to have nothing else to do but waste his money in this manner, for, apart from certain collectors who do not give themselves up to this occupation merely out of distraction it must be remembered that falsified objects find their way into public collections, where they serve a serious end, and, becoming the object of historical and learned work, they may be the cause of the gravest errors. It is therefore not useless to elucidate these frauds.

CHAPTER XIX

ARSON.

Section i.—General.

The importance of the crime of arson is as great as the difficulties which beset the Investigating Officer in detecting it. Naturally he will search for traces of the cause of ignition and attempt to establish the place of outbreak of the fire, but in the majority of cases this will be no simple matter: crimes of this kind are usually carried out so as to leave few, if any, direct clues and proof of criminality is far from easy to establish by circumstantial evidence. As a rule the culprit has approached the house on a stormy night, lit a match, and fired some inflammable portion of the edifice. The problem is still more difficult in the numerous cases where the criminal foresees that suspicion will fasten upon himself for some reason such as enmity, or jealousy, and therefore, takes the trouble of getting up an alibi in advance. So also is it in the case of the landlord himself, who, overwhelmed in debt, fires his own premises for the sake of the insurances. In these various cases the incendiary will do all in his power to prove that at the time of conflagration he was far enough away to make it impossible for the fire to be his work. To this end he endeavours to start the fire after the lapse of a certain time, and, unfortunately, the means at his disposal are many, some are simple, others very ingenious.

The most usual method is to light a candle the bottom of which rests upon some hay or other inflammable substance. Before the candle has burnt down to the hay, the criminal has time to get well away and can prove that at the time of the outbreak he was in the presence and to the knowledge of numerous witnesses, drinking in a distant house of refreshment, buying cattle at a market, or attending a ceremony.

Another common method is to join together some strips of tinder to form a train of considerable length upon the floor, one end being inserted in a box of matches surrounded with inflammable material and the other set fire to. If the tinder has been well impregnated with a solution of saltpetre its extinction is practically impossible by natural means. Such a solution is also employed to render any flaxen or hempen thread almost inextinguishable.

An intelligent criminal makes ready use of a clock which raises a hammer at any desired moment; he arranges so that the hammer strikes some explosive substance, which in turn sets fire to some matches. If need be an ordinary alarm clock suffices, especially one which lights itself. These latter are furnished with a spring to the end of which a wax match is fixed; the spring is stretched and held by a catch. At the desired moment the mechanism moves the catch, and the spring is released, carrying with it the match, the head of which rubs along a rough surface and catches fire. The convenience of this arrangement to the sleepy head in the morning is in proportion to its danger from the point of view of house firing, for its employment requires little intelligence or skill

A particularly dangerous and common method in America is to utilise an ordinary electrical bell. The sounding part of the bell is replaced by a thin, balloon-shaped glass filled with sulphuric acid. The hammer strikes on the glass and breaks it, the sulphuric acid runs into a vessel placed beneath and filled with a mixture of, for example, chloric acid and sugar. This produces fire that can easily be converted into a conflagration. Thus highly-insured warehouses can be fired in the night-time by an accomplice or even an innocent party ringing the bell, the owner being far away at the time.

In this connection a burning-glass is frequently used. In some parts there exists a popular belief that the possession of a burning-glass is forbidden by law, solely by reason of the fires it may bring about. In such a case the glass is fixed on a part of the roof where the sun strikes at a particular time and is adjusted so as to direct its rays on some sulphur, pitch, matches, straw, etc. If the glass has been placed so as to receive the sun's rays at, say, 8 a.m., the criminal can obtain twenty-four hours' start, or even longer if the following days happen to be cloudy.

In an old record the author came across an account of a fire caused by a burning-glass. A miller's boy had a grudge against a rich peasant whose house was situated opposite the mill. The youth had left his situation at the mill, and nine months later the peasant's house was burnt to the ground at mid-day when everyone was in the fields. It was suspected that this boy had arranged a burning-glass on the roof of the mill for the purpose of setting fire to the house opposite. He must have chosen for the purpose the upper part of the granary which no one ever visited. Apparently with the help of a cord, he stretched a strong iron spring in front of a skylight and stuck a ring of pitch round the end of it. Below the cord he then placed some combustibles and arranged a burning-glass so as to be struck by the sun's rays at a particular time of year and at a particular hour. Everything ready, he had waited till that time of year had gone by, then placed the glass in position, and left his situation. Nine months later the sun again came round, struck the burning glass, and ignited the fuel. This set fire to the pitch and cord, and the latter breaking released the spring, which projected the burning pitch through the skylight on to the thatched roof of the house opposite, which thus took fire and was burnt to the ground. The thing is not impossible and demonstrates how, with a little skill and ingenuity, most extraordinary things may take place.

In the majority of cases the action of the Investigating Officer is fettered by the fact that the *corpus delicti* is itself destroyed in the fire, but not always. Thus on one occasion a farmer, desiring to set fire to his large homestead for the sake of the insurances, employed the ribbon of tinder above mentioned. To make certain he arranged two trains in two different parts of the building, as far distant from each other as possible. One of the two acted but the other failed, the tinder having gone out at one of the places where it had been sewn together. The portion of the house containing this latter was saved, and the half-burnt train discovered.*

---

* This is the case where the microscope established the culpability of the farmer by proving the thread with which the strips of tinder were sewn together to be from the same piece as that employed by him in mending his fur cap. See p. 141.

When everything is consumed it must not be forgotten to investigate whether the person suspected has in his possession, or has procured articles which may be employed as fire-raisers (candle, tinder, alarm clock, burning-glass, etc). Proportionately speaking, it may be stated that few fires originate in burglaries, and this must be borne in mind. The many cases of fire caused by carelessness, stupidity, children, lightning, and spontaneous combustion, do not concern us here; but cases in which fires have been brought about from peculiar motives require notice. We must not be deceived regarding the many fires caused by young persons of undeveloped intelligence for which no normal explanation can be given. The author has himself had to deal with a case in which a boy of thirteen, remarkably well-developed both in mind and body, four times in succession started a fire, in order, as he himself confessed, to see the new fire brigade turn out. A similar case was dealt with a short time ago in Leoben (Obersteiermark), in which a young man of bad repute caused seven fires, one after the other, three of which were attended with sad results, for the simple reason that he, as a member of the Volunteer Fire Brigade had thereby an opportunity to distinguish himself by showing promptitude, courage, and ability.

An astonishing number of fires are caused by half-grown-up girls who suffer from an excess of homesickness, and who endeavour by strong and acute excitement to relieve chronic nerve-irritation.

Section ii.—Quasi-Spontaneous Combustion.

The question of spontaneous combustion is of great importance to the Investigating Officer, for on the one hand it may bring about the gravest disasters and on the other it is often the origin of fires which seem to have been lit only by the hand of a criminal. Combustion not, accurately speaking, spontaneous may be distinguished in a general way from spontaneous combustion properly so called. The former takes place through the fortuitous combustion of diverse substances, of which no one can be considered, individually, as dangerous; the latter occurs when a body catches fire by virtue of its nature and without the intervention of any other body whatever.

A. Through Physical Causes

Such causes are very numerous, we all know how a carafe of water has acted as a burning glass and set fire to articles resting behind it, such as table-cloths, curtains, paper, garments. The same effect has also been produced by photographic lenses, which is one of the reasons why they are as a rule kept covered up; metal plates, dishes, metal reflectors, etc. have also acted in this way by concentrating the rays of the sun at one particular spot.

To this category belong the numerous cases to be found in the daily papers; thus a carpenter was nailing a plank in a jute factory, the blow missed and the nail was projected into the machinery where it caused a spark which set fire to the jute. From New York we hear of a case in which a fire was caused by a fire engine. A small house was burning, the steamers were at work, and a jet of water penetrated a room of a neighbouring house where some lime and other inflammable materials were stored, the lime caught fire and so the house was burned. When Cleveland was elected President of the United States, one of his partisans arranged a set-piece of fire-works in front of the house; a squib, describing a curve, fell down a chimney of a neighbouring cotton mill to the floor, where it exploded and set fire to the building. At Verona in a train in motion the axle of a carriage became heated and set fire to the grease. At the moment when the train was passing the points, this particular carriage became derailed and was precipitated with the flaming axle into a huge oil reservoir; a violent conflagration ensued which destroyed a neighbouring factory. Here is an account given by a workman who witnessed it of the manner in which a fire broke out one day in a spinning mill. A flying beetle coming through an open window carried off a thread of flax in its flight; the insect passed close to a gas-burner, the thread took fire and fell upon a heap of flax, which immediately burned up. In this class of cases may also be cited the phenomenon observed by Dr. Hapke, whose work upon spontaneous combustion cannot be too highly recommended as a book to be studied by every Investigating Officer. He discovered that a spark might remain for weeks in damp cotton and then set fire to it. It is also noteworthy that decomposed dynamite may explode on a very slight shock, as for instance the closing of a door. All such cases should teach the Investigating Officer not immediately to jump to the conclusion that it is a case of arson solely because a conflagration cannot at first be satisfactorily accounted for.

B. From Chemical Causes.

This class of combustion is brought about by the contact of certain substances engendering heat and fire. It rarely happens that combustion of this description is fortuitous, but it may be a terrible weapon in the hands of a criminal. For this reason it would be ill-advised on our part to discuss it in detail; the Investigating Officer who desires to be well instructed in the subject had better be informed thereon by an expert. But a few well-known methods may be mentioned as their use is already fairly common and well known to criminals. For example we have liquid-fire, a solution the method of preparation of which is given in every chemistry book. If a piece of blotting paper be dipped in this solution and then waved about, the liquid evaporates and the remaining particles of phosphorus contained therein spontaneously catch fire from contact with the air. This solution appears to have been frequently employed by the Fenians and also was used to charge bombs during the American War of Independence. It is all the more dangerous in that risk remains even after the fire has been extinguished, since the phosphorus may burst into flame again at any moment. Metallic potassium also takes fire on contact with water and is sometimes made use of, whereas a mixture of chloride of sulphur with the liquid fire above mentioned catches fire on contact with liquid ammonia. Numerous other cases of fire similarly produced might be cited. For example, certain corrosive acids produce fire on contact with certain substances. Suppose a flask filled with such an acid, corked, and suspended mouth downwards above one of these inflammable substances; the acid after eating away the cork will drop upon the substance and ignite it.

Section III.—Spontaneous Combustion Proper.

The question of *spontaneous combustion*, properly so called, has been much discussed. It is now generally accepted that all bodies are susceptible of change from the solid to the gaseous state: while in the case of some the transformation takes place only at a very high temperature, with others ignition may occur at quite ordinary temperatures and thus cause disastrous conflagrations. *Boyle* (1860) has called such bodies "*Phorphori*:" and *Homburg*, *Bottger*, and others have drawn up long lists of substances possessing this property.

From our point of view the important matter is to know the particular substances in everyday use possessing this property of spontaneous combustion. This list will include all products of textile plants,—hemp, flax, cotton and tissues and thread, ropes, cords, etc., made therefrom, but this only when these substances have been treated more or less heavily with oil, especially linseed oil. The phenomenon also happens with fine carbon, especially coal dust, particularly when the latter is rich in sulphur. Whether sulphur itself can cause spontaneous combustion is still a disputed point. Cases of spontaneous combustion are known to have occurred in turf, peat, wheat, guano, powdered bones, touched grain, sponges, wood shavings, etc.; metal filings have even been known, when damped with oil, to become red hot. Zinc dust when wetted is specially prone to catch fire. In recent years benzine, now so much in demand, has been a considerable source of danger. The vapour of benzine when mixed with atmospheric air produces an explosive gas igniting at the ordinary temperature of a room. Terrible accidents by burning have been thus caused.

Numerous cases of spontaneous combustion are cited by *Collis Barry*, principally in Bombay. Of twenty-six cases given by him the majority were due to oil in contact with cotton, cotton-waste, rags, flax, jute, hemp, or sawdust. Lamp-black and coal occurred in five cases. Other cases show that woody fibre impregnated with turpentine, a mixture of resin, turpentine and tar, damp raw cotton, damp esparto grass, damp grain, dry silk, dry wool, damp hay, lime, Bengal matches and phosphorus, may all spontaneously ignite. A peculiar case is quoted by him at some length. A yellow paper lamp-shade exploded, though nowhere near a flame. On examination it was found that the paper of which the shade was made contained chromate of lead as a colouring matter. A ready method of recognising such dangerous paper is given by Dr. A. Dupré in a letter to *The Times*, May 23, 1891. "The paper is set fire to and the flame then blown out. In the case of ordinary paper it will be found that the glow along the burnt edge is very soon extinguished, whereas in the case of these chromate papers it continues until the whole is consumed, as is the case with ordinary touch-paper. I find that besides the yellow-paper, pale-green paper also contains chromate of lead, and would, no doubt, be equally dangerous and possibly there are papers of other colours containing the same material."

It has already been mentioned (see p. 324) that paper which has been quite recently burned but not completely consumed may sometimes recommence to burn on coming in contact with the open air. Care must, therefore, be taken, after a fire, before opening a safe which has been among the flames to make sure that the interior is quite cold, otherwise papers of value enclosed therein and only half-consumed may blaze up beautifully when the safe is opened. It may be noted here that the dust of grain, jute, and hemp may catch fire on a person entering with a light into a place where such substances are stored, or being worked up.

We cannot leave the subject of spontaneous combustion without a few remarks upon what is called *preternatural combustibility*. Cases have been recorded in which the human body has exhibited unwonted inflammability and burnt away rapidly, the combustion being accompanied by the presence of much inflammable gas and the production of heavy grey soot and an objectionable odour. Charles Dickens, as everybody knows, made use of this alleged property of the human body in 'Bleak House,' and there mentioned the Italian case of the Countess Carnelha Baudi (recorded by *Bianchini*), who was accustomed to bathe in camphorated spirits. One morning a servant entered the room and found a heap of ashes and the remains of her mistress on the floor, about four feet from the bed. The legs and arms were unburned and the head lay between the legs, the brain and back of the skull having been consumed by fire. There was a lamp on the floor, containing no oil and covered with ashes, and the wicks of two candles on the table were unconsumed, the tallow having melted. The bed was unburned, but everything in the room was covered with moist soot. Numerous other cases have occurred from time to time in which death by spontaneous combustion is alleged to have taken place, but to-day the possibility is not allowed by the majority of medical experts. This subject should be approached by criminal investigators with the greatest caution. Indeed, as is pointed out by *Taylor*, such a defence as spontaneous combustion might afford would, if admitted, prove most convenient to assassins. After the commission of a murder it would be the easiest thing in the world for the criminal to burn the body and ascribe the charred remains to spontaneous combustion.

The question of the spontaneous combustion of the gases of the body may also be very embarrassing to an Investigating Officer. This combustion used to be very well known to the common people, who with its help tried to explain away numerous incidents of crime; they hastened to assert the victim to be a drunkard, that the gases of the spirits he had drunk had taken fire, and that he had perished miserably. For a long time such phenomena were accepted, until the usual reaction took place and their possibility was denied altogether. Consequently many cases, otherwise inexplicable, were unexplained or explained wrongly.

The existence of inflammable gases in the stomach has been proved by medical men such as Drs *François, Kuhn, Popoff, Scott-Orr, Beatson, Schulze, Arnold*, etc., but it may generally be admitted that only gases escaping from the body by belching or otherwise can explode at a flame. Slight burns at the mouth and burning of the beard or moustache are all that observation has revealed in the majority of cases, but no doubt serious burns are possible. *Beatson* records a case where a man, while blowing out a match, set fire to his breath, the accompanying report of the explosion being loud enough to awaken his wife.

CHAPTER XX

SERIOUS ACCIDENTS AND BOILER EXPLOSIONS.

Section 1.—General Considerations.

In the latter part of this Chapter we shall offer some detailed information in connection with the explosion of steam-boilers, but, even in doing so, we treat that class of accident really as a type. The present general observations will be found equally applicable to a boiler explosion, a railway smash, a collision at sea, the collapse of a new building or any other catastrophe of a similar nature, proceeding from preventible causes. In every case what has to be done is to find the preventible cause that has not been prevented, and the person responsible for that negligence. We should permit no shifting of responsibility, we must fix it on the proper shoulders, scapegoats cannot be tolerated.

The first necessity in this connection is that the authorities should be awake to the danger and do all in their power to prevent similar accidents. So far as preventive precautions are concerned, there are plenty—sometimes, indeed, too much and too many. Take, for instance, the case of a boiler, the public tests may be too exacting and may even so weaken the boiler as to render it unfit for its work, the result being an explosion at an early date. Of course some negligence on the part of the attendants must be allowed for, but the fact remains that the boiler might have long done good work but for the injury caused by the Government trials. As to punishment it is generally wholly insufficient, at least the instances of anyone being made responsible for culpable negligence in superintendence are so rare, that we can only ask why those acts of carelessness which are always, or almost always, the cause of such catastrophes are allowed to go unpunished.

Any one of us who has been called upon to interpose officially in an accident of this nature knows how things befall. When the disaster has occurred and the experts have reported to the authorities the Investigating Officer will betake himself to the spot, but rarely will he hit the moment of the experts' visit, it will be disadvantageous, indeed, for the Investigating Officer to waste time by summoning his experts in due form and awaiting their arrival. Once the report received, the Investigating Officer ought immediately to start for the scene, leaving full instructions as to what arrangements (*bandobast*) should be made and as to summoning experts.

If the Investigating Officer remains rooted to the scene of the catastrophe, he is assailed on every side. The destruction is generally great, dead bodies lie about, the groans of the wounded are heard everywhere, the scene of the accident presents a terrible chaos, the whole is a spectacle of

GENERAL CONSIDERATION

desolation, disorder, and confusion. Then the proprietors of the works, the engineers, the traffic superintendents, the architect, the contractor, etc., are quickly in evidence and exhaust themselves in representing to the Investigating Officer, who, of course, knows nothing about it, that this disaster is the greatest chance that ever happened, or, if one of the attendant workmen has been found dead, in throwing all the blame on the negligence of the poor devil. The flood of talk never ceases until the Investigating Officer, by some apt technical questions, shows these gentlemen that they have not to do with an absolute idiot. If this succeeds, they change their tactics; instead of talking nonsense to the Investigating Officer, they furnish him with inaccurate information, the object being to clear everybody, at least those still in the land of the living. But such explanations are not protracted; there is suddenly a great hurry "to clear away," of course, for the sake of safety; the Investigating Officer is assured that no delay is permissible, to avoid a fresh explosion, a flood, a fire, the fall of a wall, etc., and, as a last resort, there is the excuse of the missing, who may be buried in the ruins and must be rescued forthwith.

But, in reality, the object is only to withdraw from the eyes of the authorities and the experts the *corpora delicti*: the rotten sleepers, the flaws in a rail or girder, the defective pieces of boiler plate, the bad setting, the overweighted safety valves—if, indeed, these are not wanting altogether; at the least, it is hoped by these proceedings to obscure and befog the whole affair, so that the experts may be unable to pronounce a definite opinion as to who is responsible. There are, of course, we admit, honourable exceptions where mistakes are frankly admitted, but they are rare enough.

By far the most difficult problem for the Investigating Officer is as to what should be done when formal permission is requested thus to clear away debris "for the sake of safety"; on the one hand, the Investigating Officer cannot take upon himself the responsibility of vetoing such operations, which may be absolutely necessary, or at least advisable, nor on the other hand can he lightly consent to the disappearance before his very eyes of the evidence necessary to bring home the guilt to the proper quarter. If the Investigating Officer has good grounds for suspecting any such design, he should boldly inform those clamouring for "clearing away" of his suspicions, and tell them straight that they will be held responsible for future developments; that a report will be prepared of everything that happens as it happens, and that the experts will be consulted later on as to this pretended urgency. In the majority of cases he will be told that these operations "are not actually so very urgent as all that," and need not be commenced at once. In the alternative, the measures announced must be carried out without fail. Every occurrence will be enshrined in a report and, above all, no object, even the most insignificant, must be permitted to disappear. The less the Investigating Officer knows about such matters, the more incumbent is it upon him to frustrate any attempt at deception. He must also be on the watch lest anything be concealed or unnecessarily mutilated, so that any subsequent inquiry may be rendered futile or at least exceptionally difficult. If everything has been carefully recorded and no material objects have disappeared, the situation will not be over-obscured by this work of clearing away, and the experts will be able to form their conclusions almost as well as if they had been there from the start and had witnessed the whole march of events. As soon as possible the Investigating Officer should interrogate, if only summarily, everyone who can furnish any information as to the occurrence, after having, of course, entrusted the *surveillance* of the scene of the accident to trustworthy subordinates. The Investigating Officer will do well not to commence his inquiry by examining managing directors, architects, contractors, engineers, and other special employés. Naturally one would wish to do this so as to possess a competent and enlightening opinion serving as a foundation for subsequent questions, most convenient but far from prudent. We thus put ourselves in the way of starting with preconceived ideas, the well-informed and scientific witness always seeks to give the affair a sort of twist, and even at times tries to coach his subordinates as to "the real cause of the accident." When these subordinates in their turn get into the witness-box, they cannot often distinguish between what they have themselves seen and what their "boss" has told them they saw.

These subordinates, assistants, workmen, chauffeurs, coolies, etc., generally desire to tell the truth and give valuable evidence, if not previously influenced; they should therefore be questioned first and quickly. They are also, naturally, those who have actually seen happenings on the spot and can give most useful hints. Otherwise the catastrophe will generally come to be laid at the door of one of these very subordinates. The primary cause, it is true, may often be brought home to one of these under-strappers, but the real question becomes,—Is he the man truly responsible? The Investigating Officer will have to find out, by his own inquiries or from experts, what the scapegoat had to do, what he was capable of doing, and how far he was competent to perform the task allotted to him.

An inquiry of this kind thus differs much from that in which the Investigating Officer is usually engaged; many things must be taken into consideration to fix responsibility on the proper shoulders. Not unfrequently it will turn out that the man was overworked, either through having to attend to his engine too many hours a day, or through having too many different things to look after. Again it may be found that while the employé was well trained for his work and had even passed examinations therein, he had not sufficient practical experience of this particular job, or was new to the engine and had not yet learned its fancies and failings. Perhaps it may come out that the man has actually reported faults and that his warnings have been disregarded. Often enough the verdict is "Boiler explosion, want of water, fault of the engineer" although the engineer may just before have complained of the deficient supply and been told to "mind his own business." In all technical undertakings, mines, factories, steam-engines and boilers by land or sea, the blame is always thrown on some wretched coolie. The real cause should be looked for in insufficient staff, lack of training, want of supervision,—and at the bottom of all we find cheese-paring and false economy. The most difficult and important task is entrusted to the cheapest workman.

Thus the Investigating Officer has far from completed his labours when he arrives at a conclusion that a workman has made a mistake. He must discover who has set the man to the job, whether he was really qualified for it, whether his knowledge, intelligence, strength, working time, have not been exaggerated, and whether there has been sufficient supervision. If the Investigating Officer can discover a gap and the person responsible therefor—that is the guilty man.

Section ii.—Technical Problems.

Apart from these general considerations we have deemed it useful, selecting boiler explosions as a type, to add a few technical details, the *same method* of inquiry will apply *mutatis mutandis*, to all serious catastrophes of the nature now under consideration.

Boiler explosions have one feature rendering them specially worthy of study, whether occurring in factories, railway trains, steamships, etc., they are, despite the march of science, exceptionally frequent and singularly destructive. German statistics, extending over eleven years, give an average of one death and two wounded for each explosion.

Our object is to assist the Investigating Officer in that critical moment when he is awaiting the arrival of the expert or interrogating the witnesses and accused. We assume that he has at least some superficial knowledge of the mechanism and treatment of boilers. In this connection we have relied mainly on the work of *Adolphe Peschka* 'Boiler Explosions and how to prevent them,'—an old work it is true, but still the clearest and most to the point we have come across. His thesis is that such explosions are not the effect of mysterious causes which we know not how to control, but really demonstrate the ignorance and gross carelessness of those interested. "The causes," he says, "can be discovered only when we know the antecedent circumstances: what was the condition of the boiler, the level of the water, the steam pressure just before the accident; in fact when we know everything about the boiler and have examined its fragments." In support of this view, we may cite the report of the *Manchester Steam Boiler Association*,—"It is difficult to imagine a case that cannot be explained by natural and well-known laws, and could not have been prevented by well-known and approved methods."

Hence it follows at once that in every explosion some human agency, some man, is at fault, any *a priori* theory as to luck or unexplainable causes must be rigorously discarded, it is also established that the cause can be determined, and that, as a rule, by very simple investigations.

The above Association, which inspects and tests all the steam boilers in England, gives the following as the primary causes of explosions: defects in construction, want of water, want of pressure gauges, over-pressure, formation of deposits in the boiler. *E. Schippe*, of *The Steam-Engine School*, Dresden, thus classifies 171 cases investigated by him: 29, faulty construction; 9, bad or worn-out material; 18, deficiency of water; 19, over-pressure; 19, weakness of the plates; 7, careless attendance; 6, incrustations; 2, explosion of a neighbouring boiler; 1, explosion of gas; 1, cause undiscovered. Other authorities, as *Paul Lagar* and *Richard Plimmer* suggest other cognate causes, but all agree on the one main point, that negligence and ignorance are the primary causes of all such catastrophes.

Section III.—Causes of Boiler Explosions.

In dealing with these we must first dismiss those false theories which ignorant and incompetent people are always pushing to the front to screen their own ignorance and incompetence

A False Theories

α *Theory of an explosive gas* This suggests that the water being decomposed by contact with the plates of the boiler, the disengaged hydrogen unites with the acid forming an explosive gas, which, catching fire from the plates of the boiler suddenly explodes

β *Theory of electricity* This is always propounded with a certain amount of mystery and is for that reason more readily accepted The suggestion is that by the contact of the steam with the boiler plates and other metals and under other influences immense quantities of electricity are produced hence the catastrophe

γ *Theory of the spheroidal state* This theory depends upon the phenomenon first recorded in 1752, that a drop of water on a red-hot metal plate preserves its spheroidal form, rotates on its axis, and evaporates very slowly as the metal cools, the rapidity of evaporation increases, and at last when the temperature has been reduced to a certain point, the liquid suddenly evaporates in a mass This is now shown as a common school experiment using an iron spoon This phenomenon has been employed to explain boiler explosions It was supposed that either through overheating or siliceous deposits a bed of vapour is formed between the water and the walls of the boiler, so that the whole mass of water may be considered as a slowly-evaporating drop Assuming that then, from some cause or other cooling—sudden or slow—supervenes, or that by some external shock the spheroidal form of the water is destroyed rapid vaporisation will ensue, followed by explosion

δ *The theory of the cold water current* This theory assumes that, in certain conditions a jet of cold water suddenly striking the hot boiler plates will cause vaporisation

Arago was the first to point out the inaccuracy of all these hypotheses, but the exertions of a long line of scientists has been necessary to complete his work, so tenacious is the grip of false theories once started *Colburn, Schwarz Schafhæutl de Burg, Kirchweggor, Hermann, Oechlhausen, Butte*, and others have shared in this task, yet we can date the general acceptance of true scientific theories only from the labours of *Paget*, (circa 1865)

B Admissible Theories.

The following may be accepted as admissible theories, and it will be seen at once that none are due to so-called bad luck or pure accident

α The chemical action of the fuel
β The chemical action of the water
γ The mechanical action of heat
δ The mechanical action of steam-pressure

α *Chemical action of the fuel* The simple heating of the boiler injures the iron but slowly, it is otherwise if, through negligence, the plates are heated red-hot In the latter case the surface of the metal is transformed into a crystallized crust, composed of oxidized iron and oxide of iron, this crust falls off and at each successive over-heating the boiler is sensibly weakened Further, when the coal contains white or yellow pyrites, the sulphur contained in the pyrites changes the surface of the iron into a friable iron sulphate, which accelerates crystallization In every case repetition of the over-heating must eventually end in a rupture of the walls of the boiler

Not unfrequently in boiler explosions we find portions of plate, thus often over-heated, breaking up under very feeble blows with a hammer. It must never be forgotten that, when a boiler becomes red-hot, the cause—always preventible—is want of water, the formation of incrustations, or sedimentary deposits

β Chemical action of the feed-water The water fed into the boiler is, for the most part, transformed into steam, but the solid matters contained in it are precipitated to the bottom or against the walls, gradually forming a solid crust, called *incrustation* Now this crust prevents direct contact between the water and the iron, and, being a very bad conductor of heat, permits the iron to become red-hot On the other hand the water, contained in this non-conducting envelope, requires the application of more heat Partial exhaust follows, whence the water may come in contact with the red-hot walls, and this partial but sudden cooling greatly injures the boiler Naturally we find to-day all kinds of inventions to prevent this evil, but none of these can remove the solid bodies from the water, at the best they can substitute for the incrustation, when forming, a sediment which is not so destructive Some present inconveniences of their own Among the many devices are enamelling apparatus for intercepting the solid particles, and countless compositions whose aim is to eliminate them Of many the components are known others are kept secret The true cure is regular cleaning of the boiler, but the Investigating Officer will also do well to inquire if any and what preventive has been employed, and to make sure that there has been no negligence in its use Solid substances are frequently contained in the water in considerable quantities a matter of some importance in certain cases The Investigating Officer should, therefore, in every instance where there is doubt as to the cause of the explosion, secure for analysis a specimen of the water used We may add that many authorities consider the presence of greasy substances in the water as most dangerous The Investigating Officer should, therefore, take note of the presence of fatty or oily matters in the condensed water

Besides the risks to which a boiler is exposed internally there are others external When the exterior walls are in direct contact with the atmospheric air, oxidation will naturally take place, but so slowly in practice as to be almost negligible But where the boiler is furnished with casings which favour the collection of water at certain points, this oxidation may become serious The water thus collected comes from outside, but in certain cases the water escapes from the inside through defects in the boiler In this instance there is continuous rusting and consequent weakening, all the more dangerous as it is concealed from view

γ Mechanical action of heat Here the metallic envelope of the boiler is in continual movement, owing to alternations of heat and cold

The degree of heat from the fire box cannot be always the same, currents of air, opening of doors, etc., continually cause new contractions and expansions, this continuous action weakens the boiler, especially if the walls be thick, as the exterior surface expands more than the interior. This is especially dangerous when the feed-water is so introduced as to pass direct into the heated chamber, at the points so touched the metal will in time crack, leading inevitably to a rupture sooner or later.

δ *Mechanical action of steam-pressure.* If the pressure of the steam in the boiler were always the same the walls would be subject to a progressive but constantly equal expansion, so that there would be no risk of giving way at any point. But the pressure varies, owing to inequalities of heating, variation in water-supply, opening doors, etc. Thus the same thing happens to the plates as occurs to a thin slip of white metal which we bend with our fingers, and which ends by breaking where thus worn out.

But an explosion can occur only when the pressure has been suddenly increased by an enormous and rapid release of steam, this takes place when the pressure on the water is suddenly diminished, thus permitting great masses of water to be vaporised. We thus arrive at the apparently paradoxical conclusion that a diminution of steam pressure increases the pressure. The explanation is simple, water boils normally at a temperature of 100°C or 212°F, but the boiling point is raised by an increase of pressure, steam or other. Suppose then a mass of water has been heated to 106°C or 222.8°F without having boiled, the sudden lowering of the pressure will produce boiling and in consequence considerable disengagement of steam.

The steps are as follow —

(a) an opening,
(b) escape of steam,
(c) lowering of pressure on the surface of the water,
(d) sudden release of large quantities of latent steam,
(e) explosion.

If it be asked how the opening is made, we can only say, in many ways, perhaps by the careless turning of a blow off cock or safety-valve, perhaps by a crack or tear in the boiler, but the primary cause in every case will be carelessness or imprudence.

INDEX.

A

Abbassi 300
Abdomen, wound to, 434, 436
Abdominal wall 421
Abortion 453
Absinthe 451
Accessories of guns 284
Accidental death 441
Accidents 582
Accomplices 200, 225, 226, 236, 249, 271, 272, 463
— in card sharping 561
— of thieves 455
Accuracy 16, 33
Accusations, False, 267
Accused
— Antecedents and records of, 77
— Examination of, 75
— Insanity of 222
Acid 579
Aconite 450
Acoustical signs 237
Actualities 201
Advertisement 200, 537
Advakatti 300
Affiliation 67
Age of horse 549
Alarm apparatus 505
Alchemy 262
Alcohol 329, 335, 368
Alibi 68, 69, 576
Alkali 527
Alhumbrictarialis 264
Almanach de Gotha 211
Almirah 455, 489
Alms 227
Alphabetical cipher 409
Aluina 264
Alum 370, 526, 527
Ammonia 233, 527, 530, 531, 579
Ammoniacal vapours 289
Ammunition 292

Amnesia 122
Anaesthetising of horse 553
Angle-writing 415
Aniline ink 528, 532
— Colours 335
Animals, Imitation of, 238
Antimony 551, 552
— Brimstone of, 335
— Sulphur of, 317
Antiphtasis, Sign of, 407
Antiquities, Frauds relating to, 564—575
Anus 550
Aphrodisiacs 449
Apoplexy 331, 421
Arangi 300
Arches (Finger-prints) 187
Arm, False, 463
Arms, Coats of, 211, 224
— Swinging of, 339
Arrow 225
Arsenic 278, 449, 551
Arson 14, 576
Art, Fraud relating to, 564
Artificial sickness 14 (see Shamming)
Ashes 233
Atropine 218, 451
Attack, Point of, in housebreaking 484
Attic thieves 480, 513
— Theft from, 518
Atzmann 266
Austrian Penal Code 566
Auto suggestion 122
Axe 401
Azote 294

B

Baker, Sign of, 226
Ballistics 151, 276
Bamboo 281
Bandy legs 352

INDEX

Bank Fraud on, 204
Banknotes, Flash, 35, 538
Bar of door Opening of, 496
Barrel 277, 280
— rings 277
— reflector 287
Battle axe 300
Bazaar thefts 474, 476, 516
Beard false 204
Bed plate 277
Beggars 215, 226, 247, 455, 457, 461, 514
Beggar stamps 535
Belching 581
Bell 155
— on shop door 514
Belladonna 217, 451
Bench 335, 580
Bertillon system of Photography, 180
Bill of Exchange 529
Bindings Falsification of ancient, 572
Bird lime 462, 495
Bitches, Employment of, in thefts, 461
Blackmail 558
Blind Removal of in burglary, 495
Blindness 217
Blood
 on body 391
 ", boots 379, 392
 of children (superstition) 261
 on clothes, 379, 392
 Colour of stains of, 129, 376
 Fetching of, 385
 of dog (superstition) 261
 — Drop of, 380
 — Effusion of, 421, 425
 — Fingerprints in, 395
 — on ground, wall, etc 388
 — on instrument and tools 392
 — Microscopic examination of, 128
 — Pool of, 379
 — Preservation of stains 399
 — Registration and description of, 382
 — Removal of, 385, 391, 393
 — Search for, 374
 — Stains of, 92, 374
 — in superstition 261—389
 — on table 378
 — Venous and arterial 130
 — on wood 386, 394
Blood-hound 380
Blotting-paper 335
Blue, washing, 335
Bodily injuries 419
Boiler explosions 582

Bolt 494
Bolts of door, Opening of, 497
Bone wounds 435, 436
Bones, Antediluvian, 567
Bones powdered 580
Book cipher 414
Books Falsification of ancient, 572
Boot 326, 331, 474
Boots, Blood on, 379
Boots as hiding place 532
Botany 153
Boundaries 312
Box
— Breaking open of, 487
— for packing 401
— Search of servant's, 516
Bracelet 512
Braces 438
Brain 436, 437
Bran 316
Branding of horses 552
Brandy 550
Bread crumb 529, 539
Breech-loaders 277, 284
— shot guns 284
— rifles 290
Bridge, Sign of, 309
Broken ground, Sign of, 309
Bronze, Imitation of old, 574
Brook, Sign of, 309
Brush 335
Brush, clothes, 318
Buck shot 278, 289
Buildings 316
Buildings, Sign of Domestic, 310
Bullet 278, 294, 435
— extractors 289
— guns 284
Bully 556
Burden
— Fact of carrying, deduced from footprints, 344, 349
Burglary 261, 456
Burglary and Housebreaking 482
— Entering by window 490
— ,, ,, door 495
— ,, ,, other ways 509
Burke's Peerage 214
Burning-glass 577
— Carafe as, 578
Burns 205
Burns to mouth, etc 581
Burnt paper 233, 324, 581
— Preserving and Deciphering of, 322
Buttocks 543

C

Calabar bean 218
Calibre 281, 285
Callosities 373
Calls and cries of warning 237
Camera lucida 314
— obscura 314
Cancellation, Sign of, 408
Candle 463
— Use of, in arson, 576
Cantharides 452
Cap (guns) 288
Capsicum seed 449
Carbolic acid 451
Carbon 294, 427, 580
Carbonate of zinc 527
Carbonic acid 294
Carbon oxide (monoxide) 294
Card cheat 225, 236, 464, 557
— cipher 417
— reading 270
Cards 225
— false 561
— marked 560
Carotid artery 437
Carriage, marks of, 372
Cartridge 284, 292
Carving letters in wood 235
Cast (fishing) 254
— of footprints 368
Castles, Sign of, 310
Castration, of horse 552
— self inflicted 14
Cat superstition 261
Catalepsy 223
Catarrh of horse 554
Caveat emptor 542, 551
Ceiling, Breaking through, 501, 510
Cement 318
— for footprints 366, 371
Cemetery, Sign of, 310
Central fire 284, 291
Certificates, Forged 208, 533
Certified copy, 524
Chain, endless, 564
Chalk 311, 318
Change of System, Sign of 408
Chapel, Sign of, 310
Characteristics, Unchangeable, of the person 206
Characters 533
Charge of gun 289
Charms 263
Chauffeurs 584

Cheating and fraud 520
— antiquities and works of art 564
— at cards 557
— Examination of false documents 524
— Falsification of documents 521
— Horse frauds 540
Chemical action in boiler explosions 587
Chemical analyst as expert 148, 448
Chemical examiner 448
Cherchez la femme 10
Child, Abandonment of, 282
Child-birth 468
Child (superstition) 251
Children 232
— Abduction of, 251
— brought into prisons 232
— Illegitimate, 517
— as sentinels 249
— as witnesses 62
Chili 449
Chimney-sweep 502, 510
Chinese ink 304, 317, 527
Chiromancy 272, 273
Chiropodist 474, 514
Chisel 488
Chloric acid 577
Chloride of cobalt 233
— of gold 530, 531
— ,, iron 329
— , potassium 531
— ,, sulphur 579
— ,, tin 530, 531
Chlorine 527, 528, 531
Chloroform 452
Choke-bore 430
Chromate of lead 580
Church, Sign of, 310
Cicatrices 113, 373, 553
Cigar in card sharping 561
Cinchonum 539
Cinnabar 335
Ciphers 403
— Alphabetical 409
— Angle writing 415
— Book 414
— Card 417
— Count Gronfeld's 412
— Count Vergenne's 417
— Deciphering, 417
— Foot-rule 416
— General Trochu's 412
— Julius Caesar's 409
— Lexicon 414
— Mirabeau's 408

Ciphers, Multiplication 410
— Napoleon's 412
— Numerical 408
— Puncture 416
— Serial 417
— Stencil or Blackline 414
— Syllabic 413
— Thread-writing 415
— Word 413
Circumcision 212
Cistern, Sign of, 310
Citric acid, 530, 531
Clay 318, 368, 495
— for footprints 371
— in pottery making 568
Clay pit, Sign of, 310
Clock, Ticking of, 489
— Use of, in arson 576
Cloth 492
Clothes 463, 474
— Blood on 379
— Hiding places in 532
— Microscopic examination of dust on, 144—145
Clue 268
Coachman 556
Coal dust 580
Coal tar 532
Coat collar as hiding place 213, 532
Cobalt 233, 526
Cobbler 298
Cobbler's wax 463
Cocaine 452
Cock, Crowing of, 238
Coffee 398
— gardens, Sign of, 310
Coining 540
Coins, Counterfeiting of, 532
— Falsification of, 569
Collection, of curios, etc., 566
Collodium 304
Colour, of horse 542, 547
— of horse, Faking of, 551, 552
— blindness 126, 127
Colours 175
Combustion Quasi-spontaneous, 578
— Spontaneous 580
Commercial traveller 458
Commission agent 455
Commissionaire 455, 457, 514
Commissioner of police 469
Communication in prison 232, 238
Compass, Points of, 303
Complaints False, 267, 269
Confession 36, 75, 78

Confession, False, 78
— of gipsy 257
— under hypnotism 125
Confrontations 232
Conjuror 513
Contour lines 316
Conveyances, Drivers of public, 9
Copper 233
— colour of horse 551
Copying (forgery) 168
Cords 580
Corn 331
Coronet of horse 554, 556
Corpse, Preservation of, 110
— Papillary lines on, 397
— Wounds to, 435
Corpses, Injuries to, 445
Corrosive sublimate 449
Cotton 580
Cotton wool 336, 492
Counterfeiting 569
— coins 540
— employment stamps 532
— seals on letters 539
— seals, stamps and coins 532
Cowardice of gipsies 244, 250
Crib biting 552
Crime, Reconstitution of, 51, 52
Cripple 331
Cross, Sign of, 309
Cross-examination of witnesses 60, 61
Crow-bar 492, 506
Cryptogram (see Cipher) 403
Curtain 495
Cut, Forced, in card sharping 562
Cutlass 229
Cutting weapons 297

D

Dagger 228, 300
Dah 300
Damascus steel 280
Datura 269, 449, 550
Dead child's bone 274
Deaf mutes 218
Deafness 318
Dealers' methods 540
Death-watch 267
Decomposition 449
Decoy 461
Deer 332
Delirium 119
Dentist 127, 206

Detective police 481
Devil 253, 274
Dialect 209
Diarrhoea 447
Dice 564
Digitalis 451
Dikatopter 314
Diplomatist as expert 404
Direction, Line of, 346
Dirt 144, 427
Discoloration of Face 437
Disguise 203
Divination 267
Documents, Falsification of, 521
Dog, Barking of, 263
— Fit of (superstition) 261
— Poisoning of, 460, 481
— stealer 479
Domestic thefts 516
Door, Barring of, in theft 249
— Fastening of, 490
— Forcing of, 496
— in theft, 455
Doping a horse 551
Dough 318
— for footprints 371
Drawing 301, 314, 315, 439
Dream books 273
Dreams 119, 272
Drill 497, 507
Drowning, Signs of death by, 444
Drum magic, 269
Drunkenness, Signs of, 120
— Shamming of, 465
Dumb alphabet 232
Dust 144, 233
Dust, footprints in, 333
Dwelling, Sketch of, 305
— Sign of, 309
Dyer's marks 201

E

Ear of horse 552
Earthenware, stone, and porcelain 571
Eczema 449
Egyptian antiquities 567
Electric bell, Use of, in arson 577
Electricity 586
Electro metallurgic process 574
Employment stamps, Forgery of, 532
Enamelling of boilers 587
Enamels, Falsification of, 471

Engravings, Falsification of, 570
Environs of house, Sketch of, 307
Epilepsy 120, 216, 475
Equipment 99
— of thieves 461
Erasures in Documents, Detection of, 526
Erotic powders 256
— sensations 452
Escape after crime 204, 248, 489
Esserie 218
Ether 329
Euphorbia lathyris 264
Exaggeration, Danger of 12
Examination
— of accused, 75
— ,, false documents 522, 524
— ,, gipsies 257
— ,, guns 288
— Precautions during 76, 77, 216
— in theft 457
— of witnesses 56
Excrement 131, 262
Expert 16, 37, 103, 331
— Artisan as, 298, 487
— Astronomer as, 105
— Blacksmith as, 298, 487
— Carpenter as, 487
— Cavalry Officer as, 540
— Chemical analyst as, 148
— in curios, etc 566
— Cutler as, 104
— Diplomatist as, 404
— in firearms 155, 276, 290
— ,, cases of fraud 520
— ,, ,, ,, housebreaking 485
— ,, handwriting 521
— Joiner as, 487
— in languages and dialects 209
— Linguist as, 105
— Locksmith as 487
— Medical, 107, 331, 426
— ,, Jurisprudents as, 107
— Microscopists as, 128
— In Mineralogy, Zoology and Botany, 153
— Numismatists as, 105
— Paper Manufacturer as, 521
— Photographer as, 521
— Physicist as, 150, 362
— Shoemaker as, 331
— Sportsman as, 331
— Turner as, 104, 105, 487
— Veterinary surgeon as, 540
— In Weapons 298

594 INDEX

Expert, Wood-carver as, 106
— examination of scene of burglary 499
Explosion 582
Explosive action 282
Eyes 217, 222

F

Face, Description of, 207
— Reconstruction of, 111, 112
Factory, Sign of, 310
Faking cards 560
Fall 421
False accusation 510
— names 208
Fares 554
Fat 265, 512
— of children 261
— dog 261
Ferrocyanide of potassium 157, 527, 530, 531
Ferrule 326, 371
Fetichism 121
Field, Sign of, 310
Files 461, 492
Filter-paper 335, 380, 390
Finger nails, Microscopic examination of dirt under, 144, 391
Finger-prints 185, 526
— in blood 395
— Chemical treatment of, 398
— on glass 296
— Illustrative cases 193
— Legal value of, 194
— Manner of recording, 195, 398
— Method of fixing, on glass 335
— Photography of, 173, 396, 399
— Practical application of, 186
Fire 583
— outbreaks of, 576
Firearms (and see Weapons), Experts in, 155, 276, 290
— Ammunition used 156
— Determination of time of firing 156
Fish hooks 255, 463
Flat 484
— foot 333
— Theft in, 468
Flax 579, 580
Flint lock 276, 283
Fly paper 463
Foot

Foot, Angle of, 348
— of horse 453
— Image of, 354
— Line of, 347
— Physiognomy of sole of, 332
— Wound to, 433
Footprints 88, 325, 483
— Age from, 329
— of bare feet 328
— Cast of, 367
— in clay 336
— Contraction of, 362
— Deduction from, 343
— Experimental, 328, 354
— Fabricated, 354
— of horse 372
— Measurements of 357
— Mould of, 367
— Observation of, 325
— Origin of, 336
— Photography of, 173, 336
— Preservation and reproduction of,
—   Dennstedt's method 370
—   General 363
—   Hodann's method 364
—   Hofmann's   ,,   367
—   Hugoulin's   ,,   365
—   Jaume's   ,,   366
—   Krahmer's   ,,   367
— Running 330, 344
— Sex from, 329
— Single, 330
— in snow 366, 371
— step, Length of, from, 327
— The "Trace" 346
— Walking, 337
Foot-rule cipher 416
Footwear, Microscopic examination of mud on, 147
Foreign Office 403
Forelock of horse, 552
Forest, Sign of, 309
Forgery 141, 164, 521
— of seals, stamps, etc 532
Fortune-telling, 247, 267
Foundation sacrifice 262
Fraud (and see Cheating)
— relating to antiquities, &c., 564—575
— relating to horse 540
French Chinese Ink 304
Frog, Croak of, 238
Frontispiece, Falsification of old, 572
Furniture, Blood on, 377

G

Gallnut ink 528, 531
Garden, Sign of, 309
Gas, Explosive, 581, 586
Gases of body 581
Gasman 502
Gelding 553
Geometrical identification 196
German Penal Code 556
Giddiness 447
— and shamming 222
Gimlet 498
Ginger 550
Gipsy, 217, 469
— Child-stealing by, 251
— Corporal characteristics of, 258
— cowardice 250
— datura, Use of, by, 263, 269
— Employment of, 245
— fire 550
— gratitude 252
— greed 251
— Homicide by 250
— Horse theft by, 251
— Housebreaking by, 489
— illnesses 258
— instruments of theft, poisoning, etc. 254
— language 243
— magic 268
— piety 253
— proverbs 260
— signs 229
— stigmata 240
— superstitions 252
— Thefts by, 247
Girl as watcher 468
Glance of sharp 558
Glanders 554
Glass 296
Glass, Breaking of, 462
— Pounded, as poison 452
Glass window, Cutting and breaking of, 494
Glassware, Fabrication of antique, 568
Gloves 463
Glue 319, 538
— in reproducing footprints, 336, 366, 371
Glycerine 512, 532
Goose-skin 444
Gout 449
Grain, Torrified, 580
Grapnels 505

Grating, Forcing of, 491
Gravity, Centre of, 339
Grazing-ground, Sign of, 310
Grease 512, 532
Greek 557
Groom 448, 555
Grosse bêtise 521
Guaic, Tincture of, 381
Guano 580
Gum 463
Gum-arabic 233, 318, 322, 329, 387, 526
Gun barrel (grooves of) 286
Gun, Bursting of 532
Gunpowder 294
Gypsum 539

H

Hair,
— Absorbing properties of, 131
— Burnt, (talisman) 256
— Decomposition of, 136
— Deductions from, 135, 136—139
— Distinctions between various kinds of, 135
— Microscopic examination of, 132
— Preservation of, 132, 134
— Superstition regarding, 266
Hairdresser 206, 514
Hakasen system 239
Hallucination, Post-hypnotic 122
— Negative, 122
— Retroactive, 74
Halter 542
Hammer 298, 401
Hand clapping 238
— False, 472, 513
— signals 231, 236
Hands 474
— of pickpockets 512
— of sharp 558
Handkerchief, Blood on, 400
Handshaking 233
Handwriting 33
— Character, etc., of, 157—164
— Dictated and copied, 162
— Expert examination of, 157, 158
— Experts in, 521
— Forged, 164
— of hypnotised persons 123
— Microscopic examination of, 139
— Peculiarities in, due to profession and traits 161
— due to illnesses 162

Handwriting of suicide 438
— under unaccustomed conditions 164
Hanging 113, 437
Harness 544
Hashish 451
Hatchet 393, 401, 402
Hay 580
Hearing 45—47
Heart 437
Hedges, Sign of, 309
Heel 326, 340, 341, 345
Height of horse 543
Hemlock 447, 451
Hemp 580
Henbane 451
Herring, Theft of, 261
Hinges 493
— Removal of, in housebreaking 487
Hinges of door, Removal of 496
Hip 274
Home-sickness 578
Homosexuality 120
Hoopoe 274
Hops 143
Horoscope 268
Horse frauds 540
— Fraud properly so called 549
— Age of the horse 549
— Broken winded, 545
— Colour, faking of, 551
— Concealing illnesses 553
— Employment of assistants 555
— Hiding defects 552
— Showing horse under most favourable conditions 542
— Special methods 541
— stealers 251
— Temperament of the horse 550
— Utilization of physiological circumstances, 545
— Utilization of psychological circumstances 547
Hotel-thief 474, 513
— Confederate of, 474
House, Plan of, 453
House-breaking (and see Burglary) 247
Hurdles, Sign of, 309
Hydrate of sodium, 531
Hydrochloric acid 233, 530, 531
Hydrogen carbonates 294
Hypnotism 121
— Effects of, 123
— Importance of, in criminology 123, 126

Hypnotism, Post-hypnotic condition 123, 125, 126
— States of consciousness, 121
— Suggestion 121, 122
Hypochlorite of soda 527, 528

I

Identification,
— by day-light 184
— ,, finger prints 186
— ,, moon-light 184
— papers 208, 214
— by photographs 180
Idols 567
Iliac bone 433
Illnesses of horses 812
— of witnesses and suspects 215
Illusions, Acoustical 45—47
— of the senses 43
— Tactile, 47, 48
— of taste and smell 49
Image of the foot 354
Imagination 61
Impressions (and see Footprints and finger-prints) 371
Incantations 265
Incendiary signs 224
Indiarubber 317
Indiarubber stamp 538
Induction in vision 42
Inebriate, Walk of, 352
Injuries to corpses, 445
Ink 438, 526, 539
— Chinese, 304
— Printer's, 398
— for stamps 532
— Sympathetic, 233
Inn, Sign of, 309
Insane persons as witnesses 119
Insanity 115—119 438
— Contagion of, 120
— Shamming, 222
— Signs of moral, 120
Inscriptions, Copying, 318
Inspection of localities 84—98
Instep 333
Instruments used in housebreaking 488, 492—498, 504, 508
Insulting police 466
Insurance cases 433
Intestines 448
— Wound in, 434

INDEX

Investigating Officer
— His clerk 84—86
— Duties of, 3, 456
— Essential qualities of, 15
— Equipment of, 99
— exaggeration, Danger of, in, 11
— The "Expeditious," 32
— General 1
— Knowledge of men by, 21—25
— Manner of constructing hypothesis by 5
— "Orientation" (finding his bearings, 25—30
— Procedure of, 3—10
— Reconstitution of the crime by, 38
Iodine 526, 529, 540
Iridescence 468
Iron in ink 526
— Powdered, 335
— wire 439
Itch 449
Ivory, Imitation of old, 574

J

Jack 486, 493
— Employment of, in burglary 493, 505
Jannal 494
Jewellers, Thefts from, 213, 476
Jewellery and precious stones 570
Jungle, Sign of, 309
Juniper berries 552
Jurymen 30, 31

K

Kassler Earth 329
Kerosine 196
Key 225, 501, 515
Key-hole 508
Keys skeleton, 445
Keyword 411
Knife 106, 300
Knots, Peculiar methods of making 106
Knowledge of men 21, 541
Korloraj 244
Kuft work 281
Kukri 300

L

Lace, Imitation of old, 574
Lameness 352

Lamp-shade 580
Lance 300
Lands of rifle 279, 285
Language, Experts in, 209
Lanoline 512
Latch 490
Laundry marks 201
Lead 551
Leading 279
Letters 403, 413
— Order of frequency of, 418
— Sealing and opening of 539
Level 505
Lexicon cipher 414
Licorice juice 570
Light, Magnesium, 176, 377
— Use of artificial, 377
Lightning powders 179
Lime 578, 580
— water 318
Linen Theft of 518
Linseed oil 233
Liquid-fire 579,
Litmus paper 527
Lividity 220
Loam 316
Localities
— Examination of objects 88
— Golden rule 89
— Inspection of 89
— ,, in the open 94
— ,, Objective and substantive systems 94
— ,, of room 90
— Photography of, 173
— Report of, 90
Locks 481
— Attacking the, in burglary, 501
— Imitation of old, 573
— Picking of, 264
Locksmith 501, 503
Logwood ink 527, 531
Lombroso, School of 80
Love charms 519
Luggage of train thieves 474
Lunar caustic 551

M

Maceration 111, 444
Magic
— divining box 258
— lantern 177
— sieve 269

Magistrate 469, *and see* "Investigating Officer"
Magnesia 317
Magnesium light 176, 377
Magnifying glass 399, 525, 536.
Maidan, Sign of, 310
Main de gloire 264
Mandrake 264
Manure, Theft of, 519
Manuscripts, Photography of, 177
— Falsification of ancient, 572
Maps 28, 308, 314, 315
March Line of, 346
Mare 553
Market thefts 475
Marks of bullets, 296
— on horses, 549
Martingale 544
Mask 463
Masochism 121
Match, Deduction from, 327
Matchlock 276, 282
Matrix 539
Meadow, Sign of, 310
Meal, In antique pottery making, 568
Measurements 302, 307, 313
Mechanical action in boiler explosions 587
Mechanograph 314
Medical Examination 212, 216
— Jurisprudence 109
— Jurisprudent, 352, 419
— „ role of, 109
Memory
— Aids to, 50
— Association of ideas 51
— Conscious and unconscious activity of, 50
— Loss of, 55
— Threefold function of, 49
Menstruation 118, 123, 392
Mental pictures 86
Mercury 449
— Fulminate of, 289
Messengers 9
Metallic fouling 279
Methods of aiming 293
Metric system 312
Microscope 529
Microscopic examination 128
— of blood 129
— clothes 146
— Cloth, woollens, linen, etc, 140, 285
— dust 144

Microscopic examination of excrement 131
— hair 131
— hand-writing 139
— mud on footwear 147
— in other medical cases 138
— of weapons and tools 142
Microscopist 360
Milk as ink 233, 234
Mineralogy 153
Mirror-bit 544
Miscarriage 453
Misspelling 522
Modelling 314
Modus operandi of thieves 478, 481
Monastery, Sign of, 310
Money, Theft of, 480
Monument, Sign of, 310
Morals, Laxity of, 262
Morse alphabet, 239
— code 562
Mosquito stings, Artificial, 513
Moulds 318, 367
Moulding 317, 487
Mouth of horse 549, 552
Mud, Footprints in, 325, 342
Multiplication cipher 407
Mummies 567
Municipality, Counterfeiting seal of, 534
Murder, 18, 173, 194, 245, 335, 375, 395, 401, 432, 437, 440, 442, 445
Murder prayers and Masses 266
Muscle 434, 435
Muscular contraction, 220
Mushrooms 447, 451
Mutes, deaf, 219
Muzzle-loader 277, 282, 287

N

Nail 420, 427, 554
— Finger, 144, 427
— of boot, 326, 359—363
— maker 225
— Removal of blood on, 390
— Rusty, 360
Name transformation 208
Napoleon 161
— Cipher of, 412
Nasal discharge of horse 813
Needle fire 291
Needle-gun 284
Needle, Use of, in forging seals, 536

Negative facts, Notification of, 90
Negro odour 248
Nerve-irritation 578
Net-glass 314
Newspaper reports 199, 213
Nick-names 228
Nicotine 451
"Night-case" 466
Nigrosine ink 531
Nipple 445
Nitrates 294
Nitrate of silver 526, 551
Nitric acid, 531
Non-values (ciphers) 407, 409
Nose 207
Numerical cipher 408
Nux vomica 460

O

Oaths, Superstitions regarding, 274
Objects hit by projectiles 295
Observation
— Differences in natural qualities, 59
— Head wounds, 55
— Strong feeling, 52
Ocular demonstration 17, 71
Ointment 368
Opal 266
Ophthalmoscope 218
Opium 449
Orchards, Sign of, 310
"Orientation" 25
Orpiment 449
Orthopædist 206
Oxalic acid 451, 527, 528, 531
Oxyhydrogen lamp 505

P

Pace, Abnormal, 352
— of horse 545
— Length of, 351
Packing 401
Padlock 481, 482, 502
Palace, Sign of, 310
Pallor 220
Panel of door, Removal of, 496
Pantograph 313
Paper (and see Tracing),
— Blotting, 318, 335
— Burnt, 322
— Cast, 318

Paper, Cigarette, 319, 387
— Filter, 335, 380, 390
— in forgery 169, 521, 525
— Packing, 401
— Piecing together of torn, 319
— Toilet, 318
Papillary lines (see Fingerprints and Footprints) 186, 396
Papyri 567
Paralysis 162
— of horse 533
— Shamming of, 221
Paralytic 331, 352
Parchment 523
Partnerships in crime 237
Passing, in card sharping, 563
Paste 318
Paste-board in papyrus making 567
Patch 285, 428
Pathological lying 74
Paths, Sign of, 308
Patina, Imitation of, 574
Pawn shops 200, 205
Peat 580
Pederast 237
Pedlar 455
Pen 100, 311
Penis 437, 445
Pentateuch 274
Peony 264
Pepper 550
Perception 40
Percussion cap 283
Percussion guns 283
Percussion, System of, 284
Personation of witnesses 67
Perspiration 266
Petroleum 318
Pewet 274
Phenyl 451
Phonetic communication in prison 238
Phosphorus, 449, 579, 580
Photography
— "Accidental," 172
— of accidents 170
— Amateur, 170
— Bertillon system of, 180
— of blood marks 385, 396
— Colour, 175
— Comparison of photographs, 182, 183, 184
— of documents 525
— Employment of, 171
— Enlargement by, 178, 525

Photographs, Examination of photographs with magnifying glass, 182
,, of faces 181
,, fingerprints 173, 179, 396, 399
,, footprints 173, 336
Hints on taking photographs, 179
of latent marks, 174, 320, 373
Lightning powders, 179
Machinery, 179
Magnesium light, 176
Microscopic 176
of manuscripts, etc., 177
of objects in relief 180
Recognition of criminals by, 180
Reproduction and reduplication, 185
Retouching 183
by Röntgen Rays 169
of scene of crime 173
of shamming persons, 175
of shining objects 179
Size, format, tone, 181
Untruthfulness of, 178, 180
Wide angle objectives, 180
of wounds 173
Phthisis 261
Physicist as expert 150
Physiognomy 79, 332
Physiology 151
Pickpockets 204, 463, 471, 474, 478, 511
Confederates of 471, 474
Picture charms and spells 266
— Taking of, 570
— writing 406
Pig 332
Pincers 513
Pine resin 526
Pin-fire 284
Pistol 291
Pitch 495
— for footprints 371
— of rifles 286
Plan 302, 311
— of dwelling 305
— ,, environs of house 307
— ,, house interior 304
Plants, Blood on, 386
Plaster 365
— cast 319
— of paris 366, 539
Poacher 98, 285
Poaching 263
Pocket 463 557
— -book 463, 472, 475

Pocket-knife, Examination of dirt in 145
— -picking 232, 500 511
— Search of, 403
Poignard 300
Poisoning cases 267
Poisoning 139, 452, 446
— by Aconite 450
— ,, Arsenic 449
— ,, Atropine and belladonna 451
— ,, Carbolic acid and phenyl, 451
— ,, Chloroform 452
— ,, Cocaine 452
— ,, Datura 449
— ,, Henbane 451
— ,, Mercury 449
— ,, Nicotine 451
— ,, Opium 449
— ,, Phosphorus 449
— ,, Pounded glass 452
— ,, Prussic acid 453
— ,, Santonine 451
— ,, Strychnine 449
— ,, Sulphuric acid 451
— ,, Sulphuric ether 452
— of watch-dog 460, 481
Police
— Choice of, 30.
— circular 456
— Duties of, 456
— Rural, 29
— Sphere of, 6—8
Police and watchers 455
Pool, Sign of, 310
Porcelain 571
Portrait Parlé 206
Post-mortem 1, 109, 446, 452
Potash 552
— Protoxide of, 335
Potassium 579
— azotate 233
— Hypermanganate of, 335
— Silicate of, 336
— sulphates and carbonates 294
— sulphurate 294
Pottery 567
Poultry stealing 254
Pounce 526
Powder 289, 294, 428
— horns 284
— Smokeless, 282
Practices of criminals 203—240
— of Disguise 203
— ,, False names 208
— ,, Shamming 215

Practices of Signs and signals 223
Preconceived theories, 10, 499
Preservation of parts of a corpse, 110
— of pieces of bone 111
Press, Sphere of, 198
Pressure of steam 588
Preternatural combustibility, 581
Prison,
— breaking 306
— Phonetic communication in, 238
— Secret writing in, 233
— Treatment of gipsies in, 259
Procedure, of pickpockets 511
— in theft cases 478
Projectiles 294, 428
Property, Pretended wrongs to, 14
Prostitutes, 9, 10
Proverbs, 260
Prussian blue 522, 526
Prussic acid 451
Psychic force 268
Psychology in horse dealing 547
Ptomaines 451
Pupil of eye 218
Puncture cipher system 416
Pus 402
Pyrogallic acid 551

Q

Quail 238
Quarry, Sign of, 310
Quasi-spontaneous combustion 578
Quis quid ubi, quibus auxiliis, cur, quomodo, quando, 87

R

Rags 304
Railways, Sign of, 308, 309
Railway thieves 235, 472
Ramrod 277
— tube 290
— plug 284
Range in shooting 434
Rape 445
— Pretended, 13
Razor 401
Reagent for finding blood 381
Receiving 475
Recognition of criminals 180
Reconstitution of the crime 37, 38
Recruits and conscripts 218
Register in theft cases 477, 482
Repair, when fraudulent, 565

Reports of crime 198, 213
Resin 463, 580
— for footprints 371
Resorcin ink 531
Retouching of photographs 183
Retroactive hallucination 74
Revolver 277, 291
Revolving chamber 292
Rheumatism 449
Rifle-butt, 279
Rifling 279, 284, 285
Rimfire 284
Ring Signet, 463, 481
Road 312, 326
Roads, Sign of, 308
Robbery from a corpse 445
Rods used for thieving 463
Roe 332
Roman ware Falsification of, 568
Röntgen rays 169, 567
Room,
— Description of, 91
— Plan of, 304
Ropes 580
Rubber stamp 538
Rubble pit, Sign of, 310
Running 344
— Mechanism of, explained, 344
Rupture of internal organ 421

S

Sabre 229
Sacramental bread 264, 274
Saddle 544, 548
Sadism 121
Safe 481, 505—11, 580
Safety bells 505
— valve 583, 588
Sailor, walk of, 347
Sahromania 121
Saltpetre 294
Salt spilling 267
Sand
— Footprints in, 368, 371
— Sign of, 309
Sandarac 526
Santonine 451
Scale 312, 316.
Scapegoat 583
Scarabs 567
Scars 205, 240
Scene of offence (*and see* Localities),
— Description of, 439

Scene of offence, Examination of, by experts 499
Scissors making 512
Scouts, sentinels and spies (theft) 249, 455
Scratches 427
Screwdriver 488
Sculptors 317
Seals,
— Counterfeiting of, 532, 534
— on letters, Copying of, 539
— Material of False 535
Seams 403
Search
— of accused person 95, 213
— in houses 95, 523
Searches in the open 96
Second hand dealers 205
Seeds 450
Senses, Illusions of 43
Serajevo, Battle of, 246
Servant as accomplice in theft 459
— falsely accused 509
Sham illnesses and pains 215
Shamming, blindness, 217
— catalepsy 223
— deafness 218
— drunkenness 465
— epilepsy 219
— fainting 221
— insanity 222
— paralysis 221
— Photography of, 175
Shamsher 300
Sharps and flats 557
Shellac 318
Shoe 354, 484
Shoemaker as expert 331
Shop thefts 476, 516
Shot 278, 279, 295
— bag 283
— Dispersion of, 430
— guns 279
Shots through glass 296
Shrine, Sign of, 310
Shuffle, False, in card sharping, 562
Shutters 494, 495, 497
Shutter cutter 507
Shying of horse 545
Sienna, Burnt, 311, 329
Sieve 323
Sight of rifle 277
Signet ring 512
Sign-post, Sign of, 309
Sign of Antiphrasis 407

Sign of cancellation 408
— ,, change of system 408
Signs and signals 223
— Gipsy 229
— Graphic 224
— Hand 224
— in plans 308—310
— of recognition 235
Silk 580
Singing in prison 239
Skeleton keys 461, 503, 515
Sketch 311, 314, 383
— of dwelling 305
— ,, environs of house 307
— ,, portion of country 311
— ,, room 304
Skin 422, 433
Skull 421, 427
Slang of criminals 242, 243
Slate 536
Slumber thumb 264
Smell 48, 248
Smoke 428
Sneak thefts 254, 514
Snow, Footprints in, 325
Soap, Use of, in horse dealing, 549, 552, 556
Soda 526
Sodium hydrate 530
Soldering 492
Soldiers, Gipsies as, 244
Somatic functions 123
Somnambulism 119, 122
Soot 335, 503
Soporiferous candles 261
Sorcery (see Superstition) 261
Spark, Fire caused by, 578
Spavins 545, 555
Spear 300
Specialists 486
— in crime 479
Spectacles (in disguise) 204
Speed from footprints 336
Spelling, Deduction of forgery by, 522, 535
Sperm 402
Spheroidal state 586
Spies
— Gipsies as, 245
— Police, 9
Spittle, Deduction from, 327
Splinter 420
Spontaneous combustion 580
Sportsman as expert 331
Spring, Sign of, 310

Spring Root 264
Squared paper 314
Squib, Fire caused by, 579
Stabbing weapons 300
Stable boy 555
Staggers 553
Stallion 553
Stamps, Counterfeiting of, 532
Stapedial bone 450
Starch 319
Statements of case in tabular form 35
— of dying persons 73
— Uncorroborated, 55
Steak, Theft of, 261
Steam boilers 582
Stearic acid (wax) 365
Stearine 304
Steatite (french chalk) 536
Steep places, Sign of, 309
Stencil cipher, 414
Step
— of invalids 531
— Length of, 327, 350
— of old persons 531
— ,, railway men 531
— ,, soldiers 531
— ,, sportsman 531
— ,, surveyors 531
Stereotyping 317
Stick 326, 401, 421
— Impression of, 356
— spells 265
Stiff arm 204
Stigmata 240
Stillborn child 261
Stock (of gun) 277, 287
Stockings, Use of, by thieves, 463
Stolen articles, Description of, 200
Stomach, Examination of, for poison, 448
Stone seekers 262
Stopping power of bullets 436
Stove 322
Strangles 554
Strangulation 437, 439
Straw 294
Street, Sign of, 308
Strychnine 449
Subordinates, Employment of, by Investigating Officer, 9
Suet for footprints 370
Suicide 431, 434, 437, 441, 446
Sulphate of copper 531
Sulphur 294, 317, 527, 580
Sulphuric acid, 233, 294, 395 451, 527 530, 531, 549

Sulphuric ether 452
Sun and burning glass 578
Superoxide of hydrogen 528
Superstition 261, 445
Superstition regarding corpses and objects abandoned 262
— Devination and fortune-telling 267
— regarding hours 267
— Interpretation of dreams and chiromancy 272
— regarding oaths 274
— ,, objects carried 263
— Treasure finding 271
— and theft 480, 518
Surgical belt maker 206
Surprise, Prevention of, by burglar, 490
Survey map 308
,, signs 308
Swamp, Sign of, 309
Swell mobsman 213
Swimming bath 333
Swindler 213, 236
Sword 225
,, arms 229
Syllabic cipher 413
Syphilis 449

T

Table of reagents for inks 531
— Blood on, 378
— Top of, as weapon, 420, 421
Tact 1, 200
Tail of horse 551
Tallow 463
Talwar 300
Tank, Sign of, 310
Tannin 527
Tannin black 532
Tapestry 376
Tar 580
Taste 48
Tattooing 112, 212
— Age of, 113
— on a corpse 113
— Importance of, 113
— when and where generally found 113
— for purpose of disguise 205
Tea gardens, Sign of, 310
Technique in housebreaking 486
Teeth 93, 127
— of horses 549

Temperature of corpses 444
Temple, Sign of 310
Testicles 553
Textile plants, Spontaneous combustion of products of, 580
Theft 267, 454
    Accomplices 463
    from attic 513
    Bazaar and shop thefts 516
    Burglary and housebreaking 482
        Attacking the lock 501
-     Entering by the door 495
-        ,, window 490
       ,, in other ways 509
- Domestic thefts 516
— from flats 513
    by gipsies 247, 254
— from hotels 514
— Instruments of, 254
    Pocket-picking, 511
- of poultry 254
— Preparations 456, 460
— Scouts and spies 455
    from shops 514
- Sneak thefts 513
- through superstition 518
    Thieves, equipment 461
Theories, Preconceived, 10
Thief 403
Thieves, Discovery of, by divination, 269
— — small 481
Thimble rigging 563
Thiosulphate of sodium 530, 531
Thorah 274
Thread 576, 580
— writing 415
Three card trick 563
Thumb 264, 399
Tinder 576
Tobacco 552
Toes, Use of, in theft, 475
Tomato 449
Tools, Microscopic examination of stains on, 142
Tope, Sign of, 310
Touch 47
Touts in horse dealing 556
Tow 294
Trace 346
Tracing and tracing paper 168, 316, 319, 322, 387
Tracks of criminals 411
Trail 346, 347
Train, Accidents to, 579

Tramps 225, 532
Transferring in cardsharping 561
Treasure finding 261, 271, 272
Tree 295, 310
Tree, Branch of, as weapon, 420
Trigger guard 277
Trouser button 274
— flap 213
Truss makers 206
Tumbler of lock 502
Tumour 453
Turf 580
Turpentine 318, 335, 381, 580
Tweezers for lock picking 515
Tympanum 401
Typewriting office 319

U

Ulceration of lungs in horse 554
Umbilical cord 445
Umbrella 510
Upholstery, Imitation of old, 572
Urine 233, 266

V

Vagabond 533
Vampires 261
Vanadium ink 531
Vaseline 512
Velocity 435
Verdigris 289
Veterinary surgeon 540, 548
Violin, Fabrication of old, 843
Virgin, Fat of, 261
— in superstition 274
Voice (disguised) 204
Vomit 447
Vowel cipher 409

W

Wad 278, 283, 294, 428, 430
— extractor 279, 290
Wale 212
Walking stick 263, 281, 393, 462
Walking
— backwards 353
— Dragged impressions in, 342
— image 346
— Impression of foot in, 341

Walking Impulsion in, 340
— Mechanism of, explained, 337
Wall 304, 306, 309, 318
— Blood on, 387
Wandering tribes (see Gipsy) 243
War Office 403
Warning, Calls and cries of, 237
— Words of, 464
Warts 205, 261
Watch 441
— chain 463
— Number of, 406
Watcher in theft 463
Watchman 464
Water
— Bodies found in, 440
— colours 311
— course 312
— Washing away blood in hot and cold, 392
Wax 266, 317, 365, 390, 463, 477
— cloth 463
— for footprints 370
Weapon
— Ammunition 294
— Axe as, 423
— Bayonet 425
— Branch of tree as, 420
— Breach loaders 284, 290
— Broken glass as, 422
— Bullet guns 285
— Carriage crossbar as, 421
— Chisel as, 427
— Construction and use of, 276
— Cutting and stabbing, 297
— Firearms 276, 428
— Gimlet as, 425
— Hatchet as, 420, 422
— Imitation of old, 573
— Knife as, 422, 425
— Microscopic examination of, 142
— Muzzle loaders 282, 287
— Objects 295
— Pistols 291
— Powder 294
— Projectiles 290
— Revolvers 291
— Scythe as, 422
— Shot guns 278
— Shovel as, 427
— Sickle as, 422
— Stick as, 421
— of stone 567
— Sword as, 420
— Top of table as, 420

Weather 331
Weidmann's ink 233
Well, 440
Whalebone 463
Wheat 580
Wheel, Marks of, 372
Whistling 238
Whorls (fingerprints) 187
Wig 207
Wind, Gipsy dislike of 258
Window 274, 296, 304
— Breaking of, 463
— Entering by 490
— in theft 455
Window-bar 490
— Breaking through, 484
— shutters 497
Winking 237
Withered hand 204
Witnesses 392
— Adults as, 65
— Boys and girls as, 63, 64
— Children as, 62
— Examination of, 36, 446
— ,, of, in theft, 457
— Illnesses of, 215
— Imaginative, 61
— Insane persons as 119
— Lying, 66
— Medical, 426
— Reserved, 62
— Shamming, 216
— Substitution of, 72
— Surveillance of, 87
— wishing to speak truth 39
Wood, Blood on, 386
— Lime, Ivy, Box, 536
Wood facing 305
Wool 368, 580
Woollens, Microscopic examination of 140
Women sentinels (theft) 249
— thieves 244
— as watchers 467
Wounded person, Walk of, 352
Wounds (and see Weapon)
— Appearance of gunshot, 434
— by blunt instruments 298, 420
— at close quarters 428, 434
— from fall 420
— by firearms 423
— on hand 378, 382
— on the head 55, 298
— Gunshot, compared with knife, 429
— Photography of, 173

Wounds, Post mortem and ante mortem, 107
— Self inflicted, 13, 14
— by sharp instruments 421, 422
Writing (see Handwriting)
— anonymous and pseudonymous, 461
— in the air 232
— Secret of prisoners 233

Y

Yataghan 239

Z

Zinc dust 580
Zoology 153

Lightning Source UK Ltd.
Milton Keynes UK
UKOW011924230512

193156UK00007BA/13/P